S0-EXB-777

WITHDRAWN

SCSU
H.C. BULEY LIBRARY

NOV 21 1988

New Haven, CT 06515

HILTON C. BULEY LIBRARY
SOUTHERN CONNECTICUT STATE UNIVERSITY
NEW HAVEN, CONNECTICUT 06515

Encyclopedia of NEW YORK

GEORGE CLINTON
-First Governor of New York State-

Encyclopedia of NEW YORK

—a volume of
ENCYCLOPEDIA OF THE UNITED STATES

SOMERSET PUBLISHERS

19722 E. NINE MILE ROAD
ST. CLAIR SHORES, MICHIGAN 48080

Ref.
F
118
.E57
1982

Library of Congress Cataloging in Publication Data
Main entry under title:

Encyclopedia of New York.

(Encyclopedia of the United States)
Edited by Beth Blenz and Thomas J. Gergel.
Bibliography: p.
Includes index.
1. New York (State)--Dictionaries and encyclopedias.
I. Blenz, Beth.   II. Gergel, Thomas J.   III. Series.
F118.E57   1982   974.7'003'21   81-85115
ISBN 0-403-09994-3

Copyright 1982 © by Somerset Publishers

All rights reserved. No part of this work may be reproduced or utilized in any form or by any means, electronic or mechanical, or by any information storage and retrieval system, without permission in writing from the publisher.

Printed in the United States of America

The Encyclopedia of New York

EDITOR AND PUBLISHER
Frank H. Gille

MANAGING EDITOR
Elizabeth Blenz

ASSOCIATE EDITOR
Timothy Gille

CONTRIBUTORS
Richard A. Clucas, *New York City*
Kenneth Spears, *Chronology*
Dr. Thomas J. Gergel, *Geography*

EDITORIAL ASSISTANT
Nancy Lambourn

PHOTOGRAPHIC SUPERVISION
Thomas Gille

PRODUCTION

Alan M. Schoff, 100 Percent Graphics

TYPESETTING
Richard Hand, Dream Electronics
Leonard Herman Typesetting

FOREWORD

Information on this state is available from many other sources. Histories and geographies abound; there are place-name books, guidebooks and biographical references; many excellent atlases provide map detail; government registers contain in-depth coverage of the political organization.

It is the existence of so many varied sources of information that makes a systematic, encyclopedic reference necessary - a single source for the most useful information about New York.

A secondary purpose of this volume is to play a part in a national reference on all of the states, a systematic approach to referencing the entire nation - an *Encyclopedia of the United States* with each volume following a planned outline that matches each other volume in the series - with exceptions in the format made only when necessary.

This goal was partly achieved during the Great Depression years with the publication of the WPA Federal Writers' Project State and City Guidebooks, which we are proud to have republished in recent years in their original form. While containing a wealth of interesting and still useful information they are outdated for most of the reference needs of today. And they were essentially *tour-guides* rather than general reference books. They were, however, very useful in the planning of this new work.

By providing consistency in format throughout the series of volumes in this Encyclopedia, researchers, whether they are academic scholars or occasional public library users, will be aided in knowing that a source exists for information on any of the states.

It is our hope that this Encyclopedia series will have a permanence through the issuance of revised editions at intervals to be determined by a careful watch on the availability of new material. Undoubtedly changes in the concept will be reflected in later editions as a result of feed back from users and the observations and introspection of our editors.

We wish to acknowledge with great appreciation the cooperation of the many state and local government offices that have furnished or reviewed material.

We are further grateful to the many librarians who have made their facilities so available during the years that this project has been in process.

Frank H. Gille

LIST OF ILLUSTRATIONS

ii —Governor George Clinton.
x-xv —Population charts and map.
Facing 24 —Map of New York Indian Tribes.
Facing 25 —Kesketoma, Chief of the Onondagas.
38 —New Amsterdam in 1626-1628.
Facing 53 — Crossing Broadway in the 1850s.
                Buffalo in mid-century.
                Seneca Falls Women's Rights convention.
                Brooklyn Bridge construction.
84 —Major drainage systems of New York--map.
85 —Physiographic regions of New York--map.
86 —Montauk Point, Long Island.
87 —Appalachian hills near Oneonta.
Facing 141 —Portraits of famous New Yorkers.
Facing 186 —Scenes of New York, Part 1.
196 —St. Lawrence Seaway.
197 —National Parks Map.
226 —Mt. Marcy, The Adirondacks.
227 —Mohawk Valley and Thomas Dewey Thruway.
Facing 360 —Scenes of New York, Part 2.

TABLE OF CONTENTS

INTRODUCTION 1
CHRONOLOGY 9
PREHISTORY AND ARCHEOLOGY 25
HISTORY 39
GEOGRAPHICAL CONFIGURATION 60
U.S. SENATORS (List) 88
NEW YORK GOVERNORS 90
BIOGRAPHIES OF FAMOUS NEW YORKERS 141
SPECIAL: ADIRONDACKS STATE PARK 187
SPECIAL: FIRE ISLAND NATIONAL SEASHORE 198
ALBANY 198
BUFFALO 204
NEW YORK CITY 208
ROCHESTER 216
SYRACUSE 220
YONKERS 224
DICTIONARY OF PLACES 229
HISTORICAL PLACES 361
DIRECTORY OF STATE SERVICES 537
CONSTITUTION OF NEW YORK STATE 543
IMPORTANT DATES 715
BIBLIOGRAPHY 719
INDEX 725

Total Population and Percent Change From Preceding Census for the State: 1900 to 1980

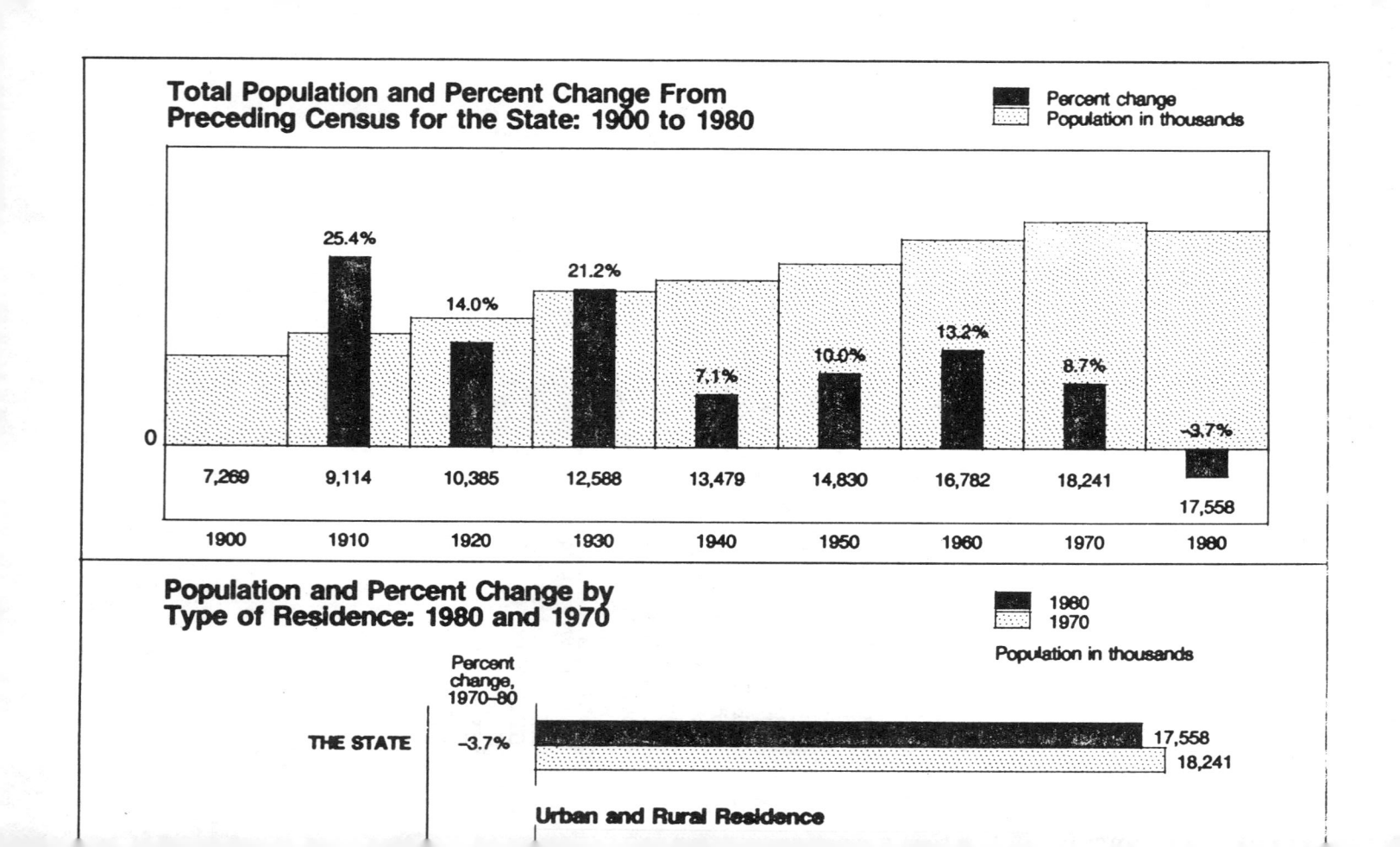

■ Percent change
▫ Population in thousands

Year	Population	Percent change
1900	7,269	
1910	9,114	25.4%
1920	10,385	14.0%
1930	12,588	21.2%
1940	13,479	7.1%
1950	14,830	10.0%
1960	16,782	13.2%
1970	18,241	8.7%
1980	17,558	-3.7%

Population and Percent Change by Type of Residence: 1980 and 1970

■ 1980
▫ 1970

Population in thousands

	Percent change, 1970–80	1980	1970
THE STATE	-3.7%	17,558	18,241

Urban and Rural Residence

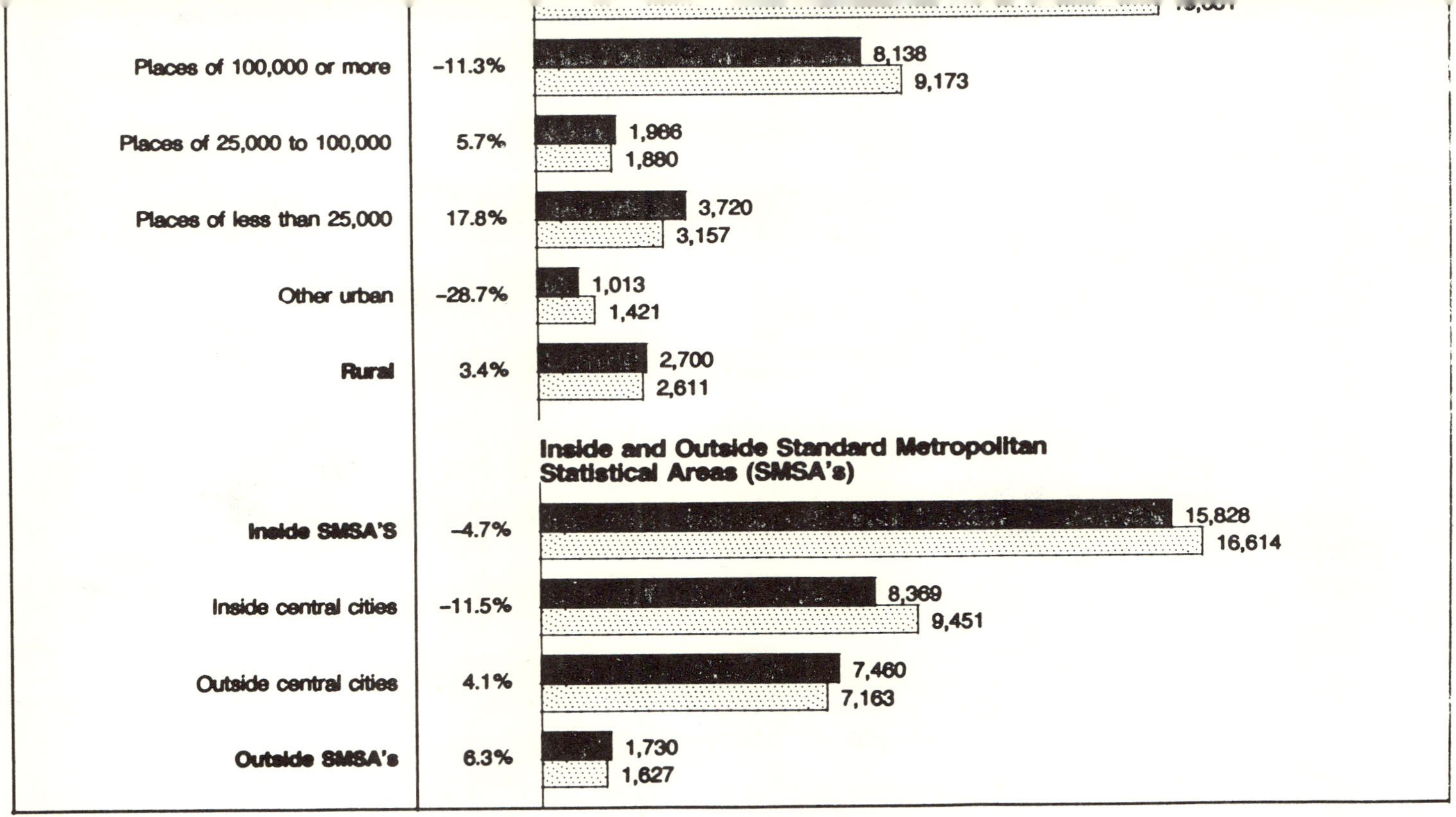

Places of 100,000 or more	−11.3%	8,138 / 9,173
Places of 25,000 to 100,000	5.7%	1,986 / 1,880
Places of less than 25,000	17.8%	3,720 / 3,157
Other urban	−28.7%	1,013 / 1,421
Rural	3.4%	2,700 / 2,611

Inside and Outside Standard Metropolitan Statistical Areas (SMSA's)

Inside SMSA'S	−4.7%	15,828 / 16,614
Inside central cities	−11.5%	8,369 / 9,451
Outside central cities	4.1%	7,460 / 7,163
Outside SMSA's	6.3%	1,730 / 1,627

U.S. Department of Commerce

BUREAU OF THE CENSUS

NUMBER OF INHABITANTS

34—4 NEW YORK

Percent Distribution by Type of Residence for the State: 1980 and 1970

A. URBAN AND RURAL RESIDENCE

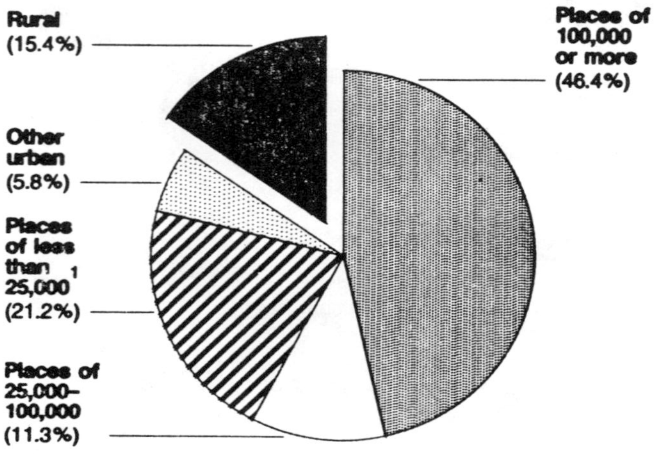

1980

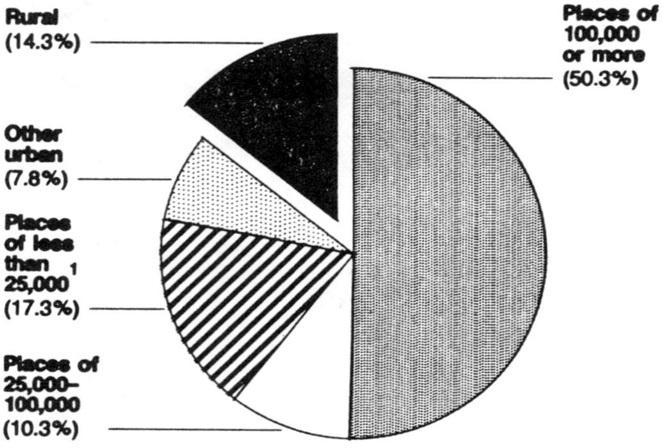

- Rural (15.4%)
- Other urban (5.8%)
- Places of less than 25,000 (21.2%)
- Places of 25,000–100,000 (11.3%)
- Places of 100,000 or more (46.4%)

1970

- Rural (14.3%)
- Other urban (7.8%)
- Places of less than 25,000 (17.3%)
- Places of 25,000–100,000 (10.3%)
- Places of 100,000 or more (50.3%)

[1] Excludes population of places in rural territory.

B. INSIDE AND OUTSIDE STANDARD METROPOLITAN STATISTICAL AREAS (SMSA'S)

1980

- Outside SMSA's (8.9%)
- Inside central cities of SMSA's (47.7%)
- Inside SMSA's, outside central cities (42.5%)

1970

- Outside SMSA's (8.9%)
- Inside central cities of SMSA's (51.8%)
- Inside SMSA's, outside central cities (39.3%)

U.S. Department of Commerce

BUREAU OF THE CENSUS

NUMBER OF INHABITANTS

NEW YORK 34–5

Standard Consolidated Statistical Area, Standard Metropolitan Statistical Areas, Counties, and Selected Places

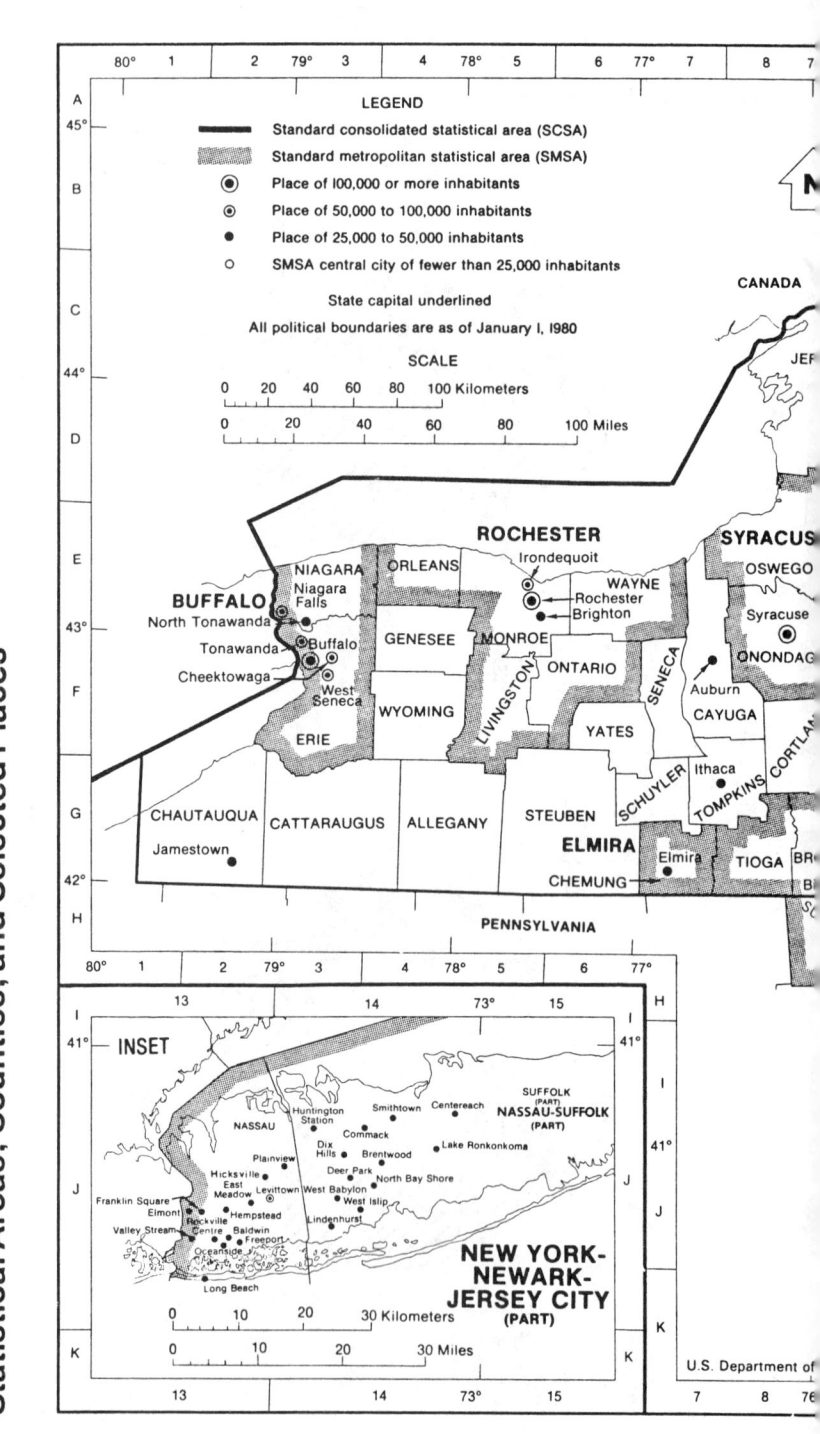

LEGEND

— Standard consolidated statistical area (SCSA)
▓ Standard metropolitan statistical area (SMSA)
⊙ Place of 100,000 or more inhabitants
⊙ Place of 50,000 to 100,000 inhabitants
● Place of 25,000 to 50,000 inhabitants
○ SMSA central city of fewer than 25,000 inhabitants

State capital underlined
All political boundaries are as of January 1, 1980

SCALE
0 20 40 60 80 100 Kilometers
0 20 40 60 80 100 Miles

INSET: NEW YORK–NEWARK–JERSEY CITY (PART)

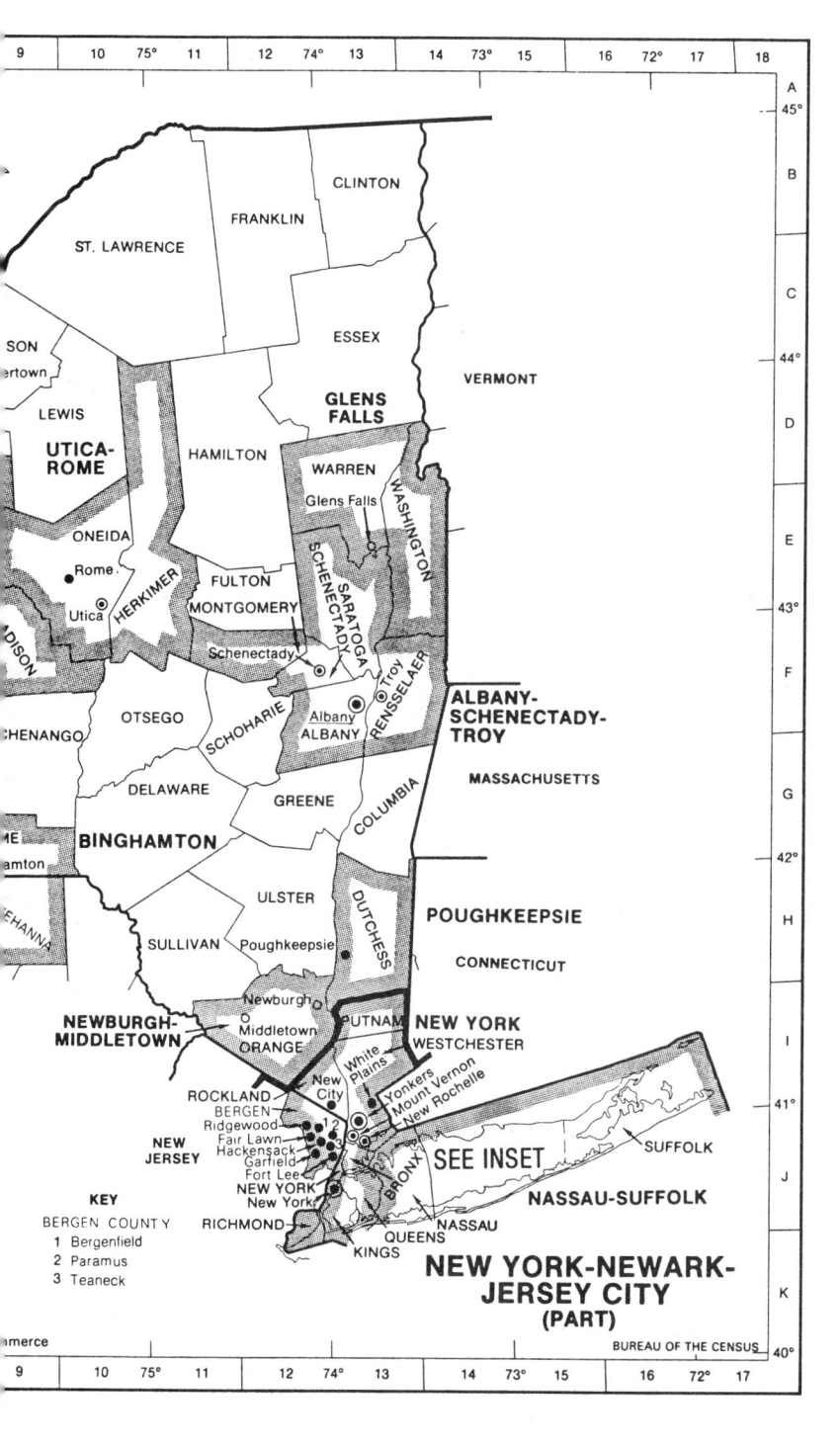

Map of New York State Regions

Counties and Metropolitan Areas shown:

- ST. LAWRENCE
- FRANKLIN
- CLINTON
- ESSEX
- LEWIS
- HAMILTON
- WARREN
- WASHINGTON
- ONEIDA
- HERKIMER
- FULTON
- MONTGOMERY
- SARATOGA
- SCHENECTADY
- RENSSELAER
- OTSEGO
- SCHOHARIE
- ALBANY
- DELAWARE
- GREENE
- COLUMBIA
- ULSTER
- DUTCHESS
- SULLIVAN
- ORANGE
- PUTNAM
- WESTCHESTER
- ROCKLAND
- BERGEN
- RICHMOND
- BRONX
- KINGS
- QUEENS
- NASSAU
- SUFFOLK

Metropolitan Areas:
- UTICA-ROME (Rome, Utica)
- GLENS FALLS (Glens Falls)
- ALBANY-SCHENECTADY-TROY (Schenectady, Troy, Albany)
- BINGHAMTON
- POUGHKEEPSIE (Poughkeepsie)
- NEWBURGH-MIDDLETOWN (Newburgh, Middletown)
- NEW YORK (White Plains, New City, Yonkers, Mount Vernon, New Rochelle, New York)
- NASSAU-SUFFOLK
- NEW YORK-NEWARK-JERSEY CITY (PART)

NEW JERSEY: Ridgewood, Fair Lawn, Hackensack, Garfield, Fort Lee

Adjacent states: VERMONT, MASSACHUSETTS, CONNECTICUT

KEY
BERGEN COUNTY
1 Bergenfield
2 Paramus
3 Teaneck

BUREAU OF THE CENSUS

GENERAL POPULATION CHARACTERISTICS

INTRODUCTION

NEW YORK
The Empire State

When Henry Hudson first saw the New York region, he probably never dreamed it would become the focal point for the world, a meeting place for people from every culture, every race. He was probably satisfied to see the first few Dutch Colonies prosper, and didn't expect the little villages along the river to become much more than outposts in a vast wilderness.

The face of New York has certainly changed since those quiet days of the Seventeenth Century. For a long time, New York was the richest and most populous state in the Union (now it is second only to the much larger state of California), and its strategic location has made it important for industry and for business, as well as transportation. Agriculture and tourism are equally important as white-collar business in this state of striking contrasts.

At last count (1980), 17,507,541 people filled the state's boundaries, with 7,035,348 of them residing in New York City. The rest live in Albany, in Buffalo, in Utica, and even in quaint places such as Tupper Lake and Canadice Corners. All of these people make up a political unit that is not easy to characterize. However, New Yorkers themselves have developed a few symbols by which the rest of us can understand them better.

State Symbols

THE NAME

When the New Netherlands was lost to the British in 1664, the King of England granted all of the formerly Dutch territory, to his brother, James, Duke of York. The province and the principle settlement were renamed New York; Beverwyck became Albany, for the region in England, and Wiltwyck, Kingston.

According to *The Story Key to Geographic Names,* "New York, (nu york) the state and the city, and also the city of York in Pennsylvania, were named after a county in England. It took a long while and many changes to simmer the word down to the short and snappy form it has now. To begin with it was *Eburacam,* a Celtic term related to *labar,* a word meaning muddy bottom. Eventually, this was changed to *Eboracum,* and then, in the Anglo-Saxon, [the name] became *Eoforwic,* which meant a 'wild boar town.' In changing the form the original meaning was forgotten." When the Danes came to England, they, finding Eorforwic clumsy to say, changed the form of the word to *Jorvik.* "From *Jorvik* to *York* was an easy change, and about as far as one could go in shortening the word."

Other accounts of the origin of the word *York* are as follows: "The old Romano-British name for York was *Eboracum.* The English, on getting hold of this name, made the *Eborac* into *Eoforwic,* which appeared to mean the *wic* or *town on the wildboar,* and from which our modern name is derived . . . Eoforwic, pronounced hurriedly, easily slides into 'York.' . . . The Archbishop of York still signs —'Ebor.' "

William Arthur, basing his information on Richard Verstegan's *A Restitution of Decayed Intelligence, in Antiquities,* derived the name of the state "from *Eure-ric* or *Eouerric,* of *Euere,* a wild boar, and *ryc,* a refuge; a retreat from the wild boars which were in the forest of Gautries. The Romans called the city *Eboracum;* it is memorable for the death of two emperors, Severus and Comstantius Chlorus, and for the nativity of Constantine the Great."

The *New English Dictionary* traces the word through the following forms: Old English Eorforwic, later Eferwic, Euerwic: Middle English, Everwik, also Yerk, . . . Latin Eboracum.

The name *New York* is composed of the prefix *New* and the name *York.* The present form of the word *new* evidently came from the Old English *niwe, niowe, neowe.* The common Aryan stem *new (j)* appears in the Greek form, *VEOS,* the Sanscrit form *navyas* or *navas,* and in the Latin form *novus,* meaning *not existing before, of recent origin or growth, young,* or *recent.*

Introduction

NICKNAME

New York is called the "Empire State" and the "Excelsior State". "Empire" is an allusion to its "commanding position" "vast wealth" and enterprise of its people. "Excelsior" commemorates the fact that the state motto is "Excelsior".

It might gratify the people of New York if they knew who first used that presumptive adjective, "Empire". It must have been a man with foresight, because in the early years of New York statehood, there was nothing imperial about the state. It was seventh in population, with New York City only two thirds the size of Philadelphia at the time, and struggling to rebuild the damage done during the British occupation. The other inhabitants were mostly isolated and rural. Clustered along the banks of the Hudson and on Long Island, there was none of the modern transportation and communication available with the rest of the new country. Up to the time of the war, Iroquois Indians held all of the northwest area of the state.

The Sullivan-Clinton campaign of 1779, which broke the Indian power, made it possible to penetrate the wilderness in peace, and in the last years of the eighteenth century settlers, chiefly from the thinner soil of New England, were wrestling with the primeval forest, planting corn and wheat between the stumps, setting up gristmills and log taverns, talking confidently of a great future. Washington, journeying thorough the new country with Governor George Clinton, hazarded a guess that New York might be the 'seat of empire'; but it was not until another generation had come to manhood and the first governor's nephew, DeWitt Clinton, had induced the state to build the Grand Canal from the Hudson to Lake Erie, giving the farmers of the new western counties an outlet for their produce, that the city on Manhattan Island was secure against the competition of Philadelphia and the state was certain of a commanding destiny.

New Yorkers are sometimes called "knickerbockers", alluding to the wide breeches worn by the early Dutch settlers of New York City. Today, a football team sporting knee-length pants are known as the "New York Knickerbockers" or "The Knicks". Washington Irving created the character Diedrich Knickerbocker in his *Knickerbocker History of New York,* and the term is German, not Dutch. *Knicker* means "a box" in German, and *bock* means "he-goat". Likewise, the nickname of "Yankees" comes from the New York City baseball team.

STATE FLAG

The arms of New York were approved by the state legislature on March 16, 1778, and are used on the state flag, approved in 1901, and described in the legislative manual as follows: Upon the center of an azure field is "a landscape, the sun in fess, rising in splendor, behind a range of three mountains, the middle on the highest". In the foreground is a lake, upon which is a "sloop under sail, passing and about to meet on a river, bordered below by a grassy shore fringed with shrubs".

Above this idyllic scene rises the crest of the arms, which is an American Eagle, with wings outspread, seemingly flying from a globe showing the north Atlantic Ocean "with outlines of its shores".

Standing on either side of this crest are two female figures. On the left is "Liberty proper, her hair disheveled and decorated with pearls, . . . a mantle descending from the shoulders behind to the feet, in the (left hand) a staff ensigned with a Phrygian cap, or the (right) arm embowed, the hand supporting the shield at the (left) chief point, a royal crown by her (right) foot dejected". To the right is "justice proper, her hair disheveled and decorated with pearls . . . mantled as Liberty, bound about the eyes with a fillet, in the (left) hand a straight sword hilted on, erect, resting on the (right) chief point of the shield, the (right) arms embowed, holding before her her scales proper".

Below this regal insignia is the state motto, *Excelsior,* in gold.

SEAL OF THE STATE

The secretary of state holds the Great Seal of the State at his office in Albany. Engraved in metal, "two and one-half inches in diameter," the seal takes the form of the coat of arms, approved by the legislature in 1778 (see "State Flag" section). In a circle surrounding the arms are the words, "The Great Seal of the State of New York".

The Great Seal has been modified five times since it was originally devised in 1778 by a Provincial Congress committee. In 1778, 1798, 1799, 1809, and 1882, attempts to find a "description in writing of the arms and the Great Seal recorded in the Secretary of State's office proved unsuccessful". In order to reestablish the original arms and to formalize it in the seal for public use, the State Legislature finally approved the present Great Seal in 1882.

All official statements and records are embossed with the state seal by the secretary of state.

STATE FLOWER

The rose is the official flower of the state in any color or combination of colors. On Arbor Day, 1891, schoolchildren of the state voted for the rose by a large majority. No particular variety of rose was specified when the vote was taken.

STATE BIRD

The bluebird *(Sialia Sialis)* is the official state bird. In 1928,

Mrs. C. Marshall of the New York Federated Women's Clubs led a campaign to adopt the bluebird as the state bird, and the public responded favorably. The bluebird is related to the robin and other American songbirds, of the genus *Sialia*. It has a blue back and reddish breast.

STATE TREE

The sugar maple (*Acer Saccharum M.*) is the official tree of New York. This stately, round-headed, gray-barked tree is fairly common in the state, and often attains heights of 120 feet. The wavy-grained wood of this tree makes fine furniture, and in upstate New York, the sap is tapped for maple syrup. The leaves of these trees turn to rich hues during the fall.

STATE SONG.

New York has no official state song.

CAPITOL BUILDING.

The Capitol Building is at Albany. Bounded by Eagle, State, and Swan Sts. and Washington Ave., is an imposing, massive granite building crowning the hill. The exterior suggests a giant French chateau, with pyramidal red tile corner roofs and long, connecting gray slate roofs, high dormers, chimneys, and balustrades, and monumental eastern staircase extending 166 feet from the building.

The New York State legislature has met in Albany since 1797. Work was started on the present building in 1867. When it was formally occupied by the legislature in 1879, it was not yet complete; and even in 1898 Governor Black was able to say only that the building was 'practically completed.' It covers three acres and cost about $25,000,000.

Because of the many years of building, 1867-1898, the influences of prevailing and passing styles of architecture, political personalities, and individual architects all found expression in the building, leaving it a mixture of styles and tastes. The exterior of the lower three floors is designed in the manner of the French Second Empire with Doric and Corinthian columns, arched windows, and rusticated stone work. The fourth floor is arched windows, and rusticated stone work. The fourth floor is Romanesque: the columns are stubby in comparison with those of the second floor, the windows have a noticeably lower arch, the stone carvings are of natural objects—birds, trees, and flowers. On the fifth floor the towers, cornices, and dormers suggest the style of Francis I, the windows lacking the arches of the lower floors. The pedestals and balustrades of the monumental front staircase and the many chimneys are French Renaissance; the chimneys are adorned with clustered columns, bases, and capitals.

The plan, exterior decorations, and general massing of the building were the work of Thomas W. Fuller. The tower which he included in the original design and partly built was eliminated because the soil and the foundations would not safely carry it. The original plans were modified and added to by Leopold Eidlitz and H. H. Richardson in the prevailing styles of their day. To Isaac G. Perry as state architect fell the duty of completing the designs of the other artchitects according to his own interpretation and subject to the needs of the state governmental departments. Eidlitz and Richardson were responsible for the executive chamber and the court of claims room; Eidlitz designed the assembly chamber and Richardson the senate chamber. The great western staircase and the main, eastern approach, with its corbels and arches, were designed by Richardson. Much of the exterior and interior stone carving and marble and wood paneling and carving was done by Perry.

The front staircase leads into the memorial rooms on the second floor, which contain Civil, Spanish-American, and World War mementos. The frescoes on the ceiling of the inner room depict military conflicts from the time of the Indian wars to World War I. The executive chambers are on this floor; the walls of the main room are wainscoted with mahogany and hung with portraits of Lafayette, Washington, and former governors of the state.

On the third floor are the senate and assembly chambers and the legislative library. The walls of the senate chamber are of Knoxville marble; the ceiling has massive carved oak beams. Two enormous fireplaces stand at one side of the room, with andirons more than four feet high. The walls of the assembly chamber are of sandstone, covered with sound-absorbing material; the ceiling is supported by four huge columns of Tennessee marble.

The building contains three notable staircases. The senate staircase in the southest corner is in the Gothic style; the assembly staircase in the northeast corner is of simpler Gothic; the famous western staircase, the most ornate, is constructed of brownstone and lighted by an immense glazed dome and many clusters of lights.

MOTTO

The motto used in almost every official symbol for New York State is *Excelsior,* a Latin word meaning "higher". It is comparable to the word *Excelses,* or "high and lofty". The first state legislature used this term to refer to the lofty mountains in New York State, Today, however, it connotes the general high quality of living in New York.

CHRONOLOGY OF NEW YORK STATE

20000 BC—Probable arrival of early man to North American continent. These early hunters were the ancestors of New York's prehistoric Indians. Ice sheets covering Lakes Ontario and Erie begin to recede.

8000 BC—Asiatic wanderers of widespread Algonquin stock arrive in New York area by way of Niagara Peninsula.

500 BC-900 AD—Owasco and other Woodland cultural tribes are prevalent in the region; these Indians were farmers, built burial mounds, and made various artifacts of native stones, metals and bone.

1300—(approx.) Algonquin Indians, original inhabitants of the New York region are conquered by the Iroquois, a more advanced, warlike tribe from regions farther west.

1497—Englishman Sebastian Cabot charts waters along the latitude and longitude of New York giving the English a thin claim to the land.

1524—Italian explorer Giovanni de Verranzo first spots the land that becomes New York City and is the first white to enter New York Bay.

1525—Explorer Gomez names Hudson River "San Antonio".

1570—Iroquois from the League of Five Nations which included the Mohawk, Oneida, Onondaga, Cayuga, and Seneca. Later they would all join the British in their fight with the French for control of North America.

1609—Frenchman Samuel de Champlain discovers Lake Champlain in present day New York coming south from Canada. Henry Hudson, aboard the *Halfmoon,* sails up the Hudson River believing it to be a passageway to the west. Though he didn't get to China, he supplied the Dutch with a claim to the New York region.

1611—Christiansen and Block sail from the Netherlands for the area near Manhattan.

1614—Netherland's ruling States General grants a trading charter in the new territory to a group of Dutch merchants, officially naming the area for the first time "New Netherland". Christiansen builds trading post named Fort Nassau near Albany at castle Island.

1615—Champlain investigates the New York region for a second time, again coming from Canada.

1620—Puritans aboard *Mayflower* denied right to settle in New Netherlands; they settle to the north at Plymouth.

1621—Control over New Netherlands for 24 years granted to the newly-chartered Dutch West India Company.

1623—New Netherlands declared a Dutch province and controlled by the West India Company out of Amsterdam.

1624—French Prostestant refugees called Waloons settle along with Dutch near Albany; Fort Orange constructed there.

1625—Manhattan Island's first white settlement established.

1626—First "Director General of New Netherlands" Peter Minuit purchases Manhattan Island for 60 Guilders (about $24) to legitimize the settlement; Fort Amsterdam Built. Later this area is known as "New Amsterdam."

1627—Friendly relations with the once outcast Puritans established.

1629—Patroon system begun with a Charter of Privileges to help spur settlement.

1630—First Patroon settlement begun by Kiliaen Van Rensselaer at Rensselaerswyck along Hudson River; Pavonia Patroonship created.

1632—Patroons and Dutch West India Company fight; English claim New Netherlands as theirs.

1640—English buy land in both Kings and Queens counties from Indians. Southold, and Southampton, Long Island settled.

1641—Director General Kieft calls for a council of people; first representative group of "Twelve Men" appointed.

1642—Kieft disbands "Twelve Men"; city tavern erected; first church at Fort New Amsterdam Constructed.

1643—Whites kill Indians, and Indians retaliate. Hempsted, Long Island settled by English from Stamford, Conn. New assembly of "Eight Men" called in New Amsterdam.

1644—New Haven and New Amsterdam join to fight Indians; Long Island Indians defeated and nearly wiped out.

1646—Yonkers settlement started; Jesuit Missionary Father Isaac Joques is killed by Mohawk Indians.

1647—Dutch and English boundaries agreed upon; Peter Stuyvesant replaces Kieft as new Director-General; New Assembly of "Nine Men" organized.

1652—Thomas Chambers settles Esopus (Kingston); Beverwyck (Albany) created by Stuyvesant.

1653—Burgher government granted at New Amsterdam (Manhattan) becoming first city government in United States.

1654—July 8, First Jewish colonist, Jacob Barsimon, comes from Holland; August 23, Jews also arrive in New York from Brazil. English plan to overthrow Dutch.

1661—Arent Van Curler settles Schenectady.

1664—Charles II grants New Netherlands to the Duke of York; Another popular assembly called; New Netherlanders surrender to the English under Colonel Richard Nicholls' demand.

1665—First English governor publishes the "Duke Laws" at Hempsted, Long Island; Governor and Council given power of taxation.

1670—New York Exchange established.

1673—New York is taken by Dutch fleet; First American postal service begun.
1674—England, by the "Treaty of Westminster" gains New Netherlands for good; Governor Andros appointed.
1679—Slavery of Indians abolished; Explorer, La Salle, builds Fort Niagara.
1683—Fort James hosts first assembly of elected representatives which approve Charter of Liberties; Thomas Dongan becomes new governor; Original twelve counties formed.
1684—The Iroquois Five Nations acknowledge the King of England.
1686—July 22, city charters granted to both New York and Albany by English governor Dongan; Peter Schuyler becomes first mayor; New England and New York join to become the Dominion of New England.
1688—French Huguenots settle New Rochelle.
1689—Discontented New Yorkers break union with English governors as Jacob Leisler seizes power with strong support from the common people.
1690—New York City site of first Colonial Congress; French and Indians massacre Schenectady settlers.
1691—English and Dutch defeat the French at La Priare, Canada; Liberal laws adopted after the call of the popular assembly; English government returns to New York.
1693—Episcopal church gains a foot hold in the colony; First printing press in colony.
1696—Trinity Church founded in New York.
1709—1712
Palatines move into the Schohaire and Hudson Valleys.
1713—British control over the Iroquois recognized by the French Treaty of Utrecht; 30 years of relative peace follow.
1731—Fort at Crown Point built by French; Connecticut-New

Chronology

York boundary dispute ended.
- **1732**—New York City opens low-cost public schools.
- **1745**—French and Indians destroy English settlement of Saratoga.
- **1748**—Albany becomes meeting place of Great Indian Council.
- **1752**—First home erected in Troy.
- **1754**—French and Indian war begins with clash at Great Meadows. Colonial union plan approved at the Albany Congress from a plan submitted by Benjamin Franklin; King's College (later Columbia University) founded.
- **1755**—Colonial governors meet in New York concerning war; Fort Edward constructed; Battle of Lake George successful.
- **1756**—Forts Ontario and Oswego taken by French.
- **1757**—British lose Fort William Henry and Indians raid rural settlements.
- **1758**—Englishman, Abercrombie, defeated at Ticonderoga; Black slave children freed; Fort Niagara rebuilt by French.
- **1759**—New York expells French as all posts are recaptured, including newly-built Niagara.
- **1760**—British take Quebec from French.
- **1763**—French and English sign peace treaty at Paris.
- **1764**—New York joins action against taxation without approval of the taxed in the colonies.
- **1765**—Stamp act passed; "Sons of Liberty" founded. New York site of Stamp Act Congress.
- **1766**—Stamp act repealed; Right of assembly denied by Parliament.
- **1768**—Colonists boycott English goods as a protest to the severe taxation on tea, glass, and paper.
- **1770**—Duties were repealed except on tea; "The Committee of One Hundred" meets; Battle of Golden Hill.
- **1771**—Tryon becomes new governor and last Royal overlord.
- **1773**—Saratoga settled.

1774—May 23, Paul Revere, sent by "The Committee of 51," goes to Boston with letter proposing a Congress of colonies; Kingston becomes sight of first academy in state.

1775—New York sends delegates to Second Continental Congress; First Provincial Congress becomes temporary state government; May 10, Fort Ticonderoga captured by Benedict Arnold and Ethan Allen; May 12, Crown Point wrested from the British by Seth Warner; July 6, Congress of New York declares necessity of war, November 13, Montreal capture by Montgomery but overall Canadian expedition fails.

1776—January 20, John Johnson forced to disarm and give his parole to General Peter Schuyler, head of the New York Department. July 4, first signature placed on Declaration of Independence. July 9, Declaration read to troops and then ratified by Provincial Congress at White Plains. August 26-29 Battle of Long Island; September 15, British take New York City; October 11, Naval battle occurs for Valcour Island, Lake Champlain, and Nathan Hale is executed; October 28, battle of White Plains.

1777—April 20, first state constitution adopted; State government established; July 27, murder of Jane McCrea; July 30, George Clinton becomes first state governor; August 6, battle of Oriskany; August 16, Battle of Bennington; August 19, General Gates takes command from Peter Schuyler; September 19, first battle of Saratoga; October 16, Kingston destroyed; Burgoyne surrenders on October 17.

1778—February 6, Articles of Confederation approved; November 11, Cherry Valley massacre results from Indian and Tory raids; Elmira settlement begun.

1779—July 16, Stony Point captured by General Wayne (later recaptured) August 29, Battle of Newton, where Indians and Tories were defeated by Generals John Sullivan and James Clinton; October 22, Loyalists lose property.

1780—Mohawk and Schohairie Valleys subjected to Indian and Tory raids; Benedict Arnold discovered to have com-

Chronology 15

mited treason; Andre executed after his capture at Tarrytown.

1781—October 25, battle of Johnstown last battle of revolution fought on New York soil; General Washington gathers new troops from New York on the way to Yorktown.

1782—New York gives up western lands to Congress and then confirms west boundary; American Army spends winter at Newburgh.

1783—Washington offered Crown at Newburgh by military group but says no; Naturalization law enacted; Treaty of Paris signed.

1784—New York City meeting place of the State Legislature and new home of the Continental Congress; May 1, legislature approves measure creating University of New York.

1786—Dominick Lynch established Lynchville (Rome).

1787—Constitution of United States formed; Tories regain rights and property; October 27, *The Federalist* first appears.

1788—Constitution ratified by 30 to 27 vote in Poughkeepsie on July 26; Massachusetts' leaders allow Phelps and Gorham to purchase two million acres in western New York; Representatives to the federal government elected.

1789—April 30, George Washington is inaugurated in New York City; Legislature set aside lands for public education.

1790—Congress moves to Philadelphia; New York relinquishes all claims to Vermont. State population: 340,120

1791—Saratoga and Rensselaer Counties formed from parts of Albany County; Holland Land Company makes purchase; Assembly and senatorial districts formed.

1792—Canals and locks to Lake Ontario and Seneca Lake contract awarded to the Western Inland Lock Navigation Company.

1793—Citizen Genet in New York.

1795—$50,000. annual fund to maintain schools for five years approved by legislature; Union College chartered; John

Jay becomes governor.

1796—American flag flown over Fort Ontario, Oswego, Fort Niagara; Oneida Lake sees first canal boats; Fitch's steamboat tried at New York.

1797—Albany made state capital; Legislature meets at Stadt Huis, Albany.

1798—Charter given to new company to build a canal from Lake Ontario to Lake Erie; July 31, state government settles in as public records are brought to Albany.

1799—Slaves are granted a slow emancipation in state by legislature; Incorporation of the Cherry Valley Turnpike.

1800—Population: 589,051.

1801—State organizes public school system; New State Constitutional Convention meets.

1802—West Point Military Academy opens.

1804—Aaron Burr and Alexander Hamilton duel, Hamilton dies; Former governor, George Clinton becomes vice-president of the United States.

1806—Original state capital building construction begins.

1807—"Clermont", Robert Fulton's steam ship goes up the Hudson, New York City to Albany in 32 hours.

1808—Importation of slaves prohibited; Clinton re-elected vice-president.

1809—Schenectady County formed from another part of Albany County.

1810—Population: 959,049.

1811—Erie Canal approved.

1812—War begins with English; New York is center of military operations; Battle is fought on Lake Erie; Hamilton College chartered.

1813—Ogdensburg is raided and taken by British; British repulsed at the battle of Plattsburg; Black Rock and Buffalo razed; Gideon Hawley becomes state superintendent of public schools.

1814—British move into northern New York, take Fort Ontario

Chronology

at Oswego; Fort Erie destroyed to avoid British capture; War nears end on Niagara frontier; Battle of Lake Champlain.

1815—Peace Treaty approved.

1816—Elkanah Watson in Cooperstown, Ostego County organizes first state fair; DeWitt Clinton organizes first state nominating convention.

1817—Proclamation prohibiting slavery in state after July 4, 1827; Construction begins at Rome on Erie Canal; Champlain canal begun.

1818—State library started at capitol; Schools number over 5,000 with over 200,000 pupils according to Superintendent Hawley.

1819—Erie Canal opens between Utica and Rome; Empire State first used to mean New York; Baptist Education Society given charter which results in forming Colgate University.

1820—Population: 1,372,812.

1821—New Constitutional Convention recognizes all white male sufferage.

1822—New York accepts second state constitution.

1823—Judicial system reorganized; Champlain Canal completed; Mormon church founder Joseph Smith has his vision revealing golden plates of the Book of Mormon in Palmyra, New York; First estimates of poor in state made.

1825—Geneva (Hobart) College receives charter; Erie Canal finished.

1826—New York House of Refuge becomes first juvenile correction center in country; Mohawk and Hudson River Railroad formed.

1827—Slaves freed within state.

1829—Working Man's Party founded by Fanny Wright.

1830—Mormon Church begins in Fayette; Seneca County and Book of Mormon first published; Population: 1,918,608.

1831—Mohawk and Hudson Railroad runs between Albany and

Schenectady; Debtor's prison abolished; Electromagnet developed by Joseph Henry of Albany.

1832—Martin Van Buren of Kinderhook becomes Vice-President of country; Buffalo and Utica get city charters.

1833—Antislavery convention held at Utica; Canal construction intensifies.

1834—Antislavery Society of New York founded; Rochester gets city charter.

1836—Van Buren elected Preseident of the country.

1839—Renters rebel and riot.

1840—Governor Seward grants asylum to black slave fugitives from southern states. Population: 2,428,921.

1841—American Express Company founded in Albany; Erie Railroad runs to Goshen.

1844—American Party formed ("Know-Nothings"); Long Island Railroad begins service.

1845—Small schools joined; Antirenters fight open war.

1846—Mexican War begins; Third state constitution adopted; University of Buffalo founded.

1847—John Humphry Noyes starts Oneida Community; Syracuse gets city charter.

1848—Seneca Falls hosts first Women's Rights Convention; Slavery extension condemned; Millard Fillmore elected to Vice-presidency; Niagara Falls Village recognized; Oswego and Auburn get city charters.

1849—Hudson Railroad opens to Poughkeepsie.

1850—President Taylor dies and Millard Fillmore replaces him: Population: 3,097,394. University of Rochester opens.

1851—Erie Railroad begins service.

1853—New York Central Railroad formed.

1854—Young Men's Christian Association (YMCA) has first meeting in Buffalo; Public Instruction made a separate department within state with superintendent as head.

1855—Suspension Bridge over Niagara Falls completed; Elmira

Chronology 19

College founded.

1856—Genesee Valley Canal from Rochester to Olean opens.

1857—Financial panic: Temperance law passed.

1858—London sends New York first cablegram.

1859—Blacks denied right of sufferage.

1860—Population: 3,880,735; South Carolina leaves union. Lincoln becomes President.

1861—Meeting for conciliation, concession, and compromise on slavery held in Tweddle Hall, Albany; Three million dollars given by legislature to uphold union; Vassar College founded; Governor Morgan asks for 25,000 troops.

1862—Ericsson's *Monitor,* the first ironclad ship, launched at Rowland's Shipyard, Greenpoint, Long Island; 120 regiments sent to war; $3.5 million paid in bounties.

1863—Anti-draft riots in New York City and Troy.

1864—State war tax implemented; Conspiracy to burn New York City found; Confederate prison at Elmira established.

1865—Cornell University founded.

1866—Public schools made free; State Constitutional Convention called.

1867—State Assembly on Women's Sufferage addressed by Elizabeth Cady Stanton.

1869—U.S. Senate hears presentation for women's sufferage as given by Stanton and Susan B. Anthony.

1870—Population: 4,382,759.

1871—Construction of new state capitol begins: Tweed Ring discovered; Syracuse University opens.

1872—Kingston chartered as a city.

1873—Financial panic caused banks to close.

1874—Women's Whiskey War; Compulsory education laws set up; S. J. Tilden elected governor.

1876—Centennial of country celebrated in New York; Samuel Tilden loses presidential election in a close race.

1878—New York City builds elevated railroads.

1879—New capitol at Albany opens.
1880—State government establishes Board of Health; Population: 5,082,871.
1883—Railroad bridge over Niagara Falls opens; Civil Service Commission created; Brooklyn Bridge opens.
1884—Buffalo's Grover Cleveland becomes President; Public park at Niagara Falls opened; New York and West Shore Railroad opens.
1886—Workers strike in state for eight-hour work day; Women permitted to join state bar; Statue of Liberty assembled in New York Harbor.
1890—Population: 6,003,174.
1892—Grover Cleveland elected to second non-consecutive term as President.
1893—Engine No. 999 of the New York Central sets world speed record of one mile in 32 seconds between Buffalo and Batavia.
1897—Greater New York receives charter: Van Wyck becomes Mayor of the Greater New York City area.
1898—Primary election law passed; War with Spain over Mexico begins.
1899—James A. Roberts becomes President of the newly formed State Historical Society.
1900—New York City begins to develop rapid transit; New Yorker Theodore Roosevelt elected to the Vice-presidency.
1901—President McKinley shot and killed in Buffalo at Pan-American Exposition making Roosevelt New York's fifth president: Pan-American Exposition; United State's first dental clinic opened in Rochester.
1903—Erie converted into barge canal with $101,000,000 appropriation.
1904—Roosevelt reelected to presidency.
1906—Nobel Peace Prize awarded to Roosevelt.
1907—Public Service Commission granted.
1908—Curtiss' airplane *Red Wing* makes trial trip; Curtiss later wins prize for flying in *June Bug* at Hammondsport, New York; Race track betting becomes illegal.

Chronology 21

1910—Curtiss flies to New York from Albany in 2 hours and 32 minutes breaking existing records; Population: 9,113,614.

1911—State capitol suffers from fire; Direct Primary Election passed.

1912—Progressive Party flourished under Roosevelt.

1913—Governor William Sulzer impeached.

1915—Plattsburg houses Citizens Military Training Camp.

1916—Plattsburg schools make physical and military training mandatory; Governor makes 18-45 years olds eligible for draft.

1917—U.S. enters World War I; 518,864 men for military and navy sign up for war; Casualties later add up to above 40,000, including 14,000 dead.

1918—State Barge Canal opens; World War I ends November 11.

1919—Prohibition amendment passed; Flying of red flags denoting communism made illegal; Commercial hydroplane makes first successful run; Ida B. Sammis of Suffold and Mary M. Lilly of Manhattan become first elected women to the New York Assembly.

1920—Five socialists are kicked out of the assembly; Soldier's bonus' adopted; Franklin D. Roosevelt runs for vice-president; Granite shaft at Antietam Battlefield dedicated to New York dead; Population: 10,385,227.

1921—Public school teachers face dismissal if found to be communist; Motion picture censorship in state begins.

1922—Children's Courts established; $20 million set aside for highways.

1923—March 3, Mullen-Gage Prohibition Law repealed.

1924—Adirondacks and Catskills have 15,000 acres burned; Alfred Smith wins third term as governor; Bear Mountain Bridge opens.

1925—With a cost of over $16,000,000 Bronx Parkway opens.

1926—State reorganization program approved for implementation following year; Short ballot used in election that gives Governor Smith fourth term in office.

1927—Sounds of Niagara Falls is played over the radio; September 12 marks New York's 150-year celebration at Kingston; Lindbergh leaves New York for transatlantic flight to Paris, France; Peach Bridge opens.

1928—Franklin D. Roosevelt becomes governor.

1929—$450 million dollar power system links major cities in state; Stock market collapses on Wall Street.

1930—Schnectady theatre site of first television feature by Dr. Alexanderson of the General Electric Company; The play *La Boheme* is presented by the Metropolitan Opera Company in Westchester County Civic Center at White Plains, first one outside of New York City; Old Age Security Act passes; Roosevelt re-elected governor; Population 12,588,066.

1931—"One Million Cubic Feet of Rock" falls at Niagara Falls; Police in 46 areas set up linking teletype alarm system; New York Temporary Relief Administration established.

1932—Winter Olympic Games held at Lake Placid; Franklin Roosevelt elected to presidency; Herbert Lehman becomes governor.

1933—March 31, 21st amendment ratified in state repealing 18th; Farmers dump milk in four counties in protest to price controls.

1934—State starts racing commission; State teachers forced to take oath of allegiance to constitution; Rock from Horseshoe Falls turmoils into Niagara; Dr. George Whipple of Rochester receives Nobel Prize in medicine; Lehman re-elected governor.

1935—Finger Lakes area devastated by floods; Legislature approves unemployment law.

1936—65 years set as age to receive pensions as Old Age Pension Bill is enacted; New state board of Welfare appointed; Roosevelt and Lehman re-elected each to their respective offices.

1937—Women allowed to serve in juries; Representation

Chronology 23

method used in election of New York City Council.

1938--State holds Constitutional Convention, ratifying new measures; Eastern New York suffers from hurricane; Lehman elected to unprecedented fourth term as governor in state.

1939—April 30, New York World Fair opens; President Roosevelt entertains King and Queen of England at Hyde Park.

1940—Peace time draft begins; Para-mutual betting starts at race tracks; Population: 13,379,662.

1941—United States enters second global conflict and New York sends.

1942—Thomas Dewey elected governor of state.

1945—War ends and New York City becomes home of The United Nations.

1949—Alger Hiss tried in New York City for allegedly supplying Soviets with secret documents and 11 heads of the Communist Party are convicted of treason in plotting to overthrow the government of the United States through violence.

1951—Julius and Ethel Rosenberg convicted and executed as Soviet spies at Sing Sing Prison, Ossing, N.Y.

1954—Averill Harriman elected Governor.

1955—College of the City of New York graduate Jonas Salk develops successful anti-polio vaccine.

1958—Nelson Rockefeller elected governor.

1959—St. Lawrence Seaway opens ports on Erie and Ontario Lakes to ocean ships, increasing shipping capabilities from the midwest to New York.

1960—Population: 16,782,304

1961—Hydroelectric power plant opens at Niagara Falls.

1964—Verranzo-Narrows, world's longest single span bridge opens; Large race riots occur in Harlem; Worlds Fair returns to New York.

1965—South Mall project begun in Albany to house new

government offices.

1966—Transit workers strike in New York City stopping buses and subways; New districts are outlined for representation in state assembly.

1967—Lottery established to help pay for public education; Ninth Constitutional Convention held, most new measures do not pass.

1968—Sanitation workers strike for nine days, letting trash pile up in New York City.

1969—Woodstock Music and Art Fair held in upstate New York as over 300,000 attend, climaxing the "hippie" movement.

1970—State of New York loses position as most populous state to California, along with two seats in the House of Representatives; Population: 18,236,967.

1917—Police strike in New York City; Assembly districts redrawn.

1972—Tropical storm causes 27 deaths and $750 million in property damage.

1973—Malcomb Wilson becomes governor replacing Rockefeller.

1975—Hugh Carey elected governor; New York City defaults on bonds and loans, faces financial crisis but is bailed out by State Legislature; The city council then approves new charter by referendum that goes into effect in 1977.

1976—United States celebrates Bicentennial with spectacular shipping display in New York Harbor.

1980—Winter Olympic Games held at Lake Placid; Democratic National Convention held in New York City. Population: 17,507,541 (decreased from 1970).

1981—Governor Carey calls two special sessions of the legislature to complete the 1982 budget. One month into fiscal 1982, the legislature approves the budget, agreeing to provide Medicaid funds for abortions and other services.

* * *

DISTRIBUTION OF HISTORICAL NEW YORK STATE INDIAN TRIBES[*]

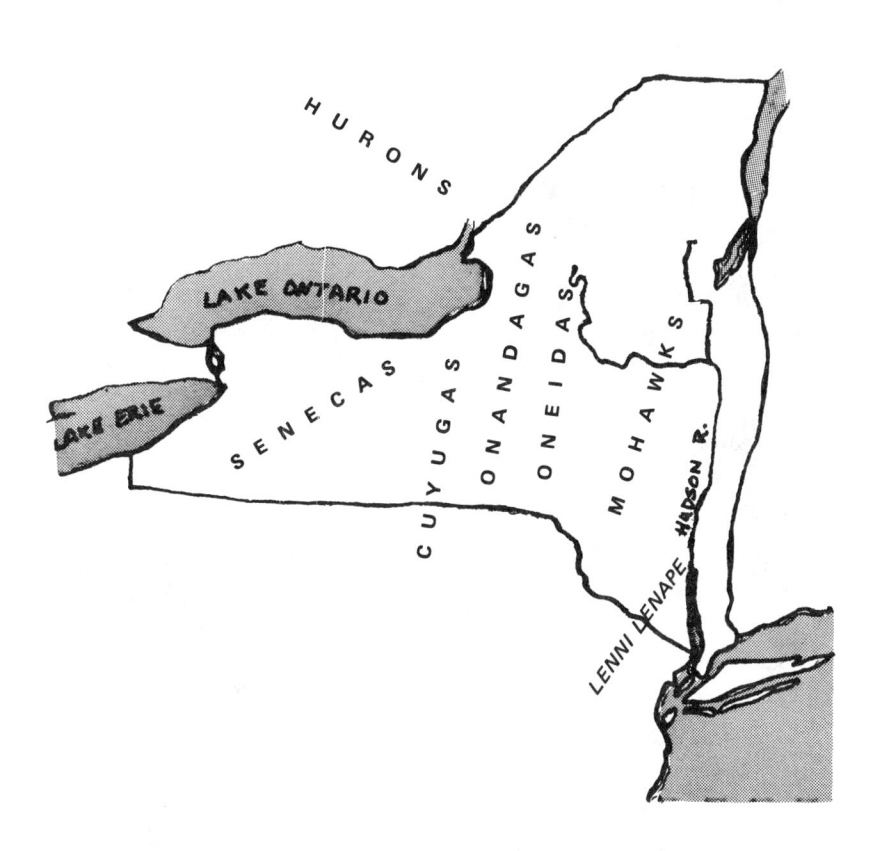

*After Smithsonian Institution Handbook of American Indians.

KESKETOMA
-Chief of the Onondagas-

PREHISTORY AND ARCHAEOLOGY

Thousands of years before the first Europeans settled in New York, the Indians found the region to be almost a paradise on Earth. The dense woods were full of wild game, the soil produced all sorts of edible plants, and the many lakes, rivers and streams were teeming with fish. An ancient Indian legend had it that the land was graced by the Great Spirit as evidenced by his hand print on the Finger Lakes.

EARLY AMERICAN CULTURES

The first persons to take advantage of this abundance were presumably the romote descendents of the Asiatic-Mongoloid wanders who migrated to America across the Bering Strait, and eventually made their way south and east. These people, known as the "Paleo-Indian Hunters" or the "Archaics" are characterized by the tools they used, especially the chipped-stone arrowheads which were long and narrow with a straight stem or faint side notches. No traces of pottery exist, and the absence of certain implements suggests that these people were nomadic hunters rather than settled farmers. This is also proven by the fact that their surface distribution is wide and scattered. No skeletons of these people have been found so the physical appearance of them is not known; but Carbon 14 dating has placed the time setting, which was from about 8000 B.C. until 1000 B.C.

Although the earliest Paleo-Indians traveled in small family groups, eventually some of them began to form larger, more territorial tribes, and encampments became more permanent. From about 4500 B.C. on, the former nomadic hunt of Northeast American Indians began to use new tools, such as choppers, beveled adzes, and stone grinding implements. This indicates a more advanced hunter-gatherer system of life. After 1300 B.C refined stone, and later, crude clay pots were first used by the early Americans. Archaeologists generally believe that people from the west brought this richer culture. Polished stone implements are more numerous in this period; crude pottery and a greater variety of bone and antler tools suggest more stable settlement, leisure, and the progress of invention. The "Vine Valley Occupation", as this period is known, was widespread along the Middle Atlantic region. After 1000 B.C. ceramics, agriculture and village life developed. The period which extends into historic times is generally regarded as the "Woodland" stage. One of the most distinguishing characteristics of this period remains in the form of pottery, which became more and more refined. The early and middle Woodland eras are known as the Owasco occupation in New York. This culture was rooted in the soil and enjoyed a high degree of cultural attainment, as indicated by the superior temper, design, and ornamentation of pottery, clay smoking pipes, triangular arrowheads, and the domestication of corn and beans. They lived in small dome-shaped houses, traded shellfish, and developed new ways to cultivate plants for food.

A well-developed ceremonial burial system is another evidence for the Woodland period. An early Woodland phase culture was discovered after an excavation of such a burial site in Monroe County, New York, and was named the "Meadowood Phase", for the estate on which it was discovered. Other sites discovered in north, central and western New York indicates that this culture clustered 35 to 40 graves in a small area, with goods such as fish nets, basketry, shells, birdstones, pipes, and stone implements accompanying the dead. A few burial mounds such as those found in abundance in the Ohio river valleys have also been found in eastern New York. These mounds contain copper articles, ornaments, pottery, fine pipes, and woven cloth. Towards the end of the Woodland phase, the ceremonial aspects of burials tapered off, and grave goods became rare.

HISTORIC INDIANS: BEGINNINGS OF THE POWER TRIBES

After the first white people came to America, the native American culture remained almost intact for a number of years. The Lenni-Lenape, or Delaware Indians greeted the first Europeans in New York, who found them banded in confederacies, tilling the soil, smoking tobacco, and inscribing rocks to denote tribal boundaries. The Lenni-Lenape dominated the southeastern part of what is now New York State. Not long

Prehistory and Archaeology 27

before the coming of the white man, the irresistable infiltration of the Iroquois had begun in the southwest, south and north. The far-spreading system of interconnected waterways made the New York regions a strategic stronghold that would endow with abundance and authority any Indian group able to win it and hold it. Although the Algonquin Lenni-Lenape were equal to the Iroquois in bravery, intelligence, and physical prowess, they lacked the Iroquois genious for political organization and their zeal for protracted warfare.

The northern group of the Five Nations, who called themselves the 'Men of Men,' in the first half of the sixteenth century cut their affiliations with the Huron-Iroquois groups of Canada, slashed their way through the vigorous but futile resistance of the Algonquins, and settled along the Mohawk River; those who came from the south and west settled in the foothills south of Lake Ontario. The conflict lasted well into the early days of white settlement; the Battle of Kinguariones was fought in 1669, though a decade or two before that the mighty Iroquois had become the virtual masters of what is now New York State and had either absorbed the Algonquins or driven them out.

One source of Iroquois power was their confederation. Late in the sixteenth century, Dekanawidah, probably of Huron blood, recognized the urgent need for peaceful unity and devised a code of laws that would bring all men together as friends and brothers. Although his dream of eternal peace was soundly ridiculed by the warriors, Dekanawidah enlisted the aid of Hayonhwatha, a Mohawk by birth, and together they launched a campaign for Iroquois solidarity which they zealously promoted for five years. Hiawatha, who began his reforms among the Onondaga, combined political strategy with eloquent oratory and finally won over Adodarhoh, powerful Onondaga opponent of the plan, by offering this fiercest of warriors the position of moderator in the league council. Legend has it that this form of flattery 'combed the snakes from the head of Adodarhoh.'

The five tribes of the Iroquois Confederacy are now known as the *Seneca, Cayuga, Onondaga, Oneida,* and *Mohawk*. These names are descendents of the appelations applied to the tribes by themselves, other Indians, the French, the Dutch, the English, and Americans over several hundred years. Each tribe has a name for itself meaning the "people of" a particular town or place. The Seneca are *Onondewagaono,* the Cayuga are *Gayokwehono,* the Onondaga are *Onontaga,* the Oneida are *Oneyotdehaga,* and the Mohawk are *Kanyengehaga.*

At the time of European contact the Seneca, Cayuga, Onondaga, Oneida, and Mohawk lived in that order from west to east in the region between the Genesee River and Schoharie Creek. Their hunters, traders, and warriors ranged from the Mississippi River to New England.

America's First Democracy

About the year 1570 the tribes were welded into the Five Nations Confederacy; and the first great council fire blazed high on what are now called the Pompey hills.

Although the founders of the league likened their new government to 'a long house where families dwell together in harmony,' the confederacy was not established without considerable jealousy; fear of supersedence and demands for special concessions were problems that had to be ironed out with a high degree of diplomacy. But the desire to control the fur supply of their neighbors to the north and west and thereby monopolize the trade in European goods finally brought about a real union; the primacy in matters of state went to the Mohawk, the Onondaga were granted custody of the permanent council fire, and the Seneca were given two war captains. These three nations together constituted the 'elder brothers'; across the fire sat the Oneida and Cayuga, 'younger brothers' of the larger nations.

The league's constitution, as it developed, consolidated a civic and social system built on the old pattern of tribal society and embracing ideas of universal peace and brotherhood, set up a policy of fraternal expansion, and provided for the appointment of the peace chiefs by the women—in effect, gave the women the right to vote.

The 'Men of Men' did not call their women squaws; to them women were 'our mothers.' Although the Iroquois woman was practically the domestic slave of her arrogant spouse, she exercised a large influence in government, shared in religious rites and festivals, arranged marriages, and authorized divorce.

All tribes recognized the descent of name and property through the female line.

The Great Law, which was transmitted orally from one generation to another, proved to be a governmental system well suited to the stage of culture for which it was designed. A federal council was established and each of the Five Nations was represented by delegates, or federal chiefs. Organization of the tribe began in the matrilineal family unit, called the *owachira,* of which the eldest woman was the nominal head; and two or more *owachiras,* believed to be related, made up a clan, which functioned within the tribe to ensure economic security and political representation for its members. Members of the clan shared certain property. The women of the clan elected its chiefs and subchiefs, who represented the clan in tribal councils. Privileges of membership included a common burial ground, the right to given childbearing women of the *owachiras* the power to elect and impeach chiefs, the right to clan personal names, help in securing a mate, and protection through 'blood revenge.'

Everyday Life of the Historic Tribes

The Five Nations spoke Northern Iroquoian languages. Each tribe's speech is sufficiently distinct to call it a separate language, but there is also enough mutual intelligibility between them that they could be called dialects of a single language. The Iroquois made pictographs, but they did not develop a written alphabet.

The Iroquois believe that the world had many supernatural spirits whose good will was needed for a bountiful life. Therefore, everyday activities were closely interwoven with religious beliefs.

The Iroquois year began in the spring. A festival was held to express gratitude to "The Creator" and "The Maple" for the sweet syrup made from sap. Spawning fish and roosting pigeons were caught. During this season clearings were made in the forests to replace old fields and also for new palisaded villages. Villages had to be moved every 10 to 20 years as firewood supplies and fields became exhausted. By May "The Three Sisters," maize, beans, and squash, were planted and a festival was held. These foods were the main sustenance of the people. Elm bark for longhouses, canoes, and containers was then gathered. Wild strawberries appeared in the woods, and a festival was held in thanks for these first fruits.

In the summer most men departed to go trading or on the warpath. Women gathered wild plants for food and medicine, worked in the fields, and harvested and stored the crops. Festivals were held to honor "The Corn Mother" and to celebrate the harvest.

In the fall deer were hunted, nuts were gathered, and fish were caught to help sustain them through the coming winter. Councils were held during this time as snow confined them to their villages for the most part. Winter was a time for socializing, storytelling, and the manufacture and repair of tools and clothing. Raw materials including stone, clay, plant fibers, and animal products were made into knives, axes, drills, bows and arrows, clubs, jars, bowls, mortars, mats, baskets, fish-hooks, needles, snowshoes, lacross sticks, dolls, and many other items.

The New Year came after winter solstice, and Midwinter, the most important festival, was held to strengthen "The Creator"

Polygamy, practiced by the Algonquin and Huron, was not encouraged by the Iroquois, although it infrequently occurred. Marriage was arranged by the mothers. The girl signified her mother's choice of a husband by placing a basket of bread at the door of the youth's home. If the lad and his mother agreed on the advisibility of the matrimonial venture, they sent back a basket of food as a token of acceptance; but if the match was not acceptable, the girl's gift was returned untouched. If both sets of parents gave their consent, the simple ceremony, consisting chiefly of a lecture on the duties of social life, was performed by the clan matrons, through the chiefs or some orator as their surrogate. A pair of impetuous lovers might ignore formal routine and stage an elopement, in which case one night away from home validated the marriage. Divorce was relatively simple, sufficient grounds being infidelity or failure to provide.

The birth of a child, male or female, was a welcome event, but female offspring were more highly valued. Most villages maintained small lodges to which women retired for childbirth; and the newborn babes were cared for in these crude maternity homes until they were ready to be shown to the family.

Comparative lack of sanitary precautions, dietary deficiencies, and the rigorous climate resulted in an extremely high rate of infant mortality.

Although the Iroquois moved their habitations every 10 or 12 years, they built their villages strong for shelter and military protection. Trees were felled, peeled, and converted into pole frameworks. Elm bark was pressed flat into sheets, laid horizontally over the frames, and tied down with cords. They built homes ranging from individual bark cabins to log communal houses 200 feet long; erected stout stockades 16 to 30 feet high, with platforms on the inside wall for fighters, weapons, and water; and dug deep moats outside the barricades.

Two Dutch travelers, Jaspar Dankers and Peter Sluyter, visited a "plantation" on Long Island in 1679 and 1680. An old woman led them to a house described as follows:

"We found the whole troop together, consisting of seven to eight families...Their house was low and long, about 60 feet long and 14 or 15 feet wide. The bottom was earth, the sides and roof were made of reed and the bark of chestnut trees; the posts, or columns, were limbs of trees stuck in the ground, and all fastened together ... On the sides or walls of the house, the roof was so low that you could hardly stand under it. In the whole building there was no line stone, iron or lead. They build their fire in the middle of the floor, according to the number of families which live in it, so that from one end to the other each of them boils its own pot, and eats when it likes, not only the families by themselves, but each Indian alone... At all hours, morning, noon, and night. They lie upon mats with their feet towards the fire, on each side of it. They do not sit much upon anything raised up, but, for the most part, sit on the ground or squat on their ankles..."

Agriculture was the chief basis of Iroquois stability. Each village had its fields and, in the 1700s, its orchards; the men cleared the land, the women planted and cultivated the fields. Corn (maize), which had been developed by deliberate breeding and was the Indians' particular grain, was planted in rows, so many kernels to the hill; and the intervals between the hills were measured by the 'long step.' These early New York farmers raised tobacco, beans, jerusalem artichokes, and squash. Exhausting the soil and the supply of firewood in a dozen years, they moved the village to a new site.

Commerce in pre-Colonial days consisted principally of direct exchange of commodities among families and tribes. The measurements used included finger width, plam breadth, finger span, and the integral fathom, just as is the case, less directly, in England and the United States today, as indicated by the term 'foot.' Wampum, arrowheads, and beaver skins were the media of exchange.

Indian warfare, before the coming of the white man, was carried on with crude weapons: bow and arrow, tomahawk, and war club were the primary equipment for offense, and round shields and slat armor for defense. War expeditions rarely numbered 100 men and only on rare occasions did the Indians assemble a force that could be considered of army proportions. Their technique called for concealment, surprise—the swift swoop from ambush. Scalping, an aboriginal custom of the Iroquois which they probably introduced to the Northeast, was encouraged by both the French and English, who offered bounties for the dripping topknots of their enemies—white or Indian. With this stimulus the practice spread rapidly and became characteristic of Indian warfare. Cannibalism was a common practice among the Huron-Iroquois, and the New York Iroquois indulged in the practice at times, under the belief that a great warrior's heart if eaten would provide increased valor and strength.

Christianity was first brought to the Indian by the Franciscan Order of Recollects in 1615 and later by the courageous Jesuits. The missionaries suffered every hardship; blamed for epidemics, crop failures, and grasshopper plagues, they were frequently subjected to extreme torture and killed. The Jesuit Relations abound with such tales.

The white man's religion was all but incomprehensible to the red man. Intimate observations of nature formed the whole fabric of his philosophy; he knew hunger, the change of seasons, the budding of flowers. To him life was practical and understandable. He envisaged a continous conflict between good and evil spirits and was perfectly willing to bribe either group with generous offerings. He believed that all living creatures possessed souls and that a supernatural force controlled all nature.

Probabably under the influence of the Jesuits, he came to believe in a land of souls, with separate villages for homicides and suicides, who were not admitted to the village of the blessed.

The white man's religion and culture was not all so easily incorporated into the Indian culture, however, Most of the Indians occupying the New York region suffered greatly as a result of contact with the white colonists, and soon succumbed to the effects of new diseases, alcoholism, and the disruption of economic life. In 1670, colonist, Daniel Denton said this about the native population of Long Island:

"To say something of the Indians, there is now but few upon the Island, and those few no ways hurtful but rather serviceable to the English, and it is to be admired, how strangely they have decreased by the Hand of God, since the English first settling of those parts; for since my time, where there were six towns, they are reduced to two small villages, and it hath been generally observed, that where the English come to settle, a Divine Hand makes way for them, by removing or cutting off the Indians either by Wars one with the other, or by some raging mortal disease..."

Denton goes on to mention the Indians' excessive use of alcohol and the crimes they committed while under the influence.

But fighting the English "Hand of God" was not the Indians' only worry. The Five Nations were continually at war with their neighbors, with the aim of controlling the fur trade. The Algonquin and the Huron, having suffered from these imperialistic tendencies, welcomed the arrival of the French, whose 'thunder poles' spoke death. In order to wreak vengeance upon the 'upstart' Iroquois secessionists, the Huron quickly formed an alliance with Samuel de Champlain and induced him to accompany a war party against the Mohawk. In the subsequent engagement near Ticonderoga, Champlain and his two musketeers introduced the use of firearms in Indian warfare, and the dumbfounded Mohawk were easily defeated. This tragic experience was symbolic of the enmity which the Iroquois developed toward the French and which helped defeat French colonization in the New World. Again the contest for domination of the trade in beaver pelts was the motivating factor.

War then blazed in earnest. The Five Nations struck their foes at every vulnerable spot. Town after town was captured; French priests were tortured, thousands of Huron warriors were slain; women and children suffered extreme hardship. With the fall of the great village of Scanenrat in 1648, the Huron confederacy was completely broken and its people fled to their allies, the Erie, the Neutrals, and the Andaste.

Determined to wipe out the last vestige of resistance, the Five Nations proceeded to conquer and absorb these neighboring tribes, which had previously rejected league membership. The Neutrals, neighbors of the Seneca on the west, were the next to be crushed. The Erie, occupying the southwestern corner of the present state, were battled into submission in 1654-5; and then the conquest of the Andaste in a bloody 10-year campaign completed the struggle for domination.

First tasting the bitter fruit of the white man's invasion at the hands of Champlain, the Iroquois established friendly relations with the Dutch and English; traded valuable beaver and mink pelts for flashy baubles, cotton, cloth, guns, and rum; and were systematically cheated by the crafty Europeans. The Hollanders, chiefly interested in the profitable fur trade, paid little attention to the Indian's lack of Christianity, but the English recognized the great power of the Five Nations Confederacy and endeavored to convert the Iroquois into loyal allies. The Episcopal Church sent out missionaries; John Stuart translated the New Testament into several Iroquoian languages; and Sir William Johnson, highly esteemed by the Indians, personally financed the publication of the Episcopal liturgy in Mohawk. Adding flattery to religion, the British formally denounced French interference with the Five Nations, and in 1687 James II issued a warrant to Governor Dongan authorizing protection of the Iroquois as subjects of Great Britain.

Proud of their new sovereignty, the Iroquois raided French settlements on the St. Lawrence with a bloodthirsty eagerness that threatened Montreal and caused bloody retaliation by Count Frontenac's vengeful hordes in the Schenectady massacre. The subsequent devastation of Iroquois villages brought the Five Nations to their knees and resulted in a treaty with the French in 1701.

Prehistory and Archaeology 35

After the cessation of war with the French, the Iroquois enjoyed a long period of ascendancy. They diplomatically played off the British and French against each other, and made their own control of the fur trade more certain. The Delaware were subdued, several Pennsylvania tribes were annexed, and in 1772 the Tuscarora were admitted to the league, which thereafter became known as the Six Nations Confederacy.

Despite their smoldering hatred of the French, many Iroquois groups joined the sporadic raids made aginst the English by motley war parties of Algonquins and Hurons during the French and Indian War. This alienation of their allegiance was evidently caused by fear of the French, distrust of English land speculators, and the dismal failure of British military efforts. But even before the final British victory the Iroquois were won back into the British fold by Sir William Johnson, who staged a grand council at Fort Stanwix in 1768. This conclave, attended by more than 3,000 Indians, marked the end of the Cherokee Wars and created a line of territorial demarcation beginning at Fort Stanwix and extending south and west to a point north of Fort Pitt, then down the Ohio River to the mouth of the Tennessee. West of this line no white settlement was to be made. It was the subsequent violation of this boundary that caused much of the Iroquois bitterness toward the colonists.

The beginning of the Revolution found the Six Nations divided in allegiance between the English and the Continentals. The Mohawk, Onondaga, Cayuga, and Seneca remained steadfast British allies; the Oneida and Tuscarora, through the powerful influence of Samuel Kirkland, were friendly to the Colonials.

Joseph Brant, full-blooded Mohawk chief whose sister had married Sir William Johnson, joined the British forces in 1776, received a captain's commission and played an important part in throughout the Revolution. A force of Iroquois under Brant and Sayenqueraghta, supporting the British and Tories at Oriskany on August 6, 1777, was outbattled by Herkimer's makeshfit militia. Smarting from this costly defeat, the Iroquois retaliated by desolating the New York and Pennsylvania frontiers. Chief Ojageght joined in Colonel Walter Butler's raids at Wyoming and Cherry Valley; Blacksnake, Little Beard, and Cornplanter left red trails of slaughter across the Unadilla hills; and

Joseph Brant defeated the Continentals at the Battle of Minisink. But the Iroquois were forced into defensive fighting in 1779 by the Sullivan-Clinton expedition, which devastated their homes and their cornfields and drove them north to seek British protection. From this blow the Iroquois never fully recovered. When the Revolution ended the Indians were entirely destitute. Joseph Brant went to England in 1785 to plead for the welfare of his people. He was cordially received in London, hobnobbed with high society, paid a formal visit to George III, and returned with a grant for a reservation on the Grand River in Ontario.

Many Mohawks, Onondagas, and Cayugas accompanied Brant to Canada, but many more remained, and their plight was entirely tragic. The Continental Congress and the State legislature passed resolutions; treaties were signed; Indian commissioners were appointed; and after 1784 reservations were established in New York State for the Oneida, Onondaga, and Cayuga. The Seneca obtained 10 tracts of land by the Big Tree Treaty in 1797, and later deeded a small section to the Tuscarora.

In this time of need and distress appeared Ganeodaio (Handsome Lake), who between 1799 and 1815 preached a doctrine of reform that became the most effective bar to the spreading of Christianity among the Indians. He organized a characteristic messianic cult, like that of Tecumseh, the Shawnee prophet. Advocating strict adherence to Indian custom, he covered hundreds of miles on foot and preached a doctrine of chastity and temperance with an eloquence that gained many converts.

With the establishment of reservations, the Indian underwent a gradual metamorphosis. He warfare was obsolete. The small area of his habitations and the decimation of wild game made hunting unprofitable. Agriculture declined with the loss of land and the weakening of morale. Missionaries erected churches, Quakers established an Indian school, and the arrogant warrior became a disciple of the white man's progress. In the nineteenth century the Quakers achieved the only real success at making the Iroquois self-sufficient farmers.

Today the Iroquois live both on and off reservations. Except for garden plots farming is generally decreasing in importance, as individuals seek wage labor. For example, Mohawks from the

Saint Regis and Caughnawaga Reserves have achieved prominence as high steel workers. On reservations many old practices and beliefs are maintained by traditional members of the community, though most Iroquois are Christians. Ceremonies for traditional foods, curing rituals, and the Midwinter Festival are still held. The League of the Iroquois continues in existence and clan mothers wield their influence in selecting chiefs. The Iroquois genius for survival has kept their cultural heritage alive through the present.

The Indian's contributions to the civilization of the New World were of inestimable value. His cultivation of corn and tobacco, his vast knowledge of woodcraft and herbs, and his technique in trapping and hunting were all vital props in bolstering the self-reliance of the pioneering colonists. Even his methods of government were freely borrowed and used in the building of empire. Most definite, and lasting into our own day, has been the Indian contribution to place names, which has stamped upon the New York State map such names as Otsego, Owasco, Canandaigua, Poughkeepsie, Schenectady, and Ticonderoga. Finally, the Indians left, hovering over brook and vale and mountain, legends of creation, of battles of gods and giants, of tragic elopements of fools and wise men,—legends which, for the initiate, animate the landscape with a beauty and an interest beyond what the senses perceive.

New Amsterdam in the 1620s.

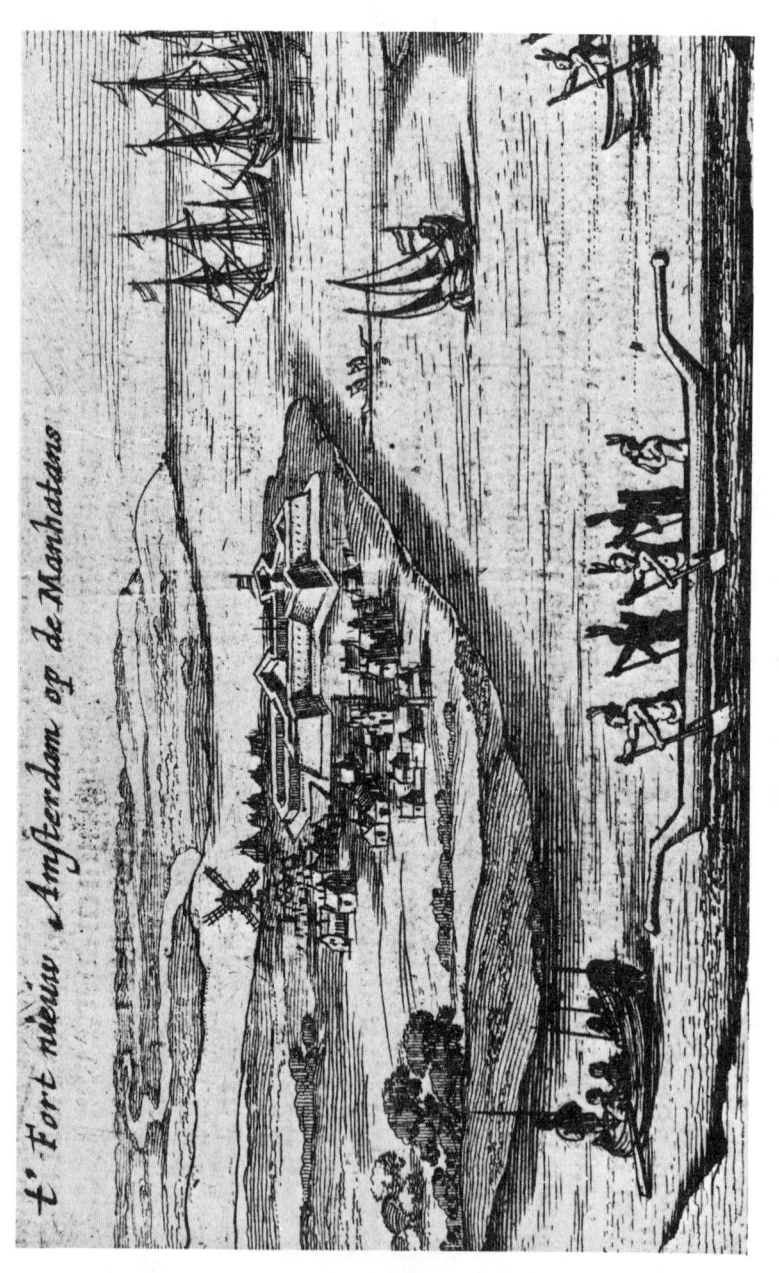

NEW YORK
—A History

In 1609, Samuel de Champlain, a Frenchman, explored southward along the valley of the lake later named for him, and Henry Hudson, an Englishman in Dutch employ, sailed northward up the river later named for him. These two expeditions, occurring within two months of each other and penetrating to points only 100 miles apart, prefigured a century and a half of struggle for control of a North American empire.

In 1614 Fort Nassau was built by the Dutch on Castle Island, south of the present city of Albany, to serve as a fur-trading post; after it was destroyed by a spring freshet in 1617, a new fort, Fort Orange, was erected on the west bank of the river near the present site of Albany. In 1621 the West Indian Company came into being. About 30 families, mostly Waloons, were transported in 1624 to New Netherland, as the area was called, and a majority of them formed the first permanent Dutch settlement at Fort Orange. The first substantial settlement on the island of Manhattan was made the following year; and after a fort was built there, the families at Fort Orange were moved down temporarily to enjoy its protection.

In order to encourage colonization, in 1629 the West India Company offered a large estate, or patroonship, in the new colony to each of its members who within four years would settle 50 colonists on the tract assigned to him. The only patroonship to survive colonial times was Rensselaerswyck, a large area on both sides of the upper Hudson, of which the site of Albany was the approximate center; it was settled by its absentee owner, Kiliaen Van Rensselaer, with Dutchmen, Germans, Danes, Norwegians, Scots, and other nationals. The nonresident patroon, through his agents, enjoyed complete suzerainty over his domain and retained ownership of the land, letting it out principally on leases.

He financed the settlers and was repaid slowly over a long period. The Fuyck, enjoying the protection of Fort Orange on the west bank of the Hudson, became the principal settlement. A quarrel over jurisdiction was ended in 1652 by the establishment of a new court at Beverwyck, which included Fort Orange and the Fuyck. This tribunal immediately overshadowed and finally absorbed the patroon's court in 1665. Other settlements in the upstate area were made during the Dutch period at Wiltwyck (Kingston) and several other points along the Hudson, and at Schenectady on the Mohawk. The settlement on Manhattan Island was designed at the city of New Amsterdam and given burgher government in 1653.

The Dutch West India Company, in common with other early trading and colonizing groups, looked upon its colony as a source of dividends. It bound the settlers by contracts that prohibited trade, change of residence, and the transfer of property; and it imposed heavy taxes, including taxes on imports, that discouraged enterprise, aroused antagonism, and insured minimum returns. It shirked all obligations of a social character, throwing on the Dutch Reformed Church the burden of education and care of the sick and the poor. This shortsighted policy, aggravated by the greed and ineptness of its officials in the colony, brought the company to virtual bankruptcy. The Directors General of New Netherland—Minuit, Van Twiller, Kieft, Stuyvesant—had trouble, much of it of their own making, with the company's business agents, with the clergy of the Reformed Church, with Van Rensselaer's agents, with the New Englanders encroaching in Westchester and on Long Island, and especially with their own people, who demanded an effective voice in the government and wider freedom.

In 1664, when Colonel Richard Nicolls at the head of a British fleet demanded the surrender of New Amsterdam, Director General Stuyvesant found himself with little support and was obliged to capitulate. The Province and the principal settlement were renamed New York, Beverwyck became Albany, and Wiltwyck, Kingston. In 1673 the Dutch recaptured the colony, but in 1674 it was restored by treaty to the English, who promptly resumed their sway.

The terms of surrender in 1664 were highly favorable to the

Dutch. Land titles were confirmed, including that of Rensselaerswyck; toleration was granted to the Dutch Reformed and other Protestant churches. Transition to English political institutions was slow; in the Albany district and along the wharves of New York City the Dutch language persisted for generations. In 1683 the Province of New York was divided into 12 counties, two of which, Dukes and Cornwall, later passed to Massachusetts and Maine; the boundaries of Albany County extended north, west, and east without fixed limits. In 1680 charters were granted to the cities of New York and Albany.

The forced abdication of James II and the accession of William and Mary (1688-9) brought discontent to the surface. Following the lead of New England, Jacob Leisler, with strong support from the common people, seized power in New York City and governed, though in Albany his authority was at first not recognized. After the arrival of Governor Sloughter in 1691, Leisler and his chief lieutenant, Jacob Milborne, were hanged for treason; but their names were later cleared in England, and for a generation the memory of Leisler served as a symbol for the discontented.

The war between Britain and France that began in 1689, known in America as King William's War, was the first of a series of four conflicts that ended in 1760 with the British conquest of Canada. In these wars, because of geography and Indian relations, the province of New York played a strategic role. In the days when natural waterways were the principal means of transportation, its lakes and rivers, connecting the Atlantic with the Great Lakes, the Mohawk and the St. Lawrence with the Susquehanna and the Delaware, and the Hudson with the Allegheny and the Ohio, made it the great crossroads of the East. The nations comprising the Iroquois Confederacy, which controlled the carries and the headwaters of this far-flung sytem of water routes, held the balance of power in the struggle. Albany was Montreal's successful rival in the fur trade, which, together with the routes to the interior, would be controlled by the side that won the friendship or the submission of the Iroquois.

On February 8, 1690, Schenectady was destroyed by one of three French and Indian war parties sent out by Frontenac, governor of Canada. Fearful lest Albany be taken and their western boundaries be open to attack, in May of that year the English Colonies sent representatives to the first intercolonial congress in New York, at which a plan for military co-operation was made; but only Connecticut and Maryland joined New York in an abortive campaign against Montreal, the New England colonies busying themselves in an equally fruitless expedition by sea against Quebec. The New York legislature, absorbed in its controversy with Leisler, failed to provide adequate defense for the Albany-Schenectady frontier, and the population in that district fell off by a third. Credit for the preservation of the Iroquois friendship in these crucial days is due Peter Schuyler of Albany, who performed heroic service in defending the frontier, in pursuing French and Indian raiding parties, and in counteracting the solicitations of French agents in the Iroquois councils. But after the first French war the English colonies never enjoyed the unanimous and wholehearted support of the Five, later Six, Nations of the Iroquois Confederacy.

After the Treaty of Ryswyck (1697) an important trade sprang up between Albany and Montreal; and the interested Albany and New York merchants were influential enough to stress the policy of neutrality in subsequent defensive wars. New England, which suffered the brunt of the attack during Queen Anne's War (1702-13)—the American phase of the War of the Spanish Succession—complained bitterly that the French Indians were shooting its people with guns bought in Albany. But Peter Schuyler learned from visiting Indians of contemplated attacks and forewarned New England authorities, and New York contributed its quota of men and money to the abortive expeditions of 1709 and 1711 against Canada.

During the 30 years of peace that followed the Treaty of Utrecht (1713), while the French strengthened their position by constructing a system of fortifications at strategic points, including Niagara (1726) and Crown Point (1731), the English colonies went their individual ways. New York's advantage in the contest for supremacy lay in the preference of the Indians for Albany goods in the barter for furs, but that advantage was sacrificed by the direct sale of those goods to the French. In King George's War (1744-8), which grew out of the War of the

Austrian Succession, New York again inclined toward a policy of neutrality, but it took part in the ineffective expedition against Canada in 1746.

During the six-year interval between the third and fourth French wars the trade of the British colonies and their prestige with the Indians declined further. There was much to alienate the Iroquois: their business as middlemen in the fur trade was spoiled by the commerce of the western tribes directly with Montreal, made possible by the Albany trade with the French merchants; France seemed to have the upper hand in a military sense; the long sojourn of the Joncaires, father and sons, among the Seneca had won that strong nation's friendship for the French; and the English were neglecting to send the Indians the customary gifts. The Albany Congress of 1754 was called in an effort to secure united colonial action and to conciliate the Iroquois, but failed to do either. Like Peter Schuyler in the earlier period, during the last two French wars Sir William Johnson possessed the confidence of the Iroquois and was able to keep them active in the British cause, or at least, in the darkest days, neutral.

The French and Indian War, the last British-American conflict with the French, begun in 1754 with the clash at Great Meadows, was marked in 1755 by Braddock's defeat and the failure of expeditions against Niagara and Crown Point. Though he did not take Crown Point, Sir William Johnson succeeded in holding the Lake George area by defeating Dieskau, for which achievement he was made a baronet and presented with 5,00 by Parliament. By taking Oswego and gaining control of the Great Carrying Place (the site of Rome) in 1756, the French dominated the important Mohawk River-Oneida Lake waterway. After these reverses all the Iroquois became neutral, with the exception of the Mohawk, who were kept loyal to the English by the efforts of Sir William Johnson. After Montcalm captured Fort William Henry and hostile Indians made successful raids on the English frontier in 1757, it required all of Johnson's influence to keep the Iroquois from going over to the enemy.

The year 1758, with William Pitt in power, proved the turning point in British affairs in North America. Encouraged by Pitt's promise of reimbursement, New York raised its quotas of men and money. The train of disasters was completed by Abercrombie's failure to take Ticonderoga (July 8), but in the same year Bradstreet with little effort captured Fort Frontenac (August 27), on the site of Kingston, Ontario. That victory enabled the English to establish themselves at Fort Stanwix (Rome) and revived the confidence of the Iroquois. As in a dramatic tragedy, once the climax was passed, the events of the denouement piled up rapidly. In 1759, while Wolfe was taking Quebec, Amherst compelled the French to abandon Ticonderoga (July 26) and Crown Point fell to his hands (July 31), while Johnson captured Niagara (July 25) and reoccupied Oswego. In 1760 Amherst took La Galette, now Ogdensburg, and at Montreal accepted the surrender of all Canada to the British. In a council at Detroit in 1761, Johnson persuaded 13 Indian tribes formerly allied with the French to sign a treaty with Britian. Though peace was not signed in Europe until 1763, for New York the menace of the French and the Indians was over, and the Province was ready to begin its rapid progress to pre-eminence.

During the English period the colony developed slowly. The Dutch occupied the Hudson and spread into the Mohawk Valley; English from New England settled along the east bank, in Cherry Valley, in northern New York, and in the vicinity of Johnstown, to which they were attracted by Sir William Johnson. In 1677 a small party of Huguenots settled New Paltz; in 1689 another group founded New Rochelle. The Palatines, comprising the largest mass immigration of the English period, came first to the Hudson Valley to produce naval stores, but with the failure of that enterprise many of them finally settled in the Schoharie and Mohawk Valleys. In 1760 the frontier settlements extended to about 40 miles north of Albany along the Hudson and about 80 miles west of Albany on the Mohawk. In that year New York ranked seventh in population among the 13 colonies.

Historians give three chief reasons for this retarded growth. The threat of French and Indian raids prevented expansion northward and westward; the Iroquois showed their displeasure at every effort to appropriate more of their land; and the prevalent system of large estates, with long-term leases preferred by the manorial lords to outright sales, discouraged settlement by immigrants to whom independence meant above all ownership of the soil they plowed. Social and economic organization still reflected the medieval inheritance. The manor was an almost self-sufficient unit, its basic agriculture supplemented by handicraft and the importation of indispensable goods; the leaseholder paid his rent in kind, and was influenced by a personal loyalty to the lord of the manor that was transmuted by the latter into political power; and the manor house was the social center of the community, in which the humble leaseholder vicariously lived a fuller life. Labor was regularly hired by contract for a term of years, and the custom of apprenticeship was widely followed. In the cities, keeping shop and practicing trades were limited to freemen; 'freedom' could be purchased, the cost to merchants being about double that to tradesmen and handicraftsmen; apprentices to freemen were admitted by registration. Negro slaves made up more than 10 per cent of the population.

In the light of subsequent Revolutionary history, the most significant aspect of the political life of the provincial period was the struggle for superemacy between the governor, representing the prerogative of the Crown and usually supported by the council, and the assembly, representing provincial interests. It was not at the time a struggle for democracy but rather an effort by the provincial aristocracy to achieve political power and by provincial business and commerce to avoid taxation and throw off the restrictions of the mercantile system. The issue was settled by control of the public purse strings. At the end of the period the assembly had established a body of precedents that gave it control of finance and established it as the dominant element in the provincial government.

It is not necessary to rehearse the conflicts between imperial policy and local self-interest and between British and colonial theories of political right, nor the series of specific clashes, that culminated in the American Revolution. In New York, as in other colonies, the situation was complicated by the effort of the propertyless class--mechanics, laborers, and tenant farmers—to bend events toward the realization of a higher economic and social level for themselves, and, at the other extreme, by the presence of a large number of Loyalists who, while willing to plead with the Mother Country, refused to follow the Patriot party into armed rebellion.. About 40,000 Loyalists left the state during and after the Revolution.

The steps involved in the actual accomplishment of revolution—the establishment of an effective insurgent government and the administration and financing of the war—were undertaken by a system of local committees. These appointed delegates to a provincial convention, which in turn sent representatives to the Continental Congress. Until the establishment of state and local governments, the committees 'had to enact law and enforce it, perform judicial and police duties, suppress the Loyalists, raise funds, recruit soldiers, furnish military supplies and perform a thousand other duties.'

On July 9, 1776, the Provincial Congress of New York, meeting at White Plains, ratified the Declaration of Independence, and on the next day named itself 'the Convention of the Representatives of the State of New York.' The first state constitution was adopted and proclaimed in Kingston on April 20, 1777. That document represented a victory for the aristocratic group of the Patriot party in that it set up property qualifications for the franchise. George Clinton, chosen by the ballots of free-holders, took the oath of office as first governor of the state on July 30; and on September 10 in the Kingston courthouse the House of Assembly of the State of New York began its initial session. In the interval affairs were administered by an extralegal Council of Safety. Local governments were set up under the supervision of the Revolutionary committees.

In the military history of the Revolution, New York State bulks large: '. . . out of the 308 battles and engagements of the Revolution, 92, or nearly one third, took place on New York soil.' In the spring of 1775 Arnold made a dash on St. Johns, Canada. The artillery captured at Ticonderoga was transported by General Knox to Boston and enabled Washington to drive the British from that city. Later in the same year Montgomery took Montreal. In the successful attack on Quebec on December 31, 1775, Montgomery was killed and Arnold was wounded.

In 1776, in the northern part of the state, Carleton defeated Arnold in the Battle of Valcour Island (October 11), one of the first engagements between a British and an American fleet, and

History 47

thereby regained control of Lake Champlain, but failed to take Ticonderoga. In the southern part of the State, Howe drove Washington from Long Island and Manhattan and followed him northward. After the Battle of White Plains, Howe captured Fort Washington. Thereafter the scene of the campaign shifted to New Jersey. The British held New York City until the end of the war.

Under the British plan of campaign for 1777, Burgoyne was to move south along Lake Champlain and the upper Hudson; St. Leger was to land at Oswego, take Fort Stanwix, and march down the Mohawk Valley; Howe was to ascend the Hudson from New York City; and the three forces were to meet at Albany, thus establishing control over New York and separating New England from the other colonies. St. Leger was halted at Fort Stanwix (Rome) and settled down to a siege. On August 6, General Herkimer and his Tryon County militia, marching to relieve the fort, were ambushed at Oriskany, six miles east, but held the field against a Loyalist, British, Hessian, and Indian force in one of the bloodiest battles of the war. On the same day Colonel Marinus Willett made a bold sortie from Fort Stanwix into St. Leger's camp. This successful resistance, together with the arrival of reinforcements under Arnold, caused St. Leger to raise the siege on August 22 and retreat to Oswego. Arnold was left free to join in the campaign against Burgoyne.

Burgoyne moved south along Lake Champlain in June, took Ticonderoga (July 6), and advanced to Sekensborough (Whitehall) at the head of the lake. His continued advance was slowed by his heavy baggage trains and by Schuyler's strategy of obstructing the road by every possible means. During the delay the defending force was strengthened by thousands of volunteers, especially after the murder of Jane McCrea. At Walloomsac, in the Battle of Bennington (August 16), Stark defeated two detachments of German dragoons on their way to take the supplies stored at Bennington. In the first Battle of Saratoga, at Freeman's Farm on September 19, the British held their ground; but in the second battle on October 7 they were defeated, largely by an assault, in defiance of orders, led by Benedict Arnold and powerfully supported by Daniel Morgan's sharpshooting riflemen. Burgoyne fell back to

Schuylerville, where, finding his retreat cut off, he surrendered on October 17.

In the meantime, Howe, not having received specific orders to move up the Hudson, went south to take Philadelphia. Sir Henry Clinton started up the Hudson on October 3 and advanced as far as Kingston, which he burned on October 16; but his messages to Burgoyne were intercepted, and, upon hearing of Burgoyne's surrender, he returned to New York.

Within 24 hours after receiving the news of Saratoga, the French government decided to come to the aid of the colonies and to declare war on Great Britain.

The years 1778 and 1779 saw a deadlock between Washington, defending West Point, and Clinton, holding New York City, neither strong enough to attack the other. The events of those years in New York took place on and beyond the frontier. In 1778 Loyalist and Indian bands under Sir John Johnson (Sir William's son), John Butler and his son Walter, and Joseph Brant—names that are to this day anathema to central New York State residents—raided a number of frontier settlements. In 1779 the carefully planned Sullivan-Clinton campaign, a punitive expedition into the central and western Iroquois country, struck a blow at the Confederacy from which it never fully recovered, though in 1780 retaliatory raids were made in the Schoharie and middle Mohawk Valleys. On October 25, 1781, six days after Cornwallis's surrender at Yorktown, Willett checked a combined force of British, Loyalists, and Indians in the Battle of Johnstown. In the pursuit after the battle, on October 30, Walter Butler was killed.

Following the surrender of Cornwallis, Washington made his headquarters at Newburgh until after the peace was signed. Here he rejected a crown offered him by a military faction, and here he prevented an uprising by the disgruntled army. In the intervals he found time to make a tour of the battlefields in the upper Hudson and Mohawk Valleys and to invest in New York real estate. On May 6, 1783, he met with the British commander to plan the evacuation of New York; on November 25 he marched into the city.

The final act of the drama in which a unified nation was molded was the adoption of the federal constitution. In New York the sharp conflict between the Clintonian faction, opposed to ratification, and the Hamiltonian faction, in favor of it, reflected the clash of interests between tenants and their manorial lords, between workers and their employers, and between the agricultural back country, which preferred state autonomy, and the city with its dominant commercial interest, which desired a strong central government to support commerce and provide a sound currency. The campaign for election of delegates to the ratifying convention was the occasion of the writing of the *Federalist* papers by Hamilton, Jay, and Madison. Two thirds of the delegates, elected by universal free male suffrage, were committed to vote against the Constitution; but the Federalists were aided by the march of events. The convention met in Poughkeepsie in June 1788. After New Hampshire ratified as the ninth state, and Virginia as the tenth, the fear of losing the lucrative trade with the other states, of the possible secession of the southern New York counties, and of having land claims in the present state of Vermont invalidated by the federal government, swung the convention over to ratification. The final vote, after more than a month of bitter debate, was 30 to 27. Four delegates, including Clinton, failed to vote.

After the Revolution, settlement extended northward and westward. The menace of the Indians was gone; the state purchased the titles to their lands and sold them to speculators: land speculation became the favorite form of financial gambling. In 1789-90 the Military Tract of more than 1,500,000 acres east of Seneca Lake, reaching from the southern tip of that lake to the shore of Lake Ontario, was set aside for Revolutionary veterans; but many of them sold their allotments to speculators. The classical names assigned to the townships of the Military Tract form a well-known characteristic of central New York.

Title to the western area of the state was disputed between New York and Massachusetts. By the Hartford Treaty of 1780, Massachusetts was awarded ownership and New York jurisdiction of the land west of the Pre-emption Line drawn through Seneca Lake. In 1788 Massachusetts gave two speculators, Oliver Phelps and Nathaniel Gorham, an option on the entire tract; but they obtained Indian title to only the land east of the Genessee River and about 200,000 acres on its western shore up from its mouth, and surrendered their option on the rest. They sold a large part of their holdings in 1790 to Robert Morris of Philadelphia, who resold it to the London Associates, headed by Sir William Pulteney. Morris bought the remaining land from Massachusetts in 1791 and sold all but a tract along the Genesee River to a Dutch group known as the Holland Land Company, which became the proprietor of about 3,300,000 acres in western New York. After Indian title was obtained in 1797, the company sent surveyors under Joseph Ellicott to mark out townships, and sales began at the land office in Batavia in 1801.

In the North Country the Macomb Purchase, 1791, including nearly 4,000,000 acres, was soon divided into small tracts. The Delaware, Susquehanna, and Champlain Valleys, and the territory north and south of the Mohawk River was taken up by innumerable small purchases.

A few pioneers had settled on some of these lands immediately after the Revolution, but once clear titles were available the migration took on the proportions of a stampede. A large majority of the settlers came from New England by way of the Mohawk and Cherry Valley routes, transporting their belongings—many now treasured in historical museums—by water and in large, boat-shaped covered wagons. Some came up the Delaware Valley from New Jersey, others up the Susquehanna from Pennsylvania. Eastern New Yorkers in large numbers sought their fortunes on the new western lands; and when the Holland Tract was opened up, some moved from central New York for a fresh start. New Englanders, French Canadians, and French *emigres* settled the North Country.

The years just preceding and following the turn of the century were New York's frontier period. Many of the trial blazers, some of whom have become part of local folklore, moved farther west before the wave of permanent settlers. Clearings were made in the forests, log cabins were erected, and the land was brought under the plow. Gradually the clearings were enlarged and the homes improved. The New Englanders built villages in the image of Lexington and Concord. Churches were formed; schools were erected, then academies were organized, and finally colleges were founded. By 1820 the population of the new settlements totaled 500,000, and that of the state 1,372,812, representing an advance since 1790 from fifth to first place among the states.

In the first years the new settlers could produce no more than enough to meet their own needs. Then the demand for supplies during the War of 1812 brought a period of prosperity, for which trade with the enemy was responsible in a substantial degree.

Most of the land fighting of the War of 1812 occurred along the Canadian border within the state. Repeated invasions of Canada failed because of the inefficiency of troops and their commanders, aggravated by the difficulties of co-operation between the state militia and the national army. In 1813 the Americans burned York (Toronto), and the British burned Lewiston, Black Rock, and Buffalo; but the end of the war found the opposing armies holding almost their original positions along the Niagara frontier. The British attack on Plattsburg (September 11, 1814) was turned back by Macdonough's naval victory on Lake Champlain.

Long before the War of 1812, the need for improved means of transportation was recognized, and by the time of the war the construction of turnpike roads was in full swing. But the war provided vivid proof that land haulage was too costly: it cost $400 to haul a gun weighing about three tons from the place of manufacture to Sackets Harbor. Prohibitive transportation rates made it impossible for farmers in the Finger Lakes and Genesee Valley regions to compete with those along the Hudson and the Mohawk. Without an available market for its products, western New York was retarded in its development. Surplus grain was turned into the more portable form of whisky, of which large quantities were consumed on the spot. Crop surpluses were also used to raise livestock, and for a period of years drivers clogged the turnpikes with herds bound for the slaughterhouses of Albany and New York. The commerce of the central and western parts of the state followed the natural waterways to market—down the Delaware to Philadelphia, down the Susquehanna to Baltimore, and down the St. Lawrence to Montreal. Farsighted leaders like DeWitt Clinton saw that a canal connecting the Hudson with the Great Lakes would provide relief for the western farmer and, by deflecting the commerce of the area down the Hudson, would make the state an economic unit and raise New York City to commercial pre-eminence. But when the bill authorizing construction of the Erie Canal was up for passage in 1817, the representatives of the city in the legislature, uninterested in 'upstate' improvements, voted against it as one man. The bill, however, was passed, the canal was dug, and the stream of commerce thus stimulated became the decisive factor in determining the rapid growth of a ton of freight from Buffalo to New York City was $120; on the canal it was reduced to $14.

The canal and its feeders created a strong economic bond between the eastern and western sections of the state to the profit of both. The drastic reduction in transportation costs opened the eastern market to western grain, and a prosperous west bought the products of eastern factories, to which more capital was steadily drawn. Inland ports grew up along the canal, serving as transportation and shopping centers and providing local markets for agricultural products.

As the influence of canal extended beyond the borders of the state and accelerated the development of the Great Lakes region, especially Ohio, midwestern grain entered the eastern market and New York farmers turned to dairying, truck gardening, and fruit-growing; and the cities, aided by inventions, available capital, an adequate labor supply, and access to power sources and markets, became industrial centers.

The railroads, extending their lines in the years following the completion of the canal, hastened the process of change; the Erie reached Lake Erie at Dunkirk in the fifties, supplying the Southern Tier with modern transportation for its products to New York City.

By 1850 the state had achieved a pre-eminent rank in industry and commerce and was still among the leaders in agriculture. In that year 'New York possessed one seventh of the true valuation of the property of the whole country.'

The twenties, thirties, and especially the forties (the period of the Great Irish Famine and abortive revolution on the continent) were marked by a large foreign immigration, principally Irish and German. The former dug the canals, then remained to build the railroads, and finally settled in large numbers in the urban centers. The German provided skilled workers and professional people and became a stimulus to an expanding cultural life.

Coincident with this economic development arose a struggle for political democracy. The Revolution and the ratification of the Federal Constitution left the landed aristocrats and commercial princes in power, and political leadership was largely identified with names like Van Cortlandt, Schuyler, Livingston, Hamilton, Jay, Morris, Van Rensselaer, and Clinton. The Hamiltonian principle of property prevailed, and the franchise was accordingly limited by property qualifications. But democratic doctrine had been rapidly gaining strength, especially in the newly settled western and northern counties and among the mill and factory workers of the cities. The constitution of 1821 represented substantial progress toward universal male suffrage, and the subsequent series of democratic reforms was completed by the constitution of 1846, which provided for direct election to high state executive and judicial offices. Other evidences of the growth of the democratic spirit were the gradual abolition of imprisonment for debt, and universal education; and the antirent wars, in which leaseholders on the large estates resorted to force in resisting the feudal inequities of the leasehold system of land tenure.

The same period was characterized by an epidemic of reform movements concentrated in central and western New York and probably attributable to the New England antecedents of the population. A strong anti-slavery sentiment expressed itself in political organization and in the activities of the Underground Railroad. The woman's-rights movement began in Seneca Falls. Temperance societies multiplied rapidly in the twenties and thirties, and total abstinence was endorsed by the state temperance society in 1835. The anti-Masonic movement was another Western growth. And a number of novel religious sects, including the Mormons and the Millerites (Seventh Day Adventists), sprang up.

The detailed history of the political strife of the period is characterized by the multiplication of factional groups brought about by conflicts of personalities, interests, and issues. The robust nature of the politics is suggested in the names of the factions—Coodies, Bucktails, Hunkers or Hard Shells, and Barnburners or Soft Shells. The Native American Party gave expression to antiforeign, anti-Catholic sentiment in the state, caused mainly by the economic pressure arising from the new immigration. The anti-Masonic party developed in the western counties out of the disappearance of one Morgan, who had threatened to expose the secrets of the order. In the Albany Regency and in the political leadership of Thurlow Weed, New York State gave the country early examples of the thorough efficiency of the modern political machine based on patronage. The Tweed Ring, the Canal Ring, and the Railroad Lobby were active in Albany.

Its population and wealth made New York a pivotal state in the national elections, enabling it to play a significant role in national politics. By 1850 it had given the nation two Presidents, five Vice Presidents, and many cabinet officers and ambassadors. The slavery issue in the Civil War period crystallized political lines into the present Republican and Democratic Parties. To the Union cause in the Civil War New York contributed its full share of men and money: the total number of New York troops engaged was nearly 500,000, of whom about one tenth were killed.

In the Civil War period capitalism was introduced, with machine production, absentee ownership, corporate management, and the wage laborer. The railroads brought the raw materials to the industrial centers and carried away the finished products; the canals declined in importance and many an inland port, once bustling and prospered, became a sleepy milk station and a Saturday-afternoon shopping center for farmers. The factories attracted young people from the country, and the cities grew rapidly at the expense of the rural areas. Later, as the heavy industries moved closer to the sources of raw materials, New York State turned to the manufacture of intermediate products and consumers' goods. In the recent past the state gained new industries resulting from scientific advance, especially the production of radio equipment, electrical supplies, chemicals, and airplanes. New York City became the center of the nation's banking, finance, and wholesale and retail merchandising; and Wall Street became the barometer, and to a growing extent the control center, of the nation's business. In recent years, the city has developed into the greatest seaport in the world. While

—*Harper's Weekly*, 1859

Seneca Falls Convention on Women's Rights, 1848.

-Harper's Weekly, 1883

Brooklyn Bridge was built by 1883.

Crossing Broadway, New York City, in 1850s.

Buffalo, New York at mid-nineteenth century.

agriculture in the state remained economically important, its character changed: cultivation of grain was superseded by dairying and the growth of fruits and vegetables for markets close at hand. Thus the wealth of the state today, one of the largest in the Union, is securely founded on eminence in specialized agriculture, manufacturing, and commerce.

Urbanization and industrialization created problems that became the political issues of the post-Civil War period. In the late seventies bad harvests in Ireland drove thousands of Irish to New York. In the eighties began a stream of immigration, ending only with the World War, that brought new racial elements in large numbers to the state—Italians, Poles, Russians, and others, all from southern and eastern Europe—and that created new problems in economics and citizenship. The growing cities needed workers to lay streets, sidewalks, and sewers to construct water, light, power, and rapid transit systems. Politicians in control of political machines were able, in granting contracts and franchises, to enrich themselves by betraying the public interest to the contractor or the public-utility promoter. Through the boss, Big Business controlled politics. The temptation of proffered graft was too strong to be universally resisted by elected representatives. Tilden achieved national renown, and all but won the Presidency, as a result of his exposure of the Tweed Ring and the Canal Ring. Conditions reached such a pass that a reputation for honesty and steadiness in local administration was sufficient, as in the case of Grover Cleveland, to place a public figure in the White House. Charles Evans Hughes first attracted wide public attention as a result of his investigations into gas and electricity rates and the financial practices of insurance companies.

In World War I New York State contributed to the military and naval service more than 500,000 men, about 10 per cent of the entire national force. The number of casualties was about 55,000, including 14,000 deaths. Its financial and industrial contributions were commensurate with its wealth.

In the twentieth century the rapid development of machine industry and the recurring cycles of prosperity and depression gave emphasis to another set of social problems: women and children in industry, conditions of work in factories, workmen's compensation, the rights and duties of organized labor, unemployment insurance, and old-age security. In many of these fields New York State legislation has served as a model for other states. The same period saw a rapid extension of state activity and support in the fields of roadbuilding, education, conservation, and the care of its wards in penal institutions and asylums. Through its financial policy of offering grants-in-aid to local units for schools, highways, and public welfare, the state has been able to secure adoption of its standards by local governmental bodies. State expenditures increased from $59,000,000 in 1916 to $396,000,000 in 1938-39; but its credit remained strong throughout the years of depression.

Early efforts to regulate public utilities by special legislative acts failed. The principal activities of the Public Service Commission in recent years have been regulation of gas and electric rates and of bus lines and elimination of railroad grade crossings. The problems of determining a just valuation of utility property as a basis for rate-making purposes and of exercising an effective control over holding companies are still largely unsolved. Public ownership as a substitute for regulation in New York State has largely been restricted to waterworks; some of the smaller cities, notably the city of Jamestown, Chautauga County, own their electric generating and distributing systems.

In the determination of policy in regard to the state's water-power resources the issue was clear-cut between state development and operation, espoused by Governors Alfred E. Smith, Franklin D. Roosevelt, and Herbert H. Lehman, and private development under state supervision, supported by the Republican majorities in the legislature. In 1930, after a long struggle, possession of the state's water power was reserved to the people; but the issue was reopened by the constitutional convention of 1938.

As it extended the sphere of its activities, the state government expanded into an uncoordinated mass of bureaus and departments without centralized responsiblity; and reorganization became another issue. The political conflict was complicated by opposition between the metropolis and the upstate area and by the demand for city home rule. The present system of representation, adopted in 1894, prevents New York City, though containing more than half of the population of the state, from securing a majority in the legislature. In 1927, largely as a result of the efforts of Governor Alfred E. Smith, all administrative functions were consolidated in a small number of departments, with final responsibility in the hands of the governor; in 1929 the executive budget system was instituted, with responsibility again vested in the governor. Since 1938 the governor is elected for a term of four years. On November 8, 1938, Governor Herbert H. Lehman was re-elected to serve the first four-year term in the history of the state. (See *Governors* section).

National interest in New York politics is always large; the governor of a state that has 47 votes in the Electoral College is always a potential candidate for the presidency. In the early twentieth century this national interest was increased by the careers of Governors Alfred E. Smith and Franklin D. Roosevelt. Both men fought for popular program—Governor Smith for reorganization of the state government, workmen's compensation, a six-day week for all workers, health insurance, improved hospitals and penal institutions, a better and larger state park system, a repeal of the prohibition amendment; Governor Roosevelt for old-age pensions, reform of local government and the courts, relief for agriculture, and public control of hydroelectric power: and the opposition of one or both of the houses of the legislature, Republican-controlled, served as a sounding-board to arouse nationwide interest in these programs and their sponsors. The administration of Governor Herbert H. Lehman followed the same pattern, with, however, a more circumspect opposition from the Republican Party. He was elected to three terms until Thomas Dewey, another presidential candidate, took office in 1942.

The 1940's also brought on the second World War, and thousands of young men cheerfully signed up for the armed forces. Even as the "World of Tomorrow" fair in Flushing was winding down, the real world was gearing up for a bloody future. In New York, millions of people bought war bonds and began to ration goods like metal and rubber. The Curtis-Wright Factory in Buffalo, Ford, General Motors, and other plants in the state built thousands of planes and tanks, and the large cities of New York became vital centers for arming the Yanks. More than half of the men and supplies sent overseas during the war left from New York Harbor.

When World War II ended, New York City became the home of the United Nations, which has since become the symbol of an international watchdog as well as reconciler. At the same time, a fear of Communism spread throughout the state, especially in New York City where Alger Hiss was tried for allegedly supplying secrets to the Soviet Union. Julius and Ethel Rosenberg were convicted as Soviet spies and executed at Sing Sing Prison in Ossing, New York in 1951.

But the period was mostly one of enormous growth. Many miles of state-funded highways were built, schools were established, and the St. Lawrence Seaway was gouged out to provide New York and the midwest with more direct access to major European ports. As the economy grew, more and more people were able to own homes, and the vast suburban metropolises around New York City and other areas began to creep outward.

This era of growth continued through in 1960's but slowed during the 1970's as many manufacturers moved from the state because of high taxes, rents, union regulations and general congestion in the cities. The state population stopped growing in 1970 when it reached 18,200,000. New York City itself lost over 700,000 people in the 1970-1980 decade, as many moved to the suburbs or to neighboring cities in New Jersey and Connecticut. Others moved completely out of the northeast, resettling in the new growth areas of the south and southwest U.S. Still, New York leads the nation in finances, production of many manufactured goods as well as dairy products, maple syrup, and the vital industrial minerals, zinc, talc, titanium, and emery.

New York is also a leader in education and the arts. Since the 1940's, when artist moved back from Paris to reform a cultural center in New York City, many new facilities have opened there. In 1948 it was the New York City Ballet; in 1959 it was the world-famous Metropolitan Opera House, and in 1962 the

Philharmonic Hall held its first performance. Governor Nelson Rockefeller was a major patron of this artistic revival, often supporting cultural foundations with his private funds. During his 15-year term in office, the state universities increased from 28 to 71 institutions. Today New York has 285 institutions of higher learning—more than any other state, and probably a higher concentration than any other area in the world.

These developments, together with a growing need for welfare support for the poor put New York State into a massive financial tangle. When Rockefeller left office in 1973, he had chalked up so many debts for the government that the new governor, Hugh Carey, was forced to cut state departments and programs for the first time since 1942. In 1975, Carey tried to organize a coalition of northeast governors to try to obtain more federal funding for social programs. The CNE's reasoning is that the northeast pays more in federal taxes than it gets back in welfare programs.

Most of the welfare funds are needed in New York City, where unemployment among young minorities has reached as high as 40 percent. During and after World War II, a large influx of blacks from the south and Puerto Ricans provided cheap unskilled labor, but left a surplus of resources with the advancement of technology and the return of the white, male workers from the war. Tensions among the races have erupted into violence many times; property crimes are commonplace; and for many New Yorkers, survival is the big question. Still a majority of people in the city would claim they are proud to be from New York, according to a mid-1970's poll.

But New York state cannot be represented only by its major city. Thousands of acres of relative wilderness still exist in the state, as in the Adirondacks, the Catskills along the Hudson River, and Long Island shoreline. Many New Yorkers are not plagued by urban problems at all, but live a similar life to that of the earliest settlers in this middle Atlantic region. Throughout the state, one sees reminders of a history that is difficult to characterize, except to say it is *diverse*.

GEOGRAPHICAL CONFIGURATION: A DESCRIPTION OF THE NATURAL LANDSCAPE

by Thomas J. Gergel
State University of New York, Oneonta

The natural landscape of New York State is a beautiful mosaic of physically diverse regions. From the subdued majesty of the Adirondack Mountain region of northern New York State southward to the sublimity of eastern Long Island and westward through the rolling hills and Finger Lakes to the vineyard-clad shores of Lake Erie, one cannot help but be impressed at the physiographic changes created by the processes of nature. The distinctive landscapes encountered are the result of particular associations of landforms and climate and, less noticeably, of vegetation and soil variation. Overlaying these natural patterns are those cultural imprints of man - fields, cities and towns, roadways and fence lines - still evolving and changing as they have since colonial days. Few regions in the United States possess such steep physical and cultural gradients over comparable distances as those found in New York State.

New York State with an area of 47,940 square miles is the largest state in northeastern United States, approached in size only by Pennsylvania. The state is roughly shaped like an isosceles triangle tipped on its side. Its base extends northward from Staten Island in the harbor of New York City, northward to the Canadian border and Montreal, a distance of just over 300 miles. From this baseline, which closely parallels the border New York State shares with the New England states of Connecticut, Massachusetts, and Vermont, the apex of the triangle points westward to the Midwest and Great Lakes states a distance of nearly 325 miles. Long Island is appended to the southeastern corner of this triangle and extends into the Atlantic Ocean a further 120 miles.

To the south, New York State is bordered for the most part by

Pennsylvania and in the vicinity of New York City, by New Jersey. A substantial portion of the state's border is made up of more than 825 miles of ocean coastline and Great Lakes shoreline. Long Island is entirely surrounded by waters of the Atlantic Ocean and Long Island Sound, and the East River which separates it from Manhattan Island of New York City. Along virtually its entire northern boundary the St. Lawrence River and Lake Ontario functions as an international boundary with Canada as does Lake Erie and the Niagara River to the west. Proximity to these large bodies exerts a profound effect on regional the climate and culture of large areas of the state.

Until recently New York State was the most populous state in the United States. Even today it is surpassed in this regard only by California. New York City remains pre-eminent among U.S. cities in such things as wealth, culture and manufacturing. Taken together, these and other facets of New York State create a tendency to think of the region as highly-urbanized, densely-populated and heavily-industrialized - not an all together inaccurate impression. However, its industry and population is concentrated in a handful of major population centers. To the person who travels widely throughout the state an impression is quickly gained of spaciousness, rural tranquillity, and ever-changing natural beauty. Rich farmland, forested hills, unblemished beaches and forever-wild trackless wilderness exists within a two-hour drive of any urban center in the state, including New York City.

A number of markedly distinct cultural and physical regions exist within the state. Culturally, New Yorkers divide the state into "upstate" (that area north of New York City exclusive of Westchester and Rockland counties), "downstate," "the City" and "Long Island." Other quasi-cultural appellations exist such as the Southern Tier (of counties) extending along the New York-Pennsylvania border, the North Country (including the Adirondacks, Lake Champlain and the St. Lawrence River Valley) as well as others. Yet, it is the physical landscape upon which the drama of human endeavors are enacted; and, a description and better appreciation of the state's natural regions serves as a more suitable prelude for a description of cultural, historic and economic aspects of the state.

Geologic History

To know, even briefly, the geology or earth history of what is now New York State, is to better understand the marked regional differences in landforms that occur.

Approximately 550 million years ago much of eastern North America was an almost featureless plain (or *peneplain*) underlain by a crystalline, granite-like rock. Highlands existed but with the exception of the Adirondack region rising 5,000 feet above its surroundings as a dome of ancient rock over two billion years old, (see Adirondack State Park section), the remainder of New York State appears to have been a low-lying, gently rolling plain only slightly above sea level. Mystery shrouds the events of the indeterminantly long period of time leading up to this time in earth history, but 550 million years ago a shallow sea advanced across this eroded lowland, surrounding but not rising over the Adirondack dome. For the next 325 million years, sediment washed from the eroded ancient rocks of the Adirondacks and other high lands to the east into the shallow seas lying to their west and south, depositing successive flat-lying layers of mud, sand and coarser materials. Crustal movement and the weight of the accumulating sediment caused the shallow sea bottom to progressively sink making room for further material carried in by rivers from the adjacent land masses. In places these sediments accumulated to a depth of over 10,000 feet and hardened into conglomerates, sandstones, shales and limestones. During this time the Adirondacks were, in effect, an island of ancient rock to be surrounded by sediments later to be hardened into much younger, largely undisturbed sedimentary rock.

Climatic changes also occurred during this protracted period causing fluctuations in sea level. When dry climatic conditions prevailed the shallow lagoons along the coastal margins accumulated thick layers of salt, gypsum and carbonates. These, as well as petroleum and natural gas formed during this same period are minerals of economic importance that are mined in quantity today.

Beginning about 200 million years ago the upper layers of this vast thickness of sediment were gradually raised to a height of more than 3,000 feet above sea level. The original, nearly horizontal attitude in which the sediment had been deposited (dipping gently from the slopes of the Adirondacks from which much of the sediment had come) was undisturbed in the New York State region by this uplift. Farther south, however, from central Pennsylvania southward to Alabama the layers were folded and buckled into the youthful Appalachian Mountains.

South of the Adirondacks and south of a general line through the northern ends of the present Finger Lakes, drainage on the new land surface persisted southward to the Atlantic Ocean. These ancestral drainage networks are today represented by the Delaware and Susquehanna river systems. North of the present Finger Lakes it is presumed that drainage was toward Hudson Bay. Thus a drainage divide existed along a line trending southwestward from the southwestern corner of the Adirondacks.

Following a relatively uneventful period of 100 million years a second uplift of the land took place with an upward bulging along this established drainage divide. North and south of this axis stream gradients were steepened and their erosive powers were effectively increased. The streams which coursed southward, however, deeply dissected the uplifted peneplain. Subsequent glaciation has failed to erase their effects and the hill country that characterizes much of New York State west from the Hudson and south from a line through the north end of the Finger Lakes still bears the imprint of stream erosion during this period.

Beginning approximately 2,000,000 years ago the last, and in many ways most important, period of earth history began for New York State. The time of the most recent of Ice Ages had come. The last 2,000,000 of earth history called the *Pleistocene* epoch was ushered in by the spreading of vast ice sheets over much of northern North America and northern Eurasia in the Northern Hemisphere. At its maximum extent ice sheets emanating from three centers in Canada spread, covering nearly 4,000,000 square miles of North America. Beginning as a number of small glaciers on Baffin Island, Labrador and eastern Quebec, the Laurentide or Labradorean ice sheet spread southward over New England and all of New York State except the southern margin of Long Island and a small area in the southwestern corner of the state. As it spread over the state, the tendency for this inexorable current of glacial ice was to divide into two streams, one of which passed southwestward up the low, broad St. Lawrence Valley pushing into and excavating the present Lake Ontario basin. The other lobe pushed due south into the Lake Champlain basin continuing down the Hudson Valley. With the lowlands filled the relentlessly advancing ice sheet climbed over even the highest peaks of the Adirondacks and Catskills and over the hills of the Appalachian Upland until virtually the entire state was buried under a continuous sheet of ice, in places, over 5,000 feet thick. Along its southern margin where the rate of ice advance was equalled by the rate of ice melt, the limit of glaciation was reached.

At present, the cause or causes of worldwide cooling that would cause such ice sheets to form can only be guessed at. What factors would cause a general warming, retreat and disappearance of such ice sheets are equally unknown. The record clearly shows that in New York State two such ice advances separated by a much longer warm interglacial period have occured in the past 1,000,000 years of the Pleistocene epoch. Less than 10,000 years ago a warming of earth climates began and New York State emerged from the last of the two ice sheets. Antarctica and Greenland on the other hand are still covered by remnants of Plesitocene glaciation. In New York State, even the smallest of residual alpine glaciers have long since disappeared but evidence of Pleistocene glaciation is everywhere. The bedrock over much of the state is carpeted by an uneven blanket of glacial debris often hundreds of feet thick laid down by the last ice sheet as it withdrew. Long Island remains as a 120-mile long accumulation of material dumped along the glacier's stagnant southern margin. The Great Lakes basins, formerly broad river valleys have been scoured, enlarged, deepened and left water-filled. Over 95,000 square miles of lakes in area, this connected series represents the largest fresh water area in the world. Spectacular Niagara Falls, the long, deep sparkling waters of the Finger Lakes, the gorges and waterfalls of Watkins Glen, Montour Falls and Taughannock Falls, near Ithaca, the highest waterfall east of the Mississippi at 215 feet, are but a few obvious examples of the legacy left by the Ice Ages. Less obviously but contributing to the regional distinctiveness of landscapes was the work of glaciers in smoothing of the hills and mountains, removing soil and in places exposing mineral-rich bedrock as in the Adirondacks, and depositing over 10,000 cigar-shaped hills called drumlins in a broad belt from Rochester to Syracuse. The best known of these drumlins is Hill Cumorah where the Mormon Joseph Smith received divine inspiration.

Landform Regions

Because of its long and diverse geological history, New York State, today, possesses an almost endless variety of landforms. To bring some sense of order from the continuously changing array one encounters travelling often only short distances, geographers have divided the state into eight fairly distinct landform or physiographic regions. Even the casual traveller will notice geographic differences, some of them quite striking, within any one of these eight regions. A number of the regions possess not only unique assemblages of landforms but often their own particular climate, vegetation, soils, or cultural features, further adding to the distinctiveness of the region's landscape.

The *Adirondack Upland* in northeastern New York has two distinct subdivisions. The most spectacular section of the Adirondacks and New York State is in the east-central part of the Upland and is a 1200 square-mile mass of old, resistant anorthosite, 40 to 50 miles across. Mt. Marcy, the state's highest peak (5,344 feet), and Algonquin Peak (5,114 feet) are surrounded by dozens of other glacially-rounded summits more than 4,000 feet high. This section of high peaks dominates the lower hills 2,000-3,000 feet high that compose the remainder of the Adirondack Upland. The recent glaciation disrupted pre-existing drainage patterns so that innumerable lakes such as Lake Placid, Saranac Lake and Tupper Lake attract summer vacationists from the entire Northeast. The snowy, winters attract equal numbers of winter sports enthusiasts. The permanent population, however, is very small, and highly dependent on tourism for income. Mining and the cutting of timber for the pulp-paper mills continues to be important to the region economically but employs relatively few people.

The *St. Lawrence-Lake Champlain Lowland* curves around the northern edge of the Adirondack Uplands. The limestone and sandstone rock that underlies these lowlands is younger and softer than the crystalline, granitic rock of the Adirondacks. Stream and ice erosion has worn this rock away creating, especcially in the St. Lawrence Valley a broad valley with extensive areas of good agricultural soils. Dairy farming, the location of several fine colleges, proximity to Canada and a degree of remoteness from the rest of the state gives this region its own flavor. The Champlain lowland is largely filled with the waters of the nearly 500 square mile, 125-mile long Lake Champlain, but funnelling through the narrow valley is the Northway a major interstate highway from Montreal, Canada south to Albany, New York City and eastern United States. Recently judged one of America's most scenic highways, this roadway has done much to renew the vitality of this region and the eastern Adirondack Mountains. The entire area is especially rich in Revolutionary War history as the lowland was a natural route followed both by British and Colonial armies.

Between the Hudson River and the west and the state border with New England on the east, is the *New England Upland,* an area of rock, in places as old as the two billion years old rock of the Adirondacks. Predominantly, a hilly, forested region 1,500-2,500 feet above sea level the upland stretches south to and includes the island of Manhattan in New York City. Steep hillsides and thin rocky soils permit only marginal farming. Many old farmhouses have become country homes and full-time residences for commuters who are within easy reach of Albany, New York City and other smaller cities of the lower Hudson Valley, and western Massachusetts and Connecticut. Natural lakes and reservoirs dot the region and with the hilly topography, provide welcome contrast within a short distance from New York City.

The *Hudson-Mohawk Lowland* is one of the nation's most historically important routes of migration and commerce. The Hudson River which starts at ". . . a minute pretending tear of the clouds as it were, - a lonely pool shivering in the breezes of the mountains . . ." is named for the Dutch explorer Henry Hudson who discovered it in 1609. Though they controlled the region for only a short time, Dutch settlement of the lower Hudson and what is now New York City imparted a definite European flavor to the region that persists today. Washington Irving's two short stories *Rip van Winkle* and *Legend of Sleepy Hollow* has preserved in the minds of generations of school children aspects of the Dutch colonial period. In *Rip van Winkle* there is a particularly beautiful description of the Hudson as seen by Rip from his vantage point in the nearby Catskill Mountains.

The Hudson Valley is really a series of low hills through which the Hudson River flows. It is a valley only in the sense that along most of its course it is bordered to the west by the higher Catskill Mountains and to the east by the Taconic Mountains of the New England Upland. Near West Point, where the U.S. Military Academy is located, the Hudson is bordered on both sides by sheer cliffs over 1,000 feet high, causing some to refer to this stretch of nearly 15 miles as the "Rhine Valley of America."

The Mohawk River which starts on the Tug Hill plateau north of Rome, New York, and the valley through which it flows joins the Hudson Valley near Albany. The Mohawk Valley is less than five miles wide at its broadest, but like the Hudson Valley with which it connects, served as an important route for post-Revolutionary War Americans moving west. Today the Thomas E. Dewey Thruway, U.S. Route 5, the New York State Barge (Erie) Canal-Mohawk River and Conrail railroad all squeeze through this natural conduit between the Adirondack Uplands on the north and the low mountains of the Appalachian Upland on the south. Carl Carmer's *Drums Along the Mohawk* and the works of other novelists bring alive in fiction the history of the Mohawk Valley for many Americans. Today, driving through the largely rural beauty of the scenic Hudson-Mohawk lowland one continually encounters historic sites and markers like pages of a history book.

The *Appalachian Upland* is the largest of New York State's landform regions, occupying near half the state. Originally a high plateau, hundreds of millions of years of stream erosion and more recent glacial erosion has sculpted the surface into a succession of hills and low mountains.

The eastern end of the region includes the Catskill Mountains, where the resistant sandstones that cap the softer underlying layers of sedimentary rock have preserved portions of an elevated peneplain that unprotected elsewhere have been eroded to much lower elevations. The Catskill region though has been deeply dissected by stream action. Here are found the highest elevations of the Appalachian Upland, ranging from 2,000 to 4,000 feet above sea level. It is a coarse-textured topography with bulky mountains and their glacially-rounded summits separated by few, often ravine-like valleys. Slide Mountain at 4,205 feet is the highest peak in the region.

Like the Adirondacks, the Catskill region is not traversed by any major highways. Agriculture and dairy farming that formerly took place on the good soils limited to the few narrow valley bottoms, and the marginal land of the hillside slopes, has largely disappeared. The close proximity of the New York City conurbation has caused many of these farms, which would otherwise have been abandoned, to become summer and often year-round country residences for "downstaters." A large section in the center of the region has been purchased by the state as the Catskill Forest Preserve. Again, as with Adirondacks, the large resort hotels of the late 19th and early 20th centuries have disappeared. A number of smaller modern hotels closest to New York City draw on cosmopolitan artists and showmen and continue to prosper. Overall, the region retains much of the wild, mountain ruggedness captured effectively and almost poetically by Washington Irving in his story *Rip van Winkle*. Bordering the Catskills on the east and north with spectacular views over the Hudson and Mohawk Valley, respectively, is the prominent Helderberg Escarpment, made of thick resistant limestone.

To the west of the Catskill Mountains the resistant sandstone caprock disappears and is replaced at the surface by weaker, more easily eroded shale. Westward to the shores of Lake Erie the landscape becomes one of lower hills and broader valleys. Elevations at the north edge of the upland rise only an average of 500 feet above the Ontario Lake Plain but gradually climb to 1500-2500 feet above sea level along the New York-Pennsylvania border. Considerable quantities of salt from sub-surface mines and brine wells is shipped from the region. The salt museum in Syracuse testifies to the claim this city long held as "salt city of the United States."

"Pennsylvania crude" oil, reputedly the world's best natural lubricating oil, has been pumped for well over a century from wells in the southwestern corner of the state. Escalating world petroleum prices have stimulated not only increased exploration and drilling of new petroleum wells but for natural gas as well. Successful natural gas exploration has continued through the entire Appalachian Upland, into Lake Erie and onto the Ontario Lake Plain to the north. The forests of oak, maple and dozens of other hardwood species which still cloak the hillsides continue to be a regional resource of considerable importance.

Numerous small cities with population of 10,000-20,000 occur throughout the upland, a number of major four-lane highways criss-cross the region; and the broad, flat-floored valleys are intensively farmed. The recreational and scenic attractiveness of the Finger Lakes and the Letchworth gorge cut by the Genesee River, aptly named the "Grand Canyon of the East," further add to the attractiveness of the area. A general air of prosperity and contentment characterizes most parts of this region.

The narrow lake plain between the western end of the Appalachian Upland and Lake Erie and the broad plain between Lake Ontario and the upland is referred to as the *Erie-Ontario Lake Plain*. Most of this plain was formerly the bottom of Lakes Erie and Ontario when, immediately following the retreat of the last ice sheet from New York 10,000-8,000 years ago these lakes were larger than they are today. The lakes have shrunk due to the melting of the ice that once blocked their drainage through the St. Lawrence River and a springing upward of the land released from the tremendous weight of the ice. As a result of recently having been lake bottom, much of the plain's surface is very flat with large poorly-drained swampy areas common. In one portion of the lake plain, approximately between Rochester and Syracuse, are hundreds of oblong hills called *drumlins* less than 100 feet high and from several hundred feet to a mile long and all strongly oriented north-south. Formed by the last continental ice sheet that covered the area, these hills are made of bouldery-clay material and provide the only notable section of low hills on the otherwise exceptionally flat plain. The major upstate cities of Syracuse, Rochester and Buffalo as well as a number of small, old industrial cities stretch across the lowland. First the Erie Canal, later the railroad and now super highways connect these cities to New York City, New England, Canada and the Midwest. Agriculturally, this area ranks only behind eastern

Long Island in value per acre of crops raised but because of its large size outproduces Long Island by a considerable amount. As one passes through the region, constant change between urban to rural landscapes takes place and one senses the dynamism of the Erie-Ontario Lake Plain.

The *Tug Hill Upland* at the eastern end of Lake Ontario is a small plateau rising 1,800 to 2,000 feet above the surrounding lowlands. Geologically, it is an extension of the Appalachian Upland to the south from which it is separated by the Mohawk Valley. It is bordered by the Black River Valley to the east, and the St. Lawrence Valley to the north. As a result of disruption of the drainage systems by Pleistocene glaciation much of the gently undulating surface is poorly drained and swamp-covered. Until about 1920 dairying and cheesemaking was important to this region, but the marginal quality of the soils, the short, cool growing season and the long, exceptionally snowy winters drove what farming there was from the area. Today spruce forests have reclaimed much of the land and few roads serving only a handful of people cross this region beautiful in its desolation.

Long Island is a small part of the *Atlantic Coastal Plain* which stretches from Cape Cod southward through Florida. The highest point, on the island's western end, is slightly over 400 feet above the waters of Long Island Sound. The island marks the southern margin of the last continental ice sheet as it moved down from Canada across New England. Along this portion of its southern margin, the melting glacier deposited a long line of glacial clay, sand, cobbles and boulders. This line of low hills running through central Long Island out to Montauk Point on the island's southeastern tip is knows as the *Ronkonkoma moraine*. Near the end of its existence the ice sheet began to retreat northward but momentarily re-advanced depositing a second line of hills knows as the *Harbor Hill moraine*. The Harbor Hill moraine now forms the north shore of the island and terminates at the northeastern end of the island as Orient Point. The island is divided into two counties; Nassau County shares the island's western end with New York City. Suffolk County takes up the eastern half of the island. Nassau County and the western part of Suffolk County are very densely populated and little open space exists. The eastern part of Suffolk County has large tracts of prime farmland and open space. Even here, though, economic pressure for urban and suburban development is intense. Only through progressive legislation have individuals and municipalities been able to preserve here and along the south shore the last vestiges of natural landscape and rural character which once typified most of the island. Long stretches of tidal marsh, open water lagoon and sandy barrier beach from Brooklyn eastward along the south shore to Montauk Point have been preserved for public use.

The Nature of Climates and New York Climatic Regions

Large bodies of air originating in Canada and moving southeastward under the prevailing westerly winds of the middle latitudes frequently bring to New York State dry, cool refreshing spells of weather in summer, and very cold, dry arctic weather in winter. Alternating with such Canadian air masses are warm, humid air masses moving north and eastward from the Gulf of Mexico, across New York State. In summer such air results in muggy, showery, uncomfortable weather. In winter, however, this humid, and quite mild air is welcomed by New Yorkers for such air will bring relief from the bitterly cold Canadian air that might have been dominating much of the state for a week or more. With air masses from these two source regions, as well as modified air masses from western United States alternating with one another and crossing the state in periods varying from a day or two, to a week or more New York State experiences highly variable weather conditions in all seasons of the year.

Lake Erie to the west of New York State, and Lake Ontario to the north and west are large sources of moisture for the comparatively dry Canadian air masses. Particularly in winter, when these Great Lakes are relatively warm and do not freeze over completely, dry Canadian air moving eastward across them becomes charged with moisture and brings precipitation to the state. The precipitation falls as rain in summer and fall and as snow in winter and early srping. Long Island, New York City and eastern New York including the Catskill Mountains receive additional precipitation annually from occasional *nor' easters* which are North Atlantic storms which sometimes extend westward through New England and into eastern New York State; and, from the weak remnants of hurricanes moving up the

Atlantic coast in late summer and early autumn. The humid climate of the state is further characterized by seasonally wide ranges in temperature resulting from the state's location on the eastern margin of the large North American land mass from which come air masses highly variable both in moisture and especially temperature. Complaints about the weather are often met with the remark "If you're not happy with today's weather just wait for the change that's coming tomorrow."

The famous geographer Ellsworth Huntington wrote extensively with regard to a concept he referred to as "climatic determinism." It was his conviction that a whole set of cultural and physical traits related to climatic differences were to be attributed to various cultural and racial groups. Further examination of this idea has shown that Huntington overstated his case. Yet within limits one can see within New York State differences in the life styles and means of livelihood engaged in by the people, aspects of which can be attributed to variations in climate. Under the combined influence of differences in terrain, particularly in elevation, and promixity to or distance from large water bodies, a number of distinct climatic regions exist within the state.

Annual precipitation averages 35-45" across the state. In the vicinity and to the south of Rochester, however, is an area where precipitation is as little as 30-35", annually. An even drier area, where annual precipitation amounts to only 25-30" is found in the Lake Champlain-Lake George lowland. This results from the Tug Hill and Adirondacks immediately to the west exerting a blocking or "rain shadow" effect on storms which come predominantly from the west. In contrast, the southeastern Catskills annually averages 45-55" of precipitation much of it coming from the very wet air of coastal storms being cooled and yielding copious rainfall as the air attempts to rise up over the only notable highlands in the Long Island-New York City coastal area.

With the exception of Long Island and the "downstate" portion of the state most of the winter precipitation is in the form of snow across the remainder of the state. Several remarkable snowbelts exist on the slopes of highlands bordering the lee shores of Lakes Erie and Ontario. In winter, Canadian air masses which absorb moisture as they move south and east across the lakes encounter either the prominent escarpment at the northern edge of the Appalachian Upland or the Tug Hill Upland at the eastern end of Lake Ontario. Forced to rise, these air masses cool and much of their moisture falls in intense, heavy snowstorms. Thus along a line from south of Rome and Utica westward to just southeast of Buffalo, then southwestward to the Pennsylvania state line is one such continuous snowbelt. Eastward moving air following along the east-west axis of unfrozen Lake Ontario become especially moisture laden; the Tug Hill Upland at the eastern end of the lake intercepts such storms resulting in the snowiest region in all of eastern North America. In the winter of 1971-72, Sears Pond in the Tug Hill south of Watertown received 345″ of snow. That same winter Buffalo received almost 200″. The heavy winter snowfall contributes to the high annual precipitation of over 50″ that much of the Tug Hill like the southeastern Catskills, receives. To the east, the Adirondack Mountains receive, over most of its area, snowfall in excess of 100″ annually. This is reflected in the large number of ski resorts and winter sports centers found here, including the internationally reknowned facilities at Lake Placid which hosted both the 1932 and 1980 Winter Olympics. The remainder of "upstate" New York receives intermediate amounts of snow; nevertheless, snow clearing and removal remains a significant item in the budgets of villages, towns and cities throughout the state. The New York City-Long Island region receives several major snowstorms each winter but alternating mild air soon arrives and such effects, as beautiful as they are exasperating, are short-lived.

Temperature variation within New York State especially in winter is very pronounced. Summer temperatures average from 68-72°F for the warmest month except for some of the highland areas within the Adirondacks and Catskills where they may be several degrees cooler. Heavily-urbanized New York City and the western end of Long Island away from the shore will average one or two degrees warmer.

There is no place in the state other than a few locations in eastern Long Island that has not experienced a temperature of 0°F. The coolest sustained winter temperatures though are found in late January to mid-February in the heart of the Adirondacks when clear, dry Canadian air frequently settles over the region for long spells. The remainder of the state will have such spells broken by the aperiodic invasion of mild Gulf of Mexico air. Thus these areas outside the Adirondacks experience intense cold less frequently and for shorter periods of time. The Atlantic Coastal lowland of New York State dominated by the marine influence of Long Island Sound and the Atlantic Ocean has temperate winter conditions without the extreme fluctutations in temperature that characterizes much of upstate New York. The shore zones of the Great Lakes do not have as mild winter conditions as one might presume, due to the extension of shore ice some considerable distances out from the shores. Such a surface behaves little differently than a snow covered land surface.

The growing season, along with the presence of suitable soils, strongly influences the geographic distribution of New York State's agriculture. From the last frost of spring until the first killing frost of autumn is a period of 180-220 days in the agricultural region of eastern Long Island. The climate, well-structured glacially-derived soils and proximity to the large New York City urban market leads to very intensive efforts to maximize the agricultural production of this region. As a result, the dollar value per acre of cropland, here, is the highest of any comparable area in the United States. High value truck garden crops, strawberries, and flowers arrive on the New York City area very early in the year as farmers benefit from a climate as equable in the spring as that of the Delmarva peninsula and southern New Jersey farther to the south. The nearby ocean waters warmed through the long, warm summer provides abundant heat energy during the autumn nights preventing damaging frosts from occurring until late November. Large quantities of potatoes are also grown for the U.S. market on the sandy, well-drained soils.

The tree and small fruit industry of upstate New York is also concentrated in areas having an abnormally-long growing season that results from the nearby presence of large water bodies. Along the Erie-Ontario Lake Plain, the Finger Lakes and the Hudson Valley, the large volumes of water, which during the summer have been heated by the sun, retain this energy more efficiently than do equal volumes of earthen material. Consequently, as the shorter days and longer, cooler nights of autumn approach the air above farm fields and orchards away from the water bodies loses heat to the ground. The moisture in the air condenses on leaf and fruit surfaces as dew, but freezes as frost when the air temperatures drop below 32°F. The air over fields and orchards close to the lakes and in the Hudson Valley, on these same nights, however are warmed by the waters below. Frosts do not occur until much later in the season when there is insufficient heat left in the water to keep air temperatures above freezing.

As it takes more sun energy to heat the water bodies in the spring, air over and near the large lakes while above freezing, is cooler than air over inland fields that warm more rapidly. This cool air over the vineyards of the Finger Lakes and orchards of the Erie-Ontario Lake Plain and Hudson Valley, retards the blossoming of the plants until all danger of a late frost has passed. Inland, blossoms might have appeared due to a succession of warm days and nights, only to be killed or severely damaged by a late spring frost. The Erie-Ontario Lake Plain and Finger Lakes have a growing season of 160-180 days. In contrast, places in the valleys of the Adirondack highlands have a growing season of less than 100 days precluding agriculture on a commercial scale.

Five basic climatic regions exist in New York State. **Region 1:** the Long Island-New York City-lower Hudson Valley region is a region of mild, rainy winters and hot, humid summers. **Region 2:** the Adirondack Mountain region has long, extremely cold, snowy winters and short, cool, cloudy and wet summers. **Region 3:** the St. Lawrence-upper Lake Champlain basin in an area that has cold, snowy winters but cool and sunny summers ideal for hay-growing to support the regions numerous dairy farms. **Region 4:** Erie-Ontario Lake Plain extends down into the Finger Lakes region. Here the winters are temperate and snowy. Summers are sunny and warm with a tendency for droughty conditions to prevail. The growing season is long and suited to fruit and vegetable production. **Region 5:** the Appalachian Upland of New York excluding the lower Finger Lakes, and the Taconic highlands along the state's eastern border. In this region the winters are cold, quite long and snowy. Summers are cool with spells of cloudy, wet weather alternating with mild to warm, partly sunny conditions. The growing season's shortness is suited to hay and varieties of feed corn for dairy farms, but precludes more intensive forms of agriculture.

Natural Vegetation

Wetlands occur where the water table is at or very near the surface for most of the year and vary in their primary vegetative cover. Those wetlands that are covered by trees are referred to as *swamps;* those covered by grass or grass-like vegetation are *marshes;* and those with grass-like vegetation mixed with thick, leather leafed vegetation are called *bogs.* In addition to possessing literally thousands of wetland sites of an acre or less, New York State has a number of major ones increasingly protected by the state as wildlife refuges, natural groundwater recharge areas for domestic water, and areas of interest for scientists and citizens with ecological interests. Major portions of the south shore of Long Island, the Montezuma and Cicero swamps near Syracuse and the Bergen swamp southwest of Rochester are several examples of major wetlands in the state.

The most widespread natural vegetation, however, are the mature forests and woodlands that are reclaiming marginal farmland that has been abandoned. The peak of cleared land in New York State was reached in the period 1880-1900. Since that time, particularly in the hill lands of the Appalachian Upland, the Tug Hill and the St. Lawrence-Champlain lowland, the steeper slopes with their thin soils located farthest from the farm buildings and access roads have been abandoned to the shadowy claim of the forest. In an as urban, industrialized state as New York it surprises many that more than 58 per cent of the land is in forest or woodland.

New York in colonial history was a major supplier of forest pro-products: lumber, cooperage, fence posts, bark for tanning, pulp for paper, firewood, and potash from wood ash ("black salts"). From its rich forest, the volume of products grew. In 1850, the state was ranked first in lumber production, accounting for over 30 percent of the lumber cut in the U.S. Lumber barons bought the land cheaply, rapaciously cut over the virgin timber, then allowed the state to repossess the land by defaulting on taxes. While this kept the state in the forefront among forest producers the loss of wildlife such as the timber wolf and moose, and the loss of valuable immature timber and scenery were significant. They were replaced instead by silt-laden streams, a general decline in mammalian, water fowl, bird and fish habitats and frequent forest fires set by sparks from the timber-hauling, narrow gauge railroad engines. Such despoliation led to the Law of 1885 passed by an irate New York State legislature. This act, antedating the Federal Act of 1891 authorizing the creation of national forests for much the same reasons underlying the Law of 1885, laid the framework of the Adirondack Forest Preserve which now stands as a 2.4 million acres, forever-wild legacy to future generations.

Far-sighted, imaginative state and private management typifies the state's forest resources, and the forest products industry of the state contributes significantly to the economy. Much of the harvested timber is used as pulp in the manufacture of paper but the diversity of products from the state's forests range from traditional items such as lumber and industrial pallets to baseball bats and maple syrup.

The "mixed" forest of New York is composed of *hardwood* and *softwoods*. The hardwoods are broadleafed, deciduous trees which include the sugar maple, oaks, birches, black walnut, tulip, ash, hickory and many others. Both the beech and beautiful American elm have recently been badly decimated by difficult to control diseases. *Softwoods* are mostly needle-leafed, evergreen trees such as the valuable eastern white pine, hemlock, spruce, and fir. Hardwood species are valuable for handles, veneer woods and cabinet woods. Softwoods supply most of the lumber and pulp coming from the forests. Increasingly today, as the popularity of wood-burning stoves increases one sees neatly cut and stacked piles of firewood outside urban as well as rural homes. As a compartively cheap and renewable source of heat, firewood is regaining the popularity it had before the railroad introduced Pennsylvania coal as a cheap source of fuel for New Yorkers.

Some regional variation occurs in the forests of the state. Oaks are prominent in the forests of southeastern New York, and on Long Island oak and pitch pine. The central Adirondack and Tug Hill forests have a predominance of spruce and fir mixed with some northern hardwoods. In a broad zone encircling the lower slopes of the Adirondacks, in the Catskills and eastern Appalachian Upland and in the southwestern corner of the state, northern hardwoods with a minor occurrence of white pine are widespread. The Finger Lakes and Hudson River-Lake Champlain lowland have a predominantly oak forest though other northern hardwoods occur. Like Long Island, forest cover on the Erie-Ontario Lake plain is limited to forest preserves, wetlands and woodlots but here red maple, and until recently elms, mixed with northern hardwoods typified the woodlands.

Soils of New York State

The soils of New York State form the resource base for the state's dynamic agricultural economy. The variation in the pattern of soils one finds anywhere is the result of differences in the materials from which soil forms, the slope of the land, differences in climate, drainage and vegetative cover, cultural practices, and the length of time since deglaciation.

The cool humid climate and the luxuriant natural and domesticated vegetation cause New York's soils to be moderately to strongly acid. Few agricultural crops prefer acid soils, thus "sweetening" the soil by adding lime is a common agricultural practice. Some soils, underlain by limestone or glacial debris rich in limestone, are less acid and naturally suited to a wider variety of crops. All berries, many tuberous root crops such as potatoes and turnips, and tree fruit such as apples, cherries and plums prefer an acid soil. Most other vegetables and grain, however, do not.

The pattern of New York soils is complex but several basic soils regions are to be found. There are: the thin, acid soils of the Adirondacks, Catksills and Hudson Highlands; the deep soils of former glacial lake and sea bottom sediment found in the Erie-Ontario Lake Plain and St. Lawrence Valley; the deep soils of the Applachian Uplands forming from glacial debris; and, the alluvial soils of river valleys in the hilly regions of New York State, and on Long Island.

The soils of the Adirondacks generally are thin and stony. The rock from which they are forming are hard granites which break only slowly into small soil-sized particles. During the cool, humid summers of the region, water filters through a thick mat of pine, fir and spruce needles creating a very acid soil solution. Coupled with the short-growing season and the lack of connections to major markets these soils contributed to the non-agricultural nature of the region. Similar conditions exist in the Hudson Highlands. The non-granite soils of the Catskills and Tug Hill are somewhat better but with other negative physical and economic conditions prevalent, the two regions have very limited agricultural potential.

The Erie-Ontario Lake Plain and the St. Lawrence Valley are regions where large post-glacial water bodies existed. Sediment brought into them by rivers and streams settled to the bottom. The Great Lakes have since shrunk to their present size and marine water has disappeared from all but the lower St. Lawrence estuary below Quebec City and the land, released from the tremendous weight of ice, continues to spring upward. The sediment of these former bottoms are the thick, rich farm soils of today. Coupled with the long growing season, especially of the lake plain and the good connections to urban markets, these soils are intensively used.

When the last ice sheet which had covered virtually all of what is now New York State retreated, the Appalachian Upland on the southern margins of the ice sheet was left buried under a thick layer of glacial debris. In the valleys this debris has subsequently been reworked by running water and has received new sediment from the hillsides. The slopes and tops of the Appalachian hills, however, retain much of this glacial mantle. The glacial debris originated mostly from the local shale that underlies most of the Appalachian Upland and as a result soils have a high clay content. Such clayey soils are difficult to plow, prone to wetness in spring and have brick-like hardness in dry periods. The moderately developed transportation system of the Appalachian hills imposes some limits on access to major urban markets by farmers. The growing season of only 110-130 days further restricts agriculture. Only along the northern edge of the Appalachian Upland and in the Hudson Valley where soils are evolving atop limestone outcrops, and glacial debris is rich with limestone material is agriculture more intensive. Proximity of the northern edge of the Upland both to the major transportation routes of the lake plain which connect to downstate and New York City via the Mohawk-Hudson corridor, and to the lake plain with its longer growing season are added advantages.

Equal to the lime-rich soils along the northern edge of the Appalachian Upland, and nearly as good as the soils of the lake plain, are the deep alluvial soils of the broad river bottoms within the Appalachian Upland. The valley floors of the Delaware, Susquehanna, Allegheny, Chemung and Genesee Rivers and their major tributaries are intensively farmed. The short growing season of the Appalachian region of the state limits the growing of the more sensitive vegetable and fruit crops but hay, corn and oats to support widespread dairy farming grow extremely well. The location of the region's transportation routes in the valleys further encourages the full utilization of these soils.

Good soil conservation and land management practices will ensure that New York State remains one of the nation's leading agricultural states. Alternate land usage, however, is removing large areas of the state's best soils from agricultural production, especially on Long Island. The identification and preservation of its best agricultural soils is one of New York's most important tasks.

New York's Lakes and Rivers

The humid climate of the Northeast results in the annual precipitation over the region exceeding the annual evaporation by a considerable amount. Geologically recent continental glaciation has dammed water courses and created numerous water-filled hollows and basins. As a result, the landscape of New York is dotted today with thousands of lakes and ponds which are fed and drained by uncountable streams creating a dense network of major rivers. Man has further integrated these natural water features through a system of canals. The government of the state maintains 524 miles of navigable waterways used jointly for commerce and recreational cruising. This enhanced system is also used as a water source for domestic and industrial consumption and for hydroelectric power generation.

Geographical Configuration

Lakes Erie and Ontario on the northern and western boundaries of the state are the two smallest of five Great Lakes. Lake Erie has an area of 9,910 square miles and is the shallowest of the lakes with a mean depth of less than 100 feet. Because of its small volume, Lake Erie has suffered most severely among the Great Lakes from industrial and municipal pollution. Drainage from the upper Great Lakes has added pollutants from such major industrial cities as Toledo and Sandusky, Ohio; Erie, Pennsylvania and Buffalo, New York, all of which are located along the Lake Erie shoreline. Major efforts by the federal and responsible state governments have been reflected in a tremendous improvement in water quality and the predicted "death of Lake Erie" forecast in the early 1970's has been avoided.

The Niagara Escarpment is a prominent limestone belt which arcs in a great semi-circle west from Rochester, New York around northern Lakes Huron and Michigan into Wisconsin. The Niagara River crosses it and is eroding back the limestone at a rate of 4-5 feet per year but has been unable to remove the rock entirely. Water cascading over this wall of rock and eating away the softer rock at its foot, has created Niagara Falls, 167 feet high. The more than 1,500,000 gallons of water plunging over the falls each second creates a spectacle millions of people come to witness. The obstacle it creates to Great Lakes shipping has been by-passed by the 27-mile long Welland Canal just to the west in Ontario, Canada.

The Niagara River draining Lake Erie and the upper Great Lakes flows into Lake Ontario, the smallest of the Great Lakes with an area of 7,550 square miles. Like Lakes Erie, Huron, and Superior, Lake Ontario is shared internationally with Canada. Lake Ontario and the entire Great Lakes system drains via the St. Lawrence river which begins just north of Watertown, New York. The Thousand Islands in the St. Lawrence River between New York State and Canada has resulted from the inability of the river over tens of millions of years to completely erode away the hard, crystalline rock that connects the Canadian Shield and Adirondack Mountains. In June, 1959, the enlarged St. Lawrence Seaway was opened and featured several sets of locks which now permits 80 per cent of the ocean-going ships to sail from the Atlantic to the westernmost tip of Lake Superior and

Duluth, Minnesota in the very heart of North America, a distance of 2,300 miles.

The Finger Lakes of central New York State consist of eleven lakes. The four small, western lakes drain west to the Genesee River which in turn flows north through Rochester and empties into Lake Ontario. The seven eastern lakes drain to the Seneca River which also flows north into Lake Ontario. All the lakes are nearly parallel and oriented north-south, have precipitously steep walls both above and below lake level and are linear in form. They occupy preglacial stream valleys that were overdeepened and oversteepened during the Ice Ages. Lakes Cayuga and Seneca are the longest and largest of the lakes, each about 40 miles long and 2.5 miles wide. In many respects, these beautiful lakes resemble fjords. On the slopes of many of the western Finger Lakes especially Keuka Lake and Seneca Lake are the vineyards which grow the grapes for the distinctive wines of New York State. Orchards and vegetable farms extending down from the moderate climate and rich soils of the Erie-Ontario Lake Plain cloak the slopes of all the Finger Lakes. The Seneca-Cayuga Canal with four locks permits pleasure craft and other small boats to move between these two lakes and the New York State Barge (Erie) Canal.

Lake Champlain and Lake George are two large lakes along New York's eastern border with Vermont. Proceeding north on the Hudson River from Troy, New York (near Albany) boaters can pass through eleven locks of the Champlain Canal into Lake George and Lake Champlain at the Canadian border, 172 miles further north and then via the Richelieu River into the St. Lawrence River.

In 1825, Governor DeWitt Clinton opened the 364-mile long Erie Canal. Barge traffic was then able to move between the Great Lakes and Buffalo, New York, to Albany, then down the Hudson River to New York City, a distance of 505 miles. The development of railroads followed soon after and diminished the commercial influence of this and other canals in eastern United States. The state continues to maintain the canal which with its 34 locks forms a network of waterways connected to the Lake Champlain system, to Lake Ontario via the Oswego River, and to the Finger Lakes, the Great Lakes and Hudson River.

Such an integrated system is a delight for pleasure craft owners who can reach the Mississippi River and Gulf of Mexico, and the Atlantic Ocean via either the St. Lawrence or Hudson Rivers using this link.

In addition to the major lakes mentioned, literally thousands of smaller lakes dot the landscape, especially in the Adirondack Mountains. The ecology of many of these lakes is being damaged by acid precipitation. Sulfur and nitrogen pollutants put into the air by industry in the Midwest combine with atmospheric moisture to be carried eastward by the wind and to fall over the Northeast as acid rain, and snowfall. Canadians and Americans are presently seeking a solution to this problem.

A number of scenic and historically important rivers arise within or cross New York State. The Great Lakes-Niagara-St. Lawrence River system is the largest river system flowing through New York State. A number of other rivers, smaller in size but nationally known arise in the state's highlands. The Hudson River flows southeast from the Adirondacks. The Mohawk originates in the Tug Hill Upland and flows east to join the Hudson near Albany. The Susquehanna and Delaware Rivers form within the Catskill Mountain region and flow southward into Chesapeake and Delaware Bays, respectively. In the western part of the state the Allegheny River which begins in northern Pennsylvania briefly arcs into New York before curving southward towards Pittsburgh and the Ohio River. The broad, rich farmland of the Genesee Valley is drained by the Genesee River which also originates in northern Pennsylvania but flows for most of its length northward across the state to Rochester and Lake Ontario.

Dr. Gergel has been a member of the Geography Department at S.U.N.Y., Oneonta, for the past 13 years. In 1980 he was awarded the Chancellor's Award for Excellence in Teaching by the State University of New York. He is co-author with Dr. George Langdon of West Chester, Pennsylvania of an 18-filmstrip series entitled *New York State and Its Resources*.

MAJOR DRAINAGE SYSTEMS OF NEW YORK STATE

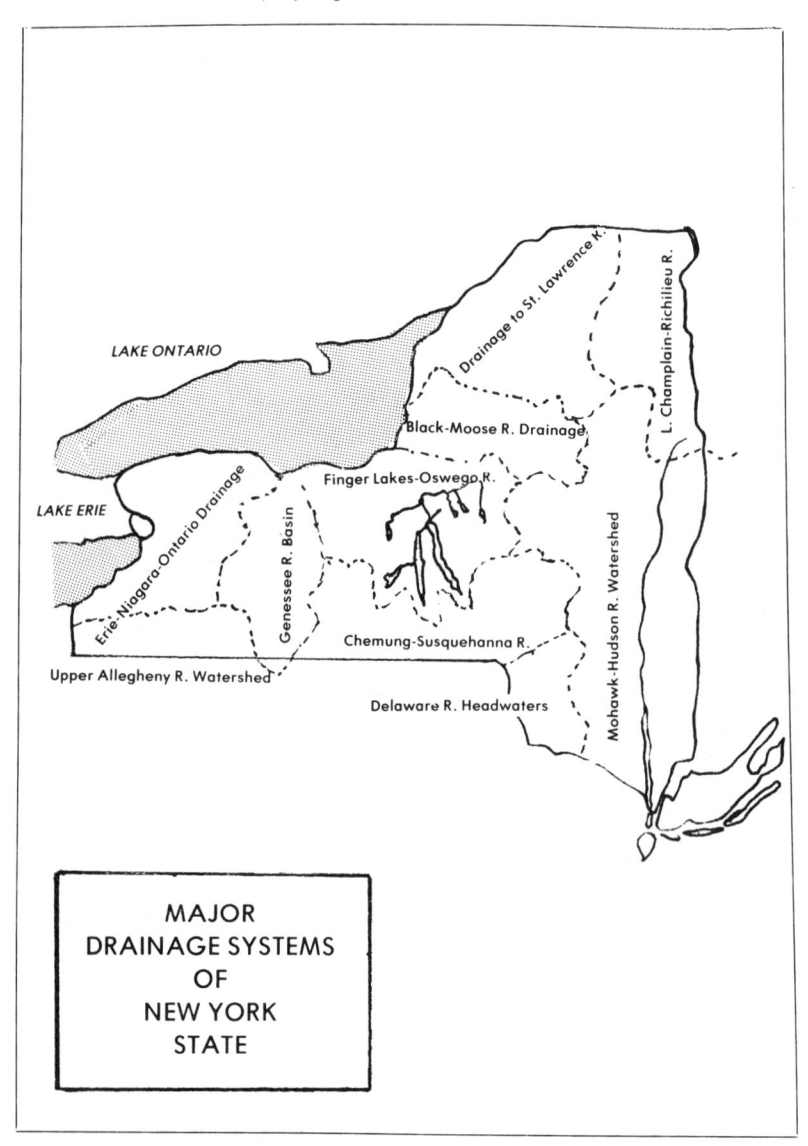

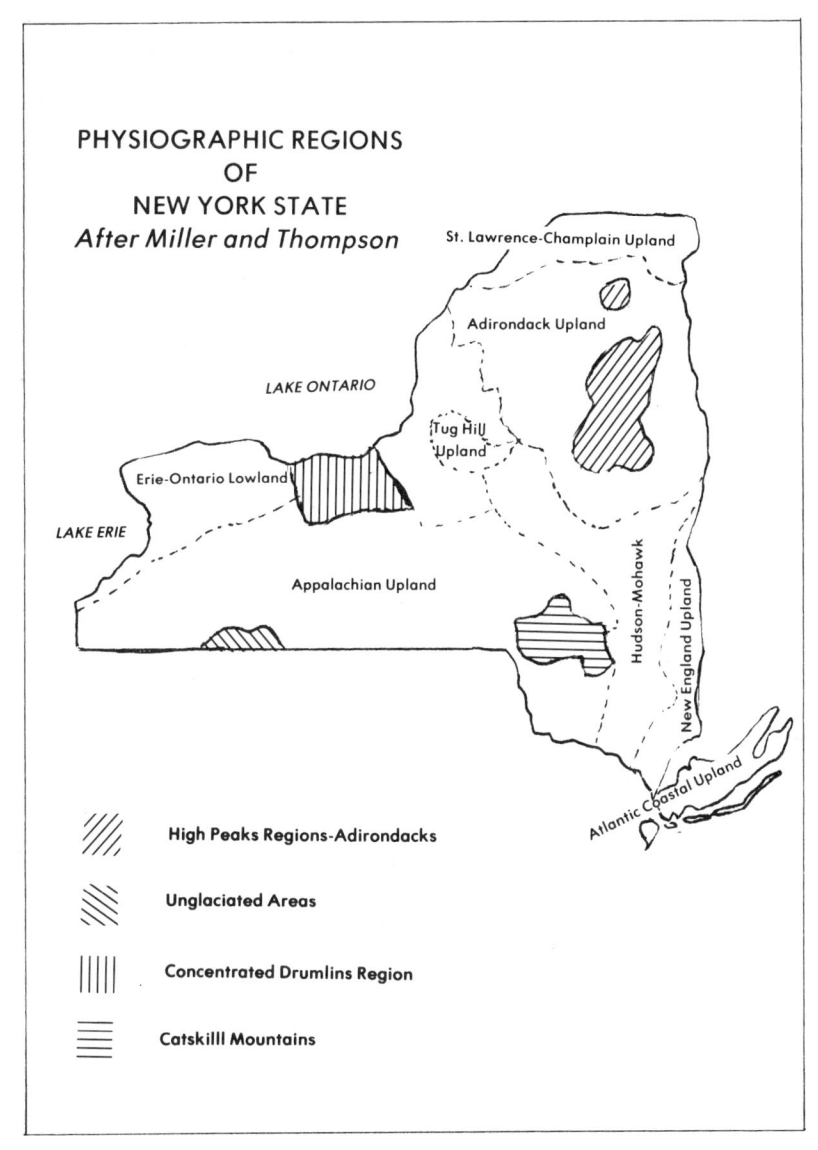

Geographical Configuration

PHYSIOGRAPHIC REGIONS OF NEW YORK STATE
After Miller and Thompson

- High Peaks Regions-Adirondacks
- Unglaciated Areas
- Concentrated Drumlins Region
- Catskilll Mountains

Montauk Point, southeastern tip of Long Island and the Ronkonkoma moraine.

Geographical Configuration 87

Hill Country-farmland of the Appalachian Upland near Oneonta.

United States SENATORS

Schuyler, Phillip J.	1789-91; 1797
King, Rufus	1789-96; 1813-25
Burr, Aaron	1791-97
Laurance, John	1796-1800
Hobart, John S.	1798
North, William	1798
Watson, James	1798-1800
Morris, Gouverneur	1800-03
Armstrong, John	1800-02; 1803-04
Clinton, DeWitt	1802-03
Bailey, Theodorus	1803-04
Mitchill, Samuel L.	1804-09
Smith, John	1804-13
German, Obadiah	1809-15
Sanford, Nathan	1815-21; 1826-31
Van Buren, Martin	1821-29
Dudely, Charles E.	1829-33
March, William L.	1831-33
Tallmadge, Nathaniel P.	1833-44
Wright, Silas Jr.	1833-44
Dicinson, Daniel S.	1844-51
Foster, Henry A.	1844-45
Dix, John A.	1845-49
Seward, William H.	1849-61
Fish, Hamilton	1851-57
King, Preston	1857-63
Harris, Ira	1861-67
Morgan, Edwin D.	1863-69
Conkling, Roscoe	1867-81
Fenton, Rueben E.	1869-75
Kernan, Francis	1875-81

United States Senators

Lapham, Elbridge G.	1881-85
Platt, Thomas C.	1881
Miller, Warner	1881-87
Evarts, William M.	1885-92
Hiscock, Frank	1887-93
Hill, David B.	1892-97
Murphy, Edward Jr.	1893-99
Platt, Thomas C.	1897-1909
Depew, Channcey M.	1899-1911
Root, Elihu	1909-15
O'Gorman, James A.	1911-17
Wadsworth, James W., Jr.	1915-27
Calder, William M.	1917-23
Copeland, Royal S.	1923-38
Wagner, Robert F. Sr.	1927-49
Mead, James M.	1939-47
Ives, Irving M.	1947-59
Dulles, John Foster	1949
Lehman, Herbert H.	1949-57
Javits, Jacob K.	1957-
Keating, Kenneth B.	1959-65
Kennedy, Robert F.	1965-68
Goodell, Charles E.	1968-71
Buckley, James L.	1971-77
Moynihan, Daniel P.	1977-

New York
GOVERNORS

Clinton, George	1777-95; 1801-04
Jay, John	1795-1801
Lewis, Morgan	1804-07
Tompkins, Daniel	1807-17
Tayler, John	1817
Clinton, DeWitt	1817-23; 1825-28
Yates, Joseph Christopher	1823-25
Pitcher, Nathaniel	1828-29
Van Buren, Martin	1829
Throop, Enos Thompson	1829-33
Marcy, William Learned	1833-39
Seward, William H.	1839-43
Bouck, William C.	1843-45
Wright, Silas	1845-47
Young, John	1847-49
Fish, Hamilton	1849-51
Hunt, Washington	1851-53
Seymour, Horatio	1853-55; 1863-65
Clark, Myron	1855-57
King, John Alsop	1857-59
Morgan, Edwin D.	1859-63
Fenton, Reuben Eaton	1865-69
Hoffman, John Thompson	1869-73
Tilden, Samuel Jones	1873-77
Robinson, Lucius	1877-80
Cornell, Alonzo	1880-83
Cleveland, Grover	1883-85
Hill, Davis Bennett	1885-92
Flower, Roswell Petibone	1892-95
Morton, Levi Parsons	1895-97
Black, Frank Swett	1897-99

Roosevelt, Theodore	1899-1901
Odell, Benjamin Barker, Jr.	1901-05
Higgins, Frank Weyland	1905-07
Hughes, Charles Evans	1907-10
White, Horace	1910-11
Dix, John Alden	1911-13
Sulzer, William	1913
Glynn, Martin Henry	1913-15
Whitman, Charles Seymour	1915-19
Smith, Alfred E.	1919-21; 1923-29
Miller, Nathan L.	1921-23
Roosevelt, Franklin Delano	1929-33
Lehman, Herbert H.	1933-42
Poletti, Charles	1942-43
Dewey, Thomas E.	1943-55
Harriman, William Averell	1955-59
Rockefeller, Nelson A.	1959-73
Wilson, Charles Malcom	1973-75
Carey, Hugh	1975-

GOVERNORS OF NEW YORK

CLINTON, GEORGE—(1739-1812), was the first and third governor of New York (1777-95 and 1801-04). A native of Ulster County, New York, his parents were Elizabeth Denniston and Charles Clinton, colonists from Ireland. At the age of 16, he ran away from home to fight the French alongside the British, and when he returned he joined his father's regiment in the attack on Fort Frontenac. Although he didn't attend college, Clinton studied law in New York City and began a law practice that spread over Ulster County in the 1760's. His reputation gained him a seat on the New York Assembly in 1768, and he served there until the revolution was in sight. In 1775, he was a delegate to the Second Continental Congress and increasingly demonstrated his anti-British sentiments. Soon afterwards, he was called home to command a brigade against the invading Redcoats, and in 1777 he helped write New York's first State Constitution. When it was accepted by the electorate, Clinton was also accepted as the first state governor. In the following elections, he won over other candidates by increasing margins.

During his long term, Clinton was faced with a large proportion of the states' population which still favored the King. For this reason, the British maintained New York as a prime target in 1777, and Clinton was continually working to drive them out. Once he even cancelled a meeting of the legislature to defend American forts in the state. In 1780, the final British troops left New York City, and Clinton rode on horseback through town next to George Washington.

By the end of the 1780's, however, Clinton had lost some of his popularity. He was against the 1787 Federal Constitution, so Alexander Hamilton and the federalists of the time tried to prevent his reelection from 1789 on. Although Clinton won in a tight race in 1792, the people of the state were beginning to scrutinize his long term of power and the political patronage system he had gradually built up.

In 1795, Clinton decided not to run for governor again because of poor health. For five years he remained in private practice.

In 1801, he was once more convinced to vie for the governorship. During this last term, he was an advocate of civil liberties, opposing the removal of civil servants because of political beliefs. This term was not a successful one, but when he left office, President Jefferson chose him as Vice President under the new Republican party. He remained in that position under President Madison as well.

Clinton, probably the most prominent figure in early New York State History, died while holding the Vice Presidency in Washington, D. C.

JAY, JOHN—(1745-1829), second governor of New York, (1795-1801), was another prominent man in early state politics as well as the Revolutionary War. Born in New York City, his parents were Hanna McVickar and Peter Jay, a West Indies trader. He spent his childhood in Westchester County, New York, and attended school in New Rochelle before entering Kings College (the future Columbia University). After graduation in 1764, he studied law for four years and was admitted to the bar.

For a few more years, he practiced law in the city, remaining a loyalist until the British Government imposed the infamous taxes of 1773. He was a delegate to the Continental Congress in 1774-77, serving on the committee of correspondence in charge of communications with Great Britain. Jay served on the New York Provincial Congress in 1776 and helped write the State Constitution of 1777. In the next year, he was elected Chief Justice for all the areas of New York not held by the British. As President of the Continental Congress (1778-79), he was also considered worthy to act as U. S. Minister to Spain, although he received no recognition on a trip there. He was one of the Americans sent to Paris in 1781-82 to negotiate the treaty which ended the Revolutionary War.

When he returned home, Jay discovered he had been elected Secretary of Foreign Affairs by Congress, and in the following years he was involved in much of the Federal organization. Although he did not help write the 1787 constitution, he was chosen to uphold it two years later when he was named the first Chief Justice of the U.S. Supreme Court.

Jay tried unsuccessfully for the New York governorship in

1792. Three years later, Clinton's resignation allowed him to be elected into the State Capitol by a large majority. Although his two terms in office were less dramatic than his previous career, Jay did witness the moving of the State Capitol to Albany, as well as the construction of the Cherry Valley Turnpike. Also, slaves were freed in New York State under an act which Jay signed.

He did not try for reelection in 1801, but retired to a private life of Bible study and some law practice. He died at his country home in Bedford, New York.

LEWIS, MORGAN—(1754-1844), fourth governor of New York (1804-07) and soldier, was born in New York City. His parents were Elizabeth Annesly and Francis York, one of the signers of the Declaration of Independence. He was sent to local schools and graduated from the College of New Jersey (the future Princeton University) in 1773. As with most statesmen, he studied law after college, but did not begin a law practice until after his activities during the Revolutionary War. He led a regiment of the New York Army as captain to the battle of Germantown, and in 1776 was named Quartermaster General under General Gates in Saratoga and later General Clinton in northern New York. John Jay, Lewis's law instructor, had a great influence on him, and his reputation helped him to a seat on the State Legislature in 1789-90. Soon afterward, he was appointed judge of Dutchess County. His career catapulted under Governor Clinton when he was chosen Attorney General of the state (1791-92) and Chief Justice of the New York Supreme Court (1801), after serving as one of the subordinate judges for nine years. His wide range of experiences as well as his connections with both of his predecessors allowed him to win an easy victory in the 1804 gubernatorial elections.

While Lewis was in office, his main goals were to improve education and defense within the state. The United States Military Academy at West Point opened during his term.

Lewis did not win a second term, however. He remained active in politics, serving on the State Senate (1810) and leading troops during the War of 1812, commanding both the frontier near Niagara Falls and New York City at different times. Lewis was also a founder of New York University and an active

Freemason (president: 1821).

He retired to private life after 1815, but was not idle; in 1832-36 he headed the New York Historical Society, and in 1839-44 he was President-General of the state's Society of the Cincinnati. He died in New York City.

TOMPKINS, DANIEL D.—(1774-1835), fifth governor of New York (1807-17) and later Vice President of the U. S., was born in present-day Scarsdale, New York, to Sarah Hyatt and Jonathan Tompkins. He was raised on the family farm before going to Columbia College. After graduation in 1795, he studied law and moved to New York City to practice in 1797. He served as a delegate to the State Constitutional Convention in 1801, was an assemblyman, and in 1804 was elected a member of Congress. However, he resigned the House seat before taking office when he was appointed Justice of the State Supreme Court. He left this office as well in 1806, when he was elected for the first of four times as governor.

During his terms, Tompkins was known for his liberal treatment of education, prison codes, black people's welfare as well as the militia. In 1812, he opposed the closure of the United States Bank and the subsequent Bank of North America, established in his state. During the War of 1812, he concentrated on improving the state militia, taking command of the Third Military District in 1814. Just before Tompkins left office in 1817, he saw the state legislature totally abolish slavery in New York.

Tompkins had won the Vice Presidency along with President James Monroe as a liberal member of the Republican party. Although he won a second term in Washington, he tried unsuccessfully for the governship in 1820. His popularity in New York had waned considerably; many accused him of excessive spending during the revolution, and cited inexplicable discrepancies in the state budget records from his term.

Tompkins took the criticisms to heart despite the discovery that the discrepancies were the fault of his inaccurate and confused accounting rather than dishonesty. After several years of excessive drinking, he died at Staten Island, New York.

CLINTON, DEWITT—(1769-1828), sixth and eighth governor of New York State (1817-23, 1825-1828), was born in Little Britain, New York to James and Mary DeWitt Clinton. His father was an important soldier in the Revolutionary War. He was educated at a local Presbyterian school and at Kingston Academy before entering Columbia College in New York City. He graduated at the head of the class in 1786 and remained in the city to study law. However, he did not practice this profession, since his uncle, Governor George Clinton, hired him as his personal secretary in 1790. Following his uncle's antifederalist sentiments, the young Clinton garnered enough support to be elected to the state assembly and senate in 1797 and 1798 respectively. Before that he was a secretary to the University of New York regents, and was involved in fortifying the New York City Harbor. All of these appointments were lost, however, when John Jay took over the governorship, and he decided to return to the city and start a law partnership. In 1802, he was appointed a U. S. Senator, upon John Armstrong's resignation, and became the youngest man to do so at that time. The next year, however, he quit when he was elected New York City's mayor. It was a position he held off and on for 12 years while serving simultaneously as a state senator (1806-1813). He tried unsuccessfully for the Presidency in 1812 against James Madison.

His nomination for governor of New York came more easily, however, after Governor Tompkins resigned. He was elected as a Democratic-Republican and three years later he defeated governor-turned Vice President Tompkins by a narrow margin. During these first terms, Clinton continued his earlier concern for canal development in the state, but he made many enemies in the process. In spite of the protests from a hostile legislature, "Clinton's Big Ditch" progressed steadily, and soon the 362-mile Erie canal was completed. He also supervised construction of the Champlain Canal (1826). Both elevated New York City above all others on the eastern seaboard and gained tremendous popularity for him among the people, if not the legislature. He declined a third consecutive term in 1822, but returned with a 16,000 majority over his opponent three years later.

Clinton's popularity was also due to his commitment to

building free public schools and religious freedom in the state. He also promoted historical research and preservation while in office.

Successful but unhealthy because of an old leg injury that never healed, Clinton lived as a semi-invalid during his last years at the Capitol before dying suddenly.

YATES, JOSEPH CHRISTOPHER—(1768-1837), seventh governor of New York (1823-25), was a native of Schenectady, New York. His parents were Jane Gradt and Christopher Yates, who hired a private tutor for young Joseph and then sent him to an academy and law study in Schenectady, and Albany. Soon, he opened his own law office in his hometown and became the first mayor of the city in 1798. Although he was a Republican, he was not active in party politics at that time, and was elected to the state senate in 1805 because of his reputation. Three years later he was appointed a Justice of the state Supreme Court, which he held for 14 years. In the meantime he was a regent of the University of New York, but fastidiously refrained from political involvement.

However, when favor for the Governor Clinton waned in the legislature, Yates was urged to run for the seat in 1822. He won nearly unopposed and took office under a new constitution of 1821, which directed him to appoint an increased number of public officers. He was overwhelmed by the decisions, especially as throngs of place-seekers harassed him daily. His confusion caused him to lose popularity. Also, his opposition to a popular new electoral law caused disfavor among the legislators. He retired after his term and returned to Schenectady to live out the rest of his life privately, disillusioned with politics.

PITCHER, NATHANIEL—(1777-1836), temporary governor of New York (1828-29), was born in Litchfield, Connecticut, but moved to Sandy Hill, New York when he was young. His parents were Nathaniel, Sr. and an unnamed mother who died at his birth. Unlike his predecessors, Pitcher received little formal education and was a member of the state militia before entering politics. He was a state assemblyman in 1806, 1815, and 1817, and took part in the State Constitutional Convention in 1821. He was a Jacksonian Republican, and served from 1819 to 1822 in Congress. In the state election of 1826 he was a member of the "bucktail" faction with Martin Van Buren and was elected lieutenant governor along with a party rival, Governor DeWitt Clinton. When Clinton died, Pitcher took over and served out the remainder of his term. He was not popular enough to win the next gubernatorial election, probably because of his Masonic connections.

Pitcher was a member of Congress again in 1833-35, but did not campaign again because of failing health. He died at Sandy Hill.

TAYLER, JOHN—(1742-1829), temporary governor of the state (1817), was born in New York City, but moved to Albany when he was 17. Tayler was active as a soldier, businessman, and statesman during the Revolution and early organization of the federal government, serving on the Provincial Congress in 1776 and 1777. After serving five sessions on the state assembly, he was appointed Canal Commissioner of New York in 1792, and Recorder of Albany in 1793. He served various other state positions during the next few years before being elected Lieutenant Governor of New York alongside Tompkins in 1811 and then 1813-17. When Tompkins resigned the governorship to take office as Vice President, Tayler succeeded him and filled out the remaining term.

Besides his executive duties, Tayler was active as a regent for the University of New York. Afterwards, he was a vice chancellor and chancellor of the university. He remained in Albany until his death.

VAN BUREN, MARTIN—(1782-1862), was ninth governor (1829), and President of the United States (1836-40). He was born at Kinderhook, New York, the son of Maria Hoes and Abraham Van Buren, farmers. His formal education was sparse, but he was able to teach himself enough to enable him to study law at the office where he worked since he was 14. After admission to the bar (1803), Van Buren moved to Hudson, New York and began his long career in politics. As a Jeffersonian Republican, he was elected a surrogate of Columbia County in 1808, which he served until 1813. That year, he took office as a state senator from his area and simultaneously served as attorney-general (1815-19). He was a key leader in the "Albany Regency" in state government, and advocated all the antislavery measures passed through the legislature. Before his election as a U. S. Senator, Van Buren was also active in the formation of the 1821 State Constitution. As a senator in Washington, he presided over the Judiciary Committee and urged the abolition of slavery and debtors' prisons in the country. He resigned the seat in 1828 when he was elected governor of New York.

Van Buren served only three months, however; the main reason he tried for the office was to open the governor's seat to his party. He was not concerned with the petty affairs of a state government. However, he did insure the passage of a safety-fund banking system before leaving office to take an appointment as President Jackson's Secretary of State. He soon became a nationally-known leader in U. S. Politics, and was elected Vice President under Jackson in 1832 before his nomination for the Presidency four years later.

Van Buren's Presidency was plagued by overwhelming financial difficulties brought on by poor management of the previous administration. Although he tried to secure bills to buy up the budget, he was blamed for the country's disasters. He lost the next election amidst the famous "Log Cabin" campaigns and was unsuccessful in his later attempt at national political offices.

He returned to Kinderhook, and lived on his 200 acre estate until he succumbed to an asthma attack.

THROOP, ENOS THOMPSON—(1784-1874), tenth governor of New York (1829-33), was born in Johnstown, New York. His parents were Abiah Thompson and George B. Throop, a teacher. Enos was educated at local grammar schools and began to study law in Albany before opening a practice at Poplar Ridge. In 1807, he moved to Auburn where he practiced law until 1811. He was a county clerk in 1811-14 and was then elected to the U. S. Congress. There he gained valuable legislative experience, but outraged his constituents with some of his actions. When he was not reelected, he resumed his law practice and then became Circuit Court Judge under Governor Yates. He gained popularity in this position when he presided over the case involving the kidnappers of anti-Masonite William Morgan. In 1828 he was elected lieutenant-governor with Martin Van Buren, with the understanding of his party that he would soon be governor. He succeeded him and filled out his term, and in 1830 he was formally elected to the position.

During his term, he signed a bill to build the Chicago Canal although he opposed further canal building because of the state's debt. When he left office in 1833, the budget was solvent and his party was popular in the state. However, political infighting caused him not to run for reelection, and he returned to lesser political positions, such as naval officer of the port of New York (1833-38), and diplomatic officer to the Kingdom of the two Sicilies. From 1842 until 1846, he lived near Auburn, but moved to a new farm near Kalamazoo, Michigan. His health failing in 1857, Throop moved back to New York, and he lived a leisurely life until his death near his old home at Auburn.

MARCY, WILLIAM LEARNED—(1786-1857), was eleventh governor of New York (1833-39). He was born in Southbridge, Massachusetts to Ruth Learned and Jedediah Marcy II, farmers. He studied at Leicester Academy and graduated from Brown University in 1808, with a specialization in the classics. In Troy, New York, he studied law and began practicing in 1811, but was soon called away by the Troy Militia to serve as a lieutenant in the War of 1812. Although he only participated in two minor battles before the war was over, Marcy remained in the service until 1821, during which time he was named Lieutenant General. In 1816, he was appointed recorder of the city of Troy and became interested in state politics. Opposed to Governor Clinton, Marcy joined the Bucktails movement, supporting Martin Van Buren for governor with his daily newspaper, the Troy *Budget*.

Marcy got his first taste of state government when he was appointed comptroller in 1823 and became a member of the new "Albany Regency", which represented a powerful political force in the state for several years during this period. He was appointed as a Justice to the Supreme Court of New York in 1829. Soon afterwards, he was elected to a U. S. Senator and was made chairman of the Judiciary Committee of that Body. His political favor led to the nomination and election as governor in

1832, and his spiralling career continued upwards in the 1836 election.

Eliminating debts and establishing an independent Treasury were Marcy's main commitments during his term. As his party was newly defined as the "Whigs", it also was newly defined as a "Hard-money", conservative line of politics. In 1835, he recommended a law to limit the amount of bank notes under five dollars and refused to allow any new bank charters in the state. He opposed the growing abolitionist movement because he feared a split between north and south. He also sponsored the first state geological survey, which settled a New Jersey border dispute.

Marcy lost the 1838 election, but remained active in national affairs. President Van Buren named him a commissioner in the Mexican claims disputes in 1839-42. For awhile, he retired to private life, but soon was involved in the Democratic Party's National Convention (1843) and was named Secretary of War under President Polk during the war with Mexico. When Polk's term ended, he practiced law for a while, but returned to Washington as President Pierce's Secretary of State, a position he held in 1853-57.

After public service, Marcy went to his home at Ballston Spa, New York, where he died while reading in his library.

SEWARD, WILLIAM H.—(1801-1872), twelfth governor of New York (1839-43) and U. S. Secretary of State, was born in Florida, New York. His parents were Samuel S. and Marry Jennings Seward. After private schooling, he studied and graduated from Union College in Schenectady in 1820. He taught school before studying law and entering a practice in 1822, with Judge Elijah Miller, whose daughter he married two years later. A liberal reformer before his time, Seward became a champion of the Greeks living near him, who were poor and suffering from prejudices (1827). In 1830, he was elected to the State Senate and after two terms tried for the governorship unsuccessfully. However, while in office he advocated the abolition of debtors' prisons and lessening of prison punishment as well as the breakup of corporate monopolies. As a Whig, he was elected governor of New York by a 10,000 majority after several years of private law practice. He was reelected two years later.

Reform measures were passed one after the other while Seward was governor. Everything from banking and the militia to laws regarding blacks, women, and Indians were brought into a more liberal light. New York City's school system changed under Seward's direction when the children of Catholics and immigrants were given better treatment. Although some of his liberal promises brought smaller results, Seward did steer New York in the union direction in the critical years before Civil War. He declined a third term, but in 1948 he was elected a U. S. Senator from New York. In Washington, Seward continued his work for the abolition of slavery and other reforms. He was a United States Judge for several years, and traveled extensively in Canada's wilderness, Europe, Egypt, and the Middle East. He was defeated by Abraham Lincoln in the 1860 Republican Convention, but served as the President's Secretary of State. In 1865, assassins attempted to kill him, but he returned to national politics as President Johnson's Secretary of State and one of President Grant's leading assistants. He made an extensive tour of North America in 1869, touring as far north as Alaska and as far south as Mexico before beginning a journey around the world. After writing *Travels Around the World,* published in 1873, he died at his home in Auburn, New York.

BOUCK, WILLIAM C.—(1786-1859), thirteenth governor of New York (1843-45), was born in Schoharie Valley, New York. The son of Margaret Borst and Christian Bouck, he had little formal education in between working on the family farm and fighting off the Indians. He was elected clerk of his hometown in 1807 and supervisor in the two following years. Governor Tompkins appointed him sheriff of his area in 1812, but the next administration removed him shortly afterwards. He served on the assembly in 1813-20, and subsequently was named a colonel in the militia and Erie Canal Supervisor (1821). After the Erie was completed, Bouck continued to supervise canal construction in general and became involved in the expansion of railroads in the state soon thereafter. He was Canal Commissioner until 1840. He was elected governor on the Democratic ticket two years later. Bouck found no favors during his only term, however, and he was not reelected. Factional splits in the Democratic party tormented Bouck's two years in office. Many of the radical faction joined the Whigs on legislative votes, opposing the governor. Bouck declined further in popularity when he sent out the state militia to settle an anti-rent conflict in Columbia County and arrested some of the protesting tenants.

Bouck was assistant treasurer of New York City after the governorship, serving from 1846 until 1849, when presidential politics changed. He retired to his farm at Schoharie where he lived quietly for 10 years until his death.

WRIGHT, SILAS—(1795-1847), fourteenth governor of New York (1845-47), was born in Amherst, Massachusetts. He was the son of Silas and Eleanor Goodale Wright, who sent him to private school in Middlebury, Vermont, and then to college there. After graduation in 1815, he studied law in New York and was admitted to that state's bar in 1819. While engaging in private practice in Canton, Wright was appointed brigadier-general of the state militia (1827) and St. Lawrence County's surrogate (1821-24). He was also a state senator during the 1823-27 term. After a session in Congress, Wright took the position of New York's Comptroller in 1829, and held it for four years. During these years he was active in Democratic party Conventions and other activities, and in 1833 he was asked to fill out Governor Marcy's unexpired term in the U. S. Senate. There he supported Clay's compromise bill, and opposed the rechartering of the controversial United States Bank. He was elected for two terms in Washington before resigning to take on the New York governorship in 1844.

With the Democratic Party still in turmoil, Wright's term was far from easy. Also, although he sympathized with the tenants' grievances in Delaware County, he called out the state army to quell the uprisings of violence there. However, Wright did achieve some beneficial measures during his term in the field of public education. Also, the Hudson Railroad Company and the University of Buffalo were founded. Just before leaving office, he ensured a bill to tax income from all rents and leases in the state, which pleased the exploited renters in Delaware County.

A third constitutional convention was held during his term and the new document he approved in 1846. After office, Wright moved back to his home in Canton, where he died a few months later of a heart attack.

YOUNG, JOHN—(1802-1852), fifteenth governor of New York (1847-49), was born to Thomas and Mary Gale Young in Chelsea, Vermont. When he was young, the family moved to Conecus, New York, where he attended the local school in between helping on the farm. Afterwards, he studied law at the nearby large town of Genesee. His eventual law practice there was very successful, and soon he was elected to the state assembly in 1831 as an anti-masonic candidate, the party which was overtaking the state at that time. He was reelected to that position in 1833 and 1844-45, and won three terms to the U. S. House of Representatives in the meantime (1836-37, 1841-43). He was an advocate of the constitutional convention in New York beginning in 1844. He also opposed the distress and long-term binding leases inflicted in 1844. He also opposed the distress and long-term binding leases inflicted on renters in the state. After his election as governor, in fact, one of his first actions was to release all the leading anti-renters from the imprisonment imposed upon them by Governor Wright's administration.

Also during his term, Young was not allowed the appointive powers of his predecessors because of the 1846 constitution, but he was able to make a few appointments of fellow Whigs. He was a strong opponent of the Mexican War, which led to unpopularity. Although he did not seek reelection, he did not retire from public life. His support for Zachary Taylor in the previous election led to his post as U. S. Assistant Treasurer at New York City, where he lived and worked until his death three years later.

FISH, HAMILTON—(1808-1893), sixteenth governor of New York (1849-51), and U. S. Secretary of State, was born in New York City, the son of Elizabeth Stuyvesant and Nicholas Fish. He graduated from Columbia College in his home town in 1827 and read the law before gaining admission to the bar in 1830. After beginning law practice, he became the city's commissioner of deeds (1832-34). He made one unsuccessful attempt for a state assembly seat as a Whig the next year, and then stayed out of politics for almost a decade. During the 1843-45 Congress, he won a seat in Washington, but was less successful in 1846 in his attempt for lieutenant governor of New York. Two years later conditions were more favorable for both the Whigs and Fish, and he was elected by a large majority as lieutenant governor of

New York. This post in turn led to the governorship after an election later in the year.

The term was relatively uneventful, although Fish was known for his anti-slavery position. A significant expansion of canals, railroads, and education occurred while Fish was governor, however. He left office at the end of his second year to take the position as U. S. Senator from New York, which he filled for one term.

A union sympathizer, and a Republican during the Civil War, Fish was later called upon by both Presidents Lincoln and Grant to help deal with the difficult issues of the country at that time. He was Secretary of State under President Grant, and was one of his closest friends.

In New York, Fish was active in the Historical Society and the Society of the Cincinnati, serving as president of both organizations at different times.

After his work in Washington, Fish returned to New York City to practice law. He died in Garrison, New York.

HUNT, WASHINGTON—(1811-1867), was seventeenth governor of New York (1851-53). He was born in Windham, New York to Sanford and Fanny Rose Hunt. Determined to follow the most respected profession of his time, despite a sparse common school education, Hunt began reading law as a boy and was admitted to the bar when he was 23. Two years later, he was appointed judge of the frontier area of Niagara County. His constituents there later elected him to Congress, where he served in 1843-49. Before winning the governorship the next year, Hunt served for a time as the New York State Comptroller.

As a Whig, Hunt was an outspoken promoter of progress and public works within the state. He was concerned with government economy and efficiency, and articulated the problems of the nation's new wave of immigrants. However, a legislative disagreement over the Erie Canal led to his defeat in the 1852 election.

Hunt became a Democrat after the Whig party broke up, although many of his peers became Republicans. He was often a delegate in national party conventions and was active in Episcopal religious organizations. He died in New York City.

SEYMOUR, HORATIO—(1810-1886), eighteenth and twenty-second governor of New York (1853-55, 1863-65), was born in Pompeii Hill, New York. His parents were Henry and Mary Forman Seymour, who sent him to the local academy and then a military school in Connecticut. In Utica, he studied law but was too tied up in the affairs of the family estate to practice the profession. He also worked as military secretary under Governor Marcy beginning in 1833. Having established favor in the Democratic Party, Seymour was elected to the state assembly after his job as an executive advisor had ended (1841). When he returned to Utica, he was elected mayor. In the following years, he was again in the assembly, serving as speaker in 1845, and he tried unsuccessfully for governor. Although he had lost to the successful Whig party's candidate, Washington Hunt, he won over him in the next election.

Seymour's first two years in office were tumultuous, as the old Democratic party conflicts still boiled in the legislature. The governor vetoed a measure for prohibition of liquor sales in the state. He also worked for reforms in the prison system but the temperance groups had grown strong enough to oust their enemy, Seymour, in the next election.

During the interval between terms, Seymour was a delegate in the 1856 Democratic National Convention and spent several years tending to private business at his farm. He was a strong union supporter, although he tried to put off the Civil War by persuading the federal government of the south's persistence. Many leaders in the north believed the war should only last about 90 days. After a stirring address to northern Democrats about the "wickedness of opposing the best government the world has ever seen," Seymour regained popularity in New York and was reelected to the governorship.

The second term was more volatile than the first, however. When the Federal Draft Laws were posted for the state militia, forcing all poor men to join while allowing those with $300 to buy a substitute, riots broke out in New York City. Seymour tried to revoke the draft law, but was too late; it had already been posted. However, he went to New York, declared a state of insurrection, and after demanding a return to law and order, the city quieted down.

Seymour lost the next election, but was nominated for president by his party in 1868. General Grant won over him, however. Afterwards, Seymour refused to run for any other public office, and retired to his new farm near Utica, where he studied and devoted himself to agriculture. He died there.

CLARK, MYRON—(1806-1892), was nineteenth governor of New York (1855-57). His parents were Mary Sutton and Maj. Joseph Clark, who raised him in Naples (Ontario County), New York, and sent him to local district schools. He was a lieutenant colonel in the state militia before beginning a public career as sheriff of his home county. After that two-year post, he moved to Canandaigua, a village where he was elected president of the small populace (1850). His constituents then elected him to the state senate in 1852. Once there, he was a member of the temperance contingency which pushed through a prohibition bill in 1854. However, Governor Seymour vetoed the legislative measure. Myron Clark's strong anti-slavery and temperance position proved more popular in the next gubernatorial election. He won the governorship by a tight 305 votes, however.

Clark was able to secure the prohibatory liquor law soon after taking office, but it was repealed after less than a year. He also approved a bill funding the Albany Bridge. His party, the Republicans, did not think Clark would be reelected, however, and he left public service for several years until President Lincoln appointed him a tax collector for the Port of New York. He tried again for the governorship in 1874 on the Prohibitionist Ticket, but lost. He died after many years of private life in Canandaigua, New York.

KING, JOHN ALSOP—(1788-1867), twentieth governor of the state (1857-59), was born in New York City. His parents, Mary Alsop and Rufus King, sent him to school in Harrow, England and afterwards, he studied law in New York. After serving in the War of 1812 as a lieutenant of Cavalry, King moved to a farm in Jamaica, New York, and became active in state and local politics. He was an assemblyman in 1819-21 and a state senator in 1823-25. Although he opposed Governor DeWitt Clinton politically, he did support his Erie Canal project. Meanwhile, King's father was appointed Secretary of Legation to the Court of St. James in England, and his son accompanied him in London until the new minister took over.

King returned to state politics in 1839 as a legislator, and 10 years later he was elected to Congress. As a Whig, he opposed all attempts at compromise when it came to the slavery issue; he was for the emancipation of blacks in all states. He also urged the admission of California into the Union while in Washington. After he presided at the first convention of the new Republican Party in New York, King was an easy winner for governor.

While in office, King found little turmoil and little to do. He did approve the expansion of the Erie Canal, and helped to improve the public education system as well as found the state agricultural society. When the next election came, he declined renomination because of his advanced age. His only other public office was a delegate to the 1861 Peace Conference in Washington. King died at home in Jamaica, New York.

MORGAN, EDWIN D.—(1811-1883), was twenty-first governor of New York (1859-63). Born in Washington, Massachusetts, his parents were Jasper A. and Catherine Copp Morgan, who moved the family to Hartford, Connecticut, after young Edwin finished grammar school. There he worked in his uncle's store as a clerk for a few years until he became a full partner in the business. He was also a member of the Hartford City Council. Soon, he struck out for New York City to try his fortunes and he founded a general store there in 1836. His grocery business soon evolved into a banking and investment firm as well, and Morgan was well on his way to becoming a wealthy and influential New Yorker. His financial assistance during the city's cholera plague of 1849 gained respect for him as well, and the next year he was elected to the state senate. He remained in that position until 1855, at which time he was appointed to the New York State Commission on immigration. As a Republican, he became active in the party's conventions and other activities, and in 1858 he was nominated for governor.

As one of the "war governors", Morgan concentrated his efforts on building up the state militia for "the impending crisis". He was a popular governor; the canal toll system he designed helped reduce the state debt considerably and he saw to it that every county delivered its quota of volunteers for the union side.

In 1861 when the state was made a military department, Morgan was named Major-General of the volunteers, and was reelected for a second term in Albany.

Declining a nomination for a third term, Morgan left office to take over the fortification of New York Habor. The state legislature then elected him to the U. S. Senate, where he served until 1869. In the meantime, he was temporary chairman of the Baltimore Convention of 1864 and the Philadelphia convention of 1866. In 1872, he was chairman of the Republican party, which gained President Grant's election. An unsuccessful candidate for the U. S. Senate in 1875, Morgan also lost the New York gubernatorial race the next year.

In his later years, Morgan declined President Arthur's offer of a post as Secretary of the Treasury. He donated millions to philanthropic causes, and died at his home in New York City.

FENTON, REUBEN EATON—(1819-1885), twenty-third governor of the state (1865-69) was born in Carroll, New York. His parents were George W. and Elsie Owen Fenton. He attended local schools until he was 17, when his father's business was failing and he had to help support the family. He worked in logging camps and clerked in stores until he could study law at Jamestown. However, he became ill and had to abandon this pursuit at the age of 20. When he regained his health, he opened a small mercantile business which soon blossomed into success. He was elected by his neighbors to be colonel of the local regiment of the state militia. He was also investing in his own lumbering business, moving his first raft of timber down the Ohio to Kentucky at a large profit. When he was young, he was a member of the Democratic party, elected Supervisor of Carroll and state assemblyman in 1849. In 1852, the Democrats elected him to Congress, where he served until 1855 and again in 1857-64. However, Fenton soon grew tired of the party's compromise solutions to the issue of slavery, and became one of the founders of the abolitionist Republican party. His second term in the House was served as a Republican, and afterwards he was elected Governor of New York under that party by a large majority. His terms were characterized by popular measures such as regulations on corporations, relief for war veterans and widows and orphans of union soldiers who had died during· the war.

Also, public schools were made free of charge for the first time and service in the military could not be used against a person who sought suffrage under a new measure approved by Fenton. He left office after his second term when he was elected to the U. S. Senate. There he continued his career as one of the leading Republicans of his time. He took part in an international money conference in 1878 in Paris, but for the most part remained in private business from his home at Jamestown. He died there while holding the position of President of the First National Bank of Jamestown.

HOFFMAN, JOHN THOMPSON—(1828-1888), twenty-fourth governor of New York (1869-73), was born in Sing Sing (the present Ossining), New York to Jane Ann Thompson and Adrian Hoffman, a physician. He graduated from Union College in New York in 1846 and went on to study law at an office in Sing Sing. He was admitted to the bar on his twenty-first birthday and then moved to New York City to share in a law partnership. A Democrat, Hoffman was soon involved in the Young Men's Tammany Hall General Committee and later the Tammany Society (1854 and 1859). He was U. S. District Attorney of New York City in 1859 and the next year he was elected recorder of that city, the youngest man who had ever filled the post. While there he was charged with dealing with the rioters of 1863, and his successes led to his election as Mayor of New York City in 1865 after the Tammany Hall Democratic Nomination. From 1866-68 he also served as that party organization's "grand sachem". Although he was unsuccessful against Governor Fenton in 1866, two years later he resigned the mayorship to take his place as governor of New York.

While he was in office, the great wave of popular indignation and opposition to the Tammany Democratic Organization swept the state, and although Governor Hoffman was elected for a second term, he was soon connected with the party machine scandals. His connection with the infamous "Tweed Ring" of Tammany Hall ruined his political career, although no concrete evidence could be raised against him. He practiced law for a while in New York City. However, his health began to fail him and he went to Europe in search of a cure. He died in Wiesbaden, Germany.

TILDEN, SAMUEL JONES—(1814-1886), twenty-fifth governor of New York (1873-77), was a native of New Lebanon, New York. His parents were Eliam and Polly Y. Jones Tilden. As he was often ill as a child, Tilden was mostly educated by tutors, although he attended an academy in Massachusetts before entering Yale University. He only studied there for one term, and attended the New York City University intermittently before graduating from law school there in 1841. He devoted much of his college years to political writing, however. His works were published by prominent Democratic journals under the pseudonym of "Amicus" as his father was a friend of Martin Van Buren. After clerking in a law office in New York City, Tilden opened his own practice there, but soon began his favorite business as publisher and editor of the New York *Morning News*. From 1844, he owned this publication, but stopped editing it the next year when he was elected to the state assembly. He was a member of the 1846 Constitutional Convention and also invested in other lucrative businesses such as canal, railroad, and mining which eventually brought his worth to six million dollars. He was not a member of the Democratic "Tammany Hall" faction as was his predecessor and in fact was a leader in the prosecution against the "Tweed Ring" in New York City. He was a member of the freesoil "Barnburners" movement within his party but sided with Republican Abraham Lincoln and the union cause during the Civil War. In 1869, when he was helping to break up the Tweed machine, William "Boss" Tweed himself complemented him by saying "He wants to bring the hayloft and the cheesepress down to the city and crush out the machine. He wants to get a crowd of country reformers in the legislature...when he gets everything fixed to suit him, he wants to go to the U. S. Senate". Indeed, Tilden did have political ambitions. After serving for eight years as the New York State Democratic Committee Chairman, he was elected governor of the state by a large majority over Governor Dix.

During Tilden's tenure, the state capitol at Albany was begun, and New York's canal system underwent a series of improvements and repairs. He helped to break up the fraudulent "canal ring" which controlled the canal system funds, and carried out a number of other streamlining efforts which led to less state taxes and expenditures. He did not run for reelection because he was nominated for president by his party. Although it originally appeared that he had won more electoral votes than Rutherford B. Hayes, several states' votes were disputed. An electoral commission of 15 was called upon by Congress to decide the outcome, and by a strict bi-partisan vote of eight to seven, these electoral votes went to Hayes.

Tilden reluctantly accepted the decision, and retired from public life to travel abroad and live in his newly-acquired estate "Greystone". When he died there, he willed five million to found a free public library in New York, but his greedy heirs claimed the will was invalid and set aside a much smaller amount for the library.

ROBINSON, LUCIUS—(1810-1880) was the twenty-sixth governor of the state (1877-80). He was born in Windham, New York, where his father Eli sent him to common schools. He studied law after academy training and set up practice at Catskill, New York. Starting in pulbic life as district attorney for Green County, Robinson was also made master in charge for New York City in 1843. Originally a Democrat, he switched to the Republican party at its founding in 1856. Three years later he was elected to the state assembly, and then was appointed comptroller of the state for two years. The Democrats still liked him and tried to elect him to the comptroller post again in 1865 but they were unsuccessful. His leaving of the party never made much difference as the Democrats supported him again in 1875 for comptroller, this time successfully. In the meantime, Robinson was a member of the State Constitutional Commission, which enacted a document designating three-year gubernatorial terms. He was elected under this law, and served one term.

As governor, Robinson approved establishment of a state reformatory and was the first to set up an office in the new capitol at Albany. Most of his administration was uneventful, however, and he was not reelected for a second term. In the following years, he lived at his residence at Elmira where he died.

CORNELL, ALONZO B.—(1832-1904), twenty-seventh governor of New York (1880-83), was born in Ithaca, New

York. His parents were Mary Ann Wood, and Ezra, founder of Cornell University and the Western Union Telegraph Company. His education was sparse since he quit school at an early age to help in his father's telegraph company. Eventually, he became the company's superintendant. He also worked at an Ithaca bank and saved enough of his earnings to purchase a line of steamboats on Cayuga Lake. In 1869, the President appointed him U. S. surveyor of customs in New York, and the next year he was promoted to assistant treasurer of the U.S. in New York, although he preferred to remain in the customs department. He was a member of the state Republican Committee in 1870-78, which helped him gain election to the state assembly in 1872, of which he became speaker. In the next few year, he devoted his time to the management of the Western Union Company, but he kept his hand in politics sufficiently to allow his election as governor in 1879. He served one three-year term.

Cornell's business training with Western Telegraph proved valuable when he administered the new state usury laws and corporation tax laws during his term. Appealing to the popular voters, he also vetoed legislation that many considered scandalous. He signed an act making women eligible to be school electors and school officers, and he approved the construction of a public restaurant in Central Park, New York City. A state railway commission was organized and a women's prison was constructed during his term as well. Although he was extremely concerned with the state's welfare, fellow Republicans did not like his policies. He was not renominated for a second term, which caused an outcry among the voters, who chose a Democrat for their next governor.

Cornell returned to his investments and the telegraph company after office. He lived in New York City until his death.

CLEVELAND, STEPHEN GROVER—(1837-1908) twenty-eighth governor of New York (1883-85) and U. S. President (1885-89, 1893-97), was born in Caldwell, New Jersey. His parents were Reverend Richard Falley and Anne Neal Cleveland. When Grover was three, the family moved to Fayetteville, New York. As soon as he was old enough to attend school, he worked in the village grocery store. In 1851, the Clevelands moved again, to Clinton, where the boy was obliged to help support the family when his father died. He worked with his brother at the Institute for the Blind in New York City, and at the same time engaged in ardent self-tutoring, mostly in history. He also studied law books, but it was not until he moved to Buffalo in 1855 that he was able to study in a law firm. He worked in Buffalo with his uncle, who was editing "The American Shorthorn Herd Book". Cleveland was admitted to the bar in 1859, and immediately became the chief clerk at the prominent law firm of Rogers, Bowen and Rogers. In 1863 he resigned to accept the appointment of assistant district attorney of Erie County. So vigorously did he prosecute crime and so efficiently administer the office that he was nominated for district attorney in 1865, but was defeated by a Republican opponent. The next year he formed his own law firm with Issacc Vanderpoel, and then joined another firm. He was elected sheriff of the county in 1870. In 1874 he became head of another law firm, with which he practiced until his election as mayor of Buffalo in 1882. A Democrat, Cleveland was elected governor of New York later in the year by a majority of 192,000, the largest ever given at that time in any state in the union. His efforts went towards ending the system of patronage and corruption that had often ruled state government. In 1884, Cleveland was nominated for President, beginning a long and bitter campaign against Republican James G. Blaine. In his inaugural address, Cleveland declared support of the Monroe Doctrine, the protection of Indians, and the fight against Mormon polygamy, a fiery issue of the day. The President accepted responsibility for every act of his administration. His cabinet officers, though men of great ability, were little more than private secretaries. He brought on enmity of many groups when he took action without consulting anyone, including Civil War veterans, large manufacturers, and members of the Democratic party establishment. He lost in the next election, but was once again elected in 1892, although he had carefully disassociated himself from the party politicians opposed his renomination, Cleveland had become somewhat of a folk hero, and he carried many unlikely states in the next election. In his second term, he had to deal with a widespread "financial panic", equivalent to a depression, which devastated many banks. The treasury surplus was devastated by the panic, and to Cleveland there was just one cause: the worldwide fear of the U. S.' inability to maintain a gold standard was draining off the supply of the precious metal. He successfully pushed for a repeal of the Sherman Silver Purchase Act, but this did not stop the outflow of gold. Also, in 1895, the income tax was declared unconstitutional, which further depleted federal funds. Cleveland left office in 1897 to return to his private law practice. He became a trustee of Princeton University, and he died near the University after many years of private life. He was the author of *Principles and Purposes of our Form of Government,* 1892; *Self Made Man in America,* 1897; *Independence of the Executive,* 1900; and *Presidential Problems,* 1900.

HILL, DAVID BENNETT—(1843-1910), twenty-ninth governor of New York (1885-92), was born in Havana, New York, the son of Caleb, a carpenter, and Eunice Durfey Hill. After attending the academy in his native town, he went to Elmira in 1862, where he studied law at the office of Erastus P. Hart. Two years later he was admitted to the state bar and gained his first public post as city attorney of Elmira. He soon gained a large practice and became prominent in his profession. His dealings led to politics, and in 1868 and 1871 he was a delegate to the Democratic party's state conventions. In 1871 he was elected to the New York assembly. During his first term he introduced a bill abolishing the contract system in the state prison, which passed in the assembly but failed in the conservative senate. Along with Samuel J. Tilden, he also worked to uncover the corruption of the so-called ring judges in New York City, which resulted in the impeachment of several judges. After his legislative term, he returned to activities with the Democratic party; he was elected an alderman in Elmira from 1880-81 and Mayor of the city in 1882 as a result of his support from his party. His term as mayor didn't last long, however, as he was elected Lieutenant Governor later in 1882. When Grover Cleveland resigned the governorship in 1885, Hill took over the seat in his own right and began an administration that was known for its efficiency and spirit of reform. He personally supervised the state's finances, law-making, and changes in the state's archaic civil and criminal codes. He advocated the use of electrocution instead of hanging as a more humane form of capital punishment, and continued his efforts to stop the use of contracted labor for prisoners in the state. Governor Hill's support from Democratic party leaders helped him gain a second term in Albany in which he continued to work for labor and criminal reforms. He decided not to run for a third term, instead returning to the legislative branch of government—this time in the U. S. Senate. The next year he was unsuccessful in his attempt for the Presidency, but served out his senatorial term. In 1897 he returned to Albany to practice law where he was successful until his death at his suburban home.

FLOWER, ROSWELL PETIBONE—(1835-1899), thirtieth governor of New York (1892-95), was a native of Theresa, Jefferson County, New York. His parents were Nathan Monroe, a wool-carder and clothmaker, and Mary Ann Boyle Flower. When his father died in 1843, young Roswell was forced to work on a farm, at a brickyard, and at a country store while attending the local school. After his graduation from high school, he began teaching local children as well as working at the Watertown, New York, post office. He became involved in a jewelry store business in town, and eventually was able to buy it. He married Sarah M. Woodruff in 1859. He continued this business until 1869 when he was called to New York to manage the estate of Henry Keep, the millionaire railroad magnate, for his widow. Mrs. Keep was Mrs. Flower's sister, and her estate grew from four to ten million dollars under Mr. Flower's management. In New York he joined the banking firm of Benedict, Flower & Company, which dissolved in 1872. Later he and his brothers organized a commission form in the city. His reputation in the financial world allowed for his election to the U. S. Congress in 1881. After a break, he was reelected in 1888. A democrat, he opposed McKinley's tariff and Force bills but supported measures to increase irrigation and aid to Civil War veterans in the nation. He had also worked on the organizational committee for the World's Columbian Exposition while in the House, and when he took the seat of New York Governor in 1892, he witnessed the grand event in New York City. Also during his term, Governor Flower organized a new banking code, and worked to abolish the state debt. In his first year, a cholera epidemic brought to America on European steamships threatened the state, and Flower's energetic efforts helped keep it under control. Despite his power in the party, Flower was not renominated for the governorship in 1894. He returned to his business interests which were connected to the strongest financial interest in New York City. He returned to Watertown just before his death. The city remembered him with a library named in his honor.

MORTON, LEVI PARSONS—(1824-1920), thirty-first governor of New York (1895-97), was born in Shoreham, Vermont, to Daniel Oliver and Lucretia Parsons Morton. He received a public school education and at age 15 began working for a merchant in Hanover, New Hampshire. In 1843, he moved to Boston and seven years later to New York, becoming more and more occupied with his mercantile trade until he organized an investment bank in New York City. The firm underwent several reorganizations in a few years until 1873 when it became the financial agent of the U. S. Government. He also became active as a Republican in politics, trying unsuccessfully for a congressional seat before gaining it in 1878. He was reelected two years later by an increased vote. He was also nominated as minister to France by President Garfield, which caused him to leave the Congress in 1881 and move to Paris. During his residence in France, he gained the offical decree revoking the prohibition of American pork products in 1883, but the prohibitive decree was subsequently renewed by the nation's parliament. He also secured recognition of American corporations in France and drove the symbolic first rivet into the Statue of Liberty, given to New York City by the French Government in 1884. He left France when President Cleveland took office, but in 1889 he tried again for public office and was nominated by the Republicans and Benjamin Harrison to become Vice President of the U. S. After his uneventful term, he ran for New York governor and won. Morton worked for civil service reforms and a more cohesive government in New York City. He often disagreed with the state party platforms in his actions, but in 1896 the Republicans brought his name up as a possible presidential candidate. Instead, he returned to his private investment, The Morton Trust Company, which in 1909 was reincorporated as the Guaranty Trust Company. Morton spent his later years at his estate in Rhinecliff, where he died on his ninety-sixth birthday.

BLACK, FRANK SWETT—(1853-1913), thirty-second governor of New York (1897-99), was born in Limington, Maine, one of many sons of Jacob and Charlotte Sweet Black, farmers. The family moved to Alfred, Maine, in 1864 when the father took a job as county jailkeeper there. Young Frank studied at local public schools and excelled so that he was able to attend a private academy in Massachusetts. He graduated from Dartmouth College in 1875 after working his way with various enterprises. Journalism occupied his time for awhile in Johnstown, New York, but the *Journal* publisher fired him when he supported a Republican for president in 1876. Later in Troy, New York, he continued newswriting and completed his studies in law. After his admission to the bar in 1879 he became a member of the law firm of Smith-Wellington, and a year later established an independent practice. He was soon considered one of the leading lawyers in Rensselaer County. He and his wife, the former Lois B. Hamlin settled in Troy and raised their one son as he built up his consultation practice. In 1894 he was elected to Congress largely as a result of his activity as counsel for the Committee of Safety. He was well respected as an orator and election law reformer and in 1896 he was nominated for the governorship of New York. Once elected, he began his efforts to reclaim the Adirondack forests and establish a school of forestry. He also pressed for the completion of the state capitol, which had been under consruction for 25 years amid scandals of every kind. Black also advocated biennial sessions of the legislature. His two-year term (changed in the constitutional convention of 1893 from three years) ended and he returned to his law practice in New York City. He died at his home in Troy of heart disease.

ROOSEVELT, THEODORE—(1858-1919), thirty-third governor of New York (1899-1901), was born in New York City, the son of Theodore Sr. and Martha Bulloch Roosevelt. He was sent to a preparatory school before studying history at Harvard University. He graduated in 1880 and studied law at Columbia University for one year. He also married Alice Hathaway Lee in 1880, but she died giving birth to their first child in 1884. In the meantime, Roosevelt wrote histories, *The Naval War of 1812,* (1882) and *The Winning of the West,* published in several volumes through 1889-96. He was elected as a Republican to the

New York state assembly serving three terms (1882-84). In 1886, while in London, he remarried Edith Kermit Carow, with whom he later had Theodore Jr. and four other children. Before that he had spent considerable time in North Dakota, on a ranch, where he did much of his writing and recovered from the loss of his first wife. He tried for the mayorship of New York City in 1886 but failed. His first political job was as a member of the U. S. Civil Service Commission (1889-1895) until he resigned to become president of the Board of Police Commissioners in New York City. He was also assistant secretary of the navy during the McKinley administration (1897-98) becoming a major promoter of war with Spain. When the war began, he was colonel of the "Rough Riders", leading the group to victory in Cuba. When he returned to New York he found that his Republican friends had nominated him for governor and he won against the Democrat Augustus Van Wyck. Roosevelt proved a strong labor sympathizer, approving restrictions on financial institutions and large corporations and promoting stricter regulations on sweatshop businesses. He also supported inspections of factories, minimum wage protection and a tax on public utility profits. His liberal leanings caused the Republican establishment to ease Roosevelt out of New York politics by propping him up for Vice President of the U.S. When President McKinley was assassinated in 1901, Roosevelt succeeded him in office. He was reelected in 1904. The President continued his "trust buster" politics in the White House, creating a Bureau of Corporations to investigate those companies involved in interstate commerce. Roosevelt was also a great conservationist; he traveled throughout the west and signed vast tracts of land over for national forests and parks. In 1906, he pushed for the Pure Food and Drug act, a much needed reform that inflamed his capitalistic peers. Roosevelt was also concerned with foreign affairs. An imperialist as well as humanist, the President funded a revolution in Panama that allowed a U. S. takeover of a strip of land for the future interocean canal. He also proposed a "corollary" to the Monroe Doctrine that would allow the U. S. government to intervene in Latin America if there was a danger that a European country might take over. He was awarded the Nobel peace prize in 1905 for his mediation efforts in the war between Russia and Japan.

When he left the Presidency, Roosevelt took a safari tour of Africa and then toured Europe. He was against the conservatism of the Republican party and for a time was a member of the Progressive Party. He was unsuccessful in his presidential ambitions in 1912, and returned to the Republicans in 1916, supporting Governor Hughes. Roosevelt strongly supported American intervention in World War I. He was considered a likely candidate for President in the 1920 election, but died in early 1919 of an embolism. His grave is at the family home in Sagamore Hill, Oyster Bay, New York.

ODELL, BENJAMIN BARKER, JR.—(1854-1926), thirty-fourth governor of New York (1901-05), was born in Newburg, New York, the son of Benjamin Barker and Ophelia Bookstaver Odell. He attended public schools and then the Newburgh Academy, and then studied at Bethany College in West Virginia as well as Columbia College, New York for three years. He returned home to help in his father's ice delivery business, and then became involved in the electric lighting industry. He was president of the Newburgh Electric Light Company as well as treasurer of the Central Hudson Steamboat Company, and was identified with several railroad enterprises. His first wife, Estelle Crist, drowned in the Hudson River, and he married her sister, a widow, in 1891. They had three children with them. In 1895 he was elected to Congress as a Republican. He had been representative of the executive committee of the state party. Before the end of his second term as a Representative, he was elected Governor of New York, and he resigned his congressional seat upon his inauguration. He was reelected in 1902. Early in his gubernatorial career he made his influence felt in reconciling the several opposing factions among the Republicans in the state, assuming virtual control over the party's organization. He advocated indirect taxation, and eventually the state stopped almost all direct taxation of goods. In the meantime, he completed his studies of law and received an L. L. D. degree from Syracuse University in 1901. The Erie Canal received much-needed improvements during his terms, and he saw the first dental school in the United States open at Rochester, New York, in his first year in office. Odell remained active as a Republican leader for many years after leaving Albany. He died in his native town and was buried at the Woodlawn Cemetery in New Windsor, New York.

HIGGINS, FRANK WEYLAND—(1856-1907), thirty-fifth governor of New York (1905-07), was born in Rushford, Alleghany County, New York, the son of Orrin Trall and Lucia Hapgood Higgins. His father was a successful realtor and owner of a number of grocery stores in rural New York. His mother died when he was a small boy. Young Frank attended private academies in Rushford and in Poughkeepsie, New York, and then took business courses for a short while. He was western sale agent for an oil refinery in Denver, Colorado, and Chicago, Illinois, and in 1875 became partner of a mercantile firm, Wood, Thayer and Co., of Stanton, Michigan. Higgins purchased the interests of his partners in 1876, and conducted the business for three years before selling out and rejoining his father in business. Investments in northwestern timberlands made him wealthy, and he was able to buy total interests in his father's firm within five years. He also operated an investment banking firm in Olean, New York. He first became prominent in politics when elected a delegate to the Republican National Convention in Chicago, 1888. Five years later he was elected to the State Senate where he served until 1902. With Benjamin Odell, he was Lieutenant Governor of New York, elected by a large plurality. His success in office led to his nomination and election as governor, and began an administration that carried Odell's policies of tight economy and tax reforms. He also supervised changes in the state's election laws and insurance programs. He did not run for reelection as he was in poor health. He died of a heart attack soon after his term ended at his home in Olean.

HUGHES, CHARLES EVANS—(1862-1948), thirty-sixth governor of New York (1907-10), and Supreme Court Justice (1910-16) and (1930-41), was born in Glens Falls, New York, the son of David Charles and Mary C. Connelly Hughes. His father, a Baptist minister, moved the family to various congregations in New York, New Jersey, and Pennsylvania. Young Charles was sent to Madison College at the age of 14 and was graduated with an A. B. at Brown University in 1880. For a year afterwards he taught Greek and math at a private academy in Delhi, New York.

In 1882 he entered Columbia Law School where he won a fellowship, and graduated with an L. L. B. in 1884. Later in the year he also received his master's degree from Brown. He joined the firm of Chamberlain, Carter, and Hornblower in New York City, and later became a junior partner. In 1888 Hughes married Antoinette Carter, daughter of the senior member of his law firm, and soon afterwards he became a full partner in the new firm of Carter, Hughes and Dwight. One of the first cases he undertook required that he spend a long period on the Pacific Coast of Oregon in the interests of a railroad company. In 1893-1901 he worked in New York and was a special lecturer on general assignments and banking at the New York Law School. The New York Legislature appointed him as a special counsel to an investigative team on public utilities. He also was chief counsel in a committee to investigate insurance companies in the state which made him many enemies in the corporate world. In 1906 he was appointed special assistant to the attorney general in a coal mining investigation and later that year, while he was on tour of Europe, he was nominated for the governorship. A Republican, he won after a tough contest with Democrat William Randolph Hearst. Hughes' terms were notable for the reforms and liberal legislation that occurred. He organized state regulation of all public utilities, and he supported legislation dealing with insurance, banking, water power, conservation, improved highways, agricultural education, employee welfare and corrupt campaign contribution practices. Hughes was reelected to a second term in 1908 in which he approved a Workmen's Compensation Act and the Moreland Act which authorized the governor to carry out investigations into all public agencies and governments within the state. In 1910, however, Hughes' term was cut short when he was appointed to the U. S. Supreme Court by President Taft. In one well-known case, Hughes pushed for restrictions on the authority of invidiual states over intrastate railroad rates. In 1916 he was nominated as the Republican candidate for President, which prompted him to resign from the Supreme Court. He was defeated in a tight race against Woodrow Wilson but continued to criticize the government's policies in World War I from the sidelines. When President Harding came into office in 1921, he became Secretary of

State remaining under the administration of President Coolidge until 1925. He made two notable pronouncements in 1923 regarding American foreign policy. The Monroe Doctrine was to him opposed to any non-American action encroaching upon the political independence of North and South American states under any guise, but that the doctrine did not infringe upon the independence of these other American nations such as those in Latin America. He was very wary of the new Russian government and warned against allowing propaganda in non-Russian territory. In 1925 Hughes returned to his private law practice. For the next few years he often argued cases before the Supreme Court and was chosen as a delegate to several international conferences and arbitrary groups. President Hoover then honored him in 1930 by naming him chief justice of the Supreme Court, where he remained until retirement in 1941. His last years were actively spent with the Legal Aid Society and the World Council of Christians and Jews. He was also a trustee of the University of Chicago and a fellow of Brown University. Honorary L. L. D. degrees were bestowed upon him by Knox, Dartmouth, Amherst, and Lafayette Colleges, as well as Brown, Columbia, George Washington, Yale and Princeton Universities. His books include *The Pathway of Peace and Other Lectures,* 1925, *Our Relations to the Nations of the Western Hemisphere,* 1928, and *Pan American Peace Plans,* 1929. Mr. Hughes was buried at Woodlawn Cemetery in New York beside his wife.

WHITE, HORACE—(1865-1943), thirty-seventh governor of New York (1910-1911), was a native of Buffalo, New York. His parents, Horace K. and Marion Strong White, sent him to public schools in Syracuse and he was able to attend Cornell University. He graduated from Cornell in 1887 with honors for his oratory abilities, and soon afterwards he began law studies at Columbia University in New York City. He was admitted to the state bar in 1890. In partnership with Harry F. King and then Jerome Cheney, he gained a good legal reputation. In the meantime he fell in love with Jane Lines Denison and married her in 1903. He served on the state senate from 1895 until 1908 acting as chair of the committee on cities and working to revise the civil service, tenement house and state fair laws of New York. In 1909 he was elected Lieutenant Governor of the state, and when Governor Hughes resigned his seat, White automatically took over to finish the term. He only served three months, but he supported a uniform charter for all cities in New York of a certain classification and a highway commission act during that time. He also gave financial support to the drafting of a rapid transit act under which the present subway in New York City was built. White resumed his law practice in Syracuse after his brief term, and he served as a trustee of Cornell University from 1916. When he died, he was the director of the Metropolitan Trust Company of New York and publisher of the Syracuse *Post-Standard*. He is buried in the Oakview Cemetery in Syracuse.

DIX, JOHN ALDEN—(1860-1928), thirty-eighth governor of New York (1911-13), was born in Glens Falls, New York, the son of James Lawton and Laura Stevens Dix. His father, a prominent foundry owner in town, sent his son to the local academy and to Cornell University where he received an A. B. degree in 1883. He returned to his hometown to work with his father in a black marble manufacturing firm. Four years later he worked with Lemon Thomson in an Albany lumber business and the firm developed into one of the largest wallpaper concerns in the country. To supply his mills, Dix acquired a tract of 17,000 acres of timberland and made it a rule that for every tree felled, another should be planted. He soon became president of the Iroquois Pulp and Paper Company and the Moose River Lumber Company and director of another wallpaper firm in Hudson Falls, New York. He also became a banker with the Albany Trust Company and the city's First National Bank as vice president. He achieved a noteworthy reform by securing an increase in the rate of interest on the state's bank deposits in 1906. His political career began in 1904 with his election as a delegate to the Democratic National Convention and he rose in prominence in the party so that in 1910 he was chosen the chairman of the state committee. In the meantime he had been nominated for governor (1906) and lieutenant governor (1908) and had served as a county chair for the party. In 1910 he was once again nominated for governor and this time won over the Republican nominee. Dix worked on reform and tight budgeting during his administration. His more important actions were a new primary elections law, a $50 million state highway improvement plan, a factory inspection commission, and conservation laws. A deficit of over $1.5 million was turned over into a surplus of $4 million by the end of his term. Dix also had to deal with the disastrous effects of a large fire that swept the State Capitol building. The governor stepped down to return to his business holdings in upstate New York. He was a trustee of Cornell University and had received an honorary L. L. D. degree from Hamilton College in 1912. He was married to the former Gertrude Thomson, daughter of his former partner, Lemon, and the two retired to Santa Barbara, California, in his later years.

SULZER, WILLIAM—(1863-1941), thirty-ninth governor of New York (1913), was born in Elizabeth, New Jersey, the son of Thomas Sulzer and Lydia Jelleme Sulzer. He attended public schools in the city and then entered Columbia College (now University). In order to attend college, he had worked on farms and then in a wholesale grocery in New York City. His taste for study caused him to seek a clerkship in a law office. When he turned 21, he had learned enough to be admitted to the bar. A Democrat, he began taking an active part in politics. In 1884 and 1888 he made many speeches for the party and in 1889 was elected to the State Assembly. He served five terms working to pass bills for the state care of the insane and better accomodations for free lectures in the city for the working class. He also worked to indict corpoations for violations of the law and to compel them to plead in court the same as individual citizens. In 1895 he took a seat in the U. S. House of Representatives where he remained until 1912. In the meantime he married Clara Rodelheim and was a delegate to all of the Democratic party's national conventions. He left Congress in 1912 to campaign for governor of New York. After inauguration Sulzer ordered an investigation of the infamous "Tammany Hall" judges in New York City. The organization was found to be fraught with corruption, patronage, and poor administration policies. Tammany Hall continued to control much of the state politics during Sulzer's term, however. Vengeful legislators led an investigation of their own which uncovered diverted campaign contributions in Sulzer's records. They moved for impeachment, and Governor Sulzer was forced to leave office less than a year after he started. However, his law practice did not suffer, and Sulzer remained active in politics as an Independent and a member of the short-lived American party in the teens. He was also involved in gold mining enterprises in Alaska. The former governor died in New York City. He is buried at Evergreen Cemetery in Hillside, New Jersey.

GLYNN, MARTIN HENRY—(1871-1924), fortieth governor of New York (1913-15), was born in Kinderhook, New York. His parents, Martin and Anne Scanlon Glynn, were of Irish descent. He attended local school and then graduated, with honors, from St. John's College of Fordham University in 1894. He then worked for the Albany *Times-Union* of which he became managing editor and later the editor-publisher. In the meantime he studied law and was admitted to the bar in 1897. His private law practice always remained second to his journalistic interests, however. He decided to enter politics in 1898 and won a seat in Congress which he held for one term. In 1901 he married Mary Magrane and became vice president of the commission of the Louisiana Purchase exposition. In 1906 he was elected comptroller of New York. In that post, he tried to divorce politics from the administration of state finances and conducted two of the most successful bond sales in the history of the state while increasing corporate and inheritance taxes. The Democrat Glynn was elected Lieutenant Governor in 1912 and following the impeachment of Governor Sulzer, he automatically took his place. During his administration Glynn worked on a number of progressive measures including the state's first workman's compensation law, a state land bank to aid farmers by extending short term loans, a free bureau of employment, and a statewide direct primary system. At the same time, the state budget was reduced to 25 percent. However, Glynn was not popular enough to be elected to a second term. He remained active in politics and was a temporary chairman of the Democratic National Convention in 1916. Glynn also had a part in the settlement of an age-long fight for Irish freedom. While he was in Europe in 1921, the critical negotiations between David Lloyd George and Roman de Valera were taking place, and Glynn was able to initiate a series of conferences between the two which eventually brought peace and the establishment of the Irish Republic. Glynn also continued publishing the Albany *Times-Union* selling it to William Randolph Hearst shortly before his death.

WHITMAN, CHARLES SEYMOUR—(1868-1947), forty-first governor of New York (1915-19), was a native of Hanover, Connecticut, and the son of John and Lillie Whitman Seymour, of prominent New England familes. Young Charles attended a local academy and then a normal school in Canfield, Ohio, before studying at Adelbert College and graduating with an A. B. from Amherst College in 1890. He then studied law at New York University and after receiving his L. L. B., began a law practice in the city in 1894. In 1901-04 he was an assistant corporation counsel assigned to represent the City of New York at the State Capitol and was then legal advisor to Mayor Seth Loe of New York City. In 1904 the mayor made him a city magistrate, and later Whitman was the chairman of the Board of City Magistrates. While in that post, he drafted the bill to create a night court in the city, the first in the world. Governor Hughes chose him to be judge of the Court of General Sessions in 1907 and for a time afterwards he resumed his private practice. In 1909 he was elected district attorney of New York County. His achievements during that term included the trial and conviction of police lieutenant, Charles Becker, and four other gunmen in the murder of New York gambler Herman Rosenthal (1912). He also helped convict members of the "Poultry Trust". In 1914 he was elected governor and began a term that was characterized by reforms in education, labor, and law enforcement. A bureau of labor statistics was organized, a township school system adopted, and new narcotics controls were enacted. Whitman was governor during World War I, and had to enact many wartime regulations. Whitman was the Republican candidate for a third term in 1918, but lost to Democrats. Afterwards, he was a member of the New York law firm of Whitman, Ransom, Coulson, & Goetz. He was also Commander of the Port of New York Authority board in 1935 until his death. His wife, Olive Hancock Whitman died in 1927; their son and daughter survived them.

SMITH, ALFRED E.—(1873-1944), forty-second and forty-fourth governor of New York (1919-21 and 1923-29), was born in New York City. His parents were Alfred E. and Catherine Mulvehill Smith, who sent him to parochial schools in the city, but when his father died in 1885, young Alfred was forced to leave the eighth grade and find work. He sold newspapers, worked in a fish market, and as a shipping clerk for a Brooklyn steam pump firm. Early in his career he became interested in politics, joined a Democratic club, and before he was 21, made campaign speeches. In 1895 he became a clerk in the commissioner of jurors office in New York City, and in 1903 his associations with Tammany Hall led to his election to the state legislature. He served in the legislature for 12 years becoming the majority leader and chair of the Ways and Means committee in 1911 and minority leader later on. As a member of the Constitutional Convention of 1915, he introduced an amendment repealing an article that prohibited the state from using its credit or money for parochial schools. Later that same year, Smith was elected sheriff of New York county. He was president of the Board of Aldermen of New York City in 1918 resigning his office upon nomination for governor. After defeating Governor Whitman, Smith had to contend with the general hostility of the Republican assembly members. Also during the first term, strikes, unemployment, disorganization in industry, and inadequate housing plagued the state. Smith worked to pass a new Workmen's Compensation Law, and approved various public facilities including a tunnel for cars between New York and New Jersey. His non-partisan reconstruction committee proposed a new income tax to offset growing costs in state government. Smith also worked for women's suffrage in the state during his first term. However, Smith did not win reelection in 1900 mainly because of accusations from William Hearst that he protected the "milk trust barons" which produced watered-down and sour milk at that time. For the next two years, Smith worked as chair of the United States Trucking Corporation and as a member of the Port of New York Authority. In 1922 Smith was again drawn to the political arena, and he was elected over his former Republican opponent by a 386,000 margin. In 1924 he won again against Republican Theodore Roosevelt, Jr. Smith advocated the expansion of water power in the state by creating a state power authority to sell the power to private companies and civic authorities. He also advocated $100 million in funding for public institutions as well as a reorganization of state government that reduced the number of elective state officers to four and the number of state departments from 180 to 18. Smith, an advocate of a four-year term for governors, won a fourth term in 1926. He was a Democratic candidate for President in 1928 but opposition to his election was based on three grounds: that he favored modification of the Prohibition Act, that he was a Roman Catholic, and that he had been a member of Tammany Hall. When he was defeated for nomination by Herbert Hoover, Smith was for a time engaged in business in New York City with the New York Trust Company which handled the construction of the Empire State Building, and as a curator of a $6 million trust fund left by Conrad Hubert. During the 1930's Smith was regarded as a prominent opponent of fellow Democrat Franklin D. Roosevelt. He tried to run against the New Dealer in 1936 but failed. In the next few years he remained in New York with his wife, the former Catherine A. Dunn, and their five children. He died there and was buried in the Calvary Cemetery in Long Island City. In 1928 he published his autobiography, *Up to Now.*

MILLER, NATHAN L.—(1868-1953), forty-third governor of New York (1921-23), was born in Solon, New York, to Samuel and Almera Russell Miller. He attended local public schools and then the state normal school at Cortland. Upon graduation in 1887, he taught school himself for awhile and eventually began studying law at Cortland. In 1893 he began his practice in that town and was school commissioner for his district in 1894-1900. In 1901 the City of Cortland named him corporation counsel, and in 1902 he became state comptroller. Miller was made a justice on the New York Supreme Court in 1903 where he sat for 10 years. After serving as Associate Judge of the Court of Appeals for three more years, he returned to his private law practice in Cortland. A Republican, he was also active in politics and in 1920 secured the nomination for governor. He won against Alfred Smith in a tight race and immediately set about a conservative course in his administration. He cut the state government by 2,000 employees and reorganized several commissions. He also organized a Motion Picture Censor Commission and a State Department of Purchase and Supply to control the budget. His policies did not succeed in the public's eye, however, and he was defeated soundly by Smith in the next election. Miller then joined with another lawyer in a law firm which came to be known for its promotion of welfare work among employees of large corporations. He was a legal advisor to the U. S. Steel Corporation, Mutual Life Insurance Company, and director of the Delaware and Hudson Railroad Corporation. Miller was buried in his native town.

ROOSEVELT, FRANKLIN DELANO—(1882-1945), forty-fifth governor of New York (1929-33), and President of the United States (1933-45), was born near Hyde Park, New York. His parents were James and Sara Delano Roosevelt, prominent members of the community who provided private tutors for their son and sent him to the preparatory Groton School until 1900. He then graduated from Harvard University, got married to his distant cousin Anna Eleanor, and received his L. L. B. in 1907. His first practice was with the New York law firm of Carter, Ledyard, and Milburn. A Democrat, he ran successfully for the state senate in 1911 and served for one term opposing the Murphy political machine in New York City. He was appointed assistant secretary of the Navy under President Wilson in 1913-20 and made an unsuccessful bid for Vice President the next year. He also became vice president of the Fidelity and Deposit Company of Maryland and continued his law practice. In 1921 he contracted polio, which paralyzed his legs. Confined to a wheelchair for the rest of his life, Roosevelt was undaunted. He continued to be an active Democrat and in 1928 was elected Governor. He supported old age pensions, a $450 million water power project, and other public welfare legislation. He also attended the 1932 Olympic Games at Lake Placid, New York, as an honored guest. His second term saw the beginning of the devastating effects of the Great Depression in New York. As a result, he instituted a New York Temporary Emergency Relief Administration. His successes led to his nomination and election as President in 1932 and he left office mid-term. In order to control the financial chaos of the nation, he ordered banks closed and stopped gold transactions until Congress passed the Emergency Banking Act and another act creating an insurance plan for savings deposits. He also began working for a "New Deal" in government creating several programs to employ workers in public projects. His Civilian Conservation Corps employed young males, his Public Works Administration employed construction workers, and his Works Projects Administration employed not only manual workers but artists and writers and musicians as well. He also tried to halt the depression by paying farmers not to grow so many crops and by allowing the secretary of agriculture to fix prices on produce and meat. He also authorized the massive Tennessee Valley Authority to build dams, power plants, and flood control facilities. He also began to regulate the stock market through the Exchange Commission Act of 1934. Roosevelt, a charismatic speaker who appeared to sympathize with the poor who suffered during the Great Depression, was elected to four consecutive terms and may have been elected to another one had he not died in 1945. He was widely respected for his diplomatic abilities when America entered World War II in 1941. He worked with Stalin and Churchill to formulate a United Nations Charter before his death at Warm Springs, Georgia. He was the author of *Government, Not Politics,* 1932; *Looking Forward,* 1933, and *On Our Way,* 1934, and is still regarded as the leader of modern liberalism.

LEHMAN, HERBERT H.—(1878-1963), forty-sixth governor of New York (1933-42), was born in New York City, the youngest son of Mayer and Babette Newgass Lehman. His father was a former cotton dealer who had organized the investment banking firm of Lehman Brothers and the New York Cotton Exchange. The privileged Herbert was sent to Dr. Sach's Collegiate Institute and then studied at William College in Massachusetts from which he received his A. B. in 1899. His first job was with the J. Spencer Turner Company where he eventually became vice president and treasurer of the textile manufacturer to work with his father's investment company. He married Edith Altschul of San Francisco in 1910 with whom he had three children. During World War I he worked with the Joint Distribution Committee which administered the disbursement of $75 million in relief to European Jews. He was a captain in the officers Reserve Corps of the U. S. Army from 1917 and attained a colonelship in 1919. Under Roosevelt he also served as Assistant Director of Purchase, Storage, and Traffic for the War Department for which he was awarded a Distinguished

Service Medal. In 1921 he received an M.A. degree from Williams College and eight years later achieved his law degree from that institution in additon to his many honorary degrees. Lehman was made chair of the citizen's committee on finances for New York City in 1926 and also worked for Alfred Smith's gubernatorial campaign that year. A Democrat, he was chair of the party's national finance committee in 1928 and was a delegate to all of the National Conventions through 1956. He was elected Lieutenant Governor of New York in 1928 and reelected in 1930. When Roosevelt left office to become President, Lehman was elected governor by a large margin. He also won in the 1934, 1936, and 1938 elections for an unprecedented four terms. Roosevelt appointed him to head his new Office of Foreign Relief and Rehabilitation Operations in 1942 and Lehman left Albany. As Governor, he had approved the repeal of Prohibition, and pushed for such reforms as Old Age Pensions and unemployment insurance. He also advocated allowing women in jury duty. His last term had been extended two years by a new amendment ot the state constitution. When Lehman left to go to Washington, he saw his duty to "feed and clothe and find shelter for the millions whose lives have been disrupted by war". In late 1943 the United Nations joined the relief activity and Lehman was named director-general of the program. He resigned this post in 1946 because of poor health but ran for U. S. Senate unsuccessfully later that year. In 1948 he was a member of the Economic Cooperation Administration's advisory board until his election to the U. S. Senate in late 1949 (he was to fill the unexpired term of Senator Robert Wagner). While in Congress, Lehman agreed with most of President Truman's "Fair Deal" policies. He served in Washington through 1956. When he turned 75, the *New York Times* reported that Lehman had led three careers: in business, philanthropy, and in government. "To all that he has done he has brought a keen intelligence, a humane spirit, and an urgent sense of responsibility," the paper added. Lehman lived 10 years longer and died at his home in New York City.

POLETTI, CHARLES—(1903-   ), forty-seventh governor of New York (1942-43), was a native of Barre, Vermont, and the son of Dino, a granite cutter, and Caroline Gervasini Poletti, who were Italian immigrants. He said later that he "learned at first hand, in a taught school, the problems of the poor and underprivileged". He attended local public schools but spent much of his time working on a farm, in a bakery, and at a grocery store run by the stonecutter's organization. He excelled at school and won enough scholarships to attend Harvard University where he received a B.A. in political science and history in 1924. With an Eleanora Duse scholarship, he was able to study at the University of Rome for one year and then in 1928 he studied at the University of Madrid, Spain. Poletti returned to Harvard and received his L.L.B. later that year. He immediately began working with the law firm of Davis, Polk, Wardel, Gardiner, and Reed, but did not gain admittance to the New York bar until 1930. That year, he was chosen to be legal counsel for the St. Lawrence Power Development Commission. Politics did not hold a large place in his life until 1932 when he was hired as counsel to the Democratic National Committee. Future governor Herbert Lehman met and liked Poletti enough to name him to be his private counsel in 1933-37. In 1937 he was appointed to be justice of the state Supreme Court. Despite the fact that he would make less than $15,000 less per year, Poletti ran for Lieutenant Governor in 1938 because he believed he could "render more valuable service" in that position. The altruistic man won the seat and remained there until 1942 when he was defeated by Thomas W. Wallace in a close race. However, in December 1942, Governor Lehman resigned to take a federal post and Poletti was chosen to hold the seat until Dewey's inauguration one month later. During that month, the governor ordered increased farming and industrial production and led an investigation of the destruction of Jewish property in the Adirondacks. His "New Deal" approach did not appeal to the conservative press in New York, but *Time* magazine characterized his political actions as "first rate". After his short term, Poletti was an advisor to War Secretary Stimson. He was then made a Lieutenant Colonel in the Army, and he served from 1943 to 1946 in Italy. Since then, he has practiced law in New York City.

DEWEY, THOMAS E.—(1902-1971), forty-eighth governor of New York (1943-55), was a native of Owosso, Michigan, and the son of George Marin, postmaster of the town and publisher of the local newspaper, and Annie Thomas Dewey. He attended local public schools and graduated with an A. B. from the University of Michigan in 1923. Two years later he received his law degree from Columbia University and was admitted to the New York State bar in 1926. He worked in the New York law firms of Larkin, Rathbone, and Perry and then MacNamara and Seymour. He was with the latter firm in 1931 when he was appointed chief assistant to George Z. Medalie, U. S. district attorney for southern New York. In 1933 he took over the D.A. post himself and served there for a few months until President Roosevelt appointed a Democrat to succeed him. Dewey returned to his private practice in New York City and in 1935 was special prosecutor in a case investigating a policy racket in the city. During the next two and a half years, Dewey and his staff obtained convictions against 72 organized crime leaders. In 1937 he ran for district attorney of New York County on the Republican ticket and won by a large plurality. He continued his prosecution of rackets in the city as well as corrupt judges and city leaders. He ran unsuccessfully for governor the next year but won in 1942 by a 600,000 margin. He was reelected to a second term by an even larger majority in 1946 and to a third term in 1950. Meanwhile, he ran for President in 1944 but was defeated by Roosevelt. He lost the Presidential election again in 1948 against Democrat Harry S. Truman. Governor Dewey supported the organization of a commission against Discrimination in 1945, the first government agency in the nation established to protect the rights of individual against discrimination in employment because of race, creed, color or national origin. He also pushed for massive highway improvements and established a Labor Mediation Board. At the end of his terms, Dewey and his wife, the former Frances E. Hutt, moved back to New York City where he accumulated wealth with the law firm of Dewey, Ballantine, Bushby, Palmet, & Wood. He remained active in the Republican party but declined a nomination by President Richard Nixon to become Chief Justice of the Supreme Court (1968). Dewey wrote *The Case Against the New Deal* (1940), *Journey to the Far Pacific* (1952), and *Thomas E. Dewey on the Two Party System* (1966). He received several honorary law degrees from prominent universities while holding office.

HARRIMAN, WILLIAM AVERELL—(1891-), forty-ninth governor of New York (1955-59), was born in New York City to Edward and Mary Averell Harriman, of a wealthy family. His father, a banker and financier who headed several railroad companies, sent him to the Groton School and then to Yale University from which he graduated in 1913. During summer vacations he worked in Omaha, Nebraska, as a clerk and manual laborer in a railroad yard. He eventually became vice president in charge of purchasing and supplies for the Union Pacific Railroad in 1915. That same year he married Kitty Lanier Lawrence, with whom he later had two daughters. In 1917 he bought a small shipyard in Pennsylvania that became one of the largest producers of partially prefabricated ships and was eventually known as the Merchant Shipping Corporation. In 1920 he was accused of tax evasion but the federal government eventually dropped charges. His first marriage split up, however, and he remained single until 1930 when he married the former Mrs. Marie Norton Whitney. Harriman's private bank merged with the Brown Brothers in 1931, and the next year he became chairman of the board for the Union Pacific Railroad. He was also on the executive committee for the Illinois Central Railroad in 1931-42 and was named to the Business Advisory Council of the U. S. Department of Commerce in 1933. The depression at its peak, he was named to the National Recovery Administration in 1934 as a special assistant and was administrative officer after Hugh Johnson's resignation. While maintaining his own interests, he was Defense Expediter and liaison between Britain and America in 1941 and then was appointed ambassador to the Soviet Union in 1943-46 as well as ambassador to Great Britain in 1946. President Truman named him U. S. Secretary of Commerce at the end of 1946, and in 1948 he became director of aid to Europe under the Marshall Plan. The President made him a special assistant in 1950-51, and he was a representative to the NATO commission on Western Defenses in 1951. For the next two years he was director of the Mutual Security Agency. His long experiences in government led to the Democratic party nomination for governor in 1954 and he won the seat. The governor sought to help the middle income familes in New York by approving housing and highway construction in their neighborhoods. He instituted the first consumer agency and approved an antidiscrimination commission in the state government. To provide more tax money, he approved a Two Track Racing Bill and legalized bingo. When he was not reelected in 1958, Harriman left office at the end of his term to continue his business. He was made United States Ambassador-At-Large in 1961 and 1965 and was Assistant Secretary of State for Far Eastern Affairs in 1961-63. During the Vietnam War, he was a member of the U. S. delegation to the Paris Peace talks of 1968-69. The powerful man retired in 1969, and died at home.

ROCKEFELLER, NELSON A.—(1907-1978), fiftieth governor of New York (1959-73), was born in Bar Harbor, Maine, at the family retreat of John D. Rockefeller, Jr. and Abby Greene Aldrich Rockefeller. He graduated from the Lincoln School at the Teacher's College in New York City and then studied at Dartmouth College until his graduation in 1930. That year he married Mary Todhunter Clark with whom he had five children. He began helping manage the family's extensive holdings, including the Rockefeller Center in New York City and the subsidiaries of Standard Oil. Under President Roosevelt, he was coordinator of the Office of Inter-American Affairs in 1940-44 using his experience with the Creole Petroleum Corporation in Venezuela. He was then Assistant Secretary of State for Latin American Affairs in 1944-45 helping to organize the Chapultepec, Mexico, conference of the governments of the Americas. At this time, he also worked for the formation of the United Nations donating Rockefeller land to the project. After 1945 he organized several agencies including the American International Association for Economic and Social Development. President Truman named him chair of the International Development Advisory Board in 1950, and in 1953, Eisenhower appointed him Under-Secretary of the Department of Health, Education, and Welfare. He was also chair of the President's Advisory Committee on Government Organization until 1958 when he ran for the New York governorship. Rockefeller, a liberal Republican, won four terms in Albany and saw an enormous amount of social change in the state. He attempted to streamline the government bureaucracy and supported civil rights legislation. He worked for urban renewal in the state's aging cities and increased the public universities and colleges by 44 institutions and billions of dollars. In the meantime, his first marriage ended in divorce, but he remarried Margaretta Fitler

Murphy in 1963 and had two more children by her. Rockefeller appeared to be a friend to the liberal groups representing underprivileged Jews, Italian, women, and blacks in New York, but he also showed a conservative side in his support of the involvement in Vietnam and his approval of large military spending. He was a member of President Nixon's advisory board on Intergovernmental Relations in 1965-69 and was a member of the Foreign Intelligence Advisory Board to the President in 1969 to 1974. He resigned the governorship in 1973 ostensibly to form the U. S. Commission for Critical Choices, but his true ambitions were seen in 1976 when he sought the Republican nomination for President. His fellow party members thought he represented too liberal a viewpoint and elected incumbent Gerald Ford instead. He served as Ford's Vice President since 1975. When he left office, Rockefeller returned to manage his family's holding and to set up several foundations. He was treasurer, president, and chair of the Museum of Modern Art, founder of the Museum of Primitive Art, and used personal funds to help build the new Empire State Plaza in Albany when he was governor. Rockefeller died in his New York City Office.

WILSON, CHARLES MALCOM—(1914-   ), fifty-first governor of new York (1973-75), is a native of New York City and the son of Charles H., an attorney, and Agnes Egan Wilson. The family moved to Yonkers, New York, when he was six, and he spent many of his summers in the dairy regions of the state helping on his uncle's farm in Oneida County. He also worked as a guide at Fort Niagara in between terms at the local parochial schools. He received his B.A. from Fordham University in 1933 and immediately began to study law. After admittance to the bar in 1936, he worked with the White Plains firm of Kent, Hazzard, and Jaggar, which eventually took him in partnership. He entered formal political life as a Republican state assemblyman although he recalled that "as a youngster I can remember spending every election day at the polls, handing out pamphlets." He had also taught parliamentary procedure at a General Motors plant to union members before election. He served 10 consecutive terms with each election bringing an increasing margin of votes from his district. It was during this time that he developed his hard-line conservative approach. He opposed a Metcalf-Baker bill banning housing discrimination because he believed that owners should be able to "do with their property what they wish to do", and he worked to halt unemployment insurance increases. Wilson had served in the Navy on an ammunition ship in the Atlantic during World War II and continued his law practice during this time. In 1958 Rockefeller chose Wilson as his campaign manager, and the next year he was made lieutenant governor serving during all of Rockefeller's terms. He often disagreed with the Governor, supporting such ultra-conservative measures as a proposed constitutional amendment making it more difficult to obtain a divorce or annulment. When Rockefeller resigned, Wilson automatically rose to fill out the term. He repealed a state income tax surcharge and dealt with the energy crisis of 1974 by instituting a gas rationing plan. At a time when many in the state were suspicious of the Republican party as a result of Watergate, Wilson attempted to win the governorship in his own right. However, Democrat Carey won, and Wilson returned to his law practice as well as business interests in White Plains.

CAREY, HUGH—(1919-   ), fifty-second governor of New York (1975-1983), was born in Brooklyn, New York, the son of Dennis J. and Margaret Collins Carey. His older brothers are Edward M. and Dennis J., and his younger brothers, John R. and Martin T., all of New York City. The youngest brother, George G., died in an airplane accident in New York City in 1959. Carey was graduated from St. Augustine's Academy and High School in Brooklyn. He took on several part-time jobs then and later during college to help pay school expenses. After high school he attended St. John's University, but his studies were interrupted by World War II. In 1939, he enlisted as a private in the 101st Cavalry, Squadron C, of the New York National Guard. In 1941, the unit was activated and Carey remained in uniform for five years. He rose quickly in the ranks and became a lieutenant and a company commander, helping train reservists and new draftees in the 104th Timberwolf Division, which later became one of the hardest fighting units of the war in Europe. He was among the troop leaders who crossed the Rhine on the Remagen Bridge, participated in the capture of Cologne, and liberated the Nazi concentration camp at Nordhausen.

Returning to the U. S. in 1946, Carey became active in a statewide effort to involve younger people and veterans in political affairs. He married Helen Owen in 1947, with whom he eventually had 14 children, and then returned to St. John's University to complete his education. He received a J.D. in 1951 and was admitted to the bar that same year. Carey first won elective office in 1960. He ran for Congress, in support of President John F. Kennedy, and defeated a four-term Republican incumbent in a major upset. He won seven successive terms despite a number of efforts to defeat him by gerrymandering his Congressional district. Carey's first major committee assignment was to the House Education and Labor Committee. He was a principal architect and floor manager of the historic Elementary and Secondary Education Act of 1965, the first Federal law in history to aid children in all schools. President Johnson, in his biography, gave credit to Congressman Carey for breaking the 20-year logham which had blocked legislation to help local schools. Congressman Carey chaired a special Sub-committee on Education of the Handicapped during his tenure on the House Education and Labor Committee. During this time, he was responsible for more legislation to aid the disabled and handicapped than any other member of Congress. An example of his work in this State was the founding of the National Technical Institute for the Deaf, at Rochester, in 1968. It is the nation's only technical college for the deaf. In 1970, Congressman Carey was assigned to the powerful House Ways and Means Committee on which he had a leading role in passage of the historic Revenue-Sharing law which provides Federal funds for state and local government.

He was serving his seventh term in the House of Respresentatives when he became a candidate for Governor in the spring of 1974. His Democratic and liberal stances helped him win over his more conservative opponent. In his inaugural address, he said, "We shall find in the hard work of building a better society, the best that is within us". In pursuing the betterment of society, Governor Carey has run into severe financial difficulties in recent years. New York City faced bankruptcy and Carey created a Municipal Assistant Corporation. He noted that "in this era of limits and economic uncertainty, we must focus our energies on managing our resources and our governments better". He has also supported offshore oil leasing and opposed an oil tariff in the state. He believes that the greatest deterrent to crime is swift and sure punishment and has approved stiffer prison sentences for violent criminals as well as tougher Board of Parole guidelines. In recent years he has also supported large tax cuts and was able to balance the budget. Carey was reelected in 1978 and his current term expires in January 1983. He has decided not to run for reelection.

CUOMO, MARIO M.-(1932-), current governor of New York (1983-), is a native of Queens, New York City, the son of Italian immigrants Andrea and Immaculata Cuomo. He attended the local Catholic grammar school and graduated with a B.A. from St. Johns College in 1953. Three years later he finished his law studies at that college and began practicing in New York. His first job was as an assistant to Judge Adrian Burke of the New York Court of Appeals (1956-58), and then he joined a Brooklyn law firm in 1958. After 1963 he was a partner in the firm. Cuomo was recognized as one of the best appellate lawyers in the state during this time. When he was not practicing law, he was teaching it at St. Johns College, or working with various community groups in the New York City area on such issues as affordable housing and minority problems. Governor Hugh Carey appointed Cuomo secretary of state in 1975, a position he held until 1979. He was elected lieutenant governor in 1978 and served in that position until taking his place as governor in January 1983. During the 1970s, Cuomo had been involved as a mediator in several controversial situations. He represented community groups in Brooklyn and Queens in 1974, which he documented in his best-selling book, *Forest Hills Diary: The Crisis of Low Income Housing* (1974). In 1977, he mediated between the state goverment and the Mohawk Indians, who were making claims to their traditional lands in upper New York state. He also ran unsuccessfully for New York City mayor in that year. In his 1982 campaign, Cuomo was perceived by the press as a clear opponent of conservative Lew Lehrman. Some accounts compared him to Massachusetts Senator Teddy Kennedy because he combined 1960s liberalism with 1970s realism, referring to his support of social programs but not of higher taxes. He won only after a close race against Lehrman. Governor Cuomo promised in his campaign not to raise business, income or sales taxes during his term. Cuomo is married to the former Matilda Raffa, a teacher, and has four children.

BIOGRAPHIES OF FAMOUS NEW YORKERS

ABERCROMBIE, JAMES (1706-1781), British general during the French and Indian War period, was famous for his ill-fated attack on Fort Ticonderoga in New York. Born in Scotland to a well-to-do family, he followed his father's example and joined the army at a young age. In 1734 he was chosen to represent Banffshire in Parliament, and in 1746 he became lieutenant colonel of the army. Just before the first stirrings of revolution were heard from the colonies, Abercrombie was appointed general of the Royal Scots.

However, his career was not one of success despite his honors. As a major-general, the government sent him to America to command the British and colonial forces until General Loudoun arrived. He trained troops at Albany, and after Loudoun was recalled in 1858, he assumed control of the Royal American Regiment. In July of that year, he led 15,000 men to Fort Ticonderoga, where the French had an impregnable stronghold. Unable to make decisions himself, Abercrombie took a young engineer's advice on strategy, and the result was one of the bloodiest British defeats in history, Abercrombie survived the ordeal, but 2,000 of his men were bayoneted to death in the unnecessary battle.

Afterwards, Abercrombie was recalled by the government, but the customary rules of seniority continued to bring him up through the ranks of the military until he was appointed a general. He lived most of the remainder of his life in Glassaugh, Scotland. As a Member of Parliament, he also voted for many of the tax measures that led to the American revolt. He died while holding the position of deputy governor of Stirling Castle, Scotland.

ALLEN, ETHAN (1737-1789), Revolutionary War soldier and essay writer, was a native of Litchfield, Connecticut. As one of the famed "Green Mountain Boys", Allen was almost a legendary figure of that era. Forced to abandon his formal education

Edward Koch

James Abercromby

DeWitt Clinton

Jay Gould

Peter Stuyvesant

Samuel Tilden

Samuel De Champlain

Joseph Brant

Franklin D. Roosevelt

Nelson Rockefeller

Fiorello LaGuardia

George Eastman

S. Grover Cleveland

Theodore Roosevelt

Susan B. Anthony

Anna Eleanor Roosevelt

Alexander Hamilton

Benedict Arnold

Robert Fulton

Andrew Carnegie

John D. Rockefeller

Alexander G. Bell

Samuel F.B. Morse

John Brown

Joseph Smith

Sojourner Truth

at a young age, because of his father's death, he managed an iron foundry near home and began silver and iron prospecting in Massachusetts, New Hampshire, and Vermont. In the meantime he grew active politically and wrote treatises dealing with his opposition to New York's claim to Vermont. He also fought in the French and Indian War at Fort William Henry in 1757. In 1769, he organized the rebellious "Green Mountain Boys" to oppose the New York authority in Vermont. The New York government put a price on Allen's head, but the unflustered outlaw replied "They may sentence us to be hung, but how will the fools manage to hang a Green Mountain Boy before they catch him?"

At the call for American independence, Allen and his band of outlaws were ready for action. He led 300 men to Ticonderoga, New York, in 1775 joined by Benedict Arnold and his men. Once there, however, there was little need for military strength as Allen's imperious manner suprised the British Captain de la Place and resulted in an immediate surrender.

Fighting like an Indian, Allen was successful in other war pursuits which helped his former enemies in New York to forget their complaints. However, he was captured and imprisoned for two years after attempting a surprise attack on Montreal. In 1778 he was taken to New York, exchanged for British prisoners, and consequently named a colonel by General Washington.

Allen had not forgotten his complaint against New York, however. When attempts for Vermont's claim were unsuccessful through Continental Congress legislation, he took it upon himself to command a Vermont militia which wreaked havoc upon New York settlers in the region. Abondoning his efforts for the American Revolution, he concentrated on defending Vermont as a separate territory until he died on his farm at Burlington.

In addition to behaving outlandishly, Allen wrote such essays as "Vindication of Vermont and her Right to Form an Independent State", "A Brief Narrative of . . . New York Relative to Their Obtaining the Jurisdiction of that Large District of Land to the Westward from Connecticut River" (1774), and "A Narrative of Ethan Allen's Captivity" (1779).

Perhaps a more curious article was his "Reason, the Only

Oracle of Man; Or A Compenduous System of Natural Religion'' (1784), which condemned as atheistic by the printer.

AMHERST, JEFFERY (1717-1797), colonial soldier during the French and Indian War, entered the British Army at the age of 14. He left his native Kent, England, and served as an aide-de-camp in the Austrian War and later fought in other European wars.

In 1758, he was ordered from the continent to set sail for America and capture the fort at Cape Breton Island. This rapid takeover of the stronghold constituted the first British victory of the Seven Years' War. Sailing southward to New York, Amherst and his men sought to hold Quebec for another year. After Abercrombie's defeat at Fort Ticonderoga, New York, however, he did not proceed with attack but settled in the territory for the winter. The next year he managed to conquer the French stronghold at Ticonderoga and moved northward to Lake Champlain. He learned of Quebec's defeat after building a strong fort at Crown Point. For these successes, George II named Amherst governor of Virginia although he later resigned the job when George III decreed that he would have to reside in the colony permanently.

Amherst spent the next few years leading successful raids on the French in Quebec and Montreal, and after a visit to England in 1786, he was given a grant of 20,000 acres in New York. He was raised to commander-in-chief of all the British forces in America during the Revolution.

The highly-respected military man was raised to the English peerage in 1776 as ''Baron'' Amherst. He retired to his estate, ''Montreal'', in Kent, after the unsuccessful Revolutionary War and participated in a few other military ventures until his death at home.

ANTHONY, SUSAN BROWNELL (1820-1906), reformer and feminist. As one of the leaders in the cause of women's rights during the nineteenth century, Susan B. Anthony is known today as the forerunner of modern feminism; her portrait has been honored on a recent commemorative silver dollar issuance.

Born in South Adams, Massachusetts, Susan was brought up in a liberal household where both male and female children were well educated. In defiance of his Quaker heritage, her father,

David, took pleasure in music and dancing, and married a Baptist woman, Lucy Read. When her father retired from his cotton manufacturing trade, young Anthony learned for the first time what it was like to earn a living for herself. She taught school in Philadelphia and from her letters of the time, showed no interest in pursuing the traditional female role of homemaking.

Her reforming zeal was evident at a young age, first with the temperance movement. After moving to her family's new home in Rochester, New York, Anthony tried to become involved in the Sons of Temperance organization at Albany. When she tried to contribute to the discussion, members told her that "the sisters were not invited there to speak but to listen and learn." Infuriated, she found that in this movement, as well as her everyday teaching associations, that women had to have an equal chance at participation if they were to be effective workers.

As an editor of the New York weekly paper, *The Revolution*, and a well-known lecturer, Anthony advocated abolition of slavery, temperance, and the inclusion of women in the suffrage clauses of the Fourteenth Amendment. Although she was usually a very austere, almost prudish woman, Susan Anthony joined her friend, Amelia Bloomer, in wearing trousers. However, she soon stopped when she discovered that when she spoke to groups of people, they were "fixed upon my clothes instead of my works . . . a successful person must attempt but one reform."

Women's suffrage was the single reform Susan B. Anthony devoted the rest of her life to. In 1869 she helped organize the National Woman Suffrage Association, and three years leater, she and a group of other women tested the legality of women's suffrage under the Fourteenth Amendment. Two weeks after they had voted in the November elections at Rochester, New York, she was arrested and after a lengthy trial, was fined $100. However, she never paid a cent saying she "would ignore all laws to help the slave," meaning women.

For the next decade, she devoted her time to lecture on suffrage throughout the country. In 1880, she pled her case before the judiciary committee of the U.S. Senate, the first woman to speak in Congress.

Although she was disregarded by the senators, Miss Anthony did live to see women's suffrage granted in four states. She died at her home in Rochester, willing her small fortune of $10,000 to the suffragette cause.

ARNOLD, BENEDICT (1741-1801), was an American Soldier during the Revolutionary War but was later uncovered as a traitor for the British side. He was born to an old family in Norwich, Connecticut. His father was a shipowner and sea captain, and tried to educate young Benedict in strict religious thinking although he rejected it. When he was only 15, he ran away from home to fight in the French and Indian War along with colonial army; but after a few months, the romance of camp life wore thin and he deserted his company. Only his youth saved him from legal prosecution. Afterwards he apprenticed at an apothecary's shop in New Haven and soon opened his own druggist and bookshop there (1767). He grew more prosperous, and with his earnings bought ships and began a mule and horse trading enterprise between the West Indies and Quebec.

Once called by a British sea captain a "damn Yankee", Arnold was anxious to join the colonial effort after the battle of Lexington in 1775. He managed to bring a small volunteer company from New Haven to Cambridge, Massachusetts where he was assigned to try to capture Fort Ticonderoga in New York. On the way he met Ethan Allen, and the two captured the stronghold by surprise without bloodshed. Soon after, he left Allen and sailed around Lake Champlain to conquer the fort at St. Johns. Later in the year, however, he was unsuccessful in his attempt to conquer the fort at Quebec, and after a bloody battle in the snow, he was wounded and forced to retreat.

By this time Arnold was well respected for his courage in these battles and he won favor from General Washington. In the next few years he supervised the construction of a fleet of ships and defended Connecticut against British invaders. But his favor from Washington did not help him when it came to his promotion in the army; several of Washington's enemies in Congress promoted officers of a lesser rank than Arnold to major-general positions over his head. When not even his pleading before the Congress and several letters of recommendation from General Washington helped his case for rank, Arnold grew infuriated and contemplated resigning from the army. Partly because of this embitterment, Arnold decided to take an offer from the British officials to become their informant.

Having moved to an estate near Philadelphia, Arnold had been court martialed for allegedly using his military office for private gain. Although the judges found him not guilty of most of the charges, they reprimanded several of his actions. This too caused Arnold's ultimate disavowal of the American government.

From 1779 on he gave the British information on the number of American troops advancing on what forts and at what time they planned to attack. After he gained the strategic post as commander of the fort at West Point, he plotted with the British to allow them to overtake it for a fee of 20,000 pounds. However, British Major John Andre, who was to meet with Arnold during the capture, was caught and the plot was discovered. Hearing of his failure, Arnold escaped to British lines and served the rest of the war on the British side. After 1781 he resided in London, although he was not particularly popular there either. He died there 20 years later.

ASTOR, JOHN JACOB (1763-1848), was a pioneer merchant in early America. Disliking his father's trade of butchery, he set out from his native Waldorf, Germany to work in his brother's piano factory in London. Once there, his objectives were to learn English, never to cheat, gamble, or be idle, and to learn everything he could about America. In 1783, he began his long hoped-for journey to the New World, and became friends with another German immigrant before his arrival in New York City in 1784. In the next few years, he began a thriving fur trade with the American Indians. By 1786, he had his own trading house where he alone bought, cured, beat, sold, and packed his skins for market in London. Fourteen years later, Astor had amassed $250,000, a large fortune for his time.

Astor essentially retired from the fur business after this but began selling sandalwood to a Chinese trader, the only merchant to do so in New England. He also began investing in large plots of New York City real estate. In later years this would constitute the bulk of his fortune, as he built the Astor House hotel on Broadway, a building larger and costlier than any previously in the city. During the War of 1812, he tried to establish a trading post with the Orient, which he called Astoria. It was on the Pacific coast in Oregon territory, but the government was unable, during wartime, to send an armed vessel to the young settlement and it failed. "But for the war," Astor said, I would have been the richest man who ever lived."

When Astor died, he left funds to build an Astor Library in New York City as well as an orphanage in his native town of Waldorf. He died at his house on Broadway.

BELL, ALEXANDER GRAHAM (1847-1922), inventor of the first telephone and pioneer worker with the deaf. Born in Edinburgh, Scotland, he learned the scientific values of experimentation from both sides of his family, which specialized in medicine on the one side and in elocution and the mechanisms of speech on the other. From his mother he also acquired a talent in music, and at the age of 16 he took a position as a pupil teacher at the Weston House Academy at Elgin for elocution and music. After studying Latin and Greek at the University of Edinburgh, he taught at several schools in England and Scotland then attended anatomy and physiology courses at the University College, London. He was unable to complete his medical education, however, as his father feared that he would die of tuberculosis as did his two brothers. The family moved to a country home in Canada near Brantford, Ontario, where Alexander soon regained his health from outdoor living.

From an early age, the young Bell had shown an aptitude for mechanical objects. In his teens, he had devised a method to remove wheat husks from the kernel and invented a speaking automation along with his brother. His studies of the resonances of vowel sounds led to its application to electricity and telegraphy. In addition, he began to work with the deaf. At Miss Susannah Hull's school for deaf children in Kensington, he taught "visible speech" and his successes prompted the Boston School Board to found a special day school for the deaf which used Bell's methods. In 1873-76, however, Bell began to devote most of his time to the transmission of audible speech through electric wires. He invented the harmonic multiple telegraph (1874) and the magnoelectric speaking telephone in 1875. In the next 30 years, revolutionary phonic inventions came out of

Bell's laboratory in succession. In 1877 he also formed the Bell Telephone Company after many claimants to his invention had plagued him over patent rights.

Around the turn of the century, Bell also turned his attention to aerodynamics, and with the help of motor-builder Glenn H. Curtiss, he built the "June Bug", and airplane that flew from Albany to New York City in 1908. In 1915 he opened the first transcontinental telephone line from New York to San Francisco. He was an early president of the National Geographic Society and helped develop the phonograph record and player.

Bell spent most of his last years at his home on Cape Brenton Island in Nova Scotia, where he died.

BERLIN, IRVING (1888-   ) composer, was born Israel Baline in eastern Russia to Moses and Leah Lipkin Baline who were prominent in their local synagogue. His father was a cantor, and taught Israel to appreciate music. When the family moved from Russia during the pogroms and resettled in New York City's lower east side, young Irving sang for a living at local theaters and cafes. With only two years of formal education and no musical training, Berlin soon learned how to pick out tunes on the piano by ear. Consequently, he was only able to compose songs in F sharp, a drawback which he eventually overcame by playing on a piano that could be transposed to any desired key. His first published work was the lyrics for "Marie from Sunny Italy" (1907), as a staff lyricist. He then appeared in vaudeville shows and made his debut on Broadway in 1910.

However, Berlin did not achieve fame until 1911, when he published his "Alexander's Ragtime Band" which sold a million copies, and popularized ragtime music in the nation. He eventually formed Irving Berlin, Inc. to sell his music and wrote the scores for the Ziegfield Follies, and the Music Box Review. His "A Pretty Girl is Like a Melody" became the theme song of the follies. Thereafter, he wrote musical comedies for which he is most famous: *The Cocoanuts,* a Marx Brothers movie made in 1925, *As Thousands Cheer* (1933), *Annie Get Your Gun* (1945), *Call me Madam* (1950), and such musicals as *Top Hat* (1933), and *There's No Business Like Show Business* (1954). Perhaps he was best known for the songs "White Christmas" and "Easter Parade", which were in two of his musical movies during the

1940's. "The time has to be right" Irving Berlin once said about patriotic songs, and he seemed to be able to pick out the choicest moments. During World War I, he wrote the score for *Yip, Yip, Yaphank,* a popular soldier's show that sold out 32 performances at the Century Theater. On Armistice Day 1939, he sat by while Kate Smith sang his "God Bless America" for the first time. Since then, the song has become almost a national anthem, and has gleaned millions in royalties for Berlin's family.

BLOOMER, AMELIA JENKS (1818-1894), feminist and reformer, was born in Homer, New York. She is probably best known for sporting the billowy pants that were named after her at a time when women were confined to strict fashion rules.

After attending local schools, Amelia Jenks taught classes herself and hired out as a private tutor. She married Quaker newspaper editor Dexter Bloomer in 1840 and afterwards lived in Seneca county. Her exposure to the newspaper made her more interested in public affairs and she was soon writing articles for the paper as well as participating in reform groups such as the Ladies' Temperance Society. Although she wasn't particularly interested in the suffrage movement of the time, she did attend the Seneca Falls women's convention in 1848, which inspired her to begin a newspaper for women called *Lily.* Articles by temperance reformers and women's rights advocates filled pages, and Mrs. Bloomer soon became a noted spokeswoman for the movement. She delivered lectures in New York City and elsewhere in the state and gradually her emphasis was apparent —women's clothing of the day was bulky and confining and something had to be done about it. She began wearing full-cut pantaloons instead of bustling skirts which drew much ridicule, if not notice, for her dress-reform cause. Her "turkish trousers" were soon known as "bloomers" and appeared in several cartoons and jokes in the popular press. Instead of helping her efforts, the bloomer experiment drew only laughter.

Nevertheless, Amelia continued to publish *Lily* in Seneca Falls where she was a deputy postmistress. She and her husband moved to Council Bluffs, Iowa, and Ohio, where she helped edit the *Western Home Visitor.* She was continously interested in reform movements until her death at Council Bluffs.

BRANT, JOSEPH (1742-1807) was a noted chief of the Mohawk who served as a British military officer during the American Revolution, but later worked constructively to end frontier warfare with the United States. From his earliest years, Brant (whose Mohawk name was Thayendanegea) had close ties with the British. His older sister married the British superintendent for northern Indian affairs, Sir William Johnson, and Brant fought under Johnson's command during the French and Indian War. Johnson, in turn, sent the young Mohawk to a charity school for Indians located at Lebanon, Connecticut.

Brant learned to speak and write English during his two years (1761-63) at the school, but perhaps more important to the course of his future career, he became a convert to the Anglican Church and served as interpreter to a missionary. An indication of how thoroughly anglicized Brant had become was his participation on the British side against Pontiac's Indian confederation of 1763-64.

Around 1765 Joseph Brant married the daughter of an Oneida chief and settled down to a peaceful life in the Mohawk Valley of New York. He assisted in the translation of several Anglican religious works into Mohawk, and in 1774 he received an appointment as secretary to the new superintendent of Indian affairs. After a trip to England in 1775, Brant returned to win the support of the Iroquois League to the British crown during the American Revolution. Commissioned a colonel in the British army, Brant was quite successful in aligning all but the Oneida and Tuscarora (out of six member nations) on the side of Great Britain.

During the War of Independence, Brant's followers—including some Tories—terrorized the Mohawk Valley, southern New York, and northern Pennsylvania. When his arch-rival Red Jacket, chief of the Seneca, attempted to have the Iroquois sign a separate peace with the Americans, Brant had the emissary killed and his papers taken, thereby frustrating Red Jacket's plans. Although apologists for Brant claim that he was not cruel to civilians during the war, there is evidence to indicate the contrary, many innocent settlers were slaughtered by warriors under his command.

Brant settled in Canada after the Peace of Paris in 1783

Biographies

officially concluded the American Revolution. He retained his commission in the British military service, but he also attempted to arrange a settlement between the Mohawk and the United States. Unsuccessful in that attempt, Brant nevertheless sought to end hostilities between the Mohawk and the Indians and whites, working with government agents to secure treaties with the tribes of the old Northwest Territory. He settled his followers on a tract of land along the Grand River near Brantford, Ontario, and spent a great deal of his time and energy opposing the land speculators who were anxious to acquire Mohawk territory. He ruled peacefully until his death, devoting himself to missionary work and religious translations.

BROWN, JOHN (1800-1859), abolitionist, waged "violent warfare" upon slavery while living in Ohio, New York and Pennsylvania. Born in Torrington, Connecticut, he spent most of his life as a wanderer, moving between his father's home in Hudson, Ohio, and Richmond, Pennsylvania. His trade was tanning, but he also studied for the ministry for a time in Massachusetts, surveyed land in Hudson, and served as postmaster for the little town of Richmond. His land speculation and wool-growing attempts brought him deeper into debt which wasn't aided by the fact that he had fathered 20 children.

The year 1849 was a turning point in his life. He left his business pursuits to settle in the Adirondacks of New York on land set aside for free blacks. Two years later, he returned to Ohio to help in the underground railroad and to form freed slaves into military companies. The antislavery and slavery conflicts in Kansas lured him there in 1855-56 and with two of his sons he became a Free-Soil leader and was knows as "Old Brown of Osawatomie". In 1856, believing himself to be inspired by a divine calling, Brown and seven others murdered pro-slavery settlers in what has been called the "Potawatomie Executions". In the next few years he continued his military involvements to this end and sought support for an abolitionist guerilla base in Maryland and Virginia in order to attack slaveholders. Although the fort was never built, Brown did receive money from several prominent Bostonians to continue his slave-freeing raids. The culmination of these took.place in the fall of 1859 when he crossed the Potomac at Harper's Ferry,

Virginia and held hostage 16 militarymen while releasing many black slaves. Instead of escaping, Brown and his men remained at the government armory exchanging shots and wounds. Brown himself was stabbed several times, but he survived to face trial a few days later in Charleston, where he was convicted of murder and treason and was sentenced to be hung. In response, Brown defended himself by saying "the Bible . . . teaches me 'to remember' them that are in bonds as bound with them . . . I say I am yet too young to understand that God is any respecter of persons. I believe that to have interfered as I have done . . . in behalf of the despised poor was not wrong, but right . . . if I should forfeit my life for the furtherance of the ends of justice and mingle my blood further with the blood of millions in this slave country whose rights are disregarded . . . I submit!".

His execution made him a hero in the north, where the song "John Brown's Body" became a legend. Lincoln's Emancipation Proclamation a few years later was largely in response to the national sentiment for John Brown.

CARNEGIE, ANDREW (1835-1919), industrialist and author, was a native of Dunfermline, Scotland, but moved with his family to Allegheny City, across from Pittsburgh, Pennsylvania, in 1848. There, at the age of 13, Andrew began work in a cotton factory, earning a little over a dollar per week. When the factory manager learned he could read and write, he took the boy into his office, but young Andrew discovered the work was not less arduous at a desk. His ambitions for wealth were begun at an early age, and he constantly strove for better-paying work. He met Thomas A. Scott of the Pennsylvania Railroad in the early 1850s, and in 1853 he was hired on as a private telegraph operator and personal secretary. Six years later he was promoted to be superintendent of the western division, which in turn led to his appointment in 1861 as superintendent of military transportation and director of telegraph communications when Scott became a Union colonel. At the Battle of Bull Run, he had charge of the railway communication and was the last official to leave for Alexandria.

After the war, Carnegie became interested in the possible uses of cast iron, especially in bridge-building, and he borrowed money in order to buy stock in Adams Express Company and join in the formation of the Keystone Bridge Company. Soon, his investments paid off and he took stock in more ventures, such as the Western Union Telegraph Company in New York and oil speculation.

During the 1870s, Carnegie invested in steel, and his use of the Bessemer process raised the quality of his product so much that his profits from it allowed him to expand his operations to include controlling interest in iron ore mining, transportation, manufacturing, and distribution. By the turn of the century, Carnegie controlled America's steel industry. His employment practices were revolutionary; the workers were paid on a sliding scale according to the current price of steel, thus forming a profit-sharing system. Carnegie's "association" of partners were all active managers and part owners of the company which led Carnegie to claim he was only one of many bosses in the firm. However, he maintained a 58 percent holding in the company throughout its existence.

In 1901 he sold the newly named United States Steel Corporation and devoted his life to philanthropy, writing, and intellectual associations. He financed many endowments for learning and teaching, and built the Carnegie Institute in Washington D.C., as well as numerous public libraries for towns and colleges. He was the principal stockholder in the Carnegie Music Hall, built in New York. Before his death, he wrote *Triumphant Democracy* (1886), *Wealth* (1886), and many other newspaper and magazine articles on his life and "How to Get Rich" (1891, New York Tribune). He died in Lenox, Massachusetts at a time when he claimed "the age of competition is over".

DOUBLEDAY, FRANK NELSON (1862-1934), publisher, was trained in the printer's trade and gained success because of his sharp appreciation of good writing. Born in Brooklyn, New York to William Edwards and Ellen M. (Dickinson), who sent him to the borough's Polytechnic Institute. He began to work at Charles Scribner's sons publishing house when he was only 15, where he advanced to publisher and manager of the *Scribner's Magazine* when it was first published in 1886. Ten years later, he left the company to organize his own publishing company with Samuel S. McClure.

The new company became successful during the first year,

after it published Rudyard Kipling's *The Day's Work* and several trade books. In 1900, Walter H. Page joined the firm to make it Doubleday, Page and Co., which published the magazines, *World's Work, Country Life in America,* and *Garden and Home Builder.*

Doubleday's first business was to deal with the fiction writers and poets of the day. He developed a close friendship with Rudyard Kipling, and helped the careers of Frank Norris, Edna Ferber, Sinclair Lewis, Joseph Conrad, and O. Henry. A bit of a writer himself, he wrote *A Plain American in England* in 1910 under pseudonym Charles T. Whitefield.

As the company progressed, Doubleday expanded his operations. He moved the printing and business facility to Garden City, New York. He also began a chain of bookstores, which numbered 30 by the time of his death. In 1927, he purchased the George H. Doran publishing house, to make his company Doubleday, Doran and Company. It wasn't until 1946, after Doubleday's death, that the corporation was known as Doubleday and Company.

He died in Cocoanut Grove, Florida.

DOWNING, ANDREW JACKSON (1815-52), landscape architect, was the creator of many New York gardens and grounds, and ended his career by drawing plans for the White House and Capitol landscapes. He was born in Newberg, New York in an Elizabethan-style mansion along the Hudson. There, he grew up learning about horticulture and personally cared for the lawns and shrubbery while attending the local academy. His mother sent him for a time to apprentice with a dry goods store owner, but he soon returned to join his father and brother in a nursery.

He became interested not only in trimming and pruning, but in the sciences of botany and mineralogy, and his spare time was spent exploring the countryside for natural examples of plant layout. From these experiences, Downing was inspired to write descriptions, which he sold to the New York *Mirror* and a Boston periodical on botany. Shortly after taking over the family nursery, Downing published a work based on his studies, *A Treatise on the Theory and Practice of Landscape Gardening, Adapted to North America* (1841). The book was considered an authority on the subject for over a hundred years.

Downing continued to write during the next decade, and in 1850 he toured the country homes and gardens of England. While there, he made a business partnership with Calvert Vaux, an English architect, and upon his return to New York, the two designed and landscaped several estates on Long Island. The next year, he was commissioned to design the grounds for the White House, Capitol, and Smithsonian Institute in Washington, D.C. However, he did not live to complete the plans; he drowned when the steamer *Henry Clay* caught fire on the Hudson.

CHAMPLAIN, SAMUEL DE (1570-1635), was a French geographer and New World explorer born in Brouage. He served under the Protestant army of Henry IV from 1593 to 1597, and two years later he entered service under the Spanish flag in hopes of adventure overseas. He commanded a vessel sailing to the West Indies, Mexico and Panama and returned to France in 1601 before recording the voyage. In 1603 he was commissioned by the governor of Dieppe to colonize and begin fur trading in Canada's French territories. He explored the St. Lawrence River area and then in 1604 traveled to Nova Scotia to found a colony at Port Royal. Champlain and his crew charted the coast in that area down as far as Cape Cod. Although the first winter was an exceptionally long and cold one, Champlain survived the epidemic of scurvy that attacked many of the colonists. He returned to France for awhile in 1607, but within a few months he was appointed to be lieutenant of another expedition to the St. Lawrence River area. This time, the crew built a fort at the site of what is now Quebec City, and in 1609 Champlain made an alliance with the Huron Indians by joining in battle against the Iroquois Indians. In this way, the continued supply of furs from the Hurons and the Algonquins was insured.

After a few more trips back and forth across the Atlantic, Champlain began his epic voyages into the interior of Canada in 1615. He was probably the first white man to see the French River and Lake Huron. Indians also led him into the northern Adirondacks to the lake that was eventually named for him. After meeting up with some Huron Indians, the group continued down the Trent River system to Lake Ontario, and nearby in a battle with the Iroquois, Champlain was wounded and had to be carried back to a Huron village. While nursing himself back to health, Champlain was able to record one of the first descriptions of Indian ways of life.

Champlain returned once again to France in 1616 and stayed there for four years. He then took his wife to New France, and they helped fortify the settlement at Quebec. In 1627 Cardinal Richilieu of France named Champlain the governor of the colony. He was compelled to surrender to the English in 1629, however, and was held captive in England for several years. When England restored Quebec to France in 1632, Champlain returned to New France to continue his service as governor.

He died at Quebec, the town he had founded.

BURROUGHS, JOHN (1837-1921), author, was born on a farm near Roxbury, New York, where he grew up surrounded by the nature he later described in his books and poems. As a young boy, he delighted in taking long walks through the Catskills, especially to watch birds. He received enough formal schooling to allow him to become a teacher at a country school in Tongore, New York. In 1863, he was appointed as a vault keeper for the Treasury Department in Washington, D.C., where he remained for 10 years. In the meantime he had begun writing essays which were transcendentalist in tone. His "Expression" was published in *Atlantic Monthly* (1860), and a series entitled "From the Back Country" appeared in the *New York Leader*. In Washington, he met Walt Whitman, who was to be the most influential on Burroughs' future life and writings. "I owed more to him than any other man in the world" Burroughs said later. In 1867, he wrote notes on *Walt Whitman as a Poet and Person*, while imitating his style in his articles about nature in *Atlantic Monthly*. In 1871, the same year that he published a book about birds, *Wake-Robin* (so titled by Whitman), Burroughs was sent to London to exchange $3 million in U.S. bonds. While there, he accumulated the four essays published in *Winter Sunshine*, acclaimed by critic and author Henry James as a "more humorous, more available, more sociable thorough." Now in the national literary limelight, Burroughs had quit to work in banking and bought a fruit farm in West Park on the Hudson. Here and at "Woodchuck Lodge" on the old family farm near

Roxbury, Burroughs wrote in natural solitude. He also traveled extensively to the western and southern U.S., as well as Jamaica, Bermuda, Hawaii, Canada, and Europe. He joined the 1903 Harriman expedition through Alaska, as well as the Theodore Roosevelt-John Muir campout in Yosemite a few years later. All of these experiences inspired him to write and Burroughs was indeed a prolific writer. His later works included *Far and Near* (1904), *Camping and Tramping with Roosevelt* (1907), and an article against flowery naturalists, *"Real and Sham Natural History"*, which appeared in Atlantic in 1903. Before he died, he became friends with such modern scientists as Henry Ford and Thomas Edison, which led to his interest in the achievements of man and the book *The Summit of the Years*.

Often called the founder of the "Nature Essay" as a literary general, Burroughs continued to write in his characteristically simple prose until his death on a train taking him home from a trip to the west coast.

CLEMENS, SAMUEL LANGHORNE ("MARK TWAIN") (1835-1910), novelist and humorist, was born in Florida, Missouri, and raised in Hannibal. He spent much of his life traveling the U.S. Author of several books and essays about frontier life, he has been called "the father of American literature" because of his closeness to the country's consciousness and language.

When his father died in 1847, young Samuel was forced to leave school and learn the printer's trade at the local newspaper in Hannibal. The town was situated on the Mississippi River and provided much of the background for his books. At the newspaper he learned the rules of good composition in writing, and soon he was a reporter for his brother, Orion's, newspaper in Hannibal. His skill as a printer took him to St. Louis, New York, Philadelphia, and Iowa in the early 1850's. He dreamed of traveling to South America to deal in cocoa but only made it to Cincinnati (1956). The next year he traveled on a flat boat down the Mississippi to New Orleans and apprenticed as a river boat pilot. For two more years he operated a boat as a licensed pilot. After a weeks' stint as a Confederate soldier he deserted and set out with his brothers for Nevada where he tried unsuccessfully at prospecting and began his successful career as a writer. In Virginia City he began to write for the *Enterprise* under the pseudonym "Mark Twain", a river term meaning "two fathoms deep". With no rules of form to follow he adopted the burlesque style of frontier journalism which he adapted to his own form of humorous writing. In 1864 he was encouraged to move to San Francisco where he worked for the *Call*. The next year the New York *Saturday Press* published his short story, "The Celebrated Jumping Frog of Calaveras County", and he received almost instant national attention. After a few years as a correspondent on the Sandwich Islands and in the Mediterranean countries, he wrote *Innocents Abroad* (1869) in which he displayed a defiantly American spirit while scorning awed American tourists with guide books in the old country. American readers loved Twain's attitude and received him warmly upon his return to the states. After marrying Olivia Longdon in Elmira, New York, he settled in Hartford Connecticut, in 1871 to begin a decade of writing humorous, social commentaries. *Roughing It* (1872) described life in Carson City, Nevada, *The Gilded Age* (1873) poked fun at the land speculation rush of the times, and *Tom Sawyer* (1876) evoked a lasting image of life in the Mississippi River towns. In his last book, as well as the classic, *Adventures of Huck Finn* (1884), he displayed his uncanny ability to reproduce the language, manners, and social organization of the south. Besides writing, Twain was well known as a humorous lecturer, and he was invited on an international tour in 1896 which he described in *Following the Equator* (1897). As he grew older, however, Twain grew less optimistically humorous and more caustically comical. Some of his fortune had been lost in unsuccessful publishing and typesetting machine investments, and he wrote more rapidly in order to make money. Not one for classical philosophy or superstitious beliefs about immortality, he began to pity mankind in his writings. His *What is Man* (1908), written shortly after his wife's death, asserted that man is basically and hopelessly selfish. His disillusionment is clearly evident in a book published posthumously in 1916, *The Mysterious Stranger*. In in he writes that life may be "all a dream—a grotesque and foolish dream". When Twain died at his "Stormfield" estate in Connecticut, tributes to him were made worldwide. His *Autobiography,* published in 1924, is regarded as a revelation of Twain's anger and frustration in life as well as the motivations for his humor.

COOPER, JAMES FENIMORE (1789-1851), author, was born in Burlington, New Jersey, but moved with his family at the end of the Revolutionary War to Cooperstown, New York, a settlement named for his father. After schooling in Albany, the boy entered Yale in 1806. He soon quit the college, however, to enter the Navy. For three years he was a midshipman all through the Northern Atlantic and then returned to New York in 1811 to run a sizeable firm in Westchester County. There he also began to write romantic stories set in the northern frontier and the high seas. In 1822, he moved to New York City in the interest of his writing career and began to work on *The Pioneers* (1823), which began his famous series of "Leatherstocking Tales" featuring the frontiersman character, Natty Bumpo. The first book was largely based on his recollections of Cooperstown which had been built at the edge of the vast primeval forest that still covered northeastern America at that time. That year he also wrote *The Pilot,* set on the seas. Cooper founded the "Bread and Cheese" literary club in New York in 1824 which allowed him to meet many of the writers and other dignitaries of the day. After a poor attempt at writing the histories of the 13 original states, he returned to the adventures of Natty Bumpo in *The Last of the Mohicans (1826),* and *The Prairie* (1826), after a few years of traveling in Europe and writing more sea romances. When he returned he discovered even such frontier villages as Cooperstown had become far too crowded and commercial for him, and he moved further into the countryside of New York. His disillusionment and longing for a return to the country gentleman style of living were apparent in his *Homeward Bound,* (1835), and *The American Democrat* (1838). The snobbish aristocrat in Cooper overtook the rugged pioneer in him, and he was criticized vehemently by the press and ignored by his former readers. Still Cooper had the presence of mind to delve into a work such as *The History of the Navy of the United States* (1839). The next two years volumes of the *Leatherstocking Tales,* which brought back some of his old fame. Still, the public demand for romances had waned, and Cooper's later sea stories and historic novels did not fare as well as his first. His last books, *The Sea Lions* (1849) and *The Ways of the Hour* (1850), were largely angry diatribes against contemporary New

England. For most of his later life, Cooper lived in Cooperstown, where he died.

CORNELL, EZRA (1807-1874), capitalist and founder of Cornell University, received no college education himself, although he was one of the most successful businessmen of his time. Born near the Bronx River at Westchester Landing, New York, Cornell learned his father's pottery and carpentry trades before setting out on his own lumbering enterprises. In Ithaca, he worked after 1828 as a carpenter and millright and decided to make the place his home. In 1841, he was commissioned to build a machine to lay the wires for Morse's new telegraph between Baltimore and New York City. Finding this successful, Cornell then devoted most of his time to the telegraph industry, laying lines to points all over New England until he had accumulated enough capital to organize the Erie & Michigan Telegraph company (1847), and then the New York and Erie T. Company and other short lines. In 1855 he and other line-owners formed the Western Union Telegraph company, which quickly grew into the largest operation in the U.S. and Canada. In the next decade, Cornell simply lived off his Western Union profits. Settling on a farm near Ithaca, he bred short-horn cows and became active in the state agricultural society and college. When that institution, based at Orid, began to fail, Cornell donated his own farm lands and $500,000, thus forming Cornell University. In order to prevent this land grant from being sold, Cornell also agreed to pay all taxes and other expenses of the land and bound himself to locate one million more acres to be sold for the benefit of the University. Today the university is one of the most respected and secure institutions in the nation. For years after Cornell opened its doors in 1867, Cornell lived in his farm house adjacent to the campus and was a familiar figure in his frock coat and stovepipe hat. He died there leaving his wife, Mary Ann, and his son, Alonzo (q.v.) who would become governor of New York.

EASTMAN, GEORGE (1854-1932), photographic equipment inventor manufacturer, was born in Waterville, New York, to Maria Kilbourn and George W. Eastman, who founded the Eastman Commercial College in Rochester, where the family moved in 1861. Young George only attended school through the seventh grade, however, and took a job first as a bookkeeper and then as a clerk in the local bank. By the age of 21, he had saved enough money to pursue a nagging interest, photography. Frustrated by his failure with the bulky and sloppy camera equipment he had bought, he experimented with dry plate emulsions which he had studied in the *British Journal of Photography*. He soon invented his own method of gelatin dry plates which he patented in Britain and then the United States. In 1880 he was making the photographic plates and other goods full time which quickly amassed a fortune for him. His new plant at Rochester began making Kodak cameras in 1888, carrying a 100 exposure roll of paper-backed film, but when the company introduced celluloid film the next year, a true monopoly on the country's photographic industry had begun and the way was paved for motion pictures.

The Eastman-Kodak Company was incorporated in 1901, and capitalized at $35 million, and that figure rose 700 times by Eastman's death in 1932. His policy of buying out patents, keeping the product unit cost down, and spending a large percentage of the profits on advertising proved successful; about 80 percent of the American photographers used Kodak goods by the 1930's. Government contracts during World War II also helped Eastman's business along.

George Eastman retired as president of the corporation in 1925, but remained as chairman of the board of directors until his death. He donated $35 million to the University of Rochester, and $20 million to the Massachusetts Institute of Technology, and several fortunes more to other educational and medical institutions. Although he was essentially the father of modern photography, Eastman was himself rarely photographed and was shy of public gatherings. He lived alone, devoting his later years to art and horticulture at his Rochester estate. Although he was still active in the company, he took his own life, leaving a note to his friends saying only, "My work is done. Why wait?".

FARGO, WILLIAM GEORGE (1818-1881), freight entrepreneur and founder of the American Express Company, began his career as a mail carrier. He was born in Pompey, New York, and received some formal education before starting work at the age of 13. After carrying the mail in his rural area, he worked in a grocery warehouse, and then became a messenger for the Pomeroy and Company express firm, operating between Albany and Buffalo for the company. During the next few years, he became more involved in the business and joined with a fellow employee, Henry Wells, to begin the Western Express from Buffalo to Cincinnati, Chicago, and St. Louis. In 1850 he merged this enterprise with others to form the American Express Company of which he became secretary. Wells joined Fargo the next year to open New York to San Francisco ship and stage lines which they called Wells, Fargo and Co. That enterprise soon spread to points all over the West coast and Nevada as the gold rush gained momentum. Fargo became the proud proprietor of the most successful express company in the west, and in 1866, with the purchase of the Overland Mail and Express Company, he helped control a virtual monopoly on express mail and cargo transportation. He was also mayor of Buffalo in 1862-66, and was president of the American Express Company from 1868 until his death at Buffalo.

FILLMORE, MILLARD (1800-1874), New York senator and thirteenth president of the United States (1850-52). Born in Locke, New York, Fillmore was the son of Nathaniel and Phebe Millard Fillmore, who sent him to learn the clothier's trade in town when he was only 15. His first interests were in reading and study, however, and after meeting a lawyer in Cayuga County, he was able to devote his time to reading law. After admittance to the bar, he moved to Aurora, New York, and then to Buffalo to begin a law partnership which would become the most respected in western New York.

Soon, he grew interested in politics. As a mild-mannered man, it was curious that he should join the fiery anti-masons, but that party elected him to the state assembly in 1828 and to the U.S. House of Representatives in 1832 and 1837-43. While there, he was the Whig floor leader and chairman of the House Ways and Means committee. His peers respected his quiet ways, and in 1844 they tried to gain his nomination for vice president and then for New York governor but were unsuccessful in both. "I was nominated much against my will, and although not insensible to the pride of success, yet I feel a kind of relief at being defeated," Fillmore wrote later to his friend Henry Clay.

Three years later, however, he knew the pride of success when he won the vice presidency alongside Zachary Taylor. When Taylor died in 1850, Fillmore became President. Although he owned slaves himself, Fillmore opposed slavery extension while in office by signing the fugitive slave bill into law. This was an unpopular move at the time, and it cost him the renomination. However, he did approve cheap postage rates and was a firm adherent to the "Monroe Doctrine" of nonintervention into foreign affairs.

After his defeat in 1852, Fillmore returned to Buffalo and lived a largely private life, except for his attempt as a "Know Nothing" candidate for president in 1856. He lost the nomination again, but was respected as Buffalo's first citizen until his death there.

FULTON, ROBERT (1765-1815), inventor of the first practical steamboat, was a Pennsylvania native and began his skill as a painter before taking up technical drawing and inventions. He attended school in Lancaster where he exhibited an aptitude for mechanical knowledge, but as his father had died, he decided to try his fortune at portrait painting. At the age of 17 he went to Philadelphia to sell his works, and his small business soon provided him with support and savings. He was able to buy a small farm in Washington County, Pennsylvania, at the age of 21, and then went to England to study under the famous painter Benjamin West for a few years. There he met the Duke of Bridgewater and Earl of Stanhope who were interested in the possibilities of inland navigation. Soon Fulton was more concerned with canals than paintings and he devised a way to raise and lower canal boats in order to make them congruous with surface railroad systems. He also worked on applying a train's steam engine to a ship, and after making the acquaintance of John Watt, who also had that idea, the two worked on an engine to be applied to navigation. Before returning to the U.S., Fulton also came up with an invention for a submarine and a torpedo. The torpedo was to be in a copper case charged with gunpowder which could be fired at any time by depressing a special lock. However, both the British and French governments refused to patronize the project.

When he arrived back in the U.S. in 1801, however, Robert, R. Livingston, the Minister to France, offered to finance Fulton's steam engine project, and the two experimented with it at Plombieres, France, until he had created a working model and begun a large scale steamroller boat.

Livingston had gained the sole right to steam navigation on the inland waters of New York, since the government believed the boat would never be produced. But by 1807 Fulton's boat had one of Watt's steam engines fitted onto it, and it was ready to roll under the name of the *Clermont.* On August 11 the *Clermont* chugged from New York City to Albany in 32 hours, remarkable time since it took four days by the usual sloop passage. Soon thousands of people clamored to ride the *Clermont,* and by the time of Fulton's death, five of his boats navigated the Hudson and the Mississippi Rivers.

Fulton died in New York City shortly after his first warship motored around the New York Harbor, protecting the city from attack during the War of 1812. He was elected to the Hall of Fame in 1900.

GANSEVOORT, PETER (1749-1812), Revolutionary War general, was born in Albany, New York, to parents of Dutch descent who helped settle the town during its early colonial days. He began his military career as a major when he signed into the 2nd New York regiment in 1775. In the next year he progressed from lieutenant-colonel and then as commander of Fort Stanwix, later called Fort Schuyler. At that stronghold, near the present site of Rome, New York, Gansevoort upheld the American claim against St. Legerx after a long and seemingly hopeless fight. For his excellence in commandeering, he was honored with the title of "hero of Fort Stanwix", and he was given more prestigious assignments. Between 1778 and 1780 he commanded Albany and then returned to Fort Schuyler with relatively little activity taking place. He helped capture an encampment of Mohawk Indians and then tried to halt a rebellion of his own men in Albany before he retired from the line. In 1781, however, the state of New York commissioned him as brigadier-general of the militia. He continued to serve in the military until his death in Albany.

Biographies

GOULD, JAY (1836-1892), railroad entrepreneur, was born in Roxbury, New York. At age 16 he left home and school to pursue a business career because "I did not make very much at farming while I was at it, and I thought I could succeed better at something else." He was a clerk in a general store and then a surveyor's assistant before forming his own surveyor's company in 1853. Engaged in mapping Albany and Ulster Counties for the next three years, Gould also wrote a *History of Delaware County, New York,* in 1856. By that time he had accumulated $5,000 in savings and was able to form a partnership with Zadock Pratt to start a tannery business. When Pratt discovered a few months later that Gould was investing a large share of the profits in personal real estate and banking, he withdrew from the company. Gould continued to embezzle company funds during his partnership with Charles M. Leupp and David Lee, however, and with the financial crash of 1857, Leupp was forced into bankruptcy while Lee was expelled by Gould's armed workers from his own company. Lee eventually regained the tannery business after legal action against Gould, but Gould had drained much of the resources.

With his ill-gained profits Gould was able to buy and sell railroad companies at an amazing rate. He made large sums from his dealings with the Cleveland and Pittsburg Railroad, the Pennsylvania Railroad, and the Erie Railroad. As a memebr of the Erie Railroad's Board of Directors, he joined in the selling of $8 million in watered stock, but Cornelius Vanderbilt charged the company with contempt of court. After Gould bribed New York legislators to authorize the stock issuance, however, he became president of the Erie Railroad. After two years more of selling stockholders short, Gould was ousted from the board of directors by the major interest-bearers (1872).

In the meantime, Gould had conspired with others to make money off the unstable American currency after the Civil War. He tried to corner the gold market supposing that the U.S. Treasury would keep its reserves out of the free market. Just as President Grant belatedly released the federal gold in 1869, Gould and his partner, Jim Fisk, sold short, turning a profit of $11 million.

Between 1874 and 1878 Gould was director of the Union

Pacific Railroad and then transfered his interests to the Kansas-Pacific and other southwestern railroads. He also continued to preside over his stock brokerage firm until his death in New York City.

GRANT, ULYSSES S. (1822-1885), general and eighteenth President of the U.S. was born in Ohio, son of Jesse R. and Hannah (Simpson) Grant. When he was one year old, the family moved to Georgetown, Ohio, where he was brought up. His father was a tanner and farmer, and though Ulysses detested tanning, he helped on the farm in the summer and attended school in the winter. After two years at private seminaries and academies, Ulysses was sent to West Point Military Academy (1839). His farm training at horseriding helped him display excellent horsemanship at the academy, and upon graduation he was appointed second lieutenant in the Fourth United States Infantry (1843). He served under Zachary Taylor during the Mexican War in Texas (1845), and later was stationed at Detroit, California, and Fort Vancouver. In 1854, however he resigned from the army and returned to his family in St. Louis where he tried to make his fortune in real estate and farming as well as storekeeping, without success. His work at his father's tanning business in Galena, Illinois (1860) gave him an annual salary of $800, however, until the outbreak of the Civil War.

He began his service in the war as a colonel to an Illinois regiment but wasn't satisfied, saying, "I have been a captain of the regular army. I am fitted to command a regiment". His ambition and several petitions to the War Department landed him the colonelcy of the Seventh District Regiment (1861), even though he had to borrow money to buy his uniform. He served in Missouri for the summer of that year, and in August Lincoln appointed him brigadier-general of volunteers. From that point on throughout the war, Grant led the army to victory (despite early setbacks) against the south, and in 1864 he was made Lieutenant General to carry the merciless drive through southern cities that ended at Appamottox where General Lee surrendered. The terms of surrender were lenient on the south, and Grant said later that he "felt like anything rather than rejoicing at the downfall of a foe who had fought so long and valiantly and had suffered so much for a cause." He returned to the north as a national hero, receiving numerous gifts and honorary degrees.

Grant toured the south in 1865, soon after Lincoln's death, to report on the reconstruction efforts. He believed that "the mass of thinking men of the south accept the present situation of affairs in good faith," and took no active part in President Andrew Johnson's reconstruction campaign. He was commissioned General of the Armies of the United States in 1866 and was chosen as the Republican party leader and presidential nominee two years later.

Having come from relative obscurity to international fame in a short period of time, Grant was not fluent in matters of politics, but he was elected to two terms as President. His administration was characterized by inexperience and lack of finesse, but also by strong patriotism and will. He was concerned with South and Central American affairs, a financial panic, and the problems with reconstructing the South. He insisted that paper money should be made payable in gold and that Santo Domingo should be annexed as a black state which aroused protest from a group calling themselves "liberal Republicans" When he ran for a second term, Grant was accused of nepotism for hiring many relatives and millionaires to his cabinet and of taking bribes from wealthy businessmen. However, he won easily. His second term in office has been interpreted as a success story gone sour; that the aging general wandered dazed through the wonderland of politics and dined with designed plutocrats without realizing their intent. The last years of Grant's presidency were indeed the lowest with several national scandals and fraud cases causing much protest from the public. Grant did not receive the Republicans nomination in 1876.

The next year he took his family on a world tour, and three years later he was once again unsuccessful in the nomination for President, partly because of many people's protest against the idea of any President serving three terms. Grant was then involved in business interests in New York City where he generally failed. In 1885, Congress restored him to the rank of general (he had resigned to take the Presidency), and he retired on full pay.

His memoirs concentrated on his military pursuits. They were completed while he fought against cancer which finally killed him at his home in Saratoga, New York.

HAMILTON, ALEXANDER (1757-1804), early American statesman and first U.S. Secretary of the Treasury, studied grammar at Elizabethtown, New Jersey, although he was born on an island in the West Indies. Originally intending to become a physician, he studied at King's College (now Columbia University), New York (1773-74) until the Revolution interrupted his studious interests. In 1774, he attended a public meeting near school and although he was only 17, he addressed the crowd as to the importance of the colonies' cause. In that year he also published a pamphlet against the "calumnies of the enemies" and began writing for Holt's *New York Journal* against British measures. He was soon looked upon as an intellectual prodigy and was dubbed the "Vindicator of Congress." Soon afterwards, he studied military tactics and received a commission in 1776 to command an artillery company authorized by the colonial convention. His success in drilling the men led to an introduction to General Washington, who asked him to become a member of his staff. In 1777, Hamilton was made aide-de-camp and private secretary to Washington with the rank of Lt. Colonel. Although he fought physically throughout New England with the general, his true weapon was his pen, and he used it in correspondences with Congress as well as in his military advice to the most prominent patriots of the time.

In 1780 Hamilton exhibited the first signs of his exceptional financial ability when he brought forth a plan for a U.S. bank, with a main purpose of supplying the army with provisions and ammunition. In a letter to Robert Morris, he also pushed for a constitutional convention, and a representative government. Washington appreciated his foresight and granted him a commandership of an infantry regiment in Lafayette's corps. At the Seige of Yorktown, he helped bring down an important British regiment.

After the war, he rented a house in Albany, New York and studied law with the intention of retiring to private life. Before admission to the bar, he wrote a *Manual on the Practice of Law*. However, he was soon to return to the new nation's politics, and sat in the Continental Congress of 1782. While thre he devoted his time to energizing the new government, especially by establishing a permanent national revenue. He looked for a centralization of the government, writing to Washington, "I have an indifferent opinion of the honesty of this country and ill foreboding of its future system." Although he retired from Congress, he soon reentered public life when in 1786 the convention he had called for all along was held in Annapolis, Maryland. He began writing the greater protion of *The Federalist.* and when Washington was elected president under the new constitution in 1789, he was chosen secretary of the treasury. His quick work and judgement led to the rapid creation of a public credit system by uniting the federal government's properties interests; he also gave the country a currency system, banking facilities and important new idnustries.

However, Hamilton was not modest about his abilities and importance to the government, and this caused conflict with Thomas Jefferson. Hamilton said of Secretary of State Jefferson in 1792, that he was a man of "profound ambition and violent passions," Jefferson condemned Hamilton's Treasury Department as a "corrupt squadron." At the 1796 election, Hamilton supported John Adams, but when Jefferson was elected four years later, Hamilton left government concerns to retire in New York.

Hamilton also opposed Aaron Burr's attempt for the governorship of New York, causing Burr to challenge him to a duel in revenge for his unsuccessful campaign. In the early morning of July 11, 1804, Hamilton fell at the first shot near the banks of the Hudson and died the next day.

HIAWATHA (1525-1590), was an apostle of peace and brotherhood, who devoted his life to ending the bloodshed among the Mohawk, Oneida, Cayuga, Seneca, and Onondaga and to uniting these five tribes into the League of the Iroquois (the Confederation of Five Nations) in the region encompassing New York.

Possessing exceptional oratorical powers, Hiawatha was a medicine man and magician among the Onondaga, and—like them—he probably practiced cannibalism. Distressed at the constant warfare and never-ending feuds among the five tribes, though, Hiawatha emerged as a reform leader, advocating the unification of the tribes and the cessation of blood revenge.

His bitter opponent, the Onondaga chief Wathatotarho, did all he could to prevent the reformers from achieving their objectices, including having one of Hiawatha's daughters murdered. Unable to overcome Wathatotarho's opposition, Hiawatha left the Onondaga to preach his message of peace and brotherhood to the Mohawk, Oneida, and Cayuga—all of whom agreed to unite and abandon bloodshed among fellow Iroquois on the condition that Wathatotarho and the Onondaga did likewise.

Apparently defeated in his reform efforts once again, Hiawatha was about to abandon hope when he fell under the influence of a mystical peacemaker and prophen named Dekanawida. The latter converted Hiawatha from cannibalism and convinced him that the obstinate and evil Wathatotarho could be won over to what would later be called The Great Peace. Together, Hiawatha and Dekanawida persuaded the Onondaga chief to join the league. During the negotiations Wathatotarho won certain concessions, but the League of the Iroquois became a reality, cannibalism was outlawed (except in times of war), and blood revenge was ended among the five tribes.

Hiawatha now turned missionary, carrying Dekanawida's confederation ideas and moral principles to other tribes. He roamed far from his home territory, traveling as far away as Lake Superior and the Mississippi River, Although he had some success in winning converts to the Great Peace, no other tribes joined the confederation until the white man had advanced so far that various tribes were forced to seek sanctuary on the lands of the Five Nations. The remnants of the conquered Tuscarora, for example, became the sixth nation in the league about the year 1715.

Meanwhile, the Iroquois were committed to warring against tribes who rejected their overtures of peace and brotherhood, with the ironic result being that the whites came to know the Confederation of Five Nations only as cruel and bloodthirsty warriors—the very antithesis of the pacifistic principles to which Hiawatha had devoted his life. The apostle/missionary himself probably spent his last days as an elder statesman among the Mohawk. The confederation he had helped to forge, however, lasted until the American Revolution, inspiring the colonists in their dream of creating a stable federal union. In the second quarter of the 19th century, Henry R. Schoolcraft, an early U.S. ethnologist, collected some of the Iroquois legends and published them in such a way that Hiawatha became identified as the greatest of the Iroquoian gods, Teharonhiawagon ("The Master of Life"), which Schoolcraft apparently assumed was just another way of spelling Hiawatha. He went on to identify this same god with the chief deity of the Chippewa (Ojibwa) Indians, who lived farther west in the Great Lakes region. The ethnologist referred to the Chippewa deity Manabozho as Hiawatha in a series of Chippewa myths which he published. This error was compounded by Henry Wadsworth Longfellow. Fascinated by Schoolcraft's Chippewa legends, Longfellow based his famous poem, written in 1855, on them, and the name Hiawatha became identified with a fictionalized Chippewa god and hero.

HOWELLS, WILLIAM DEAN (1937-1920), novelist, was born in Belmont County, Ohio, to William Cooper Howells and Mary Darn Howells. The son of a poorly paid journalist, Howells had little time as a child to go to school. He began setting type at his father's print shop in 1846, to help support his family. Although he had little formal education, the young Howells spent much of his free time reading classical literature and studying several languages. As a newspaper reporter inthe late 1850's and the early 1860's, he began writing poetry. At 22 he published a volume of poetry with a friend. *Atlantic Monthly* published five of his better poetic works shortly afterwards.

During the 1860 presidential campaign, he was asked by the Republican party to write a biography of Abraham Lincoln. After the election the nation's new president thanked Howells by naming him to a consulship in Venice. In 1862 he married Elinor Gertrude Mead, and at the end of his counsulship, the two moved to New York in 1865 where, a year later, William was named as an assistant editor for *Atlantic Monthly.* Writing novels and poetry during his free time, Howells quickly advanced at the young magazine until the was named editor-in-chief in 1871. The next year his first novel, *Their Wedding Journey,* was published. Remaining with *Atlantic* until 1881, Howells is recognized as one of the most productive writers of the late 19th century and early 20th century. In 1885 he wrote *The Rise of Silas Lapham,* his best-known work, and throughout his life, he wrote 35 novels, many short stories, and poems, some dramas, and some critical essays. His achievements earned him the title "Dean of American Letters". Although his education was poor by society's standards, he was awarded six honorary degrees and was offered posts at several univerisities. He served as the first president of the American Academy of Arts and Letters for many years until his death. Like many other authors during that period, Howells was a realist.

HUDSON, HENRY (?-1611), explorer, was born in England to unknown parents. He left no record of his early life, but he was a proficient sailor and navigator by 1607 when he was hired by the Muscovy Company, and English merchant's enterprise, which had the purpose of finding a shorter route to the Orient that the one around Africa in use at that time. Hudson had been married to a woman named Catherine who bore him a duaghter and a son, John, sho joined him on his voyages. After sailing north on the *Hopewell* from London in May, 1607, Hudson and his crew touched off at Greenland, stopped at a tiny island, which he named Hudson's Tutchers (now Jan Mayen Island), and continued east to Spitsbergen, Norway. His reports on the northern Greenland sea, sparked a new route to the Orient. On his second recorded voyage, Hudson commanded the *Hopewell* again, this time to find a route between Spitsbergen and Novaya Zemlya, in Russia, or to find a route to the Kara Sea. However, after many weeks of icy exploring, the crew returned to Gravesend, England, with a negative report. In 1609 the Dutch East India Company hired him for the same task but the huge ice packs and freezing winds kept him from his goal. Instead he and the crew chose to sail the *Half Moon* west to America in order to find a northwest passage to the Orient. The crew sailed along the coast of Newfoundland and as far south as Chesapeake Bay. Returning north, the *Half Moon* sailed into the Delaware Bay, took some soundings, and up the Delaware River until he was convinced that his was not the route to Asia. They then sailed into present-day New York Harbor, anchored near the southern tip of Manhattan, and for four days sailed up the river that now bears his name. The ship got as far up as Albany and then to the Troy area before turning back for England. The Crown demanded that Hudson leave the Dutch service and serve only his own country, but his reports of the *Half Moon* voyage were sent to the Dutch East India Company soon after his return. His next voyages were for English companies on the *Discovery*. On his fourth and last recorded voyage, he passed just south of Greenland and decided to enter the strait that bears his name and subsequently entered the great bay that was also named for him and which he called the "Sea to the Westward". However, excitement of the discovery was dimmed by the excessive cold that had begun to set in and the dwindling food supply. Foraging expeditions had failed to produce anything. When Hudson decided to take the *Discovery* out of its anchorage in the James Bay, mutiny broke out and Hudson, his son, and seven others were set adrift in a small dinghy with no food or sufficient clothing. Hudson most certainly died as a result of exposure and the unlucky crew returned in far dwindled numbers to England where they were tried and acquitted for their part in the mutiny. Hudson's remains were never discovered.

KOCH, EDWARD I. (1924-   ), mayor of New York (1978-   ), was born in the city, son of Louis and Joyce Silpe Koch, Polish immigrants. The family moved to Newark, New Jersey during the Depression when his father lost his furrier business, and young Edward attended high school there. He worked a variety of jobs; as a hat checker, a deli counter attendant, and a babysitter as a teenager. After honors graduation, Koch began studies at the City College of New York, while working as a shoe salesman.

In 1943, Koch enlisted in the United States Army, and saw combat with the infantry. He won two battle stars, one for service in Northern France, one in the Rhineland, and seved as a "deNazification specialist" in Bavaria after VE Day. He was discharged with the rank of Sergeant in 1946.

Returning to New York, he attended New York University Law School, receiving a Bachelor of Laws (LL.B.) degree in 1948. He was admitted to the New York State Bar the next year, and started his first law practice in Brooklyn. At the same time, he became politically active, working locally for the election of

Adlai Stevenson in the 1952 Presidential campaign.

In 1956, he moved to Greenwich Village, and became a charter member of the Village Independent Democrats, a reform group. Koch first ran for elective office in 1962, as a candidate for the State Assembly, but was unsuccessful. The following year, however, he defeated Carmine DeSapio, New York County Democratic Leader, by 1,300 votes in a contest for District Leader. He defeated Mr. DeSapio twice again in party contests, in 1964 and 1965, ending Mr. DeSapio's tenure as County Leader. That same year, he helped register more black voters in Mississippi.

In 1966, he won a seat on the New York City council—the first Democrat to represent his district since 1928. Two years later he was elected to the U.S. House of Representatives from Manhattan's 18th "Silk Stocking" District. He was reelected four times. His fellow city representatives voted him their "most effective Congressman" in 1976, and he served several terms as Secretary of the State's bipartisan delegation. He was a member of the House Transportation subcommittee, committee on Banking, and later Committee on Appropriations. He helped obtain $2.3 billion in Federal loans for the City of New York during its 1975 fiscal crisis. Governor Carey then appointed him to the Emergency Financial Control Board. Koch was also a supporter of military and economic aid to Israel when he was a member of the House Foreign Operations subcommittee.

In 1977, Koch announced his candidacy for mayor of New York. After a long campaign that included a race against incumbent mayor John Lindsay, he won 50 percent of the vote. In his inaugural address, he was hopeful about New York City, which many observers saw to be on the decline. "New York is a city where a hundred different cultures have been woven together into a tapestry of tradition and teamwork. Today, the great challegnes that confront this country lie in a different direction. Today, it the city of New York where the urban pioneers of this generation are to be found," he said after arriving at City Hall in a public bus. Although he is a Democrat, Koch has in recent years seemed to neglect programs for the poor in favor of balancing the city budget. This has made him extremely popular with the white middle class in the city, but has drawn heated criticism from black and Puerto Rican leaders. In fact Koch has been following the general conservative swing in American politics with his budget slashing measures. He has Republican supporters as well as Democratic (he invited candidate Ronald Reagan to Gracie Mansion during the 1980 campaign). David Rockefeller, head of Chase Manhattan Bank, has said of Koch, "I think he's probably the best mayor since La Guardia (q.v.)."

LA GUARDIA, FIORELLA (1882-1947), Mayor of New York City (1934-46), was born in that city to Italian immigrant parents. He began high school in Prescott, Arizona, and then worked as a reporter for the St. Louis *Dispatch* before gaining a position with the United States Consulate in Budapest when he was only 16. He continued his consulate work in Italy, before returning to New York and interpreting for Italian immigrants on Ellis Island. In 1910, he completed his law studies at New York University, and began legal aid service for poor immigrants. A Republican, the popular lawyer was elected to represent these immigrants in Congress in 1916 and 1918. Then he returned to New York City affairs as an alderman, serving as president of that board in 1920-21. The next year he was back in the House of Representatives, where he continued to fight for liberal reforms that belied his political party. He was co-author of the 1932 Norris-LaGuardia Anti-Injunction Act which made it easier for workers to strike, boycott and picket. By this time, La Guardia was a popular hero in New York City, and he won easily over the Tammany Hall-controlled candidate in 1933 for mayor. He served for three terms, a total of 22 years in office. Mayor La Guardia cracked down on organized crime in the city, funded public housing projects, urban renewal, and new health and recreational facilities. The new airport built along the East River near Rikers Island was named for him before he left office. He came to be known as the "Little Flower" to the people he had helped in the disadvantaged areas of New York, and he did much to alleviate the suffering of everyone as the worst of the Great Depression set in. In 1941, he was appointed the head of the U.S. Office of Civilian Defense, and when his last term was over in 1946 he worked as director of the United Nations Relief and Rehabilitation Agency for nine months. He died the next year.

MILLAY, EDNA ST. VINCENT, (1892-1950), author and women's right advocate, was born in Maine. She studied at Vassar College, receiving her B.A. degree in 1917, and her first poems were printed during those years. "Renascence" and other verse appeared in the pamphlet, *Lyric Year* when she was 20 years old. She also was a member of the Provincetown Players as a dramatist and actress before she became known as a poet. Upon graduation, she moved to Greenwich Village, New York City, and published a full volume of poems under the title of *Renascence,* narrated in simple diction as an allegorical adventure. Her *Figs from Thistles* won the Pultizer Prize in 1922, a volume of rakish ballads and impish songs mocking love.

Millay's dramatic ability was evident again in 1921 when she published *Aria da Capa,* about the war in Europe and the impossibility of understanding its folly. In 1927, the New York Metropolitan Opera produced a lyric drama, the *King's Henchman,* for which Millay wrote the libretto. The text is an example of her ability to present action, climax and mood effectively.

She continued writing poems in he characteristic style of flaunting love and rejoicing in the bohemian lifestyle of her contemporary literary world. A blunt exponent of sexual equality, she championed women's demands to be admitted to the mainstream of life and adventure.

Her works include 15 volumes of original poetry, several translations of Baudelaire and Dillon, short ficton and essays such as *Justice Denied in Massachusetts* (1928), lamenting the execution of Sacco and Vanzetti.

She died in Austerlitz, New York on her farm.

MORGAN, JOHN PIERPOINT (1873-1913), banker and financier, was born in Hartford, Connecticut, the son of a wealthy banking family. Young John was sent to a finishing school in Switzerland after high school and then on to the University of Gottingen, Germany, to study history and political economy. When he returned to the U.S. in 1857, he was hired as an assistant accountant in a New York City firm. After 1860 he was the New York agent for his father's London-based bank. Having learned the principles of capitalism to the extreme, Morgan loaned Simon Stevens $20,000 in 1861 to buy obsolete carbines and sell them to the Union Army at a 700 percent markup. Although Morgan was eventually judged innocent in the dealing, his connections with the "Hall Carbine Affair" was never forgotten.

During the next few years, however, Morgan was known as a friend to the government. In partnership with Anthony Drexel, he was a leading floater of government bonds, and controller of railroad company annexations. Through a process of "Morganization", he reorganized a number of lines by providing new capital and placing himself on the board of directors in order to insure sound financial management. By the turn of the century, several millions of Morgan's dollars were invested in all of the country's railroad lines. After both his father and Mr. Drexel died in the 1890's, Morgan controlled upward of a billion dollars in government and industry operations. He also became director of the Western Union Telegraph Company, Pullman Car Company, and the General Electric Company because of his reorganization and financial abilities.

Although the J.P. Morgan Company lost some of its control over railroad financing after 1900, he joined in the Consolidation of the U.S. Steel Corporation which proved to be the largest corporation in the country with the biggest profits going to Morgan. He soon personified Wall Street and monopoly finance although there were richer men than he in New York City and was called in as a witness during the anti-trust investigations of 1912.

As his fortune accumulated, Morgan spent more on art and philanthropic activities. Many of his artworks and sculptures were willed to the New York Metropolitan Museum of Art, and his large collection of priceless books and manuscripts were set up in the Morgan Library founded by his family in 1924 in the City.

He died in Rome, Italy, and his son, J.P. Jr., inherited the business.

MORSE, SAMUEL F., (1791-1872), artist and inventor of the electromagnetic telegraph, was born in Massachusetts. At the age of eight, he began studies at Phillips Academy, Andover, where his father was a trustee. However, he disliked the strictness of the school and ran away from it two times. In 1805 he entered Yale College, and after a break, he graduated in 1810.

While there, he began carving miniature figures in ivory, but his father discouraged him from art. However, he began painting, and his "Marius on the Ruins of Carthage" and "The Landing of the Pilgrims at Plymouth" gained the attention of Washington Allston and Gilbert Stuart. In 1811 he went with Allston to London after his father finally consented, and he lived the next four years at the Royal Academy there. In 1815 he returned home, married, and painted portraits of his neighbors most of the time, except for one invention of an improved pump. From 1823 to 1829 he lived in New York City before another trip abroad to study art once again. He had become interested in electricity before this, and it was on the sail back home from France that he began the invention of the electromagnetic telegraph. He met Charles T. Jackson on the ship, who had been studying electricity in Paris and had heard of experiments by which electricity had been transmitted long distances. During the rest of the trip, Morse designed the apparatus and devised an alphabet for it. He continued experimenting in New York City, and in 1835 the first "instrument" was completed. At that time, he accepted a professorship at the University of New York, and in 1837 exhibited his new machine to hundreds of visitors.

Not until 1843 did the U.S. Congress agree to allocate funds for developing the new machine. By 1862, however, about 15,000 miles of telegraph lines were operating. Morse's life at this time was frought with litigation in spite of his successes, and he had made many enemies out of patent disputes. He did become rich from the invention, and helped found Vassar College in 1861. His attempts at painting again were unsuccessful later in life, but New York City honored his name just months before his death with a statue erected in Central Park. Morse died in the city after a long illness.

POE, EDGAR ALLAN, (1809-1849), poet of the bizarre and horrifying as well as editor of Burton's *Gentleman's Magazine* in Philadelphia (1839), was left an orphan at two years of age when both his parents died. He was raised in Richmond, Virginia by the rich gentleman John Allan, who sent him to England and the University of Virginia for his education. In 1827, he moved to Boston and sought a publisher for his early verses. He also served two years in the U.S. Army while he wrote, mainly poems, and formed his ambition for literary achievement. Although most of his early work was in verse, Poe began writing mainly prose in 1831, and in 1832 his story, "Metzengerstein" was published in the *Saturday Courier* of Philadelphia. In 1835, he returned to Richmond to edit the *Literary Messenger,* and his stories and criticisms appearing in the Philadelphia *Graham's Magazine* helped that publication's circulation to increase from 5,000 to 52,000. After a time of writing in New York City, Poe moved to Philadelphia to become associate editor of Burton's *Gentleman's Magazine,* in which soon appeared *The Fall of the House of Usher.* In 1841 he became editor of *Gentleman's and Graham's.* While publishing such short stories as *The Murders in the Rue Morgue,* he also compiled his works into books, such as *Tales of the Grotesque and Arabesque.* He was fond of secret codes, inclined to depression, and is said to have had "a strange lesion on the side of his brain". He habitually wore black.

In the fall of 1849, he was failing in health, but hopeful to start his own literary magazine, *The Stylus.* He visited old friends in Philadelphia who might be willing to help him. In October, he was found semi-conscious outside of a tavern in Richmond and transferred him to Washington Hospital where he died after four days of delirium.

ROCKEFELLER, JOHN D. (1839-1937), capitalist and early investor in western Pennsylvania oil, was born in Richford, New York, to German immigrant parents. His father was an itinerant merchant on the frontier who taught young John elementary business practices. The boy learned his first dollar at the age of seven when he began digging potatoes for a nearby farmer. At the age of 10, he lent $50 to a neighbor, and when it was repaid with interest, he realized his profits were worth more than the pay for three days' labor. In 1853 his family moved to Cleveland, Ohio, and he took a college business course there soon after high school graduation. In 1859 he formed a produce and commission business with M.B. Clark, an Englishman, and by 1861 the firm divided $17,000 between the partners in profit. Clark and Rockefeller decided in 1863 to invest in the new oil wells near Titusville, Pennsylvania, which laid the foundation for Rockefeller's future millions. In 1865 Rockefeller bought Clark's shares in the oil business and joined with oilman Samuel Andrews to capitalize $200,000 by the end of the year. Although this made Rockefeller a rich man at age 26, he continued to invest and build new wells and refineries in Cleveland and Pennsylvania as the oil business boomed. More than anything else, Rockefeller wanted a monopoly on the oil business. In 1870 with two partners, he formed the Standard Oil Company to which he added numerous smaller companies in the following years. As the need for better rail transportation of oil across the Alleghenies grew, Rockefeller and 16 other entrepreneurs took stock in the South Improvement Company of Pennsylvania which would have been a contract between the largest oil refiners and the carriers designed to stifle smaller competition. However, when the state and federal governments heard of the plan, the company's charter was repealed (1872). Despite this setback, Rockefeller's Standard Oil continued to increase its influence and diversity until in 1882 when it was established as a trust, controlling 95 percent of the country's oil refining business. It was also the largest business organization in the U.S., with assets of over $73 million.

Rockefeller's ambitions for control of all oil industry led to frequent attacks on the business by the press and the government which eventually led to Congress' passage of the Sherman Anti-Trust Law (1890). But Standard Oil continued to grow at an amazing rate when Rockefeller came up with the idea of a "holding company" for all his interests. By 1906 the company had assets of over $350 million.

Rockefeller himself had retired from the actual management of the company operations in 1897, but he continued to serve under the title of president and invested his $900 million fortune in industries all over the U.S.

He also began to donate money to charity, establishing a number of charitable corporations with trustees charges with pin-pointing the needs for public service. Universities, scientific experiments, hospitals, religious organizations, and social settlements received Rockefeller endowments, and he was always concerned with health research.

After the turn of the century, J.D. Rockefeller was concerned with his own health, and in the 1930's he retired to his mansion in Ormond Beach, Florida. There he hoped to maintain his health in order to achieve his ultimate goal to reach 100 years of age. He died two years short of it, however, at the Ormond Beach estate.

Rockefeller was the author of *Personal Reminiscences,* (1909).

ROOSEVELT, ANNA ELEANOR (1884-1962), Activist, author, and wife of President Franklin D. Roosevelt, was born in New York City, the daughter of Elliott and Annal Hall Roosevelt and the niece of former President Theodore Roosevelt. She was taught by private tutors until age 15 when she went to Europe and studied at Allenswood, a school for girls in England. She lived with cousins after returning to the United States and taught at the Rivington Street Settlement House in New York. In 1905 she married Franklin Roosevelt. She followed her husband where his political career led him, bore children, and "fit pretty well in the pattern of a fairly conventional, quite, young society matron," as she said later. Eventually, though, she became interested in politics, too, and joined the League of Women Voters. She also learned shorthand and typing in her spare time. When her husband was paralyzed from polio in 1921, she leaped further into political activities in order to inspire her husband to resume an active life. In addition to inspiring her husband, she increased her own interest in active political involvement with the Women's Trade Union and the Democratic Party. A leader in the Progressive Movement, Mrs. Roosevelt was a pioneer in the fight for minority rights, consumer issues, and various welfare programs. In 1924-28 she was chair of finance for the women's division of New York's Democratic party committee. In the meantime she bought the Todhunter School for Girls with two other women and became the vice-principal as well as sociology teacher at the New York academy. As a New York Governor's wife, she was an active advisor. When discussing political issues, Governor Roosevelt would always refer to "Eleanor and I". In 1933 when he was elected President, Franklin Roosevelt's consultations with his wife became increasingly important. She was the most active

First Lady in American history. Since the President was physically not able to visit as many political functions and New Deal programs as he would have liked, Eleanor was sent as his representative, and she traveled hundreds of thousands of miles to observe America and to speak out on New Deal programs. Her syndicated newspaper column, "My Day", and various radio programs began as a political discussion on topics of the day. However, her political beliefs soon surfaced, and often her positions were far to the left of those demonstrated by her husband's administration. The White House was no longer a place of top-secret decision-making and monarchic diplomacy; Anna Eleanor Roosevelt almost single-handedly transformed it into a place where the working class and the underprivileged could voice their issues. She was never a neutral figure; Americans either loved her or hated her. When World War II broke out, she was named as assistant director of the Office of Civilian Defense. However, public criticism of her policies and appointments was so strong that she resigned, saying, "No individual is more important than a good program." She continued to represent the President during the war, visiting servicemen in the Pacific (1943), and the Caribbean (1944), as well as officials in Britain, Australia, and military bases in the U.S. When her husband died in 1945, she didn't stop her own involvements. President Truman appointed her U.S. delegate to the United Nations, and she served as a chair of the Human Rights Commission as well as an auxiliary of the Economic and Social Council for many years. She headed the commission which drafted the Universal Human Rights Declaration after tangled deliberations. Although she was never elected to a political office, Mrs. Roosevelt remained active in many liberal organizations in federal and New York government. She won several honorary degrees and wrote the books, *My Days* (1938), *It's Up to Women,* (1933), *The Moral Basis of Democracy* (1940), *This is My Story* (1937), and *This I Remember* (1949). She also ran several family business enterprises until her death in New York City. Five children survived her.

SINCLAIR, UPTON B. (1878-1968), novelist and political figure, was born in Baltimore, Maryland, to an old, formerly wealthy family. His father, a liquor salesman, moved the family to New York when Sinclair was a boy, and at 14 he entered the City of New York College receiving his bachelor's degree in 1897. He also worked his way through graduate school at Columbia University by writing adventure stories for pulp magazines as well as jokes for comic periodicals. His earliest writings were romances, *Springtime and Harvest* (1901), and *The Journal of Arthur Stirling* (1902), as well as a Civil War novel, *Manassas.* (1904). However, he lived in poverty with his wife in the country during those years which may have brought him to his belief in socialism and his involvement in the Socialist party. This belief inspired him in the rest of his writing making him an internationally-known controversial figure. His novel, *The Jungle,* written in 1906 as a result of his studies of the Chicago meatpacking industry for the party was meant to attack all of capitalism. However, it had most of its effect on the meatpackers who were under immense attack from the public and press for producing the spoiled and often poisonous food Sinclair described in the novel. President Roosevelt and the Congress soon pushed through pure-food laws which required much more stringent packing standards. Only his novel written in 1927, *Oil!,* approached *The Jungle's* influence on the nation.

His later novels were not so concerned with muchraking as with stories about modern-day heroes, such as Lanny Budd in the *World's End* series. These 10 volumes covered American and European history through the life of Budd from 1913 to 1946, and the 1942 volume, *Dragon's Teeth* won a Pultizer Prize for its treatment of Nazism in Germany. He also wrote treatises on his political beliefs, including "The Industrial Republic." He died in New Jersey.

SMITH, JOSEPH (1805-1844), Mormon prophet and church leader, was born in Vermont and moved to Palmyra, New York, where he spent most of his childhood. His family and neighbors were semi-illiterate and superstitious. In 1820 he claimed to have seen his first vision, which was repeated in 1823, with two heavenly messengers telling him not to join any church sect. A second vision in 1823 brought the Angel Moroni who told him of a book of gold plates inscribed with "the fullness of the everlasting gospel". Smith was to find these plates at the Hill Cumorah in Manchester, New York, and use them to restore the church of God on earth. In 1827 he claimed to retrieve the plates which he spent three years translating from an ancient language, which Smith referred to as "reformed Egyptian." In 1830 he published the results as *The Book of Mormon* and established a Church of Jesus Christ of the Latter-Day Saints in Fayette, New York. He established a following who acknowledged him a prophet of a new age, and the group lived together following contemporary communistic principles. Smith led the group to Kirtland, Ohio, in 1831, and then further west where they founded a town called Nauvoo, in Illinois in 1838. The town, ruled by a clerical oligarchy including Heber C. Kimball and Brigham Young, was situated on the Mississippi River and was declared by the church as the site of the Garden of Eden. In the following years, Smith was involved with the state and federal government on behalf of his "Saints" in order to preserve the settlement and gain a charter for the town. In 1842 the Mormons nominated a full ticket for offices in Hancock County elections, which alienated the other citizens of western Illinois and angered the political establishment there. In 1844 he ran for U.S. President, but he was shot in a riot on the town of Nauvoo by mobs protesting Smith's megalomania as well as the Mormons' practice of polygamy and scandalous business handlings.

STANTON, ELIZABETH CADY (1815-1902), early feminist and reformer. Born in Johnstown, New York, she was given a good education from her father, a lawyer, and at the Johnstown Academy and Emma Willard's Female Seminary. However, her father's profession held the most interest for her especially as she sat and watched him advise married women of their lack of rights to their property and children. Early on, the cries of these unfortunate women led to her resolve to reform the second-class status of women in her society.

When Elizabeth Cady married the abolitionist Henry B. Stanton in 1840, she refused to use the word "obey" during the ceremony. The couple attended an international abolitionist convention in London later that year, and Cady was outraged at the leaders' attitudes towards the women in attendance, who were not allowed to participate in discussion or debate. Afterwards, she began to associate with the leading American liberals of the day in Johnstown, and then in Seneca Falls where she moved in 1847. She and Lucretia Mott held a women's right convention the next year in Seneca Falls which essentially launched the suffragette movement in the United States. Her "Declaration of Sentiments" outlined the inferiority of women in society and called for broad reforms. However, even her suggestion that a woman should be able to divorce a brutal husband was denounced as "radical" by men and women alike. Still, working alongside Susan B. Anthony (q.v.) and others, she was able to influence enough legislators and voters to secure a New York Law to grant women joint guardianship of children and the right to own property separate from their husbands.

Cady-Stanton's later years were filled with lectures and writings pertaining to her lifelong case. In 1869 she helped organize the National Woman Suffrage Association. Ten years later she wrote her federal suffrage amendment proposal which was introduced to Congress at every session until it was accepted in slightly different form in 1919. Although she did not live to see her dream fulfilled, she did see some success after her sixth volume *History of Woman Suffrage* (1881-1922), was begun. She edited and published articles in Miss Anthony's *Revolution* newspaper as well as more mainstream publications. Her two-volume *Women's Bible* appeared in 1895 and 1898, and her *Eighty Years and More* appeared in 1898 when she was 83 years old and still fighting. She died several years later in New York City.

TRUTH, SOJOURNER (1797-1883), abolitionist and women's rights leader, was born a slave to a Dutch patroon in Hurley, New York. The youngest of James and Elizabeth Baumfree, she was named Isabella at birth and learned Dutch as her first language. She is said to have picked up her religious and mystic beliefs early in life from her mother. However, she was sold while still a young girl not settling until 1810 in the household of John J. Dumont of New Paltz, New York. There she had at least five children by Dumont and a fellow slave named Thomas. The New York State Emancipation Act of 1827 set her free, and she settled with her children in New York City working as a maid and laundress. Her mystic powers became more developed during this time as she joined a religious sect which at first helped poor street people in New York but degenerated into a personality cult. When the group was charged with "immoral" sexual activity and broke up, Isabella returned to her quiet life of domestic work. Not until 1843 did she again hear the voices which she believed came from God. This time the voices commanded her to take the name Sojourner Truth and to set out to preach the Good Word to the world. She traveled on foot throughout New England and eventually became more and more concerned with the growing abolitionist movement in the country. Abolitionists were impressed with her inner strength and sense of purpose and published stories of her travels in their journals. One of them, Olive Gilbert, wrote a Narrative of her life in 1850. That same year she began traveling west. Soon she was known for her great oratorical ability. People listened despite the fact she was illiterate, black, and had a heavy Dutch accent. Her speeches primarily were for abolition, but she also began supporting women's rights. She had a deep, strong voice which led many to mistake her for a man. At a women's rights convention in Indiana, she strikingly disproved this mistake by baring her breast. It was at another woman's suffrage meeting in Ohio that she made her famous "Ain't I a Woman" speech (1852). A few years later she settled with her three daughters and their families in Battle Creek, Michigan. The Civil War found her active in the Underground Railroad network in Michigan. She also toured the state trying to gain support for the Negro regiments fighting the union side. President Lincoln gave her a diplomat's greeting at the White House in 1864. After the war she continued to work for development for blacks in the country. She asked for a land grant to establish a "Negro State" in the west for former slaves. She also continued speaking before women's rights groups. In 1875 she settled in Battle Creek for good; she would not leave the town until her death in 1883. After a large funeral, she was buried in the Oak Hill Cemetery in town.

Scenes
of
New York

--Part 1.

The Statue of Liberty, symbol of liberty to the world of America and New York City.

The Empire State Building is shorter than World Trade Towers, in background.

Over seven million people live in New York City today.

The World Trade Center Towers were built between 1970 and 1977.

photo by Richard Clucas

Frank Lloyd Wright designed the spiral staircase and dome of the Guggenheim Museum, New York City.

photo by Richard Clucas

Macy's department store, a Manhattan institution.

Many of the world's famous artists have performed at Radio City Music Hall.

Aerial view of downtown Buffalo.

photo by Richard Clucas

The United Nations, organized after World War II, is a place for people of all languages to communicate.

Work was begun on the New York state capitol in 1867, but it was not completed until 1898.

Albany's modern civic center, supported by former Governor Nelson Rockefeller.

The Alia T. Miner Colonial Collection of historical artifacts is housed in this colonial house at Chazy.

Roadside stand offers fall wares in Schuyler County.

Famed Niagara Falls retreat about one foot per year.

Bear Mountain provides perfect view of the Hudson.

The Thousand Islands dot the St. Lawrence River.

photo by Harry Thayer

George Boldt erected this "castle" for his wife at the turn of the century.

Dairying is an important industry for much of upstate New York.

ADIRONDACKS STATE PARK

Only about 200 miles north of the smog and concrete congestion of New York City, the Adirondack State Park is six million acres of mountainous wilderness with only a few thousand year-round residents "crowding" within its boundaries. The largest park, state or national, in the Continental United States, the Adirondacks cover most of northern New York State, an area roughly the size of Vermont.

How did an area of land this size manage to stay so unspoiled and underpopulated in one of the most crowded states in the nation? The answer comes in part from Article XIV of the State Constitution, added in 1894, which declared the Adirondack Forest Preserve "shall be forever kept as wild forest lands". But the main reason the Adirondacks stayed undeveloped, is simply because the natural environment was not particularly hospitable to human beings.

The chain of mountains and valleys comprising this region were formed long before human beings first saw North America. Adirondack rock was molten deep in the earth over two billion years ago. As early as 350 million years ago, that igneous rock was pushed up from the lower layers of the earth, as deep as 18 to 30 kilometers down. This uplifting continued gradually for many years. In this way, new mountains were created out of old rock. This geologic history is much different from other areas in New York (see Geographical Configuration), and is much more similar to the story of the Canadian shield. After this uplift of basement rock, the true shaper of the Adirondacks—the glacier—crept across North America. The last of a series of ice sheets, the Wisoncin glacier, retreated only 10,000 years ago. At its peak, it covered the Adirondack region at least six thousand feet thick at some points. The Wisconsin glacier carved out the sedimentary rock that had developed over the uplifted basement rock, and "sanded down" the harder rock as it advanced and receded. Cracks and faulting also occured as a result of the glacier's weight, and the melting ice left large pools of water in the valleys, making the foundation of today's many lakes and streams in the region. Glaciers also dumped huge boulders along their way; many of these dwarf all of their surroundings in the Adirondack Forests today.

When the Ice Age finally ended and the climate began to warm up, the first plants appeared, lichens and mosses, clinging tenuously to the rocks. There wasn't much fertile soil left after the scraping action of the glaciers, so it took many years of the primitive plants' growing and dying, layering more and more organic debris over the rocks so that more complex plants could establish their roots. After a time, the northern pines crept down to the Adirondacks, and the hardiest varieties established themselves in the region. From the south crept the deciduous trees, the sugar maple, the birch, beech, northern red oak and other northern hardwoods which today make up about 50 percent of the forest. Only in the highest reaches of the mountains, above 4900 feet, did the trees stop and an Arctic-like ecology begin.

Hardy mammals followed the trees, and more than 200 species of birds made the new forest their home. For these animals, the muggy summers and cold, wet winters suited them just fine. Even the black flies, which give such a nasty bite to humans, didn't drive other creatures away.

But when the first human beings entered the mountain forest, they found it uninhabitable; a "howling wild" that was harsh on those who attempted to tame it. The first Indians probably related to the Algonquins, and later the Mohawks sometimes camped in the region regarding it as their territory, but no permanent settlements were ever built. When Champlain first saw the area around the present Lake Champlain, he was amazed to report that "the country becomes more and more beautiful as you advance." He didn't have time or resources to explore the mountains further, but was impressed by the rough landscape. No other records appear for many years about the region except that fur trappers soon advanced into the area after depleting the lowlands of beavers. A 1756 map shows the Adirondacks as "Couchsachrage, and Indian Beaver Hunting Territory." As the demand for pelts grew in Europe, so did the trapping in the Adirondacks until the early 1800's when the fashion went out for felt hats, and the beavers were nearly extinct in the region. One of the better-documented early settlements in the Adirondacks was by the family of William Gilliland, an Irish immigrant turned merchant who put all of his profits into 4,000 acres near the Bouquet River near Lake Champlain. In 1765 he began his settlement with men of all trades and a small group of livestock. The next year he brought his family, and although one of his daughters drowned in the Hudson River along the way, the rest made it to the new plantation and began the most successful settlement in the Adirondacks thus far. In fact, he created three villages out of the area: Willsboro, Elizabethtown, and Bessboro. His feudal system was eventually made more democratic on demand of the tenant farmers, and he organized his own army to serve on the American side when the Revolution began. However, Benedict Arnold claimed Gilliland was a British spy causing him to be sent to jail. When he returned, six years later, the plantation had fallen into disrepair: "more desolate than when he first penetrated the wilderness . . . Bushes and wild vegetation now unsurped fields which toil and expense had wrested from the forest . . ." according to Gilliland's biographer and brother, Watson. The broken man died several years later, possibly by suicide.

The famed abolitionist, John Brown, also had a settlement in the Adirondacks, this time in the more rugged reaches of the forest near present Lake Placid. He became associated with Gerrit Smith, another abolitionist who owned vast tracts of land in the Adirondacks and wanted to give it away. Brown moved his family there in 1849. He brought former slaves to the settlement offering free farms and land to those willing to till the soil. The venture failed, however, because the land was unsuited for cultivation, and the blacks from the warm southern states could not adjust to the freezing winters. But to John Brown the place remained home, and he returned to it between his tours on behalf of abolition. When John Brown was hung in 1859 for smuggling slaves, this once promising settlement also fell apart.

Meanwhile, the New York state government was doing something about the fact that this region had not been adequately explored and mapped in spite of the fact that many wildernesses in the Rocky Mountains and the west had already been settled. In 1836, geologist, Ebenezer Emmons, took on the job of a geological survey in this forbidding land. Emmons was the one who first named the region as he reports in his chapter of the *Natural History of New York* published in 1842: "This cluster of mountains in neighborhood of the Upper Hudson and Ausable rivers I propose to call the Adirondack Group, a name by which a well-known tribe of Indians who once hunted here may be commemorated". Since then scientists are not sure the name is correct, but the name has stuck.

This extensive plotting of the Adirondacks made Easterners more aware of the resources at their back door. By the hundreds, investors came to look at the forest and decided that there was indeed money to be made from the trees, the soil, and the rocks. As the nation grew, so did the demand for wood, and soon the region was booming with the sound of axes and falling trees. By 1850 the first groups of white pine had been cleared and hauled away; 50 years later much of the former woods were denuded. Mining also began full scale during and after the Civil War. More than 200 iron forges were operating in the Adirondacks during the nineteenth century, but the difficulties of transportation and simple survival in the harsh wilderness turned many away after a short time. In 1880, nevertheless, 15 percent of all ore mined in America came from the region around Lake Champlain.

Franklin B. Hough, while supervising the state census of 1865, became alarmed at the denudation of the northern hills by the miners and lumbermen, and then, after promoting interest in scientific forestry under public control, not only influenced State Legislation but ultimately organized the Forest Administration of the federal government. Verplanck Colvin, a lawyer and topographical engineer, whose name is now borne by an Adirondack peak, spent his summers exploring the mountains in 1872 ascended Mount Marcy and discovered Lake Tear-of-the-Clouds, which he determined to be the high source of the Hudson. "It was the lake, and it flowed, not to the Ausable and St. Lawrence, but to the Hudson, the loftiest lake spring of our haughty river! . . . First seen as we then saw it . . . dripping with the moisture of the heavens it seemed, in its minuteness and its prettiness, a veritable Tear-of-the-Clouds, the summit water as I named it." Colvin reported. In 1880, he had completed a thorough topographical survey of the region and hoped to further delineate the regions of private and public domain. However, as this work went on, he became discouraged by the number of newcomers to the Adirondacks—the casual tourists, "determined to see all that has been recorded as worth seeing". All of a sudden, Colvin stopped his work, perhaps afraid of what the mapping might do to his beloved forests and mountains. In his later years, he could be found wandering the streets of Albany muttering to himself.

But the tourist trade grew, encouraged by such romantic poems as *The Adirondacks* (1858) by Ralph Waldo Emerson, new paintings which showed the region in a majestic light, and by a kind of religious ectasy in the wilderness as espoused by William Henry Harrison Murray, better known as "Adirondack" Murray. This revivalist minister preached that God was in nature and that those who communed with the wilderness were also communing with the Creator. The spirit in contact with the beauty of the woods "escaped the bonds of formal worship, and for the first time tasted of freedom and tested [the soul's] capacity to soar . . . In the mountains, you see him," he said. In 1869, his book *Adventures in the Wilderness; or Camp Life in the Adirondacks* caused a sensation among the city dwellers down south and at last the hardworking urbanites had a reason to relax. Before, few New Yorkers thought of summer, much less winter vacations in the country; most people lived in the country anyway, and a vacation was simply a few days off for fishing and hunting, and even this had to be justified in terms of economic benefit.

Next to this, the American conscience accepted ill-health as a basis for compromise with leisure, and when nature withheld this excuse to "go up to camp" in the Adirondacks, it had to be spuriously affected. One of the more famous resorts for the truly ill in the Adirondacks was Dr. Edward Livingston Trudeau's sanatorium for tuberculosis victims. The New York physician had come to the Saranac Lake region to die in 1876 when he discovered he had the disease himself. However, he was so benefited from the climate, he established the first outdoor sanatorium for the treatment of tuberculosis, and also the first laboratory for scientific study of the disease. For more than half a century, patients came to Trudeau's resort, and the research carried out there helped bring about a cure for the disease.

By the late nineteenth century, however, many people discovered the pleasures of hunting, fishing, hiking, skiing, or generally relaxing in the Adirondacks. New hotels were built, and many settled in cabins in the region, making a living as guides for tourists. By 1932, leisure had been institutionalized in the region, as evidenced by the large turnout at the Winter Olympic Games in Lake Placid.

In the meantime, these vacationers were becoming increasingly aware of the preciousness of the rugged landscape in the Adirondacks. Logging and mining were endangering that fragile environment, and soon many were as concerned as Verplanck Colvin about the future of the region.

The 1894 amendment to the state constitution was the direct outcome of this concern; hence, half of the new park would remain "forever wild". Leasing, selling, logging, and mining were thereby prohibited, and strict controls were placed on the businesses allowed to remain. The rest of the land was left over for private ownership, and today much of it is as wild as the state-owned property. The dividing lines cannot be determined by the air or by land in many cases, and even the large paper companies are careful about pollutants which would harm the fragile woodland ecology. In 1968, New York Governor Nelson Rockefeller set up a study group of the Adirondacks. The chair of the commission, Harold K. Hochschild, reported, "If the Adirondacks are to be saved time is of the essence." He feared the encroachment of out-of-state developers which planned to erect condominiums and gaudy ski resorts in many areas of the park. Also the swelling summer population in the park (up to nine million as opposed to 125,000 year round) endangered even the most "wild" reaches. As a result, strict controls were placed on land use in all areas of the Adirondacks; snowmobiling and other motor driven travel was forbidden in most areas, and construction was halted in others. Only in the "Intensive Use Areas" could already existing recreational facilities be used.

"The Adirondack Park is just about the only place in the nation where people can live in a park . . . I think the idea of private land inside this park is a marvelous one." said Richard Lawrence Jr., chair of the New Adirondack Park Agency, soon after the measures were passed. "But this great concept presents an enormous challenge. For what we have to do is preserve the park environment. A false issue has grown up—an issue that looks upon people and the environment as adversaries. The implication is that if environment takes priority, people will somehow be deprived. That's nonsense. It's possible to have both."[1]

Possible perhaps, but not easily preserved amid mounting difficulties. Many of the problems come not just from within the park itself but also from hundreds of miles away—the industrial cities to the south and west. Air currents generally travel from west to east, and the Adirondacks suffer air pollution from the factories in Syracuse, Rochester, Buffalo, and even as far away as Detroit and Chicago. This smog often drops to the ground in the form of acid rain. In the 1930's, the pH of the lakes here was at around 6.25, but today, the acidity of rain falling in the region has reached 4.5 or even lower. At this stage, many of the native fish cannot live any longer in many lakes and ponds. There are, at present, at least 180 fishless ponds in the Adirondacks, about six percent of all the lakes and ponds in the mountains. Today, scientists are trying to combat the problem by artificially breeding more hardy trout with a greater acidity tolerance, but even these have trouble surviving the shock that comes every spring with increased rain and melted snow. Some lakes survive the acidic upheaval better than others, and corporation-financed research teams are discovering how.

The advance of science and technology, has in many ways, damaged the Adirondack wilderness. Ironically, it is science and technology which can now analyze and potentially reverse the damage, saving the natural beauty for future "explorers".

---

1. Barnett Lincoln, *The Ancient Adirondacks,* Time-Life Books· Inc. 1974. p. 165.

FIRE ISLAND NATIONAL SEASHORE

Within a hour's drive from the frenzy and congestion of New York City, and a short ferry ride from suburban Long Island, Fire Island stretches out as an oasis of nature in both its serenity and fierceness. One of the few relatively unspoiled barrier beaches on the Atlantic Coast, Fire Island was purchased by the National Park System to preserve its delicate and ever-changing ecosystems as an outdoor laboratory and recreational area.

The 30-mile long and one-half mile wide barrier island today shields Long Island from the pounding of Atlantic Ocean waves, but this was not always so. About 11,000 years ago, the great ice sheet that had covered much of North American began to melt and recede. Great masses of rock material borne in and on that glacier were carried far beyond the end of the ice by glacial streams and were deposited in fan-shaped formations at the stream mouths. Before the ice began to melt, so much of the Earth's water was tied up in the ice sheets that the ocean was a hundred or so meters lower than it is today, and Long Island looked like a low ridge on a plain where the glacial outwash was dumped. About 4,000 years ago, the water reached today's level, and a thousand years later, Fire Island began to take shape. In gradual succession, high waves, too large to roll in the shallow waters of the Great South Bay, crashed into each other before reaching Long Island's beaches. With each collision, sand and vegetation were scooped up from the ocean floor and were piled layer by layer upon each other to form several sandbars. Eventually, a series of small islands rose from the water, and as more of the great waves from longshore currents broke into each other, a spit connected them into one long beach that grew westward at a rate of about 25 meters per year. More wind and waves deposited glacial sediments onto the spit, so that it grew higher and wider, forming the duns and sheltered beach behind them on the Great South Bay side.

Fire Island is far from static even today. It is not only growing longer every year, but the continued storms that hit the island cause it to move closer to Long Island every year. The wild and "fiery" behavior of the land here may live up to its name, but

Fire Island's title derives from the people who once lived there. Centuries ago, islanders built huge fires here, either to warn ships or to lure them aground for looting. Others say whalers built fires to render blubber into oil. But the most humorous story is of a land surveyor for the governor of New York, who, in 1690, was sent to inspect the area after a bad storm. The swollen water levels had left five islands standing, and so the surveyor returned with a report of the "Five Islands". However, his handwriting was illegible, and the next time a surveyor visited the beach, it had rejoined into one island, which he read as "Fire Island" in the records.

Two plant and animal ecosystems are evident on Fire Island. On the shallow, calm, bay side, rushes and marshy plants thrive in the tidal zone, and several types of crabs and shallow water fish, such as flounder, abound. Moving further inland, a maritime forest of holly, sassafras, and juneberry trees, as well as small forest shrubs, grow—but stop short at a leven even with the dune crest. This large, secondary dune area along the middle range of the island protects the bay side from searing salt-laden winds, which will kill any of the plant life on this side. Over the dunes, however, another community of wildlife exists. Unprotected from the Atlantic Ocean, the beach on this side is dry and sandy, with burrowing crabs and sanderling birds living off small insects and some of the beach grasses. Seaside goldenrod and beach plum also grow along the harsher ocean side, and some of the less hardy plants, such as pitch pine, and beach heath, grow in the semi-protected area between first and smaller rows of dunes and the secondary, central range of dunes. Many insects, foxes and rabbits like this "dune and swale" region as well.

Wildlife is not confined to the plants and animals on Fire Island. A popular resort among New Yorkers, the small towns along the bay side are alive with artists, boaters, fishermen, clammers, and other fun-lovers during most of the summer months. Camping is also popular, although spaces are limited, and a series of nature walks add to the visitor's wilderness experience.

Eisenhower Locks St. Lawrence Seaway, Massena.

SELECTED PARKS AND POINTS OF INTEREST: NEW YORK

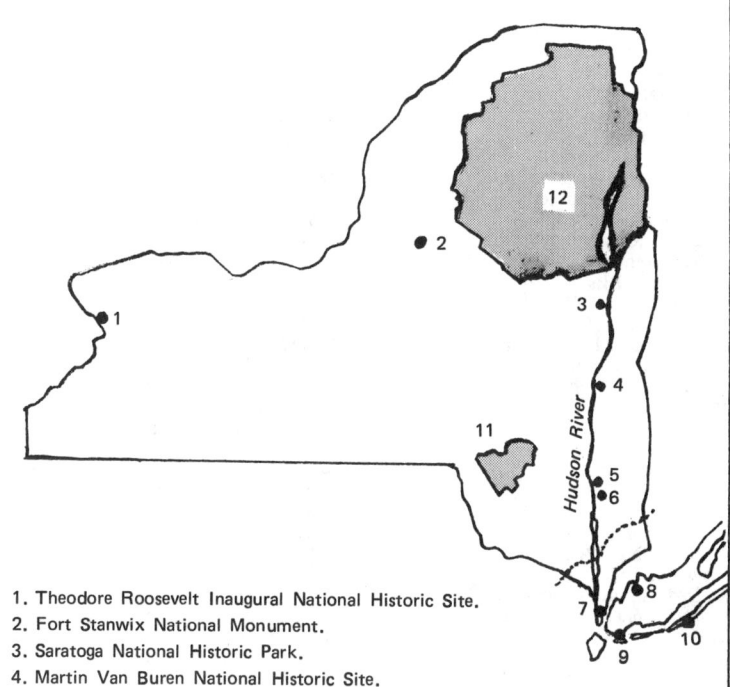

1. Theodore Roosevelt Inaugural National Historic Site.
2. Fort Stanwix National Monument.
3. Saratoga National Historic Park.
4. Martin Van Buren National Historic Site.
5. Vanderbilt Mansion National Historic Site.
6. Franklin D. Roosevelt Home National Historic Site.
7. St. Paul's Church National Historic Site.
8. Sagamore Hill National Historic Site.
9. Gateway National Recreation Area.
10. Fire Island National Seashore.
11. Catskill Mountains State Park.
12. Adirondack Mountains State Park.

MAYORS OF ALBANY

1686 Pieter Schuyler
1694 Johannes Abeel
1695 Evert Bancker
1696 Dirck Ten Broeck
1698 Hendrick Hansen
1699 Pieter Van Brugh
1700 Johannes Bleecker
1701 Johannes Bleecker, Jr.
1702 Albert J. Ryckman
1703 Johannes Schuyler
1706 David Schuyler
1707 Evert Bancker
1709 Johannes Abeel
1710 Robert Livingston, Jr.
1719 Myndert Schuyler
1721 Pieter Van Brugh
1723 Myndert Schuyler
1725 Johannes Cuyler
1726 Rutger Bleecker
1729 Johannes De Peyster
1731 Johannes Hansen
1732 Johannes De Peyster
1733 Edward Holland
1741 Johannes Schuyler
1742 Cornelis Cuyler
1746 Dirck Ten Broeck
1748 Jacob C. Ten Eyck
1750 Robert Sanders
1754 Johannes Hansen
1756 Sybrant G. Van Schaick
1761 Volckert P. Douw
1770 Abraham C. Cuyler
1778 John Barclay
1779 Abraham Ten Broeck
1783 Johannes Beeckman
1786 John Lansing, Jr.
1789 Abraham Yates
1796 Abraham Ten Broeck
1799 Philip S. Van Rensselaer
1816 Elisha Jenkins
1819 Philip S. Van Rensselaer
1821 Charles E. Dudley
1824 Ambrose Spencer
1826 James Stevenson
1828 Charles E. Dudley
1829 John Townsend
1831 Francis Bloodgood
1832 John Townsend
1833 Francis Bloodgood
1834 Erastus Corning
1837 Teunis Van Vechten
1838 Jared L. Rathbone
1841 Teunis Van Vechten
1842 Barent P. Staats
1843 Friend Humphrey
1845 John K. Paige
1846 William Parmelee
1848 John Taylor
1849 Friend Humphrey
1850 Franklin Townsend
1851 Eli Perry
1854 William Parmelee
1855 Charles W. Godard
1856 Eli Perry
1860 George H. Thacher
1862 Eli Perry
1866 George H. Thacher
1868 Charles E. Bleecker
1870 George H. Thacher
1874 John G. Burch
1875 Edmund L. Judson
1876 A. Bleecker Banks
1878 Michael N. Nolan
1883 John Swinburne
1884 A. Bleecker Banks
1886 John B. Thacher
1888 Edward A. Maher
1890 James M. Manning
1894 Oren E. Wilson
1896 John B. Thacher
1898 Thomas J. Van Alstyne
1900 James H. Blessing
1902 Charles H. Gaus
1909 Henry F. Snyder
1910 James B. McEwan
1914 Joseph W. Stevens
1918 James R. Watt
1922 William S. Hackett
1926 John B. Thacher II
1941 Herman F. Hoogkamp
1942 Erastus Corning II

ALBANY

Population: 101,767; Area Code 518; Elev.: 18-300

Albany sits in the middle of one of the most populated areas in the country. Although it would seem little more than a country town without the presence of state and local government, Albany possesses a varied cultural life that supports both the historic and the ultramodern.

Founded in 1609 as Fort Orange, the city is the oldest continuous settlement in all of the original 13 states. Some of the colonial buildings are still preserved. But the towering presence of the stark, white, harshly geometrical cultural and office buildings of the Nelson A. Rockefeller Empire State Plaza symbolize the city's recent efforts at eliminating some of the more outdated and decaying parts of Albany.

Many of those older buildings reflect the Dutch influence in Albany's history. Although French explorers saw the area as early as 1540, *Henry Hudson*, sailing in for the Dutch West Indies Company, claimed the land in 1609. United Netherlands Company traders built temporary Fort Nassau in 1614 on the site, and it was replaced in 1624 by Fort Orange. The first permanent settlers, who came shortly afterwards, were 18 families, mostly Walloons from Holland. They formed friendly alliances with the Indians, which helped *Kiliaen Van Rensselaer* to buy land on both sides of the Hudson and establish the patroonship of Rensselaerswyck in 1630. Although the patroon himself never visited the colony, he did attract hundreds more settlers with the sawmills, gristmills, homes and barns he built for them.

Jesuit priest Isaac Jogues described the settlement in 1643 as "composed of about 100 persons who reside in some 25 or 30 houses built along the river as each found most convenient... All their houses are of boards and thatched, with no mason work except the chimmneys."

Friction developed early between the patroonship and the Dutch West India Company, each claiming jurisdiction over the land on which Fort Orange was built. In 1652, *Peter Stuyvesant*, sent out by the West India Company as director general of New Netherland, set up a court and laid out space around Fort Orange for a new village called Beverwyck (Dutch town of the beaver), and forbade the patroon to erect buildings near the fort. The Van Rensselaer agent tore down the proclamation and posted another maintaining the rights of the patroon. When the English threatened New Amsterdam (now New York City) in August-September 1664, Stuyvesant called on Rensselaerswyck for aid, but was refused. Under the new English rule the Van Rensselaers still claimed Beverwyck as part of their manor, but relinquished their claim to the village in 1685. *Governor Dongan* converted their patroonship into an English manor.

The British permitted the Dutch to retain their own language, customs, religion, local courts, and institutions, and admitted them to the governor's council. Their leaders, represented by such names as *Van Rensselaer, Schuyler, Hendrick*, and *Winne*, were joined by British tradesmen and officials, led by the *Clintons, Yateses, Livingstons*, and other families prominent in the Nation's history. In 1686 Albany, chief fur trading center of the English Colonies, was given a charter by *Governor Dongan*. For a quitrent of one beaver skin a year the king granted the city control of the fur trade to "the eastward, northward, and westward as far as His Majesty's dominion may extend."

Peter Schuyler was appointed the first mayor, and aldermen were also chosen to govern the trade.

Soon, Abany rivaled Montreal in the fur trade, causing friction with the French. In 1689, one of the first inter-colonial conventions was held at Albany to discuss the crisis of the French movements into English territory. Delegates from Massachusetts Bay, Plymouth, Connecticut and New York made agreements with the Five Nations of Indian tribes for the common defense against the French. Although there was a temporary truce in 1701 when Albany attempted to take a neutral stance between the French and New Englanders, a second meeting of the colonies here in 1754 was held in anticipation of war.

The Iroquois, angered by Albany traders' dealings with the French and French-dominated tribes, gave upon the English cause. In 1754 the British Lords of Trade finally realized the danger and called a congress of all the colonies at Albany to make a treaty with the Indians and to consider colonial defense. The Indians were slow in arriving; their temper was expressed by *King Hendrick*, chief of the Mohawk, when he thundered, "Look at the French; they are men, they are fortifying everywhere - but, we are ashamed to say it, you are all like women . . ." *Benjamin Franklin's* plan of union was adopted by the congress but was rejected by the colonies because it unduly limited their independence and by Britain because it impaired the royal prerogative.

During the French and Indian War, Albany served as point of departure for colonial and British forces under *William Johnson, Abercrombie, Bradstreet*, and *Lord Amherst* on their way north and west against the French. After the Anglo-French treaty of 1763 the city was ready for peace, but farmers were disgruntled by taxes, merchants and lawyers were gauging anew the possibilities of Franklin's 1754 proposal, and young men back from the wars were restive under British rule. The break came with Stamp Act riots, the organization of the Sons of Liberty, and the burning of the city mail sleigh. *Philip Schuyler* proposed a censure of *George III* in the 1775 session of the Provincial Assembly, which carried 7 to 2 after the Loyalists had left the chamber.

Although the British planned to capture Albany during the 1777 campaign, they failed when *General Burgoyne* was defeated at Saratoga. The whole city was committed to the colonial side, and money, men and supplies were donated from its citizens for the Revolution.

Soon after the war, Albany looked ahead to its role as a major port and transportation center for a new nation. As early as 1783, pioneers moving west stopped here along the way, and within a decade, 500 oxcarts on their way to the frontier passed through town. The first steamboat, the *Clermont*, chugged up to the city port in 1807, and in succeeding years the Champlain Canal and Erie Canal provided navigation all over the state and surrounding territories.

In 1797, the city was named the state capital, and ever since then, its character has been dominated by what's happening in the Capitol. Legislative action in successive years made possible the canals and the first railroad lines that reached out from the city; in 1831 the *DeWitt Clinton* (named for the state's sixth governor) ran to Schenectady. Newspapers, such as the *Argus* and the *Evening Journal* (1830), served as forums for not only local and state political discourse, but also for issues that developed into national concerns. *Martin Van Buren's* Albany Regency group eventually ran the White House, and the *Journal's* editor *Thurlow Weed* did much to promote the Whig and then the Republican Party into prominence during the pre-Civil War days.

Industries such as paper, felts and blankets, dyes, iron, and beer began before the Civil War, but they did not gain much importance until after 1865. The latter part of the 19th century saw Albany as a major commercial center, to which new immigrants traveled every day. The former lumber industry fed by the primeval forests around Albany died out with the turn of the century, but a legacy of papermaking lived on in the city economy. A group of Albany industrialists had formed the American Express Company in 1841, and 40 years later it was a major enterprise. After a century of progress, the population also grew from about 3,000 in 1790 to over 90,000 in 1880.

The new century brought new industries, such as meatpacking, pharmaceuticals, chemicals, industrial fabrics, steel, castings and other machinery into the city. It also brought new faces.

Theodore and Franklin D. Roosevelt, as well as *Alfred E. Smith* and *Nelson Rockefeller* began their political careers in the Capitol here, which was completed in 1898. Since it was such an old town, many areas were suffering from neglect and disrepair, by the third quarter of the twentieth century. A large area of the downtown was officially condemned by the state, and a large "South Mall Project" materialized as a focal point for govenment, culture, and recreation.

Education is served in Albany by the State University of New York, which took over the old New York State Teachers College (1844) in the mid-1960s. SUNYA offers over 100 degree programs in all the major fields to 14,000 students. The Rensselaer Polytechnic Institute focuses on the sciences and architecture, with students from all over the world. The private Union University colleges of medicine (1839), law (1851), and pharmacy (1881) are also important here. Siena College (men) and St. Rose College (women) were founded by Roman Catholics in 1924.

Other points of interest in Albany are historical: the Van Rennsselaer home of Cherry Hill is restored, as are the Schuyler Mansion (1762) and Quackenbush Square, site of the oldest house (1730) in Albany. The Albany Institute of History and Art and the New York State Museum also display cultural and historical artifacts from the city. The port of Albany, one of the largest inland sea ports, was deepened and widened in the 1960's so that fully-loaded ships could be accomodated and turned around.

POINTS OF INTEREST

THE PARKER DUNN MEMORIAL BRIDGE
Named in honor of *Parker J. Dunn* (1890-1981)--Crosses the Hudson River; Opened 1933.

JOHN V.L. PRUYN LIBRARY
Modified Dutch Renaissance style; built 1901 at birthplace of lawyer and congressman.

THE SCHUYLER MONUMENT
Memorial to *Phillip Schuyler* (1733-1804), Revolutionary War commander.

THE STATE CAPITOL
In Capitol Park, styled like a French chateau; started 1867, completed 1898.

ALBANY INSTITUTE OF HISTORY AND ART
Contains collections of American, English and Dutch paintings.

THE DUDLEY OBSERVATORY
Founded in 1846, part of Union University; building erected 1893.

WASHINGTON PARK
Established in 1865, occupies 90 acres.

KING FOUNTAIN
(*J. Massey Rind*, sculptor); the figures represent Moses and followers at the rock of Hebron.

MAYORS OF BUFFALO

1832 Ebenezer Johnson
1833 Major A. Andrews
1834 Ebenezer Johnson
1835 Hiram Pratt
1836 Samuel Wilkeson
1837 Josiah Trowbridge
1837 Pierre A. Barker
1838 Ebenezer Walden
1839 Hiram Pratt
1840 Sheldon Thompson
1841 Isaac R. Harrington
1842 George W. Clinton
1843 Joseph G. Masten
1844 William Ketchum
1845 Joseph G. Masten
1846 Solomon G. Haven
1847 Elbridge G. Spaulding
1848 Orlando Allen
1849 Hiram Barton
1850 Henry K. Smith
1851 James Wadsworth
1852 Hiram Barton
1853 Eli Cook
1856 Frederick Stephens
1858 Timothy T. Lockwood
1860 Franklin A. Alberger
1862 William G. Fargo
1866 Chandler J. Wells
1870 Alexander Brush
1874 Louis P. Dayton
1876 Philip Becker
1878 Solomon Scheu
1880 Alexander Brush
1882 Grover Cleveland
1882 Marcus M. Drake
1882 Harmon S. Cutting
1883 John B. Manning
1884 Jonathan Scoville
1886 Philip Becker
1890 Charles F. Bishop
1895 Edgar B. Jewett
1898 Conrad Diehl
1902 Erastus C. Knight
1906 James N. Adam
1910 Louis P. Fuhrmann
1918 George S. Buck
1922 Frank X. Schwab
1930 Charles E. Roesch
1934 George J. Zimmerman
1938 Thomas L. Holling
1942 Joseph J. Kelly
1946 Bernard J. Dowd
1950 Joseph Mruk

1954 Steven Pankow
1958 Frank A. Sedita
1962 Chester W. Kowal
1966 Frank A. Sedita
1971 Stanley Makowski
1977 James Griffin

BUFFALO

Population: 357,384; Area Code 716; Elev.: 600

One cannot consider the character, history, or economics of the city of Buffalo without considering its geographic location. Lying on the eastern tip of Lake Erie at the source of the Niagara River, Buffalo has long been an inland seaport because of its connection to Lake Ontario, the St. Lawrence Seaway, and the Atlantic Ocean. It is also connected by land to the rest of New York state and the Midwest by a complex web of railroads and highways. No wonder the snow-storm that crippled the city in the winter of 1977 raised national concern.

The second largest city in New York, Buffalo lies on a wide plain. From the air, the streets and rail lines seem to radiate outward from the Lake Erie shoreline like a series of spokes. Outlying communities connect indistinguishably with Buffalo and spread out fanlike as well; in the past two decades, the population of Buffalo proper has declined by hundreds of thousands as former residents move to the residential suburbs. However, settlement in Buffalo and the "Niagara Frontier" began as a slow, inward movement over many decades.

Although *Joseph Ellicott* chose and mapped the site of Buffalo for the Holland Land Company in 1799, it was not until 1803-4 that he divided the land into lots and offered them for sale. He modeled the city plan after that of Washington, D.C., which his brother, *Major Andrew Ellicott*, had helped draw up several years before. Ellicott called the place New Amsterdam, but settlers preferred the old creek name.

That old name, according to local historian *Roy W. Nagle*, is enigmatic, because no buffalo ever existed in the area. Nevertheless, Buffalo Creek appeared on one early map on the Niagara Frontier as "Beaver Creek". In error, an Indian interpreter at a meeting between chiefs of the Six Nations and three U.S. commissioners referred to the creek as "Buffalo". A few years earlier, a British military engineer, who had been stationed at a place called Buffalo Creek in Pennsylvania, made a map of the Niagara Frontier in which he referred to the present Buffalo River as a "Creek called Buffalo".

The first road leading into Buffalo was the Genesee (presently Route 5), built for settlers' wagons in 1798. This road and the Great Lakes water routes made it easy for the British to attack the area during the War of 1812. However, even though much of the town was burned in 1814 by the British, Buffalo's

1,500 American residents quickly rebuilt it and were able to incorporate as a village by 1816.

In 1821, Buffalo became the seat of Erie County, and (four years later, the opening of the Erie Canal through town changed the course of its history. Boatmen congregated here after the long haul from the Hudson, joined Great Lakes and sea-going ships crews, and created songs about their lives which have enriched the country's folklore. For almost 100 years afterwards, Buffalo reigned as the largest community between Philadelphia and Chicago, so it was natural that once railroads became practical, Buffalo would be chosen as a departure and destination point for many rail companies. By 1832, Buffalo was incorporated as a city, with a population near 12,000.

At first, the city so firmly rooted in the Erie Canal and Great Lakes trade did not welcome the railroads. It appeared that the railroads would supersede water and turnpike transportation and Buffalo would lose the advantage of its location at the break in the east-west trade route. The city sought a solution by diverting its capital and energy into the industrial field, and in 1860 the Association for the Encouragement of Manufactures in the City of Buffalo was organized. But these fears proved unfounded. The Civil War, by deranging the lines of communication and transportation in the middle states, threw a vast amount of commerce to the northern routes. Trade with the expanding West grew rapidly during and after the war, and Buffalo became one of the great grain and livestock markets of the world. The railroads, attracted by existing markets and established trade routes, converged upon Buffalo and made it a railroad center. With 11 main railroad lines served by five passenger terminals and 14 freight cars clearing every 24 hours, it is today the second largest railroad center in the United States.

The stimulus to manufacture had its effect and Buffalo industry grew rapidly. In 1872 there were more than 800 small industries employing 18,000 workers out of a population of 150,000. Railroad connections were completed with the anthracite coal fields of Pennsylvania in 1873. Pennsylvania coal and Lake Superior iron ore, transported by lake boats, provided the necessary elements for large-scale manufacture of metal products.

Grover Cleveland became mayor of this bustling boomtown that liked to call itself the "Dodge City of the East" in 1881. His strict streamlining and anti-corruption administration were popular, and his reputation in this city helped him gain the fame that would lead to his election as President three years later. By the turn of the century, his town held 250,000 inhabitants.

Another President, *Millard Fillmore*, was the first chancellor of the University of Buffalo, (now New York State University at Buffalo) when it was founded in 1846. By the turn of the century, this institution boasted colleges of medicine, dentistry, and law, and other places of education and culture experienced rapid growth. Private associations opened libraries, sponsored public art shows, and built grammar and high schools. In 1901, the city hosted the Pan-American Exposition, a triumphant event in most aspects, except that *President William McKinley* was assassinated by a member of the anarchist movement.

A new economic resource was discovered when Niagara Falls' waterpower was harnessed. Only a few miles up the Niagara River, the falls gave Buffalo 11,000,000 horsepower, allowing many new industries to open and attracting thousands of workers from Europe and the eastern U.S. Grain elevators were built. The first iron ships pulled in from other Great Lakes ports. The First World War introduced the manufacture of dyes and airplanes into Buffalo's economy.

With the popularization of automobiles came new paved roads and the International Peace Bridge to Fort Erie, Canada (1927). In 1932, a large centennial celebration was held, and the opening of the St. Lawrence Seaway in 1957 made Buffalo a world port.

Today that port handles many of the city's products, such as flour, steel, industrial and automotive equipment, rubber, chemicals, televisions, radios, and clothing. A month-long cold spell froze the river and stopped trains and trucks from normal transportation. Since much of the city's economy depends upon the automobile industry, many of the workers have suffered from the recent decline in demand for American-made autos. New facilities such as aerospace plants and the nearby state Nuclear Facility for reprocessing nuclear fuels offer some promise for future industsry.

POINTS OF INTEREST

ALBRIGHT-KNOX ART GALLERY
It has a large contemporary art section.

KLEINHANS MUSIC HALL
A modernistic structure housing the Buffalo Philharmonic Orchestra.

BUFFALO & ERIE COUNTY HISTORICAL MUSEUM
Downtown.

THE MCKINLEY MONUMENT
At center of Niagara Square, erected Sept. 5, 1907, unveiled by *Governor Charles E. Hughes* in honor of *President William McKinley*.

BUFFALO CITY HALL
Completed in 1932. Designed by *John J. Wade*, an earlier example of a skyscraper as municipal offices (32 stories).

MAYORS OF NEW YORK CITY

1665 Thomas Willett
1666 Thomas Delavall
1667 Thomas Willett
1668 Cornelius Steenwyck
1671 Thomas Delavall
1672 Matthias Nicolls
1673 John Lawrence
1675 William Dervall
1676 Nicholas De Meyer
1677 Stephanus Van Cortlandt
1678 Thomas Delavall
1679 Francis Rombouts
1680 William Dyre
1682 Cornelius Steenwyck
1684 Gabriel Minvielle
1685 Nicholas Bayard
1686 Stephanus Van Cortlandt
1689 Peter Delanoy
1691 John Lawrence
1692 Abraham De Peyster
1694 Charles Lodwick
1695 William Merritt
1698 Johannes De Peyster
1699 David Provoost
1700 Isaac De Reimer
1701 Thomas Noell
1702 Philip French
1703 William Peartree
1707 Ebenezer Wilson
1710 Jacobus Van Cortlandt
1711 Caleb Heathcote
1714 John Johnston
1719 Jacobus Van Cortlandt
1720 Robert Walters
1725 Johannes Jansen
1726 Robert Lurting
1735 Paul Richard
1739 John Cruger
1744 Stephen Bayard
1747 Edward Holland
1757 John Cruger, Jr.
1766 Whitehead Hicks
1776 David Matthews
1784 James Duane
1789 Richard Varick
1801 Edward Livingston
1803 De Witt Clinton
1807 Marinus Willett
1808 De Witt Clinton
1810 Jacob Radcliff
1811 De Witt Clinton
1815 John Ferguson
1816 Jacob Radcliff
1818 Cadwallader D. Colden
1821 Stephen Allen
1825 William Paulding

1826 Philip Home
1827 William Paulding
1829 Walter Bowne
1833 Gideon Lee
1834 Cornelius V. Lawrence
1837 Aaron Clark
1839 Isaac L. Varian
1841 Robert H. Morris
1844 James Harper
1845 William F. Havemeyer
1846 Andrew H. Mickle
1847 William V. Brady
1848 William F. Havemeyer
1849 Caleb S. Woodhull
1851 Ambrose C. Kingsland
1853 Jacob A. Westervelt
1855 Fernando Wood
1858 Daniel F. Tiemann
1860 Fernando Wood
1862 George Opdyke
1864 C. Godfrey Gunther
1866 John T. Hoffman
1868 T. Coman (Acting)
1869 A. Oakey Hall
1873 William F. Havemeyer
1874 S.B.H. Vance (Acting)
1875 William H. Wickham
1877 Smith Ely
1879 Edward Cooper
1881 William R. Grace
1883 Franklin Edson
1885 William R. Grace
1887 Abram S. Hewitt
1889 Hugh J. Grant
1893 Thomas F. Gilroy
1895 William L. Strong
1898 Robert A. Van Wyck
1902 Seth Low
1904 George B. McClellan
1910 William J. Gaynor
1913 Ardolph L. Kline
1914 John P. Mitchel
1918 John F. Hylan
1926 James J. Walker
1932 Joseph V. McKee
1933 John P. O'Brien
1934 Fiorello H. La Guardia
1946 William O'Dwyer
1950 Vincent R. Impellitteri
1954 Robert F. Wagner
1966 John V. Lindsay
1978 Edward Koch

NEW YORK CITY

Population: 7,035,348; Area Code 212

Located along the southeastern point of New York state where the East and Hudson Rivers merge with New York Bay is the most prominent city in the United States. Originally settled in the early 1600's by Dutch fur traders, New York has become the heart of the nation's cultural, political and financial life. It is the largest city in the nation and one of the most diverse.

Before Dutch traders settled in the area, New York City was occupied by several tribes of the Wappinger Confederation of Indians. The Rechgawawane (or Manhattans) lived in much of Northern Manhattan, Bronx and Westchester (which they shared with the Wecquaesgeek Indians). The Canarsie Indians occupied Brooklyn, southern Manhattan, and parts of Governors and Staten Islands. In Queens, the Rockaways were the predominate tribe.

The first non-Indian is believed to have visited the area in April, 1524, when *Giovanni da Verrazano* sailed the French ship *Dauphine* into New York Bay. The Florentine sailor remained in the bay for only a short time, however, before returning home.

It was not until 1609, when *Henry Hudson* sailed the *Half Moon* into lower New York Bay in search of a northwest passage to the far east, that the land was visited again by Europeans.

After sailing up the Hudson River to a place near present day Albany, Hudson, an employee of the Dutch East India company, returned to the Netherlands with a cargo of valuable furs. Dutch merchants soon began exploring plans to commercially exploit the new lands. Within a few months, cargo ships were on their way to the New World.

The first non-Indian made permanent residence in New York in 1612 when *Jan Rodriguez*, a mulatto, was left ashore by the explorer *Adrian Block*. The first large group of settlers to come to New York were protestant Walloons who arrived in 1624. The 30 families were brought by the Dutch West Indies Company to Fort Orange (Albany) on the ship *New Netherlands*. The ship's captain, *Cornelius May*, was named the first governor of the settlement. With the arrival of more settlers and the appointment of *William Verhulst* as governor in 1625, the settlement was moved to the southern tip of Manhattan and named "New Amsterdam".

In 1626, a new Dutch governor, *Peter Minuit*, purchased

Manhattan from the Canarsie Indians for a mere 60 gilders. Over the next several years, immigrants from France, England, Ireland, the Netherlands and elsewhere began arriving in the small Dutch settlement. When *Father Isaac Jogues*, a French Jesuit, arrived in New Amsterdam in 1643 he reported that there were 18 languages spoken among the island's 500 residents.

The colony remained in Dutch control until 1664, when *Col. Richard Nicolls* seized the town for *King Charles II* of England and renamed it "New York".

Under British dominance, the colony continued to grow. The population of New York by the early 1680's when *Thomas Dongan* was named governor was well over 3,000. Under the Donegan Charter, which was adopted in 1684, the city was divided into six wards to allow for the election of a common council while New York citizens were also given their first grant of civil liberties.

By the turn of the century, New York resembled most of the other British colonies in the New World as the Dutch influence had almost entirely vanished. When *John Montgomerie* was named governor in 1731, he established a municipal government system which was heavily British influenced. As with other British colonies, New York merchants exchanged agricultural goods for slaves from Africa, rum and coffee from the West Indies, and manufactured products from England.

In 1725, the city's first newspaper, the *New York Gazette*, was founded by *William Bradford*, a Philadelphia Quaker. Eight years later, *John Peter Zenger* began the New York *Weekly Journal*. Zenger was a poor writer and printer but a staunch idealist. His desire to report the truth soon landed him in jail as he was charged with libelling *Governor William Crosby*. With the help of *Benjamin Franklin*, Zenger got *Andrew Hamilton*, the renowned Philadelphia lawyer to successfully defend him. To this day, Zenger's case remains an important landmark in the nation's fight for a free press.

King College (today known as Columbia University), the first school of higher learning in the city, was chartered in 1754, only a few months after the city's first library had been established.

During the Revolutionary War, members of the Sons of Liberty actively revolted in New York against the British rule. When Britain passed the Stamp Act, city residents gathered at City Hall and drafted a Declaration of Rights. When fighting broke out revolutionaries were able to hold off the British troops for a while with the help of *George Washington* and several regiments of troops, but within a few months the British were in control again.

When Britain surrendered at Yorktown, New York remained virtually the same as it was as a colony. For a time after the war, New York served as the capital of the state and the nation. It was at New York City Hall (named Federal Hall) that the Congress of the Confederation convened in 1785 to draft the nation's constitution. When *George Washington* was unanimously elected President, several New York residents including *Alexander Hamilton, James Duane, John Jay* and *Robert Livingston* were named to leading governmental posts.

Although New York continued to grow, it was not until the early 1800's that it started to become the nation's leading trade center. Up to the turn of the century, New York was no more than a major regional trade center, an equal to Philadelphia, Boston, Newport, and Charleston. With the removal of the capital from Philadelphia to Washington in 1800 and the completion of the Erie Canal in 1825, New York gradually became the dominant trade center on the east coast. Towards the end of the 19th century, as technology improved and ship size grew, it became economically more feasible to concentrate trade at one port. Because of New York's location along the coast and the physical makeup of the harbor, New York became the leading port in the nation. The city had only nine percent of the nation's foreign trade in 1800. By 1850, it was carrying 57 percent of the nation's foreign trade.

While the city's economy boomed, so did its population and culture. The city grew northward as immigrants from around the world entered the United States through Ellis Island looking to begin a new life. New York University City opened in 1831. *Horace Greeley* established the New York *Tribune*, one of four newspapers to begin publishing in the city. Leading literary and artistic figures were drawn to the European atmosphere of the big city. Magazines such as *Harper's* and *Atlantic* were born. The wealthy had free time for opera, music and other forms of recreation. In 1853, the city's common council under the suggestion of *Frederick Law Olmstead* and *Calvert Vaux* set aside several acres of land for a large park. Today, Central Park is one of New York's most well-known landmarks.

New Yorkers were somewhat ambivalent towards joining the conflict during the Civil War. The south was one of the main buyers of the city's imported goods, but when Fort Sumter was fired upon, numerous citizens signed up for duty. When the draft law was enacted in 1863, however, rioting erupted in the streets. *Fernando Wood* unsuccessfully suggested New York withdraw from the union and form a free city. After four days of rebellion and destruction, Union troops quelled the outbreak.

After the war, New York continued to expand outwards, while also beginning to expand upwards. With new advancements in steel structures, New York's solid granite floor made it a prime location for building skyscrapers.

New immigrants began arriving, this time from Italy, Germany and Russia, giving the city a steady stream of cheap labor while the nation's industrial revolution was at its peak. The textile industry soon became one of New York's leading industries.

In addition, banking, insurance and exchange markets, and corporate managment grew rapidly. Despite the economic boom of the period, labor conditions were at their worst. Young children and women were forced to work in filthy factories and sweatshops for hours a day only to receive a pittance in wages. It was not until the early 1900's that a state factory commission was formed and necessary reforms were instituted.

In politics, *William M. Tweed* rose to power after gaining control of Tammany Hall. As mayor of the city, Tweed is believed to have received over $1 million in bribes while stealing as much as $200 million from the city. Arrested in office, he fled the country, only to return later and be convicted.

Until the first World War, New York continued to be the main artery in the nation's foreign trade, but its predominance began to weaken after the war. It was not that New York was doing less business, but other areas in the nation were beginning to catch up.

The city survived the great Wall Street crash of 1929 and the Depression which followed, but today it is suffering similar economic ills which it suffered in the 1930's. Crime in New York is the highest in the country, its slums are some of the nation's worst, while its fisal problems have become so bad that the city was forced to accept federal loans from *President Jimmy Carter* in the late 1970's to pay its bills.

Despite the city's economic problems, private industry continues to flourish. New York has been such an important American city for so many years, that it has become one of the most important cities in the world. Within the city's skyscrapers, which are among the tallest in the world, are offices for many of the world's largest corporations. Wall Street is considered by many as the financial center for the western world, while the United Nations is an integral part of world politics.

Since 1898, Greater New York has been composed of five boroughs; Bronx, Brooklyn, Manhattan, Queens and Staten Island (formely Richmond). Although Manhattan is considered the financial center of the city, many neighboring cities in New York state and New Jersey are integral elements of the megalopolis. Of the five boroughs, only the Bronx is not located on an island.

As one of the most active seaports in the nation, New York has continued to serve as a major entry port for immigrants. The vast influx of immigrants over the years has given the city the title "the melting pot of the nation". Throughout each borough, there are numerous ethnic sections and neighborhoods where English is virtually a second language and where the people and their lifestyles reflect the countries from which they came. Today the cross-section of people gives the city a cosmopolitan flavor comparable only to the major cities of the world.

For many artists, New York continues to be the artistic

Mecca of the world. Along the 16-mile Broadway Avenue are some of the nation's leading theatres and museums. The Metropolitan Opera, which performs regularly at its home on Broadway, is considered one of the world's best. The New York City Ballet is directed by *George Balanchine*, one of the greatest choreographers of all time. On the other end of Manhattan in Harlem is the Dance Theater of Harlem, a talented and unique all-black classical dance company. The Hispanic society of America, a vast library devoted to the study of Hispanic people, and the Museum of American Indians can also be found on Broadway.

The New York Philarmonic, conducted by the Bombay-born *Zubin Mehta*, is one of the nation's best, while much of America's modern jazz and rock-n-roll was born in nightclubs around the city. During the 1920's, *Duke Ellington* made jazz famous in Harlem as he performed regularly at the Cotton Club. In the 1950's and 60's, young intellectuals crowded into Greenwich Village to write poetry and books. In the same village area where *Eugene O'Neill* established the first off-broadway theatre in the first half of the 20th century, musicians such as *Bob Dylan* were performing to the youth culture in the 1960's and 1970's.

POINTS OF INTEREST

BEDLOE'S ISLAND - STATUE OF LIBERTY
Executed by *Frederic Auguste Bartholdi*, French sculptor, presented by people of France to people of the U.S. (1886).

ELLIS ISLAND
One mile SW of the Battery in Upper New York Bay--from 1892 an immigration station.

GOVERNORS ISLAND
About 500 yards off Battery Park in Upper New York Bay. Departure point for troops in Civil and foreign wars.

BROOKLYN BRIDGE
(1883)-In this bridge, with its Gothic pylons, *John A. Roebling* and son *Washington* introduced new bridge engineering methods.

GEORGE WASHINGTON BRIDGE
Built by *O.H. Amman* and *Cass Gilbert* (1931); links Manhattan with Fort Lee, N.J. over the Hudson River.

TRIBOROUGH BRIDGE
Built by Triborough Bridge Association; links Manhattan with the Bronx and Queens.

HOLLAND TUNNEL
Completed 1927; twin tubes under the North Hudson River.

LINCOLN TUNNEL
Built 1938; twin tubes under the North Hudson River.

Broadway
Sixteen-mile street, starts as a shipping lane at tip of Manhattan, through Wall Street financial center, moves diagonally through the 34th-39th street garment district, as "The Great White Way" between 42nd and 53rd streets, through Automobile Row from 53rd street to Columbus Circle, parallels the Hudson River apartment houses, reaches Columbia University at 114th street, the museums at 155th street ending in nondescript fashion at the city's limits.

NEW YORK AQUARIUM
In Battery Park, contains the largest collection of marine life in the country.

METROPOLITAN OPERA HOUSE
Built 1883; New York's premier home of the grand opera.

AMERICAN MUSEUM OF NATURAL HISTORY
Opened 1877; one of world's largest institutions devoted to natural science exhibits.

HAYDEN PLANETARIUM
Gift of *Charles Hayden* main attractions are Hall of the Sun and Theater of the Sky.

CATHEDERAL OF ST.JOHN THE DIVINE
Designed by *Heins and La Farge and Cram and Ferguson* ; Romanesque and Gothic style.

AMERICAN ACADEMY OF ARTS AND LETTERS
National Institute; offers permanent exhibit of sculpture, paintings and manuscripts.

MUSEUM OF THE AMERICAN INDIAN
Heye Foundation; contains extensive collection of artifacts of Indians of the entire Western Hemisphere.

THE CLOISTERS
At Fort Tryon Park, a branch of the Metropolitan Museum of Art, contains collection of medieval architecture, sculptures and tapestries.

WALL STREET
Local point of the financial district; contains the New York Stock Exchange and clearing houses for commodities and other exchanges.

CHINATOWN
West of Chatham Square and the Bowery, includes curio shops, markets, and restaurants featuring Chinese imports.

THE LOWER EAST SIDE
Stretches east of Chinatown, from the Brooklyn Bridge to 14th St. Includes the Bowery and is well known as an impoverished area.

GREENWICH VILLAGE
Long known as the Latin Quarter or the Bohemia of New York City. Home of the avante-guards, haven of poets and artists.

WASHINGTON SQUARE
Near the center of Greenwich Village, dominated by an arch erected in 1892 in memory of Washington's inauguration.

THE GARMENT DISTRICT
Center of New York's famous garment industry; located between 30th and 42nd streets and Sixth and Ninth Avenues.

TIMES SQUARE
Broadway here becomes the Great White Way; once impressive and stimulating, now cheap and tawdry.

THE EMPIRE STATE BUILDING
Designed by *Shreve, Lamb and Harmon*, was long known as the tallest building in the world (1,250 ft.).

NEW YORK PUBLIC LIBRARY
At Fifth Ave. and 42nd St., designed by *Carrere and Hastings* has eclectic styling based mainly on classical concepts. The pair of crouched lions at entrance are well known landmarks.

CHRYSLER BUILDING
Completed 1929, designed by *William Van Alen*; 1,048 ft.high; is considered by many to be most beautiful in New York; notable is its metal dome terminating in a spire.

ROCKEFELLER CENTER
Designed by *Reinhard and Hofmeister, Corbett, Harrison and MacMurray and Hood and Fouilhoux*; comprises 14 buildings on 12 acres.

ST.PATRICKS CATHEDERAL
Completed 1879, at Fifth Ave. and 50th streets; designed by *James Renwick*; an example of Gothic Revival architecture, suggestive of the Cathederal of Cologne.

CENTRAL PARK
Designed by *Frederick Law Olmsted*; contains lakes, fields, playgrounds, an ice-skating rink, a zoo and the Belvedere, a meteorological observatory. Tavern on the Green is an exotic restaurant in the park.

METROPOLITAN MUSEUM OF ART
At Fifth Ave. and 82nd St.; contains the most comprehensive collection in America.

GRANT'S TOMB
Designed by *J.H.Duncan*; the burial place of *Ulysses Simpson Grant* and his wife.

CONEY ISLAND
In Brooklyn, offers a bathing beach, two mile board-walk, amusement parks, carousels and many other entertainment features.

ROCHESTER

Population: 241,539; Area Code 716; Elev. 500

Lying along both banks of the Genesee River near where it empties into Lake Ontario, Rochester began its history with a gristmill and continued growing to its status today as a major industrial center of New York state. Often considered synonymously with the Eastman Kodak Company, which employs 30 percent of the city's workers, Rochester is also a large producer of clothing, automobile parts and fine optical and photographic supplies, from independent companies.

The Indians of the Lake Ontario region never thought much of the area, however. Their chief villages were located on hilly lands 20 miles southeast of the present site, and during hunting and fishing expeditions they found the Genesee Falls here too large an obstacle. Most of the early white New York pioneers moved further west and south to the Ohio River Valley, but in 1788, *Oliver Phelps* saw the potential power source of the Genesee Falls and set about to claim the land surrounding it. He commissioned *Ebenezer Allen* to build and operate one of the mills along the falls in return for a grant of 100 acres of land at the present Four Corners site.

Allen's 100 acres, a dismal swamp infested with snakes and mosquitoes that threatened settlers with "Genesee fever", after changing hands several times was purchased in 1803 by *Colonel William Fitzhuh*, *Major Charles Carroll*, and *Colonel Nathaniel Rochester*, all from Maryland. In 1811 Colonel Rochester offered lots for sale; on May 5, 1812, *Hamlet Scrantom* moved with his family into a house on the site of the Powers Building and became the first permanent settler. *Abelard Reynolds* built a two-story home on the site of the Reynolds Arcade in 1813; in 1815 he opened a tavern; the first newspaper was published in 1816; the next year the village was incorporated as Rochesterville.

By that time the settlement was one of eight along the last 12 miles of the course of the Genesee. Most promising among these was Carthage, which in 1818-19 built a great bridge across the river to attract trade; but after 15 months the bridge buckled and fell. The ultimate supremacy was determined in 1823 by the construction of the Erie Canal through Rochester along what is now Broad Street; and eventually Rochester absorbed all her former rivals.

By drastically reducing transportation costs the canal opened eastern markets to the Genesee farmer. Flour mills multiplied along the river banks, and Rochester became the Flour City. It also became an important center of canal boat construction, and more than half the stock of the transportation companies operating on the canal was owned or controlled in Rochester. The cornerstone of the first Monroe County courthouse was laid in 1821; in 1822 the first sidewalks were voted and the name Rochester was legally adopted; in 1826 the population was 7,669; schools, churches, and bridges were built; and in 1833 Rochester applied for a city charter.

The city's success lasted only a short time before the population exceeded the job opportunities. With the help of some foresighted civic leaders, massive rebuilding and enlarging of railroads and the Erie Canal as well as a sorely-needed new Genesee Aqueduct (the old one collapsed a few months after the new one was completed in 1842), were undertaken. Because of the fertile land left by prehistoric glaciers in the region, the entrepreneurs of the mid-nineteenth century found they could make more of a profit from the ornamental plants and shrubs that grew so well here rather than flour. Many visitors were impressed with the proliferation of tulips and other flowers which set the acreage around Rochester ablaze with color, and a new nickname, "Flower City" stuck. The Ellwanger and Barry nursery established here became well-known throughout the world.

Although many of Rochester's early inhabitants carried the Puritan values of frugality and temperance into town, the newer immigrants such as the Germans brought a sense of recreation and amusement to the city consciousness. Parks were planted; numerous theaters were built, and music and chorales filled the air on many summer nights during the mid-century. But industry continued to play an important role as *Jesse W. Hatch* adapted the new sewing machine to the making of shoes. German Jews especially helped in the advancement of both the shoe and clothing industries, which grew to world-wide renown after the Civil War.

During the same period, 1850-80, Rochester's specialized industries took root. In 1851 *George Taylor* and *David Kendall* began manufacturing thermometers and selling them from house to house. *John Jacob Bausch* opened his optical store in Rochester in 1853 and a few years later began grinding his own lenses. His friend *Henry Lomb* bought a half interest in the business for $60. In 1876 *William Gleason* invented the first commercially successful machine for cutting bevel gear teeth, and his son James later added other inventions and improvements that made possible the development of the Gleason Works.

In 1880, after successful experiments in his mother's kitchen, *George Eastman* began the manufacture of photographic dry plates. His great work was the invention and manufacture of films for cameras. The invention by *Edison* of the moving picture machine resulted in a large demand for Eastman film. In 1888 the first Kodak was put on the market and brought photography within the reach of amateurs.

By the turn of the century, Rochester was known as "Kodak City", and the economy of the city was closely tied with that of the Eastman Kodak Company, although *George Eastman* himself was not often recognized on the street. Nevertheless, Eastman's money enabled many educational, artistic and social institutions to exist.

Physically, the city began to change with its unexpected rise to fame. Horsedrawn streetcars first transported commuters in 1863; electrification began in 1889. More and more long-distance rail lines traversed the city. Real Estate developed into a business and the first labor unions were organized before the turn of the century.

The early twentieth century was dominated by the growing popularity of *George Eastman's* little box cameras, but the nonstop growth of the "teens stopped shortly thereafter". Rochester's shoe industry, already faced with competition from New England and the Midwest, suffered a severe blow in the 1922 strike over the worker's union recognition. For months, most of the plants were idle in the city. When the Great Depression hit, many Rochesterians were not as worried as most people in the nation because of their faith in the city's productivity. However, they soon discovered they could not overlook the growing number of unemployed workers and city work-relief programs had to be instituted. City voters were strong in their support for former *Governor Roosevelt*, and increasingly they looked to Washington to get them back to work. Many public utility improvements were made during this time, and once war was declared, the Defense Department's factory orders put nearly everyone at a job.

After the war, Rochester, like many other American cities, became the hub of an ever-expanding ring of suburbia. The 10 largest suburbs experienced a growth of 100,000 during the 1950's while the city itself lost 16,400 inhabitants. The city continued to be the nation's specialist in the field of photography, and technological advances in textiles and food processing led to new and larger businesses. Enrollments in local schools and colleges increased so much that many new public schools and two new colleges were constructed: Nazareth College (1942) and John Fisher College (1951). The University of Rochester, founded a century before, received large grants from the government in the fields of optics, physics, chemistry, and medicine, transforming the institution into a "think tank" of science.

Today, Rochester is the third largest city in New York state, and continues to stand as a major industrial center. Besides photographic supplies and clothing, the city's workers make office equipment and supplies, thermometers, barometers, steel machinery, horticultural supplies, radios, telephone equipment, furniture, and railroad signals. Close to both Syracuse and Buffalo, as well as the ocean link of Lake Ontario, Rochester is also a shipping port for coal and other cargo.

Rochesterians recreate in seven large parks, and two city-owned bathing beaches. They study at Nazareth College (1942), St.Barnard's College (1893), Colgate-Rochester Divinity School (1928), and the Rochester Institute of Technology (1944), as well as at the University of Rochester (1850).

POINTS OF INTEREST

CITY HALL
Built in 1875, designed by *A.J. Warner* in a variation of Victorian Gothic style.

THE FREDERICK DOUGLASS MONUMENT
Designed by *Sidney W. Edwards*, dedicated 1899 by *Theodore Roosevelt* then Governor of N.Y. Douglas (1807-95) was born a slave in Maryland; his home here served as Underground Railroad Station. He later served as minister to Haiti under *President Harrison*.

THE OLD CHARLOTTE LIGHTHOUSE
Erected in 1822 of sandstone and bricks. Octagonal, ivy-covered, it stands 2,000 ft. from mouth of the Genesee River.

SYRACUSE

Population: 170,292; Area Code 315

Syracuse is not so much a city but a metropolitan area. It spreads out through three counties in central New York state, with the growth spreading north to Liverpool, west to Auburn and east to Chittenango. Perhaps this great central urban area grew out of its favorable geography. the city itself occupies the flatlands at the head of Onondaga Lake, and the new residential sections are nestled in valleys between the Onondaga Hills, as well as in the continuing glacial flatlands and moraines toward Lake Ontario, approximately 30 miles to the north.

Growth has a 400 year history in Syracuse. Since 1570, when the five Indian tribes of the Iroquois confederacy joined here for the first time, the area has been a focal point for activity in both New York state and the American-Canadian northeast. When the five Nations, the Cayuga, Mohawk, Oneida, Seneca and Onondaga Indians, met on the east shore of Onondaga Lake, one of the most sophisticated political organizations of the time was formed, and the site of Syracuse was the main headquarters.

However, what the French soldiers and Jesuits -the first white men to visit the site of Syracuse (1654) - saw, was a swamp. The salt springs were discovered by *Father Simon LeMoyne*, who reported that the Indians believed the water to be infested by a demon, rendering it fetid. The first white settler was *Ephraim Webster*, who came from Oriskany in 1786 and opened a trading station near the mouth of Onondaga Creek. Webster won the friendship of the Indians by his courage and his readiness to adopt their ways, even to marrying their daughters. Stories associated with his life are part of the folklore of the region; it is believed that *James Fenimore Cooper's* character Natty Bumppo owes much to the historical figure of *Ephraim Webster*. Webster's first Indian wife died shortly after their marriage in 1789. According to tradition, he promised his second Indian wife that he would live with her as long as she kept sober. After 20 years, Webster, reacting to the conventionalizing influences of the already large white settlement, began to desire a white wife and set out to make his Indian spouse drunk. For a long time she resisted every attempt but finally succumbed to the camouflage of milk punch. The next morning she left without uttering a word and soon therafter died of grief. Webster married a white woman and raised a white family.

While on a hunting trip in Montgomery County, Webster slept in the barn of *Major Asa Danforth* in Johnstown. Webster's praise of the Onondaga country was so convincing that *Major Danforth*, his wife, his son Asa, Jr., and *Comfort Tyler* emigrated, and on May 22, 1788, erected the "first Christian home" in the county. Asa's brother John followed him and began the manufacture of salt on the lake shore. In 1794 *James Geddes* settled on the west shore of the lake and in 1796 dug the first salt well in the present township of Geddes. The Indians claimed the springs west of the lake, but they adopted Geddes into their tribe and allowed him to continue to make salt. Other settlers came; little clusters of log houses were built around the scattered salt works along the lake shore, and for 70 years this industry formed the nucleus around which the activities of the communities revolved.

Production and packing of salt from the springs surrounding Onondaga Lake began in 1800 and changed the area immeasurably. The state had taken over the salt lands three years before, leasing portions of it on a royalty basis to miners. Small villages dependent upon the salt trade sprang up all along these briny waters, such as Salina and Webster's Landing as well as Geddes. Increasing production caused a need for better transportation of the product, and in 1804, Geddes encouraged *Governor George Clinton* to subsidize a road to the salt springs by selling the state owned land in the area. *Abraham Walton* purchased 250 acres of the reservation from the state for $6,650, and after extensive draining of the swamps and clearing of the marshes, he named the area Syracuse, after the ancient Greek city in Sicily. In fact, the landing continued to be known by several names until 1820 when a post office was built and the name Syracuse officially adopted. Saw and gristmills also appeared in the settlement, and across Walton's land, Geddes laid out a 10 mile turnpike which later became the Genesee Turnpike.

From the time of the commercial beginnings of the salt industry, th central New York waterways served as principal means of transportation. But these natural water routes were uncertain, difficult, and limited, and portages were slow and expensive. Syracuse salt manufacturers, especially *Joshua Forman* and *James Geddes*, were early propagandists on behalf of the Erie Canal project. With the lower freight rates on the canal, the production of salt increased rapidly, reaching a high point of 8,000,000 bushels annually during the Civil War period. Syracuse and Salina, situated on the canal halfway between Albany and Buffalo, and at the junction with the Oswego Canal opened in 1838, became important canal ports.

At the town grew, so did the means of transportation. *John Wilkinson*, postmaster, banker, and assemblyman at various points in his Syracuse career, supported the construction of railroad lines from the city beginning in 1838. The Syracuse and Binghamton Railroad opened in 1854, bringing coal up from Pennsylvania to be used as fuel in salt refining. This also allowed the last great boom in Syracuse's salt industry; during the Civil War, the demand peaked, only to decline rapidly with the introduction of rock salt and the discovery of more profitable uses of the land around Onondaga Lake. The presence of gypsum, limestone, ready money, and a large labor supply all combined to attract more varied industries. The acres once devoted to salt mines were now more valuable as factory sites and the old industry was forced out.

By 1880 Syracuse had several small foundries, machine shops, and factories producing agricultural implements, boots and shoes, furniture, saddlery, hardware, and silverware. The Irish, who came in large numbers to dig the canal and lay the railroads, remained to man the new factories. The Germans came between 1825 and 1850 and founded several of the industries that made Syracuse noteworthy in the nineteenth century. One group settled in the heart of the salt reservation, at the present village of Liverpool, and developed the willowware industry, which enjoyed wide fame for 50 years. In 1855, *Anthony Will*, a carpenter who had served his apprenticeship in Bavaria, melted wax over the family cook stove and started the candle industry in Syracuse.

John D. Gray moved his shoe factory from Little Falls to Syracuse in 1866. The pottery industry, which dug some of its clay near east Syracuse, was firmly organized in 1871. In the same year *William Sweet* started the first steel mill in the city. *Harry Wiard*, descendant of *Thomas Wiard*, invented the chilling process in plow manufacture, and in 1876 production of the improved plow was begun by the Syracuse Chilled Plow Company.

In 1887 the Smith-Premier, the first typewriter to bear the Smith name, was manufactured in *Lyman C. Smith's* gun factory on South Clinton Street. *Alexander T. Brown*, an employee, invented the machine, and *Wilbert Smith*, brother of Lyman, financed the construction of the model. Today the manufacture of typewriters ranks high among the industries of Syracuse.

H.H.Franklin opened a die-casting shop in 1894. In 1898 *John Wilkinson*, grandson of the first postmaster of Syracuse, was perfecting an automobile with an air-cooled motor. the facilities of the Franklin foundry were put at his disposal, and in 1902 the first Franklin stock car was turned out. As the automobile industry developed, Syracuse turned to the manufacture of gears and other parts requiring specialized labor skill.

As the city's industry developed, so did a need for cultural and educational institutions. The first public schools were erected; parks and hospitals were open to the public, and Syracuse University opened its doors to students in 1870. In the early twentieth century, civic facilities such as schools for the handicapped and adult education were initiated.

Although some of the wealthiest of Syracuse's families can trace their fortunes to the city's early salt industry, today's

Syracuse

economics depend upon a much wider base which originated at the turn of the century. The principal industries today are machinery, metal products, paper, and tableware.

In the field of arts, the College of Fine Arts of Syracuse University, the Syracuse Museum of Fine Arts, and the Everson Museum exert definite influence. A new Civic Center is growing into the focal point for art, however, with its concert theater (home of the Syracuse Symphony Orchestra), and stuido theater, where the Syracuse Ballet, and a number of musical and theatrical groups stage their works. The Syracuse Stage and Salt City Playhouse are two other theater groups with their own facilities.

However, much of Syracuse's character is evident in the surrounding communities and countryside, and because of that, local government tends to focus more on county or metropolitan issues. Over 40 other colleges and universities serve the area besides the city university, and the boating, camping, swimming and fishing facilities of nearby Onondaga Lake are well used by city residents. Eight state parks as well as the Adirondack Mountains are also within easy reach of the "Salt City."

POINTS OF INTEREST

VANDERBILT SQUARE
Named for *Commodore Cornelius Vanderbilt* ; for many years city life revolved around this site.

SYRACUSE PUBLIC LIBRARY
Built in 1902; designed by *James A. Randall* ; limestone, granite and brick in Baroque Revival style.

STATUE OF COLUMBUS
Centered in St. Mary's Circle, donated by Syracuse Italian societies (1934); *Lorenzo Baldi* , sculptor.

MUSEUM OF FINE ARTS
Organizedt..qt9m.TZY *Dr. George F. Comfort* ; first U.S. museum with permanent collection of American artists.

THE REPUBLICAN TREE
Historic elm under which met *Vivus W. Smith, Horace Greeley, Thurlow Weed* , and *William Seward* to form the Republican Party.

THORNDEN PARK
Considered most beautiful in the city with rose garden featuring 7,000 plants in 150 varieties.

YONKERS

Population: 194,601; Area Code: 914; Elev. 30

Yonkers plays the dual role of residential suburb of New York City commuters and industrial center for a wide variety of products. Lying along the east bank of the Hudson to the north of the Bronx, Yonkers is the largest city in Westchester County and the fifth largest city in the state.

Yonkers workers are famous for producing elevators and escalators as well as liquid sugar. Other products are clothing, plastics, drugs, metal products, aerosol valves and electrical equipment. It is connected to Manhattan by the northern terminus of the New York subway system, but many residents in this maze of single family homes remain in Yonkers for work.

An Indian village - Nappeckamack - stood on the site of Yonkers, which was part of the Kekeskick Purchase (1639) made by the Dutch West India Company from the Indians. The city site was included in a grant of land made in 1646 by the company to *Adriaen Cornelissen Van der Donck*, the first lawyer and the first historian of New Netherland. By reason of his wealth and social position Van der Donck enjoyed the courtesy title of "jonker," the Dutch equivalent of "his young lordship," from which was derived the name of the city.

Van der Donck's colony, called Colendonck, was broken up into smaller holdings shortly after the British took possession in 1664. In the 20 years after 1672, *Frederick Philipse*, merchant trader and member of the Provincial Council, by a series of purchases acquired a tract of land extending along the east bank of the Hudson from Spuyten Duyvil Creek on the south to the Croton River on the north and eastward to the Bronx River. In 1693, by Royal charter, this domain became the Manor of Philipsburgh and its proprietor the lord of the manor. He erected the original Manor Hall, established mills, rented land to tenants, and soon had a flourishing colony, important in the eighteenth century for its iron mines. His great-grandson, the third and last lord of the manor, supported the Tory side in the Revolution, and the estate was confiscated in 1779.

In the early years of the nineteenth century, Yonkers was a village inhabited mainly by farmers; the land was well watered, the growing metropolis to the south provided a market, and transportation by boat was cheap. Development was accelerated by the opening of the Hudson River Railroad in 1849. In 1855 the village was incorporated with a population of 7,554. With the passing of the turnpike era, stagecoaches and taverns disappeared.

Cheap transportation and the water power of the Nepperhan River attracted industries, such as *Elisha G. Otis's* elevator works in 1854, *David Saunders's* machine shop in 1857, and *Alexander Smith's* carpet mill in 1865.

In the second half of the nineteenth century, Yonkers enjoyed a national reputation for the products of its looms, spindles, and machine shops. New industries were added and attracted Irish, English, Scottish, and German immirgrants, later to be followed by Poles, Hungarians, Italians, Americans, and Russians. The city was chartered in 1872. In 1892 several dams, which at one time crossed the Nepperhan at seven levels, were torn out, industry turned to electricity for power, and the river, reduced to trickle, disappeared beneath highways and buildings. Water transportation steadily decreased until it is no longer a factor; and the Hudson River docks, which once bustled with the traffic of sea-going craft, are practically deserted.

During World War II the submarine pipeline used to transport gasoline on D-Day was manufactured in Yonkers. The Alaskan Distant Early Warning system (DEW) was also made here.

Today industry is served by several major highways, the New York Central Railroad, and ocean-going vessels of the Hudson River. Sarah Lawrence College for women is here as is St. Josephs's Seminary. Yonkers is also famous for its golf facilities and the Yonkers Raceway, a harness racing track.

The rolling hills and forests of the Adirondacks.

Mohawk Valley, where the New York State Barge Canal runs alongside the Thomas E. Dewey Thruway.

A DICTIONARY OF PLACES

--New York

*It is our intention in this section to list every **place** in the state. These places include political and administrative units, civil divisions, physical and cultural features. Since this is a totally new editorial creation without prior model to follow and with the necessity to meet a deadline, it must be expected that there will be minor omissions. By the time this first edition is circulated, our editors will have already started updatings for the next edition. All populations are taken from either the preliminary or final counts of the 1980 Census. We believe this dictionary of places provides the basis for what will be a continuously evolving guide to all the 'places' in New York.*

•**ACCORD**, Village; Ulster County; Pop. 500; Area Code 518; Zip Code 12404; Elev. 250'; SE New York; 15 m. SW of Kingston.

•**ACRA**, Village; Greene County; Pop. 400; Area Code 518; Zip Code 12405; Elev. 668'; E. N.Y.; is surrounded by apple orchards. Local cider is distilled to potent Catskill applejack. In the last years of the prohibition era, *Jack (Legs) Diamond* moved his gang headquarters here. *Thurlow Weed* (1797-1882) was born in a log cabin east of the village.

•**ADAMS**, Village and Town; Jefferson County; Pop. 1,699 and 4,368; Area Code 314; Zip Code 13605; Elev. 600'; N N.Y. 15 m. S of Watertown just E of Interstate 81; is where *Charles Grandison Finney* in 1823 claims the Lord appeared before him and gave him a "mighty baptism of the holy spirit." Later in 1841, Mormons led by *Prophet Joseph Smith* arrived here in covered wagons and started a drive for converts which caused bitter dissension, often splitting families. A year later some farmers sold their holdings and moved to Ohio with *Prophet Smith* .

•**ADDISON**, Town and Village; Steuben County; Pop. 2,751 and 2,053; Area Code 607; Zip Code 14801; on the Canisteo River in S New York on Hwy. 15.

•**ADIRONDACK MOUNTAINS**, Mountain Range; in several counties but mainly in Clinton, Essex, Hamilton and Franklin Counties in northeastern New York. The mountains supply the source of the Hudson and AuSable Rivers via lakes named Long, Racquette, Placid, Saranac and Tupper. Mount Marcy is the highest peak at 5,344 feet. The Forest Preserve encompasses five million acres for public use such as campsites and other recreational facilities. In 1859 *Paul Smith* erected his hotel on St. Regis Lake which tempted others to follow catering to the hunters, fishermen and families. See special feature *The Adirondacks* for further information.

•**AFTON**, Village and Town; Chenango County; Pop. 982 and 2,742; Area Code 607; Zip Code 13730; Elev. 974'; S N.Y. on the Susquehanna River 25 miles NE of Binghamton.

The village attempts to preserve the moral fervor of the days when *Joseph Smith*, the Mormon prophet, worked his miracles in the neighborhood.

Smith's early struggles to found the Mormon Church are closely intertwined with this countryside. West of Afton, in 1827, he dug up one of the plates which later became a part of the Book of Mormon. In nearby Colesville, Smith worked the first miracle of his faith - the casting out of the devil. *Knewell Knight*, who attended Smith's meeting but refused to pray, was stricken. Smith's own report described Knight's condition: "His visage and limbs were distorted and twisted in every shape and appearance possible to imagine; and finally he was caught up off the floor, and tossed about most fearfully." Smith commanded the devil to leave, and in the prophet's own words, Knight's "countenance became natural, his distortions of the body ceased, and almost immediately the spirit of the Lord descended upon him. So soon as consciousnes returned, his bodily weakness was such that we were obliged to lay him upon a bed!"

News of the miracle spread, shocking the community out of its rural complacency; Smith was arrested, charged with using his "priestly powers on credulous men to get their property away from them." After spending the night in Bainbridge jail, he was tried and freed. At the trial Knight said that he was sure the devil had seized him but refused to tell what the devil looked like "because it was a spiritual sight."

•**AKRON**, Village; Erie County; Pop. 2,970; Area Code 716; Zip Code 14001; NW N.Y. on State 93, 15 m. E of Buffalo in W N.Y.

•**ALABAMA**, Town; Genessee County; Pop. 1,923; Area Code 716; Zip Code 14003; 35 m. W of Buffalo on State 63 in NW N.Y.

•**ALBANY**, See major cities article.

•**ALBANY COUNTY**, E N.Y.; 526 sq. miles; Pop. 285,770; Seat - Albany; Est. November 1, 1683; Named after the *Duke of York* and Albany, *James II*, King of England, Scotland and Ireland.

•**ALBION**, Village and Town; Seat of Orleans County; Pop. 4,898 and 6,425; Area Code 716; Zip Code 14411; NW N.Y. at the junction of State 98 and 31 60 m. NE of Buffalo.

•**ALDEN**, Village and Town; Erie County; Pop. 2,490 and 10,101; Area Code 716; Zip Code 14004; 20 m. NE of Buffalo in NW N.Y.; is a summer resort, known for its paper products. Discovered in 1869, black waters used for baths are said to be four times stronger than the waters of Aix-les-Bains, France. Patients still come from many lands for treatments in the private sanatoriums.

•**ALEXANDER**, Village and Town; Genesee County; Pop. 483 and 2,639; Area Code 716; Zip Code 14005; Elev. 940'; NW N.Y. 30 m. E of Buffalo at the junction of State 98.

•**ALEXANDRIA BAY**, Village; Jefferson County; Pop. 1,265; Area Code 315; Zip Code 13607; N N.Y.; resort center and near the Thousand Islands in the St. Lawrence River.

•**ALFRED**, Village and Town; Allegany County; Pop. 4,957 and 6,193; Area Code 716; Zip Code 14802; Elev. 1,760'; 10 m. SW of Hornell in SW N.Y.

•**ALLEGANY**, Village and Town; Cattaragus County; Pop. 2,078 and 8,560; Area Code 716; Zip Code 14706; Elev. 1,425'; on the Allegany River in SE N.Y. 5 m. W of Olean; is the home of St. Bonaventure College and Seminary, a Franciscan institution chartered in 1875.

•**ALLEGANY COUNTY**, SW N.Y.; 1,047 sq. miles; Pop. 51,646; Seat - Belmont; Est. April 7, 1806; Named for the Allegewi Indian tribe.

•**ALLEGANY RESERVATION**, Cattaraugus County; Pop. 3,497; Seneca Nation of Indians; Tribal Headquarters: Saylor Building, Irving, New York 14081; Total area 30,189.40 acres.
   All land is jointly owned by the Seneca Nation. The 1794 Pickering Treaty established the boundaries of the Seneca Nation of which the Allegany Reservation is a part. As agreed in the treaty, the State continues to pay the tribe an annual payment of cloth and a small amount of cash. The reservation land is owned by the Seneca Nation and may not be sold without consent of the United States. By custom, the Seneca Nation grants assignments

or surface rights to individual members of the tribe. Nearly 10,000 acres, or 32 percent of the reservation, are leased on a 99-year basis to the villages of Salamanca, Kill Buck, Vandalia, and Carrollton. These leases will expire in 1991. Salamanca leases a total of 3,774 acres. An estimated 2,000 acres have been taken from the reservation for rights-of-way for utilities, highways, and railroads. Approximately 10,500 acres were taken on permanent easement for the Dinzua Dam and Reservoir built for flood-control purposes. Presidents of the Allegany Reservation are members of the Seneca Nation. This reservation, along with the Cattaraugus and Oil Springs Reservations, is jointly owned by the Seneca Nation. The Seneca Nation's headquarters alternate between the Allegany and Cattaraugus Reservations every 2 years. Although the Allegany and Cattaraugas are shown as state reservations, the federal government renders limited services to the Seneca Nation under the provision of Public Law 88-533, 88th Congress, August 31, 1964.

The Iroquois tribes of central, northern and western New York were members of the Six Nations of the Iroquois League, which was founded by the leaders *Dekanawida*, the Peace Maker, and *Hiawatha*. The league was originally formed by five tribes, the related Tuscarora not joining until 1716 when they moved to the area from the Carolinas. Although formed originally for mutual defense, the league became a powerful Indian empire, the force behind much of the intertribal pressures in the West and Midwest. The league evolved into a federated government and was an important model for the crafters of the American Constitution. The league's decline after two centuries of prominence was largely the result of involvement in the disputes between the entering European powers and their participation in the Revolutionary War. Most of the members of the league supported the British as they had in the French and Indian Wars. Their alliance gave Britain the necessary advantage over France, but proved fatal to the league's negotiating base following the victory of the Colonies. The State of New York has responsibility for Indian education, health, welfare, and legal protection.

•**ALLEGHENY RIVER**, River; Cattaraugus County; Originates in Pennsylvania and is located in SW N.Y. The Allegheny River is 325 miles in length.

•**ALMA**, Town; Allegany County; Pop. 925; Area Code 716; Zip Code 14708; SW N.Y. just north of the Pennsylvania border.

•**ALMOND**, Village and Town; Allegany County; Pop. 564 and 1,665; Area Code 716; Zip Code 14804; on the border of the county 7 m. W of Hornell on State 21 in S N.Y.

•**ALTMAR**, Village; Oswego County; Pop. 345; Area Code 315; Zip Code 13302; on the Salmon River in N central N.Y. just off State 13 nine miles east of Pulaski and Lake Ontario.

•**ALTAMONT**, Village; Albany County; Pop. 1,277; Area Code 518; Zip Code 12009; 8 m. W of Albany in E N.Y. at the junctions of State 397 and 156.

•**ALTON**, included in Sodus; Wayne County; Pop. est. 450; Area Code 315; Zip Code 14413; Elev. 380'; N N.Y. 50 m. e of Rochester on Hwy. 104. The area has varied farming and food packaging as agriculture and industry.

•**ALTONA**, Town; Clinton County; Pop. 2,082; Area Code 518; Zip Code 12910; in the northern corner of the state.

•**AMAGANSETT**, Included in East Hampton; Suffolk County; Pop. 1,800; Area Code 516; Zip Code 11930; SE N.Y.; is a fishing village. It has no harbor, but the tradition of seafaring dates from its settlement in 1650 and from the inhabitants who, led by Indians, first attacked the basking whales beyond the surf. As late as 1907 the old cry "whale off" rang in Gansett streets, and a crew of veterans went out with harpoon and lance to bring in a right whale, the bones of which now rest in the American Museum of Natural History, New York City.

•**AMENIA**, Town; Dutchess County; Pop. 6,266; Area Code 914; Zip Code 12510; Elev. 573'; E N.Y. at the junctions Hwy. 82 and State 343, just miles from the Connecticut state line. It is the home of *Lewis Mumford*, critic and author. His *Herman Melville* did much to revive interest in the neglected author of *Moby Dick* ; later he published penetrating studies of cultural development, including *Technics and Civilization* and *The Culture of Cities.* J.E. Spingarn (1875-1939), one of the leaders in the "new literary criticism" and author of several books on literature, spent his later years here.

•**AMES**, Village; Montgomery County; Pop. 224; Area Code 518; Zip Code 13317; N central N.Y. on State 10, NW of Albany.

•**AMHERST**, Town; Erie County; Pop. est. 1,300; Area Code 716; Zip Code 14226; W N.Y.

•**AMITYVILLE**, Village; Suffolk County; Pop. 9,085; Area Code 914; Zip Code 11701; on Great South Bay on the south shore of Long Island in SE N.Y.; a quiet village with a large commuting population, is on the dividing line of Nassau and Suffolk Counties. Several houses in this community are more than a century old.

Also, there is a "haunted house" of book and movie fame located here.

•**AMSTERDAM**, City; Montgomery County; Pop. 21,838; Area Code 518; Zip Code 12010; Elev. 289'; 28 miles NW of Albany in N N.Y.; straddles the Mohawk River at the mouth of Chuctanunda (Indian, "stony, or stone house") Creek, which has supplied water power to local industries since the first settlement by *Albert Veeder*, who came from Schenectady in 1783. It was called Veedersburg for a time.

The village of Amsterdam, so named in 1804, began to grow in size and industrial importance after the Erie Canal was opened in 1825 and the Utica & Schenectady Railroad was constructed through it in 1836. The local carpet industry traces its beginnings to 1838, when *William E. Greene* established the ancestor of the present Bigelow Sanford mills.

•**ANCRAM**, Town; Columbia County; Pop. 1,326; Area Code 518; Zip Code 12502; E N.Y. near the Massachusetts border; home of the principal iron mine of Livingston Iron Mines.

•**ANDES**, Village and Town; Delaware County; Pop. 373 and 1,316; Area Code 518; Zip Code 13731; Elev. 1,600'; Central N.Y. 7 m. NW of the Catskill Mts. on State 28; was the scene of the 1845 anti-rent war in Delaware County. When undersheriff *Caman N. Steele* attempted to evict a farmer for unpaid taxes, his neighbors, dressed as "Indians", with leather capes over their heads, cowhorns on their caps, and cowtails tied on behind, came to his aid, and in the struggle the sheriff was shot.

•**ANDOVER**, Village and Town; Allegany County; Pop. 1,119 and 1,949; Area Code 716; Zip Code 14806; S N.Y. on the western county border near the junction of State 21 and Hwy. 417.

•**ANGELICA**, Village and Town; Allegany County; Pop. 981 and 1,436; Area Code 716; Zip Code 14709; S N.Y. in the central section of the county just W of Hwy. 17.

•**ANGOLA**, Village; Erie County; Pop. 2,295; Area Code 716; Zip Code 14006; Western coast of N.Y., approx. 22 m. S of Buffalo just off Interstate 91.

•**ANTWERP**, Village and Town; Jefferson County; Pop. 747 and 1,841; Area Code 315; Zip Code 13608; N N.Y. on Hwy. 11 at State 283.

•**ARCADE**, Village and Town; Wyoming County; Pop. 2,060 and 3,719; Area Code 716; Zip Code 14009; 33 m. SE of Buffalo in western N.Y; It is mainly a dairy center.

Dictionary of Places 235

•**ARDEN**, Orange County; Area Code 914; Zip Code 10910; Elev. 520'; SE N.Y. at the west entrance Bear Mtn. State Park on Hwy. 17.

•**ARDSLEY**, Village; Westchester County; Pop. 4,162; Area Code 914; Zip Code 10502; SE N.Y. SW of White Plains and N of Yonkers; is 21 m. N of New York City. The village is mainly residential.

•**ARGYLE**, Village and Town; Washington County; Pop. 322 and 2,856; Area Code 518; Zip Code 12809; N N.Y. at the junction of States 40 and 197.

•**ARKPORT**, Village; Steuben County; Pop. 813; Area Code 607; Zip Code 14807; S N.Y. on State 36; 6 m. N of Hornell and Interstate 17.

•**ASHLAND**, Town; Greene County; Pop. 739; Area Code 518; Zip Code 12407; E N.Y. at the northern foothills of the Catskill Mountains, 30 m. W of Catskill on Hwy. 23.

•**ATHENS**, Village and Town; Greene County; Pop. 1,728 and 3,411; Area Code 518; Zip Code 12015; on the Hudson River across from Hudson on State 385; was settled in 1686 by *Jan Van Loon*, a Hollander. The village was the third in the state to incorporate in 1805.

The ice-harvesting industry once flourished here, as at other points along the river, ice cakes were cut and stored in huge icehouses along the water front and shipped to New York City during the summer. But mechanical refrigeration killed this chilly occupation and for a time the great icehouses stood empty. Then it was discovered that these windowless, well-insulated structures made ideal places for the mass production of mushrooms.

New Englanders who settled the outskirts between 1790 and 1840 called the village Esperanza, after an unrealized dream of the *Livingstons - Edward, Brockholst, and John* - who lived across the river. Envious of the Nantucketers who were making Hudson a prosperous town, they planned a rival city on the west side of the river, envisioning it as a great market for western produce, and even speculating that it might become the terminus of a canal across the state to the Great Lakes.

•**ATLANTIC BEACH**, Village; Nassau County; Pop. 1,773; Area Code 516; Zip Code 11509; at the western point of Long Beach on western Long Island in SE N.Y.

•**ATTICA**, Village and Town; Wyoming County; Pop. 2,658 and 5,690; Area Code 716; Zip Code 14011; NW N.Y. on State 98; here at the State Prison there was a riot in the 1970s.

•**AUBURN**, City; Seat of Cayuga County; Pop. 32,442; Area Code 315; Zip Code 13021; on the end of Lake Owasco, 25 miles southwest of Syracrause in central New York; is a manufacturing city. Auburn was first settled in 1793. In 1805 became the county seat and a city in 1848.

In 1793 *Colonel John Hardenbergh*, surveyor and Revolutionary veteran, built the first cabin on the present site of Auburn and a year later erected the first gristmill on the Owasco Outlet. At a meeting in 1805 the present name was taken from *Goldsmith's The Deserted Village*, In 1810 *Governor DeWitt Clinton* reported that Auburn had 90 dwellings, 17 mills along the Outlet, and an incorporated library of 200 volumes. The opening of the state prison in 1817 and of the theological seminary four years later stimulated growth. In the 1840's Auburn was a rallying point for politicians. With *William H. Seward* and other national figures as adopted sons, it had hopes of becoming the state capitol; Capitol Street is a reminder of that unrealized ambition.

Transportation facilities, abundant water power, and the practice, which was not abolished until 1882, of hiring out prison labor at ridiculously low rates, attracted industry. In 1818 *Joseph Wadsworth* transferred his scythe factory from Massachusetts to Auburn; in 1852 *Carhart & Nye* began the manufacture of carpets; in 1858 *David Munson Osborne*, a native son, founded the D.M. Osborne Company, which was absorbed in 1903 by the International Harvester Company. After 120 years existence, the Auburn Theological Seminary, chartered by the Presbyterian General Assembly in 1819, was merged with the Union Theological Seminary, New York City.

•**AURORA**, Village; Cayuga County; Pop. 454; Area Code 315; Zip Code 13026; Elev. 436'; on Cayuga Lake, 12 m. SW of Auburn in central N.Y.; Settled in 1789; was named by *General Benjamin Ledyard*, who was impressed with the splendor of the site revealed in the first rays of the morning sun. The impressive campus of Wells College rises from the lake shore. *Henry Wells*, co-founder of the Wells-Fargo Express Company, established this college for women in 1868.

•**AUSTERLITZ**, Town; Columbia County; Pop. 12,017; Area Code 518; Zip Code 12017; Elev. 1,210'; on the eastern border of N.Y. on State 22; was settled about 1750 by *Judah Laurence* and others from Connecticut and Massachusetts. *Martin Van Buren*, an ardent admirer of *Napoleon*, was incensed when a town in Seneca County was named Waterloo and moved to name this town Austerlitz.

•**AVA**, Town; Oneida County; Pop. 2,382; Area Code 315; Zip

Code 13301; in north central N.Y. 15 m. directly north of Rome on State 26.

•AVOCA, Village and Town; Steuben County; Pop. 1,153 and 2,240; Area Code 607; Zip Code 14809; Elev. 1,191'; SW N.Y. on state 415 just west of junction of Interstate 390 and Hwy. 17 at exit 36.

•AVON, Village and Town; Livingston County; Pop. 3,009 and 6,185; Area Code 716; Zip Code 14414; on the Genesee River, in western N.Y. 18 miles S of Rochester on Hwy. 20; is a farming and canning center with a considerable milk industry. The region is a horse-breeding area, and the annual Avon Horse Show, conducted by the Genesee Valley Breeders Association, draws a large gallery of spectators.

•BABYLON, Village; Suffolk County; Pop. 12,380; Area Code 516; Zip Code 117 + zone; on the S shore of Long Island on the Great South Bay in SE N.Y. on State 27A.

•BAINBRIDGE, Village and Town; Chenango County; Pop. 1,597 and 3,343; Area Code 607; Zip Code 13733; Elev. 1,000'; on the Susquehanna River in S N.Y. at the junction of State 7 and 206, 15 m. NE of Binghamton just off Interstate 88.

•BAKERS MILL, Unicorporated; Warren County; Area Code 518; Zip Code 12811; Elev. 1,580'; in the Adirondack Mountains in NE N.Y. on State 8; in the shadow of Eleventh Mountain (3,303 alt.).
Samuel M. Coplon, self-appointed Santa Claus of the Adirondacks (1936) had his headquarters here. In 25 years, he distributed more than 20,000 gifts to poor mountain children.

•BALDWINSVILLE, Village; Onondaga County; Pop. 6,434; Area Code 315; Zip Code 13027; Elev. 423'; on the Seneca River and the Barge Canal 14 m. NW of Syracruse.
Revolutionary veterans were the first settlers but died off rapidly because of the prevalent malaria in this swampy area. The malaria was brought under control when the lowlands around the River were flooded in. Close by are natural gas deposits among the lumber industry.

•BALLSTON, Town; Saratoga County; Pop. 7,707; Area Code 518; Zip Code 12019; located in E N.Y.

•BALLSTON SPA, Village; Seat of Saratoga County; Pop. 4,712; Area Code 518; Zip Code 12020; six miles SW of Saratoga Springs in E N.Y. on Hwy 50. The village was founded in 1787. Today the main attractions are the mineral springs and resort area.

Before the Civil War, Ballston Spa outranked Saratoga Springs as a resort area until Saratoga Springs built a race track and casinos.

•**BANGOR**, Town; Franklin County; Pop. 1,966; Area Code 518; Zip Code 12966; in NE N.Y. on State 118, six m. SW of Malone just N of the Adirondack Park.

•**BARKER**, Village; Niagara County; Pop. 541; Area Code 716; Zip Code 14012; in NW N.Y.

•**BARNEVELD**, Village; Oneida County; Pop. 398; Area Code 315; Zip Code 13304; in central N.Y. at the junction of State 65 and Hwy. 1228; 15 m. NE of Rome and 13 m. N of Utica.

•**BARTON**, Town; Tioga County; Pop. 8,696; Area Code 607; Zip Code 13734; in S central N.Y. on State 17C just N of the Pennsylvania border.

•**BATAVIA**, City; Seat of Genesee County; Pop. 16,667; Area Code 716; Zip Code 14020; elev. 890'; in NW N.Y. just S of Interstate 90; 35 m. SW of Rochester and 30 m. W of Buffalo. Batavia was first settled in 1801 and incorporated in 1904.

Batavia is noteworthy as the capital of the Holland Land Purchase. In 1801 *Joseph Ellicott*, surveyor and subagent for the company, built a land office at the junction of the old Genesee Road and Tonawanda Creek, where two great Indian trails crossed, and where four state highways meet today. Ellicott proposed naming the place Bustia or Bustiville, for *Paul Busti*, the company's general agent; but the latter objected to the ferocious sound of the word and proposed Batavia, the name of the Dutch republic to which the proprietors belonged.

Despite the rapid growth of neighboring Rochester and Buffalo, Batavia prospered, first as a farm trade center, later, with the development of railroads, as an industrial city and distribution point.

The Wiard Plow Plant, Swan St. between the New York Central and Erie Railroads, manufactures plows, rakes, weeders, harrows, wheelbarrows, lawn mowers, and other farm machinery. The company was organized in 1804 by *Thomas Wiard* in East Avon; his first invention, the "bull plow", a wooden plow with wrought-iron points, was made by hand for pioneer farmers in western New York. The factory was moved to Batavia in 1876.

The Richmond Mansion (now the Children's Home), E. Main St., a large, gray-painted brick building by *Dean Richmond* (1804-66), bluff, forceful native of Vermont, grain elevator operator, banker, politician, and president of the New York Central Railroad. In his day the lavish interiors included a

Dictionary of Places   239

dining room famous for its yellow damasked walls and yellow velvet carpets; one of the baths had solid silver fittings. One of Richmond's emoluments as railroad president was to have all trains of the road, even the fastest express, stop at Batavia. According to tradition, Richmond's handwriting was so illegible that a dismissal notice written by him, with only the signature easily legible, was used by the dismissed employee as a free pass on the railroad.

The Cary Mansion, corner of Main and Bank Sts., is a gray-painted post-Colonial brick house built in 1817 by *Trumbull Cary* a Batavia pioneer. The three-bay central block is flanked on each side by wings that are masked by the two-story Ionic-columned porches of the Greek Revival period. The graceful, elliptical-arched doorway exhibits the Scamozzi Ionic caitals favored in the earlier style.

The Genesee County Courthouse, Main St., erected in 1841, is a Greek Revival structure in Lockport limestone which eschews the temple form for a square cupolaed mass, probably reflecting the design of the first frame courthouse, which stood to the east of the present building until it burned in 1918.

The Holland Land Office Museum, W. Main St., erected by *Joseph Ellicott* in 1804, is a simple gray limestone building with a white wooden portico with four Roman Doric columns. Ellicott himself probably designed this graceful Roman Revival structure; its quiet dignity is closely akin in spirit to the Ellicott mansion (Goodrich House) built in Buffalo in 1823. Owned by the Holland Purchase Historical Society, the museum contains among its exhibits period rooms, early farming tools, uniforms, and local records.

The Holland Purchase included practically all of New York State west of the Genesee River, some 3,300,000 acres, sold in 1793 by *Robert Morris* to a group of Dutch capitalists who in turn financed the undertaking by selling shares. In 1797 Morris extinguished the Indian title by the Big Tree Treaty, and the sale was consummated. *Joseph Ellicott* was hired to survey the territory and lay out townships and in 1800 was appointed company agent. He was instrumental in the founding of scores of towns and villages, including Buffalo, but his especial pride was Batavia; "I intend to do all I can for Batavia," he said, "because the Almighty will look out for Buffalo."

The New York State School For The Blind (open 10-12, 2:30-5 daily), corner of State St. and Richmond Ave., comprises a group of victorian buildings set in landscaped grounds. Originating as an asylum under the State Department of Charities, it now is a school of regular academic standing under the State Education Department.

•BATH, Village and Town; Seat of Steuben County; Pop. 6,038 and 12,278; Area Code 607; Zip Code 14810; Elev. 1,104'; in S N.Y.

at the junction of State 54 and 415 just NW of Hwy. 17; is in a rich farming area; is the site of the first clearing in Steuben County made in 1793 by *Colonel Charles Williamson* (1757-1808), agent for the Pulteney Estate. Believing that the settlement and trade of central New York would follow the Susquehanna to Baltimore, Williamson chose the site of Bath on the Cohocton River as the location of the future metropolis that was to be the trading, industrial, and distribution center for the entire region. But he was too energetic to wait for the normal processes of settlement; his plan was to build the city first, which would then attract settlers. He set out to induce wealthy and socially prominent country gentlemen from Virginia and Maryland to buy land for either speculation or development.

•**BAYVILLE**, Village; Nassau County; Pop. 7,019; Area Code 516; Zip Code 11709; on the NW tip of Long Island in SE N.Y.

•**BEACON**, City; Dutchess County; Pop. 12,908; Area Code 914; Zip Code 12508; Elev. 150'; on the Hudson River across from Neaburgh in SE N.Y. just S of Interstate 84 at the foot of Mt. Beacon.

•**BEDFORD**, Town; Westchester County; Pop. 15,085; Area Code 914; Zip Code 10506; in SE N.Y. just W of the Connecticut border; is mainly a residential section.

•**BELFAST**, Town; Allegany County; Pop. 1,488; Area Code 716; Zip Code 14711; in S N.Y. on State 19.

•**BELLEROSE**, Village; Queens County; Pop. 1,186; Area Code 212; Zip Code 114 + zone; at the W end of Long Island in SE N.Y.

•**BELLPORT**, Village; Suffolk County; Pop. 2,815; Area Code 516; Zip Code 11713; on the S shore of Long Island on Great South Bay in SE N.Y. 13 m. SE of Islip.

•**BELMONT**, Village; Seat of Allegany County; Pop. 1,024; Area Code 716; Zip Code 14813; in SW N.Y., 3 m. off Hwy. 17. The village is named after *August P. Belmont*, financier and sportsman.

•**BEMUS POINT**, Village; Chautaugua County; Pop. 444; Area Code 716; Zip Code 14712.

•**BERGEN**, Village; Genesee County; Pop. 977; Area Code 716; Zip Code 14416; Elev. 600'; in NW N.Y. on State 19, 19 m. SW of Rochester.

•**BERKSHIRE**, Town; Tioga County; Pop. 1,318; Area Code 607;

Dictionary of Places 241

Zip Code 13736; in S central N.Y. on State 38, approx. 25 m. NW of Binghamton.

•BERLIN, Town; Rensselaer County; Pop. 1,703; Area Code 518; Zip Code 12022; on the E border on State 22, 28 m. E of Troy.

•BERNE, Town; Albany County; Pop. 2,515; Area Code 518; Zip Code 12023; in E N.Y. at the junction of State 156 and 443, 19 m. due W of Albany; was settled in 1750; and named for the native Swiss city of *Jacob Weidman*, leader of a party of Palatine immigrants who made the first settlement.

•BETHEL, Town; Sullivan County; Pop. 3,358; Area Code 914; Zip Code 12720; in SE N.Y. 7 m. W of Monticello.

•BINGHAMTON, City; Broome County seat; Pop. 55,745; Area Code 607; Zip Code 13901; Elev. 845'; S central New York; 150 m. NW of New York City; Near Catskills State Park on the Susquehanna River.

Appalachian uplands and the Susquehanna River provide the setting for Binghamton, a mid-sized industrial city near the Pennsylvania border. Once the site of three Indian villages, this ever widening metropolitan area began its story as a mill-town. Today it is the seat of 200,000 population Broome County and the leader of the "Triple Cities", which include Endicott and Johnson City. Thousands of workers here produce business machines, computers, shoes, aviation training and wiring, while their more rural counterparts from the surrounding countryside give the cities dairy goods, poultry, lumber, and wood pulp.

Little is known of the Binghamton area before the Revolution. The site was ceded to the whites by treaty at Fort Herkimer in 1785, and was sold in 1786 to *William Bingham*, a Philadelphia merchant. *Joseph Leonard*, first permanent settler, built his log cabin nearby in 1787, and was soon joined by other pioneers, who called the new settlement Chenango. The following year *Joshua Whitney* learned that a bridge was to be built across the Chenango River near its confluence with the Susquehanna. At his suggestion a "chopping bee" was organized, and land near the designated bridge site was cleared of timber. Several buildings were moved from the old village and the new settlement was called Chenango Point. In 1816 the first stagecoaches began weekly trips from Newburgh and Owego. Later the name was changed to Binghamton in honor of *Binham*, who made liberal donations of land to the settlement. In 1834 Binghamton was incorporated as a village.

Completion of the Chenango Canal in 1837, establishing an important link between the coal regions of Pennsylvania and the Erie Canal at Utica, began an era of progress in transportation and industrial development. During this period the manufacture of photographic apparatus was begun by the E.&H.T. Anthony Company, progenitor of the Agfa-Ansco Corporation. In 1848 the Erie Railroad brought direct connection with New York and shortly thereafter with Buffalo and the Great Lakes. In 1851 the Delaware, Lackawanna & Western Railroad opened the way into Pennsylvania, and was followed by the Delaware & Hudson, which established a direct route to New England.

At the time of its incorporation as a city in 1867, Binghamton had a population of 11,000. Cigar making, its first important participation in manufacture for other than local consumption, was firmly established by 1870 and its rapid growth put the city in second place in the tobacco industry of the country. But the popular shift to cigarette smoking, combined with a cigarmakers' strike in 1890, caused a permanent slump. The manufacture of shoes, modestly begun in 1854 by *Horace N. Lester* and his brother *George*, developed into an industry that caused the founding of Johnson City and Endicott, brought a large-scale immigration of foreign factory workers, and resulted in the building factories, six tanneries, and two rubber mills located in Binghamton, Johnson City, Endicott, and Owego.

Immigrants to Binghamton also provided the labor force which made *Thomas J. Watson's* International Business Machines bloom into international importance. Begun in 1888 as the Bundy Time Recorder Company, IBM grew with Watson's salesmanship in the early years of the twentieth century. Today it is headquartered in Endicott, with several factories in the area and tens of thousands on the employment rolls.

During the last decade the population in Binghamton proper has declined to 1930 levels. Many industries moved in the late 1960s to the outlying suburbs, and urban renewal programs resulted in a replacement of homes by high-rise office buildings.

The boundaries of the Triple Cities end abruptly at the hills. Only a few homes are scattered among the highlands and valleys, and parks, lakes and skiing areas are nearby. The State University of New York at Binghamton (1965) is just outside the city limits, as is Broome Technical Community College. The Robertson Center, built in 1968, houses scientific, historic and artistic displays under the roofs of several museums, an observatory, a theater, several galleries and classrooms. Such divergent fields as opera and golf find supporters i in the community as well. Of particular architectural interest is the Court House, built in 1898, and several preserved nineteenth century homes.

•**BLACK RIVER**, Village; Jefferson County; Pop. 1,385; Area Code 315; Zip Code 13612; in N central N.Y., 5 m. NE of Watertown on Hwy. 3.

•**BLACK RIVER**, River; Herkimer and Jefferson Counties; in N central N.Y. is 120 m. long and flows N and W into Lake Ontario by Watertown.

•**BLASDELL**, Village; Erie County; Pop. 3,290; Area Code 716; Zip Code 14219; in the W shore of N.Y. on Lake Erie, 18 m. S of Buffalo on Hwy. 5.

•**BLOOMINGBURG**, Village; Sullivan County; Pop. 328; Area Code 914; Zip Code 12721; in SE N.Y.

•**BLOOMINGDALE**, Village; Essex County; Pop. 609; Area Code 518; Zip Code 12913; in NE N.Y. in the Adirondack Park at the junction of State 3 and 192, 9 miles NE of Saranac Lake.

•**BLOOMING GROVE**, Town; Orange County; Pop. 12,395; Area Code 914; Zip Code 10914; in SE N.Y.

•**BOLIVAR**, Village and Town; Allegany County; Pop. 1,348 and 2,499; Area Code 716; Zip Code 14715; Elev. 1,609'; in S N.Y. on Hwy. 417, 7 m. N of the Pennsylvania border; inhabited chiefly by workers in the oil fields, was named for *General Simon Bolivar* when the South American patriot was a popular hero.

•**BOMBAY**, Town; Franklin County; Pop. 1,249; Area Code 518; Zip Code 12914; in N N.Y. on State 95, SE of the St. Regis Indian Reservation and 7 m. from the Quebec border.

•**BOONVILLE**, Village and Town; Oneida County; Pop. 2,356 and 4,113; Area Code 315; Zip Code 13309; Elev. 1,121'; in N central N.Y. at the junction of Hwy 12 and State 294, 46, and 120, 23 m. N of Rome. The place for investors from Holland in 1791. Today still engages in the dairy industry. It was here in 1933 where the great milk strike happened. The strike was violent including 400 to 800 farmers.

•**BOSTON**, Town; Erie County; Pop. 7,691; Area Code 716; Zip Code 14025; Elev. 727'; in W N.Y. on Hwy. 219, 12 m. SE of Buffalo; in the decades of handlebar mustaches, derby hats, and gold-headed canes, bare-knuckle fighters would doff their shirts and stage gory battles. The most famous of those encounters was the one between *Yankee Sullivan* and *John Morrissey*. Sullivan, who won, was killed soon afterward.

•**BOVINA CENTER**, Town; Delaware County; Pop. 559; Area Code 518; Zip Code 13740; in S N.Y., 15 m. NW of the Catskill State Park.

•**BRADFORD**, Town; Steuben County; Pop. 722; Area Code 607; Zip Code 14815; in S N.Y.

•**BRANT**, Town; Erie County; Pop. 2,433; Area Code 716; Zip Code 14027; on the W edge of N.Y., just W of Interstate 90, 20 m. S of Buffalo.

•**BRENTWOOD**, Suffolk County; Area Code 511; Zip Code 11717; on central Long Island is an urban community. It was in 1851 the scene of an experiment in communism led by *Joseph Warren* and others. Labor certificates passed for currency, as the group believed that all wealth was created by labor.

•**BREWSTER**, Village; Putnam County; Pop. 1,628; Area Code 914; Zip Code 10509; in SE N.Y.

•**BRIARCLIFF MANOR**, Village; Westchester County; Pop. 7,100; Area Code 914; Zip Code 10510; in SE N.Y., 31 m. from N.Y. City and E of the Hudson River. The village is mainly residential and commute to N.Y. City.

•**BRIDGEWATER**, Village and Town; Oneida County; Pop. 583 and 1,457; Area Code 315; Zip Code 13313; Elev. 1,180'; in central N.Y. at the S border of the county on Hwy. 20 17 m. S of Utica; was first settled in 1790.

From this town have come two important figures in American agriculture. *Dr. Stephen M. Babcock*, born here in 1843, invented in 1890, while professor of agricultural chemistry in the University of Wisconsin, the Babcock milk test for accurately determining the percentage of butter fat in milk and cream. In 1830 *Hiram Hunt* and *Albert Brockway*, local farmers, invented the rotary rake, a machine for gathering hay.

•**BRIGHTON**, Town; Monroe County; Pop. 35,749; Area Code 716; Zip Code 146 + zone; Elev. 470'; Suburb of Rochester.

•**BRIGHTWATERS**, Village; Suffolk County; Pop. 3,290, Area Code 516; Zip Code 11718; on Great South Bay on Long Island, 39 m. E of N.Y. in SE N.Y.

•**BROADALBIN**, Village and Town; Fulton County; Pop. 1,426 and 4,095; Area Code 607; Zip Code 12025; Elev. 820'; settled in 1770; was named by its Scottish population when the post office was established in 1804. The first white settlers came in 1770, but the village developed slowly because of its comparative inaccessibility and the frequent Indian raids.

The Home of novelist *Robert W. Chamber* (1865-1933) is on a large estate.

•**BROCKPORT**, Village; Monroe County; Pop. 9,767; Area Code 716; Zip Code 14420; Elev. 539'; 18 m. W of Rochester in W N.Y.; was the home of *Mary Jane Holmes* (1825-1907), popular post-

Civil War novelist.

•BROCTON, Village; Chautauqua County; Pop. 1,402; Area Code 716; Zip Code 14716; Elev. 740'; celebrates the memory of *Deacon Elijah Fay* by holding a grape harvest festival each Autumn, with pageants, street fairs, and dances. Deacon Fay, born September 9, 1781, began experimenting with grape culture, trying several varieties that failed, but was finally successful with the Isabella and Catawba, and late with the Concord variety, which has since become the favorite of the region.

•BRONX, Borough, Seat of Bronx County; Pop. 1,162,632; Area Code 716; Zip Code 104 + zone; in N part of N.Y. City on the mainland; settled 1641; became county in 1913; is 41 sq. miles and is both residential and industrial.

•BRONX COUNTY, SE N.Y.; 41 sq. miles; Pop. 1,162,632; Seat - Bronx; Est. April 19, 1912; Named after one of the first settlers of the area north of Harlem, *Jonas Bronck*.

•BRONXVILLE, Village; Westchester County; Pop. 6,266; Area Code 914; Zip Code 10708; 17 m. N NE of New York City in SW N.Y.

•BROOKFIELD, Town; Madison County; Pop. 2,015; Area Code 315; Zip Code 10708.

•BROOKHAVEN, Town; Suffolk County; Pop. 364,764; Area Code 516; Zip Code 11719; E of Patchogue, on Long Island in SE N.Y.

•BROOKLYN, Borough; Seat of Kings County; Pop. 2,218,441; Area Code 212; Zip Code 112 + zone; a residential borough located in SW Long Island that forms part of New York City; incorporated city 1834 and Borough in 1898.

The borough is the largest in population and is 71 sq. miles in size. Settled by the Dutch and Walloons in 1636 along the Gowanus and Jamaica Bays. The Battle of Long Island was fought here.

•BROOME COUNTY, S N.Y.; 714 sq. miles; Pop. 213,346; Seat - Binghamton; Est. March 28, 1806; Named after *John Broome*.

•BROWNVILLE, Village and Town; Jefferson County; Pop. 1,101 and 5,123; Area Code 315; Zip Code 13615; N N.Y.

•BRUSHTON, Village; Franklin County; Pop. 576; Area Code 518; Zip Code 12916.

•**BUCHANAN**, Village; Westchester County; Pop. 2,041; Area Code 914; Zip Code 10511; SE N.Y., on Hudson River, 37 m. N of New York City.

•**BURDETT**, Village; Schuyler County; Pop. 410; Area Code 607; Zip Code 14818.

•**BURKE**, Village and Town; Franklin County; Pop. 226 and 1,244; Area Code 518; Zip Code 12917.

•**BYRON**, Town; Genesee County; Pop. 2,246; Area Code 716; Zip Code 14422.

•**CAIRO**, Town; Greene County; Pop. 4,619; Area Code 518; Zip Code 12413; Elev. 340'; Resort town in the Catskills.

•**CALEDONIA**, Village and Town; Livingston Cosunty; Pop. 2,189 and 4,042; Area Code 716; Zip Code 14423.

•**CALLICOON**, Town; Sullivan County; Pop. 2,987; Area Code 914; Zip Code 12723.

•**CAMBRIDGE**, Village and Town; Washington County; Pop. 1,822 and 1,850; Area Code 518; Zip Code 12816; Elev. 500'; E N.Y.

•**CAMDEN**, Village and Town; Oneida County; Pop. 2,643 and 4,908; Area Code 315; Zip Code 13316; 16 m. W NW of Rome in central N.Y.

•**CAMERON**, Town; Steuben County; Pop. 912; Area Code 607; Zip Code 14819.

•**CAMILLUS**, Village and Town; Onondaga County; Pop. 1,300 and 24,320; Area Code 315; Zip Code 13031; 9 m. W of Syracuse in central N.Y.

•**CAMPBELL**, Town; Steuben County; Pop. 3,794; Zip Code 14821.

•**CANAAN**, Town; Columbia County; Pop. 1,663; Area Code 518; Zip Code 12029.

•**CANAJOHARIE**, Village and Town; Montgomery County; Pop. 2,401 and 4,133; Area Code 518; Zip Code 13317; on Mohawk River, 21 m. W of Amsterdam in E N.Y.; settled in 1730.

The name, from the Indian meaning, "the pot that washes itself", refers to a large pothole at the entrance to Canajoharie Gorge, south of the village, where the water boils endlessly; about a mile up the creek is a waterfall which drops 45 feet into

Dictionary of Places 247

the gorge. The village, settled by Dutch and Germans about 1730, was in 1779 the concentration point for *General James Clinton's* army.

•**CANANDAIGUA**, City; Seat of Ontario County; Pop. 10,361; Area Code 315; Zip Code 14424; Elev. 766'; at N end of Canandaigua Lake 26 m. SE of Rochester in W N.Y.; settled in 1789. After purchasing from Massachusetts all of New York State west of Geneva and extinguishing the Indian title to a large part of the tract, *Oliver Phelps* (1749-1809) and *Nathaniel Gorham* appointed *William Walker* as their agent and he opened the first office for land sales in America here. The first party of settlers, led by *General Israel Chapin*, arrived in May, 1789.

The region and its inhabitants have been romanticized by *Carl Carmer* in *Listen for a Lonesome Drum*.

Jesuit missionaries wrote about burning springs with flames on the surface of the water, which they found in the Bristol Hills and which the Seneca Indians worshipped. The explanation is natural gas, which now lights the streets of many villages in the region.

•**CANANDAIGUA LAKE**, Lake; Yates and Ontario Counties; one of the Finger Lakes located in W N.Y. The lake is 15 m. long and 2 m. wide.

•**CANASERAGA**, Village; Allegany County; Pop. 698; Area Code 716; Zip Code 14822.

•**CANASTOTA**, Village; Madison County; Pop. 4,765; Area Code 315; Zip Code 13032; on N.Y. State Barge Canal 22 m. E of Syracuse in central N.Y.

•**CANDOR**, Village and Town; Tioga County; Pop. 911 and 4,909; Area Code 607; Zip Code 13743; S N.Y.

•**CANEADEA**, Town; Allegany County; Pop. 2,426; Area Code 716; Zip Code 14717; SW N.Y.; name is Indian for "where heaven meets earth."

•**CANISTEO**, Village and Town; Steuben County; Pop. 2,679 and 3,967; Area Code 607; Zip Code 14823; on Canisteo River 6 m. S SE of Hornell in S N.Y.

•**CANTON**, Village and Town; Seat of St. Lawrence County; Pop. 7,064 and 11,576; Area Code 315; Zip Code 13617; 30 m. SE of Ogdensburg in N N.Y.

•**CAPE VINCENT**, Village and Town; Jefferson County; Pop. 782 and 1,822; Area Code 315; Zip Code 13618; Elev. 370'.

•**CARLISLE**, Town; Schoharie County; Pop. 1,416; Area Code 518; Zip Code 12031; Elev. 1,250'.

•**CARMEL**, Town; Seat of Putnam County; Pop. 27,867; Area Code 914; Zip Code 10512; Elev. 520'; 20 m. E SE of Newburgh in SE N.Y.; is a leisurely village with solid old homes and streets shaded with elms and maples along the shore of a Lake Glendia.

•**CARTHAGE**, Village; Jefferson County; Pop. 3,659; Area Code 315; Zip Code 13619; Elev. 742'; 16 m. E of Watertown in N N.Y. on the Black River; important paper-making town.

•**CASSADAGA**, Village; Chautauqua County; Pop. 820; Area Code 716; Zip Code 14718; resort.

•**CASTILE**, Village and Town; Wyoming County; Pop. 1,131 and 2,861; Area Code 716; Zip Code 14427.

•**CASTLE CLINTON**, National Monument; New York City, New York; Authorized 1950; Occupies 100 acres; Structure built 1808-11; used for defense later served as immigrant landing depot.

•**CASTLE-ON-HUDSON**, Village; Rensselaer County; Pop. 1,619; Area Code 518; Zip Code 12033.

•**CASTORLAND**, Village; Lewis County; Pop. 277; Area Code 315; Zip Code 13620.

•**CATO**, Village and Town; Cayuga County; Pop. 476 and 2,139; Area Code 315; Zip Code 13033.

•**CATSKILL**, Village and Town; Seat of Greene County; Pop. 4,699 and 11,337; Area Code 518; Zip Code 12414; Elev. 75'; on W side of Hudson River, 30 m. S of Albany in SE N.Y., it crowds the narrow valley of Catskill Creek.

Catskill mountain-brewed applejack was a staple during the prohibition era. This trade and the inaccessibility of the hills to the west attracted the leaders of New York City gangsterdom, who established their hideouts in and near Catskill; as a result the village was associatd with the careers of *"Legs" Diamond, Vincent Coll*, and others of the gun fraternity; Diamond was tried in the Green County courthouse in Catskill.

Originally known as Catskill Landing, the settlement on the river was subsidiary to the old Dutch hamlet of Kaatskill, still hibernating in the hills to the west, at the fall in Catskill Creek. Mountains, creeks, and villages were named by the Dutch for the wildcats that occasionally came down from the hills, where they roamed in large numbers.

Dictionary of Places   249

•CATSKILL MOUNTAINS, Mountains; Delaware, Greene, Sullivan and Ulster Counties; Located in SE N.Y. are part of the Appalachian Mountains. The wooded area is located on the W bank of the Hudson River and is mainly a resort area. The highest point is Slide Mountain at 4,204 feet.

•CATTARAUGUS, Village; Cattaraugus County; Pop. 1,192; Area Code 716; Zip Code 14719.

•CATTARAUGUS COUNTY, SW N.Y.; 1,334 sq. miles; Pop. 85,466; Seat - Little Valley; Est. March 11, 1808; Named for the Seneca Indian word for "bad smelling banks".

•CATTARAUGUS INDIAN RESERVATION, Cattaraugus, Erie and Chautauqua Counties; Pop. 2,400; Seneca Nation of Indians; Tribal Headquarters: Irving, N.Y. 14081; Total Area: 21,680 acres.

All the reservation land is jointly owned by the Seneca Nation. The reservation was established in the Pickering Treaty of 1794. As provided in this treaty, the state continued the annual payment of cloth and a small amount of cash. The land is owned by the Seneca Nation and may not be sold without consent of the United States. According to custom, the Seneca Nation grants assignments or surface-use rights to individual members of the tribe. Residents of the Cattaraugus Reservation are members of the Seneca Nation. This reservation and the Allegany Reservation are jointly governed by the Seneca Nation. The Seneca Nation's headquarters alternate between the Cattaraugus and Allegany Reservations every two years. Although the Allegany and Cattaraugus are shown as state reservations, the federal government renders limited services to the Seneca Nation under the provisions of Public Law 88-533, 88th Congress, August 31, 1964.

The Iroquois Tribes of central, northern, and western New York were members of the Six Nations of the Iroquois League, which was founded by the leaders *Dekanawida*, the Peace Maker, and *Hiawatha*. The league was originally formed by five tribes, the related Tuscarora not joining until 1716 when they moved to the area from the Carolinas. Although formed originally for mutual defense, the league became a powerful Indian empire, the force behind much of the intertribal pressures in the West and Midwest. The league evolved into a federated government and was an important model for the crafters of the American Constitution. The league's decline after two centuries of prominence was largely the result of involvement in the disputes between the entering European powers and their participation in the Revolutionary War. Most of the members of the league supported the British as they had in the French and Indian Wars. Their alliance gave Britain the necessary advantage over

France, but proved fatal to the league's negotiating base following the victory of the Colonies. The State of New York has responsibility for Indian education, health, welfare, and legal protection.

•**CAYUGA**, Village; Cayuga County; Pop. 603; Area Code 315; Zip Code 13034.

•**CAYUGA COUNTY**, Central N.Y.; 698 sq. miles; Pop. 79,194; Seat - Auburn; Est. March 8, 1799; named for Cayuga Indian tribe.

•**CAYUGA LAKE**, Cayuga, Seneca and Tompkin Counties; located in W central N.Y. and is ne of the Finger Lakes and is part of the N.Y. State Barge Canal System. At the northern point of the Lake is Seneca Falls and the woutherm point Ithaca. The lake is two miles wide and 66 miles long with a depth of 435 feet.

•**CAYUTA**, Town; Schuyler County; Pop. 566; Area Code 607; Zip Code 14824.

•**CAZENOVIA**, Village and Town; Madison County; Pop. 2,591 and 5,866; Area Code 315; Zip Code 13035; 18 m. E SE of Syracuse in central N.Y.

•**CEDARHURST**, Village; Nassau County; Pop. 6,190; Area Code 516; Zip Code 11516; on Long Island 17 m. E SE of New York City in SE N.Y.

•**CELORON**, Village; Chautauqua County; Pop. 1,404; Area Code 716; Zip Code 14720.

•**CENTERVILLE**, Town; Allegany County; Pop. 690; Area Code 716; Zip Code 14029.

•**CENTRAL SQUARE**, Village; Oswego County; Pop. 1,414; Area Code 315; Zip Code 13036.

•**CHAMPLAIN**, Village and Town; Clinton County; Pop. 1,400 and 5,845; Area Code 518; Zip Code 12919; NE N.Y.

•**CHATEAUGAY**, Village and Town; Franklin County; Pop. 866 and 1,859; Area Code 518; Zip Code 12920; Elev. 972'; named for the adjoining Canadian land grant owned by *Charles Lemoyne*, founder of an eminent Canadian family, the village was settled by French Canadians in 1796. a blockhouse was erected here at the outbreak of the War of 1812.

•**CHATHAM**, Village and Town; Columbia County; Pop. 2,001

and 4,286; Area Code 518; Zip Code 12037.

•**CHAUMONT**, Village; Jefferson County; Pop. 609; Area Code 315; Zip Code 13622.

•**CHAUTAUQUA**, Town; Chautauqua County; Pop. 4,734; Area Code 716; Zip Code 14722; on Chautauqua Lake in SW corner of N.Y.

•**CHAUTAUQUA COUNTY**, SW corner N.Y.; 1,081 sq. miles; Pop. 146,600; Seat - Mayville; Est. March 11, 1808; Named for the Seneca Indian word for "where the fish was taken out".

•**CHAUTAUQUA LAKE**, Lake; Franklin and Chateauqay Counties; is mainly a resort area in NE part of the state. There are two lakes - Upper and Lower Chautauqua Lake.

•**CHAZY**, Town; Clinton County; Pop. 3,777; Area Code 518; Zip Code 12921; near Lake Champlain about 13 m. N of Plattsburg in NE N.Y.

•**CHEEKTOWAGA**, Town; Erie County; Pop. 109,385; Area Code 716; Zip Code 142 + zone; E of Buffalo in W N.Y.

•**CHEMUNG**, Town; Chemung County; Pop. 2,424; Area Code 607; Zip Code 14825.

•**CHEMUNG COUNTY**, S N.Y.; 415 sq. miles; Pop. 97,586; Seat - Elmira; Est. March 29, 1836; Named after the Delaware Indian village.

•**CHENANGO BRIDGE**, Broome County; Area Code 607; Zip Code 13745.

•**CHENANGO COUNTY**, S central N.Y.; 909 sq. miles; Pop. 49,309; Seat - Norwich; Est. March 15, 1798; Named for the Onondaga Indian word meaning "large bull-thistle".

•**CHENANGO RIVER**, River; located in S central N.Y. and begins at the Oneida-Madison County lines. The river is 100 m. long and runs into the Susquehanna River near Binghamton.

•**CHERRY CREEK**, Village and Town; Chautauqua County; Pop. 676; Area Code 716; Zip Code 14723.

•**CHERRY VALLEY**, Village and Town; Otsego County; Pop. 684 and 1,205; Area Code 617; Zip Code 13320; Elev. 1,322'; 50 m. W of Albany; in 1740, when the spot was settled, the *Reverend Samuel Dunlop* became preacher and teacher in a log church that also served as a schoolhouse. In the Cherry Valley Massacre of 1778, *Mrs. Dunlop* was killed, but her husband and daughters were saved by *Little Aaron*, an Indian Chief.

•**CHESTER**, Village and Town; Orange County; Pop. 1,910 and 6,845; Area Code 914; Zip Code 10918; SE N.Y.

•**CHITTENANGO**, Village; Madison County; Pop. 4,281; Area Code 315; Zip Code 13037; 16 m. E of Syracuse in central N.Y.

•**CHURCHVILLE**, Village; Monroe County; Pop. 1,399; Area Code 716; Zip Code 14428.

•**CICERO**, Town; Onondaga County; Pop. 24,431; Area Code 315; Zip Code 13039.

•**CINCINNATUS**, Town; Cortland County; Pop. 1,155; Area Code 607; Zip Code 13040.

•**CLAREDON**, Town; Orleans County; Pop. 2,149; Area Code 716; Zip Code 14429.

•**CLARENCE**, Town; Erie County; Pop. 18,126; Area Code 716; Zip Code 14031; W N.Y.

•**CLARKSON**, Town; Monroe County; Pop. 4,015; Area Code 716; Zip Code 14430; Elev. 427'; is the birthplace of *George B. Selden* (1846-1922), called the "father of the automobile". In 1872, possessed with the idea of a "horseless carriage", Seldon gave up the practice of law and constructed small engines to be propelled by steam, by ammonia gas, and by bisulphite of carbon. The following year he discarded the idea of steam for power, devoting his experiments to an internal combustion engine. In 1877 he made his first successful experiment with a "lightweight, high-speed, three-cylinder gasoline compression engine". Granted a patent in 1895, Selden received a royalty on all automobiles made until *Henry Ford* broke his monopoly in 1903.

•**CLAVERACK**, Town; Columbia County; Pop. 6,095; Area Code 518; Zip Code 12513.

•**CLAY**, Town; Onondaga County; Pop. 52,046; Area Code 315; Zip Code 13041; Central N.Y.

•**CLAYTON**, Village and Town; Jefferson County; Pop. 1,803 and 4,004; Area Code 315; Zip Code 13624; on St. Lawrence River in Thousand Islands region in N N.Y., 20 m. N NW of Watertown.

•**CLAYVILLE**, Village; Oneida County; Pop. 470; Area Code 315;

Zip Code 13322.

•**CLEVELAND**, Village; Oswego County; Pop. 859; Area Code 315; Zip Code 13042.

•**CLIFTON PARK**, Town; Saratoga County; Pop. 23,990; Area Code 518; Zip Code 12065; E N.Y.

•**CLIFTON SPRINGS**, Village; Ontario County; Pop. 2,036; Area Code 315; Zip Code 14432; 29 m. E SE of Rochester in W N.Y.

•**CLINTON**, Village; Oneida County; Pop. 2,106; Area Code 315; Zip Code 13323; 9 m. W SW of Utica in central N.Y.

•**CLINTON COUNTY**, NE corner N.Y.; 1,059 sq. miles; Pop. 80,659; Seat - Plattsburg; Est. March 7, 1788; Named after *George Clinton*.

•**CLINTONDALE**, Ulster County; Area Code 914; Zip Code 12515; Elev. 552'; is a fruit-raising center named in honor of the *Clinton family*. Orchards extend almost to the back doors of the homes. In 1830 *William Cornell* of Clintondale invented and patented a waterproof overshoe.

•**CLYDE**, Village; Wayne County; Pop. 2,498; Area Code 315; Zip Code 14433; on N.Y. State Barge Canal 18 m. NW of Auburn in W N.Y.

•**CLYMER**, Town; Chautauqua County; Pop. 1,481; Area Code 716; Zip Code 14724.

•**COBLESKILL**, Village and Town; Schoharie County; Pop. 5,257 and 7,030; Area Code 518; Zip Code 12043; SW of Amsterdam in E N.Y.

•**COCHECTON**, Town; Sullivan County; Pop. 1,327; Area Code 914; Zip Code 12726.

•**COEYMANS**, Town; Albany County; Pop. 7,878; Area Code 518; Zip Code 12045; E N.Y.

•**COHOCTON**, Village and Town; Steuben County; Pop. 887 and 2,454; Area Code 607; Zip Code 14826.

•**COHOCTON RIVER**, River; Steuben, Chemung, Tioga Counties; located in S central N.Y. and is approx. 60 m. long. Along with Tioga River it forms the Chemung River.

•**COHOES**, City; Albany County; Pop. 18,158; Area Code 518; Zip

Code 12047; at confluence of Mohawk and Hudson Rivers near E terminus of N.Y. State Barge Canal, 10 m. N of Albany in E N.Y.

•COLD BROOK, Village; Herkimer County; Pop. 402; Area Code 315; Zip Code 13324.

•COLDEN, Town; Erie County; Pop. 3,127; Area Code 716; Zip Code 14033; named for *Cadwallader Colden*, historian.

•COLD SPRING, Village; Putnam County; Pop. 2,161; Area Code 914; Zip Code 10516; on Hudson River 20 m. S of Poughkeepsie in SE N.Y.

•COLLINS, Town; Erie County; Pop. 5,044; Area Code 716; Zip Code 14034.

•COLONIE, Village and Town; Albany County; Pop. 8,835 and 74,534; Area Code 518; Zip Code 12212; NW of Albany.

•COLTON, Town; St. Lawrence County; Pop. 1,293; Area Code 315; Zip Code 13625.

•COLUMBIA COUNTY, SE N.Y.; 645 sq. miles; Pop. 59,267; Seat - Hudson; Est. April 4, 1786; Named after *Christopher Columbus*; hilly region.

•CONESUS, Town; Livingston County; Pop. 1,972; Area Code 716; Zip Code 14435.

•CONKLIN, Town; Broome County; Pop. 6,210; Area Code 607; Zip Code 13748.

•CONSTABLE, Town; Franklin County; Pop. 1,218; Area Code 518; Zip Code 12926.

•CONSTABLEVILLE, Village; Lewis County; Pop. 330; Area Code 315; Zip Code 13325.

•CONSTANTIA, Town; Oswego County; Pop. 4,306; Area Code 315; Zip Code 13044.

•COOPERSTOWN, Village; Otsego County Seat; Pop. 2,336; Area Code 518; Zip Code 13326; Elev. 1,240'; E central New York; 60 m. W of Albany; On S tip of Otsego Lake at origin of Susquehanna River; Residential and resort.

Judge William Cooper bought land here in 1785, and soon founded the settlement which bears his name. His son, *James Fenimore Cooper*, wrote several of his romantic novels here, such as *The Deerslayer*. At that time, Cooperstown was a small

Dictionary of Places

outpost in the wilderness, from which *James F. Cooper* derived the background for his *Leatherstocking Tales*. Cooper is buried here in the family plot at Christ Church, built in 1810.

Before the Cooper settlement, *General James Clinton* and his army camped here in 1779, en route to joining *General Sullivan's* regiment. *Abner Doubleday* invented the game of baseball here in 1839 and the National Baseball Museum in town commemorates ball players. Several other museums in town house historical displays from the area.

•**COPAKE**, Town; Columbia County; Pop. 2,336; Area Code 518; Zip Code 12516; Elev. 620'; E N.Y.; Resort.

•**COPENHAGEN**, Village; Lewis County; Pop. 655; Area Code 315; Zip Code 13626.

•**CORFU**, Village; Genesee County; Pop. 698; Area Code 716; Zip Code 14036.

•**CORINTH**, Village and Town; Saratoga County; Pop. 2,698 and 5,199; Area Code 518; Zip Code 12822.

•**CORNING**, City; Steuben County; Pop. 12,894; Area Code 607; Zip Code 14830; on Chemung River 14 m. W of Elmira in S N.Y.; Corning is divided by the Chemung River.

Corning is largely a one industry town, depending on the manufacture of glass. It was settled in 1789.

The village began to grow after the completion of the Chemung Canal in 1833. *Erastus Corning* of Albany had organized a company to speculate in local real estate and promoted the building of a railroad to carry Pennsylvania anthracite here for transshipment down the canal. In 1868, when the Flint Glass Company of Brooklyn determined to move its plant to a place where the cost of fuel and raw materials would be lower, it was induced to come here. Corning Community College was established here in 1956.

•**CORNWALL**, Town; Orange County; Pop. 10,756; Area Code 914; Zip Code 12518; on Hudson River S of Newburgh in SE N.Y.

•**CORNWALL ON HUDSON**, Village; Orange County; Pop. 3,176; Area Code 914; Zip Code 12520; acquired renown in the 1840's as the home of *Nathaniel Parker Willis* (1806-69), poet, essayist, and historian, and later as the home of *Edward Payson Roe*, best-selling novelist of the 1880s.

•**CORTLAND**, City; Seat of Cortland County; Pop. 20,094; Area Code 607; Zip Code 13045; 30 m. S of Syracuse; was first settled in 1792. *Elmer Ambrose Sperry* (1860-1930), inventor, was born here. Sperry is credited with 400 patents, including the gyroscopic compasses and stabilizers used in ships and airplanes, high arc searchlights, and designs for improvements on electric street railway cars and electric automobiles.

•CORTLAND COUNTY, Central N.Y.; 502 sq. miles; Pop. 48,839; Seat - Cortland; Est. April 8, 1808; Named after *Pierre Van Cortlandt, Jr.* .

•COXSACKIE, Village and Town; Greene County; Pop. 2,761 and 5,976; Area Code 518; Zip Code 12051; on Hudson River 22 m. S of Albany in SE N.Y.

•CRANBERRY LAKE, Lake; Elev. 1,502'; St. Lawrence County; located in N N.Y. and is six m. in length. The lake is a summer resort.

•CROGHAN, Village and Town; Lewis County; Pop. 709 and 25,066; Area Code 315; Zip Code 13327.

•CROTON-ON-HUDSON, Village; Westchester County; Pop. 6,896; Area Code 914; Zip Code 10520; on Hudson River in SE N.Y.

Croton-On-Hudson came into existence as the home of Irish and Italian laborers who were building the dam that created Croton Reservoir. About the time of World War I, *Max Eastman* and several others who had to live economically and wanted to escape from Greenwich Village tenements, acquired land on the wooded hills above Croton and built small houses; in time they were joined by *Edna St. Vincent Millay*, poet; *Dudley Field Malone*, lawyer; *Doris Stevens* militant feminist; *Mabel Dodge* and her husband *Maurice Stern*, the artist; *Floyd Dell*, novelist; *John Reed*, radical journalist; *Boardman Robinson*, cartoonist and painter; *Stuart Chase*, economist; and others.

•CROWN POINT, Town; Essex County; Pop. 1,825; Area Code 518; Zip Code 12928; Elev. 126'; NE N.Y.

It was here that *Sir William Johnson* commanded the 1755 expedition. For his victory he was rewarded with baronetcy. In 1759 the town fell to *Gen James Wolfe*. Some of the military ruins remain.

•CRUGER'S ISLAND, Ulster County; *Robert Fulton's Clermont* tied up here on its initial trip to Albany. *Chancellor Robert R. Livingston*, who had financed Fulton's experiments, held a monopoly covering the making and operating of all boats propelled by "force of fire or steam" on the waters of the state. That monopoly was broken in 1824 by *Thomas Gibbons*, who operated a steamboat between New York and New Jersey and whose case was successfully argued before the Supreme Court by

Daniel Webster. After his victory, river commerce turned rapidly to steam.

•**CUBA**, Village and Town; Allegany County; Pop. 1,701 and 3,394; Area Code 716; Zip Code 14727; 13 m. NE of Olean in SW N.Y.

•**CUDDEBACKVILLE**, Orange County; Area Code 914; Zip Code 12729; was named for *Abraham A. Cuddeback*, believed to be the first white settler, who arrived here about 1792.

•**CUYLER**, Town; Cortland County; Pop. 851; Area Code 607; Zip Code 13050; Elev. 600'; the largest Seneca village in the Genesee Valley. *John Sullivan* found fields of corn, squash, and beans and many fruit orchards, all of which he destroyed along with the village. The place marks the westernmost limit of his expedition.

•**DANNEMORA**, Village and Town; Clinton County; Pop. 3,767 and 4,709; Area Code 518; Zip Code 12929; Elev. 1,400'; 13 m. W of Plattsburg in NE corner N.Y.; named for the city in Sweden because of the high quality of its iron deposits.

•**DANSVILLE**, Village; Livingston County; Pop. 4,973; Area Code 716; Zip Code 14437; NW of Hornell in W N.Y.; a nursery center and manufacturing village producing heating equipment, textbooks and magazines, tissue paper, and shoes. Here on Augus 22, 1881, *Clara Barton*, while recuperating from an illness at the Jackson Sanitarium, founded the first local chapter of the American Red Cross.

•**DAVENPORT**, Town; Delaware County; Pop. 1,971; Area Code 518; Zip Code 13750.

•**DAYTON**, Town; Cattaraugus County; Pop. 1,976; Area Code 716; Zip Code 14041; Elev. 1,322'.

•**DEFERIET**, Village; Jefferson County; Pop. 326; Area Code 315; Zip Code 13628; Elev. 641'; N central N.Y.; sprang up almost overnight after a paper mill was erected in 1900 by the St. Regis Paper Company. The place was named for *Baroness Jenika de Derriet*, who about 1830 built a beautiful mansion, called the Hermitage on the bank of the Black River. Here she lived with her servants, entertained other French emigres including *Joseph Bonaparte*, cared for her flowers and played on the first grand piano in the North Country. Shortly after her return to France in 1840 the house burned down.

•**DE LANCEY**, Delaware County; Area Code 518; Zip Code 13752; is named after the *Etienne de Lancey* a wealthy Huguenot. A relative later married the novelist *James Fenimore Cooper* in 1811.

•**DELANSON**, Village; Schenectady County; Pop. 444; Area Code 518; Zip Code 12053.

•**DELAWARE COUNTY**, S N.Y.; 1,458 sq. miles; Pop. 46,807; Seat - Delhi; Est. March 10, 1797; Named after *Thomas West* - the third Baron of De La Warr.

•**DELEVAN**, Village; Cattaraugus County; Pop. 1,124; Area Code 716; Zip Code 14042; Elev. 1,422'; S N.Y. on the Delaware River; was a favorite training place or pugilists and wrestlers. Many Buffalo fighters have trained here, among them the former heavyweight wrestling champion, *George Nichols*. The place was named in 1892 in honor of *Jack Delevan*, a trainer and hotel keeper.

•**DELHI**, Village and Town; Seat of Delaware County; Pop. 3,377 and 5,302; Area Code 518; Zip Code 13753; on the Delaware River in S N.Y. on State 10; home of a State School of Agriculture, is a neat, modern town. Shortly after the Revolutionary War *Ebenezer Foote* was so influential locally and as a member of the state legislature that he was nicknamed "the Great Mogul". At the suggestions of facetious citizens the community was named for Delhi, India, the capitol city of the real Great Mogul.

•**DENMARK**, Town; Lewis County; Pop. 2,448; Area Code 315; Zip Code 13631; N central N.Y.; named after the Kingdom in Northwestern Europe.

•**DEPAUVILLE**, Jefferson County; Area Code 315; Zip Code 13632; Elev. 297'; was named for *Francis Depau*, early settler, who in 1834-5 built the stone Depauville Union Church.

•**DEPEW**, Village; Erie County; Pop. 19,819; Area Code 716; Zip Code 14043; Elev. 680'; an industrial suburb located 9 m. E of Buffalo in W N.Y.

•**DEPEYSTER**, Town; St. Lawrence County; Pop. 896; Area Code 315; Zip Code 13633; was named after a wealthy New York merchant.

•**DEPOSIT**, Village; Broome County; Pop. 1,884; Area Code 607; Zip Code 13754; Elev. 1,000'; 25 m. E of Binghamton in S N.Y.; is a summer resort.

•**DE RUYTER**, Village and Town; Madison County; Pop. 539 and 1,345; Area Code 315; Zip Code 13052.

Dictionary of Places

•**DEWITT**, Town; Onondaga County; Pop. 26,729; Area Code 315; Zip Code 132 + zone; Central N.Y.

•**DOBBS** (alt. Dobbs Ferry), Village; was named for *Jeremiah Dobbs*, who in 1698 hollowed out a log and started the first river ferry. Across the river the Palisades begin their 14-mile march. This front of solid trap rock separates the valleys of the Hudson and Hackensack Rivers, which flow parallel for 30 miles. The Mahican Indians believed the Great Spirit raised this rampart to protect his favorite abode from man.

When *Benedict Arnold* was planning the betrayal of West Point he made an appointment to meet *Major Andre'* at "Dobbs Ferry", which may have been either at the landing here or at the one on the other side of the river.

The village is one of the line of towns along the river that provide fashionable addresses.

•**DOLGEVILLE**, Village; Herkimer County; Pop. 2,607; Area Code 315; Zip Code 13329; Elev. 800'; was named in 1881 for *Alfred Dolge*, a businessman who transformed the village of Brockett's Bridge into a factory town of several thousand workers. His factory, established here in 1875, was one of the first to manufacture felt in the United States and one of the pioneers in employee profit-sharing that provides group insurance, pensions, disability benefits, and a mutual benefit society.

•**DRESDEN**, Village; Yates County; Pop. 379; Area Code 315; Zip Code 14441.

•**DRYDEN**, Village and Town; Tompkins County; Pop. 1,758 and 12,138; Area Code 607; Zip Code 13053.

•**DUANESBURG**, Town; Schenectady County; Pop. 4,710; Area Code 518; Zip Code 12056; Elev. 720'; was named for *James Duane* (1733-97), jurist, land speculator, and mayor of Manhattan (1748-9). He sat on the Continental Congress almost continuously until 1783, serving chiefly in connection with financial and Indian affairs and in assisting with the final draft of the Articles of Confederation.

•**DUNDEE**, Village; Yates County; Pop. 1,551; Area Code 315; Zip Code 14837.

•**DUNKIRK**, City; Chautauqua County; Pop. 15,255; Area Code 716; Zip Code 14048; Elev. 600'; in SW N.Y. on Lake Erie, 35 m. SW of Buffalo. A port of entry also.

Its water and electric systems were among the first in the country to be municipally owned and operated.

•**DURHAM**, Town; Greene County; Pop. 2,296; Area Code 518; Zip Code 12422.

•**DUTCHESS COUNTY**, SE N.Y.; 814 sq. miles; Pop. 244,141; Seat - Poughkeepsie; Est. November 1, 1683; Named after the elder daughter of *Sir Edward Hyde, Anne, Duchess of York*.

•**EARLVILLE**, Village; Madison County; Pop. 987; Area Code 315; Zip Code 13332.

•**EAST AURORA**, Village; Erie County; Pop. 6,824; Area Code 716; Zip Code 14052; Elev. 926'; 15 m. E SE of Buffalo in W N.Y.; in violation of its name, lies 90 m. W of Aurora. It was first settled in 1804. In the early 1900s East Aurora was made famous by *Elbert C. Hubbard* (1856-1915) as the home of his Roycrofters. Here *Albert Hubbard* printed his *Philistine* and *A Message to Garcia* and made artistic book covers.

•**EAST BLOOMFIELD**, Village and Town; Ontario County; Pop. 585 and 3,327; Area Code 315; Zip Code 14443; Elev. 1,060'; is the original home in this country of the Northern Spy apple; *Herman Chapin* planted the first seed about 1800 and sprouts from the original tree were taken by *Roswell Humphrey*, who set them in his orchard. The original tree died but the cuttings flourished. The name Northern Spy grew out of the abolitionist movement rampant at the time; the apple was considered an interloper, hence a spy.

•**EASTCHESTER**, Town; Westchester County; Pop. 32,521; Area Code 914; Zip Code 10709; SE N.Y.

•**EAST GREENBUSH**, Town; Rensselaer County; Pop. 12,903; Area Code 518; Zip Code 12061; E N.Y.

•**EAST HAMPTON**, Town and Village; Suffolk County; Pop. 14,044 and 1,845; Area Code 516; Zip Code 11937; on Long Island, on Atlantic Ocean 20 m. W of Montauk Point in SE N.Y.; was settled in 1648. Kentish yeomen who settled here named it Maidstone. *Lyman Beecher*, progenitor of a remarkable family which included *Henry Ward Beecher*, noted orator and preacher, and *Harriet Beecher Stowe*, author of *Uncle Tom's Cabin*, was pastor of the Presbyterian Church here from 1799 to 1810. It was also the birthplace of *John Howard Payne* (1791-1852), author of "Home, Sweet Home".

•**EAST OTTO**, Town; Cattaraugus County; Pop. 931; Area Code 716; Zip Code 14729.

•**EAST RANDOLPH**, Village; Cattaraugus County; Pop. 650;

Area Code 716; Zip Code 14730.

•**EAST RIVER**, River; the strait that connects Upper N.Y. Bay with Long Island Sound also divides the Bronx and Manhattan from Queens and Brooklyn on Long Island and has many numerous port facilities.

•**EAST ROCHESTER**, Village; Monroe County; Pop. 7,556; Area Code 716; Zip Code 14445; 7 m. E of Rochester in w N.Y. Primarily engaged in various types of manufacturing.

•**EAST ROCKAWAY**, Village; Nassau County; Pop. 10,886; Area Code 516; Zip Code 11518; on Long Island 20 m. E of New York City. Mainly known as a resort area.

•**EAST SYRACUSE**, Village; Onondaga County; Pop. 3,406; Area Code 315; Zip Code 13057; in N central N.Y.; manufactures steel products of various kinds.

•**EATON**, Town; Madison County; Pop. 5,169; Area Code 315; Zip Code 13334.

•**EDEN**, Town; Erie County; Pop. 7,337; Area Code 716; Zip Code 14057.

•**EDMESTON**, Town; Otsego County; Pop. 1,723; Area Code 617; Zip Code 13335.

•**EDWARDS**, Village and Town; St. Lawrence County; Pop. 564 and 1,211; Area Code 315; Zip Code 13635.

•**ELBA**, Village and Town; Genesee County; Pop. 751 and 2,501; Area Code 716; Zip Code 14058.

•**ELBRIDGE**, Village and Town; Onondaga County; Pop. 1,098 and 5,876; Area Code 315; Zip Code 13060; Central N.Y.

•**ELIZABETHTOWN**, Village and Town; Seat of Essex County; Pop. 654 and 1,262; Area Code 518; Zip Code 12932; Elev. 550'; S of Plattsburg about 32 m., in Adirondack Mts. in NE N.Y.; hemmed in by the Adirondacks, lies at the head of a mile-wide flat land created by the Bouquet River. Lumbering reached its peak here about 1870, then rapidly declined. The rambling hotels were built when the invasion of summer visitors began in the seventies.

•**ELLENBURGH**, Town; Clinton County; Pop. 1,750; 518; Zip Code 12933.

•**ELLENVILLE**, Village; Ulster County; Pop. 4,407; Area Code

914; Zip Code 12428; Elev. 360'; located between the Shawangunk Mountains and the Allegheny Plateau, 25 m. W of Poughkeepsie, is a center of the resort district of Sullivan and Orange Counties.

•**ELLICOTTVILLE**, Village and Town; Cattaraugus County; Pop. 716 and 1,671; Area Code 716; Zip Code 14731; Elev. 1,549'; was named for *Joseph Ellicott*, Holland Land Company surveyor. In 1859 three Franciscan Fathers, *Pamfilio, Milan, and Sextus*, established themselves here to administer to the spiritual needs of the Irish railroad workers. They remained for three years and then moved to Allegany, where they founded St. Bonaventure's College in 1859.

•**ELLINGTON**, Town; Chautauqua County; Pop. 1,672; Area Code 716; Zip Code 14732.

•**ELLIS ISLAND**, Island; approx. 3 m. wide forming the mouth of the Hudson River.

•**ELLISBURG**, Village and Town; Jefferson County; Pop. 306 and 3,306; Area Code 315; Zip Code 13636.

•**ELMA**, Town; Erie County; Pop. 10,579; Area Code 716; Area Code 14059; W N.Y.

•**ELMIRA**, City; Chemung County seat; Pop. 35,363; Area Code 607; Zip Code 14901; Elev. 860; S central New York; 85 m. SW of Syracuse; Near Pennsylvania border; On Chemung River in Appalachian foothills; Named for *Elmira Teall*, daughter of an early settler.

The first white men to see the region were soldiers of the *Sullivan-Clinton* regiment in 1779. Originally, the site was the Seneca Indian village of Kanaweola, destroyed during the Battle of Newtown. First settler was *John Hendy* and his family (1788), and the town was incorporated in 1828. Four years later, the Chemung Canal was completed and the local lumber industry boomed. Woolen mills and metal industries moved into town with the coming of the railroads, and prospered during the Civil War. In 1864, the year the town received a city charter, one of the Union Army barracks here was turned into a prison camp, and local merchants made profitable contracts for food. Local dairies began transporting milk, butter and cheese to New York City in 1882.

Mark Twain lived on a nearby farm during some of his most prolific years, and his study was removed and preserved at Elmira College. He and his family are buried at Woodlawn Cemetery. The college was founded for women in 1855, at a time when education for females was considered ridiculous.

Today, clothing, metal and dairy products are still important industries in Elmira, as are electrical euqipment, business machines, processed foods and greeting cards.

•ELMIRA HEIGHTS, Village; Chemung County; Pop. 4,242; Area Code 607; Zip Code 14903; N suburb of Elmira in S N.Y.

•ELMONT, Nassau County; Pop. (Urban) Area Code 516; Zip Code 11003; on Long Island SW of Garden City.

•ELMSFORD, Village; Westchester County; Pop. 3,327; Area Code 914; Zip Code 10523; 26 m. N of New York in SE N.Y.

•ENDICOTT, Broome County; Pop. 14,457; Area Code 607; Zip Code 13760; Elev. 840'; 8 m. W of Binghamton in S N.Y. on Susquehanna River; known as one of the Triple Cities with Binghamton and Johnson City.

•ERIE COUNTY, W N.Y.; 1,058 sq. miles; Pop. 1,014,926; Seat - Buffalo; Est. April 2, 1821; Named after the Erie Indians.

•ERIN, Town; Chemung County; Pop. 2,047; Area Code 607; Zip Code 14838.

•ESOPUS, Town; Ulster County; 47,584; Area Code 914; Zip Code 12429; at the mouth of Roundout in the Catskill Mts. in SE N.Y.

In 1615 Dutch traders established a trading post at the mouth of Roundout Creek and named it Esopus. A group of Dutch colonists from Alban made the first permanent settlement in 1653. The Indians attacked the place on two occasions and took many lives. In 1658 *Director General Peter Stuyvesant* erected a stockade and blockhouse and in 1661 granted a char-ter to the village, which he called Wiltwyck (Dutch, "wild retreat").

•ESPERANCE, Village and Town; Schoharie County; Pop. 362 and 1,940; Area Code 518; Zip Code 12066.

•ESSEX, Town; Essex County; Pop. 884; Area Code 518; Zip Code 12936; NE N.Y.; caters to a large summer tourist trade, and from here a ferry crosses the lake to Charlotte, Vermont. At the north village line is the junction with Split Rock Road.

•ESSEX COUNTY, NE N.Y.; 1,823 sq. miles; Pop. 36,094; Seat - Elizabethtown; Est. March 1, 1799; Named for Essex County, England.

•EVANS MILLS, Village, Jefferson County; Pop. 653; Area Code 315; Zip Code 13637; Elev. 431'; N. N.Y.; a farm center at the junction of West and Pleasant Creeks. *Ethni Evans*, New Hampshire millwright, who settled here in 1803, gave his name to the hamlet.

•**FABIUS**, village and Town; Onondaga County; Pop. 367 and 1,821; Area Code 315; Zip Code 13063.

•**FAIRFIELD**, Town; Herkimer County; Pop. 1,433; Area Code 315; Zip Code 13336.

•**FAIR HAVEN**, Village; Cayuga County; Pop. 947; Area Code 315; Zip Code 13064.

•**FAIRPORT**, Village; Monroe County; Pop. 5,958; Area Code 315; Zip Code 14450; 10 m. E of Rochester in W N.Y.

•**FALCONER**, Village; Chautauqua County; Pop. 2,786; Area Code 716; Zip Code 14733; SW N.Y.

•**FALLS**, Niagara County; Area Code 716; Zip Code 143 + zone; W N.Y.; named for Niagara Falls.

•**FALLSBURG**, Town; Sullivan County; Pop. 9,801; Area Code 914; Zip Code 12733; SE N.Y.

•**FARMINGDALE**, Village; Nassau County; Pop. 7,940; Area Code 516; Zip Code 11735; 30 M. E of New York City on Long Island in SE N.Y.

The first village in American history to be "blacked out" for a mimic night air raid, lies on the plain at the foot of Mannetto Hills. The village economy was founded on the surrounding farms. Silk dyeing and airplane manufacturing are recently added activities.

•**FARNHAM**, Village; Erie County; Pop. 404; Area Code 716; Zip Code 14061.

•**FAYETTE**, Town; Seneca County; Pop. 3,556; Area Code 315; Zip Code 13065; W central N.Y.

•**FAYETTEVILLE**, Village; Onondaga County; Pop. 3,556; Area Code 315; Zip Code 13066; Elev. 500'; 10 m. E of Syracruse in central N.Y.

•**FILLMORE**, Village; Allegany County; Pop. 563; Area Code 716; Zip Code 14735.

•**FINE**, Town; St. Lawrence County; Pop. 2,243; Area Code 315; Zip Code 13639.

•**FINGER LAKES**, Lakes; Ontario, Yates, Steuben, Seneca,

Cayuga, Onondaga Counties; located in W N.Y.; lie in north-south valleys in central N.Y. Geologists believe that the lake valleys once contained southward-flowing rivers which were backed up by dams of glacial debris formed during the Ice Age, and that the new or post-glacial drainage was forced to seek the northward course it now takes. The sides of the valleys rise abruptly to the broad back of the Allegheny Plateau. Tributary streams, tumbling down the steep slopes, have cut glens and produced many waterfalls. Taughannock Falls near the head of Cayuga Lake plunges 215 feet, the highest waterfall east of the Rockies. The main lakes are Canandaigua, Owasco, Seneca, Cayuga, Keuka and Skaneateles.

•**FIRE ISLAND**, Island; Suffolk County; consists of a state park, beach and a national seashore in Suffolk County. Located on S central Long Island in SE N.Y. is approx. 30 m. long and 1/2 m. wide. Mainly a summer resort but is also used as a signal station and a lighthouse.

•**FISHERS ISLAND**, Island; Suffolk County; located on the NE point of Long Island and S of Connecticut.

•**FISHKILL**, Village and Town; Dutchess County; Pop. 1,733 and 15,668; Area Code 914; Zip Code 12524; Elev. 200'; on the Hudson River. Though some Dutch settlers were living on the lowlands soon after 1700, at the time of the Revolution the village had only a dozen or so houses, two churches, a tavern, and a schoolhouse.

•**FLEISCHMANNS**, Village; Delaware County; Pop. 350; Area Code 518; Zip Code 12430; Elev. 1,515'; in S N.Y. in the Catskill Mts. 30 m. NW of Kingston; is one of the major summer resort centers of the Catskill region. The village is built around its busy and colorful main street.

•**FLORAL PARK**, Village; Nassau County; Pop. 16,778; Area Code 516; Zip Code 110 + zone; in S N.Y. on Long Island. New York City is 15 m. to the W.

•**FLORIDA**, Village; Orange County; Pop. 1,932; Area Code 914; Zip Code 10921.

•**FLUSHING**, Queens County; Area Code 212; Zip Code 113 + zone; SE New York; was once a village; since 1898 part of Queens Borough in Queens County; located on Long Island in S N.Y. Mainly a residential area also was home of the Worlds Fair of 1939-40.

•**FONDA**, Village; Seat of Montgomery County; Pop. 1,006; Area Code 518; Zip Code 12068; Elev. 300'; on Mohawk River 12 m. W of

Amsterdam in E N.Y. Settled early in the eighteenth century by the Dutch, the place was known as Caughnawaa (Indian, "On the rapids"). During the Revolution it was the scene of sharp and bloody conflicts among neighbors divided on the issue of revolution. On May 21, 1780, the village was burned by a raiding party under *Sir John Johnson*, but was rebuilt and became an important stopover point on the turnpike. Construction of the Utica & Schenectady Railroad in 1836 brought it prosperity and designation as Montgomery County Seat; in 1851 it took its present name.

•**FOREST HILLS**, Residential; Queens Borough; Queens County; Area Code 212; Zip Code 113 + zone; on Long Island. The home of the U.S. Open tennis tournaments held annually.

•**FORESTPORT**, Town; Oneida County; Pop. 1,371; Area Code 315; Zip Code 13338.

•**FORESTVILLE**, Village; Chautauqua County; Pop. 804; Area Code 716; Zip Code 14062; Elev. 875'; in an amphitheater of hills, was the birthplace of *George Abbott*, playwright and producer, author of *Boy Meets Girl* and other plays.

•**FORT ANN**, Village and Town; Washington County; Pop. 510 and 4,436; Area Code 12827; Elev. 150'; NE N.Y.; on the low divide between the Hudson River watershed and Lake Champlain, was the site of a series of Colonial and Revolutionary forts. A brief encounter between an advance British force and the Americans on July 8, 1777, is called the Battle of Fort Ann.

•**FORT COVINGTON**, Town; Franklin County; Pop. 1,812; Area Code 518; Zip Code 12937; Elev. 166'; on the N tip of N.Y. near the Quebec border on Hwy. 11. In the autumn of 1812 *General Wade Hampton*, guarding the border, built a blockhouse here.

•**FORT EDWARD**, Village and Town; Washington County; Pop. 3,563 and 6,476; Area Code 518; Zip Code 12828; Elev. 147'; on Hudson River 38 m. N of Troy in E N.Y.; is a paper-making village.

As the Great Carrying Place, where Indians and white toted their canoes between the Hudson and Lake Champlain, the site of Fort Edward was fortified throughout the French and Indian and Revolutionary wars. In July 1777, when *Burgoyne* was advancing a mile a day from the head of Lake Champlain, the American forces were stationed here.

•**FORT JOHNSON**, Village; Montgomery County; Pop. 647; Area Code 518; Zip Code 12070; Elev. 300'; N N.Y.; was the scene of many important Indian councils - as many as 1,000 Indians camped in the vicinity at one time; and it figured in the British

Army movements up the Mohawk Valley to Canada. During the French and Indian War a palisade was built around it - hence the "Fort" in its name. *Sir William Johnson* ranks as one of the great empire builders of North America.

•**FORT PLAIN**, Village; Montgomery County; Pop. 2,538; Area Code 518; Zip Code 12229; Elev. 320'; on the Mohawk River, 23 m. W of Amsterdam in E N.Y.; at the confluence of Otsquago Creek and the Mohawk River, Fort Plain has a bird sanctuary in Fish and Game Park where native wild birds are fed in Winter and protected during the nesting season.

•**FRANKFORT**, Village and Town; Herkimer County; Pop. 2,989 and 7,652; Area Code 315; Zip Code 13340; Elev. 400'; 10 m. E SE of Utica in NE central N.Y.; industrial past includes parentage of the American match industry. In 1843 *William A. Gates* began the manufacture of wooden matches in a tiny village shop and peddled them from house to house along the river. The matchsticks were cut by hand from strips of wood three feet long and then dipped into a sulphur composition and allowed to dry. The process was slow and exacting; but later Gates invented a machine, made at the Remington plant in Ilion, that did away with much of the hand labor. After his death in 1877 the plant was merged with the Diamond Match Company and in 1893 was moved to Oswego.

In the 1890s, on what is called the Balloon farm, near Frankfort, *Carl and Carlotta Myers*, intrepid pioneer balloonists, equipped a building with laboratory and shop for the manufacture of balloons, including small hydrogen balloons used for Federal weather experiments. In their spare time Myers and his wife toured the country fairs with a balloon, taking awed spectators on flights.

•**FRANKLIN**, Village and Town; Delaware County; Pop. 442 and 2,431; Area Code 518; Zip Code 13775.

•**FRANKLIN COUNTY**, NE N.Y.; 1,674 sq. miles; Pop. 44,876; Seat - Malone; Est. March 11, 1808; Named after *Benjamin Franklin*.

•**FRANKLIN SQUARE**, Nassau County; Area Code 516; Zip Code 11010; in SE Long Island W of Hempstead.

•**FRANKLINVILLE**, Village and Town; Cattaraugus County; Pop. 1,874 and 3,085; Area Code 716; Zip Code 14737; Elev. 1,549'; 16 m. N of Olean in SW N.Y.; was settled shortly after 1800 by *Joseph McClure*, who surveyed for the Holland Land Company.

•**FREDONIA**, Village; Chautauqua County; Pop. 11,071; Area

Code 716; Zip Code 14063; Elev. 740'; SW corner of N.Y., near Lake Erie 23 m. N of Jamestown; was called by *Chauncey M. Depew* "the most beautiful village in New York State." Natural gas was discovered early in the nineteenth century and exploited almost immediately for lighting; the streets of the village are said to have been the first in the world to be lighted by gas. It is known for grape juice and wine.

•**FREEDOM**, Town; Cattaraugus County; Pop. 1,842; Area Code 716; Zip Code 14065.

•**FREEPORT**, Village; Nassau County; Pop. 38,168; Area Code 516; Zip Code 11520; on S shore of Long Island 25 m. E SE of New York City in SE N.Y.; is the largest of the south side Long Island villages.

•**FREEVILLE**, Village; Tompkins County; Pop. 449; Area Code 607; Zip Code 13068.

•**FRIENDSHIP**, Town; Allegany County; Pop. 2,151; Area Code 716; Zip Code 14739.

•**FULTON**, City; Oswego County; Pop. 13,274; Area Code 315; Zip Code 13069; Elev. 400'; 24 m. NW of Syracuse in central N.Y.; ships milk and fruit and makes woolen goods, candy, paper containers, food products, ventilators, and linoleum felts. Settlement began because it was necessary to unload cargoes here and haul them in oxcarts around two falls in the river.

•**FULTON COUNTY**, E N.Y.; 498 sq. miles; Pop. 55,089; Seat - Johnstown; Est. April 18, 1838; Named after *Robert Fulton*.

•**FULTONVILLE**, Village; Montgomery County; Pop. 763; Area Code 518; Zip Code 12072.

•**GAINESVILLE**, Village and Town; Wyoming County; Pop. 334 and 2,140; Area Code 716; Zip Code 14066; W N.Y.; Farmers of the region about Gainesville, during the 1938 season delivered 90,000 pecks of potatoes, all bagged and ready for sale, to a single grocery store chain. *David Starr Jordan* (1851-1931), Biologist and President of Leland Stanford University, was born on a farm a quarter of a mile east of the village; *Belva Ann Lockwood* (1830-1917), lawyer, suffragist, and first woman candidate for President, was head of the Gainesville Female Academy in 1858; and *Isabella McDonald Alden* (1841-1930), author of moral tales for young people, wrote many of her stories in this vicinity.

•**GALLOO ISLAND**, Island; Jefferson County; in NE Lake Ontario in N N.Y.

Dictionary of Places 269

•**GALWAY**, Village and Town; Saratoga County; Pop. 246 and 3,020; Area Code 518; Zip Code 12074.

•**GARDEN CITY**, Village; Nassau County; Pop. 23,019; Area Code 516; Zip Code 11530; 18 m. E. N.Y. City on Long Island in SE N.Y.; a planned town, one of the wealthiest residential communities on Long Island, the realization of the dream of *Alexander Turney Stewart*, Manhattan merchant prince. Stewart bought 8,000 acres for $55 an acre and built the necessary railroad connection. Wide streets, shaded by trees of mature growth, are laid out in checkerboard pattern. Imposing residences stand on spacious plots; parks embellish the village, It is something of a social center and largely free from the turmoil of trade, although some fashionable city shops have branches here.

•**GARDINER**, Town; Ulster County; Pop. 3,550; Area Code 914; Zip Code 12525.

•**GARDINERS BAY**, Bay; Located NE of Long Island and Peconic Bay in Long Island Sound; SE New York.

•**GARDINERS ISLAND**, Island; Suffolk County; located in E Part of Long Island in Gardiners Bay. Also, located W of Montauk Point. The island was first settled in 1639 and owned originally by *Lion Gardiner*. In 1693 was made part of Easthampton Township and Long Island. Supposedly is where the famous pirate *Capt. Kidd* buried his treasure.

•**GASPORT**, Niagara County; Area Code 716; Zip Code 14067.

•**GEDNEY**, Westchester County; Area Code 914; Zip Code 106 + zone.

•**GENESEE COUNTY**, W N.Y.; 501 sq. miles; Pop. 59,369; Seat - Batavia; Est. March 30, 1802; Named for the Indian word meaning "beautiful valley".

•**GENESEE RIVER**, River; located in W N.Y. The river actually begins in Pennsylvania and runs N to Lake Ontario not far from Rochester. The river is 144 miles long.

•**GENESEO**, Village and Town; Seat of Livingston County; Pop. 6,744 and 8,670; Area Code 716; Zip Code 14454; Elev. 800'; in Genesee Valley in W central N.Y. The name is from the Indian word meaning beautiful valley. A farm trade village best known for its association with the Wadsworth family and the Genesee Hunt.

•**GENEVA**, City; Seneca and Ontario Counties; Pop. 15,068; Area Code 315; Zip Code 14456; at N end of Seneca Lake in W N.Y.
Geneva is on Seneca Lake. The city includes the site of the Indian settlement Kanadesaga, a name also applied to Seneca Lake, destroyed by the *Sullivan-Clinton* expedition in 1779.
The outskirts of Geneva are fringed with the field of nurseries, growing fruit trees, berry bushes and ornamental plants and shrubs. Foundries turn out ranges, furnaces, radiators, and high-grade cutlery; mills produce cereals, and canneries preserve the fruit of the countryside; factories make optical goods and enamelware. The township of Geneva (1897) adjoins the city but is not part of it.

•**GENOA**, Town; Cayuga County; Pop. 1,921; Area Code 315; Zip Code 13071.

•**GEORGETOWN**, Town; Madison County; Pop. 779; Area Code 315; Zip Code 13072.

•**GERMANTOWN**, Town; Columbia County; Pop. 1,920; Area Code 518; Zip Code 12526; Elev. 180'; about 1,200 of the German Palatines brought over in 1710 by *Governor Hunter* to make tar and other naval stores were settled on Livingston land in this area. It was then called East Camp.

•**GERRY**, Town; Chautauqua County; Pop. 2,022; Area Code 716; Zip Code 14740.

•**GHENT**, Town; Columbia County; Pop. 4,627; Area Code 518; Zip Code 12075; SE N.Y.

•**GILBERTSVILLE**, Village; Otsego County; Pop. 443; Area Code 617; Zip Code 13776.

•**GILBOA**, Town; Schoharie County; Pop. 1,083; Area Code 518; Zip Code 12076.

•**GLEN COVE**, City; Nassau County; Pop. 24,516; Area Code 516; Zip Code 11542; NE of N.Y. City on Long Island's N shore in SE N.Y.; is one of Long Island's two incorporated cities and the business center of Cove Neck. Its narrow and hilly streets hum with activity in summer when vacationers at Lattingtown, Glen Cove Landing and Bayville, nearby seaside colonies, do the weekend marketing. *Charles A. Dana*, who served with *Greeley* on the *New York Tribune* and organized the old *New York Sun*, came to Glen Cove in 1873 and died here in 1897.
In 1982, Glen Cove's City Council voted to ban Soviet diplomats residing in the town from public beaches and recreational areas. The ban came after the Soviets were accused of spy-

ing on Long Island defense industries.

•**GLENS FALLS**, City, Warren County; Pop. 15,884; Area Code 518; Zip Code 12801; Elev. 343'; in E N.Y.; was part of the Queensbury Patent, 23,000 acres of land granted in 1759 to 23 men. The water power provided by the 60-foot falls in the Hudson, which the Indians called *Chepontuo* (a difficult place to get around), determined the location of the settlement. During the Revolution the village was in direct path of invasion and in 1780 it was destroyed by the British. In 1788 *Colonel John Glen* of Schenectady acquired land and built mills here.

•**GLOVERSVILLE**, City; Fulton County; Pop. 17,751; Area Code 607; Zip Code 12078; Elev. 800'; 12 m. NW of Amsterdam in E N.Y.; Named for its outstanding industry. While the manufacture of heavy gloves and mittens has spread into every state, the making of fine kid gloves remains a Fulton County specialty.

•**GORHAM**, Town; Ontario County; Pop. 3,722; Area Code 315; Zip Code 14461.

•**GOSHEN**, Village and Town; Seat of Orange County; Pop. 4,869 and 10,475; Area Code 914; Zip Code 10924; Elev. 439'; S N.Y.; The settlers who came to this place in the early decades of the eighteenth century believed that the fertility of the rich soil would rival that of the Biblical land of Goshen. The solid prosperity of this tree-shaded town attests to the soundness of their choice. It exports dairy products and garden trucks in large quantities. *Claudius Smith*, the bandit was hanged on the village green.

•**GOUVERNEUR**, Village and Town; St.Lawrence County; Pop. 4,287 and 6,655; Area Code 315; Zip Code 13642; Elev. 428'; N N.Y.; is on both banks of the Oswegatchie (Indian, "black water flowing out") River. *Gouverneur Morris* purchased land here in 1798, and seven years later the village was settled. In 1867 talc (magnesium silicate) was discovered in this region and it has since become an important product.

•**GOVERNORS ISLAND**, Island, New York County; Area Code 212; Zip Code 10004; at the end of the East River in the N.Y. Bay, is an old fort named Castle William that was built 1807-1811. Headquarters of the Second Corps Area, lies about 500 yds. off Battery Park in Upper New York Bay. Troops have left this island for the Seminole Wars, the Mexican War, the Civil War, the Spanish-American War, and World Wars I and II.

•**GOWANDA**, Village; Erie and Cattaraugus County; Pop. 2,718; Area Code 716; Zip Code 14070; Elev. 760'; in SW N.Y.; Cattaraugus Creek attracted New England settlers in 1810, and they raised sawmills and gristmills. The intrepid *Ahaz Allen* built the first frame house in 1814. In 1830 *Horace Greeley*, who had hiked as a journeyman printer from Vermont to Erie County, came to Lodi, as the place was then known, in search of a job. In 1848 Lodi became Gowanda; three years later the Erie Railroad came through and brought industries.

•**GRAFTON**, Town; Rensselaer County; Pop. 1,622; Area Code 518; Zip Code 12082; located in W N.Y.

•**GRAND ISLAND**, Town; Erie County; Pop. 16,766; Area Code 716; Zip Code 14072; W N.Y.

•**GRAND ISLAND**, Island; Erie County; in W N.Y. in the Upper Niagara River. The river is eight miles long. In 1833 *Lewis F. Allen* - purchased several thousand acres of land on Grand Island in the Niagara River, on which he planted peach trees and grew large crops. Eventually yellows destroyed these orchards; and the fruit industry moved from Grand Island to the mainland of Niagra County, which now produces more than twice as many peaches as any other New York county.

•**GRANVILLE**, Village and Town; Washington County; Pop. 2,689 and 5,527; Area Code 518; Zip Code 12832; Elev. 400'; in E N.Y.; was originally called Bishop's Corners when its first settlers, many of them Quakers, arrived from Vermont in 1781. The site of the village was part of the hunting and fishing grounds of the St. Francis Indians of Canada, who made hatchets and arrowheads from slate and enjoyed friendly relations with the Mohawk.

•**GREAT NECK**, Village; Nassau County; Pop. 9,045; Area Code 516; Zip Code 110 + zone; in S N.Y. on the S shore of Long Island is mainly residential. Also nearby are the Great Neck Estates and Plaza.

•**GREAT SOUTH BAY**, Bay; E coast of N.Y. is a lengthy and thin inlet between the south shore of Long Island and Fire Island.

•**GREAT VALLEY**, Town; Cattaraugus County; Pop. 2,009; Area Code 716; Zip Code 14741.

•**GREECE**, Town; Monroe County; Pop. 81,316; Area Code 716; Zip Code 14616; W N.Y.

•**GREENE**, Village and Town; Chenango County; Pop. 1,762 and 5,736; Area Code 607; Zip Code 13778.

•**GREENE COUNTY**, SE N.Y.; 654 sq. miles; Pop. 40,495; Seat -

Dictionary of Places   273

Catskill; Est. March 25, 1800; Named after *Nathanael Greene*.

•**GREEN ISLAND**, Village and Town; Albany County; Pop. 693; Area Code 518; Zip Code 12183.

•**GREENPORT**, Village; Suffolk County; Pop. 2,288; Area Code 516; Zip Code 11944; between Gardiner Bay and Long Island Sound on the N tip of Long Island in SE N.Y.; is the principal commercial center of the north fluke. The village is laid out in squares that slow down to the harbor; high bluffs face the Sound.

In the days of deep-sea whaling Greenport rivaled Sag Harbor, and the seafaring tradition lives in the multiplicity of relics in the old houses of the town. The village is now a center of the oyster trade. Since the local bivalve is held inferior in the market to that of Great South Bay, 400,000 bushels are sent yearly to Sayville for a finishing course that gives them the bulk and flavor of "Blue Points". Building of small boats is an auxiliary industry.

•**GREENVALE**, Nassau County; Area Code 516; Zip Code 11548; W Long Island in SE N.Y.

•**GREENVILLE**, Town; Green County; Pop. 2,820; Area Code 518; Zip Code 12083.

•**GREENWICH**, Village and Town; Washington County; Pop. 1,955 and 4,278; Area Code 518; Zip Code 12834.

•**GREENWICH VILLAGE**, Now is a part of Manhattan Borough; was once a village on Manhattan Island; in S N.Y. bordering the Hudson River.

The streets, turning abruptly or crossing where they should be parallel, express the antic spirit of the community. For the Village has performed some amazing mental acrobatics. Not for nothing is it called the Latin Quarter, the Bohemia of New York City. Free love, Freudianism, Socialism, imagist poetry, and fads of all shades have waxed and waned here. Today the burden of its incessant talk is economics. The Village retires late, rises late. In eccentric night clubs visited by the curious, it listens to a crapulent poet melodramatically reciting his effusions. Its Main Street, is a bazaar of art objects and second-hand books, odd tearooms and studios cheek-by-jowl with drug and grocery stores, movie houses, tailor shops. The real-estate boom of the 1920s, with its intrusion of tall, ostentatious apartment buildings, added a Midas touch.

•**GREENWOOD**, Town; Steuben County; Pop. 882; Area Code 607; Zip Code 14839.

•**GREENWOOD LAKE**, Village; Orange County; Pop. 2,820;

Area Code 914; Zip Code 10925.

•**GREENWOOD LAKE**, Lake; Orange County; in SE N.Y. and N N.J. is mainly a summer resort and measures nine m. in length.

•**GREIG**, Lewis County; Pop. 1,135; Area Code 315; Zip Code 13345.

•**GROTON**, Village and Town; Tompkins County; Pop. 2,294 and 5,195; Area Code 607; Zip Code 13073; Elev. 1,026'; 26 m. S SE of Auburn in S central N.Y.

•**GROVELAND**, Town; Livingston County; Pop. 2,123; Area Code 716; Zip Code 14462.

•**GUILDERLAND**, Town; Albany County; Pop. 26,462; Area Code 518; Zip Code 12084; Elev. 210'; E N.Y.

•**GUILFORD**, Town; Chenango County; Pop. 2,441; Area Code 607; Zip Code 13780.

•**HADLEY**, Town; Saratoga County; Pop. 1,348; Area Code 518; Zip Code 12835.

•**HAGAMAN**, Village; Montgomery County; Pop. 1,329; Area Code 518; Zip Code 12086.

•**HAGUE**, Town; Warren County; Pop. 767; Area Code 518; Zip Code 12836; Elev. 330'; on Lake George in E N.Y.

•**HALESITE**, Suffolk County; Area Code 516; Zip Code 11743; SE N.Y. on Long Island; was named for the American martyr, *Nathan Hale*.

•**HAMBURG**, Village and Town; Erie County; Pop. 10,591 and 53,292; Area Code 716; Zip Code 14075; Elev. 826'; 10 m. S of Buffalo in W N.Y.

Hamburg was settled by German immigrants about 1808. During the Canadian uprising of 1837-9 the villagers were sympathetic to the rebel cause and 400 recruits planned to cross Lake Erie one wintry night to invade Canada; but this heroic undertaking was stopped by New York State militia.

The undulating hills and hummocks south of Hamburg are the outposts of the Allegheny Mountains. This part of the state was settled by New Englanders; the soil has been cultivated by their descendants for generations, and the hardy New England influence is still in evidence: the zigzag rail fence, the solid stone or brick house, the neat flower garden.

•**HAMDEN**, Town; Delaware County; Pop. 1,281; Area Code 518; Zip Code 13782.

•**HAMILTON**, Village and Town; Madison County; Pop. 3,719 and 6,031; Area Code 315; Zip Code 13346; Elev. 1,216'; SW of Utica in central N.Y.; Settled 1792; settled by New Englanders and incorporated in 1816, the village is built around a green reminiscent of New England.

•**HAMILTON COUNTY**, NE central N.Y.; 1,735 sq. miles; Pop. 5,058; Seat - Lake Pleasant; Est. April 12, 1816; Named after *Alexander Hamilton*.

•**HAMLIN**, Town; Monroe County; Pop. 7,676; Area Code 716; Zip Code 14464.

•**HAMMOND**, Village and Town; St. Lawrence County; Pop. 271 and 1,091; Area Code 315; Zip Code 13646.

•**HAMMONDSPORT**, Village; Steuben County; Pop. 1,054; Area Code 607; Zip Code 14840; Elev. 718'; at S end of Keuka Lake 25 m. E of Hornell in S N.Y.

Located at the head of Keuka Lake, it is a center of the New York State champagne industry. In the early 1900s it was the aviation center of the Nation and it is proud of the title, "Cradle of American Aviation".

Glenn Hammond Curtiss was born here in 1878. As a builder of motors, he was sought out by *Dr. Alexander Graham Bell* to build a motor home for a kite. Curtiss, *Lieutenant Thomas Selfridge* of the U.S. Army, and others began their work of building "a practical aerodrome driven by its own motive power and carrying a man". On July 4, 1908, on Stony Brook Farm, Curtiss flew the June Bug 2,000 yards. In 1910 he flew an airplane from Albany to New York, with two stops. In 1917 he joined with *John N. Willis*, automobile manufacturer, to supply airplanes for World War I. Later he designed and manufactured the *Wasp*, which established records for speed, climbing, and altitude.

•**HAMPTON**, Town; Washington County; Pop. 545; Area Code 518; Zip Code 12837.

•**HANCOCK**, Village and Town; Delaware County; Pop. 1,523; Area Code 518; Zip Code 13783; Elev. 920'; S N.Y. on the Delaware River on State 97; a summer resort at the junction of the East and West Branches of the Delaware River.

•**HANNAWA FALLS**, Hamlet; St. Lawrence County; Area Code 315; Zip Code 13647; Elev. 560'; 2 m. S of Potsdam on the Racquette River in N N.Y.; spreading from the falls of the same name. Here the Raquette River, 300 feet wide, falls 85 feet. A masonry dam forms a pool almost three miles long that covers 200 acres.

•HANNIBAL, Village and Town; Oswego County; Pop. 667; Area Code 315; Zip Code 13074; Elev. 330'; central N.Y.; is a fruit-growing and dairy hamlet.

•HARFORD, Town, Cortland County; Pop. 855; Area Code 607; Zip Code 13784.

•HARPERSFIELD, Town; Delaware County; Pop. 1,491; Area Code 518; Zip Code 13786; Elev. 1,752'; central N.Y. on Hwy. 23; was the scene of Indian-Tory raids during the Revolution, and later was one of the principal stops on the old Catskill Turnpike. Settled in 1771 by *Colonel John Harper* from Cherry Valley, the settlement, on the Indian trail between the Schohorie and the Susquehanna Valleys, was attacked in the spring of 1780 by Indians led by *Joseph Brant* ; three settlers were scalped and eight taken captive. *Timothy Murphy* avenged the loss in a single-handed attack on a camp of 27 Indians. When he left the camp, six Indians were dead and the rest scattered in the hills.

•HARRIMAN, Village; Orange County; Pop. 788; Area Code 914; Zip Code 10926.

•HARRISON, Village and Town; Westchester County; Pop. 23,046; SE N.Y.

•HARRISVILLE, Town, Lewis County; Pop. 938; Area Code 315; Zip Code 13648.

•HARTFORD, Town; Washington County; Pop. 1,754; Area Code 518; Zip Code 12838.

•HASTINGS-ON-HUDSON, Village; Westchester County; Pop. 8,550; Area Code 914; Zip Code 10706; Elev. 140'; on Hudson River 18 m. N of New York in SE N.Y.; named for the English birthplace of *William Saunders*, a local manufacturer, has chemical, copper, and paving-block factories along the river front. Mustard gas for the American Expeditionary Forces in World War I was manufactured here. Hastings, like Yonkers, began to grow after construction of the Hudson River Railroad in 1849. *Horace Greeley* was one of the commuters of the Civil War period; in 1862 a drunken mob, blaming him for having incited the draft riots in New York City, started down from Sing Sing Valley (Ossining) to blow up his house, but it was dispersed before it accomplished its purpose. It is a residential area.

Dictionary of Places 277

•**HAVERSTRAW**, Village and Town; Rockland County; Pop. 8,826 and 31,923; Area Code 914; Zip Code 10927; Elev. 20'; on W shore of Hudson River 32 m. N of New York in SE N.Y.; squats on the edge of the Hudson with its back propped against High Tor, Little Tor, and Pyngyp. Its main industry is the manufacture of brick and cement. Here *James Wood* discovered the modern system of burning brick and set up brickyards in the town, the beginnings of an industry which at the peak included 40 brickyards, producing 326,000,000 bricks annually.

In 1825 the Franklin Community was established here by followers of *Robert Owen* ; they wished to discard "absurd and immaterial systems of religion" and the form of marriage based on them. But local antagonism soon put an end to this Utopia.

•**HECTOR**, Town; Schuyler County; Pop. 3,769; Area Code 607; Zip Code 14841.

•**HEMPSTEAD**, Village and Town; Nassau County; Pop. 40,377 and 737,903; Area Code 516; Zip Code 115 + zone; 20 m. E of N.Y. City on Long Island in SE N.Y.; is one of the largest population centers on Long Island. In the early days it was called the "Town Spot"; local partisans now lean to "hub of Nassau County". In 1644 the first settlers found a well-watered grassy plain on which their cattle grew fat; the virgin soil was excellent for timothy, rye, wheat, and maize; the score or more families who made up the settlement prospered. Not before 1801, however, did the village begin to grow appreciably. At the end of World War I *Hempstead* was in aspect still a country town. After 1920 the automobile expanded the radius of the territory from which it drew its trade, and large concerns established branches in the village.

•**HENDERSON**, Town; Jefferson County; Pop. 1,310; Area Code 315; Zip Code 13650.

•**HENDERSON HARBOR**, Jefferson County; Area Code 315; Zip Code 13651; N N.Y.; a popular summer resort with hotels, and inns overlooking Horse Island in the Bay. During the War of 1812, sharpshooters were stationed here to harass the British in their attempt to reach the mainland from Horse Island.

•**HENRIETTA**, Town; Monroe County; Pop. 36,084; Area Code 716; Zip Code 14467; W N.Y.

•**HERKIMER**, Village and Town; Seat of Herkimer County; Pop. 8,339; and 10,975; Area Code 315; Zip Code 13350; NE central N.Y.

Herkimer was settled by a group of Palatines in 1725 and was long known as German Flats. During the French and Indian

War the place suffered from raids by the enemy. In 1776 Fort Dayton, a wooden structure surrounded by a stockade, was built.
In 1777, *General Nicholas Herkimer* marched to the Battle of Oriskany. In 1778 *Joseph Brant* and his Indians attacked the settlement, but the celebrated run by *Adams Helmer*, *Ranger Scout*, described in *Walter D. Edmond's Drums Along the Mohawk*, prevented a large-scale massacre.
Its main industry is office furniture.

•**HERKIMER COUNTY**, NE central N.Y.; 1,435 sq. miles; Pop. 66,432; Seat - Herkimer; Est. February 16, 1791; Named after *Nicholas Herkimer*.

•**HERMON**, Village and Town; St. Lawrence County; Pop. 488 and 1,079; Area Code 315; Zip Code 13652.

•**HERRINGS**, Village; Jefferson County; Pop. 172; Area Code 315; Zip Code 13653.

•**HEUVELTON**, Village; St. Lawrence County; Pop. 776; Area Code 315; Zip Code 13654.

•**HIGHLAND FALLS**, Village; Orange County; Pop. 4,215; Area Code 914; Zip Code 10928; Elev. 200'; on Hudson River 5 m. S SW of Newburgh in SE N.Y.; in 1862, *John Burroughs* discovered *Audubon's Birds*; the pictures so fired his imagination that he began his lifelong study of nature. Families of infantrymen, cavalrymen, and bandsmen stationed at the West Point Reservation have their homes here. For a century small boys of the village earned pocket money by selling "smokes" to cadets during practice marches.

•**HILLBURN**, Village; Rockland County; Pop. 915; Area Code 914; Zip Code 10931.

•**HILL CUMORAH**, Hill Cumorah, a glacial drumin, is the Mormon Mount Sinai, where *Joseph Smith* unearthed the gold plates that were the source of the Book of Mormon. "Convenient to Manchester", Joseph Smith wrote, "stands a hill of considerable size, the most elevated of any in the neighborhood. On the west side of this hill, not far from the top, under a stone of considerable size, lay the plates, deposited in a stone box." He saw them the first time in September 1823 and visited the place on each anniversary, until on September 22, 1827, he took them out of their hiding place. From 1827 to 1829 he translated them and then returned them to the angelic messenger.

•**HILLSDALE**, Town; Columbia County; Pop. 1,607; Area Code 518; Zip Code 12529; Elev. 686'.
John Cowper Powys, a British novelist, lived for several

years in country "more like England than any landscape I have yet seen in the whole of America." *Arthur Davison Ficke,* author of *Sonnets of a Portrait Painter,* lived nearby on his farm, "Hardhack," named for the swamp brush that chokes the fields; here he wrote most of the poems in *The Secret,* published in 1936. In the shadows of Phudd Hill, *Alan Devoe* wrote his nature essays in the tradition of Thoreau and Burroughs.

•HILTON, Village; Monroe County; Pop. 4,152; Area Code 716; Zip Code 14468.

•HINSDALE, Town; Cattaraugus County; Pop. 2,165; Area Code 716; Zip Code 14743.

•HOBART, Village; Delaware County; Pop. 478; Area Code 518; Zip Code 13788.

•HOGANSBURG, Franklin County; Area Code 518; Zip Code 13655; Elev. 175'.

•HOLCOMB, Village; Ontario County; Pop. 951; Area Code 315; Zip Code 14469.

•HOLLAND, Town; Erie County; Pop. 3,435; Area Code 716; Zip Code 14080.

•HOLLAND PATENT, Village; Oneida County; Pop. 532; Area Code 315; Zip Code 13354.

•HOLLEY, Village; Orleans County; Pop. 1,886; Area Code 716; Zip Code 14470.

•HOMER, Village; Cortland County; Pop. 3,636; Area Code 607; Zip Code 13077; Elev. 1,140'; 28 m. S of Syracuse in central N.Y.; was first settled in 1791. It was the locale of *Edward Noyes Westcott's David Harum* and the birthplace of *David Hannum*, around whom Westcott built his chief character. *Francis Bicknell Carpenter* (1832-1918), historian, state senator, first president of Cornell University and United States Minister to Germany and Russia, was born in a two-story Victorian brick home here.

•HONEOYE FALLS, Village; Monroe County; Pop. 2,403; Area Code 716; Zip Code 14472.

•HOOSICK, Town; Rensselaer County; Pop. 6,749; Area Code 518; Zip Code 12089; Elev. 480'; on the Hoosic River, 20 m. NE of Troy near the Vermont border in E N.Y.; 3 m. W of Vermont on Hwy. 7; named from the Indian meaning "stony place".

•HOOSICK FALLS, Village; Rensselaer County; Pop. 3,611;

Area Code 518; Zip Code 12090; on Hoosick River near Vermont border 21 m. E NE of Troy in E N.Y.; incorporated as a village in 1827, has utilized the falls in the Hoosick River to build a thriving industrial town.

•HOPKINTON, Town; St. Lawrence County; Pop. 1,057; Area Code 315; Zip Code 12940.

•HORNELL, City; Steuben County; Pop. 10, 225; Area Code 607; Zip Code 14843; Elev. 1,160'; 56 m. S of Rochester in S N.Y.

In September 1850, a pigmy locomotive called the "Orange No. 4" drew the first train into Hornellsville, a village of 100 scattered houses, two churches, and two schools.

The first clearing on the site of Hornell was made by *Benjamin Crosby* in 1790. The city was named for *George Hornell*, an Indian trader who purxhased the site in 1793, built the first gristmill and the first tavern, and became the leading citizen of the upper Canisteo Valley.

•HORSEHEADS, Village and Town; Chemung County; Pop. 7,338 and 20,216; Area Code 607; Zip Code 14845; 5 m. N of Elmira in S N.Y.

•HUDSON, City; Seat of Columbia County; Pop. 7,925; Area Code 518; Zip Code 12534; Elev. 100'; on E bank of Hudson River 28 m. S of Albany in SE N.Y.; is built on a slope that rises from the Hudson River. *Jan Frans Van Hoesen* bought land here from the Indians in 1662, but there was no permanent settlement until 1783, when a number of New Englanders arrived, mostly Nantucket Quakers, whose fishing and whaling activities had suffered during the Revolution. The place has been called Claverack (Dutch, "clover reach").

•HUDSON FALLS, Village; Seat of Washington County; Pop. 7,223; Area Code 518; Zip Code 12839; Elev. 280'; on Hudson River 40 m. N of Troy in E N.Y.; a papermaking center, is at the sharp bend in the Hudson where the river changes its course from east to south. The village shares with Salem the county seat functions of Washington County. The first white settlers came in 1760 and built gristmills and sawmills on the 70-foot falls; but at first the *Burgoyne* campaign delayed development and then in 1780 *Sir Guy Carleton* burned the settlement. In the nineteenth century, pulpwood, floated down the Hudson River from Adirondack forests, established paper manufacturing as the dominant industry.

•HUDSON RIVER, E New York; The river rises in the Adirondack Mountains, and runs south for about 310 miles into Upper New York Bay at the boundary for New Jersey and New York

near New York City in SE N.Y., then into the Atlantic Ocean.
The river is named for the explorer *Henry Hudson* who discovered it in 1608 and sailed up as far as Albany on his original exploration to find China. The Hudson begins near Mount Marcy as a small river from Lake Tear of the Clouds and is known as the Opalescent River.
The river is a great asset to New York in many ways. The winding beauty of the river with its numerous falls make it a very scenic river enjoyed by all. In the earliest days and still today is a great source of transportation for business, commerce and industry. Hydro-electric power is provided from the great falls and the strength of the river.
The major tributaries are North Creek, Indian, Sacondaga, Schroon, Batten Koll, Fish Creek, Hoosic and Mohawk rivers. The Mohawk is the largest source of water for the Hudson. As far as Albany from New York City about 150 miles the river is navigable. The southern end of the Hudson forms a main section of New York Harbor and is known as the North River. At the northern end of the river is the N.Y. State Barge Canal, St. Lawrence Seaway, Lake Champlain on into the Great Lakes.

•**HUME**, Town; Allegany County; Pop. 2,034; Area Code 716; Zip Code 14745; Elev. 1,281'; marks the northern limit of the former Caneadea Reservation of the Seneca Indians, one of the 11 set aside in the Big Tree Treaty of 1797. The Indians sold the land to a group of land speculators in 1826 and settled on state reservations.

•**HUNTER**, Village and Town; Greene County; Pop. 521 and 2,278; Area Code 518; Zip Code 12442; Elev. 1,600'; is an array of boardinghouses against the mountain wall. As early as 1880 the railroad through Stony Clove was depositing Jewish families in the valley town.

•**HUNTINGTON**, Town; Suffolk County; Pop. 201,559; Area Code 516; Zip Code 11743; on N shore of Long Island in SE N.Y.; the British soldiery during the Revolution converted the old cemetery, at the eastern end of the business section, into a fort, which with grisly humor, they named Fort Golgotha.

•**HURLEY**, Town; Ulster County; Pop. 7,049; Area Code 914; Zip Code 12443; first called Nieuw Dorp (Dutch, "new village"), was renamed in 1669 for *Francis Lovelace,* Baron Hurley of Ireland.

•**HYDE PARK**, Town; Dutchess County; Pop. 20,719; Area Code 914; Zip Code 12538; Elev. 187'; on E bank of Hudson River 6 m. N of Poughkeepsie in SE N.Y.; was once called Stoutenburgh, for *Jacobus Stoutenburgh*, the first settler, who arrived in 1741. It was the birthplace (1882) of *President Franklin Delano*

Roosevelt. Franklin D. Roosevelt Library was established here in 1941.

In January, 1982, a large fire broke out in the Roosevelt summer home-museum, and millions of dollars of damage was done to the building as well as Roosevelt memorabilia.

•**ILION**, Village; Herkimer County; Pop. 9,156; Area Code 315; Zip Code 13357; Elev. 400'; on Mohawk River 11 m. E SE of Utica in NE central N.Y.; in 1800 *Eliphalet Remington*, farmer-mechanic, brought his family, including *Eliphalet, Jr.* (1793-1861), from Connecticut. Young Eliphalet inherited his father's mechanical bent; when he needed a gun for hunting he fashioned the barrel in his father's forg at Ilion Gulph and then trudged 15 miles to Utica to have it rifled. When neighbors asked for similar guns, father and son built a new forge and began the manufacture of firearms.

•**INDIAN LAKE**, Town; Hamilton County; Pop. 1,410; Area Code 518; Zip Code 12842.

•**INDIAN LAKE**, Lake; Hamilton County; outlets into the Hudson River. *Dr. Thomas C. Durant* (1820-85) and *Wiliam Durant* (1850-1934), father and son, were early promoters of this section of the Adirondacks.

•**INLET**, Town; Hamilton County; Pop. 327; Area Code 518; Zip Code 13360.

•**INTERLAKEN**, Village; Seneca County; Pop. 686; Area Code 315; Zip Code 14847.

•**IRONDEQUOIT**, Town; Monroe County; Pop. 57,585; Area Code 716; Zip Code 14617.

•**IRVINGTON**, Village; Westchester County; Pop. 5,783; Area Code 914; Zip Code 10533; Elev. 175'; on Hudson River 22 m. N of N.Y. and 3 m. S of Tarrytown in SE N.Y.

Named for *Washington Irving*, is a metropolitan suburb ringed by wooded estates. An ornate brick mansion, hidden by a wall, was built in 1918 by *Mrs. C. J. Walker* (1867-1919), a pioneer Negro businesswoman. About 1905, when Mrs. Walker was a laundress in St. Louis, Missouri, she concocted a preparation to straighten tightly curled hair.

It was also the home of *Cyrus W. Field* (1819-92) from 1868 to 1892. In 1866, after 12 years of work Field brought to completion the first transatlantic telegraph cable.

•**ISCHUA**, Town; Cattaraugus County; Pop. 774; Area Code 716; Zip Code 14746. In a pocket along Ischua Creek among quarried

Dictionary of Places 283

hills. In 1845, the settlers rose up against the Holland Land Company in the "Dutch Hill War", a bloodless affair. Farmers took to arms to defy ejection; one settler, an Irishman, accidentally discharged a gun as the militia, called by the company, approached. But that was all, and the agitated farmers returned home. The incident has been called the "first agrarian strike in America."

•ISLAND PARK, Village; Nassau County; Pop. 4,847; Area Code 516; Zip Code 11558; on Atlantic Ocean 29 m E SE of N.Y. in SE N.Y.

•ISLIP, Town; Suffolk County; Pop. 298,895; Area Code 516; Zip Code 11751; on Long Island on Great South Bay, about 10 m. W of Patchogue in SE N.Y.

•ITHACA, City; Tompkins County Seat; Pop. 28,846; Area Code 607; Zip Code 14850; Elev. 900'; S central New York; 40 m. NW of Binghamton; at S tip of Cayuga Lake; Named for legendary ancient Greek home of *Ulysses* by *U.S.Surveyor General Simeon DeWitt* ; Site of Cornell University.
 Indians inhabited this region until 1779 when *Gen John Sullivan's* expedition burned their cornfields. After the Revolution, the first settlers built cabins here in 1789, but they were forced to move when the new gvernment designated the area a Military Tract for Revolutionary veterans. The village was incorporated in 1821, but solid growth did not begin until after *Ezra Cornell*, originator of the Western Union Telegraph Company here, established Cornell University in 1868. The city was chartered 20 years later, Ithaca College in 1931.
 Ithaca is centrally located in the agricultural Finger Lakes region, and institutions such as the New York State College of Agriculture and the State Veterinary College are incorprated within Cornell University. Several statewide farmers' associations are headquartered here, as is a U.S. Plant and Soil Laboratory.
 Industry is kept to a minimum in Ithaca, but adding machines, research instruments, guns, power saws, and clothing are produced here, as are dairy products.

•JAMAICA, part of Queens Borough; Seat of Queens County; Area Code 212; Zip Code 114 + zone; on Long Island in SE N.Y.

•JAMESTOWN, City; Chautauqua County; Pop. 35,687; Area Code 716; Zip Code 14701; Elev. 1,400'; at S end of Chautauqua Lake 57 m. S SW of Buffalo in SW corner of N.Y.; the business and smoke-covered factory district of Jamestown, clusters about the outlet of Chautauqua Lake. The founder of the settlement was *James Prendergast*, who purchased 1,000 acres of land his brother had earlier bought from the Holland Land Company for $2.00 an acre. Among the early settlers were a number of skilled woodworkers, who began to make furniture to supply the needs of the pioneers in the region. In 1849 some Swedish immigrants appeared; after the close of the Civil War many others joined them. Most of the men were cabinet makers attracted by the furniture factories.

•**JASPER**, Town; Steuben County; Pop. 1,126; Area Code 607; Zip Code 14855.

•**JAY**, Town; Essex County; Pop. 2,206; Area Code 518; Zip Code 12941.

•**JEFFERSON**, Town; Schoharie County; Pop. 1,105; Area Code 518; Zip Code 12093.

•**JEFFERSON COUNTY**, N N.Y.; 1,294 sq. miles; Pop. 88,130; Seat - Watertown; Est. March 28, 1805; Named after *Thomas Jefferson*.

•**JEFFERSONVILLE**, Village; Sullivan County; Pop. 549; Area Code 914; Zip Code 12748.

•**JERICHO**, Nassau County; Pop. 14,200; Area Code 516; Zip Code 11753; on Long Island in SE N.Y.

•**JEWETT**, Town; Greene County; Pop. 722; Area Code 518; Zip Code 12444.

•**JOHNSBURG**, Town; Warren County; Pop. 2,171; Area Code 518; Zip Code 12843.

•**JOHNSON CITY**, Village; Broome County; Pop. 17,115; Area Code 607; Zip Code 13790; Elev. 847'.

•**JOHNSTOWN**, City; Seat of Fulton County; Pop. 9,345; Area Code 607; Zip Code 12095; Elev. 660'; 11 m. W NW of Amsterdam in E N.Y.; is on the Cayadutta Plateau. It was named for *Sir William Johnson*, who settled here in 1762 at the height of his picturesque life as a frontier statesman and empire builder.

•**JORDAN**, Village; Onondaga County; Pop. 1,362; Area Code 315; Zip Code 13080.

•**KEENE**, Town; Essex County; Pop. 916; Area Code 518; Zip Code 12942; Elev. 860'.

•**KEENE VALLEY**, Village; Essex County; Area Code 518; Zip

Code 12943; Elev. 860'; 39 m. S SW of Plattsburgh in NE N.Y.; boasts of the oldest school district in the Adirondacks, its school records preserved from the year 1813. Some of the most famous of America's landscape painters have studios here; among the earliest were *John Fitch, Roswell Morse Shurtlegg, A.F.Tait*, and *A.H.Wyant*. One of the most colorful Keene Valley intellectuals was *Thomas Davidson* (1840-1900), who opened the Glenmore Summer School here for his Concord School of Philosophy.

•**KEESEVILLE**, Village; Clinton and Essex Counties; Pop. 2,025; Area Code 518; Zip Code 12944; Elev. 400'; 12 m. S of Plattsburgh in NE N.Y.; was settled by Quaker *John Keese*, who arrived in 1806. Soon afterward he was joined by French Canadians attracted by the lumbering and iron-mining industries.

•**KENDALL**, Town; Orleans County; Pop. 2,378; Area Code 716; Zip Code 14476.

•**KENMORE**, Village; Erie County; Pop. 18,475; Area Code 716; Zip Code 14217; on Niagara River 5 m. N of Buffalo in W N.Y.

•**KEUKA LAKE**, Lake; Yates and Steuben Counties; located in W N.Y.; is one of the Finger Lakes; is 18 m. long and 1-1/2 m. wide; the Lake flows N into Lake Seneca; also known as Crooked Lake.

On March 12, 1908, one of the world's first flying machines was carefully set up on the ice here. Its official name was Drome No. 1, but its familiar name was *Red Wing*, because its two long kitelike wings were covered with red silk. A 24-horsepower, eight-cylinder motorcycle motor, built by *Glenn Curtiss* in his Hammondsport shop, was installed between these flimsy wings. *Casy Baldwin, John McCurdy*, and *Glenn Curtiss* drew lots to see who would pilot the craft. *Dr. Alexander Graham Bell*, who had helped to design the "aerodrome," was not present, having been forced to leave Hammondsport because of his wife's illness. *Casey Baldwin* won the drawing and cimbed into the pilot's seat. His assitants cranked the motor. Baldwin yelled, "Let go!". The *Red Wing* skimmed along on its runners for 250 feet, rose into the air six or eight feet, flew 318 feet and 11 inches, then crashed. Baldwin crawled out of the wreckage with a few bruises.

•**KINDERHOOK**, Village and Town; Columbia County; Pop. 1,365 and 7,632; Area Code 518; Zip Code 12106; Elev. 256'; E of Hudson River in SE N.Y.; Kinderhook (Dutch "children's corner") is a village whose Dutch settlers brought the village name with them. Birthplace of *Martin Van Buren*, 8th President of the U.S., who is buried in the village cemetery.

•**KINGS COUNTY**, SE N.Y.; 70 sq. miles; Pop. 2,218,441; Seat -

Brooklyn; Est. November 1, 1983; Named after *King Charles II* .

•**KINGS POINT**, Village; Nassau County; Pop. 5,208; Area Code 516; Zip Code 11024; near Great Neck, Long Island, N.Y.

•**KINGSTON**, City; Seat of Ulster County; Pop. 24,427; Area Code 914; Zip Code 12401; Elev. 150'; on Hudson River 15 m. N of Poughkeepsie in SE N.Y.; rises from the W bank of the Hudson River at the mouth of Rondout Creek.

In 1615 Dutch traders established a trading post at the mouth of Rondout Creek and named it Esopus. A group of Dutch colonists from Albany made the first permanent settlement in 1653. The Indians attacked the place on two occasions and took many lives. In 1658 *Director General Peter Stuyvesant* erected a stockade and blockhouse and in 1661 granted a charter to the village, which he called Wiltwyck (Dutch, wild retreat). In 1669 the English *Governor Francis Lovelace* gave it its present name in honor of Kingston L'Isle, his family seat in England. During the short Dutch reoccupation in 1673-4 the place was called Swanenburgh.

Industries include electronic computers, boat building, clothing and fruit.

•**KIRKWOOD**, Town; Broome County; Pop. 5,839; Area Code 607; Zip Code 13795.

•**KNOX**, Town; Albany County; Pop. 2,476; Area Code 518; Zip Code 12107.

•**LACKAWANNA**, City; Erie County; Pop. 22,730; Area Code 716; Zip Code 14218; Elev. 600'; S of Buffalo; approx. 5 m. on Lake Erie in W N.Y.; an industrial suburb, was named for the steel company that moved from Scranton, Pennsylvania, and erected its plant here in 1899; 10 years later the early hamlet of Limestone Hill, Lighting District No. 1, Town of West Seneca, was incorporated as a city. The population is of European origin, mostly Polish and Hungarian.

•**LACONA**, Village; Oswego County; Pop. 588; Area Code 315; Zip Code 13083.

•**LA FARGEVILLE**, Jefferson County; Area Code 315; Zip Code 13656; Elev. 380'; N N.Y.; settled in 1816 by *Reuben Andrus* and named for *John LaFarge*, large landholder and father of *John Lafarge*, American artist, and grandfather of *Oliver LaFarge*, author of *Laughing Boy* .

•**LA FAYETTE**, Town; Onondaga County; Pop. 4,473; Area Code 315; Zip Code 13085; Elev. 1,160'.

Dictionary of Places 287

•**LAKE GEORGE**, Village and Town; Seat of Warren County; Pop. 1,042 and 3,402; Area Code 518; Zip Code 12845; Elev. 350'; is a year-round sports center, lies in the foothills of the Adirondacks at the southern end of Lake George.

•**LAKE GEORGE**, Lake; Essex and Warren Counties; Approx. 30 miles long.

•**LAKE GROVE**, Village; Suffolk County; Pop. 9,683; Area Code 516; Zip Code 11755; 7 m. NE of Islip in SE N.Y.

•**LAKE LUZERNE**, Town; Warren County; Pop. 2,674; Area Code 518; Zip Code 12846.

•**LAKE PLACID**, Village; Essex County; Pop. 2,474; Area Code 518; Zip Code 12946; Elev. 1,880'; in Adirondack Mts. on Mirror Lake, near Lake Placid, 40 m. SW of Plattsburg in NE N.Y.

Lake Placid, built around Mirror Lake and surrounded by the highest Adirondack peaks, is a year-round sports community that has developed the surrounding natural resources for winter and summer activities: skiing, skating, bobsledding, golf, tennis, boating, swimming, fishing, and mountain climbing. Almost every sport has its annual competition, and the seasons merge in the mid-summer indoor ice carnival. The Winter Olympic Games of 1932 and 1980 were held here. In 1980, the U.S. (Amateur) Hockey Team won the Gold Medal over the Russians.

The Lake Placid Club, on the east shore of Mirror Lake, was founded in 1895 by *Melvil Dewey*, inventor of the Dewey Decimal System for library classifications and advocate of phonetic spelling.

•**LAKE PLEASANT**, Town; Seat of Hamilton County; Pop. 865; Area Code 518; Zip Code 12108; 50 m. E NE of Utica in NE central N.Y.

•**LAKEVILLE**, Livingston County; Area Code 716; Zip Code 14480; W N.Y.

•**LAKEWOOD**, Village; Chautauqua County; Pop. 3,931; Area Code 716; Zip Code 14750; on Chautaqua Lake 5 m. W of Jamestown in SW corner of N.Y.

•**LANCASTER**, Village and Town; Erie County; Pop. 13,049 and 30,130; Area Code 716; Zip Code 14086; in W N.Y. 11 m. E of Buffalo; Mainly a residential suburb.

•**LANSING**, Village and Town; Tompkins County; Pop. 3,031 and 8,301; Area Code 607; Zip Code 14882.

•**LARCHMONT**, Village; Westchester County; Pop. 6,268; Area Code 914; Zip Code 10538; Elev. 100'; on Long Island Sound in S N.Y. New York City is 20 m. to the SW.

•**LAURENS**, Village and Town; Otsego County; Pop. 276 and 1,879; Area Code 617; Zip Code 13796; Elev. 1,117.

•**LAWRENCE**, Village; Nassau County; Pop. 6,183; Area Code 516; Zip Code 11559; on Long Island 16 m. E SE of New York in SE N.Y.

•**LAWRENCEVILLE**, St. Lawrence County; Area Code 315; Zip Code 12949; Elev. 1,000'; N N.Y.

•**LEBANON**, Town; Madison County; Pop. 1,126; Area Code 315; Zip Code 13085.

•**LEBANON SPRINGS**, Village; Columbia County; Area Code 518; Zip Code 12114; Elev. 800'; near Massachusetts border about 22 m. SE of Albany in SE N.Y.; owes its existence to mineral springs. Indians who had long claimed medical value for the water brought *Captain Thomas Hitchcock*, a British officer, to the spring in 1766 after New England physicians had diagnosed his case as hopeless. The thermal waters ostensibly effected a cure. Hitchcock returned in 1771 and built a bathhouse and roads.

•**LEICESTER**, Village and Town; Livingston County; Pop. 453 and 1,880; Area Code 716; Zip Code 14481; Elev. 661'.

•**LEON**, Town; Cattaraugus County; Pop. 1,047; Area Code 716; Zip Code 14651.

•**LEROY**, Village and Town; Genesee County; Pop. 4,890 and 8,013; Area Code 716; Zip Code 14482; Elev. 869'; 24 m. SW of Rochester in W N.Y.; birthplace of the stringless bean and home town of Jello, is a thriving village on Oatka (Indian, an opening) Creek, with more than its share of fine old post-Colonial houses, most of them grouped on Main Street adjacent to the one-block business section.

In the late 1870's *Nicholas B. Keeney* and his son, Calvin, of LeRoy, by cross-fertilizing some 40 or more bean plants over a series of years, weeded out all but the stringless pods, thus bringing to the market beans minus strings.

•**LEVITTOWN**, Unincorporated village; Nassau County; Area Code 516; Zip Code 11756; SE New York; 30 m. E of Manhattan on Long Island in SE N.Y.; Residential.

Between 1947 and 1951, the development firm of Levitt and Sons built over 17,000 homes and apartments on a site of the

Hempstead plain that was formerly agricultural. Using prefabricated materials and assembly-line style construction, the development represented the prototype of post-World War II suburbia. The homes were laid out on equal plots in a geometrical pattern, with shops, schools, parks and churches interspersed systematically according to a general plan. Although each of the houses had a different facade, the floorplans and plots were essentially alike.
Since the 1950s, however, residents of Levittown have done much to reduce the mass-produced look of their neighborhood. Room additions, new landscaping and paint, as well as other modifications have helped create some diversity. The community supports the Levittown Hall, where meetings and cultural events are held.

•LEWIS, Town; Essex County; Pop. 924; Area Code 518; Zip Code 12950.

•LEWIS COUNTY, N central New York; 1,291 sq. miles; Pop. 25,06; Seat - Lowville; Est. March 28, 1805; Named after *Morgan Lewis*.

•LEWISTON, Village and Town; Niagara County; Pop. 3,321 and 16,185; Area Code 716; Zip Code 14092; Elev. 363'; W New York; along the Niagara River at the foot of a steep bluff. According to geologists, this was the site of Niagara Falls some 35,000 years ago.
In 1626 a Franciscan missionary found here a settlement of the Attawandaronk or Neuter Indians. Twenty-five years later the village was destroyed by the Seneca. In 1678 *Rene' Robert Cavelier de La Salle* and his men built a storehouse here and completed to the upper Niagara a portage trail which was used for a century and a half. Settlement did not begin until after the English troops surrendered Fort Niagara in 1796. The frontier village, named after *Governor Morgan Lewis*, was captured and burned by the British in 1813, but was rebuilt immediately.

•LEXINGTON, Town; Greene County; Pop. 807; Area Code 518; Zip Code 12452.

•LIBERTY, Village and Town; Sullivan County; Pop. 4,293 and 9,931; Area Code 914; Zip Code 12754; Elev. 1,581'; 45 m. W of Poughkeepsie; a year-round resort with toboggan slides and ski trails and a program of winter carnivals and races.

•LILY DALE, Chautauqua County; Area Code 716; Zip Code 14752; SW N.Y.

•LIMA, Village; Livingston County; Pop. 2,033; Area Code 716;

Zip Code 14485.
Genesee College was founded here in 1870, but moved to Syracuse the next year.

•**LIMESTONE**, Village; Cattaraugus County; Pop. 464; Area Code 716; Zip Code 14753.

•**LINDENHURST**, Village; Suffolk County; Pop. 26,896; Area Code 516; Zip Code 11757; 35 m. E of N.Y. On Great South Bay on Long Island in SE N.Y.; overgrown in pine and brushwood as late as 1870, it was laid out by a German and still retains something of a mid-European flavor. One of the few industrial communities on Long Island, the village contains several small factories and a brewery.

•**LINDLEY**, Town; Steuben County; Pop. 1,823; Area Code 607; Zip Code 14858.

•**LISBON**, Town; St.Lawrence County; Pop. 3,555; Area Code 315; Zip Code 13658.

•**LISLE**, Village and Town; Broome County; Pop. 351 and 2,023; Area Code 607; Zip Code 13797.

•**LITTLE FALLS**, City; Herkimer County; Pop. 6,153; Area Code 315; Zip Code 13365; Elev. 440'; 20 m. E of Utica in NE central N.Y.; Settled 1725; Inc. 1895; occupies both sides of the Mohawk River; An industrial city. In 1782 the place was burned down by Indians and Tories.

A boom town of the old Erie Canal era, the city has never outlived the influence of that waterway; and its successor, the Barge Canal, remains an integral part of industrial and mercantile life.

The population was predominently Roman Catholic as a result of the settlement of large numbers of Irish in the 1850's and the southern European invasion of the early decades of the present century.

The Mohawk Indians recognized the strategic value of the Little Falls portage; its control gave them primacy in the Iroquois councils. The few fortunate Palatines who settled along the carrying place about 1725 soon turned to the business of hauling the crude bateaux over the rocks around the falls. Thereafter every form of transport paid its toll to the community.

About 1800, Herkimer County farmers began to make "Country store," or American, cheese; and Little Falls, the natural shipping point for the region, became the largest cheese market in the country. At the same time, the opening of the Erie Canal and the completion of the Utica & Schenectady Railroad combined with the available water power to attract industries. In

1871 the New York Dairymen's Association and Board of Trade, the first organization of its kind in the country, was organized in Little Falls. The local cheese industry declined as the farmers turned to providing fluid milk for city markets.

•**LITTLE VALLEY**, Village and Town; Seat of Cattaraugus County; Pop. 1,194 and 1,822; Area Code 716; Zip Code 14755; Elev. 1,594; SW N.Y.

•**LIVERPOOL**, Village; Onondaga County; Pop. 2,844; Area Code 315; Zip Code 13088; Elev. 380'; 5 m. N of Syracuse in central N.Y.

•**LIVINGSTON**, Town; Columbia County; Pop. 3,052; Area Code 518; Zip Code 12541.

•**LIVINGSTON**, Kings County; Area Code 212; Zip Code 112 + zone; SE N.Y.

•**LIVINGSTON COUNTY**, W New York; 638 sq. miles; Pop. 56,970; Seat - Geneseo; Est. February 23, 1821; Named after *Robert R. Livingston*.

•**LIVONIA**, Village and Town; Livingston County; Pop. 1,238 and 5,753; Area Code 716; Zip Code 14487; Elev. 825'.

•**LOCKE**, Town; Cayuga County; Pop. 1,747; Area Code 315; Zip Code 13092; Elev. 800'; central N.Y.; birthplace of *President Millard Fillmore*.

•**LOCKPORT**, City; Seat of Niagara County; Pop. 24,857; Area Code 716; Zip Code 14094; Elev. 660'; grew around the series of locks built to carry the Erie Canal through the Lockport gorge. The businessman who put Lockport on the map in the 1870's was *John Hodge*, proprietor and manufacturer of Merchant's Gargling Oil, a remedy advertised to our grandparents as "good for man or beast"; one of Hodge's stunts was to send a steamer bedecked with banners over the Niagara cataract.

•**LOCUST VALLEY**, Nassau County; Area Code 516; Zip Code 11560; on Long Island in SE N.Y.; residential community, historically interesting as the spot where *Captain John Underhill* (1597-1672) acquired much land and lived his last years. Underhill came to Boston in 1630 to organize and command the Massachusetts militia. After a stormy career in New England he came here, where he fought Dutch discrimination against English settlers. He was led into wrangles with *Peter Stuyvesant* and narrowly escaped trial on the charge of sedition. The British occupation of 1664 elevated him to High Sheriff and made further belligerency unnecessary.

•**LODI**, Village and Town; Seneca County; Pop. 340 and 1,181; Area Code 315; Zip Code 14860; W central N.Y.

•**LONG BEACH**, City; Nassau County; Pop. 34,022; Area Code 516; Zip Code 11561; is an exciting mixture of Atlantic City and Coney Island. It sits on the shifting sands of the W end of the Outer Barrier, a hive of bathers and anglers in summer, a place of little movement in winter. A popular resort for city people of moderate incomes, its population varies with the season. A superb boardwalk stretches two miles along the ocean front and all the accessories of a seaside resort are at hand.

•**LONG ISLAND**, Island; Kings, Nassau, Queens and Suffolk Counties; located in S N.Y., S of Connecticut and surrounded by the Atlantic Ocean. The land mass is 1,401 sq. miles, 118 miles in length and 23 miles at its greatest width. The coastline measures 280 miles. The northland is hilly, beaches are on the S side and many smaller islands are located around the main island.

•**LONG ISLAND CITY**, Part of Queens Borough; Queens County; Pop. included in Queens Borough; Area Code 312; Zip Code 111 + znoe; on Long Island in S N.Y. At one time was a village of Astoria and did not become a city until 1898 when it became part of Queensborough. In 1640 it was settled by the Dutch. Currently is an industrial center.

•**LONG ISLAND SOUND**, Water; located N of Long Island and S of Connecticut. The Block Island Sound is to the W and East River to the E. Long Island Sound is 110 miles long and varies in width from 10 miles to 25 miles encompassing 1,300 sq. miles.

•**LONG LAKE**, Town; Hamilton County; Pop. 932; Area Code 518; Zip Code 12847.

•**LONG LAKE**, Lake; Hamilton County; Elev. 1,615'; in N N.Y. and S Hamilton County. The water flows from Raquette Lake to Raquette River. Long Lake is 14 miles in length and one mile in width. It is a long, narrow body of crystal-clear water, which is actually the widened channel of the Raquette River. During spring floods the water level is sometimes raised as much as 14 feet.

•**LORRAINE**, Town; Jefferson County; Pop. 732; Area Code 315; Zip Code 13659.

•**LOWVILLE**, Village and Town; Seat of Lewis County; Pop. 3,382 and 4,595; Area Code 315; Zip Code 13367; Elev. 865'; 26 m. SE of Watertown in N central N.Y.; is a characteristic North

Country village with tree shaded streets, frame dwellings, and a neat brick business section. In one of the largest cold storage plants in the world, cheese and other farm products are gathered from the surrounding farms for shipment.

•**LYNBROOK**, Village Nassau County; Pop. 20,500; Area Code 516; Zip Code 11563; on S shore of Long Island 18 m. E of New York City in SE N.Y.

•**LYNDONVILLE**, Village; Orleans County; Pop. 919; Area Code 716; Zip Code 14098.

•**LYON MOUNTAIN**, Clinton County; Area Code 518; Zip Code 12952; Elev. 1,753'; is near the NW base of Lyon Mt. in NE corner of N.Y. The area is engaged in mining ore. The great cables of the Brooklyn Bridge get their strength from iron mined at the bowels of the Mountain. Lyon Mt. is located in the Adirondack Mts. and its peak is 3,880 feet.

•**LYONS**, Village and Town; Seat of Wayne County; Pop. 4,160 and 6,078; Area Code 315; Zip Code 14489; Elev. 420'.

•**LYONS FALLS**, Village; Lewis County; Pop. 749; Area Code 315; Zip Code 13368; Elev. 865'; N central N.Y.

The narrow ditch of the old Black River Canal crosses and recrosses State 12; down the sharp hill slopes, the dilapidated locks, some of them still bearing their hand-operated wooden gates, appear like short stairways. The 35-mile canal was begun in 1838 and completed in 1855; it was not finally abandoned until 1926, when it was superseded in its final function as water feeder for the Barge Canal by the Hinckley and Delta reservoirs.

•**LYSANDER**, Town; Onondaga County; Pop. 13,889; Area Code 315; Zip Code 13094.

•**MACEDON**, Village and Town; Wayne County; Pop. 1,388 and 6,490; Area Code 315; Zip Code 14502.

•**MACHIAS**, Town; Cattaraugus County; Pop. 2,036; Area Code 716; Zip Code 14101.

•**MADISON**, Village and Town; Madison County; Pop. 395 and 2,315; Area Code 315; Zip Code 13402.

•**MADISON COUNTY**, Central N.Y.; 661 sq. miles; Pop. 64,983; Seat - Wampsville; Est. March 21, 1806; Named after *James Madison*.

•**MADRID**, Town; St. Lawrence County; Pop. 1,856; Area Code

315; Zip Code 13660.

•**MAHOPAC**, Village; Putnam County; Area Code 914; Zip Code 10541; Elev. 640'; on Lake Mahopac, about 10 m. NE of Peekskill in SE N.Y.; is the trading center for residents of the almost continuous line of summer cottages along the lake, named for a local Indian tribe.

•**MAINE**, Town; Broome County; Pop. 5,256; Area Code 607; Zip Code 13802.

•**MALDEN ON HUDSON**, Ulster County; Area Code 914; Zip Code 12453; Elev. 80'; SE N.Y.; during the latter part of the nineteenth century the place throve on the mining of "bluestone" for sidewalks and street curbings.

•**MALONE**, Village and Town; Seat of Franklin County; Pop. 7,645 and 11,215; Area Code 518; Zip Code 12953; Elev. 730'; 45 m. W NW of Plattsburg in NE N.Y.; straddles the Malone River. The place was settled by Vermonters in 1802; the name was bestowed by Vermonters in honor of his friend, *Edmund Malone*, Shakespearian scholar.

•**MALVERNE**, Village; Nassau County; Pop. 9,257; Area Code 516; Zip Code 11565; on Long Island 17 m. E of New York in SE N.Y.

•**MAMARONECK**, Village and Town; Westchester County; Pop. 17,501 and 28,817; Area Code 914; Zip Code 10543; Elev. 47'; on Long Island Sound 22 m. NE of New York in SE New York; Settled in 1650; Inc. in 1895; (Indian, "he assembles the people"); first settled by English farmers about 1650. It is a pleasure boat center.

•**MANCHESTER**, Village and Town; Ontario County; Pop. 1,681 and 9,039; Area Code 315; Zip Code 14504; Elev. 590'; 24 m. SE of Rochester in W N.Y., in the Finger Lakes resort area. The early residents named the place after Manchester, England.

•**MANHASSET**, Nassau County; Area Code 516; Zip Code 11030; NW Long Island in SE N.Y. at the end of Manhasset Bay; is one of the oldest settlements on the N shore of Long Island.

•**MANHATTAN**, Borough; New York Conty; Pop. 1,148,124; Area Code 212; Zip Code 100 + zone; in SE N.Y. part of New York City and Manhattan Island, 22 square miles nestled between East River and Hudson River; In 1898 was chartered as one of five boroughs (which includes the islands of Wards, Randalls and Welfare located in the East River). Manhattan is the exclusive residential part of the city of New York.

For most visitors to New York City, the center of interest is the Borough of Manhattan, the most explosive center of civilization in the New World. The borough is an island 12-1/2 miles long, shaped like an index finger pointing to the south. Broadway, the longest and most fantastic street in the world, starts its 16-mile journey from the tip of Manhattan as a shipping lane, moves a few blocks north to the Wall Street financial center, passes by the civic buildings of the city, and takes a diagonal course from Union Square through the needle-trades area between 34th and 30th Streets. Between 42d and 53d Streets, Broadway is the Great White Way -renowned as an amusement and theatrical center. From 53rd Street to Columbus Circle it cuts through Automobile Row, center of the auto retail trade. It changes its diagonal course at 79th Street to parallel the island's high escarpment facing the Hudson River. Here it is lined with hotels, apartment houses, cafeterias, beauty salons, movie houses, and churches. At 114th Street it strikes a new note in the buildings of Columbia University, and another at 155th Street in a group of museums. From this point on it is a nondescript thoroughfare, ending as a semisuburban road as it approaches the city's limits.

•MANLIUS, Village and Town; Onondaga County; Pop. 5,354 and 28,475; Area Code 315; Zip Code 13104; 10 m. E of Syracuse in central N.Y.

•MANNSVILLE, Village; Jefferson County; Pop. 431; Area Code 315; Zip Code 13661; Elev. 630'.

•MARATHON, Village and Town; Cortland County; Pop. 1,030 and 1,782; Area Code 607; Zip Code 13803.

•MARCELLUS, Village and Town; Onondaga County; Pop. 1,880 and 6,188; Area Code 315; Zip Code 13108.

•MARCY, Town; Oneida County; Pop. 6,425; Area Code 315; Zip Code 13403.

•MARGARETVILLE, Village; Delaware County; Pop. 750; Area Code 518; Zip Code 12455; Elev. 1,325'; in central N.Y. on the N border of the Catskill State Park on State 30; catering to summer residents and tourists, it is in a valley between 2,600-foot Pakatakan Mountain on the south and 2,211-foot Kettle Hill on the north, at the western boundary of Catskill State Park.

•MARILLA, Town; Erie County; Pop. 4,864; Area Code 716; Zip Code 14102.

•**MARION**, Town; Wayne County; Pop. 4,471; Area Code 315; Zip Code 14505.

•**MARTINSBURG**, Town; Lewis County; Pop. 1,504; Area Code 315; Zip Code 13404.

•**MARYLAND**, Town; Otsego County; Pop. 1,680; Area Code 617; Zip Code 12116.

•**MASONVILLE**, Town; Delaware County; Pop. 1,152; Area Code 518; Zip Code 13804.

•**MASSAPEQUA**, Unincorporated; Nassau County; Area Code 516; Zip Code 11758; on S shore of Long Island about 10 m. SE of Mineola in SE N.Y.

•**MASSAPEQUA PARK**, Village; Nassau County; Pop. 19,791; Area Code 516; Zip Code 11762; on Long Island in SE N.Y.

•**MASSAWEPIE**, Franklin County; Area Code 518; Zip Code 12986.

•**MASSENA**, Village and Town; St. Lawrence County; Pop. 12,838 and 14,842; Area Code 315; Zip Code 13662; Elev. 1,340'; near St. Lawrence River 31 m. W of Malone in N N.Y.

•**MAYBROOK**, Village; Orange County; Pop. 2,007; Area Code 914; Zip Code 12543.

•**MAYFIELD**, Village and Town; Fulton County; Pop. 944; Area Code 607; Zip Code 12117.

•**MAYVILLE**, Village; Seat of Chautauqua County; Pop. 1,629; Area Code 716; Zip Code 14757; SW corner of N.Y.; at the head of the Chautauqua Lake.

•**MC DONOUGH**, Town; Chenango County; Pop. 794; Area Code 607; Zip Code 13801.

•**MC GRAW**, Village; Cortland County; Pop. 1,186; Area Code 607; Zip Code 13101.

•**MECHANICVILLE**, City; Saratoga County; Pop. 5,481; Area Code 518; Zip Code 12118; Elev. 105'; On Hudson River 17 m. N of Albany in E N.Y.; the yards, roundhouses, and repair shops of the Delaware & Hudson and Boston & Maine Railroads and the book-paper plant of a pulp & paper company are here.

•**MEDINA**, Village; Orleans County; Pop. 6,391; Area Code 716;

Dictionary of Places 297

Zip Code 14103; 41 m. W of Rochester on N.Y. State Barge Canal in W N.Y.

•MENDON, Town; Monroe County; Pop. 5,434; Area Code 716; Zip Code 14506.

•MEREDITH, Delaware County; Pop. 1,363; Area Code 518; Zip Code 13805.

•MERIDALE, Delaware County; Area Code 518; Zip Code 13806.

•MERIDIAN, Village; Cayuga County; Pop. 339; Area Code 315; Zip Code 13113.

•MERRIMAN, Dam; Rondout Creek, Ulster County; SE New York; Completed 1949; Maximum Height 370 ft.; earth fill type; for power.

•MEXICO, Village and Town; Oswego County; Pop. 1,619 and 4,770; Area Code 315; Zip Code 13114; Elev. 384'.

•MIDDLEBURGH, Village and Town; Schoharie County; Pop. 1,356 and 2,970; Area Code 650; Zip Code 12122; Elev. 650'; founded in 1712 by *John Conrad Weiser* and the first group of Palatine pioneers, Middleburgh, first called Weiser's Dorf, is the oldest settlement in the valley. It was burned in the Johnson raid of 1780.

•MIDDLE ISLAND, Suffolk County; Area Code 516; Zip Code 11953; E Long Island in SE N.Y.

•MIDDLEPORT, Village; Niagara County; Pop. 1,999; Area Code 716; Zip Code 14105; Elev. 540'; 30 m. E NE of Niagara Falls in W N.Y.; it sprang up as a settlement upon completion of the Erie Canal in 1825, and took its name from its location midway between Lockport and Albion.

•MIDDLESEX, Town; Yates County; Pop. 1,124; Area Code 315; Zip Code 1,124.

•MIDDLETOWN, City; Orange County; Pop. 21,455; Area Code 914; Zip Code 10940; Elev. 559'; 23 m. W of Newburgh in SE N.Y.; the city grew up along what had been the Minisink Trail, which ran from the Hudson to the headwaters of the Delaware and the Susquehanna.

•MIDDLEVILLE, Village; Herkimer County; Pop. 640; Area Code 315; Zip Code 13406; Elev. 570'.

•MILFORD, Village and Town; Otsego County; Pop. 513 and

2,656; Area Code 617; Zip Code 13807.

•**MILLBROOK**, Village; Dutchess County; Pop. 1,316; Area Code 914; Zip Code 12545; 13 m. E NE of Poughkeepsie in SE N.Y.

•**MILLERTON**, Village; Dutchess County; Pop. 1,020; Area Code 914; Zip Code 12546; Elev. 700'.

•**MILL NECK**, Nassau County; Pop. 962; Area Code 516; Zip Code 11765.

•**MILLPORT**, Village; Chemung County; Pop. 441; Area Code 607; Zip Code 14864.

•**MINEOLA**, Village; Seat of Nassau County; Pop. 20,673; Area Code 516; Zip Code 11501; on Long Island 20 m. E of New York in SE N.Y.

•**MINERVA**, Town; Essex County; Pop. 781; Area Code 518; Zip Code 12851; Elev. 1,400'; caters mostly to hundreds of tourists.

•**MINETTO**, Town; Oswego County; Pop. 1,903; Area Code 315; Zip Code 13115.

•**MINOA**, Village; Onondaga County; Pop. 3,552; Area Code 315; Zip Code 13116.

•**MOHAWK**, Village; Herkimer County; Pop. 2,954; Area Code 315; Zip Code 13407; Elev. 410'; on Mohawk River 12 m. E SE of Utica in NE central N.Y.; originally a Palatine settlement, was ravaged during the French and Yankee newcomers. After the opening of the Erie Canal, the settlement boomed; near by farmers turned to making cheese, an art introduced by the Yankees, and the village was second only to Little Falls as a cheese-shipping point.

•**MOHAWK RIVER**, River; Oneida County; in E central N.Y. The river is formed by the east and west branches of the Mohawk and is the largest tributary of the Hudson River. The river is 148 miles in length, flowing south and then east into the Hudson River.

  Mohawk River encircles several large islands, locale of the legend of the passing of the last of the Mohawks. When he was called by the Great Spirit, the old Indian gave his catch of fish to a white friend and refused the usual firewater offered in return, saying, "Great Spirit call, Indian no need." He sat down in the stern of his canoe, his arms folded, and the craft moved swiftly upstream, pulled by some invisible power into the settig sun. The next day his empty canoe was found floating in the river.

•**MOHEGAN LAKE**, Westchester County; Area Code 914; Zip Code 10547; Elev. 460'; SE N.Y.

•**MOIRA**, Town; Franklin County; Pop. 2,629; Area Code 518; Zip Code 12957.

•**MONROE**, Village and Town; Orange County; Pop. 5,987 and 14,942; Area Code 914; Zip Code 10950; Elev. 610; 15 m. SW of Newburgh in SE N.Y.

•**MONROE COUNTY**, W N.Y.; 675 sq. miles; Pop. 701,531; Seat - Rochester; Est. February 23, 1821; Named after *James Monroe*.

•**MONTAUK**, Unincorporated; Suffolk County; Area Code 516; Zip Code 11954; W Long Island in SE N.Y.; is the most easterly of New York state villages. A thriving trade caters to fishermen who go out for tuna and swordfish off Montauk Point or angle for smaller fry inside Peconic Bay and Gardiners Bay. From the middle of March, when the flounders run, until the arrival of winter storms, the chase never slackens. During the summer a ferry operates to New London, Connecticut.

•**MONTAUK POINT**, Point; Suffolk County; in SE N.Y. on Long Island at the farthest point NE.

•**MONTEZUMA**, Town; Cayuga County; Pop. 1,125; Area Code 315; Zip Code 13117; Elev. 400'.

•**MONTGOMERY**, Village and Town; Orange County; Pop. 2,318 and 16,554; Area Code 914; Zip Code 12549; SE N.Y.

•**MONTGOMERY COUNTY**, E N.Y.; 408 sq. miles; Pop. 53,325; Seat - Fonda; Est. March 12, 1772; named after *Richard Montgomery*.

•**MONTICELLO**, Village; Seat of Sullivan County; Pop. 6,297; Area Code 914; Zip Code 12701; 42 m. W of Poughkeepsie in SE N.Y.

•**MONTOUR FALLS**, Village; Schuyler County; Pop. 1,791; Area Code 607; Zip Code 14865; Elev. 480'; 16 m. N of Elmira in SW central N.Y. near the N point of Seneca Lake. Nearby are seven glens, each with a distinctive claim to beauty in cascades, caverns, waterfalls, amphitheaters, and high and angular cliffs. *David B. Hill* (1843-1910), state governor (1885-92), was born here.

The village occupies the site of Catherine's Town, a Seneca village. The white settlement on the site was named Havana in 1829; in the 1890's the name was changed to Montour Falls in honor of *Queen Catherine Montour*, of Canada, by an Indian woman. Catherine, "a handsome woman of polite address who spoke French fluently," married a Seneca chief, and after her husband's death ruled the village wisely.

•**MOOERS**, Village and Town; Clinton County; Pop. 546 and 2,296; Area Code 518; Zip Code 12958; Elev. 260'; NE corner of N.Y.; the region is inhabited largely by descendants of French Canadians who came here as lumberjacks.

•**MORAVIA**, Village and Town; Cayuga County; Pop. 1,565 and 2,614; Area Code 315; Zip Code 13118.

•**MORIAH**, Town; Essex County; Pop. 5,124; Area Code 518; Zip Code 12960.

•**MORRIS**, Village and Town; Otsego County; Pop. 683 and 1,780; Area Code 617; Zip Code 13808; in central N.Y.

•**MORRISTOWN**, Village and Town; St. Lawrence County; Pop. 461; Area Code 315; Zip Code 13664; N N.Y.; bass fishing center on a peninsula jutting into the St. Lawrence; The easternmost of the Thousand Islands are visible from here.

•**MORRISVILLE**, Village; Madison County; Pop. 2,711; Area Code 315; Zip Code 13408.

•**MOUNT KISCO**, Village and Town; Westchester County; Pop. 8,017; Area Code 914; Zip Code 10549; 36 m. NE of N.Y. City in SE N.Y.; is mainly residential.

•**MOUNT MARCY**, Mountain; Essex County; Elev. 5,844'; located 5 m. S of Lake Placid in NE N.Y. The highest point in the state and part of the Adirondack Mts.

•**MOUNT MORRIS**, Village and Town; Livingston County; Pop. 3,044 and 4,482; Area Code 716; Zip Code 14510; Elev. 3,163'; 34 m. SW of Rochester in W N.Y.; The first fire observation tower in the Adirondacks was erected on Mount Morris in 1909.

•**MOUNT VERNON**, City; Westchester County; Pop. 66,023; Area Code 914; Zip Code 14075; Elev. 100'; SE New York; N New York City suburb; Named for *George Washington's* Virginia estate.

Although it is considered a commuter suburb of New York City, Mount Vernon has a story of its own to tell. It also has its own commercial and industrial enterprises, in the fields of electronics, chemicals, plastics, machinery and precious metals.

The history of Mount Vernon goes back to the story of

Eastchester, an attractive stretch of rolling countryside watered by small streams. Originally the region was known as Hutchinson's, after *Anne Hutchinson*, who found refuge here for a time after being exiled from Massachusetts. In 1664 a group of 10 families from Fairfield County, Connecticut, under the leadership of *Thomas Pell*, arrived and asserted the right of Connecticut to the territory "as far south as the sea," including Eastchester and Westchester. The settlers conciliated the Indians, but the boundary dispute between New York and Connecticut was not settled until many years later.

In 1733, New York newspaperman *John Peter Zenger* was arrested here because of his account of *Lewis Morgan's* election to the assembly of Westchester County. *William Cosby*, the royal governor of New York at the time, opposed the election, and when Zenger accused Cosby of malfeasance in office, the governor imprisoned him on charges of libel. Zenger's acquittal by jury two years later established a freedom of press precedent in America.

Modern Mount Vernon began as a planned community. In 1850 a group of New York City workmen, artisans, and others of moderate means formed the Home Industrial Association with the purpose of "protection against the unjust power and influence of capital, and against land monopoly as the prime cause of poverty." The immediate aim was to establish a home making community outside the city. Members paid into the treasury not less than $25 and not more than $75. By 1852, 300 homes had been built and Mount Vernon became a regular stop on the New York New Haven and Hartford Railroad.

The undertaking of the Home Industrial Association attracted the interest of many prominent men in the liberal circles f the day, conspicuous among whom was *Horace Greeley*. These men were accustomed to gather for discussion at Gould's Hotel, built in the new settlement by *George J. Gould*. The cuisine soon acquired a wide reputation and the guest book displayed, among others, the signatures of *Cyrus* and *Dudley Field, Frank Leslie*, and *John J. Huyler*.

Points of interest here are the Old St. Paul's Episcopal Church built in 1761 and a few homes and taverns dating to the Revolution. A co-op college center of the State University is also located here.

•**MUNNSVILLE**, Village; Madison County; Pop. 489; Area Code 315 Zip Code 13409.

•**NAPLES**, Village and Town; Ontario County; Pop. 1,226 and 2,339; Area Code 315; Zip Code 14512; Elev. 800'; 24 m. N NE of Hornell in W N.Y.

Naples is the center of an important grape-growing and wine-making region. Grape culture was introduced in 1852 and the wine industry began about 1856, attracting Germans from the

Rhine Valley, followed by Swiss and French; their descendants and more recent German and Swiss immigrants are employed in the wineries.

In 1882 the late *D. Dana Luther* of Naples discovered in Grimes Glen, in the village the "Naples tree" (Archeosigillaria primerum), which was evidence that trees grew on the earth during the Devonian period; before, scientists had believed that Devonian vegetation was limited to a species of fern. The restored fossil, 33 feet high, is in the State Museum, Albany.

•**NASSAU**, Village and Town; Rensselaer County; Pop. 1,286 and 4,489; Area Code 518; Zip Code 12123; Elev. 403'.

•**NASSAU COUNTY**, SE N.Y. (W Long I); 289 sq. miles; Pop. 1,319,726; Seat - Mineola; Est. April 27, 1898; Named after *William of Nassau*.

•**NELLISTON**, Village; Montgomery County; Pop. 691; Area Code 518; Zip Code 13410.

•**NELSONVILLE**, Village; Putnam County; Pop. 562; Area Code 914; Zip Code 10516.

•**NEVERSINK**, Town; Sullivan County; Pop. 2,850; Area Code 914; Zip Code 12765.

•**NEWARK**, Village; Wayne County; Pop. 10,022; Area Code 315; Zip Code 14513.

•**NEWARK VALLEY**, Village and Town; Tioga County; Pop. 1,189 and 3,763; Area Code 607; Zip Code 13811.

•**NEW BALTIMORE**, Town; Greene County; Pop. 3,046; Area Code 518; Zip Code 12124.

•**NEW BERLIN**, Village and Town; Chenango County; Pop. 1,371 and 2,993; Area Code 607; Zip Code 13411.

•**NEW BREMEN**, Town; Lewis County; Pop. 2,339; Area Code 315; Zip Code 13412.

•**NEWBURGH**, City; Orange County; Pop. 23,116; Area Code 914; Zip Code 12550; Elev. 160'; on Hudson River opp. Beacon; 15 m. S of Poughkeepsie in SE N.Y.; lies above the broad expanse of Newburgh Bay.   The first settlement on the site of Newburgh was made in 1709 by a group of about 50 penniless German Palatines led by *Joshua Kocherthal*, a Lutheran preacher. They settled in the vicinity of Quassaick Creek, known as "The Palatine Parish of Quassaick." As Scottish, Dutch, and English settlers moved in, the Palatines found it difficult to live in harmony with their new neighbors and sought out the larger groups of their own people up the Hudson, in the Mohawk Valley, and in Pennsylvania and Delaware. The present name was given to the settlement in 1762 in honor of the town in Scotland on the River Tay. The city was incorporated in 1865. Epiphany Apostolic College was established here in 1888, Our Lady of Hope Seminary in 1900 and Mount St. Mary College in 1930.

•**NEW CITY**, Unincorporated; Seat of Rockland County; Pop. 27,344; Area Code 914; Zip Code 10956; SE N.Y.

•**NEWCOMB**, Town; Essex County; Pop. 683; Area Code 518; Zip Code 12852.

•**NEWFANE**, Town; Niagara County; Pop. 9,274; Area Code 716; Zip Code 14108; Elev. 345'; W N.Y.

•**NEWFIELD**, Town; Tompkins County; Pop. 4,394; Area Code 607; Zip Code 14867.

•**NEW HARTFORD**, Village and Town; Oneida County; Pop. 2,323 and 21,105; Area Code 315; Zip Code 13413; central N.Y.

•**NEW HAVEN**, Town; Oswego County; Pop. 2,414; Area Code 315; Zip Code 13121.

•**NEW HYDE PARK**, Village; Nassau County; Pop. 9,875; Area Code 516; Zip Code 11040; on Long Island 17 m. E. of N.Y. in SE N.Y.

•**NEW LEBANON**, Town; Columbia County; Pop. 2,313; Area Code 518; Zip Code 12125; Elev. 720'; was the birthplace of *Samuel J. Tilden* (1814-86), who as member of the state legislature and as Governor pushed the investigations that smashed New York City's Tweed Ring and the upstate Canal Ring.

•**NEW LISBON**, Town; Otsego County; Pop. 942; Area Code 617; Zip Code 13415.

•**NEW PALTZ**, Village and Town; Ulster County; Pop. 4,906 and 10,135; Area Code 914; Zip Code 12561; Elev. 236'; 10 m W of Poughkeepsie in SE N.Y.; center for vacationers in the Shawangunk Mountains. Early in 1678, 12 families loaded their possessions in three oxcarts and established their new home, which they called New Paltz after their first refuge, the Rheinish Pfalz.

•**NEWPORT**, Village and Town; Herkimer County; Pop. 745 and 2,203; Area Code 315; Zip Code 13416.

•**NEW ROCHELLE**, City; Westchester County; Pop. 70,519; Area Code 914; Zip Code 10801; Elev. 72'; SE New York; 16 m. NE of New York City boundary; on Long Island Sound; Residential.

The city occupies the site of the villages of the Siwanoy, principal nation of the Wappinger Indian confederacy. In 1688 a small group of Huguenot refugees landed at what is now Bonnefoi Point. In 1689 they purchased from *John Pell*, second lord of the manor of Pelham, through the agency of *Jacob Leisler*, a tract of 6,000 acres and named the settlement for their old home in France, La Rochelle. In 1692 they built the first church in New Rochelle. With the passing of the years, they became communicants of the anglican church. In 1698 a census showed a total population of 232, consisting of 188 whites and 44 Negro slaves.

Highlights of the Revolutionary period were the arrival of *Paul Revere* and other messengers from Boston to New York and the overnight stay of *George Washington* in 1775 on his way to Cambridge, Massachusetts, to take command of the Continental Army. *General Philip Schuyler* rode into town with him and left the next morning to take command of the defenses on the northern New York frontier. Schuyler was familiar with New Rochelle: as a boy of 15 he had attended the school of the *Reverend Pierre Stouppe* here, and his shore estate was near Pell's Point, five miles southeast.

New Rochelle became a village in 1857 and was incorporated as a city in 1899. As early as the 1890s it began to attract theatrical people, artists, and writers. *Agnes Booth* and *Cora Tanner*, famous in their day as starts of the melodrama *The Sporting Dutchess*, from time to time made the city their home, as did *Eddie Foy*, vaudeville actor and hero of the Iroquois Theater fire on Chicago. *Francis Wilson*, of *Erminie* fame, lived here; and *Frederick Remington*, sculptor and painter of western scenes, and *Augustus Thomas*, playwright, were commuters. Here, too, lived *George Randolph Chester*, who invented that delectable character of the old school, Get-Rich-Quick Wallingford. *Faith Baldwin*, novelist, was born in New Rochelle in 1893. A contemporary resident was *Norman Rockwell*, artist and illustrator.

Today, New Rochelle has some importance as an industrial center. Although heavy industry is restricted, metals, chemicals, processed foods, clothing and books are made here. However, many of the city's residents commute to New York City, and live in the parklike setting of many neighborhoods here. Others attend classes at Iona College and the College of New Rochelle (1891), both founded by Roman Catholics.

The local historical society maintains the *Thomas Paine Memorial House* and *Paine Cottage* in town. The memorial houses relics of the American Revolution and of Paine's life. Paine's cottage is the original post-Colonial frame structure the author of Common Sense lived in (1804-09). Paine was buried on his farm here, but in 1819, English political economist *William Cobbett* had his remains transferred to England, where they later disappeared. Some residents claim they were returned and buried under the present bronze monument on Paine and North Avenues.

•**NEW SCOTLAND,** Town; Albany County; Pop. 8,960; Area Code 518; Zip Code 12127.

•**NEW WINDSOR,** Town; Orange County; Pop. 19,512; Area Code 914; Zip Code 12550; Elev. 160'; a Newburgh suburb, is the site of Washington's headquarters from June 24 to July 21, 1779, and December 6, 1780 to June 25, 1781. On July 4, 1779, in celebration of the third anniversary of American Independence, Washington granted a general pardon to all war prisoners under sentence of death, while 13 rounds boomed from the cannon at distant West Point. *George Clinton*, the first elected governor of New York State, lived here; and his nephew, *DeWitt Clinton*, also governor in his turn was born here.

•**NEW YORK COUNTY,** SE N.Y.; 23 sq. miles; Pop. 1,418,124; Seat - New York; Est. November 1, 1683; Named after the *Duke of York*.

•**NEW YORK MILLS,** Village; Oneida County; Pop. 3,528; Area Code 315; Zip Code 13417; 5 m. E of Utica in central N.Y.

•**NIAGARA COUNTY,** W N.Y.; 532 sq. miles; Pop. 226,508; Seat - Lockport; Est. March 11, 1808; Named for the Indian word meaning bisected bottom lands.

•**NIAGARA FALLS,** City; Niagara County; Pop. 71,344; Area Code 716; Zip Code 14301; Elev. 575'; NW New York; On Niagara River at the Falls; 20 m. N of Buffalo.

Named for what is undisputably the most famous natural feature in New York state, Niagara Falls' main industry is tourism, since over two million visitors come to the city each year to view the neighboring Falls. It is also a port of entry for the Great Lakes - St. Lawrence Seaway system since it is only about 110 miles south of Lake Ontario on the Niagara River. But once vessels reach the south end of the city, rushing water and the falls do not permit further inland travel. These rushing waters are the mainstay of much of the city and Buffalo metropolitan area, however. The small but thriving industrial community here converts the great power of the falls into electric power, for use in electrochemical and electrometallurgical industries. Paper products, batteries and processed foods are also made here, using the power of the river.

Control of this region was of strategic value in the Colonial period because of the seven mile portage around Niagara Falls - the only break in the all-water journey between the St.Lawrence and the upper reaches of the Great Lakes. The first published view of Niagara Falls, reproduced in a volume in 1697, was a sketch made by *Father Louis Hennepin*, who visited the falls on December 6, 1678. In 1745 and 1750 the French built two forts near the falls to supplement Fort Niagara at the mouth of the river and to guard the upper end of the portage. Before the approach of the British in 1759, *Calbert Joncaire*, French master of the portage, burned the forts and retreated across the river.

Under British occupation, *John Stedman* received a grant of land along the river from the Indians and became master of the portage. Fort Schlosser, more substantial than its predecessors, was erected by *Captain Joseph Schlosser*, a German officer in the British army. An old stone chimney, the only part of the French forts not destroyed by Joncaire, was built into the mess hall of Fort Schlosser and now stands, reconstructed, on the grounds of the Carborundum Company.

Augustus Porter visited the place in 1795, returned in 1805 or 1806, purchased the land immediately surrounding the falls, moved his family there, built a gristmill, and succeeded Stedman as master of the portage. Visioning a manufacturing center that would rival the English city, Porter named the settlement Manchester. The fighting that took place on the Niagara Frontier throughout the War of 1812 culminated in the burning of Manchester and Fort Schlosser by the British in 1813. Only a few houses escaped the flames.

When Porter realized that the Erie Canal had destroyed business on the portage, he urged capitalists to develop Niagara power. As a result, a canal between the upper and lower rivers, begun in 1852, was completed in 1862 at a cost of about $1,000,000. In 1877 the entire property was bought at auction for $76,000 by *Jacob F. Schoellkopf*, whose descendants merged their holdings with the Niagara Falls Power Comapny during World War I. Niagara water power turned the first generator in 1881; power lines reached Buffalo in 1896 and Syracuse in 1905; today they extend into western and central New York, serving a large population. The horsepower of electric current generated, not only turns the wheels of local plants producing abrasives, paper, flour, foundry materials, and machinery, but also has made possible the remarkable technological development of the aluminum, calcium, carbide, ferroalloy, silicone, and graphite industries.

In 1950, local residents feared the scenic beauty of the Falls would be ruined if no controls were placed over hydroelectric power plants. Officials on both Canadian and American sides of the River agreed to reserve sufficient amounts of water so that

Dictionary of Places   307

they might flow normally over the Falls. Many areas surrounding the Falls, including Goat Island, were set aside as state parks.

•NIAGARA RIVER, River; located in W N.Y.; the river forms the boundary between Canada and the U.S.; it also connects Lake Erie with Ontario.

•NICHOLS, Village and Town; Tioga County; Pop. 608 and 2,554; Area Code 607; Zip Code 13812.

•NORFOLK, Town; St.Lawrence County; Pop. 4,975; Area Code 315; Zip Code 13667.

•NORTH COLLINS, Village and Town; Erie County; Pop. 1,509 and 3,801; Area Code 716; Zip Code 14111; Elev. 830'; was settled about 1809 by Quakers, who in 1813 built the first meetinghouse.

•NORTH HUDSON, Town; Essex County; Pop. 181; Area Code 518; Zip Code 12855.

•NORTH NORWICH, Town; Chenango County; Pop. 1,688; Area Code 607; Zip Code 13814.

•NORTHPORT, Village; Suffolk County; Pop. 7,640; Area Code 516; Zip Code 11768; N coast of Long Island in SE N.Y.
In the days of sail, ships circled the globe in search of markets for the expanding American trade. Between 1820 and 1884, 179 vessels were built in Northport yards, and allied industries thrived. The village is known as one of the most healthful in the state and famous for the fine views from its wooded slopes.

•NORTH SALEM, Town; Westchester County; Pop. 4,562; Area Code 914; Zip Code 10560.

•NORTH SYRACUSEj, Village; Onondaga County; Pop. 7,965; Area Code 315; Zip Code 13212; 8 m. N NE of Syracuse in central N.Y.

•NORTH TARRYTOWN, Village; Westchester County; Pop. 8,254; Area Code 914; Zip Code 10591; Elev. 70'; on Hudson River 26 m. N of N.Y. City and adjoining Tarrytown in SE N.Y.; is a commuters' village. At the foot of a hill,Gory Creek, or Pocantico River is crossed on the Washington Irving Memorial Bridge. A short way upstream stood the narrow wooden bridge where *Brom Bones* threw the pumpkin head at *Ichabod Crane*.

•NORTH TONAWANDA, City; Niagara County; Pop. 35,717; Area Code 716; Zip Code 14120; Elev. 575'; 10 m. E of Niagara

Falls in W N.Y.; on the northern bank of the Barge Canal, an industrial city. In the eastern part of town is an impressive residential district, with tree lined avenues, parks, and gardens. The industrial section, with its large foreign population groups, faces the water front.

•NORTHVILLE, Village; Fulton County; Pop. 1,335; Area Code 607; Zip Code 12134; Elev. 795'.

•NORWICH, City; Seat of Chenango County; Pop. 8,070; Area Code 607 Zip Code 13815; Elev. 1,015'; 36 m. N NE of Binghamton in S central N.Y.

•NORWOOD, Village; St. Lawrence County; Pop. 1,902; Area Code 315; Zip Code 13668.

•NUNDA, Village and Town; Livingston County; Pop. 1,168 and 2,695; Area Code 716; Zip Code 14517.

•NYACK, Village; Rockland County; Pop. 6,455; Area Code 914; Zip code 10960; on W shore of Hudson River 25 m. N of N.Y. in SE N.Y.

•OAKFIELD, Village and Town; Genesee County; Pop. 1,795 and 3,210; Area Code 716; Zip Code 14125.

•OCEAN BEACH, Village; Suffolk County; Pop. 163; Area Code 516; Zip Code 11770.

•OCEANSIDE, Nassau County; Area Code 516; Zip Code 11572; W end of Long Island in SE N.Y.

The first white settlers, a group of fishermen who arrived here nearly 200 years ago, called the settlement Christian Hook but the name was changed to Oceanville in 1864 and Oceanside in 1889. Inhabitants are mostly city workers with a sprinkling of fishermen.

The wayside shrine, Church of St. Anthony, built in a hillside at the corner of Windsor Parkway and Lincoln Ave., is sunk 30 feet below a beautifully landscaped rock garden. It was designed by the *Reverend Robert Barrett*, pastor, and built with funds bequeathed by his father. In the subterranean interior an ingenious system of lighting throws the main body of the cavern into reposeful shade and brings into relief in a blaze of light a golden tabernacle.

•ODESSA, Village; Schuyler County; Pop. 611; Area Code 607; Zip Code 14869.

•OGDENSBURG, City; St.Lawrence County; Pop. 12,372; Area

Code 315; Zip Code 13669; Elev. 275'; on St.Lawrence River 55 m. N NE of Watertown in N N.Y.; is a port of entry with five miles of irregular shoreline. In 1749 *Abbe' Francois Picquet* built fort La Presentation at the mouth of the Oswegatchie River to serve as a rallying place for converted Indians, a fortification against the English, and a post for the French fur trade. In spite of the hard conditions that *Father Picquet* laid down - no more than one wife to a man and no drunkeness - the Iroquois settled here in large numbers; from Fort La Presentation came many of the Indians who helped defeat *General Braddock* in 1755. The British held the fort from 1760 to 1796. First called Oswegatchie, the town was renamed for *Colonel Samuel Ogden*, who purchased the site in 1792 and promoted its resettlement after the British evacuation.

In 1837 Ogdensburg was a base for American aid in the Patriots' War, an abortive effort by Canadian groups and American sympathizers to free Canada from the "yoke of England."

The three-story brick Remington Art Memorial, corner of State and Washington Sts., houses Indian relics, cowboy implements, paintings, statues, and books and sketches by *Frederic Remington*. The Custom House (1809-10) is officially designated (1964) as the oldest U.S. Government building.

•OIL SPRINGS INDIAN RESERVATION, State Reservation; Cattaraugus and Allegany Counties; W N.Y.; Area Code Pop. 0; Seneca Tribe; Tribal Headquarters: Irving, N.Y. 14081; Total Area:: 640 acres; All reservation land is jointly owned by the Seneca Nation.

•OLD WESTBURY, Village; Nassau County; Pop. 3,245; Area Code 516; Zip Code 11568; on W central Long Island SE of Roslyn; SE N. Y.

•OLEAN, City; Cattaraugus County; Pop. 18,188; Area Code 716; Zip Code 14760; Elev. 1,440'; on Allegheny River in SW N.Y.; is an important junction of the Erie and Pennsylvania Railroads. It is known for oilwells and dairy products.

•ONEIDA, City; Madison County; Pop. 10,779; Area Code 315; Zip Code 13421; Elev. 437'; 5 m. SE of Oneida Lake 13 m. WSW of Rome in central N.Y.; is the geographic center of the state. The establishment and early growth resulted from a bargain made by *Sands Higinbotham*, owner of the city site, with the railroad whereby it received free right of way across his land, plus ample ground for a station, on the condition that it stop every passenger train at the depot 10 minutes for refreshments. Higinbotham then built the Railroad House to serve meals to passengers.

•ONEIDA COUNTY, Central N.Y.; 1,224 sq. miles; Pop. 252,912;

Seat - Rome, Utica; Est. March 15, 1798; Named for the Oneida Indian tribe.

•**ONEIDA LAKE**, Lake; Madison, Oneida, Onondaga and Oswego Counties; located in central N.Y.

•**ONEONTA**, City; Otsego County; Pop. 14,810; Area Code 617; Zip Code 13820; Elev. 1,120'; on Susquehanna River 45 m. S of Utica in central N.Y.; (Indian for "stony place") is called the City of Hills. It is in the Catskill foothills on the Susquehanna River.

It was slow in developing until the Albany and Susquehanna Railroad established a car-building shop here in 1863.

First settled by *John Vanderwerker* (1795) and *Aaron Brink* (1780). It was first known as McDonalds Mills, later Milfordville.

Hartwick College, under the direction of the Lutheran Synod of New York, was founded in 1928.

•**ONONDAGA**, Town; Onondaga County; Pop. 17,825; Area Code 315; Zip Code 13215; central N.Y.; means "People of the Mountains."

•**ONONDAGA COUNTY**, Central N.Y.; 747 sq. miles; Pop. 463,843; Seat - Syracuse; Est. March 5, 1794; Named for the Onondaga Indian tribe.

•**ONONDAGA INDIAN RESERVATION**, State Reservation; Onondaga County; Pop. 1,594; Onondaga and Oneida Tribes; Tribal Headquarters; Nedrow, N.Y. 13120; Total Area: 7,300 acres; Central N.Y.

All the land is tribally owned. At the close of the Revolutionary War, the Six Nations, of which the Onondaga were members, held most of what is now New York state. In 1784, 1788, and 1794, the United States made treaties with the Six Nations, guaranteeing them they could live, undisturbed, in their territory. The United States pays annuities to the Six Nations each year.

The Federal Government, in 1948, gave the State of New York criminal and civil jurisdiction on the reservation, but reserved to the Indians the right to choose which laws they would use. Since the Indian territory is ruled and governed by the chiefs, and their laws and customs prevail, New York State has limited jurisdiction.

The Indians are exempt from state land, income, and sales taxes while residing within their territories.

Both Onondaga and Oneida reside on this reservation. However, the Oneida Nation of New York is classified as "non-reservation, tax-exempt land," and for that reason is not listed separately in this dictionary.

Dictionary of Places   311

The Iroquois Tribes of central, northern, and western New York were members of the Six Nations of the Iroquois League, which was founded by Dekanawida, the Peace Maker, and Hiawatha. The league was originally formed by five tribes, the related Tuscarora not joining until 1716 when they moved to the area from the Carolinas. Although formed originally for mutual defense, the league became a powerful Indian empire, the force behind much of the intertribal pressures in the West and Midwest. As the central nation in the founding of the confederacy, the Onondaga are the "Keepers of the Council Fire." The league evolved into a federated government and was an important model for the crafters of the American Constitution. The league's decline after two centuries of prominence was largely the result of involvement in the disputes between the entering European powers and their participation in the Revolutionary War. Most of the members of the league supported the British as they had in the French and Indian Wars. Their alliance gave Britain the necessary advantage over France, but proved fatal to the leagues' negotiating base following the victory of the Colonies.

•ONTARIO, Town; Wayne County; Pop. 7,452; Area Code 315; Zip Code 14519; abt. 17 m. NE of Rochester in W N.Y.

•ONTARIO COUNTY, W N.Y.; 651 sq. miles; Pop. 88,505; Seat - Canandaigus; Est. January 27, 1789; Named for the Iroquois Indian word for beautiful lake.

•ORANGE COUNTY, SE N.Y.; 833 sq. miles; Pop. 259,092; Seat - Goshen; Est. November 1, 1683; Named after *Prince William IV* of Orange.

•ORCHARD PARK, Village and Town; Erie County; Pop. 3,666 and 24,353; Area Code 716; Zip Code 14127; 10 m. SEj of Buffalo in W N.Y.

•ORISKANY, Village; Oneida County; Pop. 1,676; Area Code 315; Zip Code 13424; on Mohawk River 7 m. W NW of Utica in central N.Y.; occupies the site of the Indian village of Oriska, on Oriskany Creek near its confluence with the Mohawk. Oriskany battlefield was the scene of a Revolutionary Battle on August 6, 1777. One of the bloodiest battles of the Revolution.

•ORISKANY FALLS, Village; Oneida County; Pop. 804; Area Code 315; Zip Code 13425; Elev. 460'.

•ORLEANS COUNTY, W N.Y.; 396 sq. miles; Pop. 38,473; Seat - Albion; Est. November 12, 1824; Named for Orleans, France.

•ORWELL, Town; Oswego County; Pop. 1,024; Area Code 315;

Zip Code 13426.

•OSSINING, Village and Town; Westchester County; Pop. 20,228 and 30,722; Area Code 914; Zip Code 10562; on E bank of Hudson River overlooking Tappan Zee, 30 m. N of New York in SE N.Y.; Inc. Village in 1813.

Ossining occupies part of what was Philipsburgh, the Philipse Manor, confiscated in 1779. The earliest settlement grew up before the Revolution around the natural dock at Sparta, just south of the present-day village. After the Revolution Hunter's Landing was settled and by 1813 was the incorporated village of Sing Sing. Inhabitants grew tired of the jokes suggested by the association of their village name with the state prison and in 1901 had the name changed.

Sing Sing Prison, along the river front, was established here in 1824 with the idea of working the Mount Pleasant marble quarries with convict labor. The following year *Captain Elam Lynds* , just dismissed from Auburn State Prison because of his excessively severe discipline, was put in charge and by May 1828 had completed by the labor of 100 prisoners a stone cell block of 800 cells. The new institution was operated from the first according to the Auburn system of silent group labor by day and solitary confinement by night. The lock step, rock pile, and lash were ordinary routine; mail and visitors were forbidden. Sing Sing marble was not only used in prison buildings but for a time enjoyed considerable vogue, especially for Greek Revival structures; witness the New York Court of Appeals Building in Albany. In contrast to the harsh and repressive practices of the past, the latest cell blocks at Sing Sing have beds, desks, running water, and radio earphones for most of the inmates. Educational and recreational programs are carried on and "varsity" teams compete with outside groups.

•OSWEGATCHIE, Town; St.Lawrence County; Pop. 3,184; Area Code 315; Zip Code 13670.

•OSWEGO, Seat of Oswego County; Pop. 19,737; Area Code 315; Zip Code 13126; Elev. 295'; on Lake Ontario at mouth of Oswego River 33 m. N NW of Syracuse in central N.Y.; easternmost port on the Great Lakes and Barge Canal terminal, lies on Lake Ontario at the mouth of the Oswego River. The name, from the Indian, means "pouring out of waters". Long before settlement, the strategic importance of the site as the western terminus of the Mohawk River - Oneida Lake - Oswego river water route was recognized; and the French and English contended for control. During the Colonial wars the region was an important base of supplies and Oswego was fortified after 1722. In 1756 the fort was captured by *Montcalm* but was reoccupied by *Sir William Johnson* in 1759; the British retained control until they sur-

Dictionary of Places 313

rendered it under the Jay Treaty in 1796. *Mary Edward Walker* (1832-1919), physician and advocate of women's rights, was born in Oswego.

•**OSWEGO COUNTY**, Central N.Y.; 964 sq. miles; Pop. 113,721; Seat - Oswego; Est. March 1, 1816; Named for the Iroquois word for "the outpouring".

•**OTEGO**, Village and Town; Otsego County; Pop. 1,091 and 2,800; Area Code 617; Zip Code 13825.

•**OTISVILLE**, Village; Orange County; Pop. 940; Area Code 914; Zip Code 10963.

•**OTSEGO COUNTY**, Central N.Y.; 1,013 sq. miles; Pop. 58,789; Seat - Cooperstown; Est. February 16, 1791; Named for the Indian word meaning "place of the rock."

•**OTSEGO LAKE**, Lake; Otsego County; Elev. 1,193'; in central N.Y. in the N central part of the county. At the S side of the lake is Cooperstown and is the primary source of the Susquehanna River. The lake is one mile wide and nine miles in length. Lake Otsego is mentioned in many of *James Fenimore Cooper's* novels. Called Glimmerglass as described in "The Deerslayer" as "a broad sheet of water, so placid and limpid that it resembled a bed of pure mountain atmosphere compressed into a setting of hills and woods."

•**OTSELIC**, Town; Chenango County; Pop. 957; Area Code 607; Zip Code 13129.

•**OTTO**, Town; Cattaratugus County; Pop. 820; Area Code 716; Zip Code 14766.

•**OVID**, Village and Town; Seat of Seneca County; Pop. 669 and 2,582; Area Code 315; Zip Code 14521; W central N.Y.

•**OWASCO**, Town; Cayuga County; Pop. 3,617; Area Code 315; Zip Code 13130.

•**OWASCO LAKE**, Lake; Cayuga County; located twenty tow m. from Syracuse in N central N.Y. The lake is one of the Finger Lakes and measures one m. in width and eleven miles in length. At the N end is an outlet that runs into Seneca River.

•**OWEGO**, Village and Town; Seat of Tioga County; Pop. 4,389 and 20, 488; Area Code 607; Zip Code 13827; Elev. 818'; 20 m. W of Binghamton on the Susquehann River in S N.Y.; came into existance on the site of Ah-wah-ga (where the valley widens), one of the Indian towns destroyed by the *Sullivan-Clinton* troops in 1779. Owego was an important railroad junction.

•**OXFORD**, Village and Town; Chenango County; Pop. 1,766 and 3,967; Area Code 607; Zip Code 13830; Elev. 982'.

•**OYSTER BAY**, Town; Nassau County; Pop. 305,407; Area Code 516; Zip Code 11771; on Long Island on inlet of Long Island Sound in SE N.Y.

•**PAINTED POST**, Village; Steuben County; Pop. 2,189; Area Code 607; Zip Code 14870; Elev. 950'; 16 m. W of Elmira in S N.Y.; is at the point where the Tioga and Cohocton Rivers unite to form the Chemung. Painted Post was so named because of a red-painted oaken post that was once here, probably erected as a memorial either to an Indian victory or to an Indian chief. The first white settler arrived in 1789, 10 years after the *Sullivan-Clinton* expedition had wiped out the Indian village by the river.

•**PALATINE BRIDGE**, Village; Montgomery County; Pop. 604; Area Code 518; Zip Code 13428; Elev. 340'; in 1723 about 60 families of Palatines from the Schoharie Valley and Livingston Manor settled in this area; their leader was *John Christopher Gerlach*.

•**PALMYRA**, Village and Town; Wayne County; Pop. 3,730 and 7,651; Area Code 315; Zip Code 14522; Elev. 470'; 21 m. E of Rochester in W N.Y.; is associated with the Beginnings of Mormonism; the *Joseph Smith* farm and Hill Cumorah are close by.

•**PARIS**, Town; Oneida County; Pop. 4,458; Area Code 315; Zip Code 13429; Elev. 1,481'; central N.Y.; the cemetary contains the grave of *Issac Paris Jr*. In 1789, when local crops failed, he sent settlers provisions from Fort Plain, taking his pay in ginseng, a medicinal root that abounded in this region. In 1792 the township was named for him, and in 1880 his remains were exhumed at Fort Plain and reinterred here with elaborate ceremonies.

•**PARISH**, Village and Town; Oswego County; Pop. 533 and 2,184; Area Code 315; Zip Code 13131.

•**PARISHVILLE**, Town; St.Lawrence County; Pop. 1,951; Area Code 315; Zip Code 13672.

•**PATCHOGUE**, Village; Suffolk County; Pop. 11,300; Area Code 516; Zip Code 11772; on S shore of Long Island, on Great South Bay 53 m. E of N.Y. in SE N.Y.; three small streams in the vicinity were dammed for lumber and gristmills probably before 1750.

By 1800 the Union Twine Mill, third of its kind in the United States and the first to supply cotton carpet warp, was in operation.

•**PATTERSON**, Town; Putnam County; Pop. 7,255; Area Code 914; Zip Code 12563; Elev. 400'; SE N.Y.; squatting in a broad valley formerly part of the Patterson Great Swamp, where cattle headed for the New York market were allowed to graze. The village, originally named Franklin, was settled about 1770 by Scotsmen discharged from the British army after service in the French and Indian War. The present name - after *Matthew Patterson*, an early settler -was adopted in 1808 when the legislature passed a law abolishing the numerous "Franklins" in the state. At the time, local governmental offices included pathmasters, fence-viewers, and pound-masters, the duties of the latter including control of a large herd of hogs that roamed the neighborhood and wore rings in their noses to prevent them from burrowing the roads. A standing reward of one shilling was offered to the person who "shall return a swine to his owner having a proper ring in his nose."

•**PAVILION**, Town; Genesee County; Pop. 2,385; Area Code 716; Zip Code 14525.

•**PAWLING**, Village and Town; Dutchess County; Pop. 1,961 and 5,674; Area Code 914; Zip Code 12564; Elev. 420'; 20 m. SE of Poughkeepsie in SE N.Y.; was settled about 1740 by English Quakers. Today it is the home of many wealthy New Yorkers.

•**PEEKSKILL**, City; Westchester County; Pop. 18,247; Area Code 914; Zip Code 10566; Elev. 120'; on Hudson River 39 m. N of New York in SE N.Y.; takes its name from Peeks's Kill, the creek along its northern boundary named for *Jan Peek*, a Dutch trader who settled on its bank in 1665. During the early years of the Revolution, staff officers and troops moved back and forth through the settlement on their way between the river landing and their points of duty.
    Chauncey M. Depew Park, in the center of the village, contains a statue of Depew (1834-1928) who was a lifelong resident. In 1899 Depew was elected to the United States Senate.

•**PELHAM**, Village and Town; Westchester County; Pop. 6,825 and 12,913; Area Code 914; Zip Code 10803; Elev. 100'; 17 m. NE of New York in SE N.Y.; is on land purchased by *Thomas Pell* in 1664 from the Siwanoy Indians; the tract included what is now New Rochelle, Mount Vernon, the Pelhams, and Eastchester. *Anne Hutchinson*, rebel against Puritan conformity in Massachusetts, settled in this section in 1642 and was murdered in 1643 by Indians at Throgg's Neck, now Pelham Bay Shore.

•**PENFIELD**, Town; Monroe County; Pop. 27,154; Area Code 716; Zip Code 14526; 7 m. SE of Rochester in W N.Y.

•**PENN YAN**, Village; Seat of Yates County; Pop. 5,241; Area Code 315; Zip Code 14527; Elev. 767'; at outlet of Lake Keuka 30 m. SW of Auburn in W N.Y.; is guarded on three sides by hills and on the fourth faces the long eastern arm of Keuka Lake. The village wineries, canneries, and mills process and market the grapes, grain, fruits, and vegetables of the countryside, and small factories make grape baskets, boats, store fixture, and bus bodies. A large tourist trade provides an additional source of income. Controversy between the settlers from Pennsylvania and New England over a name for the place was compromised by combining the first syllables of Pennsylvania and Yankee.

•**PERRY**, Village and Town; Wyoming County; Pop. 4,193 and 5,436; Area Code 716; Zip Code 14530; Elev. 1,320'; 37 m. SE of Rochester in W N.Y.; which has large knitting mills and a septic and gasoline tank factory. In 1833 the *Reverend William Arthur* became pastor of the First Baptist Church in Perry. His son, *Chester Alan*, then four years old, was destined to become the 21st President of the United States.

•**PERRYSBURG**, Village and Town; Cattaraugus County; Pop. 401 and 2,173; Area Code 716; Zip Code 14129.

•**PERU**, Town; Clinton County; Pop. 5,341; Area Code 518; Zip Code 12972; Elev. 300'; NE corner of N.Y.; was named by some stretch of the imagination for the South American country because of its proximity to the mountains.

•**PETERSBURG**, Town; Rensselaer County; Pop. 1,370; Area Code 518; Zip Code 12138; E N.Y.; 20 miles E of Troy.

•**PHELPS**, Village and Town; Ontario County; Pop. 2,006 and 6,515; Area Code 315; Zip Code 14532; Elev. 522'.

•**PHILADELPHIA**, Village and Town; Jefferson County; Pop. 864 and 1,428; Area Code 315; Zip Code 13673.

•**PHILMONT**, Village; Columbia County; Pop. 1,527; Area Code 518; Zip Code 12565.

•**PHOENIX**, Village; Oswego County; Pop. 2,350; Area Code 315; Zip Code 13135; 14 m. N NW of Syracuse in central N.Y.

•**PIERCEFIELD**, Town; St. Lawrence County; Pop. 365; Area Code 315; Zip Code 12973.

•**PIERMONT**, Village; Rockland County; Pop. 2,313; Area Code 914; Zip Code 10968; on Hudson River 22 m. N of New York in SE N.Y. Piermont took its name from the mile-long pier of the Erie Railroad. When the Erie was first completed in 1851, Piermont was made the Eastern terminus because the railroad charter required the line to be constructed entirely within the boundary of New York State; connection with New York was by boat. The village was originally called Tappan Landing. *Sir Guy Carleton* came ashore here to discuss with *Washington*, then living at Tappan, peace terms and the orderly withdrawal of the British from New York City. Upon Washington's return visit to Carleton's flagship, the British for the first time saluted the flag of the United States of America.

•**PIKE**, Village and Town; Wyoming County; Pop. 367 and 992; Area Code 716; Zip Code 14130.

•**PINE HILL**, Village; Ulster County; Pop. 221; Area Code 914; Zip Code 12465; Elev. 1,500'; SE N.Y.; in the valley between Belle Ayr Mountain and Rose Mountain, is the beginning of a foot trail.

•**PISECO LAKE**, Lake; Hamilton County; located in NE N.Y. in S Hamilton County; The lake is approx. 5 m. in length and runs S to Sacandaga River into the Great Sacandaga Reservoir. Also known as the Piseco Inlet.

•**PITCHER**, Town; Chenango Conty; Pop. 732; Area Code 607; Zip Code 13136.

•**PITTSFORD**, Village and Town; Monroe County; Pop. 1,569 and 26,701; Area Code 716; Zip Code 14534; Elev. 500'; 7 m. SE of Rochester in W N.Y.; is a residential suburb of Rochester.

•**PLANDOME**, Village; Nassau County; Pop. 1,501; Area Code 516; Zip Code 11030; SE New York; on Long Island's north shore.

•**PLATTEKILL**, Town; Ulster County; Pop. 7,411; Area Code 914; Zip Code 12568; Elev. 140'.

•**PLATTSBURGH**, City; Seat of Clinton County; Pop. 12,074; Area Code 518; Zip Code 12901; on W shore of Lake Champlain, 20 m. S of Canadian border in NE corner of N.Y.; is on Lake Champlain at the mouth of the Saranac River, which has provided water power for manufacturing since 1785. It was founded by *Zephaniah Platt* in 1764.

The Battle of Plattsburgh was fought in and north of the village. On September 6, 1814, two skirmishes occurred north of Plattsburgh. The Americans retreated south of the Saranac

River and threw up fortifications. The British waited north of the river for *Commodore Downie* to clear the lake of the American fleet under *MacDonough*. On September 11, while the naval battle was in progress, the British attacked on land; but the news of the defeat on the lake caused *Prevost* to retreat during the night.

•**PLEASANT VALLEY**, Town; Dutchess County; Pop. 6,867; Area Code 914; Zip Code 12569; Elev. 200'; was settled in 1740 by Quakers and Presbyterians.

•**PLEASANTVILLE**, Village; Westchester County; Pop. 6,757; Area Code 914; Zip Code 10570; 30 m. N NE of N.Y. in SE N.Y.

•**PLUM ISLAND**, Island; Suffolk County; is located in Long Island Sound in SE N.Y. The island is three m. long and is off NE Long Island.

•**PLYMOUTH**, Town; Chenango County; Pop. 1,514; Area Code 607; Zip Code 13832; Central N.Y.

•**POESTENKILL**, Town; Rensselaer County; Pop. 3,647; Area Code 518; Zip Code 12140; near Troy in E N.Y.

•**POLAND**, Village; Herkimer County; Pop. 554; Area Code 315; Zip Code 13431; N N.Y.

•**POMONA**, Village; Rockland County; Pop. 2,424; Area Code 914; Zip Code 10970; SE N.Y.

•**POMPEY**, Town; Onondaga County; Pop. 4,512; Area Code 315; Zip Code 13138; Elev. 1,700'; was the birthplace, between 1795 and 1830, of 13 members of the state legislature, one United States senator, two state governors, mayors of five cities, three Supreme Court Justices, one major general, several authors, and at least two business geniuses.

•**POOSPATUCK INDIAN RESERVATION**, State Reservation; Suffolk County; Pop. 160; Poospatuck Tribe; Tribal Headquarters: Mastic, Long Island, New York 11950; Total Area: 60 acres.

This reservation was granted to the Poospatuck by the colonial government in the name of the King. New York State recognizes the land as a tax-free reservation and extends services to the tribe, which include health, education, and social services.

The Poospatuck were part of the Long Island tribes' Montauk Confederacy. Their economy was based primarily on fishing and whaling, and it is believed that early in the 18th century most of the men in the tribe were lost in a whaling expedition. The necessity for marriage outside the tribe could account for the present triracial appearance of the tribe. The tribe was never permitted to vote on the Indian Reorganization Act, primarily because of its mixed ancestry.

The Poospatuck are believed to have had tribal and commercial relationships with the Algonquin Indians of Connecticut. They were primarily a fishing and whaling people. At present, they are the smallest tribe on the smallest reservation in New York state, and although their problems are numerous, they receive little assistance from the state.

•PORT BYRON, Village; Cayuga County; Pop. 1,400; Area Code 315; Zip Code 13140; Elev. 400'; NW N.Y.; is a canal orphan, left high and dry when the Erie Canal was abandoned; a stagnant creek with ruins of masonry locks is all that is left of the artery of transporation.

Henry Wells (1803-78), co-founder of the Wells-Fargo Express Company and founder of Wells College in Aurora, worked in the village as a shoemaker from 1827 to 1830; *Isaac Singer* is said to have made his first model of a sewing machine in his workshop that stood near the present dam across Owasco Outlet; and *Brigham Young* lived here for a short time.

•PORT CHESTER, Village; Westchester County; Pop. 23,472; Area Code 914; Zip Code 10573; on Long Island Sound 25 m. NE of New York in SE N.Y.; first known as Saw Log Swamp and later as Saw Pit, was settled about 1650. Although mainly residential, its factories produce candy, ammonia, nuts and bolts, furnaces, coal, soft drinks and cartons.

•PORT HENRY, Village; Essex County; Pop. 1,438; Area Code 518; Zip Code 12974; Elev. 600'; NE N.Y.; summer residents double the population of Port Henry, which rises on a series of terraces above the lake. Many of the citizens work in the nearby iron mines.

One of the winter pastimes of the villagers is to fish through the ice for smelt, perch, pike, and pickerel. In the winter, innumerable movable shanties, referred to in local idiom as the "Stovepipe City", dot the gleaming sweep of ice on Lake Champlain. Inside them, heavily clothed ice-fisherman sit huddled around kerosene stoves. The fish are hungry and rise to the bait eagerly.

•PORT JEFFERSON, Village; Suffolk County; Pop. 6,673; Area Code 516; Zip Code 11777; on Long Island, on Long Island Sound abt. 13 m. N of Patchogue in SE N.Y.

•PORT JERVIS, City; Orange County; Pop. 8,680; Area Code 914; Zip Code 12771; on Delaware River 38 m. W of Newburgh in

SE N.Y.; calls itself the Tri-State City. The Minsi band of the Lenni-Lenape did not give up the bottom lands here willingly, but Dutch and Huguenot farmers, who began arriving about 1698, were able to live in peace with them until Revolutionary times. For some years after 1779, when Brant led his Tory and Indian followers on a raid that wiped out the settlement, the place was deserted by the whites.

•PORT WASHINGTON, Village; Nassau County; Pop. 15,923; Area Code 516; Zip Code 11050; SE N.Y. on N shore of Long Island. The village is built on a hill overlooking Manhasset Bay, which in summer is full of sailboats and ferries.

•PORTLAND, Town; Chautauqua County; Pop. 4,394; Area Code 716; Zip Code 14769; SW N.Y.

•PORT LEYDEN, Village; Lewis County; Pop. 738; Area Code 315; Zip Code 13433; N New York.

•PORTVILLE, Village and Town; Cattaraugus County; Pop. 1,140 and 4,487; Area Code 716; Zip Code 14770; SW N.Y.

•POTSDAM, Village and Town; St.Lawrence County; Pop. 10,676 and 17,466; Area Code 315; Zip Code 13676; 27 m. E of Ogdensburg in N N.Y.

In 1804 *William Bullard* and others came here from Massachusetts, pooled their resources, and purchased a tract of land, on which they established the "Union." Property was held in common, an accurate account of labor and materials contributed by each member was kept, and all proceeds were divided pro rata annually. The group prospered for a few years, but a demand by more indolent members for an equal division of income led to internal strife, resulting in dissolution in 1810, and the land was evenly divided among the members.

In the nineteenth century the sandstone quarries, now almost completely flooded by Hannawa Falls, employed hundreds of workers. The durable stone, of a deep, rich, lasting red color, was used in the construction of the House of Parliament, Ottawa, and All Saints Cathedral, Albany. But beginning with the late nineties, largely because of the cost of transportation, sandstone gradually lost its popularity.

•POUGHKEEPSIE, City; Dutchess County Seat; Pop. 29,677; Area Code 914; Zip Code 12601; Elev. 175; SE New York; on Hudson River; midway between New York City and Albany; Name is modified from Indian word meaning "tree-covered lodge by the little water place"; Site of Vassar College.

Dutch settlers bought land from Indians here in 1683, and although it was a small quiet town all through the seventeenth century, it was chosen as New York's first state capitol while New York City was occupied in 1777. *Governor George Clinton* lived here, and the state legislature ratified the U.S. Constitution here in 1788. For a short time, Poughkeepsie was an important port for transporting Dutchess County grain and farm products to the city, but after the Erie Canal was built in 1825, produce was transported from other areas in the state. Education took importance soon afterwards, when more than a dozen private schools were established in Poughkeepsie. *Matthew Vassar*, a local brewer, founded Vassar College in 1861, and from its opening in 1865 faculty and students were active in the campaign for women's suffrage.

Poughkeepsie was incorporated as a city in 1854. Today, its industries include business machines, cough drops, metal products and dairy machines. Marist College and Dutchess Community college are located here. Among the city's famous residents were *Henry Wheeler Shaw*, the "Josh Billings" of Yankee humor, who was a newspaperman and an alderman here in the mid-nineteenth century.

Each June, the city and Vassar College host the Intercollegiate Regatta, a rowing championship.

•**POUND RIDGE**, Town; Westchester County; Pop. 4,016; Area Code 914; Zip Code 10576; SE N.Y.

•**PRATTSBURG**, Town; Steuben County; Pop. 1,641; Area Code 607; Zip Code 14873; S N.Y.

•**PRATTSVILLE**, Town; Greene County; Pop. 658; Area Code 518; Zip Code 12468;E central N.Y.

•**PREBLE**, Town; Cortland County; Pop. 1,635; Area Code 607; Zip Code 13141; N central N.Y.

•**PROSPECT**, Village; Oneida County; Pop. 363; Area Code 315; Zip Code 13435; N central N.Y.

•**PULASKI**, Village; Oswego County; Pop. 2,417; Area Code 315; Zip Code 13142; near Lake Ontario 30 m. S SW of Watertown in central N.Y.

•**PULTENEY**, Town; Steuben County; Pop. 1,267; Area Code 607; Zip Code 14874; is named after *Sir William Pulteney*, head of the London Associates. The town was a hotbed of abolitionism before the Civil War.

•**PUTNAM COUNTY**, SE N.Y.; 232 sq. miles; Pop. 76,996; Seat - Carmel; Est. June 12, 1812; Named after *Israel Putnam*, Revolutionary general.

•**PUTNAM VALLEY**, Town; Putnam County; Pop. 8,959; Area Code 914; Zip Code 10579; SE N.Y.

•**QUEENS BOROUGH**, Queens County; Pop. 1,886,550; Area Code 212; located in SE N.Y. on Long Island. At the W section of Long Island is the largest borough in area, 121 square miles. The borough encompasses Brooklyn to Long Island Sound. The growth of this borough, dependent in large part upon subway, road, and bridge extensions, was further stimulated by the establishment of the New York World's Fair at Flushing.

•**QUEENSBURY**, Town; Warren County; Pop. 18,970; Area Code 518; Zip Code 12801; NE N.Y.

•**QUEENS COUNTY**, SE N.Y; 108 sq. miles; Pop. 1,886,550; Seat - Jamaica; Est. November 1, 1683; Named after *Queen Catherine* of Braganza.

•**QUOGUE**, Village; Suffolk County; Pop. 970; Area Code 516; Zip Code 11959; SE N.Y. on Long Island. Resort.

•**RANDOLPH**, Village and Town; Cattaraugus County; Pop. 1,393 and 2,588; Area Code 716; Zip Code 14772; SW corner of N.Y.; *Charles Austin Foskick*, under the pen name "Harry Castlemon", rivaled the popularity of *Horatio Alger, Jr.*, with his *Frank the Young Naturalist* and his *Gunboat*, *Rocky Mountain*, and *Boy Trapper* series; Foskick was born in Randolph in 1842.

•**RAVENA**, Village; Albany County; Pop. 3,092; Area Code 518; Zip Code 12143; on the Hudson River 11 m. S of Albany in E N.Y.

•**RED CREEK**, Village; Wayne County; Pop. 638; Area Code 315; Zip Code 13143; W central N.Y.

•**REDFIELD**, Town; Oswego County; Pop. 459; Area Code 315; Zip Code 13437; NW N.Y.

•**REDFORD**, Village; Clinton County; Pop. 300; Zip Code 12978; Elev. 1,100'; NE N.Y.; In Adirondack State Park along the Saranac River.

Charles Corning and *Gersham Cook* of Troy established a glass factory in 1831 and permanently abandoned it 20 years later. The secret of manufacture died with these men; white Potsdam sandstone was a principal ingredient and was melted in imported pots made of Stonebridge clay. Today the pale green Redford glass, in the form of goblets, vases and crown window glass, is a collector's item.

Dictionary of Places 323

•**RED HOOK**, Village and Town; Dutchess County; Pop. 1,686 and 8,353; Area Code 914; Zip Code 12571; SE N.Y.; Elev. 200'; was called Roode Hoeck by early Dutch navigators because of the profusion of red berries they saw growing on the hillsides. The village is a trade center for the apple growers of northern Dutchess County, and cider-vinegar mills are operated here during the fall.

•**REMSEN**, Village and Town; Oneida County; Pop. 620 and 1,617; Area Code 315; Zip Code 13438; N central N.Y.

•**RENSSELAER**, City; Rensselaer County; Pop. 9,006; Area Code 518; Zip Code 12144; across Hudson River from Albany in E N.Y.
The city, formed in 1897 by the union of the villages of East Albany, Greenbush and Bath-on-the Hudson, stands on ground that was part of Rensselaerswyck, most successful of the patroonships.
In 1758, while *Abercrombie* was preparing to attack Ticonderoga, *Dr. Richard Shuckburgh*, a British army surgeon, sat on the Fort Crailo well curb watching the provincial militia drill and wrote the derisive words of "Yankee Doodle", which later became the marching song of the Revolution. Its industries are concrete and chemicals.

•**RENSSELAER COUNTY**, E N.Y.; 665 sq. miles; Pop. 151,699; Seat - Troy; Est. February 7, 1791; Named after *Kiliaen Van Rensselaer*, Dutch patroon.

•**RENSSELAER FALLS**, Village; St. Lawrence County; Pop. 360; Area Code 315; Zip Code 13680; N N.Y.

•**RENSSELAERVILLE**, Town; Albany County; Pop. 1,780; Area Code 518; Zip Code 12147; Elev. 1,350'; E N.Y.; settled toward the end of the eighteenth century by Connecticut families who came by way of Long Island.
The village is a museum of post-Colonial and Greek Revival architecture, owing much of its charm to *Ephraim Russ* (1784-1853), who was the village carpenter-architect during its golden age and manifested an exceptional skill in adapting the trend toward the classical to the traditional New England structure.

•**RHINEBECK**, Village and Town; Dutchess County; Pop. 2,519 and 6,926; Area Code 914; Zip Code 12572; near East bank of the Hudson River 16 m. N of Poughkeepsie and 5 m. E of Kingston in SE N.Y.

•**RICHBURG**, Village; Allegany County; Pop. 489; Area Code

716; Zip Code 14774; S N.Y.

•**RICHFIELD SPRINGS**, Village; Otsego County; Pop. 1,561; Area Code 617; Zip Code 13439; Elev. 1,300'; 20 m. SE of Utica in central N.Y.; came to prominence in 1820 when the Great White Sulphur Springs became popular.

•**RICHFORD**, Town; Tioga County; Pop. 915; Area Code 607; Zip Code 13835; S N.Y.

•**RICHLAND**, Town; Oswego County; Pop. 5,553; Area Code 315; Zip Code 13144; central N.Y.

•**RICHMOND BOROUGH**, Borough; Richmond County; Pop. 349,601; SW part of New York city in SE N.Y. As of 1975 officially known as Staten Island. The borough, a roughly triangular island is 37 square miles in area; in 1898 became a borough of New York City. The borough contains a free park and long piers with 35 miles of waterfront on the Atlantic coasts there are beach resorts. The island was first granted by the Dutch West Indian Company in 1630 to Pauw. Scattered along the north and northeast shores are shipbuilding yards, lumber mills, printing and publishing plants, and a large soap and oil plant. Storage tanks and the refinery units of New Jersey oil companies rise on the lowlands of the western district.

Dutch, English, Huguenot, Italian, Scandinavian, and Poles are the major ethnic groups in the area.

•**RICHMOND COUNTY**, SE N.Y.; 58 sq. miles; Pop. 349,601; Seat - Saint George; Est. November 1, 1683; Named after the *Duke of Richmond*.

•**RICHMONDVILLE**, Village and Town; Schoharie County; Pop. 799 and 2,210; Area Code 518; Zip Code 12149; Central N.Y.

•**RICHVILLE**, Village; St.Lawrence County; Pop. 339; Area Code 315; Zip Code 13681; NW N.Y.

•**RIPLEY**, Town; Chautauqua County; Pop. 3,238; Area Code 716; Zip Code 14775; Elev. 730'; SW corner of N.Y; Elev. 370'.

•**RIVERHEAD**, Town; Seat of Suffolk County; Pop. 20,204; Area Code 516; Zip Code 11901; on the Peconic River, E end of Long Island in SE N.Y.; settled in 1690. The town depended for its prosperity largely upon the surrounding farms, the two main crops of which are potatoes and cauliflower. Within recent years the old predominant Yankee strain has dwindled and South and East Europeans, particularly Poles, have increased.

Dictionary of Places 325

•ROBERT MOSES, Dam; Niagara River (off stream), Niagara County; W New York; Completed 1962; Maximum height 389 ft.; gravity type; for power.

•ROCKLAND COUNTY, SE N.Y; 176 sq. miles; Pop. 259,576; Seat - New City; Est. February 23, 1798; Description of the county.

•ROCKVILLE CENTRE, Village; Nassau County; Pop. 25,384; Area Code 516; Zip Code 11570; on Long Island, 19 m. E SE of New York in SE N.Y.; owes its name to the Long Island Smiths, of whom there were so many that qualifying names were needed to distinguish the various clans. Hence an odd list; "Bull", "Tangier", "Wait", and "Rock" Smiths. To the last-named family belonged the *Reverend Mordecai "Rock" Smith*, for whom the village was named.

•RODMAN, Town; Jefferson County; Pop. 842; Area Code 315; Zip Code 13682; W central N.Y.

•ROME, City; Oneida County Seat; Pop. 43,732; Area Code 315; Zip Code 13440; Elev. 440'; Central New York; 20 m. NW of Utica on Mohawk River.

The industries of copper, brass and other metal products provide much of Rome's economy today, and the Rome-Utica metropolitan area is substantially filled in with homes and commercial enterprises. But for many years, the area was a small outpost of civilization.

Long before Rome was settled, its site, *De-o-wain-sta* (Ind., lifing or setting down the boat), the one-mile portage or "carry" between the upper reaches of the Mohawk and Wood Creek, formed an important link in the water route connecting the Great Lakes region with the Atlantic seaboard. Beginning in 1725 the English kept the place fortified; in 1758 Fort Stanwix replaced two earlier forts.

The first settlement, a huddle of fur traders' huts outside the wall of Fort Stanwix, was destroyed by the American garrison before the siege of 1777. The first permanent settlers after the Revolution were New Englanders. In 1786 *Dominick Lynch*, whom *George Washington* called "the handsome Irishman", purchased 2,397 acres at Fort Stanwix, parceled out his land in village lots, and founded a settlement that he called Lynchville. Completion of a canal in 1797 connecting the Mohawk and Wood Creek started a new era of progress. In 1819 Lynchville was incorporated as the village of Rome, the name being in tribute to the "heroic defense of the Republic made here".

In 1817, the Erie Canal first flowed through Rome and the little settlement soon changed into a bustling town. It soon became known as the "copper city" as many factories making wires, cables and machinery sprang up. By 1870, Rome was incorporated as a city. In 1891 the Rome Brass and Copper Company was founded, which eventually evolved into the Revere Copper and Brass Company, producing cookware. Griffiss Air Force Base opened here after the World Wars, and brought more people and industry into the city that grew 50 percent between 1940 and 1960.

The site of Fort Stanwix is preserved in Rome, as is the home of *John B. Jervis*, a chief engineer of the Erie Canal.

•ROMULUS, Town; Seneca County; Pop. 2,459; Area Code 315; Zip Code 14541; Elev. 330'; W central N.Y.

•RONKONKOMA, Village; Suffolk County; Pop. 16,000· Area Code 516; Zip Code 11779; SE N.Y. in central Long Island on W side of Lake Ronkonkoma. Its quiet waters are surrounded by resort homes and night spots.

•ROOSEVELT, Village; Nassau County; Pop. 15,008; Area Code 516; Zip Code 11575; SE N.Y. on Long Island; Residential.

•ROSE, Town; Wayne County; Pop. 2,676; Area Code 315; Zip Code 14542; W central N.Y.

•ROSEBOOM, Town; Otsego County; Pop. 609; Area Code 617; Zip Code 13450; Central N.Y.

•ROSENDALE, Town; Ulster County; Pop. 5,890; Area Code 914; Zip Code 12472; SE N.Y.

•ROSLYN, Village; Nassau County; Pop. 2,120; Area Code 516; Zip Code 11576; on Long Island abt. 4 m. N of Mineola in SE N.Y.; stretches along the curving shore of Hempstead Harbor. For many years the settlement was known as the Town at the Head of the Harbor.

William Cullen Bryant lived in Roslyn from 1843 to 1878; he came to New York in 1825 and a few years later became editor of the *New York Evening Post*, a position he held until his death.

•ROSSIE, Town; St.Lawrence County; Pop. 836; Zip Code 13646; N N.Y.

•ROTTERDAM, Town; Schenectady County; Pop. 29,445; Area Code 518; Zip Code 12303; E N.Y.

•ROUND LAKE, Village; Saratoga County; Pop. 792; Area Code 518; Zip Code 12151; E N.Y.

•ROUSES POINT, Village; Clinton County; Pop. 2,257; Area

Code 518; Zip Code 12979; at the upper end of Lake Champlain at Canadian border 21 m. N of Plattsburg in NE corner of N.Y.

•ROXBURY, Town; Delaware County; Pop. 2,286; Area Code 518; Zip Code 12474; Elev. 1,470'; 18 m. E of Delhi in S N.Y.

•RUSH, Town; Monroe County; Pop. 3,001; Area Code 716; Zip Code 14543; W N.Y.

•RUSHFORD, Town; Allegany County; Pop. 1,121; Area Code 716; Zip Code 14777; S N.Y.

•RUSHVILLE, Village; Yates County; Pop. 545; Area Code 315; Zip Code 14544; W central N.Y.

•RUSSELL, Town; St. Lawrence County; Pop. 1,634; Area Code 315; Zip Code 13684; N N.Y.

•RYE, City; Westchester County; Pop. 15,055; Area Code 914; Zip Code 10580; Elev. 47'; on Long Island Sound 24 m. NE of New York City in SE N.Y.; settled in 1660.
   The Haviland Inn was built in 1730. The inn was run by *Dame Tamar Haviland*, after her husband's death during the Revolution. In her time this was a notable stopping place on the Old Post Road.
   The Cave of John Jay (1749-1829), first Chief Justice of the US, is in a private cemetery on the Palmer Estate.

•SACKETS HARBOR, Village; Jefferson County; Pop. 1,017; Area Code 315; Zip Code 13685; on Lake Ontario 11 m. W SW of Watertown in N N.Y.

•SAG HARBOR, Village; Suffolk County; Pop. 2,483; Area Code 516; Zip Code 11963; 25 m. W of Montauk Point at the W end of Long Island in SE N.Y.; the most famous of the Long Island whaling towns. The townfolk fondly recall the days of "Thar she blows." *James Fenimore Cooper* found in Sag Harbor characters for his sea stories; and while here as agent for a whaling company he wrote part of his first novel, *Precaution*. Years later he drew, from Sag Harbor recollections, *Long Tom Coffin*, who belongs to the galaxy of John Silver and Equality Jack. *David Frothingham* began the publication of his newspaper, the *Long Island Herald*, the first on Long Island, in Sag Harbor on May 10, 1791.

•SAINT JAMES, Village; Suffolk County; Pop. 11,000; Area Code 516; Zip Code 11780; SE N.Y.; On Long Island in a residential area surrounded by farms.

•SAINT JOHNSVILLE, Village and Town; Montgomery County; Pop. 1,949 and 3,043; Area Code 518; Zip Code 13452; Elev. 360'; on Mohawk River 30 m. E of Utica in E N.Y.; founded in 1775 by *Jacob Zimmerman*, who built a gristmill by Zimmerman Creek.

•ST. LAWRENCE COUNTY, N N.Y.; 2,768 sq. miles; Pop. 114,257; Seat - Canton; Est. March 3, 1802; Named for the Saint Lawrence River.

•ST. LAWRENCE RIVER, River; located N of New York and forms the boundary between Canada and the United States.

•ST. REGIS INDIAN RESERVATION, State Reservation; Franklin County; Pop. 2,268; St. Regis Mohawk Tribe; Tribal Headquarters: Hogansburg, N.Y. 13655; Total Area: 14,640 acres.

The reservation lies in the northernmost part of New York state along the St. Lawrence River and is divided from the Canadian portion of the reservation, the Caughnawaga Reserve, by the 45th Parallel, the international boundary. The Canadian Caughnawaga Reserve encompasses 23,750 acres. Because the State of New York never ceded any land to the federal government following ratification of the Constitution, the Mohawk Reservation has never been federal territory. The Indians recently demanded recognition of the duty-free passage rights as guaranteed to them in the Jay Teaty of 1794.

An Iroquois tribe of central New York, the Mohawk were the "Keepers of the Eastern Gate" for the Iroquois League. The league, originally formed by five tribes, added a sixth in the early 1700's and was known as the Six Nations. Formed in the early 16th century for mutual defense, the league became a powerful Indian confederacy and ultimately a model for the United States government. Pressure from the Iroquois was largely responsible for the westward movement of other Indian tribes. The Iroquois fought on the side of the British during the American Revolution and consequently lost a great deal of land to the new sState government. The American Revolution marked the end of Iroquois power, as the league's organization and population fell away.

The St. Regis Mohawk were of the Eastern Woodland cultural group. They resided in permanent villages, in multifamily buildings called longhouses, and supported themselves through hunting and agriculture. The tribe was matrilineal, with chiefs inheriting office through their mothers. Property was owned by the women. Mohawk men have become widely known as excellent high-steel workers. In the past, the Canadian and United States Mohawk have been divided politically, with much confusion concerning citizenship. Recent events have resulted in an upsurge of tribalism and the native religion which centers around the longhouses.

•**SALAMANCA**, City; Cattaraugus County; Pop. 6,849; Area Code 716; Zip Code 14779; Elev. 1,380'; on Allegheny River 13 m. W NW of Olean in SW N.Y.
Salamanca is known for furniture and dairy products. The first settlers came here from what is now West Salamanca in 1862, when a sawmill was established and the Atlantic & Great Western carried its single track line to this point. When the railroad company built shops and yards here, the grateful citizens named their village in honor of one of the important stockholders.

•**SALEM**, Village and Town; Washington County; Pop. 959 and 2,381; Area Code 518; Zip Code 12865; Elev. 500'; E N.Y.

•**SALINA**, Town; Onondaga County; Pop. 37,380; Area Code 315; Zip Code 132 + zone; Central N.Y.

•**SALTAIRE**, Village; Suffolk County; Pop. 38; Area Code 516; Zip Code 11706; SE N.Y. on Long Island.

•**SAN REMO**, Village; Suffolk County; Pop. 8,700; Area Code 516; SE N.Y.; on N shore of Long Island in a residential area.

•**SAND LAKE**, Town; Rensselaer County; Pop. 6,957; Area Code 518; Zip Code 12153; E N.Y.

•**SANDY CREEK**, Village and Town; Oswego County; Pop. 762 and 3,258; Area Code 315; Zip Code 13145; W N.Y.

•**SANGERFIELD**, Town; Oneida County; Pop. 2,409; Area Code 315; Zip Code 13455; W central N.Y.

•**SARANAC**, Town; Clinton County; Pop. 3,379; Area Code 518; Zip Code 12981; NE N.Y.

•**SARANAC LAKE**, Village; Essex and Franklin Counties; Pop. 5,580; Area Code 518; Zip Code 12983; Elev. 1,540'; near Lower Saranac Lake 36 m. S of Malone in NE N.Y.; on Flower Lake and about one m. NE of the lake from which it gets its name, is a world-famed health resort.
Jacob Smith Moody, the first settler in the region, came here in 1819 and cleared 16 acres of land; while all of his sons became guides, *Martin Moody*, or Uncle Mart, guided the most distinguished list, including *Governor Horation Seymour*, Presidents *Chester A. Arthur* and *Grover Cleveland*, and the members of the Philosophers' Camp.
Captain Pliny Miller erected a sawmill here in 1827, and Saranac developed slowly as an isolated lumbering settlement. In 1876 *Dr. Edward Livingston Trudeau* (1848-1915), a New York

physician who had contracted tuberculosis, came to Saranac to die, but was so benefited by the climate that he established here the first outdoor sanatorium.
North Country Community College was established here in 1967.

•SARATOGA COUNTY, E N.Y.; 818 sq. miles; Pop. 153,735; Seat - Ballston Spa; Est. February 7, 1791; Named for the Indian word for "the side hill".

•SARATOGA LAKE, Lake Saratoga County; located in E N.Y.; popular summer resort. The Mohawk believed that the lake reflected their god's peaceful mind and that anyone crossing it would be drowned if he uttered a single sound. A white woman, to prove the superstition false, shouted while being taken across in a canoe, and nothing happened. The Indians brought her to shore and explained, "The Great Spirit is merciful. He knows that a white woman cannot hold her tongue."

•SARATOGA SPRINGS, City; Saratoga County; Pop. 23,901; Area Code 518; Zip Code 12866; Elev. 330'; in E N.Y. in the center of the county; is a resort city of the Adirondack foothills, famed for its mineral springs, its horse racing, and its old hotels, for eight months of the year is just another central New York state town. It stirs with anticipation in June, swings into preparatory activity in July, and rushes headlong into the full tumult of its summer season in August. In September the decline begins. In October the town resumes its character as a sectional trading center, settling into its winter normality, which is broken only be occasional social functions at Skidmore College and a winter sports carnival.

The growth and development of Saratoga has been closely associated with its mineral springs, the waters of which have been in systematic use since 1774. Large numbers of wild animals, attracted by the saline properties of the water, made this section a favorite hunting ground for the Indians, who called it Saraghoga (place of swift water). The Mohawk and the Oneida built hunting lodges at the springs each summer, and the Saraghoga of that era was as well known to the Indians as the modern Saratoga is to the white man today. For many centuries High Rock Spring was called by the Indians the Medicine Spring of the Great Spirit.

Father Isaac Jogues, Jesuit missionary and explorer, is believed to have visited the springs in 1643. In 1767 Mohawk braves are said to have carried *Sir William Johnson* to the springs on a stretcher, that he might benefit from the waters. Johnson's strength was improved and he returned several times. In 1775 *Dirck Schouten* built a cabin near High Rock Spring, but he heeded Indian warnings and moved away from that beneficient abode of the Great Spirit. The Revolutionary War delayed settlement further, but the curative powers of the waters were recognized and the resultant value of the land was foreseen by many colonists. In 1783 *George Washington* attempted to buy High Rock and adjacent springs. The development that has made Saratoga a place of international reputation began with arrival of the pioneer *Gideon Putnam* in 1789. In 1802 he bought the land around the present Congress Spring, cleared the heavy timber, and built the three-story frame Union Hall, "the first commodious hotel erected at the springs for the accommodation of the visitors." People were attracted to the spot, and when they came to settle they found Putnam ready to sell them lots around his inn. Thus Saratoga Springs was built around a hotel. In 1811, during the construction of Congress Hall, his second venture, Putnam was fatally injured.

The first United States Hotel was built in 1824. The second railroad in New York state, the Schenectady & Saratoga, was opened in 1832. Saratoga soon surpassed the earlier popular Ballston Spa, which had the seeming advantage of a more solid foundation in industry and commerce, but devoting itself wholeheartedly to the service of its visitors. To its natural attractions for people who were health-bent, Saratoga added man-made attractions for those who were pleasure-bent, and the spa beame the social and sporting center of the country. In 1841 a guidebook described the clientele of the hotels as a mingling of "gentlemen of the turf, connoisseurs of the odd trick, and the amateurs of poker."

•SARDINIA, Town; Erie County; Pop. 2,801; Area Code 716; Zip Code 14134; W N.Y.

•SAUGERTIES, Village and Town; Ulster County; Pop. 3,879 and 17,880; Area Code 914; Zip Code 12477; Elev. 100'; on W side of Hudson River 11 m. N of Kingston in SE N.Y.; was once an important bluestone shipping center and is backed by an imposing cluster of Catskill peaks - Overlook Mountain, High Peak, and Sugarloaf Mountain. In *James Fenimore Cooper's The Pioneers*, Natty Bumppo stood on the crest of Overlook and saw "The river . . . in sight for 70 miles under my feet, looking like a curled shaving, though it was eight long miles to its bank."

•SAVANNAH, Town; Wayne County; Pop. 1,879; Area Code 315; Zip Code 13146; W central N.Y.

•SAVONA, Village; Steuben County; Pop. 939; Area Code 607; Zip Code 14879; S N.Y.

•SAYVILLE, Village; Suffolk County; Pop. 15,300; Area Code

516; Zip Code 11782; SE N.Y.; on S shore of Long Island at the Great South Bay.

The village is an oyster center, packing the "Blue Point" for shipment world-wide. It is also a yachting center, with one of the best sailing facilities on the South Bay. *Father Divine*, a Black cultist, maintained a "heaven" in the village in 1929. A ferry connects the town with Cherry Grove on Fire Island.

•**SCARBOROUGH**, Village; Westchester County; Area Code 914; Zip Code 10510; SE N.Y.; is a commuters' village in a region of large estates.

In the 1890's and later, the 15-mile stretch along the Hudson between Scarborough and Yonkers was called the Gold Coast because of the procession of elegant estates costing in the millions and representing in their owners a total wealth easily reaching into the billions. Among the owners were the *Rockefellers, Vanderbilts, Wendels*, and *Morgans, J. Gould, Amzi L. Barber*, (asphalt), *J.Jennings McComb* (cotton), and *Daniel Reed* (copper). In recent years many of these estates have been sold or rented to country clubs an others have been cut up into high class subdivisions and apartment house sites.

•**SCARSDALE**, Village and Town; Westchester County; Pop. 17,625 and 17,625; Area Code 914; Zip Code 10583; Elev. 200'; 20 m. N NE of New York City in SE N.Y.; is a restricted residential village; many of its wealthy residents commute to the city. It takes its name from the Manor of Scarsdale, of which its site was a part, established by *Caleb Heathcote*, who came from Scarsdale, Derbyshire, England, in 1701.

•**SCHAGHTICOKE**, Village and Town; Rensselaer County; Pop. 681 and 7,134; Area Code 518; Zip Code 12154; E N.Y.

•**SCHENECTADY**, City; Seat of Schenectady County; Pop. 67,877; Area Code 518; Zip Code 123; Elev. 220'; E N.Y.

The Mohawk Indians called the present city site Schonowe (big flats). The Indian original of the name Schenectady (at the end of the pine plains) referred to the sites of both Albany and Schenectady as the termini of the aboriginal portage between the Hudson and Mohawk Rivers. In 1662 *Arent Van Curler*, with a small group of Dutchmen, emigrated from Albany to the Groote Vlachte (Dutch, big flats) and made formal application to the governor for permission to purchase the land from the Indians.

A major industrial annex of a large metropolitan area, Schenectady was born and raised alongside the great Mohawk River. The major business area of the city is still clustered near the river banks, and a great area of residential and commercial suburbs spread out in all directions from this core.

The economic life of the city depends principally upon the

Dictionary of Places 333

huge General Electric Company complex and Alco Products' diesel locomotive plants. Schenectady also produces atomic and jet machinery, insulating materials, chemicals and plastics, as well as devices for measuring different aspects of the environment. Much of the research that has brought about industrial progress in the city takes place at Union College, founded in 1795. The sedate, parklike campus is set in the middle of residential downtown, reminding Schenectady's citizens of its pioneering history. Union College was the second institution founded in New York, and was the birthplace of college fraternities. Several leading American statesmen studied here, such as *President Chester A. Arthur*, New York Governor and U.S. Secretary of State, *William H. Seward*, and *Robert Toombs*, Confederate Secretary of State. Today the school is a private liberal arts college for men, with three affiliated schools in Albany. The university uniting these schools with Union College was formed in 1873.

Today, the city remembers its achievements at the Schenectady Museum, which houses museums of art, natural history and science, as well as a planetarium. The county historical society operates a small museum of local Indian artifacts, and Revolutionary and Civil War historical items. Several churches and homes dating to colonial times have been restored throughout town.

•SCHENECTADY COUNTY, E N.Y.; 207 sq. miles; Pop. 149,769; Seat - Schenectady; Est. March 7, 1809; Named for the Mohawk Indian word meaning "on the other side of the pine lands".

•SCHENEVUS, Village; Otsego County; Pop. 613; Area Code 617; Zip Code 12155; Central N.Y.

•SCHOHARIE, Village and Town; Seat of Schoharie County; Pop. 1,015 and 3,114; Area Code 518; Zip Code 12157; E N.Y.

•SCHOHARIE COUNTY, E N.Y.; 624 sq. miles; Pop. 29,693; Seat - Schoharie; Est. April 6, 1795; Named for the Mohawk Indian word meaning "floating driftwood".

•SCHROON LAKE, Village; Essex County; Area Code 518; Zip Code 12870; Elev. 840'; lies at the head of Schroon Lake. The name is believed to have been given by French scouts in the early eighteenth century, who compared the beauty of the long slim body of water with that of the young widow of *Paul Scarron*, the dramatist, best known as Madame de Maintenon, consort of Louis XIV. Within a five mile radius are 70 lakes and ponds.

•SCHUYLER COUNTY, SW central N.Y.; 330 sq. miles; Pop. 17,636; Seat - Watlins Glen; Est. April 17, 1854; Named after

Philip John Schuyler.

•**SCHUYLER FALLS**, Town; Clinton County; Pop. 4,174; Area Code 518; Zip Code 12985

•**SCHUYLERVILLE**, Village; Saratoga County; Pop. 1,265; Area Code 518; Zip Code 12871; on W bank of Hudson River 32 m. N of Albany in E N.Y.; Elev. 140'

•**SCIO**, Town; Allegany County; Pop. 1,969; Area Code 716; Zip Code 14880; S N.Y.

•**SCOTIA**, Village; Schenectady County; Pop. 7,241; Area Code 518; Zip Code 12303; Elev. 240'; 25 m. NW of Albany in E N.Y.; the village takes its name from the Latin name of Scotland, the native land of *Alexander Lindsey Glen*, who was the first settler here.

•**SCOTTSVILLE**, Village; Monroe County; Pop. 1,788; Area Code 716; W N.Y.

•**SEA CLIFF**, Village; Nassau County; Pop. 5,351; Area Code 516; Zip Code 11579; on W Long Island in SE N.Y.; originally planned as a summer resort in the 1940's but is now a residential village on the side of a hill.

•**SELDEN**, Village; Suffolk County; Pop. 21,800; Area Code 516; Zip Code 22784; SE N.Y. on central Long Island.

•**SENECA COUNTY**, W central N.Y.; 338 sq. miles; Pop. 33,733; Seat - Ovid, Waterloo; Est. March 24, 1804; Named for the Seneca Indian tribe.

•**SENECA FALLS**, Village and Town; Seneca County; Pop. 7,481 and 9,894; Area Code 315; Zip Code 13148; Elev. 465'; on Seneca River 11 m. W of Auburn in W central N.Y.

Mrs. Amelia Jenks Bloomer (1818-94), wife of the local postmaster, did not invent the "Bloomer", that honor goes to *Mrs. Elizabeth Smith Miller*, daughter of *Gerrit Smith*, but she introduced it and advocated it as a uniform for the soldiers of the woman suffrage cause in this town.

Susan B. Anthony (1820-1906) was already interested in temperance and anti-slavery when in 1850 she met *Elizabeth Stanton* in Seneca Falls. The two women worked together for 50 years. As a militant abolitionist Miss Anthony campaigned under the slogan, "No union with slave-holders," and advocated Black suffrage. In 1872 she and 15 other women voted in Rochester in an attempt to test the legality of woman suffrage under the Fourteenth Amendment; she was arrested, but before the trial, held in

Canandaigua, she voted again. The court, however, evaded the constitutional test and fined Miss Anthony $100; she refused either to pay or to go to jail, and the sentence was never carried out. Miss Anthony served as president of the American Women's Suffrage Association until 1900, when she resigned at the age of 80.

•SENECA LAKE, Lake; Yates and Seneca Counties; located S of Geneva in W central N.Y. is one of the Finger Lakes. The lake measures 35 miles long and aprox. 2 miles in width is 67 sq. miles with a depth of 600 feet. At the southern end of the Lake is Watkins Glen. This Lake is part of the New York State Barge Canal System. At the N end the Seneca River connects Seneca Lake with Cayuga Lake.

•SENNETT, Town; Cayuga County; Pop. 2,547; Area Code 315; Zip Code 13150; W central N.Y.

•SEWARD, Town; Schoharie County; Pop. 1,566; Area Code 518; Zip Code 12043; SE N.Y.

•SHANDAKEN, Town; Ulster County; Pop. 2,912; Area Code 914; Zip Code 12480; SE N.Y.

•SHARON SPRINGS, Village; Schoharie County; Pop. 516; Area Code 518; Zip Code 13459; Elev. 1,320'; in NW section of the county in N central N.Y. 45 miles to the W of Albany.

When the pioneers first came into this region they found blazes on trees leading from all directions toward the sulphur springs around which the Great Western Turnpike from Albany and the Loonenberg Pike running from Athens across the Helderbergs brought increasing numbers of people to the spa. *David Elbredge* took the first steps to accommodate visitors when he moved a house close to the springs in 1825 and opened it to the public.

In the center of the village the WHITE SULPHUR SPRINGS, a natural sulphur-and magnesia-stained spring, poured forth at an average of four barrels a minute. A distinct, startling odor permeates the pools and bath-houses, which give hundreds of water treatments daily during the season, May to September.

•SHELTER ISLAND, Town and Island; Suffolk County; Pop. 2,060; Area Code 516; Zip Code 11964; an island in Gardiners Bay off the NE coast of Long Island in SE N.Y. As early as 1652 Quakers sought refuge on the island. Now largely a summer resort.

•SHERBURNE, Village and Town; Chenango County; Pop. 1,550 and 3,644; Area Code 607; Zip Code 13460; Elev. 1,071; in central

N.Y. at the junction 12, 12B and 80 on the Chenango River. Sherburne is halfway between Binghamton and Utica. In 1804, *Brigham Young* lived here on his father's farm.

•**SHERIDAN**, Town; Chautauqua County; Pop. 2,656; Area Code 716; Zip Code 14135; on State 20 in SW corner of the state; was named after *General Philip Sheridan*.

•**SHERMAN**, Village and Town; Chautauqua County; Pop. 778 and 1,484; Area Code 716; Zip Code 14781; in SW corner of N.Y.

•**SHERRILL**, City; Oneida County; Pop. 2,818; Area Code 315; Zip Code 13461; Elev. 500'; in N central N.Y. 2 m. E of Oneida and 22 m. W of Utica.

•**SHINNECOCK BAY**, Bay; SE N.Y.; at SE shore of Long Island; sheltered by Shinnecock Inlet from the Atlantic Ocean. Several coves reach into the mainland from this small bay, approximately 8 m. long.

•**SHINNECOCK RESERVATION**, Indian Reservation; Suffolk County; Pop. 200; Shinnecock Tribe; Tribal Headquarters: Southampton, Long Island, New York 11968; Total area: 400 acres.

The Shinnecock Tribe has retained this land since it was first reserved for them by the colonial government in the name of the King. It is a State reservation, receiving social services from New York state. The reservation is tax-free and valued at $45 million.

The Shinnecock, part of the Montauk Confederacy, were largely a fishing and whaling tribe. They had contact with the Algonquin tribes in Connecticut, traveling the Long Island Sound.

The Shinnecock today appear triracial, a probable result of intermarriage following the loss of men in whaling. Little of their former culture is evident now. Tribal members participate fairly successfully in the economy of the area around them.

•**SHIRLEY**, Village; Suffolk County; Pop. 8,200; Area Code 516; Zip Code 11967; SE N.Y.; On Long Island near the Great South Bay in a wealthy residential area.

•**SHOREHAM**, Village; Suffolk County; Pop. 556; Area Code 516; Zip Code 11786; in SE N.Y.

•**SHORTSVILLE**, Village; Ontario County; Pop. 1,717; Area Code 315; Zip Code 14548; 7 m. N of Canandaigua in W central N.Y.

•**SIDNEY**, Village and Town; Delaware County; Pop. 4,851 and

6,852; Area Code 518; Zip Code 13838; Elev. 900'; across the Susquehanna River on Interstate 88 in S central N.Y., 34 m. NE of Binghamton.

•SILVER CREEK, Village; Chautauqua County; Pop. 3,113; Area Code 716; Zip Code 14136; Elev. 640'; on Lake Erie 28 m. S of Buffalo in SW Corner of N.Y.; is a Summer Resort and is known for its missiles and textiles. It is at the northern end of the Chautauqua grape belt. *Abel Cleveland* and *David Dickinson* made the first land purchase along Walnut Creek, named for a giant tree, 31 feet in circumference. When the tree was blown down, the butt was transformed into a grocery, and the village that grew up around it took its name from another creek flowing into Lake Erie.

•SILVER SPRINGS, Village; Wyoming County; Pop. 806; Area Code 716; Zip Code 14550; N N.Y.

•SINCLAIRVILLE, Village; Chautauqua County; Pop. 772; Area Code 716; Zip Code 14782.

•SKANEATELES, Village and Town; Onondaga County; Pop. 2,777 and 7,774; Area Code 315; Zip Code 13152; at N end of Skaneateles Lake 8 m. E of Auburn in central N.Y.; in 1750 Moravian missionaries from Bethlehem, Pennsylvania, visited the Indian village on this site. *Abraham A. Cuddeback*, believed to be the first white settler, arrived here about 1792. In 1841 a water-cure sanitarium was started here by *Dr. W.C.Thomas*, who conducted the "cures" for 40 years. Before the Civil War the village was a headquarters for the abolitionist activities of *Gerrit Smith* and an important station on the Underground Railroad.

•SLIDE MOUNTAIN, Mountain; Ulster County; SE N.Y.; is the largest peak in the Catskill Mountains at an elevation of 4,204 feet.

•SLOAN, Village; Niagara County; Pop. 5,216; Area Code 716; W N.Y.; 6 m. E of downtown Buffalo in a residential area.

•SLOATSBURG, Village; Rockland County; Pop. 3,157; Area Code 914; Zip Code 10974; Elev. 320'; near New Jersey state line 31 m. N NW of New York in SE N.Y.; the Slot House is a brick Greek Revival structure built by *Isaac Clot* in the early 1800's on the front of a much older one-story house erected by his father Isaac, for whom the village was named. Smith's Tavern, built on the foundation of an old stage-coach tavern of the same name in which *Washington* stopped in June 1775.

•SMITHTOWN, Town; Suffolk County; Pop. 116,460; Area Code

516; Zip Code 11787; SE N.Y; Residential community surrounded by farmland.

•**SMITHTOWN BAY**, Bay; SE N.Y.; N of Long Island on Long Island Sound; protected by Crane Neck Point and a stretch of land ending in Eatons Neck. Extends approx. 12 m.

•**SMYRNA**, Village and Town; Chenango County; Pop. 225; and 1,145; Area Code 607; Zip Code 13464; Central N.Y.

•**SODUS**, Village and Town; Wayne County; Pop. 1,788 and 9,484; Area Code 315; Zip Code 14551; Elev. 475'; near Lake Ontario in the N section of the county, Rochester is 29 m. to the west in W N.Y.

Here as in several other places in western New York, the raising of silkworms was attempted in the 1930's. Large buildings were erected to house the worms and mulberry trees were planted to supply their food. In 1838 a newspaper declared that the manufacture of silk was "as simple as feeding pigs and very easy to perform: one in which small children could be made useful, and also decayed widows and decrepit females. . .". The attempt failed because the mulberry trees could not withstand the severe winters.

•**SODUS POINT**, Village; Wayne County; Pop. 1,343; Area Code 315; Zip Code 14555; Elev. 224'; in the Lake Ontario plain in NW N.Y., 30 m. N of Geneva; is a popular summer resort on Sodus Bay. On June 19, 1813, *Sir James Yeo*, War of 1812 commander of the British fleet on Lake Ontario, descended upon Sodus Point and landed a looting party, which overcame the defenders and burned every building but one.

•**SOLVAY**, Village; Onondaga County; Pop. 7,107; Area Code 315; Zip Code 132 + zone; 5 m. W of Syracuse in central N.Y.

•**SOMERS**, Town; Westchester County; Pop. 13,152; Area Code 914; Zip Code 10589; Elev. 300'; in SE N.Y.; is the "birthplace of the American circus." In the center of the hamlet is the wooden Statue of Old Bet, the first traveling elephant, standing on a granite shaft. In 1815 *Hachaliah Bailey* purchased the animal from a ship captain, who had brought her over from England. Bailey named her "Old Bet" and began to exhibit her about the country. He added monkeys and a bear or two, traveling from place to place at night to minimize the "free show" possibilities.

•**SOUND BEACH**, Village; Suffolk County; Pop. 5,400; Area Code 516; Zip Code 11789; Elev. 60'; SE N.Y.; On N shore of Long Island.

•SOUTH DAYTON, Village; Cattaraugus County; Pop. 659; Area Code 716; Zip Code 14138; SW N.Y.

•SOUTH GLENS FALLS, Village; Saratoga County; Pop. 3,727; Area Code 518; Zip Code 12801; 17 m. NE of Sarasota Springs in E N.Y. Across the Hudson River to the N is Glens Falls which sprang this village.

•SOUTH HUNTINGTON, Village; Suffolk County; Pop. 8,946; Area Code 516; SE N.Y. in central Long Island, 3 m. S of Huntington.

•SOUTH OYSTER BAY, Bay; SE N.Y.; at S shore, Long Island; protected from Atlantic Ocean by Fire Island and a group of small islands; extends approx. 6 m. from North Line Island W to Cedar Island.

•SOUTHAMPTON, Village and Town; Suffolk County; Pop. 4,021 and 42,796; Area Code 516; Zip Code 11968; on Long Islands S shore in SE N.Y.; is mainly a resort area. Montauk Point is 33 m. to the E. The Shinnecock Indian Reservation is a near neighbor. Settled by immigrants from Lynn, Massachusetts, in 1648, and therefore is one of the oldest villages on Long Island. Today it is a truck garden center and a fashionable resort ranking with Bar Harbor, Newport, and Mt. Desert. Many mansions of the wealthy that overlooked the beach were all but destroyed during the 1938 hurricane.

•SOUTHOLD, Town; Suffolk County; Pop. 19,140; Area Code 516; Zip Code 11971; 18 m. NE of Riverhead on the N end of Long Island in SE N.Y. The town is mainly a summer resort.

•SOUTHPORT, Village; Chemung County; Pop. 8,865; Area Code 914; S N.Y.; near Pennsylvania state line and 2 m. S of Elmira near the Chemung River.

•SPECULATOR, Village; Hamilton County; Pop. 407; Area Code 518; Zip Code 12164; NE central N.Y.

•SPENCER, Village and Town; Tioga County; Pop. 864 and 2,636; Area Code 607; Zip Code 14883; S N.Y.

•SPENCERPORT, Village; Monroe County; Pop. 3,428; Area Code 716; Zip Code 14559; Elev. 528'; 10 m. NW of Rochester in W part of the state. The area is mainly agricultural. *John T. Trowbridge* , author, was born here and lived here for 17 years.

•SPRING VALLEY, Village; Rockland County; Pop. 20,580; Area Code 914; Zip Code 10977; in SE N.Y.; is known for its fruit farms and as a resort.

•**SPRINGVILLE**, Village; Erie County; Pop. 4,271; Area Code 716; Zip Code 14141; Elev. 1,341; 27 m. SE of Buffalo in W N.Y.; was early known as Fiddlers' Green. *David Leroy*, "famous and inveterate fiddler," settled here in 1812, and he and other amateurs made it a habit to meet on the green and strike up popular tunes.

•**SPRINGWATER**, Town; Livingston County; Pop. 2,134; Area Code 716; Zip Code 14560; Elev. 970'; 40 m. S of Rochester in W central N.Y.

•**SQUAW ISLAND**, Island; Ontario County; W N.Y.; In Canardaigua Lake. According to legend, the island takes its name from its use by the Seneca as a sanctuary for their women and children during the *Sullivan-Clinton* expedition.

•**STAFFORD**, Town; Genesee County; Pop. 2,507; Area Code 716; Zip Code 14143; W N.Y.

•**STAMFORD**, Village and Town; Delaware County; Pop. 1,237 and 2,150; Area Code 518; Zip Code 12167; Elev. 1,827'; in S N.Y. at the NE corner of the county; is the largest and most pretentious resort in the Catskills. Excellent facilities for golf, tennis, swimming, riding, mountain-climbing, and fishing provide rural recreation, without sacrifice of urbanlike hotel conveniences.

•**STATEN ISLAND**, Island; Richmond County; Pop. 349,601; Area Code 212; Zip Code 103 + zone; in SE N.Y. W of Long Island in New York Bay. The state of New Jersey is to the W. Raritan Bay is to the S and Newark Bay to the N. The island is 15 miles long and 7 miles wide for a land mass of 64 sq. miles. Was formerly known as Richmond until April 1975 when it was renamed. *See also Richmond*.

•**STATUE OF LIBERTY**, National Monument; on (Bedloe's) Liberty Island in Upper N.Y.Bay; SE N.Y.; was bought by New York City in 1758 and later was given to the U.S. Government. The island occupies 58 acres. The Statue was given to the U.S. by the French people, and was sculptured by the Frenchman *Frederic Auguste Bartholdi* and was unveiled in 1886. "Liberty Enlightening the World" is the motto.

•**STEPHENTOWN**, Town; Rensselaer County; Pop. 2,049; Area Code 518; Zip Code 12168; in E N.Y.; was the birthplace of *Zaddock Pratt* the founder of Prattsville.

•**STERLING**, Town; Cayuga County; Pop. 3,264; Area Code 315;

Dictionary of Places

Zip Code 13156; in central N.Y.

•**STEUBEN COUNTY,** S N.Y.; 1,410 sq. miles; Pop. 98,978; Seat - Bath; Est. March 18, 1796; Named after *Friedrich Wilhelm Ludolf Gerhard Augustin von Steuben*.

•**STILLWATER,** Village and Town; Saratoga County; Pop. 1,586; Area Code 518; Zip Code 12170; on the Hudson River in N N.Y. about 20 m. N of Albany. The Battle of Saratoga during the Revolutionary War was fought just to the N of Stillwater.

•**STOCKPORT,** Town; Columbia County; Pop. 2,805; Area Code 518; Zip Code 12171; in SE N.Y.

•**STOCKTON,** Town; Chautauqua County; Pop. 2,316; Area Code 716; Zip Code 14784; in the SW corner of N.Y.

•**STONY BROOK,** Village; Suffolk County; Pop. 6,391; Zip Code 11790; SE N.Y.; on Smithtown Bay N of Long Island; Residential.
In 1843, 24 vessels carried loads of cordwood to New York City from here. The harbor today can accomodate only small craft. *William Sidney Mount* (1807-68) lived here for a time. He was an American genre painter. On Mill Road at the Stony Brook crossing is a gristmill, built in 1699, still doing business grinding grain. The State University of New York at Stony Brook was instituted here during the 1960s, when college enrollment soared in the state.

•**STONY POINT,** Town; Rockland County; Pop. 12,841; Area Code 914; Zip Code 10980; Elev. 120'; in SE N.Y; derives its name from the rocky bluff that projects into the Hudson. Here the Federal government erected in 1826 a lighthouse 179 feet above sea level equipped with a mechanical fog signal and a "fixed white light."

•**STRATFORD,** Town; Fulton County; Pop. 632; Area Code 607; Zip Code 13470; in E N.Y.

•**STUYVESANT,** Town; Columbia County; Pop. 2,207; Area Code 518; Zip Code 12173; Elev. 100'; in SE N.Y. *Henry Hudson* is supposed to have landed at this site and named the place Kinder Hoek. The early Dutch settlers of the place moved up the hill to get away from malaria and mosquitoes and took the name with them.

•**SUFFERN,** Village; Rockland County; Pop. 10,785; Area Code 914; Zip Code 10901; Elev. 500'; 30 m. NW of N.Y.City in SE N.Y.; is a commuters' village and the local shopping center for many city people with summer homes nearby. It was the Home of *Dan*

Beard, teacher and author, best known as the founder of the Boy Scouts of America.

•**SUFFOLK COUNTY**, SE N.Y. on E Long Island; 929 sq. miles; Pop. 1,284,091; Seat - Riverhead; Est. November 1, 1683; Named for Suffolk County, England.

•**SULLIVAN COUNTY**, SE N.Y.; 980 sq. miles; Pop. 64,950; Seat - Monticello; Est. March 27, 1809; Named after *John Sullivan*.

•**SUMMIT**, Town; Schoharie County; Pop. 911; Area Code 518; Zip Code 12175; in E N.Y.

•**SYLVAN BEACH**, Village; Oneida County; Pop. 1,234; Area Code 315; Zip Code 13157. Central N.Y.

•**SYOSSET**, Village; Nassau County; Pop. 10,200; Area Code 516; Zip Code 11791; SE N.Y. on Long Island.

•**TANNERSVILLE**, Village; Greene County; Pop. 678; Area Code 518; Zip Code 12485; Elev. 1,920'; on Lake Rip Van Winkle in SE N.Y.

•**TAPPAN**, Village; Rockland County; Pop. 6,100; Area Code 914; Zip Code 10983; Elev. 80'; SE N.Y.; 5 m. S of Nyack near the Hudson River.

This residential village is associated with the beginning and the end of the *Benedict Arnold-Major Andre'* tragedy. In the De Wint Mansion here, *Washington's* headquarters in 1780 and 1783, the general entrusted to the embittered Arnold the command at West Point. Arnold then wrote to *Sir Henry Clinton* in New York City, offering to betray the garrison to the British. Clinton sent Major Andre' to help, but Andre' was captured on the way back and the plans discovered. As soon as Arnold heard of the capture, he fled down the river to the British. Andre' was hanged on a hill outside of town.

•**TARRYTOWN**, Village; Westchester County; Pop. 10,608; Area Code 914; Zip Code 10591; Elev. 70'; on the Hudson River in SE N.Y. about 24 m. from N.Y. City.

Tarrytown, according to *Washington Irving*, was named by irate Dutch farm women who complained that their husbands lingered too long at the village tavern after depositing produce at the Philipse wharf; but more serious historians say that "tarry" is a corruption of the Dutch word "tarwe" (wheat). The first commuter to attract attention to the Tarrytown neighborhood was *Washington Irving*, who in 1835 decided to rebuild an old farmhouse as his home; he felt he could live here very cheaply, find seclusion for work, and yet be close to New York City. Central historical buildings are in town.

•**TERRYVILLE**, Village; Suffolk County; Pop. 6,000; Area Code 516; SE N.Y. on Long Island.

•**THERESA**, Village and Town; Jefferson County; Pop. 926 and 1,848; Area Code 315; Zip Code 13691; Elev. 376'; in N N.Y.
Birthplace of *Roswell P. Flower* (1835-90), governor of New York, 1892-95. Flower started as a poor working-man, employed in turn as farm boy, millhand, and teacher; and in his first campaign for Congress, against *William Waldorf Astor*, he used the slogan; "My opponent counts his rents by the millions, while I have only the rents in my clothes." But Flower grew wealthy rapidly: in the gubernatorial campaign of 1891 Tammany Hall introduced him as "the flower that will never fade"; but anti-Tammany Democrats countered: "By nominating a flamboyant millionaire you propose to make the honor and power of the Republic a mere perquisite to the rich."

•**THORNWOOD**, Village; Suffolk County; Pop. 6,000; Area Code 516; Zip Code 10594; SE N.Y.; 25 m. N of Manhattan.

•**THOUSAND ISLANDS**, Islands in St. Lawrence River; N N.Y. and partially in Canada. There are many resorts located on the islands.

•**TICONDEROGA**, Village and Town; Essex County; Pop. 2,2921 and 5,419; Area Code 518; Zip Code 12883; NE N.Y. on the neck of land connecting Lake George and Lake Champlain; is a year-round tourist spot, with historic shrines and winter sports. The name is a variation of the Indian Cheonderoga (between two waters, or where the waters meet). The French built a military road along the path of the Indian carry between the two lakes and in 1755 they constructed Fort Carillon, later called Fort Ticonderoga. It was captured by *Ethan Allen* in 1775 and later retaken by *Burgoyne* in 1777.

•**TIOGA COUNTY**, S N.Y.; 524 sq. miles; Pop. 49,724; Seat - Owego; Est. February 16, 1791; Named for the Indian tribe, it also means "at the forks."

•**TIVOLI**, Village; Dutchess County; Pop. 701; Area Code 914; Zip Code 12583; Elev. 152; SE N.Y.
Here in 1798-1802 *Peter de Labigarre*, who came to America after the French Revolution, built the Chateau de Tivoli, the first unit of a projected model community. *Charles Balthazar Julien Fevret de Saint-Memin*, an expatriate officer of the guard at the court of *Louis XVI* and an itinerant draftsman and portrait painter, drew the plan for the settlement. It was more visionary

than practical. Two extant copies show a grid-iron of 60-foot streets named Friendship, Chancellor (after Livingston), Liberty, Plenty, Peace, etc. The plan was so ill-adapted to the precipitious site that Zephyre Square, the central unit, would have been excavated in a hillside. Of the eighteenth-century dream only Flora Street, a road down to the riverside station, and Diana Street, a tiny private concrete driveway, remain. The scheme collapsed after *De Labigarre's* death in 1807, and *Chancellor Livingston* bought the property at a foreclosure sale.

•TOMPKINS COUNTY, S central N.Y.; 482 sq. miles; Pop. 87,107; Seat - Ithaca; Est. April 7, 1817; Named after *Daniel D. Tompkins*.

•TONAWANDA, City; Erie County; Pop. 18,701; Area Code 716; Zip Code 14150; Elev. 575'; 9 m. N of Buffalo in W N.Y. The city is mainly a manufacturing and shipping center.

•TONAWANDA INDIAN RESERVATION, State Reservation; Niagara, Erie and Genesee Counties; Pop. Est. 850; Tonawanda Band of the Seneca Tribe live on the Reservation. The total area of the reservation is 7,549 acres.

From proceeds realized by the relinquishment of the land west of the Missouri, the tribe purchased 7,549 acres of their original 12,000-acre reservation. The deed was taken in trust in the name of the Secretary of the Interior. In 1863, the secretary conveyed these lands to the comptroller of the State of New York in trust for the Tonawanda Band of Seneca Indians. Most of the land is allotted by the tribe to its members. Leasing and mortgaging laws generally follow those regulations applicable to federal reservations. Land cannot be alienated without the permission of the Secretary of the Interior.

Under a treaty negotiated in 1838 between the Seneca and the United States, the Seneca supposedly agreed to relinquish the Allegany, Cattaraugus, and Tonawanda Reservations in exchange, among other considerations, for land west of the Missouri. The Indians objected to the treaty, and negotiations were renewed. In 1842, a compromise treaty was negotiated by which the Seneca were allowed to retain the Cattaraugus and Allegany Reservations, but the Tonawanda Reservation was to be relinquished to a land company. Disgruntled over the treaty, the Senecas split as a tribe and became two entities. Those from the Tonawanda group refused to move from their reservation, and, in 1857, another compromise treaty relinquished their land west of the Missouri; from the proceeds they purchased 7,549 acres of the orignal 12,000 acre reservation.

With exception of the annual celebrations and the practices of the Handsome Lake Religion now carried on by an increasing number of people, the Indian culture of the Tonawanda Seneca is nil. On special occasions, even the clothing and beadwork that were once quite common must now be borrowed by the Seneca from museums. In recent years there has been a revival of lacrosse, but other sports in which the Indians participated are being largely ignored.

•TROUPSBURG, Town; Steuben County; Pop. 1,002; Area Code 607; Zip Code 14885; in S N.Y.

•TROY, City; Rensselaer County seat; Pop. 56,614; Area Code 518; Zip Code 12180; Elev. 34'; E New York, near Albany and Schenectady metropolitan area; On E bank of Hudson River at mouth of Mohawk River.

First sighted by a white man in 1609, Troy has grown into an important residential-commercial-industrial center for east central New York. Its connection to the Albany-Schenectady metropolitan areas originated by water; not only because of the Hudson River, but also by the New York State Barge Canal, which terminates here. Clothing, machinery, transportation equipment and processed foods are transported along these waterways as well as the numerous highways and railroads traversing the area.

Originally, the site was a Mohegan Indian fort erected during that tribe's war with the Mohawks. *Henry Hudson* and his crew explored the region in 1609, and for 120 years afterwards, the area was a part of the Dutch patroonship of *Kiliaen Van Rensselaer*. Even after the British and later the Americans took over leadership of the area, Dutch influence and land ownership was prevalent.

After the Revolution *Benjamin Thurber* purchased a lot at the intersection of the river and the Hoosick road and opened a general store, which he called the Bunch of Grapes. *Captain Stephen Ashley* leased the *Matthias Vanderheyden* home which stood at what is now the corner of Division and River Streets, and turned it into a tavern. *Jacob D. Vanderheyden*, owner of the middle farm, for a while opposed settlement was but finally persuaded to lay out his holding in building lots. The land was surveyed for a town site in 1786. Philadelphia, a city of regular squares, was adopted as a model, and, except for the curving of the river road, now River Street, the plan was followed. Vanderheyden insisted that the village carry his name, but the half dozen houses were popularly known as Ashley's Ferry or Ferry Hook. The name Troy was adopted at a public meeting in Ashley's Tavern on January 5, 1789. *Jacob Vanderheyden*, reconciled to town building, rebelled anew against the name, and for years gave his address as "Vanderheyden alias Troy."

After the town was incorporated, in 1798, however, Troy was the name that stuck, and once the falls of the small Poestenkill River were harnessed, several paper and grain mills sprang up in the area. A Troy-Schenectady toll road was built in 1802, and 10 years later Troy was incorporated as a city.

The next century was one of progress for Troy, as it began to host hundreds of New Englanders making their way west. Rensselaer Polytechnic Institute was founded in 1824, with early mechanical and scientific genius *Amos Eaton* as its first senior professor. *Emma Willard* brought her pioneering school for women here in 1821, and as the iron industry grew, *Henry Burden* helped it along with his inventions. Many new factories opened during Troy's golden age; between 1820 and 1830, the population more than doubled.

Although the mid 1830's to 1840's were troubled financially, Troy surged into national prominence as an industrial center during the 1850's. Canals and railroads provided most of the business, and the Civil War only intensified the demand for the city's iron products and "fancy clothes". It was during this time that women garment workers in the city developed their own union.

In 1868 the powerful Collar Laundry Workers of Troy gave $1,000 to the Troy Iron Moulders Association and $800 to striking bricklayers in New York City. Coupled with this, they forced increases in their own wages from $2-$3 to $12-$14 a week. In 1869, however, a strike split the union members into factions and the movement disintegrated.

Visiting Europe in 1864, *Horatio Winslow* purchased the rights to manufacture and sell Bessemer steel in the United States and began production at his company's Troy works. Introduction of the metal brought a new order of mass haulage by rail, and Troy became the steel center of the country. Its supremacy was doomed, however, when in 1873 *Andrew Carnegie* set up a steel mill 12 miles from Pittsburgh.

The beginning of the twentieth century promised continued success for Troy, but changing conditions in transportation as well as the recent decline in demand for American-made steel products is reflected in Troy's declining population.

However, the Rensselaer Polytechnic Institute remains an important science and engineering school, and the private liberal arts Russel Sage College offers two-year programs in nursing. The State University of New York also sponsors classes at the Hudson Valley Community College here.

•**TRUMANSBURG**, Village; Tompkins County; Pop. 1,724; Area Code 607; Zip Code 14886; Elev. 1,000'; in S central N.Y. The name was misspelled for that of its first settler *Abner Treman*, who was a Revolutionary veteran who came here in 1792.

•**TRUXTON**, Town; Cortland County; Pop. 988; Area Code 607; Zip Code 13158; Elev. 1,150'; in central N.Y.; birthplace of *John J. McGraw* (1873-1934) baseball's "master mind". Tiring of farm life at the age of 17, McGraw joined the Olean baseball team. A scrappy little lad with a passion for the game, he won the attention of baseball scouts, and was signed the following year by the Baltimore Orioles of the American Association, one of the most famous teams of all time. Among his teammates were *Miller Huggins*, later manager of the New York Yankees, and *"Connie" Mack*, later manager of the Philadelphia Athletics. On July 10, 1902, McGraw became manager of the New York Giants, holding that position until June 3, 1932, when he voluntarily retired. Called the "Little Napoleon", he ruled the Giants with an iron hand, going to the extreme of calling every pitch from the dugout. Under his guidance the team won 10 National League pennants and three world's championships.

•**TUCKAHOE**, Village; Westchester Conty; Pop. 6,274; Area Code 914 Zip Code 10707; Elev. 120'; 18 m. N NE of New York in SE N.Y.; is a suburb of Yonkers, where most of the working population are employed. The village originated around marble quarries, at one time a principal source of supply for New York City construction.

•**TULLY**, Village and town; Onondaga county; Pop. 1,065 and 2,414; Area Code 315; Zip Code 13159; Central N.Y.

•**TUPPER LAKE**, Village and Lakes; Franklin County; Pop. 4,470; Area Code 518 Zip Code 12986; Elev. 1,569'; 45 m. S of Malone in NE N.Y. in S section of the county. This village is a summer resort because of the two lakes, Big and Little Tupper Lakes.

•**TURIN**, Village and Town; Lewis County; Pop. 284 and 823; Area Code 315; Zip Code 13473; Elev. 1,264'; in N central N.Y.

•**TUSCARORA INDIAN RESERVATION**, Niagara County; Pop. 647; Tuscarora Tribe; Tribal Headquarters: Tuscarora Rural Community, Niagara County, N.Y. 14094; total area: 5,700 acres.

Tuscarora Reservation is located nine miles northeast of Niagara Falls. Slightly more than one-third of this area was acquird by gifts of 640 acres from the Seneca and of 1,280 acres from the Holland Land Company. The remainder was purchased from the latter company with money received for the release of their lands in North Carolina. Recently, approximatley 550 acres were taken by the state power authority for use as a reservoir, with approximately $850,000 paid as compensation. The entire area is collectively owned by the tribe, which rents to its individual members.

The Tuscarora are indigenous to North Carolina; however, they are of the Iroquois linguistic group. Continual pressure for land from white settlers forced the Tuscarora to western New

York, and, in 1718, they were admitted as the sixth nation in the Iroquois Confedercy. For remaining neutral during the Revolutionary War, the Treaty of 1784 secured for them the possession of the land upon which they were living.

The Tuscarora, like the majority of tribes in New York, rule and share through a system of matriarchy. There are nine clans within the Iroquois group, and the oldest mother in each clan chooses its chief. The chiefs govern for the remainder of their lifetime or until removed from their positions for misbehavior. Only those individuals born of an Iroquois mother are considered as members of the tribe, eligible to share in its resources and privileges. English is, today, the principal language of the tribe. Life on the reservation is, with some exceptions, much as it is in any relatively poor rural community. Few traditions are practiced.

•TUXEDO PARK, Village; Orange County; Pop. 812; Area Code 914; Zip Code 10987; Elev. 420'; in SE N.Y.; covers 13,000 acres around Little Wee, Big Little Wee, and Tuxedo Lakes. The beautiful tract was owned in the 1880's by *Pierre Lorillard*, the fourth, who decided to make it a refuge for America's early crop of millionaires. The land was broken up and sold in large tracts, on which were erected turreted mansions of the kind then fashionable. Proof that the Tuxedoites had reached the eminence from which they could set the styles, rather than follow them, is found in the name of the dinner jacket that is now a formal uniform of the males of the nation. For a long time *Mrs. Emily Post*, authority on etiquette, lived here.

•TYRONE, Town; Schuyler conty; Pop. 1,475; Area Code 607; Zip Code 14887; in SW central N.Y.

•ULSTER COUNTY, SE N.Y.; 1,141 sq. miles; Pop. 157,494; Seat - Kingston; Est. November 1, 1683; Named for Ulster, Ireland.

•UNADILLA, Village and town; Otsego County; Pop. 1,366 and 4,023; Area Code 617; Zip Code 13849; Elev. 1,023'; in central N.Y.

During the early years of the Revolution the Indian castles in the vicinity of Unadilla were the gathering place for Tories and Indians bent on destruction of frontier patriot settlements. In October 1778, an American force destroyed the Indian villages - "real towns of stone houses with glass windows and brick chimneys" - and burned 4,000 bushels of corn.

•UNION, Town; Broome County; Pop. 61,160; Area Code 607; Zip Code 13760; in S N.Y. 9 m. W of Binghamton; was so named because it was to this place that the forces of *Sullivan* and *Clinton* met in August 1779. Sullivan had come up from Pennsylvania and Clinton down from the Mohawk. Endicott, Union, and West Endicott were consolidatd in 1921.

•UNION SPRINGS, Village; Cayuga County; Pop. 1,201; Area Code 315; Zip Code 13160; Elev. 419'; in central N.Y.; takes its name from the numerous sulphur and salt springs in the vicinity. Rich archeological remains have been found nearby and on Frontenac Island, in Lake Cayuga. This is one of the very few islands in the Finger Lakes, a knot of land that was once an Algonquian burial ground but is now a bird and game refuge.

•UNIONVILLE, Village; Orange County; Pop. 578; Area Code 914; Zip Code 10988; in SE N.Y.

•UPPER BAY, Bay; SE N.Y.; S of Manhattan Island between Staten Island and Brooklyn. Site of the Statue of Liberty and Ellis Island; Approx. 3 m. wide forming the mouth of the Hudson River.

•UTICA, City; Oneida County seat; Pop. 75,435; Area Code 315; Zip Code 13501; Elev. 500'; Central New York; 90 m. W of Albany; On Mohawk River and New York State Barge Canal; at foothills of Adirondack Mts.

The original name for Utica was the Indian Yahnundadasis, or "around the hill", in reference to this area where trails passed through the foothills. Later, these trails were used and expanded by white pioneers.

The site was included in Cosby's Manor, a grant of 22,000 acres made by *George II* to *William Cosby*, governor of the Province of New York, and others in 1734. In 1758 the British erected Fort Schuyler on what is now Main Street, just below Second Street, close to the river. It was never garrisoned, and was abandoned in the early 1760's.

In 1772 the Cosby tract, on which the quitrents were unpaid, was bought at public sale by *Philip Schuyler, John Bradstreet*, and others for about 1,300 pounds. In 1773 the *Weaver, Reall*, and *Demuth* families, descendants of the Palatines and staunch patriots, moved from German Flats to the north bank of the Mohawk River where it is crossed by the present North Genesee Street. In 1776 their settlement was destroyed during an Indian-Tory raid. After the Revolution new homes were erected; and in the floodtide of westward migration the settlement grew rapidly as a trading and transportation center. Among the early settlers was *Peter Smith* (1768-1837), who came in 1787 and who in later years was a partner of *John Jacob Astor*.

John Post of Schenectady moved his family here in the late eighteenth century, and built an Indian trading post. He also began to trade with New Englanders, and managed to attract many new setters from Schenectady and the East Coast. In 1798, the settlement boasted 200 persons, and was incorporated as a

village. "Utica" was chosen as the name by a chance selection from a hatful of paper slips, and is derived from the name of the ancient city on the Mediterranean coast of Tunisia.
The nineteenth century boomed in Utica, as the Erie Canal was built and Irish and German immigrants arrived to man the new factories. The city was chartered in 1832, the same year engine and boiler works joined the existing plow factory, gristmill, iron foundary and pottery works. Railroads and more canals also helped bring about the city's boom. After 1840, the textile industry dominated the economy here, by after 1940, the main factories moved south and new sources of income had to be defined so that the city could survive. Today, electronics, agriculture, aeronautics and computer technology are important to Utica. Oneida County's large dairy and grain farms depend upon Utica as a distribution point, as do the makers of pneumatic tools, metal products, textiles, and beer.
Many other Uticans are students; the Utica College of Syracuse University, Mohawk Valley Community College, and the State University College at Utica/Rome are located here. Cultural attractions such as the Munson-Williams-Proctor Institute of Art are important. The Oneida Historical Society preserves such buildings as the *Horatio Seymour* Home, built in 1810 by Seymour's family before he became mayor of Utica and later governor of New York (1853-55 and 1863-65).

•VALATIE, Village; Columbia County; Pop. 1,605; Area Code 518; Zip Code 12184; in SE N.Y.

•VALHALLA, Village; Westchester County; Pop. 6,600; Area Code 914; Zip Code 10595; SE N.Y.; approx. 25 m. N of Manhattan at S tip of Kensico Reservoir.

•VALLEY FALLS, Village; Rensselaer County; Pop. 550; Area Code 518; Zip Code 12185; in E N.Y.

•VALLEY STREAM, Village; Nassau County; Pop. 35,597; Area Code 516; Zip Code 115 + zone; 18 m. from the Manhattan Bridge; SE N.Y.; It developed after the World War. New streets shot out over the flat surface and through the woodland; new bungalows and cottages sprang up like mushrooms; new people came to Valley Stream.

•VAN ETTEN, Village and Town; Chemung County; Pop. 558 and 1,516; Area Code 607; Zip Code 14889; S N.Y.

•VERNON, Village and Town; Oneida County; Pop. 1,381 and 5,364; Area Code 315; Zip Code 13476; Elev. 580'; Central N.Y.

•VERONA, Town; Oneida County; Pop. 6,652; Area Code 315; Zip

Code 13478; in central N.Y.; *Russell Sage* was born in a covered wagon here.

•**VESTAL**, Town; Broome County; Pop. 27,234; Area Code 607; Zip Code 13850; in S N.Y.; was the birthplace of *David Ross Locke* who was an author during the Revolutionary War period.

•**VICTOR**, Village and Town; Ontario County; Pop. 2,362 and 5,768; Area Code 315; Zip Code 14564; Elev. 580'; in W N.Y.; occupies the site of a battle, the only one ever fought in Ontario County, between Denonville and a Seneca force in July 1687. On June 10, 1939, a monument was unveiled in the village in memory of *Kryn*, or Athasata, "The Great Shadow," the Mohawk chief who led the Christian Indian contingent of the French force against his own people.

•**VOORHEESVILLE**, Village; Albany County; Pop. 3,310; Area Code 518; Zip Code 12186; in E central N.Y.; was named after *Walker and Gmelin Voorhees*.

•**WADDINGTON**, Village and Town; St. Lawrence County; Pop. 978 and 2,102; Area Code 315; Zip Code 13694; Elev. 250'; N N.Y.; is a terminal for Canadian pulpwood and a milk shipping center. Here the St. Lawrence flows through the ruins of an eighteenth-century lock built to permit river traffic through the Rapide Plat.

•**WALDEN**, Village; Orange County; Pop. 5,648; Area Code 914; Zip Code 12586; NW of Newburgh in SE N.Y.

•**WALTON**, Village and Town; Delaware County; Pop. 3,331 and 5,836; Area Code 518; Zip Code 13856; in S N.Y. 42 m. E of Binghamton on the Delaware River; was the birthplace of *Rev. Joel Tyler Headly* in 1813.

•**WALWORTH**, Town; Wayne County; Pop. 5,280; Area Code 315; Zip Code 145568; in W N.Y.

•**WAMPSVILLE**, Village; Seat of Madison County; Pop. 566; Area Code 315; Zip Code 13163; elev. 480'; 25 m. E of Syracuse in central N.Y.; is the smallest county seat in the state. It was selected as a compromise to settle a dispute between factions favoring Canastota and Oneida.

•**WANTAGH**, Village; Nassau County; Pop. 22,300; Area Code 516; Zip Code 11793; SE N.Y.; On Long Island near South Oyster Bay. The Wantagh State Parkway leads across the bay to Fire Island from here.

•**WAPPINGERS FALLS**, Village; Dutchess County; Pop. 5,071;

Area Code 914; Zip Code 12590; Elev. 116'; 8 m. S of Poughkeepsie near the Hudson River in SE N.Y.; named for the 75-foot cascade in Wappinger Creek that has provided water power since the place was settled. The chief industries are a bleachery and an overall factory.

•**WARREN COUNTY**, E N.Y; 887 sq. miles; Pop. 54,822; Seat - Lake George; Est. March 12, 1813; Named after *Joseph Warren*.

•**WARRENSBURG**, Town; Warren County; Pop. 3,796; Area Code 518; Zip Code 12885; Elev. 720'; is on the shore of the Schroon River; was named for *James Warren*, who settled here in 1804.

•**WARSAW**, Village and Town; Seat of Wyoming County; Pop. 3,617 and 5,050; Area Code 716; Zip Code 14569; Elev. 1,000'; 39 m. SW of Rochester in W N.Y. in the Wyoming Valley. Mainly a manufacturing city.

•**WARWARSING**, Town; Ulster County; Pop. 12,868; Area Code 914; Zip Code 12489; in SE N.Y.

•**WARWICK**, Village and Town; Orange County; Pop. 4,319 and 21,001; Area Code 914; Zip Code 10900; Elev. 558'; 40 m. NW of New York City in S N.Y.; settled in 1746 by English immigrants from Warwickshire. The area is mainly agricultural.

•**WASHINGTON COUNTY**, E N.Y; 836 sq. miles; Pop. 54,758; Seat - Hudson Falls; Est. March 12, 1772; Named after *George Washington*.

•**WASHINGTONVILLE**, Village; Orange County; Pop. 2,384; Area Code 914; Zip Code 10992; in S N.Y.

•**WATERFORD**, Village and Town; Saratoga County; Pop. 2,412 and 7,191; Area Code 518; Zip Code 12188; Elev. 38'; 10 m. N of Albany on the Hudson River in E N.Y.; is at the junction of the Champlain and Erie divisions of the Barge Canal; during the navigation season the waterfront is a maze of barges and tugboats. Textile mills and machine works provide local employment.

•**WATERLOO**, Village and Town; Seat of Seneca County; Pop. 5,297 and 7,778; Area Code 315; Zip Code 13165; Elev. 450'; 15 m. W of Auburn in W N.Y. The ashes of the Indian settlement of Skoiyase were here before the town grew.

•**WATERTOWN**, City; Seat of Jefferson County; Pop. 27,900; Area Code 315; Zip Code 13601; Elev. 478'; 10 m. E of Lake Ontario in N N.Y.; is a trading and industrial center bisected by the Black River, which falls 112 feet within the city. Manufactured products include paper, papermaking machines, air brakes, plumbing supplies, and surgical instruments.

In 1800 five New Englanders hacked their way up from the Mohawk Valley, stopped at the rocky Black River Falls, and named the site Watertown. They built sawmills and gristmills along the river, and burned piles of lumber for potash. Residents of nearby hamlets flocked to the settlement to work in carpenter and machine shops, barrel shops, and sash and blind factories.

The papermaking industry began with a rag mill in 1809 and reached its peak in the 1890's when the Black River Valley was one of the nation's leading papermaking districts. The industry started on the downgrade in the early 1900's when the supply of spruce dwindled.

The Jefferson County Museum contains collections of Indian curios, historical materials relating to the era of French settlement, and pioneer furniture. Jefferson Community College was established here in 1963.

•WATERVILLE, Village; Oneida County; Pop. 1,677; Area Code 315; Zip Code 13480; Elev. 1,231'; 13 m. SW of Utica in central N.Y.; settled before 1800 by emigrants from Waterville, Maine, was a hop-raising center until the close of the past century. With power available, industries were established and Waterville acquired a reputation for wealth and gentility. *George Eastman* was born here.

•WATERVLIET, City; Albany County; Pop. 11,322; Area Code 518; Zip Code 12189; 6 m. N of Albany on the Hudson River across from Troy in E N.Y. at the center of the New York State Barge Canal.

•WATKINS GLEN, Village; Seat of Schuyler County; Pop. 2,425; Area Code 607; Zip Code 14891; Elev. 477'; 18 m. N of Elmira in SW central N.Y.; at the end of Seneca Lake; there is an International Speedway amongst this resort town.

•WAVERLY, Village; Tioga County; Pop. 4,755; Area Code 607; Zip Code 14892; Elev. 839'; 15 m. SE of Elmira in SE N.Y. on the Pennsylvania border near the Chemung River; is contiguous to Sayre and Athens, Pennsylvania.

•WAYLAND, Village and Town; Steuben County; Pop. 1,844 and 3,875; Area Code 607; Zip Code 14572; Elev. 1,372'; 16 m. NE of Hornell in S N.Y. The area surrounding is agricultural. It was a stopping place for the stage between Elmira and Buffalo; the last "coach," a buckboard wagon, made its final trip on July 20, 1889. After the Erie Railroad was built in the 1850s, German im-

migrants settled here and gave the place a reputation for hard work and thrift.
Wayland is in the northwest corner of Steuben County, one of the greatest potato-growing counties in the country; in recent years the canneries in the village have encouraged the growing of peas, beans, and corn.

•**WAYNE COUNTY**, W N.Y.; 606 sq. miles; Pop. 84,456; Seat - Lyons; Est. April ll, 1823; Named after *Anthony Wayne*.

•**WEBSTER**, Village and Town; Monroe County; Pop. 5,486 and 28,895; Area Code 716; Zip Code 14580; 10 m. NE of Rochester in W N.Y.

•**WEEDSPORT**, Village; Cayuga County; Pop. 1,945; Area Code 315; Zip Code 13166; Elev. 425'; in N central N.Y.; is 62 m. NW of Vernon; many of the working population commute to Auburn and Syracuse. The village Whittlers' Club was formed in 1914 by local philosophers.

•**WELLS**, Town; Hamilton County; Pop. 633; Area Code 518; Zip Code 12190; in NE central part of the state.

•**WELLSBURG**, Village; Chemung County; Pop. 648; Area Code 607; Zip Code 14894; in S N.Y. near Elmira. In 1882 a resident of this village (Abner Wright shipped the first raw milk to New York City market in a felt-jacketed milk can surrounded by ice. In 1893 he and his associates organized the Chemung Valley Condensing Company which gave a new impetus to the local dairy industry.

•**WELLSVILLE**, Village and Town; Allegany County; Pop. 5,764 and 8,646; Area Code 716; Zip Code 14895; Elev. 1,517'; in SW N.Y.; settled in 1795; is an oil and dairy center. It was settled in 1795 and named for *Gardiner Wells*, early settler and chief landowner.
Wellsville was the hub of the Allegany County oil field, is a town of beautiful old homes and much wealth. The town has continued to prosper since the completion of Triangle No.1 in 1879, about four miles to the southwest. The well got its name from the fact that it was the third of a series forming a triangle.

•**WEST BABYLON**, Village; Suffolk County; Pop. 32,100; Area Code 516; Zip Code 11704; SE N.Y.; 1 m. W of Babylon near the Great South Bay of Long Island.

•**WEST BLOOMFIELD**, Town; Ontario County; Pop. 2,283; Area Code 315; Zip Code 14585; in W N.Y.

•WESTBURY, Village; Nassau County; Pop. 13,802; Area Code 516; Zip Code 11590; 2-1/2 m. E of Mineola and 23 m. E of N.Y. City on Long Island in SE N.Y.; is mainly a residential village.

•WESTCHESTER COUNTY, SE N.Y.; 443 sq. miles; Pop. 864,116; Seat - White Plains; Est. November 1, 1683; Named for Chester, England.

•WESTERLO, Town; Albany County; Pop. 2,924; Area Code 518; Zip Code 12193; in E N.Y.

•WESTFIELD, Village and Town; Chautauqua County; Pop. 3,451 and 5,065; Area Code 716; Zip Code 14787; 23 m. NW of Jamestown on Lake Erie in SW corner of N.Y.

Westfield has since 1896 been the headquarters of the Welch Grape Juice Company, the largest producer of grape juice in the world. *Dr. Thomas Branwell Welch*, graduate of Syracuse University, practiced dentistry in several cities. Both he and his son, *Dr. Charles Edgar Welch*, abandoned dentistry for the grape juice business in 1893.

•WESTFORD, Town; Otsego County; Pop. 636; Area Code 617; Zip Code 13488; in central N.Y.

•WESTHAMPTON BEACH, Village; Suffolk County; Pop. 1,626; Area Code 516; Zip Code 11978; on W half of Long Island in SE N.Y.; at the point where the Outer Barrier all but joins the mainland, leaving a small basin and Quantuck Bay. Two roads run out to the Outer Barrier, join, turn east, and continue to Southampton, passing Quogue and Shinnecock Bay and traversing Hampton and Tiana Beaches. The beaches and road suffered severe damage during the hurricane of September 21, 1938, in which about 40 persons lost their lives.

•WEST HAVERSTRAW, Village; Rockland County; Pop. 9,152; Area Code 914; in SE part of N.Y.

•WEST MONROE, Town; Oswego County; Pop. 3,489; Area Code 315; Zip Code 13167; in central N.Y.

•WESTMORELAND, Town; Oneida County; Pop. 5,454; Area Code 315; Zip Code 13490; in central N.Y.

•WEST POINT, SE N.Y.; United States Military Academy and Village; Orange County; Area Code 914; Zip Code 10996; On the •Hudson River; 50 m. N of New York City; Established March 16, 1802; Named for its position on the river.

The West Point region was one of four in the Hudson Highlands fortified during the Revolution, and the American flag has flown over forts here since 1778. The only threat came in 1780, when *Benedict Arnold* plotted to hand West Point over to the British, but his plan was foiled. After the War, *George Washington* and other military leaders recognized the need for a standardized officer's training school which offered practical and scientific education as well as military technology. A four-year curriculum was added to the engineering studies in 1812. Under *Major Sylvanus Thayer*, who presided in 1817-33, West Point grew into a military school of international recognition, as graduates demonstrated their abilities to handle the civil engineering needs of a growing nation. During the Civil War, generals on both sides -- *Lee, Grant, Jackson, Sheridan* and *Jefferson Davis* -- were West Point graduates. *Edgar Allen Poe* and the painter *James A.M. Whistler* failed to finish the stringent scientific schooling here, but went on to other fruitful fields.

Today, the four year course of study leads to the equivalent of a B.S. degree, and most graduates continue with a lifetime career as an officer of the armed services. Women graduated from the institution for the first time in 1980. Enrollment is approximately 2,500.

•**WESTPORT**, Village and Town; Essex County; Pop. 615 and 1,448; Area Code 518; Zip Code 12993; Elev. 271'; in E N.Y.

Westport lies on a natural terrace which encircles a deep bay extending in from Lake Champlain. Many of the stately homes have wide lawns, well-tended formal gardens, and iron fences with ornamental gateways. The Essex County Fair is held here annually in late August and the local yacht club puts on a summer regatta.

•**WEST SENECA**, Town; Erie County; Pop. 51,204; Area Code 716; Zip Code 14224; in W N.Y.

•**WEST WINFIELD**, Village; Herkimer County; Pop. 980; Area Code 315; Zip Code 13491; NE N.Y.

•**WHITEHALL**, Village and Town; Washington County; Pop. 3,232 and 4,414; Area Code 518; Zip Code 12887; Elev. 123'; is midway between New York and Montreal on the Hudson-Champlain trail. In 1759 the place took the name of Skenesborough in honor of *Major Philip Skene* of the British Army, who settled here with about 30 families. The settlement was razed in 1780 when *General Haldimand*, left in charge by *Burgoyne*, abandoned the place.

•**WHITE PLAINS**, City; Seat of Westchester County; Pop. 46,799; Area Code 914; Zip Code 106 + zone; Elev. 467'; on W bank of Hudson River just SE of Storm King and Crow's Nest mountains; about 50 m. by railroad N of New York in SE N.Y.; Inc. Village in

1866 and City in 1916.
White Plains is well within the commuter's belt around New York City. On weekday mornings more than half the working population leave by train and auto for business in the metropolis.

The early settlement, an established community by 1735, was the center of the county's iron mining activity, which remained important until the end of the eighteenth century, and the hub of stage routes. Troubled military conditions in New York City compelled the Provincial Congress to move to White Plains. On July 9, 1776, it met in the courthouse and ratified the Declaration of Independence, which was read for the first time in upstate New York on the courthouse steps on July 11.

From October 21 to 26, 1776, *Washington* with his army of 25,000 ragged, hungry, and poorly equipped soldiers, most of them raw recruits, arrived in White Plains on his masterly retreat from Manhattan.

After the Revolution, mining gave way to agriculture as the main source of livelihood. The railroad reached the settlement in 1844. In 1866, the village was incorporated. Then New Yorkers discovered White Plains and they moved here in large numbers.

New York School of Deaf was established here in 1817 and Good Council College (Women) in 1923.

•**WHITESBORO**, Village; Oneida County; Pop. 4,462; Area Code 315; Zip Code 13492; Elev. 140'; 5 m. NW of Utica in central N.Y. on the Mohawk River.

It has preserved the flavor of the New England of its first settlers; its industries produce knit goods, furniture, and heaters. *Judge Hugh White* (1733-1812) left his Middletown, Connecticut, home in 1784, shipped by water to Albany, overland to Schenectady, and up the Mohawk by boat to his western frontier; his son, driving a yoke of oxen, kept pace by land. The family's log house, thrown up in a hurry, was the first dwelling west of Utica on the Fort Stanwix military road.

•**WHITNEY POINT**, Village; Broome County; Pop. 1,081; Area Code 607; Zip Code 13862; in S N.Y.

•**WILLET**, Town; Cortland County; Pop. 757; Area Code 607; Zip Code 13863; in central N.Y.

•**WILLIAMSON**, Town; Wayne County; Pop. 6,275; Area Code 315; Zip Code 14589; Elev. 452'; 25 m. NE of Rochester in W N.Y.

•**WILLIAMSTOWN**, Town; Oswego County; Pop. 1,003; 5315; Zip Code 13493; Central N.Y.

•**WILLIAMSVILLE**, Village; Erie County; Pop. 6,005; Area Code 716; Zip Code 142 + zone; 10 m. E of Buffalo in W N.Y.; is mainly a residential village.

•**WILLISTON PARK**, Village; Nassau County; Pop. 8,201; Area Code 516; Zip Code 11596; 18 m. E of New York City on Long Island in SE N.Y.; is basically a residential village.

•**WILLSBORO**, Town; Essex County; Pop. 1,759; Area Code 518; Zip Code 12996; Elev. 150'; 25 m. S of Plattsburg in NE N.Y.; on the Bouquet River, has a large pulp mill, but thrives largely on its tourist trade. The district was first settled in 1765 by *William Gilliland*, a New York City merchant, who attempted to establish a feudal manor, but the Revolution put an end to the venture.

In June 1777, *General Burgoyne*, on his march toward Saratoga, encamped at Willsboro and here completed negotiations with the Indians, persuading them to take up arms against the Colonials.

•**WILMINGTON**, Town; Essex County; Pop. 1,058; Area Code 518; Zip Code 12997; Elev. 1,021'; in NE N.Y.

•**WILSON**, Village and Town; Niagara County; Pop. 1,260 and 5,793; Area Code 716; Zip Code 14172; in N N.Y.

•**WILTON**, Town; Saratoga County; Pop. 7,232; Area Code 518; Zip Code 12866; Elev. 348'; in E N.Y. eight m. N of Saratoga Springs and just SE of the Adirondack Park.

•**WINDHAM**, Town; Greene County; Pop. 1,641; Area Code 518; Zip Code 12496; in E central N.Y. at the N foothills of the Catskill Mountains on State Hwy. 23.

•**WINDSOR**, Village and Town; Broome County; Pop. 1,134 and 5,877; Area Code 607; Zip Code 13865; in central S N.Y. on Highway 17, 13 m. E of Binghamton.

•**WOLCOTT**, Village and Town; Wayne County; Pop. 1,491 and 4,019; Area Code 315; Zip Code 14590; Elev. 378'; in N central N.Y. 47 m. E of Rochester; US 104 enters the great Ontario fruit belt. Apples are the most important crop, but here and there is an orchard of pear, peach, or cherry trees. The sour cherries are picked early in July. Men, women, and children work in the orchards, living during the picking season in barns or any makeshift shelter they can find or erect. Cherries are picked stemless for the canneries, and workers must be careful not to break off the fruit spurs, from which next season's crop will grow.

•**WOODHULL**, Village and Town; Steuben County; Pop. 314 and 1,455; Area Code 607; Zip Code 14898; in SE N.Y. on State 417 just N of the Pennsylvania border.

•**WOODRIDGE**, Village; Sullivan County; Pop. 918; Area Code 914; Zip Code 12789; in S N.Y. in the western section of the county just S of the Catskill Mountains; is surrounded by ski resorts.

•**WOODSTOCK**, Town; Ulster County; Pop. 6,733; Area Code 914; Zip Code 12498; Elev. 560'; in E central N.Y. in the Catskill State Park 10 m. NW of Kingston on the New York State Thruway on State 212; Home of artists for the last century and is a ski resort village. A famous rock concert was held here in the late sixties. Dairy and fruit farming are also popular in this area.

•**WORCESTER**, Town; Otsego County; Pop. 1,993; Area Code 617; Zip Code 12197; 33 m. NE of Oneonta in E central N.Y. on State 7.

•**WURTSBORO**, Village; Sullivan County; Pop. 1,135; Area Code 914; Zip Code 12790; Elev. 560'; in SE N.Y. 15 m. SE of Monticello just 1 m. off Hwy. 17; is a picturesque region of lakes and woodlands visited by hundreds of summer resorters from New York City. S of Wurtsboro in the Shawangunks Mountains.

•**WYOMING**, Village; Wyoming County; Area Code 506; Zip Code 716; Zip Code 14591; Elev. 987; 30 m. SW of Batavia in NW N.Y.

•**WYOMING COUNTY**, W N.Y.; 598 sq. miles; Pop. 39,795; Seat - Warsaw; Est. May 19, 1841; Named for the Wyoming Indian tribe.

•**YATES COUNTY**, W N.Y.; 343 sq. miles; Pop. 21,414; Seat - Penn Yan; Est. February 5, 1823; Named after *Joseph Christopher Yates*.

•**YORK**, Town; Livingston County; Pop. 3,208; Area Code 716; Zip Code 14592; in W N.Y.

•**YORKSHIRE**, Town; Cattaraugus County; Pop. 3,629; Area Code 716; Zip Code 14173; Elev. 1,438; 37 m. SW of Buffalo in SW N.Y.

•**YORKVILLE**, Village; Oneida; Pop. 3,113; Area Code 315; Zip Code 13495; Elev. 420'; 3 m. SW of Utica in N N.Y. in the Mohawk Valley; is a suburban residential community and birthplace of *Henry Inman* who was a portrait and landscape painter and one of the founders of the National Academy of Design. Mr. Inman painted many landscapes of the Catskill Mts.

•**YOUNGSTOWN**, Village; Niagara County; Pop. 2,196; Area Code 716; Zip Code 14174; Elev. 290'; in W N.Y.; 35 m. N of Buffalo.

Scenes
of
New York

--Part 2.

Whiteface Mountain Gatehouse, Adirondack Mountains.

photo by Roger Moore

Rainbow Falls spill 75 feet over a brown rock ledge.

Blenheim Bridge, over Schoharie Creek, was built in 1855.

New York wines are becoming well known throughout the world.

Lake Placid, site of the 1932 and 1980 Winter Olympics.

Camper enjoys the Fourth Lake, one of eight in the Fulton Chain, Adirondacks.

Snow skiing attracts thousands to New York's northern mountains.

Well-trimmed sails on one of the Finger Lakes.

Whiteface Mountain shows its winter colors in background.

Driving on snowy Adirondacks roads is breathtaking and cautious.

Ancient gorge of Au Sable Chasm, in the Adirondacks.

Apples are the major produce near Peru, New York.

Children follow the boardwalk along the beach at Fire Island.

Fishing on the Genessee River.

The Spiritualist Monument, Rochester.

National Baseball Hall of Fame, Cooperstown.

HISTORICAL PLACES IN NEW YORK STATE

ALBANY COUNTY

Albany. **ALBANY ACADEMY (JOSEPH HENRY MEMORIAL)**, Academy Park, 1815-1817, Philip Hooker, architect. Brownstone, 2 stories on high basement, projecting central block with side wings, hipped roof section with balustrade, central cupola, center entrance with fan and side lights, rusticated basement, main block window bays divided by fluted Ionic pilasters, 1st-story wing window bays set in rusticated ground-floor arches, rectangular and round arched windows. Georgian. Presently a memorial for Joseph Henry, professor of mathematics and natural philosophy at the Academy. *Municipal.*

Albany. **ALBANY CITY HALL**, Eagle St. at Maiden Lane, 1881, Henry Hobson Richardson, architect. Stone, 3 1/2 stories, modified rectangle, gabled and hipped roof sections, 2 interior chimneys; slightly projecting corner tower with pyramidal roof, elongated triple arched windows, corner turret, and clock face; triple, compound arched entrance; arcaded 2nd-story loggia, 3rd-floor windows with mullions, wall dormer with Palladian window, squat rear corner tower, decorative stone carvings around arcades. Richardsonian Romanesque. Exemplary of Richardson's mature style and a key landmark in urban Albany. *Municipal.*

Albany. **ALBANY UNION STATION**, E side of Broadway between Columbia and Steuben Sts., 1899-1900, Sheply, Rutan and Coolidge, architects. Granite; tall, 1-story central block (waiting room) flanked by 2 3-story sections; rectangular, flat roof with parapet interrupted by center clock section with NY state seal and corner lion sculpture, rectangular windows divided by pilasters, rusticated ground floor and main block with 3 round arched window and entrance areas articulating its front facade, front full-width iron canopy, denticulated cornice. Second Renaissance Revival. Built as part of general railroad improvement program popular in E at this time; considered one of the most modern railroad stations featuring elevators and underground walkways. *State.*

Albany. **CATHEDRAL OF ALL SAINTS**, S. Swan St., 1883, Robert Gibson, architect. Stone (random ashlar), high nave and transepts, Latin cross plan, gabled roof sections, plain exterior with engaged buttresses, rose window by John LaFarge in center of facade, E end completed with flying buttresses and stone facing; rib-vaulted lady chapel, fine stained glass windows, iron and brass rood screen, elaborate and extensive carving, 17th C. choir stalls salvaged from Belgian church. Gothic Revival. Unfinished cathedral planned as one of largest Episcopal cathedrals in U.S.; this "provisional" shell was to be embellished into Gibson's extravagant Gothic Revival building over the years; only the interior, with carving by Louis Hinton and imported stained glass approximates Gibson's original vision. *Private.*

Albany. **CHERRY HILL**, S. Pearl St. between 1st and McCarthy Aves., 1768. Frame, clapboarding; 2 1/2 stories, rectangular, gambrel roof, interior chimney with corbel cap, 2 gabled dormers, side and front porches, center entrance. Built by Dutch colonial master builder for Col. Philip Van Rensselaer. Later home of Solomon Van Rensselaer, adjutant general of

NY, postmaster of Albany, and a member of Congress. *Private.*

Albany. **DELAWARE AND HUDSON RAILROAD COMPANY BUILDING,** The Plaza on State St., 1914–1918, Marcus T. Reynolds, architect. Stone, 4 1/2 stories, modified V shape, hipped roof sections, every other bay surmounted by gabled wall dormer; 12 1/2-story square center tower with windows set in 3 tall round arched panels on each side polygonal corner turrets with pyramidal caps, and hipped roof with tall spire; round arched window bays separated by pilasters, decorative stonework, ground-floor arcaded section; 6-story steel and concrete addition with 8-story tower. Jacobethan Revival elements. Important structure in early "City Beautiful" urban renewal plan. *State.*

Albany. **FIRST REFORMED CHURCH,** 56 Orange St., 1789–1798, Philip Hooker and Elisha Putnam, builder-architects. Brick, 2 stories, rectangular, gabled roof; triple arcaded projecting entrance section with large round arched tracery window and decorative cornice flanked by 2 3-tiered towers with louvred belfry, clockfaces, and classical detailing. Vaulted interior. 1830 expansion of rear by John Boardman, 1858 alterations by Steinwehr and Hodgins, 1859 renovation of front facade, and 20th C. addition housing parish offices and meeting rooms. Georgian. Organized, 1634; 4th church building; Philip Hooker's earliest known building. *Private.*

Albany. **FIRST TRUST COMPANY BUILDING,** 35 State St., 1904, Marcus T. Reynolds, architect. Steel frame, brick, stone 1st floor; 5 1/2 stories, quadrangular, mansard roof, dormers with segmental pediments, 5-bay rounded corner section surmounted by ornate stamped sheet-metal dome, segmental pedimented en-

Albany. **NEW YORK STATE CAPITOL,** Capitol Park, 1867-1899, Thomas Fuller, Henry Hobson Richardson, Leopold Eidlitz, Isaac Perry; architects. Stone faced with granite, 4 1/2 stories, square with open courtyard; hipped roof sections, some with cresting; numerous chimneys; elaborate gabled dormers, some with Palladian windows; 5 1/2-story corner towers, arcaded entrance porch with balustrade above and grand staircase, rusticated 1st story and quoins, round arched and rectangular windows separated by pilasters and columns; ornate interior featuring inlaid marble floors and stone carving and marble and wood paneling by Perry. Second Renaissance Revival and Chateauesque elements. Original design by Fuller abandoned after construction of basement; design reworked by Richardson and Eidlitz and completed by Perry. *State.*

Albany. **NEW YORK STATE COURT OF APPEALS BUILDING (STATE HALL),** Eagle St. trance; pilasters separating windows on 1st floor beneath frieze and shallow cornice, windows topped by hoods on 3rd and 5th floors and by cartouche panels on 2nd and 4th floors; modillion cornice, stone belt courses and quoins around windows; side wings added later to original corner section. Eclectic. Building is essential part of "Plaza" area of early-20th C. "urban renewal" program. *Private.*

Albany. **NEW YORK EXECUTIVE MANSION,** 138 Eagle St., c. 1860. Brick, 2 1/2 stories, irregular shape, gabled and hipped roofs, numerous projecting sections and towers, wrap-around 1st-story veranda, off-center entrance with elaborately carved porch with iron balustrade at deck, denticulated and modillion cornice, decorative cornice. Original Second Empire dwelling remodeled with Queen Anne elements, 1887, by architect Isaac G. Perry. *State.*

between Pine and Columbia Sts., 1842, Henry Rector, architect. Stone covered with marble blocks, 3 stories, rectangular, flat roof with low parapet, center front pedimented Ionic entrance portico, full-height pilasters dividing window bays, windows in attic above full entablature, interior dome and rotunda sheathed in copper. Greek Revival. Built as State Hall which housed the offices of the chancellor, the comptroller, and other state officials. *State:* HABS.

Albany. **NEW YORK STATE DEPARTMENT OF EDUCATION BUILDING,** Washington Ave. between Hawk and Swan Sts., 1908-1912, Henry Hornbostel, architect. Stone, 5 stories, modified T shape, metal hipped roof, front colonnade of 36 hollow marble Corinthian columns with terra cotta capitals supporting a wide entablature, ornate stone cornice, rusticated ground floor; wing added, 1960's. Interior features large vaulted reading room and rotunda under 94'-high dome. Neo-Classical Revival. *State.*

Albany. **NUT GROVE,** McCarty Ave., 1845, Alexander Jackson Davis, architect. Brick, 2 1/2 stories, modified rectangle, low hipped roof, full-width front porch on Doric columns with projecting center section, polygonal side extensions, denticulated cornice now broken by 4 wall dormers, elaborately framed entrance door, full-length windows on front facade; altered with roof raised, c. 1903. Greek Revival. Although altered, this is a fine example of Davis' "Grecian country houses." *Private.*

Albany. **OLD POST OFFICE,** NE corner of Broadway and State St., 1879-1883. Stone, 3 1/2 stories, modified rectangle, hipped roof sections with cresting; projecting 5 1/2-story square corner tower with 2nd- and 3rd-story windows set in bay, ornate 5th floor, and high hipped roof with oculus; corner pavilion with large round arched windows in slightly recessed panel, slightly projecting balustraded center portico with Doric columns, paired 3rd-floor round arched windows separated by pilasters, semicircular dormers, denticulated modillion cornice, belt courses. Second Renaissance Revival. Plays major role in central urban composition. *State.*

Albany. **PASTURES HISTORIC DISTRICT,** Bounded on N by Madison Ave., on E by Green St., on S by South Ferry St., on W by S. Pearl St., 19th C.. Commercial and residential district containing numerous brick, 2 1/2–3 1/2-story row houses with gabled roof sections, dormers, splayed stone window lintels, and adjoining stone yards. Wide variety of 19th C. architectural styles represented. Site of original Dutch communal pasture; mid-19th C. construction largely by highly skilled carpenter builders. *Multiple public/private.*

Albany. **QUACKENBUSH HOUSE,** 683 Broadway, c. 1736. Brick, painted; 2 1/2 stories, rectangular, gabled roof, interior end chimney, tin side cornice, 2nd-story and attic window entablatures; altered 1st-floor storefront; early rear extension with splayed lintels; under restoration. Oldest building in city, dating from Dutch settlement. *Municipal.*

Albany. **SCHUYLER, PHILIP, MANSION,** Clinton and Schuyler Sts., 1761–1762, John Gaborial, master carpenter-builder. Brick, 2 stories, rectangular, hipped balustraded roof with deck, 2 interior chimneys, 6 pedimented dormers; 1-story, 6-sided entrance vestibule, added, 1810; central hall plan; elaborate interior elements include scenic hall wallpaper, spiral staircase balusters, and decorative cornices; restored, 1916 and 1950. Late Georgian. Home of Gen. Philip Schuyler, political and military leader during the Revolutionary and early Federal periods. *State:* NHL; HABS.

Albany. **ST. PETER'S CHURCH,** 108 State St., 1859, Richard Upjohn, architect. Bluestone, sandstone; 1 story, modified rectangle, gabled roof with shed roof side aisles, small gabled vents, front side 5-story tower with arcaded parapet and tall corner spire; front center entrance with 2 doors, each with trefoil arch above, under compound arch; gable rose window flanked by projecting stone pier capped by spire, side entrance, pointed arched openings, semioctagonal chancel; black walnut interior details, stained glass windows; vestry room and tower added 1876; interior restored 1964. Fine example of Gothic Revival style by noted architect Richard Upjohn. *Private.*

Albany. **TEN BROECK MANSION,** 9 Ten Broeck Pl., 1797–1798. Brick, 2 1/2 stories, modified rectangle, gabled roof with stepped parapets connected by front frame balustrade, paired connected interior end chimneys; front center entrance with 1-story frame gabled and pedimented distyle portico with enclosed sides, round arched window above, attic elliptical light; side rectangular wing with parapet and denticulated cornice. Federal with Greek Revival elements. Built for Abraham Ten Broeck, noted Revolutionary War figure, state senator, and Albany mayor. Museum. *Private:* G.

Albany. **WASHINGTON PARK HISTORIC DISTRICT,** Washington Park and surrounding properties, 19th–20th C.. Attractive residential area surrounding 90-acre park; contains 2 1/2–4 1/2-story brick and brownstone row houses and detached houses in a variety of 19th C. styles; notable are the Richardsonian Romanesque Sard House by H. H. Richardson, and the Queen Anne house at No. 7 Englewood

Place. Park development (c. 1870-1890) strongly influenced by Frederick Law Olmsted who made an early consultation report; area became increasingly fashionable during this period. *Multiple public/private.*

Albany. **WHIPPLE CAST AND WROUGHT IRON BOWSTRING TRUSS BRIDGE,** 1000 Delaware Ave., 1867, Simon DeGraft, builder. Cast and wrought iron bowstring truss bridge of 110' single span; stone and concrete abutments; moved. Bridge type developed 1841 by Squire Whipple, American engineer; popular for its strength, relative light weight, and low cost. One of earliest iron bridges remaining in U.S. *Private; not accessible to the public:* HAER.

Albany vicinity. **ONESQUETHAW VALLEY HISTORIC DISTRICT,** About 10 mi. SW of Albany off NY 43, 17th-19th C.. Contains numerous archeological sites and about 25 dwellings with farm buildings. Predominantly 18th C. structures, some 19th C. architectural styles represented such as Greek Revival and Second Empire. Notable are 8 18th C. stone houses, the majority of which have 1 1/2 stories, 5-bay facades, center entrances, and 2 interior end chimneys. Originally occupied by prehistoric Indians; later settled by Dutch. Valuable Colonial agricultural area and trade point. Pro-British during Revolution. *Multiple private:* HABS.

Altamont. **DELAWARE AND HUDSON RAILROAD PASSENGER STATION (ALTAMONT VILLAGE HALL)**, Main St. and the Delaware and Hudson RR., 1887. Brick base, frame; 1 1/2 stories, flared hipped roof with projecting hipped canopy, interior chimney, cupola with bell-cast roof, eyebrow dormers, entrances with transoms, hipped bay window, overhanging eaves with deep braces, passenger canopy. Stick Style. Railroad line very important for development of Altamont, inc. 1890; passenger service discontinued 1964; now used for civic activities. *Municipal.*

Altamont. **HAYES HOUSE**, 104 Fairview Ave., 1910. Frame, 2 1/2 stories, modified rectangle, hipped roof with balustraded deck, central chimney, gabled dormers with paired windows, denticulated modillion cornice, front center double-door entrance with transom, front and side L-shaped 1-story enclosed porch with Ionic columns and balustraded deck with semielliptical front center section, 2-story-tall Ionic columns flank front entrance and support roof over 2nd-story deck with French window, 1st-story windows with stained glass transoms, side bay window, corner Ionic pilasters, rear entrance with 1-story porch; original interior features include mantels, lighting fixtures, and dumbwaiter; tool shed and garage. Under restoration. Georgian Revival. Built next to mill (destroyed by fire, 1960's) for progressive small town miller who could supervise his business from the side porch. *County:* G.

Bethlehem vicinity. **BETHLEHEM HOUSE (RENSSELAER NICOLL HOUSE)**, E of Bethlehem off NY 144, 1735. Brick, 2 1/2 stories, L-shaped, gambrel roof, 4 interior chimneys, rear dormer, late-19th C. porch with bracketed posts and modillions; original 4 bays extended, 1799; 19th C. rear additions. *Municipal:* HABS.

Coeymans. **COEYMANS, ARIAANJE, HOUSE**, Stone House Rd., c. 1716. Stone, 2 1/2 stories over full basement, rectangular, gambrel roof, interior end chimneys, front and rear center entrances; 1-story, brick side wing with stone basement and clapboarded N gable end; gambrel roof replaced original gabled roof and dormer, late-18th C. Unusual large-scale example of early area construction. *Private:* HABS.

Coeymans. **COEYMANS SCHOOL (ACTON CIVILL POLYTECHNIC INSTITUTE)**, SW corner of Westerlo St. and Civill Ave., 1873. Brick, 3 stories, rectangular, mansard roof, elaborate dormers with pedimented caps, curvilinear corner dormers, side segmental pediment above a series of 3-over-4-over-5 round arched windows, front center entrance with elaborate Ionic porch with balustrade above; decorative lintels, window trim, cornice, and quoins. Second Empire. Typical of the private school or academy built in communities during the 19th C. *Private.*

Cohoes. **HARMONY MILL NO. 3 (MASTODON MILL)**, 100 N. Mohawk St., 1866–1868, 1871–1872, D. H. Van Auken, architect. Brick, 4 1/2 stories, modified rectangle, mansard roof with dormers, central pavilion with 2 6-story mansarded towers with bracketed cornices and cresting, 5th-floor center niche with statue, quoins, label molded windows; interior cast iron columns; 1871 addition. Second Empire. Part of mill complex important in town's history; mastodon skeleton discovered here during building excavation. *Private:* HAER.

Cohoes. **LOCK 18 OF ENLARGED ERIE CANAL (DOUBLE LOCK)**, W of 252 N. Mohawk St., E of Reservoir St. near Manor Ave., 1837–1842, Holmes Hutchinson, engineer. Cut-stone lock, built to reduce the number of locks in canal between Albany and Schenectady. Part of scheme calling for the increase in size of locks and canal bed and the doubling of locks which was to make canal transportation speedier and easier, thus reducing competition from the railroad. *Municipal/private:* HAER.

Cohoes. **MUSIC HALL**, NW corner of Remsen and Oneida Sts., 1874. Brick, 4 1/2 stories, rectangular, mansard roof, interior side chimneys, hipped dormers, raised parapet with name plate, bracketed cornice, ground-floor entrances with large windows between, segmental and round arched windows; many original interior elements remain including wooden bank tellers' counters, theater ticket booth, and theater with painted canvas ceilings and walls. Commercial Second Empire. Built as business enterprise by James Masten and William Acheson; contained post office, theater, and bank offices. *Municipal.*

Cohoes. **OLMSTEAD STREET HISTORIC DISTRICT,** 19th C.. Three blocks along site of the first Erie Canal (1826-1844); contains 2-2 1/2-story brick row houses with interior chimneys and dormers, and a 3 1/2-story brick mill with gabled 4-story center section with corbeled gable cornices. Illustrates industrial community which developed along canal and mill operations. *Multiple public/private.*

Cohoes. **VAN SCHAICK HOUSE,** Van Schaick Ave. and the Delaware & Hudson RR. track, c. 1735. Brick, 1 1/2 stories, rectangular, gambrel roof, 2 interior chimneys, center entrance with late-19th C. porch with balustrade above accessible through the center dormer door. Early area use of roof; served as English military headquarters during the French and Indian War, headquarters for Gens. Montgomery, Schuyler, and Gates during the Revolution; and temporary state capitol (Aug. 22-25, 1777). *Private:* HABS.

Colonie. **WATERVLIET SHAKER HISTORIC DISTRICT,** Watervliet Shaker Rd., 1775-1938. Contains 3 clusters of buildings: Church Family, consisting of 2nd meetinghouse and several houses and shops; West Family, with a dwelling and several shops; and South Family, with office, dwelling, and several shops. First U.S.

Shaker settlement, led by founder Mother Ann Lee, who is buried here; religious sect well known for architecture, inventions, and domestic arts; declined, 20th C. *Multiple public/private.*

Green Island. **RENSSELAER AND SARATOGA RAILROAD: GREEN ISLAND SHOPS,** James and Tibbits Sts. and the Delaware and Hudson RR. tracks, 1871. Brick, 2 1/2 stories with attic and 1-story rear wing with monitor, modified T shape, gambrel and gabled roof sections, numerous interior and interior end chimneys, gabled dormers on main block; 5-bay front facade, each bay with segmental arched double-door entrance; pilasters articulate bays, oculus in front gable; interior with cast iron columns and reinforced wood trusses; 3-story octagonal brick water tower 40' high with decorative brickwork at cornice, iron tie rods; 1-story semicircular brick roundhouse. Romanesque Revival elements. One of 3 maintenance complexes for the Delaware & Hudson RR., originally built for the Rensselaer & Saratoga RR. *Private:* HAER.

Newtonville. **NEWTONVILLE POST OFFICE (FIRST BAPTIST CHURCH)**, 534 Loudonville Rd. (NY 9), 1852. Brick, 1 story, rectangular, gabled roof with end returns; front facade with 2 entrances, one with lintel; front steel lintel over bricked-in garage door, center tablet, gable blind lunette; side windows with lintels; altered. Greek Revival elements. Located on property of John Newton, who settled here c. 1840 and built structure as church in 1852. *Municipal.*

Watervliet. **SCHUYLER FLATTS,** W side of Hudson River, on NY 2, 17th–18th C.. Site of early Indian camps and of 17th C. colony. Recent investigations have located foundations of Schuyler house, cobblestone courtyards, well, 19th C. cistern, and early-17th C. structure. Settled by Dutch colonists including Philip Pietersen Schuyler and son Peter, colonial governor, first mayor of Albany, and Indian agent. Served as troop headquarters for armies heading for Canada. Important 18th and 19th C. transportation and trading area. *Multiple private.*

Watervliet. **WATERVLIET ARSENAL,** S. Broadway, 1813. Complex of military buildings involved in the development and production of weapons. Contains gun factory (1889–1891), commanding officers' quarters (1842, 1848), barracks (1843), and related structures. Established during War of 1812; stored and repaired weapons and changed small arms from flint to percussion weapons until 1889 when cannon manufacturing was introduced. *Federal/USA.*

Watervliet. **WATERVLIET SIDE CUT LOCKS (DOUBLE LOCK)**, 23rd St. at the Hudson River, 19th C.. Remains of limestone ashlar double lock with stone seawall curving in to form entrance; wooden gates demolished. Part of a lateral canal or side cut constructed to connect the Albany stem of the Erie Canal with the Hudson River at West Troy; original Erie Canal plans bypassed Troy. *State.*

ALLEGANY COUNTY

Alfred. **ALLEN STEINHEIM MUSEUM**, Alfred University Campus, 1876–1880. Stone, 1–4 1/2 stories, irregular shape; gabled, jerkinhead, and bell-cast gabled roof sections; 4 1/2-story tower with stepped parapet connected by 3-story entry section to 2-story tower with modified crenelations, 2 entrances recessed under round arches, side 1–2-story structures, rear ell; oculi, round and pointed arched windows, some with tracery. Gothic Revival elements. Building conceived by Jonathan Allen, 2nd president of Alfred University, as a showcase for his varied geological collections; internal framework includes 700 samples of local and foreign woods, and walls include more than 8,000 rock specimens. *Private.*

Alfred. **TERRA COTTA,** Main St., 1892. Brick, tile; 1 story, rectangular, gabled tile roof with rear hipped section, exterior end chimney, front off-center entrance with raised segmental arched architrave on half columns, oculus in gable; profuse use of decorative tile ornament in quoins, friezes, and window surrounds; moved. Built as office and display case for the Celadon Terra Cotta Co., Ltd., company organized 1889 to manufacture bricks and roofing tile whose greenish glaze resembled ancient Chinese ceramic work; a replica of Terra Cotta was exhibited at the 1893 Chicago World's Fair. *Private.*

Angelica. **ANGELICA COURTHOUSE (ALLEGANY COUNTY COURTHOUSE)**, Park Circle, 1819. Brick, painted; 2 stories, modified rectangle, hipped roof, interior end chimneys, central octagonal fenestrated cupola with octagonal domed roof, bracketed cornice, decorative band below plain frieze, front center projecting hipped section with recessed double-door entrance, gabled lintels over rectangular windows; 2nd-floor courtroom with open cupola base. Federal elements. Served as courthouse until 1892; now used for town offices. *Municipal.*

Belmont vicinity. **BELVIDERE,** 3 mi. N of Belmont on SR 408, 1804. Stone, brick; 2 1/2-story main block with 2-story wing; modified L shape; hipped, gabled, and modified mansard roof sections; interior and interior end chimneys, gabled dormers, denticulated modillion cornice on main block; front center entrance with fanlight and side lights, 1-story porch; riverfront with 2-story Ionic pedimented portico with oval light in tympanum; small 1-story side wing, large 2-story side wing with modified mansard roof added c. 1870; 9-sided barn and 1806 hexagonal teahouse. Design with Federal elements locally attributed to Benjamin Latrobe. First owner was John B. Church, former British Minister Plenipotentiary who adopted the American cause during the Revolution and served as commissary general to the French Army in America, and who also founded 2 American banks. *Private:* HABS.

Belvidere vicinity. **CHRIST EPISCOPAL CHURCH,** Gibson Hill Rd., SW of Rtes. 19 and 408, 1860, John Dudley, designer. Frame, vertical board-and-batten siding; 1 story, rectangular, steeply gabled roof sections, 2 gabled side entrance areas with pointed arched doorways, corner bell turret, recessed chancel in end gabled sections, shutters. Adjacent cemetery. Gothic Revival. *State.*

Friendship. **WELLMAN HOUSE,** Main St., 1835. Frame, clapboarding; 3 stories, rectangular, mansard roof, segmental arched dormers, off-center entrance with small porch; alterations include the addition of the mansard roof, the 2-story gabled rear section, and the 1-story E porch. Home of prominent local Wellman family. *Municipal.*

BRONX COUNTY

HIGH BRIDGE AQUEDUCT AND WATER TOWER (AQUEDUCT BRIDGE AND WATER TOWER), *Reference—see New York County*

New York. **BARTOW-PELL MANSION AND CARRIAGE HOUSE,** Pelham Bay Park, Shore Rd., 1836–1842. Stone (ashlar), 2 stories with 1- and 2-story wings, rectangular, flat and gabled roof sections, interior end chimneys and center chimneys with small monitor between, center entrance with raked lintel on 5-bay facade, windows outlined with projecting smooth stone frames, center niche on 2nd floor of front and 1st floor of garden facade, iron balconies on 2nd-floor French windows, smooth stone quoins; interior features pedimented doors and windows, and ceiling ornamentation. Deteriorated stone carriage house on lot. Greek Revival. Fine taut design attributed to Minard Lafever. *Municipal:* HABS.

New York. **RAINEY MEMORIAL GATES,** New York Zoological Park, 1926, Paul Manship, sculptor. Freestanding bronze gates in the form of a stylized tropical tree with animal life representing that in the zoo in the early-20th C., flanked by low bronze screens on marble bases connected to gatekeepers' lodges. Art Deco. Gates designed by noted American sculptor Paul Manship; casting done in Belgium took 2 years; gates given to the park as a memorial to big game hunter Paul Rainey. *Municipal.*

The Bronx. **NEW YORK BOTANICAL GARDENS,** Southern and Bedford Park Blvds., 1896. 250-acre botanical garden complex containing one of the world's largest herbariums and botanical libraries, a 40-acre hemlock forest, research laboratories, conservatories, and educational complex. Promoted in England by Professor and Mrs. Nathaniel Lord Britton; opened, 1896, under direction of Britton and developed into outstanding botanical facilities. *Private:* NHL.

The Bronx. **VAN CORTLANDT, FREDERICK, HOUSE,** Van Cortlandt Park at 242nd St., 1748-1749. Fieldstone, 2 1/2 stories, modified L shape, hipped roof with deck, interior chimneys, gabled dormers, center entrance with small shed porch, brick window trim with mask-like heads in keystones, rear gabled additions with porches added later, exquisite interior. Restored. Early Georgian country home. Built for prominent resident, Frederick Van Cortlandt. *Private:* NHL.

BROOME COUNTY

Binghamton. **BINGHAMTON CITY HALL,** Collier St. between Court and Academy Sts., 1897-1898, Francis R. Almirall, architect. Brick faced with sandstone, 5 stories, rectangular, mansard roof with balustrade at base, elaborate segmental arched dormers, slightly projecting corner pavilions with balconies at windows, center round arched entrance surmounted by 3 tall round arched windows framed by elaborate Ionic pilasters, rusticated ground floor and pavilion fronts, decorative classical detailing. Second Empire. *Municipal:* HABS; G.

Binghamton. **BROOME COUNTY COURTHOUSE,** Court St., 1897-1898, Isaac G. Perry, architect. Sandstone, 2 1/2 stories over high basement, Latin cross shape, gabled roof sections, interior and interior end chimneys; copper central dome on octagonal base surmounted by cupola and statue, clockfaces at dome level; front 2-story hexastyle Ionic portico with pediment and county seal in tympanum relief, center entrance; Ionic pilasters surrounding building, frieze with oculi, side end pediments with lunettes. Notable regional landmark in Neo-Classical style. *County.*

Binghamton. **CHRIST CHURCH**, Corner of Washington and Henry Sts., 1853-1855, Richard Upjohn, architect. Stone, 1 story, modified rectangle, high gabled roof, E end corner tower with spire and buttresses, lancets along sides divided by buttresses, apse on E end, gabled side entrance vestibule; spire added, 1903; modern addition to W end. Early Gothic Revival. Built by noted Gothic Revivalist for oldest congregation in Binghamton. *Private.*

Binghamton. **PHELPS MANSION (MONDAY AFTERNOON CLUB)**, 191 Court St., 1870, Isaac G. Perry, architect. Brick, 2 stories, modified rectangle, truncated hipped roof, interior end chimneys, stone frieze at cornice level, front double-door entrance with 1-story porch, granite quoins; stone architraves over segmental arched windows, hoods over 2 front windows; elaborate interiors feature marble, glass, and rare carved woods including fine black walnut staircase; 1905 auditorium addition, porte-cochere moved; 1941 3rd floor and mansard roof removed. Italianate elements. Built for ShermanD. Phelps, former mayor. *Private.*

CATTARAUGUS COUNTY

ZAWATSKI SITE, Archaic, Woodland, Historic (3000 B.C.-19th C. A.D.). Stratified, multicomponent site; contains artifacts and remains of Zawatski family house and other buildings. Investigated by State University of New York, Buffalo, 1971 and 1973. *Private.*

Ellicottville. **ELLICOTTVILLE TOWN HALL**, Village Sq., NW corner of Washington and Jefferson Sts., 1829. Brick, 2 stories, rectangular, gabled roof with stepped gable ends, interior end chimneys, central hexagonal cupola on square base; front center entrance with fanlight and side lights, 2nd-story center Palladian windows, oval medallion in gable; front recessed brick arches form 3 bays; altered; restored. Federal elements. Built as Cattaraugus County courthouse; purchased by Ellicottville in 1869 and used for a variety of civic purposes. *Municipal.*

Napoli. **GLADDEN WINDMILL,** Pigeon Valley Rd., 1890. Vertical windmill; frame; 4 stories—3 lower stories housing machinery, 4th containing revolving wind wheel. Built by farmer George Gladden. Probably only mill of its type in eastern U.S.; equipped with machinery for elevating and grinding grain, an apple grater and press, wood turning lathe, and repair shop. *Private.*

CAYUGA COUNTY

Auburn. **FLATIRON BUILDING,** 1-3 Genessee St., 1829. Limestone, 3 stories, triangular with rounded apex, low pitched roof, wooden cornice, ground-floor storefront, upper-story apartments. Illustrates innovative solution to the problem of placing a commercial structure on a triangular plot. Built by Ezekial Williams, early Auburn developer. *Private; not accessible to the public.*

Auburn. **HARRIET TUBMAN HOME FOR THE AGED,** 180-182 South St., c. 1908. Frame, clapboarding; 2 1/2 stories, rectangular, gabled roof, interior end chimneys, full-width front porch, side porch; restored 1947. Established as home for elderly blacks by Harriet Tubman, an escaped slave who is credited with leading at least 300 blacks to freedom along the Underground Railroad, and who aided the Union during the Civil War, and who also worked toward the improvement of black education and women's rights. Museum. *Private:* NHL.

Auburn. **SEWARD, WILLIAM H., HOUSE**, 33 South St., 1816. Brick, painted; 2 1/2 stories, modified rectangle, gabled and hipped roof sections, interior chimneys, center entrance with fanlight and side lights surmounted by Palladian window and center gable with fanlight, side bays and porches; N tower and rear wing added, 1847; S section added, 1860. Federal and Italianate elements. Home of William H. Seward, state senator, NY governor, and U.S. senator and Secretary of State who is most commonly remembered for his part in the purchase of Alaska, then ridiculed as "Seward's Folly." *Private:* NHL.

Poplar Ridge. **WOOD, JETHRO, HOUSE**, NY 34B, 18th-19th C.. Frame, clapboarding; 2 stories, rectangular, gabled roof, 1 exterior end and 1 interior chimney, center entrance with transom and side lights and small pedimented hood. Home of Jethro Wood, who in 1819 invented the first accepted 3-part iron plow, which featured an improved moldboard for easy cutting through soil. *Private; not accessible to the public:* NHL.

CHAUTAUQUA COUNTY

Ashville. **BLY, SMITH, HOUSE**, 4 N. Maple St., 1835. Frame, clapboarding; horizontal front flush siding; 2 stories, modified rectangle, low hipped roof, wide entablature; recessed entrance with decorative panels, transom, and side lights, framed by 2 Ionic columns supporting a frieze with ornamental lotus motifs; rectangular windows with lotus panels above, front bays articulated by fluted Ionic pilasters, 1-story side section with porch; decorative interior woodwork. Greek Revival with Egyptian Revival elements. *Private:* HABS.

Chautauqua. **CHAUTAUQUA INSTITUTION HISTORIC DISTRICT,** Bounded by Chautauqua Lake, North and Lowell Aves., and NY 17-J, 19th–20th C.. Community district contains residential and public buildings, parks, and informal open spaces; features primarily 2-story, frame residential structures with clapboarding and shingling, and brick and stone public buildings in a variety of styles; notable are the Francis Willard house with Stick Style elements, the 1881 Athenaeum Hotel and Second Empire elements, and the 1929 Art Deco Norton Hall by Otis Floyd Johnson under the supervision of Lorado Taft. The Chautauqua movement began in 1874 to provide education for Sunday school teachers in a natural environment, and developed into a center for numerous educational and cultural activities. *Private.*

Chautauqua. **MILLER, LEWIS, COTTAGE, CHAUTAUQUA INSTITUTION,** NY 17J, 1875. Frame, vertical siding; 2 stories, L-shaped, gabled roof sections with wide overhanging eaves; center double door entrance with full-width, 2nd-story balcony above; stick work under gables and balconies and along facades; remodeled and altered, 1922. Derived from Swiss Chalet. Early structure of a secular, year-round adult education program established by Lewis Miller, an OH businessman, and John Heyl Vincent, a Methodist minister. The building is complemented by the Athenaeum Hotel, Pioneer Hall, and Octagon House. *Private;not accessible to the public:* NHL.

Jamestown. **FENTON, GOV. REUBEN, MANSION (WALNUT GROVE)**, 68 S. Main St., 1863, Aaron Hall, architect. Brick, 2-3 stories, modified Latin cross shape, low pitched roof sections, interior chimneys, denticulated bracketed eaves, front 4-story tower with arched corbel tables, round arched windows, oculus, and ground-floor double-door entrance with fanlight, framed with ornamented spandrels and clustered columns; side polygonal bay, round and 5-centered arched windows with hood molds, segmental arched windows, 5 small arcaded porches with ornamented spandrels; interior with octagonal vestibule, marble fireplaces, and foliate plasterwork. Italian Villa. Built for Reuben E. Fenton, NY governor and congressman. *Municipal.*

Westfield. **BARCELONA LIGHTHOUSE AND KEEPER'S COTTAGE,** East Lake Rd., 1829. Lighthouse complex includes conical stone lighthouse approximately 50' high with octagonal lantern and detached 1 1/2-story stone cottage. Reputedly oldest existing lighthouse on Great Lakes; first public building to be lighted by natural gas; in use until 1859. *Private.*

CHEMUNG COUNTY

Elmira. **CHEMUNG COUNTY COURTHOUSE COMPLEX,** 210-228 Lake St., between Market and E. Church Sts., 19th C.. County government center featuring 1861 Italianate courthouse by architect Horatio Nelson White; a 2-story brick building with 3-story corner tower, round arched label molded windows, and battlemented roof sections. Adjacent offices and annex with similar decorative treatment, earlier old clerk's office with tetrastyle portico. Complex of buildings related both in function and treatment, serving county for a century. *County.*

Elmira. **NEWTOWN BATTLEFIELD,** 6 mi. SE of Elmira on NY 17, 1779. Site where Iroquois under leadership of Chief Joseph Brant made an unsuccessful stand against American general John Sullivan, who was leading a counteroffensive in retaliation for 1778 Indian raids against settlements in the Mohawk Valley; Sullivan's expedition covered 600 mi., destroying 41 villages and some Indian crops. *State:* NHL.

CHENANGO COUNTY

Earlville. **EARLVILLE OPERA HOUSE (DOUGLASS OPERA HOUSE)**, 12-20 E. Main St., 1890. Brick, 3-story main section with 2-story wings, rectangular, mansard-type roof and flat roof sections, ground-floor storefronts with cast iron columns, segmental and round arched windows, corbeled cornice; theater interior features gilt ornamentation, balconies; alterations; under restoration; theater and annex occupy 4 parts of 8-unit homogenous block. Eclectic. Early rural opera house that shifted from housing a variety of traveling acts to showing silent movies and talkies. *Private.*

New Berlin. **MOSS, HORACE O., HOUSE (PREFERRED MANOR)**, 45 S. Main St., 1831. Stone, 2 stories, rectangular, hipped roof with monitor, 4 interior end chimneys, center entrance porch with flat roof and balustrade, side entrance vestibule, stone lintels and quoins, center hall plan, spiral staircase along wall with paper depicting hunting scenes painted by Pierre Jacquemart. Excellent example of a Federal dwelling. Built for prosperous citizen Horace O. Moss. *Private.*

CLINTON COUNTY

ADIRONDACK FOREST PRESERVE, NE New York State (also in Essex, Franklin, Fulton, Hamilton, Herkimer, St. Lawrence, and Warren counties), 1885. About 2.5 million acres of land containing preserved forests and recreational areas. First state forest preserve in U.S., established under first comprehensive preservation program in a state. *State:* NHL.

Plattsburgh. **CITY HALL,** City Hall Pl., 1917, John Russell Pope, architect. Limestone, 2 stories over high basement, central block with dome, symmetrical flanking wings, flat roof, Doric portico, prominent stone watertable balanced by strong cornice, pilasters dividing bays, and frieze ornamented with wreaths. Greek Revival. *Municipal.*

Plattsburgh. **KENT-DELORD HOUSE,** 17 Cumberland Ave., 1797, Nathan Averell, builder. Frame, clapboarding; 2 stories, modified L shape, gabled roof with rear lean-to, 2 interior end chimneys. Home of early settler Capt. John Bailey and his daughter and her husband, James Kent, who later became a famous New York Supreme Court Chief Justice. Reputedly the oldest house in Plattsburgh. *Private.*

Plattsburgh. **OLD STONE BARRACKS,** Rhode Island Ave., Plattsburgh Air Force Base, 1838–1840. Stone, 2 stories, rectangular, gabled roof, interior end and interior chimneys, full-width 2-story N veranda, several 1- and 2-story S entrance porches. Greek Revival elements. One of 2 structures built on Plattsburgh Barracks, the military reservation where the "Plattsburgh Idea," an innovative officers' training program, was developed. *Federal/USAF.*

Plattsburgh vicinity. **PLATTSBURGH BAY,** Cumberland Bay, E of Plattsburgh, 1814. Limestone memorial to naval commander Thomas Macdonough overlooks site of Battle of Plattsburgh, Sept. 11, 1814, in which American fleet under Capt. Macdonough halted major British invasion via Lake Champlain and

Hudson River. Destruction of the British fleet forced the invading army to retreat into Canada, abandoning large stores of supplies. *State:* NHL.

Plattsburgh vicinity. **VALCOUR BAY,** 7 mi. S of Plattsburgh on the W shore of Lake Champlain, 1776. Site where American fleet under Benedict Arnold lost a naval engagement (Oct. 11, 1776), but delayed the planned British invasion of the northern colonies late enough into the winter season that the British postponed their advance until the following year, at which time the Americans were better prepared and were able to check the invasion at Saratoga (see also Saratoga National Historical Park, NY). *State:* NHL.

COLUMBIA COUNTY

Ancram. **SIMONS GENERAL STORE,** Ancram Sq., 1873-1874. Frame, clapboarding; 2-3 stories, rectangular, flat roof, square cupola, center double-door entrance flanked by a large window on each side, front 2-story balustraded veranda supported by decorative posts. Italianate. Commercial center, visual focal point, and gathering place for villagers. *Private.*

Austerlitz vicinity. **STEEPLETOP (EDNA ST. VINCENT MILLAY HOUSE)**, NE of Austerlitz on E. Hill Rd., c. 1870. Frame, clapboarding; 2 stories, L-shaped, gabled roof, central chimney, entrance with transom and side lights, projecting 1-story shed section, 1 1/2-story gabled ell with shed dormers. Home of Edna St. Vincent Millay, noted American poet, feminist, and political radical, who became a leader of the Bohemian cultural movement centered in Greenwich Village in the 1920's. *Private; not accessible to the public:* NHL.

Chatham. **SPANGLER BRIDGE,** Spangler Rd. over Kinderhook Creek, 1880. Iron Pratt truss of 138' single span, 16' wide, decorative cast iron brackets and urns at each end, stone abutments. Built by Morse Bridge Co.; provided access to nearby mill. *County.*
Chatham vicinity. **UNION STATION,** NY 66 at intersection with NY 295, 1887, Shepley, Rutan, and Coolidge, architects. Stone, 1 story, rectangular, hipped roof with large gabled dormers, central chimney, roof extension provides shelter over train platform area, front and rear entrances framed by quoins and lintels. Richardsonian Romanesque elements. *Private.*

Church Hill. **OLANA (FREDERIC E. CHURCH HOUSE)**, Church Hill, E end of Rip Van Winkle Bridge, 1874, Frederic Church, designer; Calvert Vaux, architect. Stone, brick, tile; 2 1/2 stories, modified L shape; slate hipped, pyramidal, gabled, mansard, and flat roof sections; projecting and recessed sections, polychromatic brick and tile work set in geometric and stylized natural patterns, ogee arches, balustrades, towers, minarets; roof replaced 1970's. High Victorian Eclectic. Home of prominent landscape artist Frederic E. Church, only pupil of Hudson River Valley landscape artist, Thomas Cole (see also Thomas Cole House, NY). Decorative elements of villa reflect artist's extensive exotic travels; contains numerous Church paintings. Museum. *State:* NHL; G.

Germantown. **CLERMONT,** Clermont State Park, c. 1777. Brick, stuccoed and scored to resemble stone; T-shaped, hipped roof, 5 interior chimneys with corbel caps, gabled dormers, center entrance; 3rd story and slate roof added later. Georgian. Home of Robert R. Livingston, public leader, Continental Congress leader, first Secretary of Foreign Affairs, and backer of Fulton's steamboat, *The Clermont. State:* HABS.

Hudson. **EVANS, CORNELIUS H., HOUSE,** 414-416 Warren St., 1861. Brick, painted, sandstone trim; 2 1/2 stories, rectangular, mansard roof, fancy interior chimney; pedimented dormers, tripartite center dormer; 3 1/2-story W side center tower with round arched windows, mansard roof, and oval dormers; front center entrance with flanking pilasters and bracketed hood, pediment and pilasters framing at center 2nd-story window, bracketed cornice; original open side porch enclosed, c. 1920; original interior marble mantels, stained glass, and china and brass hardware. Second Empire. Built for Cornelius H. Evans, local entrepreneur who successfully developed family brewing and bottling business into one of the city's major industries. *Private.*

Hudson. **FRONT STREET-PARADE HILL-LOWER WARREN STREET HISTORIC DISTRICT,** 18th-19th C.. Port containing numerous dwellings and commercial structures; predominant are frame and brick buildings with living quarters above a 1st-floor business. Established as a commercial venture outside of Hudson, NY by New England proprietors; commercial and simple character contrasted sharply to surrounding Dutch settlements. Retains original scale and appearance. *Multiple public/private.*

Hudson vicinity. **BRONSON, DR. OLIVER, HOUSE AND STABLES,** S of Hudson off U.S. 9, Early-19th C.. Frame, clapboarding, vertical flush siding; 2 stories, rectangular, hipped roof surmounted by pedimented block, interior chimneys, full-width 1st-floor hipped veranda with ornamental trim and supports, center entrance with fanlight and side lights, 2nd-story center tripartite window with fanlights, decorative brackets and trim. Original Federal dwelling altered 1839 and 1849 by Alexander Jackson Davis; additions; related stables. *State.*

Kinderhook. **KINDERHOOK VILLAGE DISTRICT**, Both sides of U.S. 9, 18th–20th C.. Little altered village district containing about 200 pre-20th C. buildings, largely residential but with a variety of commercial and utilitarian structures. Styles range from colonial period houses with Dutch elements through most 19th C. styles. Area originally settled in 1650's, gradually grew with farming development; fire in 1880's led to rebuilding of commercial district. Birthplace and boyhood home of U.S. Vice President and 8th President, Martin Van Buren. *Multiple public/private.*

Kinderhook vicinity. **MARTIN VAN BUREN NATIONAL HISTORIC SITE (LINDENWALD)**, E of Kinderhook on NY 9H, 1797. Brick, 2 1/2 stories, L-shaped, gabled roof sections, interior end chimneys, center gable; gabled dormers, each with a round arched window; side tower, front center entrance with side lights and Palladian window above; original Georgian structure enlarged and remodeled with Italianate elements by Richard Upjohn, 1849; fullwidth 2-story front portico added, 1958. Georgian and Italianate elements. Home of 8th U.S. President, Martin Van Buren, from end of his presidential term (1841) until his death in 1862. *Private:* NHL; HABS.

Kinderhook vicinity. **VAN ALEN, LUYCAS, HOUSE**, E of Kinderhook on NY 9H off U.S. 9, 1737. Brick, 1 1/2 stories, rectangular, steeply gabled roof, interior end chimneys on original block and wing, coped gable ends, paired windows, doors with transoms; wrought iron "beam anchor"; extended, mid-18th C.; restored 1960's; late-18th C. schoolhouse moved to property. Fine well-preserved example of Dutch Colonial architecture. Museum. *Private:* NHL; HABS.

Livingston. **LIVINGSTON, HENRY W.,**

HOUSE (THE HILL), N of Bell's Pond at Jct. of U.S. 9 and NY 82, c.1796-1803. Brick, stuccoed; 2 stories, modified T shape, flat and modified domed roof sections, front main block with bowed N and S facades and full-height Ionic portico, side wings with octagonal end sections. Neo-classical. Designed by an Italian architect for Henry W. Livingston, prominent NY resident. *Private; not accessible to the public.*

New Lebanon. **MOUNT LEBANON SHAKER SOCIETY,** U.S. 20, 1787. Remains of Shaker community; includes numerous frame 18th and 19th C. buildings, some with clapboarding and some with board-and-batten siding with simplified Federal elements; notable are the first (1785) and 2nd (1824) meetinghouses with unusual segmental arched roof sections; other buildings include original dormitory, tannery, and chair factory. Under restoration. Second Shaker community in U.S., established by Joseph Meacham after Ann Lee's death at Watervliet in 1784 (see also Watervliet Shaker Historic District, NY); one of mostsuccessful 19th C. Shaker communities; once had 600 members. Portion of land and buildings purchased 1929-1930 by Darrow School. *Private:* NHL; HABS; G.

Spencertown. **SPENCERTOWN ACADEMY,** NY 203, E of jct. with CR 7, 1847. Frame, clapboarding; 2 stories, rectangular temple-form, gabled roof, pedimented tetrastyle Ionic portico, square front belfry, corner pilasters; center door in flush-sided facade with pilasters, entablature, and transom; ' full entablature. Greek Revival. Built as private school near village green; now serves town activities. *Municipal.*

Stockport. **CHURCH OF ST. JOHN THE EVANGELIST,** Chittenden Rd., 1845-1846.

Frame, board-and-batten siding; 1 1/2 stories, Latin cross shape, gabled roof sections; front projecting castelated bell tower with louvered belfry, tracery lancet window, pinnacles, and compound pointed arched entrance; recessed lancet windows, buttresses; notable interior exposed hammer beam ceiling with carved tie-beams. Gothic Revival. Illustrates rural interpretation of ecclesiastical building requirements popularized by the Episcopal Church. *Private.*

Stuyvesant. **VAN ALEN, JOHANNIS L., FARM,** School House Rd., 1760. Farm complex containing 18th C. 1 1/2-story main brick gambrel house with center entrance with transom and side lights, frame Dutch barn, 19th C. barn, corncrib, and chicken house. Exemplifies early Dutch building in Upper Hudson Valley. *Private.*

CORTLAND COUNTY

Cortland. **CORTLAND COUNTY COURTHOUSE,** Courthouse Park, 1924, James Riley Gordon, architect. Stone, 3 stories over high basement, Latin cross shape, intersecting low hipped roof sections, parapet; large central dome on Corinthian colonnaded drum on balustraded octagonal base, surmounted by open cupola with statue above; coursed rusticated 1st floor, front Doric portico in antis, 2nd- and 3rd-story bays articulated by Doric pilasters; coffered interior dome ceiling. Neo-Classical Revival. *County.*

Cortland. **CORTLAND FIRE HEADQUARTERS,** 21 Court St., 1914, Sackett and Park, architects. Yellow-faced brick over hollow clay tiles, 3 stories, rectangular, gabled tiled roof with stepped gabled and gabled dormers, front square bell tower, 1st-floor open bays with veranda above, decorative stone trim and finials. Jacobethan Revival. Built as part of Cortland's early-20th C. modernization and expansion plan. *Municipal.*

Homer. **OLD HOMER VILLAGE HISTORIC DISTRICT,** 19th C.. Contains residential, commercial, religious, and civic structures around a New England village green plan; various architectural styles. Important structures include the large Greek Revival dwelling of Jedediah Barber and an octagon house with octagonal outbuildings. Reflects 19th C. growth. Prosperity a result of excellent location on early trade route, opening of Erie Canal, and the onset of the Industrial Revolution. 19th C. character remains. *Multiple public/private.*

DELAWARE COUNTY

Delhi. **DELAWARE COUNTY COURTHOUSE SQUARE DISTRICT,** 19th C.. Civic, commercial, and religious structures around village green. Outstanding structures include 2 1/2-story mansarded brick courthouse, the sheriff's office and jail, and the 1-story clapboard church (1831) designed by Charles Hathaway. Typical of small courthouse square with courthouse as focal point. *Multiple public/private.*

East Meredith. **HANFORD MILL,** On CR 12, 19th C.. 50-acre mill complex including raceway, spillway, 2 railroad bridges, main 2-story frame building, and other structures; steam engines, steel waterwheel, and other machinery remains. Industrial complex developed from 1825, illustrating the variety of operations and expanding technology of 19th C. milling. Products ranged from shelled corn to house ornaments, while the mill generator produced electricity for the village. Museum. *Private.*

Meredith. **MACDONALD FARM,** Elk Creek and Monroe Rds., 19th C.. Several-hundred-acre farm complex consisting of main house, barns, smokehouse, mill, and numerous other buildings. 1851 Greek Revival house is earliest structure; 1890's reinforced concrete buildings included. Buildings from working farm illustrate inventiveness of John Thomas MacDonald, who applied hydroelectric power for numerous operations in late-19th C. in reputedly first electrically powered farm in state. *Private.*

Roxbury vicinity. **BURROUGHS, JOHN, HOME (WOODCHUCK LODGE)**, 2 mi. from Roxbury 1860's. Frame, clapboarding; 1 1/2 stories, L-shaped, gabled roof sections, box cornice without original paired brackets; 1910 front porch with rustic railings; interior features furniture made by Burroughs. Summer residence, after 1910, of John Burroughs, well-known naturalist who shared Whitman's and Thoreau's appreciation of nature from a scientific outlook, and whose works include *Wake-Robin* and *Locusts and Wild Honey. Private; not accessible to the public:* NHL.

DUTCHESS COUNTY

Beacon. **HOWLAND LIBRARY,** 477 Main St., 1871, Richard Morris Hunt. Brick, shingling; 1 1/2 stories, modified rectangle, gabled and hipped roof sections, central chimney, bracketed cornice, gabled and hipped dormers, front center entrance with porch under 2nd-story projecting gabled section with half-timber effect, granite molded water table, 1st-story polychrome brick patterns and corbeling; interior reading room with 33' 9" ceiling; reading room gallery added 1895. Stick Style and High Victorian Gothic elements. Picturesque Victorian building by noted architect Richard Morris Hunt. *Private.*

Fishkill. **FISHKILL VILLAGE DISTRICT,** Roughly along NY 52 from Cary St. to Hopewell St., 18th-19th C.. Historical village center contains residential, commercial, religious, and government structures; features 1 1/2-3-story stone, frame, and brick buildings in Greek Revival, Italianate, and other 19th C. styles; notable are the Fishkill Methodist Church (1838-1841) and the house at 21 Broad St., each Greek Revival. Important 18th-19th C. transportation crossroads in the Hudson Valley; major quartermaster commissary facility and encampment during the American Revolution. *Multiple public/private.*

Fishkill vicinity. **FISHKILL SUPPLY DEPOT SITE,** 1777-1779. Site of supply depot once containing barracks, stables, blacksmith shop, and the Van Wyck-Wharton House. Served as major northern commissary facility for American forces. Excavated, 1974, by Fishkill Historical Society. *Multiple private.*

Fishkill vicinity. **VAN WYCK-WHARTON HOUSE,** S of Fishkill on U.S. 9, c. 1733. Frame, brick nogging with clapboarding; 1 1/2 stories, rectangular, gabled roof, interior end chimneys, front and rear porches; larger c. 1756 gabled W addition, frieze of vertical boards. Type of rural Dutch farmhouse with regional features including Dutch oven, Dutch door, and nogging. Only documented building remaining from 1776 military provision complex. *Private:* HABS.

Hyde Park. **BERGH-STOUTENBURGH HOUSE,** U.S. 9, 18th C.. Fieldstone, clapboarded upper-story ends; 1 1/2 stories, modified rectangle, gambrel roof, interior end chimneys, center entrance with small wooden porch; side and rear frame additions. Characteristic of 18th C. Hudson Valley stone architecture. *Private.*

Hyde Park. **HOME OF FRANKLIN D. ROOSEVELT NATIONAL HISTORIC SITE**, 2 mi. S of Hyde Park on U.S. 9, 1826. Includes the birthplace and home of Franklin Delano Roosevelt, his grave, and the Franklin D. Roosevelt Library. House served as his "summer white house" and retreat during his illness while President. *Federal/NPS:* HABS.

Hyde Park. **STOUTENBURGH, WILLIAM, HOUSE**, U.S. 9G, East Park, 1765. Limestone, 1 1/2 stories, rectangular, gabled roof, interior end chimneys, gabled dormers, front center entrance framed by fluted woodwork, clapboarded N gable end. Example of typical early area structure. *Private.*

Hyde Park. **VANDERBILT MANSION NATIONAL HISTORIC SITE**, N edge of Hyde Park, U.S. 9, 1896-1898, McKim, Mead, and White. Limestone ashlar, 3 stories, rectangular, low pitched roof with balustraded parapet, slightly projecting central block with front tetrastyle Corinthian entrance portico and rear semielliptical portico, full-width side hexastyle entrance porticos; ornate eclectic interior elements, 1st-floor oval reception hall with light well; Italianate gatehouses, pavilion that served as family's dwelling when mansion was closed during winter; extensive gardens and walks. Example of elaborate Second Renaissance Revival mansion. Country home of Frederick W. Vanderbilt, gentleman, financier, and grandson of Cornelius Vanderbilt. *Federal/NPS:* HABS.

Pawling. **OBLONG FRIENDS MEETINGHOUSE**, Meetinghouse Rd. on Quaker Hill, 1764. Frame, shingling; 2 1/2 stories, rectangular, gabled roof, central chimney, 2 adjacent center entrances, pedimented end entrance; single 2-story room with sliding partition, gallery. Large meetinghouse served prosperous 18th–19th C. Quaker settlement; used as hospital during American Revolution. *Private.*

Poughkeepsie. **CHURCH OF THE HOLY COMFORTER (EPISCOPAL),** 13 Davies St., 1860, Richard Upjohn, architect. Bluestone, red sandstone; 1 story, modified cruciform shape, gabled roof, cresting, small gabled vents, main entrance through side projecting gabled vestibule; transept on one side, tower with spire on other side; polygonal apse, trefoil windows; original pews, trusses with tracery. Gothic Revival structure by noted architect Richard Upjohn. *Private.*

Poughkeepsie. **GARFIELD PLACE HISTORIC DISTRICT,** Both sides of Garfield Pl., 19th–20th C.. Stylish residential district containing 25 dwellings and several dependencies; features primarily 2 1/2-story brick and frame dwellings built mid–late-19th C. in Italianate, Queen Anne, and other 19th C. styles. Village developed during 18th C.; first Garfield Place house built 1852; area attracted residents of social and economic prominence. *Multiple private.*

Poughkeepsie. **ITALIAN CENTER,** 225-227 Mill St., Mid-19th C.. Brick, 2 1/2 stories, irregular shape, gabled and pyramidal roof sections with finials, 2 interior chimneys, off-center front entrance set beside front pyramidal sections with large front gable and turret with shingled conical cap; wrap-around front and side porch with turned columns, decorative balustrade, and spindle work fascia; gable windows set in almost round recesses, decorative brickwork and bargeboards, stone quoins and trim, 1st-story window with stained glass transom. Original L-shaped structure enlarged and redecorated with Queen Anne elements, late-19th C. *Private.*

Poughkeepsie. **LOCUST GROVE (SAMUEL F. B. MORSE HOUSE)**, 370 South St., 1830. Frame, clapboarding; 2 stories, modified T shape, gabled roof, interior chimneys, bracketed cornice, projecting octagonal wings, 4-story stuccoed end tower with round arched windows, porch with latticework fascia and posts, carriage house extension with large round arched openings; substantially expanded during Morse's ownership. Italianate. Home after 1847 of Samuel F. B. Morse, inventor of the telegraph and a noted artist who had studied and traveled in England and Europe. *Private; not accessible to the public:* NHL.

Poughkeepsie. **MAIN BUILDING, VASSAR COLLEGE,** Vassar College campus, Mid-19th C., James Renwick, architect. Brick, 4 stories with 5-story pavilions, U-shaped, mansard roof punctuated by towers and central convex mansard section. One of the earliest Second Empire buildings in the U.S.; reputedly designed after 16th C. Tuileries Palace. School founded by Matthew Vassar, Poughkeepsie philanthropist who pioneered higher education for women. *Private.*

POUGHKEEPSIE. **MILL STREET-NORTH CLOVER STREET HISTORIC DISTRICT,** 19th–20th C.. Residential area containing primarily 2-3-story brick houses from post-Civil War period in styles ranging from Greek Revival to those of the Victorian period; notable are the numerous Second Empire structures and the Queen Anne Italian Center (see also Italian Center, NY). Eastern section became city's civic and cultural center under direction of the Vassar family. *Multiple public/private.*

Poughkeepsie. **POUGHKEEPSIE CITY HALL,** 228 Main St., 1831. Brick, 2 stories, rectangular, gabled roof, denticulated cornice, front open balustraded frame belfry with hipped roof, rear cupola with pyramidal roof, front center entrance with transom and side lights; brownstone trim including wide belt course between stories, lintels, and sills; 2 brick additions; altered. Greek Revival. Built as market and village hall, presumably with open 1st-floor market area; served as post office, 1865-1886. *Municipal.*

Poughkeepsie. **SECOND BAPTIST CHURCH,** 36 Vassar St., Mid-19th C.. Brick base, frame, flush siding; 1 1/2 stories over high basement, rectangular temple-form, gabled roof, interior end chimneys, entablature surrounding building; front tetrastyle Doric pedimented portico with balustrade, oculus in tympanum, and 2 entrances with shouldered architraves; side pilasters; side rectangular windows, each with cornice and shouldered architrave; altered. Greek Revival. Property originally purchased from Matthew Vassar's family; building has been used for Protestant and Jewish worship. *Private.*

Poughkeepsie. **UNION STREET HISTORIC DISTRICT,** About 8 blocks in downtown Poughkeepsie centered around Union St., 19th C.. Working class urban neighborhood containing 173 historical commercial and residential structures; features numerous 2 1/2-story brick buildings in styles from Federal to those of the Victorian period, long narrow lots, and backyards. City's oldest section; settled largely by German, Irish, Italian, and Slavic immigrants, and by Blacks. *Multiple public/private.*

Poughkeepsie. **VASSAR HOME FOR AGED MEN,** 1 Vassar St., 1880. Brick, 3 stories over high basement, rectangular, low hipped roof with deck, interior end chimney, gabled section rises above cornice line on each side, bracketed cornice with narrow arched corbel tables below, stairway leads to front entrance with transom; 1-story balustraded porch with slender columns, similar side and rear porches with entrances; granite banding connects granite architraves and sills. Italianate. Built on the site of Matthew Vassar's town residence as home for men 65 and over, as established by Matthew Vassar, Jr., and John Guy Vassar. *Public.*

Poughkeepsie. **VASSAR INSTITUTE,** 12 Vassar St., 1882, J. A. Wood, architect. Brick, 2 1/2 stories, rectangular, convex mansard and hipped roof sections, interior chimney, round arched dormers with raised ridge, bracketed cornice with decorative frieze, front center 3-story tower, entrance porch with paired columns, recessed brick paneling, segmental arched openings, granite trim, rear lower wing with round arched windows houses auditorium; tower dome removed. High Victorian Italianate with Second Empire elements. Built for Matthew Vassar Jr. and John Guy Vassar; contained natural history museum and library. *Private.*

Poughkeepsie. **VASSAR, MATTHEW, ESTATE (SPRINGSIDE),** Academy and Livingston Sts., 1850–1852, Andrew Jackson Downing, architect. Rural estate containing a 2-story cottage with board-and-batten siding, gabled roof, bay windows, and decorative bargeboards, shutter trim, and bracketing; a gatehouse in similar style; and the remains of an L-shaped barn complex. Picturesque Gothic Revival. Home of Matthew Vassar, Poughkeepsie brewer and Vassar College founder (see also Main Building, Vassar College, NY). Grounds also designed by early landscape architect Andrew Jackson Downing. *Private; not accessible to the public:* **NHL; HABS.**

Red Hook. **MAIZEFIELD, 75 W. Market St., 18th-19th C.**. Brick, 3 stories, rectangular main block with later additions, flat roof, 4 interior end chimneys, 1-story front entrance portico with Palladian window above, heavy cornice with block modillions. Federal. Only extant dependency-2-story, hipped roof board-and-batten cottage designed by Alexander Jackson Davis. Residence of Gen. David Van Ness, prominent military and political leader in the late-18th and early-19th C. *Private.*

Rhinebeck. **DELAMATER, HENRY, HOUSE, 44 Montgomery St.**, 1844, Alexander Jackson Davis, architect. Frame, board-and-batten siding; modified rectangle; hipped roof with cross gable, each end with finial; interior chimneys, carved scalloped bargeboards; 3 front Tudor arched openings, 1-story 3-bay-wide porch with carved flat posts and brackets forming Tudor arches, balustraded deck; center 2nd story and attic, each with rectangular window under blind pointed arch with tracery; each side with bay window; interior designed by architect to harmonize with exterior design; rear veranda enclosed and extended; board-and-batten carriage house. Excellent example of Gothic Revival cottage design advocated by Alexander Jackson Davis and Andrew Jackson Downing. *Private.*

Sylvan Lake vicinity. **SYLVAN LAKE ROCK SHELTER, 5000 B.C.-700 A.D.**. Undisturbed stratified rock shelter; served as winter camp for Archaic hunters beginning c. 5000 B.C. Excavations between 1964 and 1966 revealed numerous remains of the Sylvan Lake Culture (c. 2500 B.C.), elements of the Susquehanna Tradition (c. 1500-1000 B.C.), and Middle and Late Woodland deposits. *Private.*

ERIE COUNTY

Buffalo. **ALBRIGHT-KNOX ART GALLERY,** 1285 Elmwood Ave., in Delaware Park, 1900–1905, Edward B. Green, architect. Partially marble faced, 2 stories, modified H shape, gabled roof sections; E pedimented Ionic entrance portico flanked by colonnaded wings ending in pavilions, each with caryatids by Augustus Saint Gaudens; W semielliptical Ionic porch flanked by colonnaded sections; interior sculpture courtyard. Neo-Classical Revival. Built to permanently house the collections of the Buffalo Fine Arts Academy. *Private.*

Buffalo. **BUFFALO STATE HOSPITAL,** 400 Forest Ave., 1871–1890, Henry Hobson Richardson, architect. Random rough ashlar sandstone, brick; 3 1/2 stories above high basement, main block with 5 W wards and 2 E wards, gabled and hipped roof sections, gabled and flared hipped dormers, front entrance recessed under 3-bay arcade flanked by projecting pavilion; 2 main-block towers with steeply hipped roofs, shed dormers, and corner turrets; machicolations, rectangular and segmental arched windows, wings with projecting cross-gable sections; 3 wards removed, 1960's; 4 service buildings; site plan by Frederick Law Olmsted. Richardsonian Romanesque elements. Early development example of Henry Hobson Richardson's work. *State:* HABS.

Buffalo. **DELAWARE AVENUE HISTORIC DISTRICT,** W side of Delaware Ave. between North and Bryant Sts., 19th–20th C.. Remaining section of elite residential area of predominantly turn-of-the-century grand dwellings. Era's Neo-Classical and Georgian Revival styles represented in designs by noted architects such as McKim, Mead, and White. Reflects overwhelmingly successful economic development stimulated by Pan-American Exposition,

1901. Prominent residents included Anson C. Goodyear and Millard Fillmore. *Multiple public/private.*

Buffalo. **GUARANTY BUILDING (PRUDENTIAL BUILDING)**, Church and Pearl Sts., 1894–1895, Louis Sullivan, architect. Steel frame, terra cotta sheathing; 12 1/2 stories, U-shaped, flat roof; front and side entrances, each with large lunette at 2nd-story level; first 2 stories topped by narrow cornice form base for upper levels, upper-story fenestration organized in vertical bands under round arches, oculi in coved section below cornice, decorative terra cotta ornament in low relief covers entire building; interior lobby with cast iron and leaded glass skylight, mosaic frieze and cast iron stairway; 1st-story store windows altered 1970 to form flat plane behind piers. Sullivanesque. A milestone in modern skyscraper development by Louis Sullivan, building successfully integrates structural clarity with ornamentation. *Private:* NHL; HABS.

Buffalo. **MACEDONIA BAPTIST CHURCH**, 511 Michigan Ave., 1845. Brick, 1 story, rectangular, gabled roof, enclosed entrance vestibule flanked by round arched windows in recessed rectangular panels, rounded and inscribed stone plaque above entrance; modified meetinghouse plan with apse; 20th C. alterations. Social and religious center for Black community for 125 years. Parish of Dr. J. Edward Nash, a founder of the Buffalo Urban League and the local branch of the NAACP. *Private.*

Buffalo. **PIERCE ARROW FACTORY COMPLEX**, Elmwood and Great Arrow Aves., 1906, Albert Kahn, architect. Factory complex containing 14 major buildings mainly of reinforced concrete steel with brick and glass curtain walls; saw-tooth roof sections, large spans up to

60'; some Arts and Crafts decorative elements on Administration Building front. Represents synthesis of trends foreshadowing developments in factory design; owned and operated by Pierce Arrow Co. until 1938; buildings later converted for diversified commercial use. *Multiple private.*

Buffalo. **ST. PAUL'S EPISCOPAL CATHEDRAL**, 125 Pearl St., 1850–1851, Richard Upjohn, architect. Sandstone ashlar, 1 story, irregular shape, gabled roof sections; cornice sections, some with modillions, some with trefoil arcading; front 3-stage tower with tall spire, entrance porch, transept chapel with entrance and adjacent 3-stage bell tower with spire, nave lancet windows with label molds, buttresses; towers completed 1870's; 1888 fire destroyed interior; new interiors designed by English architect, Robert Gibson; clerestory added. Fine example of Gothic Revival building adapted to unusual triangular site. *Private:* HABS.

Buffalo. **THEODORE ROOSEVELT INAUGURAL NATIONAL HISTORIC SITE**, Delaware Ave., 1838. Site includes Ansley Wilcox house: brick, 2 1/2 stories, modified rectangle; gabled roof sections, some with end returns; interior end chimney; front full-width 2-story pedimented portico, center entrance with fanlight, Palladian window in tympanum; 1863 remodeling, portico moved; 1890's additions; 20th C. interior alterations; restored. Greek Revival. Built for officers' quarters as part of Poinsett Barracks; site of Theodore Roosevelt's inauguration Sept. 14, 1901 after William McKinley's assassination. Museum. *Federal/NPS.*

Buffalo. **U.S. POST OFFICE**, 121 Ellicott St., 1897–1901, James Knox Taylor, architect. Rock-faced granited base, granite ashlar; 4 1/2 stories over high basement, modified rectangle, gabled and pyramidal roof sections, numerous gabled dormers, modillion cornice; front center tall tower with corner turrets, gargoyles, and spire with crockets and finial; front 3 entrances recessed under 3-bay entrance porch with elaborate Gothic detailing, each side with 3-bay entry and 1–3 entrances; rear cast iron portecochere, string courses, windows grouped under pointed arches; molded and carved detail including foliate capitals and buffalo heads; 4-story-high central courtyard above 1st floor with steel and glass roof surrounded by galleries with rectangular, segmental, and pointed arched openings; 1936 remodeling included roofing of 1st floor of courtyard and skylight. Later Gothic Revival. Excellent example of late-19th C. dual-nature architecture combining revivalist style with technological innovations; designed by James Knox Taylor, Supervising Architect of the U.S. Treasury. *Federal/GSA:* HABS.

East Aurora. **FILLMORE, MILLARD, HOUSE**, 24 Shearer Ave., 1826. Frame, clapboarding; 1 1/2 stories, modified L shape, gabled roof sections, exterior end chimneys, 1-story full-width front tetrastyle Doric porch, front center entrance; moved, 1915 and 1930; altered, c. 1930. Greek Revival elements. Built by Millard Fillmore, lawyer, state and U.S. representative, and U.S. Vice President who became President upon the death of Zachary Taylor in 1850. *Private; not accessible to the public:* NHL.

East Aurora. **ROYCROFT CAMPUS**, Main and W. Grove Sts., Late-19th C.–1938. Complex containing approximately 9 structures, the majority of which feature crenelated towers, half-timbered gables, and stone or shingled exteriors. Built as part of Arts and Crafts artistic community established in late-19th C. by writer

Elbert Hubbard after visiting a similar English community organized by Arts and Crafts movement leader William Morris; utilized Medieval organization and building concepts as inspired by the writings of John Ruskin; in operation until 1938. *Multiple public/private.*

Irving. **THOMAS INDIAN SCHOOL,** NY 438 on Cattaraugus Reservation, 1900, Barney and Chapman, architects. Educational complex consisting of 9 principal brick Georgian Revival buildings and 25 dependencies; notable is the elaborate Administration Building with its ornate stone trim and decorative use of Indian related motifs and subject matter. Built by NY on reservation as a self-sufficient educational facility; school began, mid-18th C., as the Thomas Asylum of Orphan and Destitute Indian Children and developed into a successful, accredited educational institution; in operation until 1958 when closed as result of centralization of the public school system. *Tribal.*

ESSEX COUNTY

ADIRONDACK FOREST PRESERVE, *Reference—see Clinton County*

Crown Point. **FORT ST. FREDERIC,** Jct. of NY 8 and 9N, 1731. Limestone ruins of .fort established by French to guard Lake Champlain route into Canada. Abandoned in 1759 after Lord Jeffrey Amherst captured nearby Fort Carillon, which the British renamed Fort Ticonderoga (see also Fort Ticonderoga, NY), during the French and Indian War. *State:* NHL.

Crown Point vicinity. **FORT CROWN POINT,** Crown Point Reservation, SW of Lake Champlain Bridge and NY 8, 1760. Limestone walls of 5-sided fort containing 6.5-acre parade ground and 2 of 3 original barracks, and surrounded by dry moat. Constructed by British as Fort Crown Point or Amherst after Lord Jeffrey Amherst who drove French from area during the French and Indian War. Damaged in 1773 when powder magazine exploded; reconstruction interrupted by Revolution was never completed. Occupied alternately by Americans and British during Revolution. *State:* NHL.

Essex vicinity. **CHURCH OF THE NAZARENE,** W of Essex on NY 22, 1855. Frame, board-and-batten siding; gabled roof with double pitch and end returns, front shoulder arched entrance, lancet windows, trefoil in gable; interior wooden arches spring from unengaged wooden posts to form primary roof support. Gothic Revival. Simple design apparently based upon small mission chapel prototype in Richard Upjohn's *Rural Architecture,* published 1852. *Private.*

Essex vicinity. **OCTAGONAL SCHOOLHOUSE,** On Rte. 22 in Bouquet, 1826, Benjamin Gilbert, builder. Rubble sandstone, 1 story, modified octagon, polygonal roof, octagonal open belfry with polygonal roof, front entrance with shed porch, rear entrance leads to frame vestibule addition; porch added. Octagon Mode. Probably state's oldest schoolhouse; served as school until 1952. *Municipal.*

Ironville. **IRONVILLE HISTORIC DISTRICT,** 19th C.. Rural residential area includes focal Penfield Homestead (1828), other houses, church, boardinghouse, Grange Hall, inn, schoolhouse, and ruinous remains of ironworks. Est. 1807; developed major iron industry; pioneered in industrial use of electricity. Museum. *Multiple private.*

Lake Placid (North Elba). **BROWN, JOHN, FARM,** John Brown Rd., 1850. 214 acres containing 1 1/2-story gabled frame cabin, and burial plot containing grave of abolitionist John Brown. Farm bought by Brown from philanthropist and abolitionist Gerrit Smith, for the purpose of assisting Blacks in establishing farms. Museum. *State.*

Port Kent. **WATSON, ELKANAH, HOUSE,** 3 mi. E of U.S. 9, 1828. Stone (ashlar), 2 stories, rectangular, hipped roof, interior chimney, large square cupola; porte-cochere, 2-story pedimented entrance porch, and wrap-around porch with 1st- and 2nd-story balustrades; elliptical and round arched openings on 1st story, quoins; altered, late-19th C. Eclectic elements. Home of Elkanah Watson, diplomat and agriculturalist who originated the competitive agricultural fair and promoted agricultural societies and improvements. *Private; not accessible to the public:* NHL.

Ticonderoga vicinity. **FORT TICONDEROGA,** 2.5 mi. S of Ticonderoga on NY 22, 1755–1757. Reconstructed fort complex first constructed and garrisoned by French as Fort Vaudreuil and then Fort Carillon; located at junction of Lake Champlain and Lake George, controlling access to Canada and the Hudson River Valley. Captured by British general Lord Jeffrey Amherst during the French and Indian War and renamed Fort Ticonderoga; taken by Ethan Allen and his "Green Mountain Boys" in 1775 and became base for unsuccessful plan to attack Canada; restored to British control when Gen. John Burgoyne seized a strategic height overlooking the fort, forcing the retreat of American troops under Gen. Arthur St. Clair, July 25, 1775. Museum. *Private:* NHL.

FRANKLIN COUNTY

ADIRONDACK FOREST PRESERVE,
Reference—see Clinton County

FULTON COUNTY

ADIRONDACK FOREST PRESERVE,
Reference—see Clinton County

Dolgeville. **DOLGE COMPANY FACTORY COMPLEX,** S. Main St. (also in Herkimer County), 1882–1894. Factory complex including 2 large factory buildings, 1 frame and 1 limestone; a double span iron Pratt truss bridge; several smaller frame and stone buildings; and the Alfred Dolge house, a large, elaborate Eastlake structure. Factory and town est. 1875 by felt manufacturer Alfred Dolge, who attempted to create an ideal community for his workers by offering benefits that included a pension plan, and insurance and endowment plans later adapted by some U.S. railroads and corporations. Complex acquired by Daniel Green and Co. after Dolge failed financially and moved from town, May 1899. *Private.*

Johnstown. **FULTON COUNTY COURTHOUSE (TRYON COUNTY COURTHOUSE)**, N. William St., 1772–1773. Brick, 1 1/2 stories, modified rectangle, gabled roof with slight kick and pedimented gable ends, interior end chimneys, central octagonal cupola with domed roof on balustraded square base, denticulated modillion cornice, front center entrance with fanlight in projecting gabled vestibule with end returns and posts, gable fanlight; interior altered; cupola added late-18th–early-19th C.; vestibule added after 1872; rear addition (c. 1900) connects courthouse to L-shaped county office building; repairs made 1930's. Georgian elements. State's oldest remaining courthouse, attributed to Samuel Fuller. *County:* HABS.

Johnstown. **JOHNSON HALL**, Hall St., 1763, Lemal Baker, builder. Frame, imitation ashlar siding; 2 stories over basement, rectangular, hipped roof with deck, interior chimneys with corbeled caps, front and rear center entrances framed by modillion pediment and pilasters, 2nd-story center Palladian window, modillion cornice; one of 2 adjacent 2-story stone blockhouses remains. Restored. Georgian. Fine house built for Sir William Johnson, Superintendent of Indian Affairs of the Northern Colonies, 1763–1774. *State:* NHL; HABS.

GENESEE COUNTY

Alexander. **ALEXANDER CLASSICAL SCHOOL**, Buffalo St., 1837. Fieldstone, 3 stories, L-shaped, hipped roof with cupola surrounded by balustrade, 1 interior chimney, 5 bays wide, entrance with transom and side lights, quoins; central hall plan; 1-story frame N addition, W cinderblock garage; interior alterations. Federal. Built as private school, 1837; became public school, 1886; converted into town hall, 1940. *Municipal.*

Batavia. **BATAVIA CLUB (BANK OF GENESEE)**, Main and Bank Sts., 1831, Hezekiah Eldredge, builder-architect. Brick, stuccoed; 2 1/2 stories, L-shaped, gabled roof, paired interior end chimneys joined to form stepped gable ends, central chimneys; center entrance with side lights, flanking colonnettes, and ornate bracketed hood; tripartite windows with colonnettes as mullions, blind lunettes in gables, rear ell with chimney. Federal and Greek Revival elements. One of few remaining examples of Eldredge's work; built as bank; purchased by men's club, 1886. *Private.*

Batavia. **GENESEE COUNTY COURTHOUSE,** Main and Ellicott Sts., 1841–1843. Limestone ashlar, 2 stories above high basement on sloping site, square, pyramidal hipped roof with central 2-stage square cupola with small domed roof, interior end chimney; front center recessed entrance with transom and side lights, 1st-story pilasters delineate bays; basement recessed rear entrance with side lights, belt course between basement and 1st story; 1931 original front porch enclosed except for recessed entry; under restoration. Greek Revival elements. Focal point of town's central area. *County.*

Batavia. **HOLLAND LAND OFFICE,** W. Main St., 1815. Stone, 1 1/2 stories, rectangular, gabled roof, pedimented tetrastyle portico; center entrance framed by fanlight, engaged columns, and entablature; rectangular panels in wall above windows, dormers, simple entablature. Federal. Headquarters for land company organized by Dutch investors; played a vital role in the developemnt of western NY and northern PA, and typified the activities of foreign speculative enterprises on the American frontier. Museum. *County:* NHL.

Batavia. **RICHMOND MEMORIAL LIBRARY,** 19 Ross St., 1887, James Gould Cutler, architect. Sandstone (rock faced, random ashlar), 1 1/2 stories, L-shaped, gabled roof sections, front gabled off-center entrance with large Syrian arch beneath 3 round arched windows, octagonal corner tower with pyramidal roof; belt courses, decoration, and corner tower of different color stone; brick rear ell. A local example of the many libraries built in Richardsonian Romanesque style in the late century, designed by a Rochester architect who at one time was mayor of Rochester. *Municipal.*

Morganville. **MORGANVILLE POTTERY**

FACTORY SITE, Morganville Rd. off NY 237, 1829-1905. Site of pottery factory and remains of 2 pottery kilns, and pottery sherds. Probably best preserved earthenware pottery site in western part of state. Investigated by New York state, 1973. *Private.*

GREENE COUNTY

Athens vicinity. **WEST ATHENS HILL SITE,** W of Athens, Paleo-Indian (8000-9000 B.C.). Extensive Paleo-Indian quarry-workshop-habitation site. Tested between 1963 and 1965 by Robert E. Funk and William A. Ritchie of the New York State Museum, and excavated again by Funk in 1966. *Private.*

Catskill. **COLE, THOMAS, HOUSE,** 218 Spring St., 1812-1814. Brick, 2 stories over high basement, rectangular, low hipped roof, interior end chimneys, box cornice, balustraded veranda over brick basement-level piers, splayed lintels, center door with side lights. Nearby frame studio building with 2-story windows and eclectic elements. Federal. Home and studio of Thomas Cole, a notable 19th C. American landscape and allegorical painter, whose portrayal of nature and of the Catskill region in which he lived influenced the development of the Hudson River landscape painters. *Private; not accessible to the public: nhl.*

Catskill. **SUSQUEHANNAH TURNPIKE,** Beginning at Catskill, follows the Mohican Trail (NY 145) and CR 20 and 22 NW to the Schoharie County line, 19th C.. Paved 2-lane road paralleling original 25-mile route between Catskill and West Durham. Includes 2 single-arched stone bridges (no longer used), a 3-arched stone bridge, and 9 of the original 25 milestones. Convenient direct route through county; contributed to economic growth of area. *State.*

Coxsackie vicinity. **BRONCK, PIETER, HOUSE,** 2 mi. W of Coxsackie on W side of U.S. 9W, 1663. Two structures joined by passage; random fieldstone, brick; 1 1/2 stories, one structure with attic; modified L shape, steeply gabled roof sections, interior and interior end chimneys, entrance to stone structure located in rear 1 1/2-story stone wing, transom, shed hood, and balustraded stoop; brick structure with 2 front entrances, each with transom, and 1-story balustraded shed porch, shed dormers, and stepped parapet at gable ends; much original furniture; fieldstone structure built 1663; rear wing added 1685; brick structure added 1738; renovated 1938. Nice example of early dwelling with Dutch colonial elements. Museum. *County:* NHL.

Earlton vicinity. **FORESTVILLE COMMONWEALTH,** NW of Earlton off NY 81, 1826. Foundations of houses, community house, mill, and other outbuildings mark site of Utopian community founded on social principles of British reformer, Robert Dale Owen, who established several communal societies in the U.S. Disbanded after a year. *Private.*

Greenville vicinity. **PREVOST MANOR HOUSE (HUSH-HUSH FARM)**, W of Greenville off NY 81, 1793, Fitch Lanpher, builder. Frame, clapboarding; 1-2 1/2 stories, rectangular main block with side and rear wings, gabled roof sections, interior and interior end chimneys, front center entrance with transom and side lights, side wing entrance with transom; side wing built probably 1793, main block built 1794; 2 board-and-batten rear wings built later. Colonial elements. Example of early mansion of the mid-Hudson Valley frontier. *Private.*

HAMILTON COUNTY

ADIRONDACK FOREST PRESERVE,
Reference—see Clinton County

HERKIMER COUNTY

ADIRONDACK FOREST PRESERVE,
Reference—see Clinton County

DOLGE COMPANY FACTORY COMPLEX,
Reference—see Fulton County

Cold Brook. **COLD BROOK FEED MILL,** NY 8, 1857. Frame, clapboarding and flush siding; 2 1/2 stories, square, shed roof sections, exterior chimney, 1-story shed porch supported by square posts, small shed roof section projecting on 2nd floor; includes a waterpowered stone grinder and corn sheller; later additions; remains of mill dam and flume nearby. Example of early mill with some original equipment still intact. *Private.*

Danube. **HERKIMER HOUSE,** Near NY 5 S., Mid-18th C.. Brick, stone foundation; 2 1/2 stories, rectangular, gambrel roof with small end pediments, interior end chimneys, boxed cornice with end returns, front center entrance with transom and small pedimented porch, flat arched windows; remodeled, 1820's; restored, 1914–1915; altered to original appearance, 1960–1967. Georgian elements. Built by Revolutionary War general, Nicholas Herkimer; operated as tavern on Erie Canal during early-19th C. Museum. *State.*

East Herkimer vicinity. **FORT HERKIMER CHURCH (REFORMED PROTESTANT DUTCH CHURCH OF GERMAN FLATTS)**, NY 5S, 1767. Limestone, 2 1/2 stories, rectangular, gabled roof, square wooden belfry, gabled frame vestibule; segmental arched 1st-floor windows, lunette in pedimented front gable, Doric entablature with narrow triglyphs; 2nd floor added, 1812. Federal elements. Built by Palatine German settlers; part of fortification under command of Sir William Johnson during French and Indian War. *Private:* HABS.

Herkimer. **HERKIMER COUNTY COURTHOUSE**, 320 N. Main St., 1873. Brick, 3 1/2 stories, modified rectangle, gabled roof with cross gables, interior end chimney, denticulated cornice; front end 3-stage cupola with open arcaded 3rd stage, truncated polygonal roof with round arched dormers and modillion cornice; front center entrance with 1-story porch with parapet, front round arched windows with hood molds, gable oculi, recessed brick paneling, string course above 1st story; interior remodeled 1936. Romanesque Revival elements. Site of 1906 trial of Chester Gillette, the background of which formed the framework for *An American Tragedy* by Theodore Dreiser. *County.*

Herkimer. **HERKIMER COUNTY HISTORICAL SOCIETY (DR. A. WALTER SUITER HOUSE)**, 400 N. Main St., 1884. Rock-faced limestone foundation, brick; 2 1/2 stories over high basement, modified rectangle, double pitched gabled roof sections with cross gables, interior end chimneys, shed dormer, denticulated cornice sections, decorative brick corbeling below cornice, corner polygonal tower with pyramidal roof, front off-center double-door entrance with carved oak doors, ornamental terra cotta banding, front 2nd-story oriel with balcony above with turned woodwork; fine interior woodwork with different species of wood used in each room. Excellent example of Queen Anne style. *Private.*

Herkimer. **HERKIMER COUNTY JAIL**, 327

N. Main St., 1835. Limestone ashlar, 2 1/2 stories over high basement with 2-story wing, L-shaped, gabled and flat roof sections, mainblock side parapet, gable end returns, interior end chimney, bracketed cornice on wing, double stairway leads to front center entrance with fanlight and side lights, dressed stone quoins, lintels, belt course, and water table; oval gable light; front wing entrance, windows with cornices. Greek Revival and Italianate elements. *County:* HABS; G.

Herkimer. **REFORMED CHURCH, THE,** 405 N. Main St., 1835. Brick, painted; 2 stories, rectangular, gabled roof, 3-stage tower with spire, projecting pedimented entrance portico, 3 pointed arched front windows with tracery between doric pilasters; interior remodeled, 1874, 1912; rear stone chapel added, 1894. *Private:* G.

Indian Castle vicinity. **INDIAN CASTLE CHURCH,** NY 5S, c. 1769-1770. Frame, clapboarding; 1 story, rectangular, gabled roof, front square belfry with steeple above center entrance; alterations include relocation of entrance and replacement of original open Georgian cupola. Built as Indian mission church by Sir William Johnson, Superintendent of Indian Affairs, on land donated by Chief Joseph Brandt. Museum. *State.*

Little Falls. **HERKIMER COUNTY TRUST COMPANY BUILDING,** Corner of Ann and Albany Sts., 1833. Stone, 1 story, rectangular, gabled roof over main block, full-width pedimented Doric portico with entablature, center entrance; small side wing with flat roof added, 1874. Excellent Greek Revival commercial structure. *Municipal; not accessible to the public:* G.

Salisbury Center. **SALISBURY CENTER**

COVERED BRIDGE, Fairview Rd. over Spruce Creek, 1875. Frame with vertical siding, Burr arch truss of 42' single span, 16' wide, 18' ridge with 10' clearance, gabled roof; restored. Only remaining covered bridge of 7 in Salisbury; combination arch-and-truss structural system patented by Theodore Burr in 1817. *Municipal.*

JEFFERSON COUNTY

Adams vicinity. **TALCOTT FALLS SITE,** U.S. 11 at jct. with Old Rome State Rd., Prehistoric, 1825. Contains remains of Iroquois earth ring and ditch, stream and waterfall, and brick inn, presently used as a dwelling. Inn built and owned by Maj. Daniel Talcott, grist and sawmill operator. Area facilities provided excellent means of occupation throughout the years. *Private.*

Black River vicinity. **LERAY MANSION,** NE of Black River on Camp Drum Military Reservation, Early-19th C.. Stone, stuccoed; 2 stories, T-shaped, hipped roof sections, wide front 2-story tetrastyle Ionic portico; center entrance with transom, side lights, and a French window on either side; rear 1-story hipped wings; excellent interior detailing. Greek Revival. Home of James Le Ray, French immigrant whose family in France had been major supporters of the American Revolution and who made significant contributions to the development of upstate NY. *Federal/USA.*

Cape Vincent. **LERAY, VINCENT, HOUSE (STONE HOUSE)**, Broadway (NY 12E), c. 1815. Native limestone, 2 1/2 stories, rectangular; hipped roof with 2 interior chimneys, center dormer, and balustrade; splayed arches over center entrance and 1st-floor windows; 3 dependencies. Late Georgian. Built for Vincent

LeRay, son of James LeRay, who came to U.S. in 1785 to represent all private French claims against the U.S. government and whose family later emigrated and opened its immense landholdings in northern NY for development. *Private.*

Sackets Harbor. **CAMP, ELISHA, HOUSE (BRICK CAMP MANOR)**, 310 General Smith Dr., 1808–1815. Brick, 2 1/2 stories, rectangular; gabled roof with stepped gable ends incorporating paired interior end chimneys, each gable with lunette; front center entrance with fanlight and side lights, 2nd-story center Palladian window, side entrance with fanlight, splayed granite lintels, rear full-width 1-story shed wing with center frame section; breezeway and garage added 1950's; original Adamesque interior woodwork, many original furnishings; breezeway and garage added 1950's. Excellent example of Federal style dwelling, locally attributed to architect-builder Barnabus Waterman. *Private.*

Sackets Harbor. **MADISON BARRACKS**, Military Rd., 1815. Remnants of earthworks (c. 1812), several limestone buildings (1816–1819), numerous brick buildings and a stone water tower (1890's), and 20th C. brick and concrete structures span 130-year occupation of this former U.S. military facility. Site of early fortification forming part of American defense system along Lake Ontario after the Revolution; new installation begun in 1815 named for President Madison; James Fenimore Cooper, Ulysses S. Grant, and Gen. Mark Clark are among those associated with the barracks; sold, 1940's. *Private.*

Sackets Harbor. **SACKETS HARBOR BATTLEFIELD**, Coastline and area from Sackets

Harbor SW to and including Horse Island, Early-mid-19th C.. Contains ruins of 2 War of 1812 forts, farm complex on War of 1812 battlefield, 2 officers' quarters and support structures of mid-19th C. naval station, and a 20th C. stone monument commemorating Americans who repulsed 2 British attacks on important shipyards during War of 1812. Naval station established in response to British-American border tensions of 1838-1839, and abandoned in 1855. Museum and park. *Multiple public/private.*

Sackets Harbor. **UNION HOTEL,** Main and Ray Sts., 1817-1818. Limestone rubble, 3 1/2 stories, rectangular, gabled roof, interior chimneys, front center entrance with transom and side lights; ashlar belt courses, lintels, and quoins; some original interior woodwork; stepped gables removed. Federal elements. Community focal point. *Private.* G.

Watertown. **JEFFERSON COUNTY COURTHOUSE COMPLEX,** SE corner of Arsenal and Sherman Sts., Mid-19th-early-20th C.. Complex of county government structures; includes the High Victorian Gothic red brick courthouse (1862, Horatio Nelson White, architect), the simplified Chateauesque clerk's office (1884, J. W. Griffin, architect), and the greystone Second Renaissance Revival surrogate's office (1905, David Kieff, architect). *County.*

KINGS COUNTY

Brooklyn. **BOATHOUSE ON THE LULLWATER OF THE LAKE IN PROSPECT PARK,** Prospect Park, 1904, Helmle and Huberty, architects. Ashlar, 2 stories, rectangular, hipped roof, interior end chimneys, modillion cornice, 2nd-story pavilion set on larger 1st-story base; 1st story with entablature with frieze set on half columns which flank round arched fenestrated openings, each with fanlight and side lights, on water side. Example of Beaux-Arts Classicism, typical of the style that became popular following the success of the 1893 Chicago World's Fair. *Municipal.*

Brooklyn. **BROOKLYN BRIDGE,** Across the East River from Brooklyn to Manhattan (also in New York County), 1869–1883, John A. and Washington A. Roebling, engineers. Iron and steel suspension bridge, one 1,595' span with approaches of nearly 1000', 350'-high stone pylons with pointed arched openings between end and center buttresses, galvanized steel cables; strengthened, floor replaced, 1948–1953. Largest and most famous of the early suspension bridges, designed by John A. Roebling, pioneer of suspension bridges, who died from injuries suffered during construction; first use of steel cables in a suspension bridge. *Municipal:* NHL; HAER.

Brooklyn. **BROOKLYN HEIGHTS HISTORIC DISTRICT,** Borough of Brooklyn, bounded by Atlantic Ave., Court and Fulton Sts. and the East River, 19th C.. Leading 19th C. residential district composed of many fine brick and stone town houses lining tree-shaded streets on cliff over the East River. Structures are predominantly Federal, Greek Revival and Italianate styles, and often feature ornamental ironwork and elaborate interiors. Area developed beginning in 1820's when establishment of ferry to Manhattan brought Brooklyn Heights into easy commuting distance. Popular area noted both for its elegant buildings and the dramatic view of the bay. *Multiple public/private:* NHL; HABS.

Brooklyn. **CASEMATE FORT, WHITING QUADRANGLE,** Fort Hamilton, off NY 27, 1819-1826. Site of early-19th C. military facility; greatly altered and modernized but retains general rectangular plan, some original stone and brickwork in buildings, and the walled enceinte; original main building modernized and enlarged. Site occupied in 1652 by Dutch troops and in the 1770's by French forces; occupied by U.S. Army after the Revolution; one of the oldest extant U.S. military facilities. *Federal/USA.*

Brooklyn. **FEDERAL BUILDING AND POST OFFICE,** 271 Cadman Plaza, E., 1885-1891, Mifflen E. Bell, architect. Stone, 3 1/2 stories, rectangular, hipped roof sections, elaborate pinnacled gabled dormers, gabled sections, projecting 5 1/2-story square corner tower with open 5th floor, corner pavilions, gabled center block flanked by turrets, arcaded sections and ornate round arched openings, belt courses, modillion cornice, carved decoration; later 5 1/2-story extensions. Chateauesque with Richardsonian Romanesque elements. *Federal/GSA.*

Brooklyn. **FLATBUSH TOWN HALL,** 35 Snyder Ave., 1874-1875. Stone foundation, brick; 2 1/2 stories over high basement, modified rectangle, mansard roof with cross gables, interior end chimneys, front corner 3-story bell tower with truncated pyramidal roof, front side stairs lead to full-width deck with heavy stone railing, off-center entrance; pointed arched openings, front openings with label molds; stone trim and banding; original polychrome effects obscured; minor alterations;

rear 1-story wing probably added 1926. High Victorian Gothic elements. Community building served many civic purposes. *Municipal:* G.

Brooklyn. **FULTON FERRY DISTRICT,** Roughly bounded by the East River and Washington, Water, Front, and Doughty Sts., 19th–20th C.. Light industrial area containing ferry site, waterfront, and commercial and commercial/residential buildings, the majority of which are brick and 2–4 stories high in a variety of styles. Once Brooklyn's commercial hub; built to house extensive waterfront activities which developed around the Brooklyn-Manhattan ferry system, est. 1642. After construction of roadways and bridges such as the Manhattan Bridge, the ferry fell into disuse and the waterfront structures were converted into warehouses. *Multiple public/private.*

Brooklyn. **GRECIAN SHELTER (CROQUET SHELTER)**, Prospect Park near Parkside Ave., 1905, McKim, Mead, and White, architects. Marble, 1 story, rectangular, flat roof, open peristyle with Corinthian columns supporting terra cotta entablature with rinceau frieze and modillion cornice, roof balustrade; vaulted ceiling; renovated 1966. Beaux-Arts Classicism. Acts as unifying link between Park Circle and Ocean Ave. entrances to park. *Municipal.*

Brooklyn. **HOUSES ON HUNTERFLY ROAD DISTRICT,** 1698, 1700, 1702, 1704, 1706, 1708 Bergen St., c. 1830. Four small buildings containing 6 houses are frame with clapboarding and shingling; 1–2 1/2 stories, rectangular with gabled roofs, and central and interior end chimneys; shingling added; some rear additions. Federal elements. Only surviving group of houses in Bedford Stuyvesant section of Brooklyn that were built parallel to the line of a colonial road; located on the edge of Weeksville, area's first major free black settlement. *Private; not accessible to the public.*

Brooklyn. **OLD BROOKLYN FIRE HEADQUARTERS**, 365-367 Jay St., 1892, Frank Freeman. architect. Red granite base, brown roman brick; 5 1/2 stories with 7-story front side tower, rectangular, steeply hipped roof sections, eyebrow dormer; 2 front entrances, one rectangular, one under wide round arch; tower and main block with front corner full-height rounded elements topped by turrets, terra cotta ornament. Excellent example of Richardsonian Romanesque style; continuously in use as a firehouse. *Municipal.*

Brooklyn. **PERRY, MATTHEW C., HOUSE,** Quarters A, U.S. Naval Facility, 1805-1806. Frame, clapboarding; 2 1/2 stories over full stone basement, rectangular with flanking wings, gabled roof with balustraded deck, interior end chimney, dormers, simple supporting piers, off-center basement and main entrances; 1860, 1904, and 1936 additions; altered. Federal. Commanding officer's residence of New York Navy Yard since construction; home (1841-1843) of Matthew C. Perry, who is best known for his successful negotiation of a treaty opening Japan to the western nations (1853-1854), but who also made important contributions in steamship navigation and navaleducation. *Federal/USN; not accessible to the public:* NHL.

Brooklyn. **PLYMOUTH CHURCH OF THE PILGRIMS**, 75 Hicks St., 1849, Joseph C. Wells, architect. Brick, 2 stories, rectangular, gabled roof, Doric portico with entablature, slightly recessed center section beneath segmental arch, recessed end window bays, raked lintels on front windows, belt course above 2nd floor, flat window lintels on side; open interior with gallery on slender columns; stained glass windows added, early-20th C. Greek Revival elements. Built for newly formed congregational church whose first minister was Henry Ward Beecher; important center of abolitionist sentiment; remained prominent in social and cultural movements throughout latter half of 19th C. *Private:* NHL; HABS.

Brooklyn. **WYCKOFF-BENNETT HOMESTEAD**, 1669 E. 22nd St., 18th C.. Frame, clapboarding, shingling; 1 1/2 stories, rectangular, gabled roof, interior end chimneys, dormers, full-width front entrance porch, center entrance; much original interior paneling intact; 1890's alterations include the addition of the N wing, dormers, shingling, columns, and brick foundation; moved. Excellent and rare area example of 18th C. domestic architecture. *Private.*

Brooklyn. **WYCKOFF, PIETER, HOUSE**, 5902 Canarsie Lane, 1639–1641. Frame, shingling; 1 1/2 stories, modified rectangle, gabled roof with widely overhanging eaves, 2 interior brick chimneys, center entrance, gabled wing, shed addition; expanded over 17th and 18th C. Dutch Colonial. New York City's oldest house and one of oldest extant in U.S. *Municipal:* NHL; HABS.

LEWIS COUNTY

Constableville. **CONSTABLE HALL**, Off NY 26, 1810–1819. Limestone, 2-story main block on sloping site with 1-story side wings, modified rectangle, hipped and gabled roof sections, paired interior end chimneys; front side polygonal bays angled toward recessed entrance section with double-door entrance with transom and side lights, slightly projecting pedimented portico with 2-story columns; splayed stone lintels over windows; rear elevation with full exposed basement with entrance, basement and 1st-story shed porch with 1st-story balustrade, center and side entrances; original interior woodwork. Mansion with Georgian and Federal elements in frontier NY. Museum. *Private.*

Lowville. **HOUGH, FRANKLIN B., HOUSE,** Collins St., c. 1861. Brick, 2 1/2 stories, rectangular, hipped roof, interior end chimneys, central rectangular cupola, projecting gabled entrance pavilion with oculus under gable, segmental arched recessed entrance and hood molds, brick frieze with attic windows, modillion cornice under overhanging eaves. Italianate elements. Home of America's first federal forest official, Dr. Franklin B. Hough, credited with writing the first book prepared in U.S. on forestry and helping prepare the bill which created the nation's first state forest preserve (see also Adirondack Forest Preserve, NY). *Private; not accessible to the public:* NHL.

Port Leyden vicinity. **WILSON, EDMUND, HOUSE,** S of Port Leyden off NY 12 on Talcottville Rd., 1789-1803. Limestone, 2 1/2 stories, rectangular main block, gabled roof with interior end chimneys, Palladian window under each gable, 2-story front porch; small 1-story rear wing. Georgian. Residence of U.S. literary and social critic Edmund Wilson (1895-1972). *Private; not accessible to the public.*

LIVINGSTON COUNTY

Dansville vicinity. **PIONEER FARM (MCCURDY HOUSE)**, S of Dansville on NY

36, c. 1822. Brick, 2 stories, L-shaped, gabled roof with stepped gable ends, interior and exterior end chimneys, front entrance with blind fanlight and side lights, stone lintels and sills, rear wing. Federal elements. Built for James McCurdy, son of town's first settler. *Private; not accessible to the public.*

Geneseo. **HOMESTEAD, THE,** NY 39 and U.S. 20A, 19th C.. Frame, clapboarding; 3 stories, irregular massing, modified mansard roof, decorative parapet at roof deck, interior chimneys, irregularly shaped dormers, entrance portico, full-width W porch, garland panels over some 2nd-story windows, modillion and denticulated cornices; original house built, c. 1804; numerous late-19th C. additions and embellishments; little interior alterations; moved, 1874; numerous outbuildings. Eclectic. Home of locally prominent Wadsworth family, influential in developing town into agricultural community. *Private.*

Piffard. **WESTERLY,** Chandler Rd., 1850. Brick, 2 stories, L-shaped, overhanging hipped roof with deck, paired interior end chimneys, full-width portico on Ionic columns, center entrance with side lights, stone lintels and sills, side and rear wings; barns and other outbuildings, gardens. Italianate elements. Built overlooking the Genessee Valley Canal for one of the developers of the canal, Maj. William H. Spencer. *Private.*

MADISON COUNTY

Cazenovia. **LORENZO,** Ledyard St. (U.S. 20), 1807–1809 Brick, painted; 2 stories, L-shaped; low hipped roof, balustraded with front center gable; 2 pairs of interior end chimneys, center entrance with fan and side lights, front bays divided by pilasters topped by segmental arches forming a blind arcade, 1-2-story rear ell; interior spiral stairway, fine woodwork and ceiling cornices. Federal elements. Built by Col. John Linklaen, Cazenovia founder. *State:*. HABS.

Hamilton. **OLD BIOLOGY HALL,** Colgate University, 1884. Stone with brick trim, 2 stories, T-shaped, hipped roof with center intersecting gabled roof sections on each side, eyelet dormers, round arched windows, front entrance archway; alterations include addition of rectangular wing, 1906, and the division of interior space. Richardsonian Romanesque elements. *Private.*

Hamilton. **SMITH, ADON, HOUSE,** 3 Broad St., c. 1850. Brick, 2 1/2 stories, irregular shape, hipped roof sections, 4 interior chimneys, central monitor, wrap-around porch with wrought iron columns and railing, side porch, bracketed lintels; large decorative cornice brackets, some framing windows. Italian Villa. Built for realtor and bank president Adon Smith. *Municipal.*

Oneida. **ONEIDA COMMUNITY MANSION HOUSE,** Sherrill Rd., 1860. Brick, 3 stories, U-shaped; gabled, flat, and mansard roof sections; main central block with columned entrance portico with a balustraded deck, 3 arched windows, and an open hipped central cupola; 1-story balustraded porch and balcony, 4-story projecting end towers; over 400 rooms. High Victorian Italianate and Second Empire elements. Built by John Humphrey Noyes and his followers to house their perfectionist community which thrived from 1848-1880. *Private; not accessible to the public:* NHL.

MONROE COUNTY

Honeoye Falls. **LOWER MILL**, N. Main St., c. 1829. Ashlar, 3-4 1/2 stories on sloping site, modified rectangle, flat roof, several entrances, stone lintels and sills, quoins; interior with exposed beams and central hoistway; 20th C. 1-story side wing; larger side wing removed; gabled roof and one story destroyed by fire, c. 1900. Important element in area's economy during 19th C. *Municipal.*

Pittsford. **PHOENIX BUILDING**, S. Main and State Sts., Early-19th C.. Brick, 3 1/2 stories, L-shaped, gabled roof, paired interior end chimneys forming part of stepped gable ends, recessed 1st-story arches containing windows and main entrance with side lights and wide fanlight, regular fenestration, stone lintels; restored after 1963 fire. Federal. Prominent 19th–early-20th C. hotel. *Private.*

Rochester. **ANTHONY, SUSAN B., HOUSE**, 17 Madison St., Mid-19th C.. Brick, clapboarded and shingled sections under gables; 2 1/2 stories, rectangular, intersecting gabled roof sections, interior chimneys, off-center hipped entrance porch, raised basement, attic front oriel window. Combines simplified Victorian elements. Home of Susan B. Anthony (1866–1906) abolitionist, temperance worker, and leading figure in women's rights movement. *Private:* NHL.

Rochester. **BEVIER MEMORIAL BUILDING**, Washington St., 1910, Claude Bragdon, architect. Brick (Flemish bond), 4 stories, square, flat roof with parapet raised slightly over front entrance, projecting arcaded cornice, center entrance vestibule, decorative polychromatic ceramic banding above windows. Built to house Rochester Atheneaum and

Mechanics Institute School of Applied Arts. *Private.*

Rochester. **CAMPBELL-WHITTLESEY HOUSE, 123 S.** Fitzhugh St., 1835-1836, attributed to Minard Lafever, architect. Brick, 2 1/2 stories, modified rectangle, gabled roof, 4 interior side chimneys, 2-story pedimented N Ionic portico, recessed E entrance with side lights and transom; 1-story rear wing; restored Greek Revival. *Private:* HABS.

Rochester. **CHILD, JONATHAN, HOUSE AND BREWSTER-BURKE HOUSE HISTORIC DISTRICT, 37 S.** Washington St. and 130 Spring St., 1837-1838 (Jonathan Child House), mid-19th C. (Brewster-Burke House). Contains 2 houses typical of the fashionable residential district developed during city's expansion. Jonathan Child House: stuccoed brick, 2 1/2 stories, rectangular, gabled roof, N and S entrance porticos, 2-story E pedimented Corinthian portico, egg and dart cornice above frieze. Brewster-Burke House: brick, 2 stories, L-shaped, hipped roof with low cupola, wide eaves, double brackets; 1-story entrance porch with Moorish ornamentation, iron balconies, 1-story wing. Italian Villa. *Multiple private:* G.

Rochester. **CITY HALL HISTORIC DISTRICT, S.** Fitzhugh St. between Broad and W. Main Sts., 19th C.. Civic complex including 4 structures: Second Renaissance Revival county courthouse; City Hall and the Rochester Free Academy, both High Victorian Gothic structures with steep mansard towers designed by A. J. Warner, local architect; and Early Gothic Revival St. Luke's Church. Architectural highpoints of 19th C. are represented. Diverse structures comprise well-related group of buildings. *Multiple public/private:* HABS.

Rochester. **DAISY FLOUR MILL, INC.,** 1880 Blossom Rd., 19th–20th C.. Mill complex includes flour mill and 3 houses; 1848 mill is 2 1/2-story gabled structure with gabled cupola and board-and-batten siding (added 1966), 1912 addition, silo, and loading dock; houses, built 1840's–1890's, are 1 1/2–2-story gabled structures with clapboarding and board-and-batten siding. City's only remaining working flour mill; dates from era (c. 1825–1860) when Rochester was the nation's leading center for flour milling. *Multiple private.*

Rochester. **EASTMAN, GEORGE, HOUSE,** 900 East Ave., 1905, J. Foster Warner, architect. Concrete, 2 1/2 stories, modified L shape, dormered gambrel roof, numerous chimneys, front balustraded roof section with balustraded deck, 2-story pedimented Corinthian entrance portico, balustraded and columned side porticos, bay windows, quoins, modillion cornice. Georgian Revival. Built for George Eastman, whose invention and manufacture of dry plate film, flexible film, and the Kodak box camera revolutionized photography. Became photographic museum, 1948. *Private:* NHL.

Rochester. **ELY, HERVEY, HOUSE,** 138 Troup St., 1837. Brick, stuccoing; 2 1/2-story rectangular main block with 1-story side wings; gabled, flat, and low pitched roof sections; interior end chimneys, dormers, mutule cornice with triglyph frieze, front 2-story tetrastyle Doric pedimented portico, off-center entrance with transom and pilasters; real ell; original interior woodwork with plasterwork and marble fireplaces; carriage house connected to main house, 1920. Excellent example of Greek Revival house. *Private.*

Rochester. **FEDERAL BUILDING (OLD POST OFFICE)** , N. Fitzhugh and Church Sts., 1885–1889, Harvey and Charles Ellis, architects. Metal frame, brown sandstone facing; 3 1/2 stories, modified rectangle, gabled roof with cross gables, interior chimneys, connected gabled and shed dormers, modillion cornice sections, front entrance with stone porch, 2 round arched side entrances, rectangular and round arched openings; front corner polygonal towers, each with bell-cast polygonal roof; corner 4 1/2-story tower with pyramidal roof; interior rectangular courtyard with skylight surrounded by arcades with wrought iron railings, fine detailed courtroom; rear extensions 1893, 1907. Richardsonian Romanesque. Early use of metal frame in building designed by Harvey Ellis, who had worked for H. H. Richardson; Supervising Architect for the Treasury Department was Mifflin E. Bell. *Federal/GSA:* HABS.

Rochester. **FIRST PRESBYTERIAN CHURCH,** 101 S. Plymouth Ave., 1871, Andrew J. Warner, architect. Sandstone, 1 1/2 stories, modified L shape, gabled roof with iron cresting and patterned shingling, 4-story bell tower with pointed arched louvered windows and octagonal spire, recessed pointed arched entrance, large tracery window over entry; 2-story gabled church office wing; interior walnut woodwork. High Victorian Gothic. Built by prominent local architect. Third church building for city's oldest congregation. *Private.*

Rochester. **FIRST UNIVERSALIST CHURCH,** SE corner of S. Clinton Ave. and Court St., 1907–1908, Claude F. Bragdon, architect. Brick, 2 stories, modified Greek cross shape, gabled and hipped roof sections, central tower section with low octagonal clerestory and cupola, 2 arcaded and gabled entrance porches, round and segmental arched windows, stone and tile trim, corbeled cornices, rectangular rear wing. Richardsonian Romanesque elements. Outstanding example of architect's work. *Private:* HABS.

Rochester. **GENESEE LIGHTHOUSE,** 70 Lighthouse St., 1822. Limestone, 80' high, octagonal, interior iron spiral staircase leads to observation deck. Gabled 2 1/2-story brick house (1863) replaced earlier stone house. Illustrative of state's earliest light stations; in operation until 1902. *Federal/USCG.*

Rochester. **LEOPOLD STREET SHULE,** 30 Leopold St., 1886. Brick, 2 stories on high stone basement, rectangular, gabled roof, center shed entrance porch with central barrel vault, slightly projecting entrance section under segmental pediment and flanked by 2 reverse scrolls to form a curvilinear gable; gallery, basilica plan. Built to accommodate the Eastern European Jewish immigrants who formed a tightly knit neighborhood here after the Civil War. Oldest Orthodox Jewish synagogue remaining in Rochester. *Private.*

Rochester. **MT. HOPE-HIGHLAND HISTORIC DISTRICT,** Bounded roughly by the Clarissa St. Bridge, Genesee River, Grove and Mt. Hope Aves., plus the entire Highland Park properties, 19th–20th C.. Residential area including numerous large and moderate-sized dwellings and landscaped open spaces. Picturesque architectural styles of 2nd half of 19th C. represented. Notable elements are the 4 Romantic Downing cottages; the Gothic Revival Warner Castle, designed by A. J. Warner after Scotland's Castle Douglas; the Mt. Hope Cemetery; and Highland Park. Land bought by George Ellwanger and Patrick Barry and developed as Mt. Hope Botanical Gardens. Victorian character of area established by personal preferences of developers as influenced by the popular trend of the era. *Multiple public/private.*

Rochester. **OLD STONE WAREHOUSE,** 1 Mt. Hope Ave., 1822. Sandstone, 4 stories, trapezoidal, flat roof, wooden lintels over doors and rectangular windows; exposed interior wood framing and stone walls; 6-story SW addition, 1864. Built at original junction of Erie Canal and canal feeder. Built by John Gilbert and Erie Canal financier Myron Halley. Converted to foundry by 1838, reverted back to warehouse, late-19th C.–early-20th C. *Municipal:* HABS.

Rochester. **POWERS BUILDING,** W. Main and State Sts., 1869–1870, Andrew J. Warner, architect. Metal frame, stone facing; 8 stories, rectangular, flat roof, corner and side storefront entrances; 2nd–5th-floor corner bays with round or flat arches and vermiculated stone quoins, other bays with flattened arched windows and Corinthian half columns; bracketed cornice above 5th story, 6th–8th stories with shingling and 6th- and 7th-story mansard roof profile with heavy hooded dormers, off-center 3-tier rectangular tower; interior court with cast iron stairway; 7th story added 1872; 8th story added 1874; 1st story altered 20th C. Second Empire elements. City's first fireproof structure; built for financier Daniel Powers, who wanted to own the city's tallest building. *Private:* HABS.

Rochester. **ROCHESTER SAVINGS BANK,** 40 Franklin St., 1927, McKim, Mead and White, architects. Steel frame, Kato stone facing; 4 stories, V-shaped, flat roof, parapet; corner entrance recessed under tall round arch with stylized floral ornament, name inscribed above; cornice above 3rd story with 3-story-tall pilasters, 1st- and 2nd-story windows under tall round arches, 4th-story round arched arcade; interior imitates basilican plan church with side aisles and apse using many colored marbles; mosaic arch, pillars, ceiling, and glass mosaic designed by Ezra Winter. Eclectic. Fine example of the work of McKim, Mead, and White. *Private.*

Rochester. **THIRD WARD HISTORIC DISTRICT,** Roughly bounded by Adams, and Peach Sts., I 490, and both sides of Troup and Fitzhugh Sts., 19th-20th C.. Residential area containing approximately 126 structures, the majority of which are dwellings of various scale and sophistication in those styles popular during the Greek Revival and Victorian eras. Notable are the Greek Revival Campbell-Whittlesey and Hervey Ely Houses (see also Campbell-Whittlesey House, NY and Hervey Ely House, NY), and the Italian Villas on Fitzhugh St. Developed between 1830 and 1880 as Rochester's most elite residential section; home ofsuch notables as the international investor Leonard Jerome, father of Jennie Jerome Churchill, the mother of Winston Churchill. *Multiple public/private.*

Scottsville. **ROCHESTER STREET HISTORIC DISTRICT,** 19th C.. 19th C. dwellings in variety of styles including Greek Revival and the Victorian styles. Majority built between 1830's and 1840's during town's growth period. Insulated village section retains 19th C. character. *Multiple private.*

MONTGOMERY COUNTY

Amsterdam. **GUY PARK,** W. Main St., 1773. Coursed rubble, 2 1/2 stories over high basement, U-shaped, hipped and flat roof sections, paired interior end chimneys, skylight, bracketed cornice, front center entrance with transom; rear center entrance with transom and side lights; U-shaped 1-story shed porch with balustrade; rear wing entrance, stone water table, stone and brick quoins; wings added 1850's; roof and cornice altered; 20th C.

restoration; site includes a lock and structures associated with the Barge Canal. Georgian and Greek Revival elements. Built for Guy Johnson, Superintendent of Indian Affairs in 1774, and Loyalist who rallied Indians to British cause during American Revolution; located in transportation network with railroad tracks in front and canal (completed 1918) behind. *State:* HABS.

Amsterdam vicinity. **ERIE CANAL,** 6 mi. W of Amsterdam on NY 5S, 19th-early-20th C.. Ditch and only extant locks of original Erie Canal, aqueduct and lock grocery from 1840's, and lock of the 1903-1918 New York Barge Canal that followed sections of the Erie remain of the 363-mi. Erie Canal (1817-1825), which was 44' wide at top and 4' deep, with 88 locks; enlarged 1835, 1862; deepened 1897-1898. First major U.S. canal project and most important engineering undertaking of early-19th C.; established a vital and influential link between the Great Lakes and the Atlantic, between east and west, and transported people, produce, and manufactured goods throughout 19th C. *Multiple public/private:* NHL; HAER.

Fonda vicinity. **CAUGHNAWAGA INDIAN VILLAGE SITE,** 1666-1693. Mohawk-Caughnawaga village site; evidence of structure locations and shape, stockade, storage pits, and village plan. Investigated by John S. Clark, 1877; New York State Archaeological Association, 1948; John Swart, 1950 and 1957; and Thomas Grassman. Artifacts preserved and exhibited at the Mohawk-Caughnawaga Museum at the base of the village hill site. *Private.*

Fort Johnson. **FORT JOHNSON,** Jct. of NY 5 and 67, c. 1749. Stone, 2 1/2 stories, rectangular, hipped roof, 4 interior chimneys, hipped dormers, entrance portico with open pediment, triglyphs of frieze, rear entrance, 1st-story paneled shutters. Georgian. Home of soldier and Indian agent Sir William Johnson, who was largely responsible for keeping the Iroquois allied with the British during the French and Indian War. *Private:* NHL; HABS.

Palatine. **PALATINE CHURCH,** Mohawk Tpke., 1770. Stone, 1 story, rectangular, gambrel roof; 2-tiered octagonal end tower on square base, with louvered lancet opening and bell-cast roof; large round arched windows, oculus in gable end, center side entrance with fanlight, modillion cornice; altered. Georgian. Built for pioneer German settlement. Museum. *Private:* HABS.

Palatine Bridge. **WAGNER, WEBSTER, HOUSE,** E. Grand St., 1876, Horatio Nelson White, architect. Frame, flush siding; 1–2 1/2 stories, modified rectangle, mansard and gabled roof sections, interior chimney, gabled dormers, denticulated modillion cornice, front side 3-story tower with main entrance, front and side balustraded veranda with projecting section at entrance with pendants, tower with pointed arched windows, side 2-story bay, side 2-level porch with bracing, rear 2-story service wing with 1-story wing attached. Second Empire. Built for Webster Wagner, state senator, and inventor of the Wagner sleeping and drawing room cars and elevated ventilation panel for railroad car roofs. *Private.*

Palatine Bridge vicinity. **PALATINE BRIDGE FREIGHT HOUSE,** E of Palatine Bridge on NY 5, Mid-19th C. Coursed rubble limestone, 1 story, rectangular, gabled roof, end entrance, stone lintels over rectangular openings; openings altered. Example of functional mid-19th C. storage house; located on Utica and Schenectady RR. line. *Private.*

St. Johnsville. **FORT KLOCK,** 2 mi. E of St.

Johnsville on NY 5, 1750. Stone, 1 1/2 story over full basement on riverside, L-shaped, gabled roof sections, central chimney, reconstructed wooden stairs, loopholes; restored. Unusual example of mid-18th C. fur trading post and fortified stone house; used as refuge by area settlers during American Revolution; Gen. Robert Van Rensselaer repulsed combined British and Indian raiding party in adjacent field, Oct. 19, 1780. *Private:* NHL; HABS.

NASSAU COUNTY

Hempstead. **ST. GEORGE'S CHURCH,** 319 Front St., 1822-1823. Frame, clapboarding; 1 1/2 stories, modified rectangle, gabled roof, interior end chimney, front slightly projecting square tower with double-door entrance with fanlight, clockfaces and octagonal belfry with louvered openings; 2 levels of side windows, lower level rectangular, upper level round arched; interior box seats, galleries; chancel extended 1856; 2 entrances in re-entrant angles of front tower added; offices and educational facility added to rear 1949 and 1958. Federal. Design attributed to local resident, Timothy Clowes. *Private:* HABS.

Hicksville. **HEITZ PLACE COURTHOUSE,** Heitz Pl., 1894-1895. Frame, clapboarding; 2 stories, L-shaped, hipped roof sections, front gable with cornice and eave return, round arched window in gable, pedimented 2nd-floor window, open domed belfry with thin turned posts on square base above gable, front porch with turned columns and pediment, narrow applied pilasters on 1st and 2nd floors; 1-story brick jail connected to rear. Eclectic elements in vernacular building. Served community's judicial purposes until 1967; now a museum. *Municipal.*

Oyster Bay. **BEEKMAN, JAMES WILLIAM, HOUSE (THE CLIFFS),** West Shore Rd., 1863–1864, Henry G. Harrison, architect. Frame, clapboarding; 2 1/2 stories, rectangular with projections, gabled and hipped roofs, front entrance porch and separate porch section, 2nd-floor alternating hipped dormers with transverse gabled sections, 4 rear chimneys, 2 intersecting jerkinheads; interior coffered and patterned wooden ceiling, polychromatic mosaic and wood floors, and ornate woodwork. Early Gothic Revival. Formal gardens, stable, carriage house, greenhouse, archeological site with shell/black soil midden. Built for JamesWilliam Beekman, prominent state politician and philanthropist. Excellent example of the picturesque quality favored by the mid-19th C. wealthy. *Private.*

Oyster Bay. **RAYNHAM HALL,** 20 W. Main St., 18th–19th C.. Frame, clapboarding; 1 1/2–2 1/2 stories, modified L shape, gabled roof sections, interior chimneys, window bays, porches; original 1738 structure enlarged, 1851 and 1855. First structure built for Samuel Townsend, merchant and importer and descendant of early settler John Townsend. Typical domestic vernacular design. *Municipal.*

Oyster Bay. **SEAWANHAKA CORINTHIAN YACHT CLUB,** Centre Island Rd., 1891–1892, Robert W. Gibson, architect. Frame, clapboarding; rectangular, hipped roof with deck and railing intersected by 4 center gabled sections, gabled dormers, 2 chimneys, 1-story veranda with octagonal sections at entrance and front corners; portions of veranda enclosed, 1960 and 1964; frame outbuilding constructed, 1967. Georgian Revival. Founded by William L. Swan, 1871. Merged with another NY yacht club to become prominent international small boat facility. Sponsors Seawanhaka

International Challenge Cup for Small Yachts. *Private.*

Oyster Bay, Long Island. **SAGAMORE HILL NATIONAL HISTORIC SITE,** End of Cove Neck Rd., 1884-1885, Lamb and Rich, architects. Brick, frame, shingling; 2 1/2 stories, modified T shape, gabled roof sections, interior chimneys, gabled dormers, gabled portecochere with entrance, front bay window, side polygonal veranda. Queen Anne. Built for Theodore Roosevelt as his permanent home; visited by many national and international figures during and after his presidency (1901-1909); he died here Jan. 6, 1919. *Federal/NPS:* HABS.

Port Washington. **SOUSA, JOHN PHILIP, HOUSE (WILDBANK)**, 14 Hicks Lane, Sands Point, c. 1907. Brick, stuccoed; 2 1/2 stories, modified rectangle, gabled roof, hipped dormers, exterior end chimneys; painted mural in one room; garage building. Eclectic. Home of John Philip Sousa, conductor, director of the U.S. Marine Corps Band, and composer, whose works include "Stars and Stripes Forever" and the "Washington Post March." *Private; not accessible to the public:* NHL.

Roslyn. **MAIN STREET HISTORIC DISTRICT,** Main St. from N. Hempstead Tpke. to E. Broadway, including Tower St. and portions of Glen Ave. and Paper Mill Rd., 17th-20th C.. Old village section containing mostly late-19th C. residential structures, commercial building cluster, and park area. Post-Civil War architectural styles represented in frame-constructed buildings. Village settled mid-17th C. as port of entry for Hempstead; Main St. became section of connecting road between 2 settlements. Early-18th C. development due to paper industry; 19th C. building boom. Area maintains 19th C. character. *Multiple private.*

NEW YORK COUNTY

BROOKLYN BRIDGE, *Reference—see Kings County*

New York. **ADMIRAL'S HOUSE (COMMANDING GENERAL'S QUARTERS),** Governors Island, 1840. Brick, 2 stories over basement on sloping site, rectangular, gabled roof sections, interior end chimneys, denticulated cornice; frame hexastyle 2-story portico with roof balustrade on front and rear facades; rear portico supported on arched loggia with double stairway to main level, front center entrance with transom and side lights flanked by pilasters, side wing with wrap-around screened porch with iron roof balustrade, stone lintels. Federal and Greek Revival elements. Residence of U.S. Army commanders until 1966 when the island was relinquished to the Coast Guard. *Federal/USCG; not accessible to the public.*

New York. **ARTHUR, CHESTER A., HOUSE,** 123 Lexington Ave., 1881–1886. Brownstone, painted; 5 stories, rectangular, flat roof, 3 bays wide, segmental arched windows, off-center doorway, bracketed cornice; 1st- and 2nd-floor storefronts, upper floors converted to apartments. Home of Chester A. Arthur, 21st U.S. President, responsible for civil service reform; location where Arthur was sworn in as President following death of President Garfield from an assassin's bullet, Sept. 1881. *Private; not accessible to the public:* NHL.

New York. **BIALYSTOKER SYNAGOGUE,** 7–13 Willett St., 1826. Random ashlar, 2 1/2 stories, rectangular, gabled roof, wood cornice articulates pedimented end with lunette; 3 front double-door entrances, each with fanlight; round arched openings. Federal. Erected as Methodist church in semirural area; became a synagogue with influx of Jewish population in 1905. *Private.*

New York. **BLACKWELL HOUSE,** Welfare Island, 1796-1804. Frame, clapboarding; 2 1/2-story main block with 1 1/2-story side wings, modified rectangle, gabled roof sections, gabled dormers, front center entrance with 1-story balustraded shed porch; side wings, each with front entrance; rear entrance with pedimented portico; side wings and portico added. Federal elements. Island previously called Blackwell's Island for family who owned it nearly 150 years; house built for James Blackwell when the island was open country. *Municipal; not accessible to the public.*

New York. **BLOCK HOUSE, THE,** Governors Island, 1843, Martin E. Thompson, architect. Stone base, brick; 2 stories over high basement, square, gabled roof, 2 chimneys, denticulated cornice; front center entrance with transom, pediment, and pilasters within stone architrave, tripartite window above with balcony; stone lintels, sills, and water table; entrance door added. Greek Revival. *Federal/USCG.*

New York. **CARNEGIE, ANDREW, MANSION,** 2 E. 91st St., 1900-1901, Babb, Cook, and Willard, architects. Brick, 3 1/2 stories, rectangular, balustraded hipped roof, high paneled interior chimneys, projecting center pavilion with balustraded balcony over center entrance, coursed rusticated stone ground floor with round arched windows, elaborate stone 2nd- and 3rd-floor window surrounds, quoins, dormers with segmental pediments; extravagant interior which included sterling silver plumbing; altered. Georgian Revival. Built for over $1 million for Andrew Carnegie, industrialist and philanthropist who made almost $500 million through the sale of his large and successful steel company in 1901, after which he devoted his efforts to establishing public libraries and promoting research and education. *Private:* NHL.

New York. **CARNEGIE HALL,** 7th Ave., 56th to 57th Sts., 1891, William B. Tuthill, architect. Brick, 6 stories with 15-story corner tower, rectangular, flat roof with small gabled sections, parapet with balustraded sections; front center 5-bay entrance arcade surmounted by similar 2-story window arcade, each with articulating pilasters; round arched windows of different sizes arranged in groups of 2's, 3's, and 4's; decorative brick panels and blind arches and arcades, 4th-story row of pilasters surmounted by wide ornate frieze; projecting cornice with frieze above 5th story; interior auditorium with excellent acoustics, recital hall, and numerous studios and shops. Second Renaissance Revival. Built for the Oratorio Society, principally with funds invested by Andrew Carnegie; became center for American and musical activities featuring artists such as Tchaikovsky, Paderewski, Arturo Toscanini and the New York Philharmonic Symphony Orchestra, and Benny Goodman. *Municipal:* NHL.

New York. **CASTLE CLINTON NATIONAL MONUMENT,** South Ferry, 1811. Harbor fortification, adapted to numerous uses. Built just before War of 1812 to protect Ney York; served as important 19th C. immigration depot; castle garden leased by New York as place of public entertainment; housed the New York City Aquarium, 1896–1941. Restored. *Federal/NPS.*

New York. **CASTLE WILLIAMS (THE TOWER)** , Governors Island, 1807, Jonathan

Williams, engineer. Sandstone ashlar fort; 3 stories, semicircular, parapet, flat roof, open interior courtyard, 3 tiers of gunports, 2 interior stone tower staircases; repaired 1833, 1836; 1912 additions include concrete galleries facing courtyard. Impressive fortification which helped dissuade the British fleet from attacking NY during the War of 1812. *Federal/USCG.*

New York. **CENTRAL PARK,** Bounded by Central Park S., 5th Ave., Central Park W., 110th St., 1859-1876, Frederick Law Olmsted and Calvert Vaux, landscape architects. Wooded park with paths, roads, bridges, and lakes. Country's first urban park; outstanding landscape architecture provided impetus to national park movement and set example for other cities. *Municipal:* NHL.

New York. **CENTRAL SYNAGOGUE (CONGREGATION AHAWATH CHESED-SHAAR HASHOMAYIM)** , 646-652 Lexington Ave., 1870-1872, Henry Fernbach, architect. Stone, 2 stories, rectangular, gabled and flat roof sections, 2 flanking octagonal front towers with globes above, polychrome stone banding, central rose window, round arched windows with multicolor voussoirs, cornice corbeling; interior features cast iron columns, wall stencils, and Islamic details. High Victorian approach with eclectic Islamic elements. Oldest continuously-used synagogue in city. *Private:* NHL.

New York. **CHAMBER OF COMMERCE BUILDING,** 65 Liberty St., 1901, James Barnes Baker, architect. Marble, 4 1/2 stories, square, semielliptical roof sections, round arched dormers, front side entrance, 2nd front entrance recessed under segmental arch; 1st story deeply coursed, smooth marble above; 2-story-tall Ionic columns extend from 2nd-3rd stories, framing 3rd-story oculi, denticulated modillion cornice above 3rd story; interior Great Hall modeled on Guild Halls of London, contains paintings by many noted American artists; statuary removed; addition above main entrance. Erected in Beaux-Arts Classical style to symbolize the importance of the Chamber of Commerce in the community. *Municipal.*

New York. **CHAPEL OF THE GOOD SHEPHERD,** Welfare Island, 1888-1889, Frederick C. Withers. Brick, 1 story, modified rectangle, gabled and shed roof sections, square cupola with flared pyramidal roof, rear corner tower with broached spire, 2 front entrances through shed vestibule, front gable with rose window under wide arch, semicircular apse, pointed arched openings, brownstone trim. High Victorian Gothic church designed by English architect Frederick C. Withers. *Public.*

New York. **CHARLTON-KING-VANDAM HISTORIC DISTRICT,** 19th C.. Contains late-18th C. dwellings and excellent 19th C. Federal and Greek Revival town houses. Well preserved cross section of early New York architecture. City mapped, 1797; developed, 1820-1829 by John Jacob Astor on land of Aaron Burr's estate "Richmond Hill," once George Washington's headquarters and Vice-Presidential mansion for John Adams. *Multiple private.*

New York. **CHURCH OF THE HOLY APOSTLES,** 300 9th Ave., 1846-1848, Minard Lafever, architect. Brick, 1 story, cross-shaped, gabled roof sections, shed dormers; front center projecting square tower with oculi below bellcast bracketed cornice sections, louvered belfry, and tall spire; center entrance under round arch; stained glass windows by William Jay Bolton; enlarged 1854; transepts designed by Charles Babcock added 1858; 1908 alterations. Eclectic. Provides welcome contrast in scale to surrounding tall apartment complexes. *Private.*

New York. **CHURCH OF THE TRANSFIGURATION AND RECTORY,** 1 E. 29th St., 1849. Brick, 1 story, modified L shape, gabled roof sections, dormers, 3-story square buttressed tower with main entrance with semicircular glass canopy, 2-story octagonal tower located at angle between nave and transept, semicircular apse, pointed arched openings with drip molds, brownstone trim; additions and alterations begun 1852, including entrance tower and transept; Gothic Revival 4 1/2-story brick rectory (1849–1850) with brownstone front facing; lich gate designed by Frederick C. Withers, 1896; Lady Chapel, 1906; St. Joseph's Mortuary Chapel, 1908. Gothic Revival. Has played prominent role in city's life; linked to theatrical community. *Private.*

New York. **CITY HALL,** Broadway and Chambers St., 1803–1812, James Mangin and John McComb, Jr., architects. Stone, 2 stories over high basement, U-shaped, hipped roof sections, center 2 1/2-story pavilion with high central cupola and end chimneys, projecting end pavilion, round arched 1st-story and pavilion windows, pilasters between bays on pavilions, modillion cornice, balustraded roof, 1st-floor Ionic loggia; central rotunda beneath dome; restored, early-20th C., 1950's. Fine classical design based on European Renaissance and Baroque precedents. Third city hall, long considered one of the most beautiful buildings in city; scene of many of city's historic events. *Municipal:* NHL.

New York. **CITY HOSPITAL,** Welfare Island, 1858–1870, James Renwick, architect. Granite, 4 1/2 stories, U-shaped, mansard roof sections, gabled dormers, central pavilion with parapet and convex mansard roof, twin stairways lead to center entrance under Tudor arch with vermiculated voussoirs, quoins, stone lintels and sills, belt courses, side octagonal tower. Second

Empire. Designed to be the largest and most modern hospital in America by noted architect James Renwick. *Private; not accessible to the public.*

New York. **COOPER UNION,** Cooper Square, 7th St., and 4th Ave., 1859. Wrought iron frame, brownstone; 7 stories, trapezoidal, flat roof, front center tower with clock under false pediment; 2-story columned, triple arched projecting center entrance pavilion; single, double, and triple round arched windows framed by pilasters. Italian Renaissance Revival. Built to house Peter Cooper's pioneer effort to provide free public education; served for a century as public forum for important issues. Site of Lincoln address which established him as serious contender for Presidency, Feb. 27, 1860. *Private:* NHL; HAER.

New York. **DAKOTA APARTMENTS,** 1 W. 72nd St., 1884, Henry J. Hardenbergh, architect. Brick, 7 stories with 2 attic stories, rectangular, gabled and pyramidal roof sections, interior chimneys, numerous gabled dormers, entrance through archway with iron gate leads to I-shaped central courtyard with corner entrances, cornice and terra cotta belt course with diaper pattern above 2nd story, oriels, small balconies, rectangular and round arched windows, quoins; roof replaced. Eclectic. Built for Edward S. Clark, who led the development of the Upper West Side area; named after the Dakota Indian territory to reflect its distance from the city's center. *Private:* HABS.

New York. **DYCKMAN, WILLIAM, HOUSE,** 4881 Broadway, 1783. Brick, stone, partially clapboarded; 1 1/2 stories, rectangular, bell-cast gambrel roof, 3 interior chimneys, front and rear full-width balustraded porches, frame gabled wing. Dutch colonial elements. City's only 18th C. farmhouse. *Municipal:* NHL; HABS.

New York. **FEDERAL HALL NATIONAL MEMORIAL,** Wall and Nassau Sts., 1842. Stone, 2 stories, rectangular, gabled roof, full-width front and rear pedimented Doric entrance porticos, center entrances, full Doric entablature, recessed side windows, rotunda. Greek Revival. Built as U.S. Customshouse on site of City Hall (1703), later renamed Federal Hall; original building was scene of trial and acquittal of printer John Peter Zenger (1735), meeting place of the Stamp Act Congress (1765) and the Continental Congress (1785-1788), and site of inauguration of President George Washington (1789); served as first seat of the new Federal government (1788-1790). Museum. *Federal/NPS.*

New York. **FEDERAL OFFICE BUILDING (U.S. APPRAISERS' WAREHOUSE)**, 641 Washington St., 1892-1899, Willoughby J. Edbrooke, architect. Brick, granite trim; 10 stories, irregular quadrangle, flat roof, 5-tier structure with varied fenestration and string courses marking each tier, Syrian arched ground-floor openings, paired 3rd-7th-floor windows grouped in recessed round arched vertical bays, corbel tabeling, pilasters between bays, broadly rounded corners neatly recessed; interior structure of metal columns and arched floor slabs. Commercial building with Richardsonian Romanesque elements. *Federal/GSA.*

New York. **FIREHOUSE, ENGINE COMPANY 31,** 87 Lafayette St., 1895, Napoleon Le Brun and Sons, architects. Ashlar 1st story and corner tower, roman brick; 2 1/2 stories, rectangular, steeply hipped roof, iron cresting, parapet, gabled dormers with paired and tripartite windows, corner polygonal 2-story tower with polygonal roof with slight kick, front with 3 basket-handle arched openings for fire engines, pedestrian entrances; ornamental detail includes shells, dolphins, and floral wreaths. Chateauesque. One of several firehouses commissioned by city c. 1900; similar in scale and detail to contemporary private mansions on 5th Ave. *Municipal.*

New York. **FIREHOUSE, ENGINE COMPANY 33,** 44 Great Jones St., 1898, Ernest Flagg and Walter B. Chambers, architects. Coursed stone base, brick; 4 1/2 stories, rectangular, modified mansard roof with skylight, paired bracketed cornice with anthemion cresting, 2 arched entrances for fire engines, front side pedestrian entrance, center 2nd–4th-story windows recessed under round arch with stone voussoirs, drip mold and center cartouche, 2nd-story iron balcony, pediment above 3rd-story center window. Eclectic. Designed by Ernest Flagg in collaboration with his junior partner, Walter B. Chambers. *Municipal.*

New York. **FIRST NATIONAL CITY BANK (MERCHANT'S EXCHANGE)** , 55 Wall St., 1842, Isaiah Rogers (lower half); 1907, McKim, Mead, and White (upper half). Granite ashlar, 8 stories, quadrilateral, flat roof, denticulated cornices above 4th story and 8th story, parapet; 2 superimposed colonnades, each with 3-story-tall columns, Ionic below and Corinthian above; interior banking hall with coffered ceiling. Greek Revival and Neo-Classical Revival. First 4 stories built 1836–1842 for the Merchant's Exchange; upper 4 stories built for the National City Bank; fine example of unified design dating from 2 classical revival periods. *Private.*

New York. **FORT JAY,** Governor's Island, 1794. Complex of 2-story brick officers' quarters surrounding a square courtyard and enclosed by octagonal breastworks and dry moat. Built in preparation for war with France; rebuilt in 1806 as Fort Columbus; resumed original name, 1904. *Federal/USCG.*

New York. **FOUNDER'S HALL, THE ROCKEFELLER UNIVERSITY,** 66th St. and York Ave., 1905-1906, Shepley, Rutan, and Coolidge, architects. Steel frame, brick, limestone; 5 stories over high basement, flat roof, parapet, denticulated cornice, front double-door entrance with small 1-story distyle Ionic portico; Welch Hall added to rear, 1927; enclosed walkway added to connect building to isolation pavilion, hospital, and Flexner Hall. Neo-Classical Revival elements. First laboratory building of the Rockefeller Institute for Medical Research, founded in 1901 by industrialist and philanthropist, JohnD. Rockefeller. *Private:* NHL.

New York. **GENERAL GRANT NATIONAL MEMORIAL,** Riverside Dr. and W. 122nd St., 1897, John H. Duncan, architect. Granite ashlar, Neo-Classical Revival monument featuring a rectangular base with front Doric tetrastyle entrance portico and projecting cornice, and surmounted by a large colonnaded drum with modified conical roof; white marble interior contains the sarcophagi of Ulysses S. Grant, Union Army commander (1863-1865) and U.S. President (1869-1877), and his wife. *Federal/NPS:* HABS.

New York. **GOVERNOR'S HOUSE,** Governors Island, Early-18th C.. Brick, 2 stories, modified Greek cross shape, gabled and hipped roof sections with pedimented gable ends, front gable louvered lunette, interior chimney, center front entrance with 1-story square porch with denticulated cornice and Ionic columns; rear side addition with garage and pavilion. Georgian. After late-17th C. British capture of New Amsterdam, island was assigned to the English governors of the province; house probably built c. 1702 as gubernatorial mansion for Lord Cornbury. *Federal/USCG.*

New York. **GRACE CHURCH AND DEPENDENCIES,** Broadway, 10th St., and 4th Ave., 1840's, James Renwick, Jr., architect. Complex of Gothic Revival ecclesiastical buildings featuring Grace Church: marble, modified rectangle, gabled roof; square front tower with belfry, corner pinnacles, and tall octagonal spire; gabled main entrance at base of tower, crenelated parapet, pinnacled buttresses, tracery windows, stained glass; adjacent chantry added. Rectory and marble-faced brick row of dependencies (1882-1911) follow Gothic theme with pinnacles, buttresses, and tracery windows. One of the first serious Gothic Revival works in the U.S., and the first work of Renwick's career. *Private.*

New York. **HAMILTON GRANGE NATIONAL MEMORIAL,** 287 Convent Ave., 1801, John McComb Jr., architect. Frame, clapboarding; 2 stories, rectangular, hipped roof, interior chimneys, triglyph frieze; 2 front entrances at sides, each with transom; front center bay window, full-width 1-story balustraded porch; altered; moved 1889. Federal elements. Home of Alexander Hamilton, a major draftsman of the Constitution, co-author of *The Federalist*, and architect of early American fiscal policy as first U.S. Secretary of the Treasury. *Federal/NPS.*

New York. **HAUGHWOUT, E. V., BUILDING,** 488-492 Broadway, 1857, J. P. Gaynor, architect. Mason bearing wall construction, cast iron; rectangular, 5 stories, ground-floor storefronts, recessed rectangular windows set in round arched frames set between Corinthian pilasters on each level; virtually unchanged. Italian Renaissance Revival. Employed first suspended cable elevator with automatic safety devices. *Private.*

New York. **HENDERSON PLACE TERRACE,**

Henderson Pl., c. 1882. Group of 3-story town houses featuring pseudo-mansard roofs with pedimented dormers, corner towers, projecting window bays; and decorative paneling; 24 of the original 32 remain. Excellent Victorian block built to provide housing for persons of moderate means. *Private.*

New York. **HIGH BRIDGE AQUEDUCT AND WATER TOWER (AQUEDUCT BRIDGE AND WATER TOWER)**, Harlem River at W. 170th St. and High Bridge Park (also in Bronx County), 1839–1848 (aqueduct), David B. Douglas, John B. Jervis, engineers; 1872 (water tower). 1420'-long, 138'-high ashlar and steel bridge across 630'-wide Harlem River, carried on piers with arched spans of 50'–80'; 27' wide, 18' wide inside parapet walls with pedestrian walk on each side; side walls raised to accommodate a larger pipe, 1850; center arches replaced by larger steel arch, 1937; 1872 rock-faced stone octagonal water tower in Romanesque Revival style with electronic carillon installed, 1958. Part of Old Croton Aqueduct (see also Old Croton Aqueduct, NY), which provided city's first adequate water supply; structurally innovative in its system of longitudinal and transverse braced brick walls within the hollow volume enclosed by arch barrels, deck, and spandrel walls to carry heavy load. *Municipal:* HAER.

New York. **HOUSE AT 131 CHARLES ST.**, 131 Charles St., 1834. Brick, 2 1/2 stories, rectangular, low pitched roof, denticulated cornice; front off-center entrance with transom and cornice on brackets, entrance flanked by Ionic columns; front side entrance to passageway to rear, original interior woodwork; lintels and cornice added. Federal and Greek Revival elements. Well-preserved example of row house built in mid-19th C. suburban

Greenwich Village. *Private; not accessible to the public.*

New York. **INDIA HOUSE,** 1 Hanover Sq., 1852–1853, Nicholson and Galloway, architects. Brownstone, brick; 3 stories over high basement, 4–4 1/2-story side elevations; modified rectangle, flat and low pitched roof sections, interior chimney, modillion cornice, front center entrance with entablature on Corinthian columns and paneled pilasters, segmental arched pediments on brackets over 1st-story main-block windows, pediments over 2nd-story windows with shouldered architraves, 3rd-story windows with shouldered architraves, window sizes diminish in upper stories; side buildings incorporated with main block; remodeled 1924. Renaissance Revival. Originallybuilt for Hanover Bank; example of aspect of city's pre-Civil War financial district. *Private.*

New York. **J. P. MORGAN & CO. BUILDING,** 23 Wall St., 1913, Trowbridge and Livingston, architects. Steel frame, marble facing; 4 stories within 2-story facade, polygonal shape, flat roof with high parapet, modillion cornice with floral frieze, corner site with entrance in canted corner section, tall 1st-story rectangular windows with cornice with bands of molding above, 2nd-story grouped rectangular windows; large interior banking room; penthouse added 1955 to house air-conditioning equipment; interior alterations 1960's. Neo-Classical Revival. Commissioned by J. P. Morgan to house his company's banking interests. *Private.*

New York. **JEFFERSON MARKET COURTHOUSE,** 425 Avenue of the Americas, 1877, Frederick C. Withers, architect. Brick, 2–3 1/2 stories, modified triangular shape, gabled roof sections, interior chimney, entrance recessed under compound arch surmounted by crocketed gable with flanking turrets, corner tall clock tower with pyramidal roof, pointed arched openings, windows with dripstones and tracery, numerous turrets, sandstone banding, polychrome ornamentation; restored. Outstanding example of High Victorian Gothic style. Courthouse until 1945; converted for use as Greenwich Village Branch of the New York Public Library. *Municipal.*

New York. **JOHN STREET METHODIST CHURCH,** 44 John St., 1841. Brick, stuccoing; 1 story over high basement, rectangular with semicircular apse; gabled roof with pedimented front gable end with lunette, entablature below; front center double-door entrance, Palladian window above door flanked by elongated round arched windows. Federal. Site of city's earliest Methodist church; many elements reused from 1817–1818 building. *Private.*

New York. **JUDSON MEMORIAL CHURCH, CAMPANILE, AND JUDSON HALL,** Washington Sq. at Thompson St., Late-19th C., McKim, Mead and White, architects. Brick and terra cotta religious facility complex; includes 2-story Second Renaissance Revival church with pedimented ends containing decorative disks, rusticated ground floors, and bays articulated by round arched panels, some with windows; a 10-story campanile with denticulated modillion belt courses between each level and round arched panels and windows; and 6-story Judson Hall with Second Renaissance Revival elements. Church named for Edward Judson (1844–1913), important local Baptist minister interested in reforming the relationship between the Church and the urban community. *Multiple private.*

New York. **JUMEL TERRACE HISTORIC DISTRICT,** W. 160th and 162nd Sts. between St. Nicholas and Edgecombe Aves., 18th–20th

C.. Residential district surrounding 17th C. mansion contains nearly 50 row houses and 1 apartment building; features frame houses built 1882 with Italianate elements, each 2 stories over high basement, and brick and stone houses built 1890-1902 in Queen Anne, Romanesque Revival, and other late-19th C. styles; district focal point is 1765 Roger Morris-Jumel Mansion (see also Morris-Jumel Mansion, NY) with Georgian and Federal elements, built for Col. Roger Morris and used by George Washington as his headquarters during the Revolution. *Multiple private.*

New York. **KING MANOR (RUFUS KING HOUSE)**, 150th St. and Jamaica Ave., Early-18th C.. Frame, shingling; 2 1/2 stories with attic, L-shaped, gambrel and gabled roof sections, interior and interior end chimneys, main block with modillion cornice, front 1-story porch with columns; entrance with transom, 2nd-story window above with segmental arch; small side entrance porch, rear ell composed of 2 attached gabled structures; 2 sections of present ell built early-18th C.; part of main house built c. 1750; main house completed after 1805; shingling added. Colonial elements. Home (1805-1827) of Rufus King, a signer of the Constitution, U.S.senator, and ambassador to Great Britain. Museum. *Municipal:* NHL.

New York. **LIGHTHOUSE**, Welfare Island, c. 1842. Rock-faced granite octagonal shaft, 50' tall, with bracketed cornice, iron railing, and polygonal fenestrated cupola with polygonal roof and ball finial; seashell corbels below cornice, entrance with splayed keystone and gable made of stones corbeled to simulate overlapping roof tiles and with incised pointed arch, broad base tapers to main shaft size at gable level through a series of stone moldings, 2 narrow windows. Eclectic. Located on peninsula that once was a small island; allegedly built by a mental patient from the island's asylum. *Municipal; not accessible to the public.*

New York. **MADISON AVENUE FACADE OF THE SQUADRON A ARMORY,** Madison Ave. between 94th and 95th Sts., 1895, John R. Thomas, architect. Facade and corner towers of armory razed in 1966; 2 stories with front parapet rising in center gabled section; 5-story corner towers with crenelations, machicolations, and turrets of varying heights; center entrance recessed under round arched entry with terra cotta barrel vault, rectangular and round arched openings. Romantic interpretation of medieval style. City school, designed to harmonize with the facade, erected behind structure. *Municipal.*

New York. **MOORE, WILLIAM H., HOUSE,** 4 E. 54th St., 1898-1900, McKim, Mead, and White, architects. Ashlar, deeply coursed base, smooth above; 5 stories, rectangular, flat roof with balustrade, denticulated modillion cornice with scallop shell frieze, front center double-door entrance with wide architrave and center cartouche; 2nd-story balcony on consoles, each window with cornice on ancones; 3rd-story center window with segmental arched pediment and cast iron balcony, belt course above 4th story, quoins. Excellent example of Second Renaissance Revival style adapted to row house form; built for William H. Moore, a founder of the U.S. Steel Corp. and American Can Co. *Private.*

New York. **MORGAN, PIERPONT, LIBRARY,** 33 E. 36th St., 1906, Charles Follen McKim, architect. Marble, 2 stories, rectangular, hipped roof sections, parapet, front center recessed Ionic entrance portico with round arched entranceway and 6 Doric pilasters on each side; sculpture by Edward Clark Potter and Andrew

O'Connor; interior wall and ceiling murals by Harry Siddons Mowbray; interior marble columns and trim; elaborate East and West meeting rooms contain numerous personal office items of Morgan as well as vast literary and artistic collections. Second Renaissance Revival. Built as personal library for J. P. Morgan, major American financier who dominated the railroad industry after 1879, organized the U.S. Steel Co. in 1901, and helped avert a financial panic in Nov. 1907. *Private:* NHL.

New York. **MORRIS-JUMEL MANSION,** 160th St. and Edgecombe Ave., 1765. Frame, horizontal wood sheathing cut to resemble stone; 2 1/2 stories, T-shaped; hipped roof with balustraded deck, 3 interior chimneys, gabled dormers; pedimented Tuscan entrance portico with fanlight over entrance and in pediment, 2nd-story Palladian window, modilliion cornice, quoins, raised basement; octagonal rear wing; restored. Georgian. George Washington's headquarters during Battle of Harlem Heights, 1776. *Municipal:* NHL; HABS.

New York. **MOUNT MORRIS PARK HISTORIC DISTRICT,** Bounded roughly by Lenox Ave., Mount Morris Park West, and W. 124th and W. 119th Sts., 19th C.. Residential district facing city's Mount Morris Park; contains row houses, a few apartment houses, and several churches; features 3 1/2-4-story late-19th C. residences and a variety of churches in Queen Anne, Richardsonian Romanesque, and Italianate styles; notable is the row of houses on Mount Morris Park West. Opening of the "El" in 1872 made this area a suburb of New York City; speculative building began 1878; first residents were of Dutch, English, and Irish descent; German Jewish families came early-20th C.; area developed into a black neighborhood 1935–1940. *Multiple public/private.*

New York. **MUNICIPAL BUILDING**, Chambers at Centre St., 1912-1914, McKim, Mead, and White, architects. Steel frame, granite ashlar facing; 25 stories, C-shaped, low pitched roof sections with deck, antefixae, modillion cornice; central multistory tower with corner pinnacles, 2-story cupola with colonnades surmounted by copper statue, "Civic Fame," by Alexander A. Weinman; triple barrel vaulted openings based upon Roman triumphal arch form span Chambers St., at ground level multistory Corinthian columns and pilasters support entablature, 15 stories of unadorned vertically aligned windows topped by 5-story band with ornament and 3-story-tall Corinthian columns. Important example of early skyscraper style with classical elements, designed by William M. Kendall of the firm of McKim, Mead, and White. *Municipal.*

New York. **NEW YORK PUBLIC LIBRARY**, 5th Ave. and 42nd St., 1911, Carrere and Hastings, architects. Marble, 3 stories, rectangular, hipped roof with Greek cross-shaped gabled clerestory; triple arched, projecting entrance pavilion with paired Corinthian pilasters; pedimented and columned pavilion at either end of front facade, round arched 1st-story windows; classical details include quoins, columns, and sculpture. Beaux-Arts Classicism. Reference department formed by consolidation of Astor, Tilden, and Lenox libraries, 1895; circulation department made possible by gift from Andrew Carnegie, 1901. *Municipal:* NHL.

New York. **NEW YORK SHAKESPEARE FESTIVAL PUBLIC THEATER (ASTOR THEATER)**, 425 Lafayette St., 1849-1853, Alexander Saeltzer (S wing); 1856-1859, Griffith Thomas (central section) 1879-1881, Thomas Stent (N Wing), architects. Brick, stone; 4-story center block with 3-story wings, irregular shape, flat roof, stone parapet, elaborate cornice panels and molding, round arched openings articulated by cast iron columns, rusticated ground floor; skylights. Italianate. Construction illustrates progress from use of solid stone to light iron as a building material. Stylish cultural center during the 2nd half of the 19th C. *Private:* G.

New York. **OCTAGON, THE,** Welfare Island, 1839, Alexander Jackson Davis, architect. Granite ashlar, 3 1/2 stories over high basement, octagonal, flat roof, denticulated cornice with paneled frieze above 3rd story, central octagonal lantern with dome with segmental arched and gabled dormers, twin balustraded stairways lead to double-door entrance with transom, center front basement entrance; interior central cantilevered iron staircase; entrance porch and dome above lantern added 1878; alterations supervised by architect Joseph M. Dunn; brick 4th story added above cornice, frame roof now removed; 2 side wings removed 1970; under restoration. Greek Revival and Second Empire elements. Only remaining building of Alexander Jackson Davis' project for the New York City Lunatic Asylum, a prototype for his later public works. *Municipal; not accessible to the public.*

New York. **OLD MERCHANT'S HOUSE (SEABURY TREDWELL HOUSE)**, 29 E. 4th St., 1832. Brick, 3 1/2 stories, rectangular, gabled roof, 2 gabled dormers with end returns and round arched windows, modillion cornice; off-center entrance with Ionic columns in antis, rusticated surround, fanlight, and archivolt with keystone. Federal with Greek Revival elements. Building purchased 1835 by Seabury Tredwell, New York merchant, and remained in family until 1935; interior includes original furniture. Museum. *Private:* NHL; HABS; G.

New York. **PLAYERS, THE,** 16 Gramercy

Park, 1850's. Stone (ashlar), 4 stories over high basement, heavy bracketed cornice, 2nd- and 3rd-floor rectangular label molded windows, later Doric porch with elaborate iron lamps across basement and 1st floor; interior includes extensive theater library; interior and lower exterior facade redesigned for club, c. 1890, by Stanford White. Original Italianate house with Second Renaissance Revival lower floors. Residence of Edwin Booth, famous actor and founder of The Players Club, leading theatrical club in U.S. *Private:* NHL.

New York. **PUPIN PHYSICS LABORATORIES, COLUMBIA UNIVERSITY,** Broadway and 120th St., 1939. Cyclotron that first split the uranium atom in the Western Hemisphere on Jan. 25, 1939; largely unaltered, remains in operation. *Private; not accessible to the public:* NHL.

New York. **SALMAGUNDI CLUB,** 47 5th Ave., 1852-1853. Brick, smooth brownstone facing; 4 stories, rectangular, flat roof, cornice with paired acanthus leaf brackets, projecting window sills and splayed lintels, 1st-floor French windows beneath entablatures, cast iron balconies, round arched pedimented entrance, raised basement; interior includes Gothic Revival and Italianate rooms. Italianate elements. An early brownstone facade in New York, built for a wealthy executive; since 1917 served purposes of Salmagundi Club, a private artists' club to which many notable artists have belonged. *Private.*

New York. **SCHERMERHORN ROW BLOCK (NEW YORK STATE MARITIME MUSEUM BLOCK),** Block bounded by Front, Fulton, and South Sts., and Burling Slip, 19th C.. Block of brick commercial structures featuring a variety of architectural details. Notable are the block's original structures (1811-1812) on South, Fulton, and Front Sts. and the cast iron and glass storefronts of the block's later buildings. Last remaining waterfront buildings built during city's sailing era; original section built by Peter Schermerhorn, a ship's chandler; area expanded with growth of port. Under restoration. *State.*

New York. **SCOTT, GEN. WINFIELD, HOUSE,** 24 W. 12th St., 1851–1852. Brownstone ashlar, rusticated 1st story; 4 stories, rectangular, flat roof; simple front center round arched window flanked on one side by round arched entrance and on the other by a wider round arched window, each with a hood supported by consoles; segmental arched windows, each with decorative molding. Italianate. Home of Winfield Scott, general, pacificator, and 1852 Presidential candidate. *Private:* NHL.

New York. **SMALLPOX HOSPITAL,** Welfare Island, 1854–1857, attributed to James Renwick, architect. Rubble masonry, granite ashlar facing; 3 stories, U-shaped, low hipped roof sections, chimneys, corbeled crenelated parapet sections, front center 1-story entrance porch with oriel above and center crenelated section raised above roofline, 3rd-story pointed arched windows with straight jambs; central cupola and wing mansard roof sections removed; SW wing designed by York & Sawyer added 1903–1904; NE wing designed by Renwick, Aspinwall, and Owen added 1904–1905. Gothic Revival. Built as Riverside Hospital for smallpox patients; after 1886 housed the Nurses' Home and Training School. *Private; not accessible to the public.*

New York. **SMITH, ABIGAIL ADAMS, HOUSE (STABLE),** 421 E. 61st St., 1799. Fieldstone, 2 1/2 stories, H-shaped, gabled roof sections, 2-story balustraded veranda between projecting pedimented pavilions, entrance doors with side lights within original arched doorways, stone trim; converted from coachhouse and stable to residence, 1827; restored 1973-1974. Federal. Part of estate belonging briefly to Abigail Adams Smith, daughter of President John Adams; headquarters of Colonial Dames of America since 1924. *Private.*

New York. **SMITH, ALFRED E., HOUSE,** 25 Oliver St., Late-19th C.. Brick row house, 3 stories over stone basement, rectangular, flat roof, off-center entrance with transom, iron railing and 2 rear iron balconies, bracketed tin cornice; remodeled interior. Home of governor and unsuccessful Presidential candidate Alfred E. Smith, 1907-1924. *Private; not accessible to the public:* NHL.

New York. **SNIFFEN COURT HISTORIC DISTRICT,** E. 36th St., between Lexington and 3rd Aves., 1860's. Well-preserved area; 10 adjoining 2-story painted and unpainted brick structures, each with wide 2-story round arched carriage entrances, now modified; rectangular, segmental, and round arched windows. Originally stables of Murray Hill families. Area named for John Sniffen, local builder who adapted 4 standard lots to 10-lot area with common access to alley. *Private.*

New York. **SOUTH STREET SEAPORT,** Bounded by Burling (John St.) and Peck Slips, and Water and South Sts., 18th-20th C.. Five-block waterfront district containing commercial buildings and 2 piers where historic ships are moored; features predominantly late-18th-19th C. 4-5-story brick contiguous structures sited directly on the street, generally with 1st-floor commercial space with storefronts and storage and/or living space above; earlier buildings have little ornament, later 19th C. ones have some ornament including Italianate details; district under restoration. Area created mid-18th C. by landfill; 18th C. mixed wholesale/retail market became dominated by the fish market after Fulton Market opened in 1822; city's major port and commercial center late-18th–mid-19th C. *Private.*

New York. **ST. JAMES CHURCH,** 32 James St., 1837. Brick, stuccoed; 1 1/2 stories, rectangular temple-form, gabled roof, pedimented facade with Doric pillars and 2-story fluted columns in antis; 3 entrances with fine frames, full entrance; interior gallery with cast iron columns. Fine example of ecclesiastical structure of Greek Revival style, with elements derived from Minard Lafever's *The Beauties of Modern Architecture* (1835). *Private.*

New York. **ST. MARK'S HISTORIC DISTRICT,** Roughly bounded by 2nd and 3rd Aves. and E. 9th and 11th Sts., Late-18th–19th C.. Urban residential district including 2 Federal town houses, Italianate row houses, a block known as "The Triangle" attributed to James Renwick, and St. Mark's Church (see also Saint-Mark's-in-the-Bowery, NY). Area once part of Colonial governor Peter Stuyvesant's "Bouwery" or farm; retains original street pattern not conforming to city's grid and some buildings associated with the Stuyvesant family. *Multiple public/private.*

New York. **ST.-MARKS-IN-THE-BOWERY,** E. 10th St. and 2nd Ave., 1795–1799. Fieldstone, 2 stories, rectangular, gabled roof, 1-story cast iron porch with 8 Doric columns and ornamental balustraded deck, stepped square tower and spire, Florentine marble lions guarding entrance, 2 granite statues of American Indians outside porch, bull's-eye window in pediment, 2 rows of round arched windows; interior gallery; alterations include bricked-in rear Palladian windows and addition of tower (1807), spire

(1828), and porch (1854). Georgian and Italianate elements. Cemetery includes grave of Gov. Peter Stuyvesant. *Private:* HABS.

New York. **ST. PAUL'S CHAPEL,** Broadway between Fulton and Vesey Sts., 1764–1766, Thomas McBean, architect; 1794, James C. Lawrence, architect. Dressed fieldstone with brownstone trim, 2 stories, rectangular, gabled roof with balustrade, modillion cornice; giant pedimented end Ionic portico with oculi and sculptural niche in typmanum, paired pedimented entrances with Gibbs surrounds, large Palladian window; 1st- and 2nd-story round arched windows with keystones along sides; rear facade with high, ornate multitier spire; interior vaulted ceiling and galleries; tower and portico added, late-18th C. Church influenced by St. Martin-in-the-Fields, London, by James Gibbs. Georgian. Among finest examples of Georgian religious architecture in U.S. City's sole colonial church; attended by both British and American officers during Revolution. *Private:* NHL; HABS.

New York. **STATUE OF LIBERTY NATIONAL MONUMENT,** Liberty Island, New York Harbor (also in Hudson County, NJ), 1886, Frederic Auguste Bartholdi, sculptor. Copper statue of Liberty, 152' high on a pedestal approximately 150' high; 11-point star base, originally a masonry fort. Gift from France to America, commemorates the French-American alliance during the American Revolution. Includes Ellis Island, immigrant receiving station, 1892–1954. *Federal/NPS.*

New York. **STRECKER MEMORIAL LABORATORY,** Welfare Island, 1892, Frederick C. Withers and Walter Dickson, architects. Rock-faced granite, brick; 1–3 stories, T-shaped, flat and gabled roof sections, skylight, modillion cornice with bead and reel molding, curved vestibule with brick flat arch over entrance in front of gabled pavilion with end returns and large lunette, 3-story main structure, round arched side windows. Richardsonian Romanesque elements. Built to service nearby City Hospital; contained autopsy room, morgue, blood bank laboratory, animal house, and chemistry and serology laboratory. *Municipal.*

New York. **STUYVESANT-FISH HOUSE,** 21 Stuyvesant St., 1804. Brick (Flemish bond), 3 1/2 stories, rectangular, gabled roof, 2 segmental pedimented dormers, off-center entrance with side lights and transom, splayed stone lintels, iron fence; original interior. Federal. Typical early-19th C. area town house. *Private.*

New York. **SURROGATES' COURT (HALL OF RECORDS)**, 31 Chambers St., 1899–1911, John R. Thomas, Horgan and Slattery, architects. Steel frame, granite ashlar facing; 6 1/2 stories plus attic, rectangular, mansard roof, copper cresting, interior chimneys, segmental arched dormers and oculi, modillion cornice with ornamented frieze above 5th story, slightly projecting front center pavilion with entrance recessed under 3-bay arcaded porch with entablature with triglyph frieze, 3-story-tall Corinthian columns under entablature, balustrade with statues; center entrances on each side, smooth rustication of 1st 2 stories; carved ornamentation over 3rd-, 4th-, and 6th-story windows, corner pavilions; main entrance hall of marble with divided staircase and colonnaded gallery. Beaux-Arts Classicism. Design completed by Horgan and Slattery following Thomas' death. *County.*

New York. **THEODORE ROOSEVELT BIRTHPLACE NATIONAL HISTORIC SITE,** 28 E. 20th St., 1840's. Brownstone, 3 1/2 stories over high basement, rectangular row house, mansard-like roof, dormers, scalloped trim below cornice, balustraded staircase leads to 1st-floor off-center double-door entrance with transom and label mold, plaque above door; some original furnishings; reconstructed 1923. Gothic Revival. Birthplace and home (1858-1873) of Theodore Roosevelt, 26th president of the U.S. Museum. *Federal/NPS.*

New York. **TWEED COURTHOUSE (CRIMINAL COURT OF THE CITY OF NEW YORK)**, 52 Chambers St., 1858-1880's, John Kellum, architect. Granite and iron, white marble facing; 3 stories, modified rectangle, balustraded flat roof sections, center tetrastyle 2-story Corinthian pedimented portico and end pavilions projecting both front and rear; rusticated ground story, giant pilasters above between each bay; segmental pediments over 2nd-story windows, entablatures over 3rd; side pedimented pavilions. Completed and renovated by Leopold Eidlitz in 1880's. Italian Renaissance Revival. Product of reign of William Marcy (Boss) Tweed; building served the Tweed Ring's purposes of graft, costing over $13 million in inflated and fraudulent contracts. *Municipal.*

New York. **U.S. CUSTOMHOUSE**, Bowling Green, 1901-1907, Cass Gilbert, architect. Steel frame, ashlar facing; 5 1/2 stories over full basement, modified U shape, mansard roof, copper cresting, segmental arched dormers, balustraded parapet with front center cartouche bearing arms of the U.S. by sculptor Karl Bitter, entablature with stylized frieze at 4th-story level, stairway leads to front center entrance recessed under tall round arch, statuary groups by Daniel Chester French representing the 4 continents on front projecting pedestals, deeply coursed base; 3-story-tall Corinthian columns flanking windows, 1st-story windows with pediments; statuary between windows at

5th-story level; oval chamber in central courtyard with rotunda decorated with murals painted by Reginald Marsh, completed 1937. Excellent example of Beaux-Arts Classicism by Cass Gilbert in collaboration with noted artists and sculptors. *Federal/USCS.*

New York. **U.S. GENERAL POST OFFICE,** 8th Ave. between 31st and 33rd Sts., 1910-1913, McKim, Mead, and White, architects. Steel frame, granite ashlar facing; 4 stories over high basement, rectangular, flat roof with truncated pyramids over corner pavilions, parapet of stylized anthemia cresting, entablature above 3rd story; front wide flight of steps leads to Corinthian portico in antis between corner pavilions, each with central niche flanked by Corinthian pilasters; other facades with corner pavilions, pilasters, and narrower center colonnades; 4th-story windows with shouldered architraves. Designed by McKim, Mead, and White as companion piece to old Penn Station (demolished 1964). *Federal/USPS.*

New York. **WATSON, JAMES, HOUSE (MISSION OF OUR LADY OF THE ROSARY)** 7 State St., 1793 (E portion), attributed to John McComb, Jr., architect; 1806 (W portion). Brick, 3 stories over high basement, wedge-shaped, low pitched roof sections, interior and interior end chimneys, balustraded parapet, modillion cornice; front wall section curves inward behind 2-level portico, lower 1-story level with square piers and twin stairways leading to entrance with transom, upper level with 2-story-tall Ionic columns, each level with railings; belt course between 1st and 2nd stories, welsh arches over front windows; 3-bay addition including curved portico, 1806; dormers removed 1964; restored. Last of many Federal style town houses which once lined this street. *Private.*

Historical Places 465

New York. **WOOLWORTH BUILDING,** 233 Broadway, 1913, Cass Gilbert, architect. Steel frame, stone; 60 stories, rectangular, mansard roof, ground-floor arcade on 3 sides, turrets, flying buttresses, spires, gargoyles; interior richly decorated with marble, mosaics, and gold leaf; 11–20′-high ceilings. Late Gothic Revival. Built for businessman Frank W. Woolworth who originated the "five and ten" store; the "Cathedral of Commerce" remained the world's tallest building from 1913 to 1930, and was the first building with its own power plant. *Private:* NHL.

New York. **170-176 JOHN STREET BUILDING**, 170-176 John St., 1840. Granite, 5 stories, rectangular, flat roof, ground-floor window bays divided by pilasters, regular fenestration. Simple Greek Revival commercial structure. *Private.*

New York. **75 MURRAY STREET BUILDING,** 75 Murray St., 1865. Masonry with cast iron front; 5 stories, rectangular, low pitched roof, ornamented bracketed cornice and frieze, 2 ground-floor entrances in 3-bay-wide facade, engaged columns flank round arched windows with keystones and small engaged columns at jambs, modillion cornices separating stories; 1st-story facade altered for storefront and elevator door. Renaissance Revival. Excellent example of city's 1860's commercial cast iron architecture. *Private.*

New York City. **HENRY STREET SETTLEMENT AND NEIGHBORHOOD PLAYHOUSE,** 263–267 Henry St. and 466 Grand St., 1827–1834, 1915 (playhouse), 1915 (No. 466). Group of 3 adjacent town houses with playhouse located 2 blocks N; features 3–4-story brick structures with Federal, Greek Revival, and Georgian Revival elements; some with later renovations. Settlement begun by Lillian Wald, who introduced the concept of "public health nursing" to the Lower East Side in 1893, and later organized classes and clubs for local children and also provided a play area. Neighborhood Playhouse built for Alice and Irene Lewishon to carry forward their work in drama and dance with local children. *Multiple public/private:* NHL.

NIAGARA COUNTY

Lewiston. **FRONTIER HOUSE,** 460 Center St., 1824–1826. Stone, 3 1/2 stories, rectangular; gabled roof with stepped gables, paired chimneys, and balustrade; off-center and center entrances, full-width front porch with hipped roof, regular fenestration, oval windows in gables; N kitchen wings. Federal elements. Built as a tavern for Joshua Fairbanks and Benjamin and Samuel Barton, local prominent businessmen. *Private.*

Lewiston. **LEWISTON MOUND,** Lewiston State Park, Hopewellian affinities (c. 160). Oval burial mound. Partially investigated. *County.*

Lewiston vicinity. **LEWISTON PORTAGE LANDING SITE,** Prehistoric–19th C.. Gently sloping ravine leading from river remains of path used by travelers to avoid Niagara Falls. Archeological explorations yielded artifacts from Indian to British occupation, indicating this was a heavily used access point to a vital overland route. *State.*

Lockport. **LOWERTOWN HISTORIC DISTRICT,** Roughly bounded by Erie Canal and New York Central RR., 19th–20th C.. Primarily residential district, with some religious and commercial buildings and warehouses; facing the canal are 2 1/2-story brick and stone residences with Greek Revival and Italianate elements built in the 1830's; off the canal are 1-2-story frame structures with additions and modern siding built mid-19th C. and some stone structures: notable are the Gothic Revival former Christ Episcopal Church (1854) and the Italianate Vine Street School (1864). Systematic development of the village began after canal opened; district was Lockport's social, commercial, and industrial center, 1830's-1860's. *Multiple public/private:* HABS.

Lockport. **MOORE, BENJAMIN C., MILL (LOCKPORT CITY HALL; HOLLY WATER WORKS)**, Pine St. on the Erie Canal, 1864. Coursed rubble, 2 1/2 stories over basement on sloping site, trapezoidal shape, hipped roof sections with cross gables, interior chimney; front center entrance with transom and pediment on pilasters, triple round arched windows in gables, rock-faced stone lintels and sills, ashlar quoins; interior altered; rear 2-story addition 1893. Built as a flour mill, converted c. 1885 to a water pumping plant; adapted as city hall 1893; one of few survivors of 25 industrial buildings once clustered along this section of Erie Canal. *Municipal.*

Niagara Falls. **DEVEAUX SCHOOL COMPLEX,** 2900 Lewiston Rd., 1855-1888. Educational complex; contains 3 connected structures–Van Rensselaer Hall (1855-1857), Patterson Hall (1866), and Munro Hall (1888); and outbuildings–barn, shed, and gymnasium. Gothic Revival elements. Founded by Judge Samuel DeVeaux as an Episcopal school for poor and orphaned boys; later became a prominent preparatory school; closed, 1971. *Private.*

Niagara Falls. **NIAGARA FALLS PUBLIC LIBRARY,** 1022 Main St., 1902-1904, E. E. Joralemon, architect. Stone, yellow brick; 1

story, rectangular with semielliptical rear bow, flat roof with parapet, slightly projecting center entrance bay with pedimented double doorway, pedimented windows, string courses; fine interior detail intact. Neo-Classical Revival elements. One of many public libraries endowed by Andrew Carnegie. *Public.*

Niagara Falls. **NIAGARA RESERVATION,** 1885. Includes the falls, Goat Island and other islets, paths, and an observation tower. In establishing a reservation of over 400 acres, New York became the first state to use eminent domain powers to acquire land for aesthetic purposes. *State:* NHL.

Niagara Falls. **SHREDDED WHEAT OFFICE BUILDING,** 430 Buffalo Ave., 1900. Steel frame, brick; 5 stories, rectangular, flat roof, center entrance, 5 paired window bays, segmental arched basement windows, wide parapet; interior featured 4th-floor auditorium and 5th-floor cafeteria; doubled glazed windows. Commercial style. Administrative office building of original Shredded Wheat factory complex, developed by Henry D. Perky. *Private.*

Niagara Falls. **U.S. CUSTOMHOUSE,** 2245 Whirlpool St., 1863. Stone, 2 1/2 stories, square, hipped roof, arched window and door openings on W facade; built into railroad embankment, S side opens onto railroad tracks; renovated, 1928. Continues to serve as customs office for trains from Canada. *Private:* HABS.

Niagara Falls. **WHITNEY MANSION,** 335 Buffalo Ave., 1849–1851. Limestone, 2 1/2 stories, L-shaped, intersecting gabled roof sections; original section has off-center entrance with full-width Ionic portico; 19th C. side addition has front bay window and gabled dormer with 3 round arched windows. Greek Revival. Built according to 1830's design by Solon Whitney, son of Gen. Parkhurst Whitney, village founder and prominent hotel and tavern owner. *Private.*

Youngstown vicinity. **OLD FORT NIAGARA,** N of Youngstown on NY 18, 1678. Complex of stone buildings bounded by stone walls, earthworks, and a moat; restored. Original fort built in 1678; altered 1725-1726 and 1750-1759. Held alternately by French, British, and Americans in struggle for control of continent; strategically located in commanding the Great Lakes from Lake Erie to Ontario and in covering approaches to western NY. *State:* NHL.

ONEIDA COUNTY

Boonville. **ERWIN LIBRARY AND PRATT HOUSE,** 104 and 106 Schuyler St., 1890, C. L. Vivian (Erwin Library); 1875, J. B. Lathrop (Pratt House). Erwin Library: limestone, 1 story, gabled and hipped roofs; square tower with pyramidal roof contains recessed arched entrance. Romanesque. Pratt House: brick, 3 stories, mansard roof with dormers and central tower crowned with iron cresting and spire, ornate bracketed cornices and metal lintels; original interior wall coverings, fixtures, and woodwork. Second Empire. *Private.*

Boonville. **FIVE LOCK COMBINE AND LOCKS 37 AND 38, BLACK RIVER CANAL (BOONVILLE GORGE PARK)**, NY 46, 19th-20th C.. Section of the abandoned Black River Canal (built mid-19th C.) running through rugged terrain of Boonville Gorge; contains locks 37 and 38 and a 5-lock combine (locks 39-43); canal was 42' deep; locks, 90' by 15', which accommodate 70-ton boats, were built 1895-early 1900's. Canal built to connect Black River Valley to Erie Canal provided water supply for Erie Canal, allowed expansion of valley's lumbering industry, and fostered growth of towns. *State/county:* HAER.

Clinton. **HAMILTON COLLEGE CHAPEL,** Hamilton College campus, 1827, Philip Hooker, architect. Coursed rubble, 3 stories, rectangular, low pitched roof, interior chimney, modillion cornice, front and rear parapet; front slightly projecting 4-story clock tower with 3-stage frame belfry—2 stories, each with columns and entablature, surmounted by octagonal cupola; front center double-door entrance with round arched window above, flanked by tall round arched windows, blind decorative frame panels; limestone ashlar quoins, lintels, and sills; side elevations with 3 tiers of windows; apse added 1897; interior altered. Federal. Multipurpose classroom and chapel building designed by Philip Hooker; unusual 3-story interior plan attributed to John H. Lothrop, a trustee. *Private.*

Clinton. **ROOT, ELIHU, HOUSE,** 101 College Hill Rd., 1817. Frame, clapboarding; 2 stories, irregular shape, gabled roof, interior chimneys, pedimented arched portico, off-center entrance with semielliptical fanlight and side lights, 2-story pilasters dividing bays in flush-sided main facade, pedimented rear porch; side additions; restored, 1900's. Federal. Home of Elihu Root, U.S. Secretary of War largely credited with conceptual foundation for 20th C. development of American Army, Secretary of State, U.S. senator, and winner of 1912 Nobel Peace Prize. *Private; not accessible to the public:* NHL.

Rome. **ARSENAL HOUSE,** 514 W. Dominick St., c. 1813–1814. Brick, 2 1/2 stories, rectangular, gabled roof, pairs of bridged interior end chimneys above single gable steps, central pedimented gable with elliptical window, 2 vertical elliptical windows in gabled ends between chimneys, stone sills and lintels; later front porch with large modillion blocks, chamfered columns, and wooden arches with pendants; 1-story rear wings added later. Federal with Eastlake porch. Built by Federal government as part of arsenal complex for the War of 1812. *Private:* HABS.

Rome. **FORT STANWIX NATIONAL MONUMENT,** Bounded by Dominick, Spring, Liberty, and James Sts., 1758. Fort site where Iroquois treaty (1768) was signed allowing for safe westward expansion. Also scene of American garrison stand (Aug. 1777) which disrupted British strategy and contributed to the surrender of British Gen. John Burgoyne at Saratoga a few months later (see also Saratoga Historical Park, NY). Fort razed, early-19th C; site excavated, 1970–1973; fort reconstructed, 1975. *Federal/NPS.*

Rome vicinity. **ORISKANY BATTLEFIELD,** 5 mi. E of Rome on NY 69, 1777. Site of engagement between Americans attempting to relieve beseiged Fort Stanwix (see also Fort Stanwix National Monument, NY) and a combined force of Loyalists and Indians; the Americans failed to reach the fort, but forced a British retreat, foiling St. Leger's effort to provide a diversion for Gen. Burgoyne's advance along the Hudson. *State:* NHL.

Utica. **FOUNTAIN ELMS,** 318 Genesee St., 1850–1852, William J. Woolett, Jr., architect. Brick, painted; 2 1/2 stories, irregular shape, low hipped roof sections, elongated rectangular interior and interior end chimneys, bracketed cornice; front center main-block entrance with transom, 1-story balustraded entrance porch with roof balustrade and 2nd-story Palladian window; flanking front pavilions, each with bay window with balcony, gabled cornice with end returns and oculus in gable; side bay window; exterior woodwork painted brown; 2-story rear and side wings; rear wing remodeled and 2-story wing added 1883; side wing with piazza added 1908; interior alterations; restored. Italian Villa. Owned originally by the Munson-Proctor family, important investors in local industries. Museum. *Private.*

Utica. **RUTGER-STEUBEN PARK HISTORIC DISTRICT,** 19th C.. Numerous late-19th C. dwellings. Notable is Miller's Folly, an Italianate villa derived from an Andrew J. Downing design. Reflects prosperity gained between 1830 and 1890 through early transportation development and later establishment of small industries and opening of the Erie and Chenango canals. Residential area for important area merchants and industrialists. *Multiple public/private.*

Utica. **UTICA STATE HOSPITAL,** 1213 Court St., 1838-1843, William Clarke, designer. Limestone ashlar; 4-story main block with 3-story wings, all over high basement; modified rectangle, gabled roof sections; front full-height main-block hexastyle Doric portico with pediment and center entrance, full-height pilasters on front and side; side wings with projecting pedimented end pavilions with full-height pilasters. Greek Revival. First state owned and operated institution to care for the mentally ill in NY; foundations were begun for 3 other buildings to form a quadrangle, but were never completed; designed by William Clarke, a commissioner of the asylum; grounds designed by Andrew Jackson Downing. *State.*

Westernville. **FLOYD, GEN. WILLIAM, HOUSE,** W side of Main St., 1803. Frame, clapboarding; 2 stories, modified rectangle, gabled roof, interior chimneys, center entrance with hipped 1-story porch, smaller 2-story side wing with off-center entrance with small shed porch. Federal elements. Home of Gen. Wil-

Historical Places 473

liam Floyd, NY delegate to the Continental Congress and signer of the Declaration of Independence. *Private; not accessible to the public:* NHL.

Whitesboro. **WHITESTOWN TOWN HALL (COURTHOUSE),** 8 Park Ave., 1807. Brick, painted; 2 stories, rectangular, hipped roof with small octagonal domed cupola, intersecting front gable; central 3 bays of 5-bay front facade divided by pilasters and crowned by fanlighted pediment. Greek Revival. Built on land donated by Hugh White (1733-1812), one of earliest and most important settlers in central NY immediately after Revolutionary War. Courthouse for 50 years, now center of local government. *Municipal:* HABS.

ONONDAGA COUNTY

Manlius. **MANLIUS VILLAGE HISTORIC DISTRICT,** Pleasant, Franklin, North, Clinton, and E. Seneca Sts., 19th-20th C.. Dwellings, 3 churches, and a commercial building in variety of 19th C. architectural styles, and 3 20th C. buildings. Village developed around intersection of 2 early-19th C. turnpikes; inc. 1813. Buildings such as Smith Hall and the Rectory reflect the prosperity gained through turnpike trade; later, transportation routes bypassed town, ending growth. 19th C. quality retained. *Private.*

Onondaga. **HUTCHINSON, GEN. ORRIN, HOUSE,** 4311 W. Seneca Tpke., c. 1812. Coursed rubble, 2 1/2 stories, L-shaped, gabled roof with stepped gable ends, front side entrance with fanlight and side lights; rear wing with 2-story porch, 1st story enclosed and 2nd story balustraded with unusual cigar-shaped columns; rear 1-story frame wing with bay window and gabled roof section in flat roof; fine interior woodwork; restored. Regional Federal style with Dutch colonial influence in stepped gables. House on county's forested frontier may have been built as a tavern serving the newly constructed Seneca Turnpike. *Private:* HABS.

Syracuse. **CENTRAL NEW YORK TELEPHONE AND TELEGRAPH BUILDING,** 311 Montgomery St., 1895-1896, Henry W. Wilkinson, architect. Roman and red brick, 1st story laid with channels to simulate rusticated stonework; 5 stories, rectangular, flat roof, denticulated cornice with ovolo molding, front side entrance with transom with wrought iron grille, 1st-story semielliptical window; belt course above 1st, 3rd, and 4th stories; 2nd- and 3rd-story windows grouped under cornice with terra cotta ornament between and flanking wall cartouches; original open-cage passenger elevator; modillions removed. Second Renaissance Revival. First building erected in central NY area for telephone offices; purchased in 1905 by Onondaga Historical Association to house their offices. *Private.*

Syracuse. **CROUSE COLLEGE, SYRACUSE UNIVERSITY,** Syracuse University campus, 1881-1884, Archimedes Russell, architect. Sandstone, 3 1/2 stories, L-shaped, hipped roof, high front tower with pyramid roof and corner turrets; roofline with gabled dormers, turrets, and decorated chimneys; polygonal side bays, porte-cochere, foliated carving above round arched entrance, carved tympanum with musical instruments and palette, numerous string courses and corbeled arcades; interior includes large 2-story auditorium with stencilled decoration and circular and rectangular stained glass windows. Richardsonian Romanesque elements with other eclectic sources. Constructed by the Norcross Brothers firm; built to serve as the university's fine arts center. *Private.*

Syracuse. **GERE BANK BUILDING,** 121 E. Water St., 1894, Charles E. Colton, architect. Rock-faced granite 2-story base, brick; 5 stories, rectangular, flat roof, ornamented cornice with modified brackets, front side entrance recessed under round arch supported on short columns, 2nd-story windows under arcade with cornice above, 3rd–5th-story windows grouped under arcading with terra cotta ornament in spandrels and between stories; interior open elevator with bronze well screen, marble flooring, and wainscoting. Fine example of Sullivanesque style with Richardsonian Romanesque elements. *Private.*

Syracuse. **GRACE EPISCOPAL CHURCH,** 819 Madison St., 1876–1877, Horatio Nelson White, architect. Rock-faced limestone, 1 story, modified rectangle, steeply gabled roof with vents, cresting; front gabled vestibule with entrance recessed under pointed archway, rose window above within pointed arched recess, pointed arched windows; front corner 2-story tower with corner buttresses and crenelated parapets, side entrance vestibule, polygonal apse; roof supported by 6 exposed hammerbeam trusses; interior renovated c. 1891; 2 stories of tower removed 1930's. Gothic Revival. *Private:* HABS.

Syracuse. **HALL OF LANGUAGES, SYRACUSE UNIVERSITY,** Syracuse University campus, 1871–1873, Horatio Nelson White, architect. Limestone; 3 1/2-story central section, 2 1/2-story wings; H-shaped, mansard roof, 3 large cupolas (central one a later addition); molded metal cornice, stone brackets, smooth quoins, and 2 belt courses. Retains many original ornamented pressed sheet metal ceilings and woodwork. Second Empire. *Private:* HABS.

Syracuse. **ONONDAGA COUNTY SAVINGS BANK BUILDING**, 101 S. Salina St., 1869, Horatio Nelson White, architect. Limestone, 3 1/2 stories, irregular shape, mansard roof, gabled and round arched dormers, mansarded end pavilion and tall SE clock tower, rectangular and round and segmental arched windows divided by pilasters, balconies, pediments, quoins, ground-floor storefronts, rustication; 50' E addition, 1875–1876; interior remodeled, 1899. Second Empire. *Municipal:* HABS.

Syracuse. **SYRACUSE SAVINGS BANK**, 102 N. Salina St., 1876, Joseph Lyman Silsbee, architect. Steel frame, sandstone; 5 1/2 stories, rectangular; intersecting gabled, hipped, and pyramidal roof sections; tall central tower, center entrance with pointed arched light above, all set under entrance gable with crockets; rectangular and segmental arched windows in pointed arched polychromatic frames, some with trefoils; upper-story pointed arched windows divided by columns, finials, crockets, and turrets. High Victorian Gothic. First office building in Syracuse with elevator. *Private.*

Syracuse. **TEALL, OLIVER, HOUSE**, 105 S. Beech St., Early–mid-19th C.. Frame, stuccoed; 2–2 1/2 stories, irregular shape, gabled and flat roof sections, interior chimneys, hipped dormers, front main-block center entrance with blind fanlight and side lights flanked by 2-story fluted wooden pilasters; side 2 1/2-story wing with front 1-story enclosed gabled porch and rear open porch; rear 2-story full-width addition; side wing added 1920's; original clapboarding stuccoed; interior altered. Federal elements. Built for Erie Canal construction superintendent Oliver Teall, inventor of an underwater excavator for deepening the canal, and later holder of village's water franchise. *Private.*

Syracuse. **THIRD NATIONAL BANK (COMMUNITY CHEST BUILDING)**, 107 James St., 1885, Archimedes Russell, architect. Steel frame, rock-faced base, brick bearing walls; 5 1/2 stories, rectangular, gabled and pyramidal roof sections with large and small cross gables, gabled dormers, ornate brick cornice and spiral frieze, entrances on each street side, canted corner with oriel with semiconical roof and large 4th-story corbel supporting 5th-story corner projection; rock-faced stone window surrounds and belt courses; rectangular, segmental, and round arched windows; brick corbeling; wing added 1926-1940; interior renovated 1945 and 1956. Richardsonian Romanesque elements. Located in city's late-19th C. commercial center. *Private.*

Syracuse. **WEIGHLOCK BUILDING**, SE corner of Erie Blvd. E. and Montgomery St., 1849-1850. Brick, 2 1/2 stories, rectangular, gabled roof, corbel tabled cornice and end and center pediments, 8 front bays articulated by ground-floor pilasters. Third structure built for collecting canal tolls and inspecting boats; originally contained weighing lock with scales determining weight of boat and appropriate toll; canal toll abolished, 1883; scales removed, 2nd story extended over lock, and Greek Revival portico removed, early-20th C. Museum. *County:* G.

Syracuse. **WHITE, HAMILTON, HOUSE**, 307 S. Townsend St., 1845. Painted brick, 2 1/2 stories on high stone foundation, main block with N and E wings, hipped roof with cupola and 4 interior chimneys, ornately grilled frieze, projecting box cornice, 1-bay porch flanked by fluted Ionic columns; additions include N wing (1860's) and E wing (1900). Hamilton White, original owner, was a prominent local banker and businessman. *Private:* HABS.

Syracuse. **WHITE MEMORIAL BUILDING,** 106 E. Washington St., 1876, Joseph Lyman Silsbee, architect. Polychrome brick, 5 stories, rectangular, steeply hipped and gabled roof sections, interior end chimneys, cresting; front center hipped pavilion projects slightly at cornice, accentuates entry with steep gable, engaged columns, carved ornament, and memorial plaque; 1st-story storefronts with entrances, corbeled brick and limestone trim; one storefront section altered. Fine example of High Victorian Gothic. *Private:* HABS.

ONTARIO COUNTY

Canandaigua. **NORTH MAIN STREET HISTORIC DISTRICT,** Between railroad tracks and Buffalo-Chapel St., 19th–20th C.. Civic and residential section with a wide variety of 19th and 20th C. architectural styles. Outstanding buildings include the Greek Revival Ontario County Courthouse and the Federal First Congregational Church with Gothic Chapel. Settled after Revolution by MA settlers Oliver Phelps and Nathaniel Gorham; developed as focal point of area providing law offices and courts, stores, and taverns. Architecture reflects conservative nature of town. *Multiple public/private:* HABS.

Canandaigua. **SONNENBERG GARDENS,** 151 Charlotte St., 1887 (house), c. 1900 (gardens), Ernest Bowditch, landscape architect. Extensive landscaped lawns, 8 distinct gardens, and deer park clustered around rambling Richardsonian house. Main house: stone and half-timbered, 2 1/2 stories, gabled and hipped roofs with numerous dormers and chimneys; later wings and extensions. Excellent private estate; landscaping unusual for scale and location. Built for philanthropist Frederick Ferris Thompson. House and gardens conveyed to charitable non-profit corporation named Sonnenberg Gardens, 1972; gardens under restoration. *Private.*

Geneva. **GENEVA HALL AND TRINITY HALL, HOBART & WILLIAM SMITH COLLEGE,** S. Main St., 1821–1822, 1837–1838; attributed to Benjamin Hale, architect. Fieldstone, 3 stories, rectangular, hipped roof, stone quoins and window lintels and sills. Geneva Hall entrance has transom and side lights; Trinity Hall has elliptical fanlight and side lights; interiors remodeled, 1960's. *Private.*

Geneva. **PARROTT HALL (DENTON HOUSE)** W. North St. between Castle St. and Preemption Rd., 1850's. Brick, 2–3 stories over high basement, L-shaped, flat roof sections, interior end chimneys, paired bracketed cornice, front center entrance with transom and side lights, ornate 1-story cast iron balustraded veranda extending around building, cast iron window cornices and sills; 2-story rear ell; cupola removed. Italian Villa. Built for Nehemiah Denton; sold to NY in 1882 and converted to serve as agricultural experiment station; named for Dr. Percival Parrott, station's first entomologist. *State.*

Geneva. **SOUTH MAIN STREET HISTORIC DISTRICT,** Irregular pattern along S. Main St., Late-18th–early-20th C.. Mile-long district along residential street laid out in 1796 parallel to W bank of Seneca Lake. Includes over 100 structures, with over half dating from 1825–1850, featuring numerous Greek Revival houses, some Federal buildings, and a series of 1820's row houses, unusual in this area. Other buildings include 2 adobe-like structures, Gothic Revival churches and houses (including some by Richard Upjohn, his son, and grandson), and later Jacobethan and Colonial Revival style structures. Railroad brought commercial development to another part of town, leaving Main Street a residential setting widely acclaimed for its beauty. *Multiple public/private:* HABS.

Stanley vicinity. **SENECA PRESBYTERIAN (NUMBER NINE) CHURCH**, E of Stanley off NY 245 on Number Nine Rd., 1838. Frame, clapboarding; 1 1/2 stories, rectangular, gabled roof, front 3-story tower with pyramidal roof with kick, 2 front double-door entrances with wide architraves, oculi above entrances, round arched windows; interior with trompe l'oeil fresco in chancel, stencils on walls; 1863 widened to include 2 galleried side aisles; c. 1873 bell tower and front vestibule added; 1889 vestibule altered, interior decorations added. Eclectic. Site was chosen in center of township designated as Number Nine on pioneer maps; first church built by Scotch settlers, 1810; present church a center of social and community interest for rural residents. *Private.*

Victor vicinity. **BOUGHTON HILL**, c. 1675–1687. The site of Gannagaro, the "great town" of the Seneca Indians, westernmost tribe of the League of the Iroquois during the period of European contact. The town was destroyed by the French in 1687 and was never rebuilt. Unexcavated. *Multiple private; not accessible to the public:* NHL.

ORANGE COUNTY

PALISADES INTERSTATE PARK, *Reference—see Bergen County, NJ*

Campbell Hall. **BULL STONE HOUSE**, Hamptonburgh Rd., 1722–1727, William Bull, builder. Stone (uncoursed rubble), 2 1/2 stories, rectangular, gabled roof, massive interior end chimney, simple cornice, irregularly placed windows. Original barn from same period received new siding, but retains 18th C. framing. Substantial house built by owner, William Bull, an English-born immigrant who became a mason in the colonies; remains in Bull family. *Private.*

Campbell Hall vicinity. **BULL-JACKSON HOUSE (HILLHOLD), NY 416, NW** of Campbell Hall, 18th-19th C.. Stone, partially stuccoed; 2 1/2 stories, L-shaped, gabled roof sections, interior end chimneys, gabled dormers, center entrance with porch; rear ell with frame saltbox extension; outbuildings; under restoration. Agricultural complex developed by second-generation members of the Bull family; birthplace of Civil War Capt. William A. Jackson, member of the Bull family. Museum. *County:* HABS.

Fort Montgomery vicinity. **FORT MONTGOMERY SITE, S** of Fort Montgomery, just N of Popolopen Creek, 1776-1777. Site of Revolutionary War river fortification including remains of earthen walls and 8-point star-shaped foundations of barracks, storehouses, and bakehouse. One of several military installations planned by Americans to deter passage of the British up the Hudson River. Successful in preventing Gen. Sir Henry Clinton from reinforcing Gen. John Burgoyne's troops; later destroyed by Clinton. Archeological investigation 1967 by curator at New Windsor Cantonment revealed locations and features of structures within the fort. *State:* NHL.

Goshen. **HISTORIC TRACK,** Main St., 1854. Race track complex including track originally laid out in 1854 and changed several times since; 1911 steel grandstand, stables, barns, bandstand, judges' stand, and other assorted structures. Harness racing and trotting track established in major horse racing area where races have been popular since 18th C.; saved from financial ruin and redeveloped in 1890's by E. H. Harriman, railroad magnate and horse lover. Still in use. *Private:* NHL.

Goshen vicinity. **DUTCHESS QUARRY CAVE SITE,** Paleo-Indian; Archaic–Late Woodland, Midden in cylindrical limestone cave. Investigated by New York State Archeological Association, 1965–1967. *County.*

Harriman. **ARDEN (E. H. HARRIMAN ESTATE)**, NY 17, 1905–1909. Stone, 2 1/2–3 1/2 stories, modified rectangle, high hipped roof sections, numerous interior chimneys, gabled and hipped dormers, large round arched 1st-floor openings with light colored keystones, belt course above 1st floor, upper mullioned windows with quoined surrounds, entrance framed by engaged columns and segmental pediment with sculpture; wings added, 1960's. Eclectic elements in dominantly French manorial style. Built for E. H. Harriman, preeminent organizer and builder of railroads in the late-19th and early-20th C. whose holdings included the Union Pacific and Southern Pacific Railroads. *Private:* NHL.

Highland Mills. **SMITH CLOVE MEETINGHOUSE,** Quaker Rd., 1803. Frame, clapboarding; 1 1/2 stories, rectangular, gabled roof with overhanging eaves, central chimney, full-width 1-story front porch, 2 entrances; porch added, 1875; interior space once divided by sliding panels to separate men and women; wide floor planking; restored. Built for Quaker group organized 1790. First town church; in continuous use since construction. *Private.*

Monroe vicinity. **SOUTHFIELD FURNACE RUIN,** S of Monroe off NY 17, 1804. Industrial complex ruins of furnace stack, charging bridge, water race, casting room, and stamping mill. Original self-sufficient organization had ironmaster's house, blacksmith shop, store, railroad facilities, gristmill, barns, and stables. Built and operated by Peter Townsend family. First New York blistered steel made here, 1810; first cannon cast in state, 1816. Operated until 1887. *Private.*

New Windsor. **NEW WINDSOR CANTONMENT,** Temple Hill Rd., 1782–1783. Campsites, foundations, artifacts, and part of a Revolutionary soldier's hut within site of 3 large encampments used by Continental Army under George Washington as last winter quarters of Revolution, Nov. 1782–June 1783. Partially excavated, 1959–1962. *State.*

New Windsor vicinity. **HASKELL HOUSE,** W of New Windsor off NY 32, Early-18th C.. Log and frame construction, stuccoing and board-and-batten siding; 1–2 1/2 stories, L-shaped, gabled roof, interior end chimneys, gabled dormers, front entrance, entrance in lean-to ell; dormers and ell entrance added. Country home of John Haskell; unusual surviving example of early log construction applied to a manor house. *Private.*

Newburgh. **CRAWFORD, DAVID, HOUSE,** 189 Montgomery St., 1829–1831. Frame, clapboarding; 2 1/2 stories, rectangular, gabled roof, interior end chimneys, modillion cornice, front full-width 2-story pedimented Ionic portico with 2nd-story balustrade, center entrance with elaborately carved transom and side lights with elliptical lights, Palladian window in tympanum, entablatures over windows, 1-story full-width rear wing with center entrance with small arcaded porch; finely detailed interiors; formal garden restored 1968. Greek Revival elements. Built for David Crawford, member of citizen's group working to boost the economy and well-being of the community. *Private:* HABS.

Newburgh. **DUTCH REFORMED CHURCH,** NE corner of Grand and 3rd Sts., 1835-1837, Alexander Jackson Davis, architect. Stone, stuccoed; 1 story with gallery, T-shaped, gabled roof, pedimented front Ionic entrance porch, tall entrance and windows; barrel-vaulted interior with deeply recessed coffers, gallery with leaf and dart moldings. Greek Revival. Designed after the Town and Davis French Protestant Church in New York City. *Municipal:* HABS.

Newburgh. **MILL HOUSE (GOMEZ THE JEW HOUSE)**, Mill House Rd., Early-18th C.. Stone and brick, 2 stories, rectangular, gabled roof, interior end chimneys, entrance with transom, semielliptical and semicircular arches over 2nd-floor windows, heart-shaped brick design in 1 gable end; brick 2nd story added to stone 1st story, c. 1772; 19th C. kitchen wing; several outbuildings. Built as house, fortification, and trading center by Daniel Gomez, son of wealthy Jewish immigrant merchant; later 2nd story, reflecting Dutch influence in brickwork. *Private.*

Newburgh. **MONTGOMERY-GRAND-LIBERTY STREETS HISTORIC DISTRICT,** 19th-20th C., Contains numerous dwellings, 9 churches, and several public buildings; wide variety of dwelling types and sizes and architectural styles. Numerous houses influenced by Gothic Revival elements and designs popularized by Andrew J. Downing and Calvert Vaux; later Victorian styles used. Early-19th C. river trade established area as a landing waterfront; settled by town's wealthy merchants and businessmen. *Multiple public/private.*

Newburgh. **WASHINGTON'S HEADQUARTERS (HASBROUCK HOUSE),** Liberty and

Washington Sts., 1750. Stone, 2½ stories, rectangular, modified jerkinhead roof, 3 interior chimneys, entrance with transom and gabled entrance hood, segmental arched 1st-floor front windows, rear shed porch; 2 additions to original NE section by 1770; interior Georgian woodwork and 3 hood fireplaces. George Washington's headquarters, Apr. 1782–Aug. 1783, while he drafted 3 documents that reaffirmed the principal of military subordination to civilian control and helped lay the foundations for orderly transition from war to peacetime government; he also established the "Order of the Purple Heart" military award. Became first historic site to be preserved by a state in 1850. Museum. *State:* NHL; HABS.

Port Jervis. **FORT DECKER,** 127 W. Main St., 1779. Stone, 1 1/2 stories, rectangular, gabled roof, interior end chimneys, center entrance with small hipped porch flanked by simple window on either side, wide board flooring; under restoration. Built on foundation of earlier fort or blockhouse occupied as a dwelling or military trading post which burned in 1779. Housed workers on the Delaware and Hudson Canal in 1826. *Private.*

Vails Gate. **KNOX HEADQUARTERS (JOHN ELLISON HOUSE)**, Quassaick Ave. and Forge Hill Rd., 1754. Uncoursed stone, 2 stories over basement, L-shaped, hipped and gabled roof sections, interior chimneys, modillion cornice, center entrance with 5-light transom, paneled door and shutters, recessed NW corner porch; 1 1/2-story gabled E side wing added, 1799; restored 1954. Georgian. Served as headquarters for Revolutionary War generals Henry Knox, Nathanael Greene, Frederick von Steuben, and Horatio Gates. Museum. *State:* NHL.

West Point. **U.S. MILITARY ACADEMY (WEST POINT),** NY 218, 1802. Educational institution and military training complex containing numerous buildings and monuments, the remains of Revolutionary War forts Clinton and Putnam, and Constitution Island with its Revolutionary War archeological sites. Site of military garrison since 1778, training regular U.S. Army; post which Maj. Gen. Benedict Arnold commanded and attempted to betray to the British in 1780. Academy est. 1802 by Act of Congress; rebuilt in Late Gothic Revival style in early-20th C. by Cram and Ferguson. *Federal/USA.*

OSWEGO COUNTY

Brewerton. **FORT BREWERTON,** State and Lansing Sts., 1759. Flagpole and commemorative stone gates mark site of fort built to protect Mohawk-Oneida-Oswego waterways during French and Indian War; dismantled, 1767. Partially excavated by William Ennis of the Fort Brewerton Museum Association, 1965-1966. *State.*

Oswego. **FORT ONTARIO,** E. 7th St. and Lake Ontario, 1839. Stone pentagonal fort with 5 arrow-shaped bastions; oval inner courtyard with stone, frame, and brick 1-2 1/2-story structures including powder magazine (1839-1844), officers' quarters, and post headquarters. Third fort on site (others date from 1755, 1759); walls rebuilt for greater strength 1860; used actively by military until 1946. Museum. *State.*

Oswego. **MARKET HOUSE,** Water St., 1835, attributed to Jacob Bonesteel, builder. Brick, stone; 3 stories, rectangular, hipped roof, interior chimneys, ornate central cupola with mansard roof; slightly projecting front and rear center pedimented sections, each with recessed entrance; 1st-story round arched openings; minor alterations and additions. Federal. Built to accommodate the growing commercial traffic in Oswego after completion of the Oswego Canal, 1829. *Private.*

Oswego. **OSWEGO CITY HALL,** W. Oneida St., 1870, Horatio Nelson White, architect. Ashlar, 2 1/2 stories over high basement, rectangular, mansard roof, gabled dormers, stylized dentils and corner brackets, front center tower with 3-tier clock tower above cornice, center entrance, segmental arched 1st-story windows, round arched 2nd-story windows with slightly pointed archivolts, paneled stonework and quoins articulating facade, belt course; original interiors; under restoration. Prominent Second Empire style building; in continuous use as town hall since 1870. *Municipal.*

Oswego. **OSWEGO CITY LIBRARY,** 120 E. 2nd St., 1855, Hewes and Rose, architect. Brick, 2 stories, rectangular, gabled roof, crenelated machicolation, 3-story projecting entrance tower, round arched openings with label molds, full limestone basement, limestone trim; restored. Romanesque Revival. State's oldest remaining public library, donated by philanthropist Gerrit Smith. *Municipal:* HABS.

OTSEGO COUNTY

Cooperstown. **OTSEGO COUNTY COURTHOUSE,** 193 Main St., 1880, Archimedes Russell, architect. Brick, 2 1/2 stories, modified rectangle, gabled roof, exterior end chimneys, front center double-door entrance with small gabled porch with polished granite columns and carved limestone capitals, above entrance is wide pointed arched section of limestone with 2 tiers of stained glass windows, hood mold with griffin corbels; side tower with pyramidal roof and supporting pavilion, side slightly projecting gabled pavilion, decorative brickwork, polychrome stone trim; 2nd-floor courtroom with original woodwork. Design in High Victorian Gothic style was controversial when built. In continuous use as courthouse. *County:* G.

Gilbertsville. **GILBERTSVILLE HISTORIC DISTRICT**, 19th C.. Contains 2 parks, 3 bridges, 1 monument, and 69 structures, the majority of which date between 1825 and 1875. Notable are the Greek Revival frame dwellings and the transitional Federal/Gothic Revival Grange Hall. Built around the settlement of Englishman Abijah Gilbert, c. 1786; developed around local industries until arrival of the railroad. Retains 19th C. character. *Multiple public/private.*

Gilbertsville. **GILBERTSVILLE HISTORIC DISTRICT**, Bounded roughly by Marion Ave., Cliff and Green Sts., Grover and Sylvan Sts., 19th C.. District containing a monument, several parks and bridges, and 69 structures, most of which date from 1825 to 1875. Notable are the Greek Revival frame dwellings and the transitional Federal/Gothic Revival Grange Hall. Built around the settlement of Englishman Abijah Gilbert, c. 1786; developed around local industries until arrival of the railroad. Retains 19th C. character. *Multiple public/private.*

Gilbertsville. **MAJOR'S INN AND GILBERT BLOCK** , Both sides of Commercial St. near NY 51, 1893–1897. Complex of structures in similar styles, along both sides of street. Major's Inn (1893–1895) is stone, brick, half-timbering; 2-3 1/2 stories, irregular shape; gabled and hipped roof sections, some flared; interior and exterior end chimneys; numerous gabled dormers, turrets, balconies, and bands of quatrefoil ornament; porches on each side, various entrances; Gothic dining hall added 1915; companion structure is the Gilbert Block (1895-1897), a row of three 1 1/2-story attached commercial structures with gabled roof sections. Jacobethan Revival elements. Town founded 1786 by Abijah Gilbert of Warwickshire, England; 19th C. economy based upon small industry gave way to resort industry late-19th C.; these buildings form a focal point of the town. *Private.*

Oneonta. **FAIRCHILD MANSION (MASONIC TEMPLE),** 318 Main St., 1867. Brick, 3 stories, irregular massing, steep hipped roof with intersecting gables, interior end chimneys, E porch, center pedimented Ionic entrance porch, 3-story front corner tower with conical roof, bay windows, Palladian windows in gables; exterior alterations, 1891 and 1897. Italian Villa and Chateauesque elements. Home of George W. Fairchild, U.S. congressman and an original promoter of the IBM corp.; birthplace of Sherman M. Fairchild, Fairchild camera inventor. *Private.*

Springfield. **HYDE HALL,** Glimmerglass State Park, E of CR 31, 1817-1835, Philip Hooker, builder-architect. Stone, brick; 1-story main block with raised attic pavilion and 2-story wings, modified U shape, hipped and gabled roof sections, interior chimneys, front center entrance with Doric portico with balustraded deck and gabled pavilion with gable pediment, rear family and kitchen wings, central courtyard; 2 large rooms with coved ceilings, circular mahogany stairs, much original furniture, early central heating system (c. 1833); stone and frame outbuildings. Greek Revival. Country seat of landowning family, the Hyde Clarkes; designed by architect Philip Hooker and owner George Clarke. Museum. *State:* HABS.

PUTNAM COUNTY

Brewster vicinity. **OLD SOUTHEAST CHURCH,** N of Brewster on NY 22 off Putnam Lake Rd., 1794. Frame, clapboarding; 1 1/2 stories, rectangular, gabled roof, square belfry with louvered openings over W end, W double-door entrance, W gable semielliptical blind lunette, 1st- and 2nd-story end and side windows; interior with galleries and pulpit between 2 entrances from W vestibule, box pews; 1830 alterations after fire included moving entrance from side to W end, belfry addition, gallery alterations, clapboarding, and partial dismanteling of 2 chimneys. Georgian and Federal elements. An important landmark of early Doanesburg settlement, the principal hamlet of E Putnam Countyuntil the railroad diverted population and enterprise to Brewster. *Private.*

Cold Spring. **WEST POINT FOUNDRY,** Foundry Cove between NY 90 and NY Central RR. tracks, 1817. Foundry area includes a few 19th–20th C. structures and a large archeological site; notable are the Italianate brick 2-story office building (1865) with slightly projecting center tower with octagonal arcaded cupola, a cinder block industrial building, and the Greek Revival brick Chapel of Our Lady at Cold Spring (1833), currently under restoration. Construction of the iron and brass foundry was begun (1817) by the West Point Foundry Association as a result of the federal government's decision to promote the establishment of foundries to improve the country's ordnance; consideredthe largest of its kind in mid-19th C. U.S.; produced the unusually accurate Parrott gun, credited with enabling the Union to win the Civil War. *Private.*

QUEENS COUNTY

Flushing. **FLUSHING TOWN HALL,** 137-35 Northern Blvd., 1862. Brick, painted; 2 stories, modified rectangle, gabled roof sections, elongated arched corbel tables; front center 3-bay arcaded entrance porch with balustraded deck, bays articulated by paneled buttresses that rise above cornice; windows, each with double round arched lights with oculus above and drip mold; side wing; rear wing added 1938; interior alterations; under restoration. Italian Villa elements. Focal point of important town functions, 1862-1900. *Municipal.*

Flushing. **KINGSLAND HOMESTEAD,** 37th St. and Parsons Blvd., 1774. Frame, shingling; 2 1/2 stories, modified L shape, gambrel and gabled roof sections, central chimney, dormer, front full-width shed porch with side entrance with small projecting vestibule, gable end with round and quadrant arched windows; gabled side wing; interior paneling and mantels; original beaded clapboarding covered; rear ell added; moved. Dutch and English colonial elements. City's 2nd oldest residential structure. *Municipal.*

Flushing. **OLD QUAKER MEETINGHOUSE,** S side of Northern Blvd., 1695. Frame, shingling; 2 stories, rectangular, hipped roof, interior chimney, 1-story S porch with separate entrances for men and women; interior contains beamed ceiling and hand-made unpainted benches. Served continuously as a meetinghouse except during the Revolutionary War. *Private:* NHL; HABS.

New York. **HUNTERS POINT HISTORIC DISTRICT,** Along 45th Ave., between 21st and

23rd Sts., 19th C.. Well-preserved residential district exhibiting diverse styles of the 1890's, but with uniform character; many retain original stoops, cornices, and detail. Included is "White Collar Row," group of stone town houses with pedimented doorways and slightly arched lintels on brackets; most other structures in area were frame. *Multiple private.*

RENSSELAER COUNTY

Rensselaer. **AIKEN HOUSE**, NE corner of Riverside and Aiken Aves., c. 1816. Brick, 2-2 1/2 stories, L-shaped, flat and gabled roof sections, paired end chimneys connected with high parapets forming stepped gable ends; off-center entrance with semielliptical fanlight, paneled sandstone architrave with keystones, splayed window lintels, round and elliptical windows in S gable end; cornice added, late-19th C., with jigsawn frieze and brackets; fine interior woodwork; later frame addition. Federal. Attributed to Philip Hooker; built for city's founder, William Aiken. *Private; not accessible to the public.*

Rensselaer. **FORT CRAILO**, S of Columbia St. on Riverside Ave., c. 1700. Brick (Dutch crossbond), 2 1/2 stories with attic, L-shaped, gabled roof with elbows, interior end chimneys, front center slightly recessed entrance with transom, flat arched front windows, loopholes in 1st story, gable end mouse-tooth brickwork, rear 2 1/2-story ell with center entrance; 1740 additions included cross hall and dining room; mid-18th C. ell addition; early-19th C. alterationa; restored. Dutch Colonial. Manor house of Kiliaen Van Rensselaer served as administrative center for the Rensselaerswyck, the first and only successful patroonship established by authority of the Dutch West India Co. *State:* NHL; HABS.

Schaghticoke. **KNICKERBOCKER MANSION,** Knickerbocker Rd., c. 1770. Brick, frame; 2 1/2-story main block with 1-1 1/2-story wing, modified rectangle, hipped and gabled roof sections, interior and interior end chimneys, gabled dormers with gable pediments, bracketed cornice, front center entrance with gabled frame porch with carved ornament, cornices over front and side windows, rear entrance; frame side wing with lean-to sections at front and rear, side and rear entrances; wing, entrance porch, window cornices added 19th C. Georgian and Greek Revival elements. Occupied by descendants of original owner, Johannes Knickerbocker II, until 1946; family prominent in county for nearly 2 1/2 centuries. Museum. *Private:* G.

Schodack. **MUITZES KILL HISTORIC DISTRICT,** An irregular pattern on both sides of Schodack Landing Rd., 18th-19th C.. Rural community center containing residences, barns, and a variety of other buildings; many 18th and 19th C. styles, for the most part fairly simple vernacular structures. 18th C. hamlet of farmers; developed into 19th C. milling and trading center; declined in late-19th C. *Private.*

Troy. **BURDEN IRONWORKS OFFICE BUILDING,** Polk St., 1881-1886. Brick, 1 story over high basement, Greek cross shape, gabled and hipped roof sections, interior chimneys with corbeled caps, central octagonal cupola with onion dome, skylight on hipped roof, denticulated cornice, ornamental brickwork forms window surrounds and quoins. Brick interpretation of Richardsonian Romanesque. Built as office building for company which originated in 1809 and became the Troy Iron and Nail Factory Co. in 1813; Henry Burden became superintendent in 1822, invented several machines to increase output, and later became sole proprietor. *Private:* HAER.

Troy. **BUSSEY, ESEK, FIREHOUSE,** 302 10th St., 1891-1892, H. P. Fielding, architect. Brick, 2 stories, rectangular, flat roof, dressed and rusticated stonework trim, corbeled brick frieze, terra cotta pedimented detailing; retains general layout and wooden wainscoting and ceiling. *Municipal.*

Troy. **CANNON BUILDING,** 1 Broadway, 1835, Alaxander Jackson Davis, architect. Brick, 5 stories, rectangular, mansard roof with end and center pavilions, triangular and segmental pedimented dormers, simple cornice with paired brackets, ground-floor entrances and storefronts with Greek Revival pilasters and entablature; mansard added, 1870's. One of a few remaining commercial structures designed by Davis in the country. *Private.*

Troy. **CHURCH OF THE HOLY CROSS,** 136 8th St., 1840's. Random ashlar, 1 story, modified rectangle, gabled roof, entrance through vestibule next to corner 3-tier tower with crenelations, buttresses, water table, trefoil openings, rose window; antechapel and tower added 1859; contiguous with the church is the 3-story stone manse (1857) with grouped pointed arched windows; connected to the church by a passageway is the stone Mary Warren Free Institute (c. 1863). Gothic Revival. Alexander J. Davis designed the chapel in 1843; Richard Upjohn drew plans to enlarge the church c. 1847; plans for the institute, which was tooffer religious instruction and musical training, are attributed to Nathan Warren, son of Mary Warren, who established the church in the early-1840's. *Private:* HABS.

Troy. **FIFTH AVENUE-FULTON STREET HISTORIC DISTRICT,** Bounded by Grand, William, and Union Sts., and Broadway, 1862-1894. Urban district containing 37 residential, commercial, industrial, and religious buildings constructed in a consistent scale and building height. Dominant is the 3-story brownstone row house with basement and a variety of brownstone and cast iron details. Area rebuilt after city's great fire of 1862; structures influenced by designs from pattern book *Architecture Designs for Street Fronts, Suburban Homes and Cottages* (1865), by noted Troy architect, M. F. Cummings. *Multiple private.*

Troy. **GLENWOOD (TITUS EDDY MANSION)** Eddy's Lane, Mid-19th C.. Brick, 2-2 1/2 stories over high basement, modified L shape; hipped, gabled and flat roof sections; interior end chimneys, denticulated cornice and blind frieze with windows, front center entrance with transom and cornice on pilasters, full-height tetrastyle pedimented Ionic portico, brownstone window sills and lintels, side entrance with 1-story Ionic porch, rear 2-story wing forms a courtyard. Greek Revival. Built for Titus Eddy, who manufactured the ink used through early-20th C. for U.S. government currency, bonds, and stamps. *Municipal.*

Troy. **GRAND STREET HISTORIC DISTRICT,** Grand St. between 5th and 6th Aves., Late-19th C.. Small downtown district containing residential and a few commercial structures; buildings are 2-3-story brick and brownstone row houses with wood and brick cornices, many with dentils and/or modillions and brackets, and windows and doors trimmed with cast iron or stone lintels and sills; buildings constructed late-1860's–early-1870's in Italianate style. One-block district of contiguous structures located close to the street is good example of late-19th C. urban architecture. *Multiple private.*

Troy. **HART-CLUETT MANSION,** 59 2nd St., 1827, attributed to Philip Hooker, builder-architect. Limestone, marble; 2 1/2 stories over high basement, L-shaped, gabled roof sections, interior end chimneys, modillion cornice, balustraded parapet, gabled dormers, slightly off-center entrance with doorway with fanlight and side lights recessed within facade entry with fanlight on columns and vermiculated keystone and quoins on archivolt, paneled window surrounds; much original decorative wood and plasterwork; rear additions c. 1847, 1911; coach house. Excellent example of Federal home. Museum. *County:* HABS.

Troy. **ILIUM BUILDING,** NE corner of Fulton and 4th Sts., 1904, M. F. Cummings and Son, architects. Brick, 5 stories, rectangular, flat roof with stone cornice, curved SW corner with ground-floor round arched entrance, 1st-story storefronts, decorative terra cotta trim, similar window treatment to that of the National State Bank Building (see also National State Bank Building, NY). Second Renaissance Revival. Built during Troy's early-20th C. building boom (see also McCarthy Building, NY). *Private.*

Troy. **MCCARTHY BUILDING,** 255-257 River St., 1904. Iron, terra cotta, glass; rectangular, flat roof, carved parapet with center swan's neck pediment on pilasters; full-width 2-story glass arch with storefronts and center entrance, all framed by decorative terra cotta paneling; three 3rd- and 4th-story window bays divided by 3-sided banded pilasters, upper-story window arcade. Decorative Commercial style. Built during Troy's early-20th C. building boom (see also National State Bank Building, NY and Ilium Building, NY). *Private.*

Troy. **NATIONAL STATE BANK BUILDING,** 297 River St., 1904, M. F. Cummings and Son, architects. Metal frame, stone; 5 stories, rectangular, flat roof with cornice, rusticated ground floor with round arched openings; 2nd-, 3rd-, and 4th- story windows set under arched sections divided vertically by pilasters and horizontally by low relief stone panels; upper-story window arcade. Second Renaissance Revival and Beaux-Arts Classicism. Built during Troy's building boom during early-20th C. (see also Ilium Building, NY and McCarthy Building, NY). *Private.*

Troy. **OLD TROY HOSPITAL,** 8th St., c. 1870, attributed to Marcus F. Cummings, architect. Sandstone, 4 stories, Greek cross shape, mansard roof, gabled dormers, round and segmental arched windows, 3-bay front projecting section articulated by 3-story pilasters, enclosed gabled entrance porch; extensive interior alterations. Built as private Catholic hospital; converted to Catholic high school, 1923; became West Hall at Rensselaer Polytechnic Institute, 1953. *Private.*

Troy. **POWERS HOME,** 819 3rd Ave., 1846. Frame, clapboarding; 2 stories, L-shaped, flat and gabled roof sections, interior chimneys, Ionic entrance portico, 1-story rear entrance portico, recessed off-center entrance framed by pilasters and denticulated broken pediment; 1883–1884 wings added in conversion to a nursing home, Classical decorative motifs, interior and exterior renovations. Greek Revival. *Private; not accessible to the public.*

Troy. **SECOND STREET HISTORIC DISTRICT,** Both sides of 2nd St., 19th–20th C.. District including numerous 2–3 story town houses and commercial buildings of various mid- and late-19th C. styles, several larger freestanding buildings of more monumental character, and several works by local architect Marcus Cummings, and one by George B. Post. Street has been little altered and retains scale of late-19th C. through successful adaptive use of the former private residences. *Multiple public/private.*

Troy. **TROY GAS LIGHT COMPANY: GASHOLDER HOUSE,** NW corner of Jefferson St. and 5th Ave., 1873, Frederick A. Sabbaton, engineer. Brick, 2 stories, circular, shallow domed roof, central cupola, corbeled brick and metal cornice, 2-story piers projecting every 3 bays; pilasters and label molded round arched blind windows on each level; 2-lift iron gasholder removed. Italianate elements. Built to store coal gas before distribution; pressure generated by weight of the iron gasholder. One of few remaining examples of structure once common in urban areas. *Private:* HAER.

Troy. **TROY PUBLIC LIBRARY (HART MEMORIAL LIBRARY)**, 100 2nd St., 1896–1897, Barney and Chapman, architects. Marble, deeply coursed base, finely dressed above; 2 stories, U-shaped, low pitched roof, partially balustraded parapet, denticulated modillion cornice, end and side center round arched entrances, cornice between stories, belt courses, side 2nd-story 5-bay arcade with loggia, end 2nd-story ornamented window grouping; original interior features carved woodwork, ornamental plaster ceilings, and a Tiffany window; under restoration. Excellent example of Second Renaissance Revival structure. *Private:* G.

Troy. **W. & L. E. GURLEY BUILDING,** 514 Fulton St., 1862. Brick, 4 stories, U-shaped, flat roof; corbel brick cornice with heavily bracketed sheet metal cornice above; raised center relief name panel above cornice; compound 1st-, 2nd-, and 3rd-story round arched windows and 4th-story segmental arched windows; decorative string courses. Renaissance Revival. Built to house the operations of W. & L. E. Gurley Co., surveying and mathematical instruments manufacturers, and the minor manufacturing activities of smaller companies. *Private:* HAER; G.

Troy. **WASHINGTON PARK HISTORIC DISTRICT,** Washington Park and adjacent properties on 2nd, 3rd, and Washington Sts. and Washington Pl., 19th-20th C.. District located near city's center contains park with facing residential and religious buildings; dwellings are primarily 3-story, brick and brownstone town houses, semidetached, and detached homes erected 1840's–late-19th C. in Greek Revival, Italianate, and other 19th C. styles, many with rear gardens and carriage houses; central private park is surrounded by an iron fence and sidewalk. Park was laid out in 1840, based on the late-18th C. English tradition of private residential squares used and maintained by the adjoining residents. *Multiple private.*

Walloomsac vicinity. **BENNINGTON BATTLEFIELD,** NY 67, on VT state line, 1777. Site of Aug. 16, 1777, Battle of Bennington, where Colonial troops under leadership of Gen. John Stark defeated British forces composed in part of German mercenaries and Indians. Victory helped to defeat Burgoyne at Saratoga 2 months later by cutting off supplies, and by showing the ability of American forces and encouraging volunteers. Museum. *State:* NHL.

RICHMOND COUNTY

New Brighton. **SAILORS' SNUG HARBOR NATIONAL REGISTER DISTRICT,** Richmond Ter., 1839-1880. Residential complex of 5 connected, well-executed, 2-story Greek Revival ashlar and brick structures, built 1839-1880; middle and end structures feature front full-height hexastyle Ionic entrance porticos, others have small pedimented front porches; buildings connected by small 1-story corridors; extensive grounds, walkways, outbuildings. Housing complex bequeathed by Capt. Robert R. Randall (1750–1801) for retired seamen. *Private.*

New York. **NEW DORP LIGHT**, Altamont Ave., Staten Island, 1854. Frame, clapboarding; 2 stories, rectangular with porch wing, gabled roof with square light tower and interior end chimneys, tower room with cantilevered balcony, pyramidal roof topped by fixed beam light beacon. *Federal/GSA; not accessible to the public.*

Rosebank. **AUSTEN, ELIZABETH ALICE, HOUSE**, 2 Hylan Blvd., 18th–19th C.. Stone, frame, clapboarding; 1 1/2 stories, T-shaped, gabled roof, gabled dormers with decorative bargeboards, full-width front porch supported by 6 openwork piers, center entrance, diamond-paned windows; original late-17th or early-18th C. structure enlarged, 18th–19th C.; Gothic Revival detailing added, 19th C., reputedly by James Renwick. Home of Alice Austen, early photographer. *Private;* HABS.

Staten Island. **BATTERY WEED (FORT RICHMOND)**, Fort Wadsworth Reservation, 1847–1861. Waterfront fort built of granite in irregular trapezoidal shape; consists of inner courtyard with 3 facing sides 3 stories high with segmental arched galleries and corner octagonal towers; 4th side is a low wall with center 2-story gatehouse with pedimented entrance on landside and end 4-story blockhouses. Area previously fortified by Dutch (1663) and British (1707) before American requisition during Revolution. *Federal/USA.*

Staten Island. **FORT TOMPKINS QUADRANGLE**, Building 37, Fort Wadsworth,

1847-1861. Granite, brick and earth; 2-story hollow irregular quadrangular fortification, approximately 500' by 250', with inner and outer walls, moat between them, central yard; ashlar exterior walls include narrow vertical gun slits, pedimented entrance; interior walls with arched entrances to vaulted storerooms; both structures covered with earth. First fortified by the Dutch in 1663, later served the British. Museum. *Federal/USA.*

Staten Island. **KREUZER-PELTON HOUSE,** 1262 Richmond Ter., 1722. Stone (partially clapboarded) and brick; 1 1/2-2-story sections, rectangular, gabled roof sections, interior chimneys, dormers, bracketed cornice on center block, gabled vestibule with round arched entrance; 18th and 19th C. additions to original 1-room cottage. *Private.*

Staten Island. **VOORLEZER'S HOUSE,** Arthur Kill Rd., opposite Center St., 1690. Frame, novelty siding, shingling; 2 1/2 stories, rectangular, gabled roof with slight cant in front; interior end chimney, partially exposed on exterior; front side entrance with hood; staircase altered. Dutch Colonial elements. Believed to be oldest elementary school building in U.S., part of a 17th C. Dutch settlement. *Private:* NHL.

Tottenville, Staten Island. **CONFERENCE HOUSE,** Hylan Blvd., 1680. Stone, 2 1/2 stories, rectangular, gabled roof, interior end chimneys, wooden stoop and railing, segmental arched 1st-floor openings, coped end gables with end parapets, center entrance with transom, rear shed extension. Site of Revolutionary War conference between British admiral, Lord Richard Howe, and Colonial representatives, Benjamin Franklin, John Adams, and Edward Rutledge, Sept. 11, 1776; the Americans reiterated their commitment to independence in reply to Howe's offer of amnesty to all repentant rebels. *Municipal:* NHL; HABS.

ROCKLAND COUNTY

PALISADES INTERSTATE PARK, *Reference—see Bergen County, NJ*

Sloatsburg. **SLOAT HOUSE,** 19 Orange Tpke., Late-18th–early-19th C.. Stone, brick, and frame, clapboarding; 2 1/2 stories, modified rectangle, gabled roof; full-width front porch with paneled columns, denticulated cornice, and turned railing; door with transom and side lights flanked by paneled pilasters; 18th C. rear wing of stone and frame, clapboarding; 1 1/2 stories, with a double gabled roof; barn included. Federal and Greek Revival elements. Used by Sloat family as a meeting place, inn, and center of political activity. *Private; not accessible to the public.*

Stony Point vicinity. **STONY POINT BATTLEFIELD,** N of Stony Point on U.S. 2 and 202, 1779. Extensive earthworks and historic markers designate site where Americans led by "Mad" Anthony Wayne captured a fort located near West Point from the British garrison under Gen. Clinton, allowing Washington to regain control of the Hudson River. Interpretive museum. *State:* NHL.

Tappan. **DE WINT HOUSE,** Livingston Ave. and Oak Tree Rd., 1700. Brick and stone, 1 1/2 stories, rectangular, gabled roof, interior end chimneys, stone end walls and rear facade, brick front facade and gable ends, overhanging box cornice, 2 small blind oculi on front facade; restored. Georgian elements. Early Dutch colonial building; housed George Washington 4 times during Revolution, including the period during the trial and execution of John Andre, Sir Henry Clinton's adjutant who helped Benedict Arnold plan his treason. Museum. *Private:* NHL.

West Haverstraw. **GARNER, HENRY, MANSION,** 18 Railroad Ave., c. 1845. Brick, 2 stories, irregular shape with rear ell (1907), gabled roof, full-height Corinthian portico, flanking 2-story octagonal tower with octagonal belvedere; highly decorative interior plasterwork, 9' doors with silver hardware. Greek Revival. Residence of Henry Garner, wealthy industrialist, benefactor, and builder. *Private; not accessible to the public.*

West Nyack. **TERNEUR-HUTTON HOUSE,** 160 Sickelton Rd., 1731. Stone, 1 1/2 stories, modified rectangle, gabled roof sections with shingled gable ends, interior end chimneys, shed dormers; 2 front entrances, each with transom; full-width shed porch with Ionic columns, side 1-story wing. Example of pre-Revolutionary house with Dutch Colonial elements, erected originally as 2 separate dwellings, 1731 and 1753. *Private.*

SARATOGA COUNTY

Albany vicinity. **SARATOGA NATIONAL HISTORICAL PARK,** 30 mi. N of Albany via U.S. 4 and NY 32, 1777. Site of Gen. John Burgoyne's surrender to Gen. Horatio Gates after battle of Saratoga, Oct. 17, 1777. Victory was followed by French recognition of American Independence; thwarted British invasion of the North, considered the turning point of the Revolutionary War. *Federal/NPS.*

Mount McGregor. **GRANT COTTAGE,** CR 101 N of Rte. 9, 1872. Frame, clapboarding; 2 stories, rectangular, gabled roof, central and interior chimneys, off-center entrance, N and W porch on deck surrounding house. Place where

Gen. Ulysses S. Grant spent the last 5 weeks of his life. Museum. *State.*

Saratoga. **CASINO-CONGRESS PARK-CIRCULAR STREET HISTORIC DISTRICT,** Bounded by Broadway, Spring, and Circular Sts., 19th–20th C.. Residential district contains 33-acre Congress Park, Canfield Casino, and 10 surrounding dwellings; features 2–4-story frame and brick structures erected primarily in the late-19th C. with one earlier Greek Revival example; notable is the Renaissance Revival Canfield Casino (1866–1869, with additions 1902–1903), and the High Victorian Italianate Batcheller House (1870's); designers of the basin-shaped park included Frederick Law Olmsted and Jacob Weidenman in 1875, and Charles Leavitt and Henry Bacon in 1914. Town's fame as a health spa and gambling center stemmed from discovery of Congress Spring in the late-18th C. in the present park, and from the casino built by John Morrissey and taken over c. 1894 by Richard Canfield. *Multiple public/private.*

Saratoga Springs. **DRINKHALL, THE,** 297 Broadway, 1915, Ludlow and Peabody, architects. Concrete, stuccoed; 2-story central block with 1 1/2-story flanking side wings, modified U shape, tiled hipped roof sections; triple arched entrance section, each section containing pedimented doorways with glass panels above, and side lights; low relief panels, decorative arrowhead frieze, rear porch served as trolley platform. Beaux-Arts Classical elements. Built as railroad trolley station, later used by state to dispense mineral waters to public. *Municipal; not accessible to the public.*

Saratoga Springs. **FRANKLIN SQUARE HISTORIC DISTRICT,** In an irregular pattern from Beekman St. along both sides of Grand Ave., Franklin, and Clinton Sts. to Van Dam,

19th C.. Residential area with dwellings in wide range of 19th C. architectural styles including Greek Revival, Italianate, and Second Empire. Notable are the Second Empire row houses on Clinton Pl. with elaborate dormers, iron roof cresting, and front carved porches and the Greek Revival house at 1 Franklin Sq. with a 2-story Doric entrance portico and 2 1-story wing porticos. Popular 19th C. resort area. *Multiple private.*

Saratoga Springs. **TODD, HIRAM CHARLES, HOUSE (MARVIN-SACKETT-TODD HOUSE)**, 4 Franklin Sq., c. 1837. Frame, clapboarding; 2 stories, T-shaped; low pitched, gabled, and hipped roof sections; interior and paired interior end chimneys, central cupola with pilasters and parapet, main-block parapet, front center 2-story pedimented tetrastyle Doric portico; center entrance with transom, side lights, and entablature; portico flanked by polygonal bay windows, corner pilasters; side 1-story enclosed hipped porch with Doric columns, entrance with transom; side rear pavilion with pediment, entrance with small porch and full-height pilasters; rear 2nd-story porch, side enclosed porch; interior central hall leads to double curving staircase that converges to a single staircase; side porch enlarged 1928; porch on rear pavilion added 1940's. Built for Thomas Marvin, joint proprietor of the United States Hotel, one of a number of large hotels built to accommodate the city's influx of summer visitors which occurred beginning in the 1820's-1830's. *Private.*

Waterford. **PEEBLES (PEOBLES) ISLAND,** At jct. of Mohawk and Hudson rivers, 16th-20th C.. Natural crossroads, habitation site, and fortress for Indians and white settlers. Occupied by troops of Gen. Philip Schuyler and Polish patriot Gen. Thaddeus Kosciusko during

Revolutionary War. Traces of breastworks visible. *State.*

SCHENECTADY COUNTY

Delanson vicinity. **CHRISTMAN BIRD AND WILDLIFE SANCTUARY,** Schoharie Tpke., 1888. 105-acre rural tract containing hiking trails, 2 frame dwellings, and farm buildings. Developed from winter bird feeding program of W. W. Christman, nature lover and conservationist who advocated Daylight Savings Time and who reforested his land. Area designated as bird and wildlife sanctuary by the New York State Conservation Department and the Mohawk Valley Hiking Club, 1931. *Private.*

Schenectady. **NOTT MEMORIAL HALL, UNION COLLEGE,** Union College campus, 1872–1876, Edward Tuckerman Potter, architect. Random ashlar, 2 stories, 16-sided base, polygonal roof, modillion cornice, 16 low interior chimneys, central 16-sided cupola with clerestory and domed roof with Hebrew inscription; 4 entrances, 2 closed; 1st story with triple-grouped windows with cinquefoil arches, each with single pointed arched window above; 2nd-story triple-grouped pointed arched windows with small trefoil windows above, polychrome trim; interior with cast iron structural system; porches removed; 1902 renovation under supervision of William Appleton Potter included addition of 2nd story by extending a 2nd balcony, and completion of dome clerestory. High Victorian Gothic. Originally conceived as a circular neo-classic structure in J. J. Ramee's 1813 plan for the campus; foundation laid in 1858, shortage of funds stopped construction until 1872–1876; designer was grandson of Eliphalet Nott, president of Union College (1804–1864), for whom building was named. *Private.*

Schenectady. **STOCKADE HISTORIC DISTRICT,** Roughly bounded by Mohawk River, railroad tracks, and Union St., 17th–20th C.. Wedge-shaped downtown waterfront district contains residential, commercial, religious, and public buildings, railroad bridges, and remains of a wooden suspension bridge; featured are brick and frame structures in a wide variety of styles with many Federal, Greek Revival, and Italianate examples; notable is the Gothic Revival David Forrest house. Dutch village of Schenectady was established 1664; served as transportation center before building of the Erie Canal; later prominent for production of broom corn and brooms; citizens formed a private association in 1962 to promote restoration in the area. *Multiple public/private.*

Schenectady vicinity. **DELLEMONT-WEMPLE FARM,** W of Schenectady on Wemple Rd., c. 1790. Brick (English bond), 2 stories, rectangular, gambrel roof, end chimneys, center entrance with transom, symmetrical fenestration; original window sashes, interior mantels, and staircase replaced; barn, chicken house, burial ground. Georgian with local Dutch building influence. Residence of early Dellemont family. *Private; not accessible to the public.*

SCHOHARIE COUNTY

Blenheim. **NORTH BLENHEIM HISTORIC DISTRICT,** Both sides of NY 30, beside Schoharie Creek, Mid-19th C.. Village community comprised of about 30 structures, dominantly of Greek Revival origins, and including a fine church with Ionic columns in antis and a square peristyle belfry; also a covered bridge (see also Old Blenheim Covered Bridge, NY). District has been little changed since development as local trading center. *Multiple public/private.*

Blenheim vicinity. **LANSING MANOR HOUSE,** 2 mi. S of North Blenheim on NY 30, c. 1818. Frame, clapboarding; 2 stories, rectangular, hipped roof, interior end chimneys, center entrance with fanlight, front and side wraparound 1-story shed porch with balustrade; numerous outbuildings including well, outhouse, barn, and silos. Federal elements. Land was part of Blenheim Patent granted by King George III in 1769; scene of anti-rent activity in 1840's; working farm through 19th–20th C. *State.*

Breakabeen. **BREAKABEEN HISTORIC DISTRICT,** 19th–early-20th C.. Small rural town with about 35 largely 19th C. buildings along crossroads. Majority of structures on tree-lined streets are Greek Revival variations of frame houses, with several temple-form residences and a nice Greek Revival church. Area settled 18th C. by Palatine Germans, expanded over 19th C. *Multiple private.*

North Blenheim. **OLD BLENHEIM BRIDGE,** NY 30 over Schoharie Creek, 1855, Nicholas Montgomery Powers, builder. Frame with vertical siding, modified Long truss of 210′ clear span, 2 lanes, 26′ wide, stone and concrete abutments; reinforced, 1953. The longest single span covered bridge; one of few in the country with 2 lanes. *State:* NHL; G.

Schoharie. **OLD LUTHERAN PARSONAGE,** Adjacent to Spring St. in Lutheran Cemetery, 1743. Frame, clapboarding and shingling; 1 1/2 stories, rectangular, gabled roof, interior chimney, small 1-story entrance porch, original half-timbered end walls with clay and straw daub exist behind later lath and plaster walls; chimney added; under restoration. Colonial elements. Built as a parsonage for a Lutheran preacher from Germany who came to serve the Palatine German community of Schoharie

Creek; has served as residence for several church sextons. *Municipal:* G.

Schoharie. **SCHOHARIE VALLEY RAILROAD COMPLEX,** Depot Lane, c. 1875. Remains of rural railroad line include former passenger station, freight/locomotive house, mill building, and coal silos; features 1-2 1/2-story brick and frame buildings constructed c. 1875; under restoration. Railroad served as link to Albany and Susquehanna RR.; transported tourists to the valley and crops (hops, milk, apples, and grain) to markets in Albany and Binghamton; operations ceased 1942. *Municipal.*

SCHUYLER COUNTY

Tyrone vicinity. **LAMOKA,** Archaic (c. 3500 B.C.). The classic Archaic type site in the NE. Excavated by W. A. Ritchie. *Private; not accessible to the public:* NHL.

Watkins Glen. **SCHUYLER COUNTY COURTHOUSE COMPLEX,** Franklin St., 19th C.. Three-building county government complex; includes the 2-story brick Italianate Schuyler County Courthouse built in 1855, the sheriff's residence and jail, and the clerk's office. Courthouse served as focal point of community for over 100 years. *County.*

SENECA COUNTY

Fayette vicinity. **ROSE HILL,** W of Fayette on NY 96A, 1837-1839. Frame, clapboarding and flush siding; 2-story main block with 1 1/2-story wings, modified U shape, gabled roof sections, interior end chimneys, central cupola with parapet on balustraded square base, front full-width pedimented hexastyle Ionic portico; center entrance with transom and side lights slightly recessed behind entablature on pilasters with 2 freestanding Ionic columns framing door, carved moldings; side wings, each with front porch on Ionic columns; rear facade recessed behind balustraded 2-story porch with posts, 1st-story entrance with transom and side lights, 2nd-story entrance; interior plasterwork andcarved woodwork; cupola removed c. 1940, later reconstructed; restored 1968–1969. Excellent example of Greek Revival house; purchased by Benjamin L. and Robert J. Swan in 1850, the estate was a model of advanced agricultural methods for 40 years; Robert Swan was an incorporator of the State College of Agriculture (1853) and president of the NY State Agricultural Society (1881). Museum. *Private:* HABS.

Seneca Falls. **FALL STREET-TRINITY LANE HISTORIC DISTRICT,** Off NY 414 at Van Cleef Lake, Mid-19th–early-20th C.. 19th C. industrial district remains on 3 islands and part of mainland. Contains Late Gothic Revival Trinity Episcopal Church by Brown and Dawson and its parish house; a frame machine shop; a bandstand; and underwater sites of several small private residences, Rumsey Bridge, and many previously standing industrial structures, including large pump-manufacturing complexes, which were flooded and demolished to their foundations to create a navigable barge canal pool in 1914. *Multiple public/private.*

Seneca Falls. **STANTON, ELIZABETH CADY, HOUSE,** 32 Washington St., 19th C.. Frame, rectangular shingling and shingling in imbricated pattern under front gable; 2 stories, L-shaped, gabled roof, interior chimney, raised stone basement; enclosed front entrance porch added. Home of feminist Elizabeth Cady Stanton at time of the Seneca Falls Convention, which formally launched the women's rights movement and at which she read the Declara-

Historical Places 511

tion of Sentiments, advocating the ballot for women, 1846. *Private; not accessible to the public:* NHL.

ST. LAWRENCE COUNTY

ADIRONDACK FOREST PRESERVE, *Reference—see Clinton County*

Canton. **HERRING-COLE HALL, ST. LAWRENCE UNIVERSITY,** St. Lawrence University campus, 1869 (Herring Library); 1902, Paul Malo, architect (Cole Reading Room). Sandstone, 1 1/2 stories, T-shaped, intersecting gabled roof sections, pedimented and columned E main entrance portico, original gabled W entrance pavilion with arched doorway, E rose window; Cole addition designed by architect Paul Malo. Second building of St. Lawrence University. (See also Richardson Hall, St. Lawrence University, NY). *Private.*

Canton. **RICHARDSON HALL, ST. LAWRENCE UNIVERSITY,** St. Lawrence University campus, 1855-1856. Brick, 3 stories, rectangular, flat roof with central square cupola, 12 interior chimneys, front and rear Corinthian entrance porticos, side entrance porticos, bracketed cornice, 2nd- and 3rd-story stained glass center windows; interior renovations, 1906 and 1961. Classical elements. First building of St. Lawrence University which began as Universalist theological school and added the College of Letters and Science (see also Herring-Cole Hall, St. Lawrence University, NY). *Private.*

Ogdensburg. **U.S. CUSTOMSHOUSE,** 127 N. Water St., 1809-1810. Stone, 2 1/2 stories over full basement, rectangular, gabled roof, interior and exterior end chimneys, 3 entrances; 1937 additions and alterations include clapboard shed dormers, porch, segmental arched windows, and denticulated cornice. Focus of area's 19th C. St. Lawrence River shipping trade. *Federal/GSA.*

STEUBEN COUNTY

Corning. **JENNING'S TAVERN (PATTERSON INN),** 59 W. Pulteney St., 1796. Frame, clapboarding; 2 stories, L-shaped, gabled roofs, 2 interior chimneys; center entrance framed by pilasters, side lights and molded entablature; 2 early-19th C. rear additions. Federal. Erected by land agent Charles Williamson, who came to U.S. in 1791, and opened SW New York for settlement; built Lycoming Road and inn for early settlers. Benjamin Patterson, frontier scout and Revolutionary soldier, was first innkeeper, 1797 to 1804. *Private.*

Corning. **MARKET STREET HISTORIC DISTRICT,** Market St. from Chestnut St. to Wall St., 19th C.. Contains about 130 structures, mostly 1- and 2-story brick commercial buildings with molded brick, terra cotta, cast iron, and stone decorative elements; under restoration. Commercial center of important industrial community noted for glassworks. *Multiple public/private.*

SUFFOLK COUNTY

Cutchogue. **OLD HOUSE, THE,** NY 25, 1649. Frame, clapboarding; 2 1/2 stories, rectangular, gabled roof, interior chimney; exceptional extant 3-part casement windows; moved 1659; restored 1940. Good example of English colonial domestic architecture. Museum. *Private.* NHL; HABS.

Cutchogue vicinity. **FORT CORCHAUG SITE,** c. 1640-1661. Site of rectangular Indian log fort. Evidence of European contact and prehistoric occupation. Investigated, 1936-1948. *Private.*

East Hampton. **EAST HAMPTON VILLAGE DISTRICT,** Bounded by Main St. and James and Woods Lanes, 17th-19th C.. Residential Main Street area defined by tree-lined streets surrounding a village green; contains 1-2 1/2-story frame structures, a windmill, and a burying ground. Typical are the John Howard Payne House and the Thomas Moran House (1883). Settled as farming community; grew into popular seaside resort by 1870's. Maintains rural atmosphere. *Multiple public/private.*

East Hampton, Long Island. **MORAN, THOMAS, HOUSE,** Main St., 1884. Frame, shingling, 2 stories, rectangular, gabled roof with jerkinhead ends, interior chimney, front gables, off-center double-door entrance, front bay window and corner polygonal bay with pyramidal cap; full-width front interior studio. Eclectic. Home of American painter Thomas Moran, whose paintings depict the natural splendors of the West; notable are *The Grand Canyon of the Yellowstone* and *The Chasm of the Colorado,* both of which hang in the U.S. Capitol. *Private; not accessible to the public:* NHL.

East Hampton vicinity. **MONTAUK POINT LIGHTHOUSE,** Montauk Point, 1797. Stone, octagonal, 108' high; outbuildings rebuilt and structure altered, 1860. One of the earliest lighthouses built by the federal government; marks entrance to Block Island Sound. *Federal/USCG.*

Great River vicinity. **CUTTING, BAYARD, ESTATE (WESTBROOK),** N of Great River on NY 27, 19th C., Charles Haight, architect; Frederick Law Olmsted, landscape architect. Frame, half-timbering, and shingling; 2 1/2 stories, irregular massing, transverse gabled roof, 5 prominent brick chimneys, decorative stick work. English Tudor elements. Outbuildings include gatehouse, cottage, carriage house, and various farm buildings. Major portion of present complex built for wealthy entrepreneur and philanthropist, W. Bayard Cutting. *State.*

Great River vicinity. **SOUTHSIDE SPORTSMENS CLUB DISTRICT,** NE of Great River, off NY 27, 19th C.. Contains club facilities and extensive outdoor recreational areas and structures including woodland, ponds, brooks, bridges, dams, and footpaths; frame and shingled inn, height varies by section, 2-3 1/2 stories, gabled roof with cross gables; numerous alterations since construction of original inn, 1820's-1836. Built by Eliphalet Snedicor on New York City stage route; social and political gathering place of Islip residents. Club organized after Snedicor family's retirement in 1866; membership included the wealthy and prominent such as Charles Tiffany, William K. Vanderbilt, and Theodore Roosevelt. *State.*

Huntington. **EATONS NECK LIGHT,** Eatons Neck Point at Huntington Bay and Long Island Sound off NY 25A, 1798, John McComb, Jr., architect. Octagonal stone lighthouse approximately 60' high with iron lantern with domed roof, 1-story gabled wing; altered; light automated 1972; original complex included keeper's dwelling, now demolished. One of 3 lighthouses known to have been designed by John McComb, Jr. *Federal/USCG.*

Sag Harbor. **SAG HARBOR VILLAGE DISTRICT,** 18th-19th C.. Waterfront business and residential district; wide variety of 18th-19th C. building styles represented. Architectural highlights include Greek Revival Benjamin Huntting House, presently the Whalers Museum, and the Whalers Presbyterian Church, both attributed to Minard LaFever. Developed as whaling center until mid–late-19th C. when growth centered around watchcase manufacturing and other industries. *Multiple public/private.*

Saint James. **SAINT JAMES DISTRICT,** On NY 25A, 18th–19th C.. Community of estates built around early-19th C. Timothy Smith House, the Gothic Revival St. James Episcopal Church with stained glass by L. C. Tiffany, and Deepwells, a Greek Revival dwelling. Area first settled in 17th C. by Richard "Bull" Smith. Development as farming settlement during 19th C. resulted in larger and more sophisticated dwellings. Retains 19th C. character. *Multiple private.*

Smithtown. **HALLIOCK INN,** 263 E. Main St., 18th C.. Frame, shingling; 2 1/2 stories, L-shaped, 2 interior chimneys; 20th C. front porch, 1 1/2-story rear ell. Colonial elements. Center for town's social and political activities for nearly a century. Museum. *Private.*

St. James vicinity. **BOX HILL ESTATE,** NW of St. James on Moriches Rd., 19th C., Stanford White, architect. Pebble-dashed stucco, 2 1/2 stories, rectangular, gabled dormered roof with 3 cross gables, 1-story front veranda; Neo-classical exterior details; wide variety of styles on interior; formal gardens. Enlarged 3 times by Stanford White who also designed several shingled outbuildings including orangerie, water tower, and carriage house; enlarged once by son, Lawrence Grant White. Summer residence of Stanford White. *Private.*

St. James vicinity. **MILLS POND DISTRICT,** W of St. James on NY 25A, 17th–19th C.. Area containing cultivated open land, woodland, 2 ponds, and 9 structures including 18th C. Wegrzyn and Dougherty Houses and 19th C. Mills Homestead, built for William Wickham

Mills by Calvin Pollard. Area originally settled by Timothy Mills and developed as an agricultural complex by family. *Multiple private.*

Stony Brook. **MOUNT, WILLIAM SYDNEY, HOUSE,** Gould Rd. and NY 25, 1725. Frame, shingling; 2 1/2 stories, rectangular, gabled roof, interior and interior end chimneys; 2 front entrances, one with transom and small shed porch; ordinary constructed 1725; front portion constructed 1810; later addition; 2 barns. Vernacular style. Home (1836-1868) of William Sydney Mount, whose fine genre paintings reflect his attachment to the people and land of his local environment. *Private:* NHL.

SULLIVAN COUNTY

DELAWARE AND HUDSON CANAL, *Reference—see Orange County*

TIOGA COUNTY

Owego. **TIOGA COUNTY COURTHOUSE,** Village Park, 1871-1872, Miles F. Howe, architect. Brick, 2 stories with 3-story corner towers, rectangular, low pitched roof, modillion cornice sections; front and rear entrances, each with 1-story porch with iron railing around deck; side entrance with pedimented hood on brackets, limestone trim, corner buttresses, brick paneled sections with grouped segmental and round arched windows; original interior chestnut and black walnut woodwork; 2 towers lowered in height; 1969 renovations. High Victorian Gothic elements. Important local landmark designed by Owego resident, Miles F. Howe. *County.*

TOMPKINS COUNTY

Ithaca. **BOARDMAN HOUSE,** 120 E. Buffalo

St., 1867. Brick, 2 1/2 stories, modified rectangle, hipped roof with wide overhanging eaves, interior chimneys, central cupola, center entrance with fanlight and Ionic portico; front and 4 side windows, each with decorative segmental hood on consoles; side entrance porch. Italianate. Home of George McChain, Ithaca publisher; purchased by Judge Douglas Boardman, New York Supreme Court Justice and prominent businessman. *County.*

Ithaca. **CLINTON HOUSE,** 116 N. Cayuga St., 1828–1830, attributed to Ira Tillotson, architect. Brick, stuccoed; 3 stories over high basement, modified rectangle, low hipped roof with center cross gable, balustraded parapet, modillion cornice, wide frieze, front center pedimented hexastyle Ionic portico with balustraded 2nd- and 3rd-story balconies and tympanum Palladian window; front center 1st-, 2nd-, and 3rd-story entrances, secondary round arched ground-floor entrances; stone sills and projecting lintels; rear wing; restored, 1974. Federal and Greek Revival elements. One of the earliest luxury hotels built in America. *Private.*

Ithaca. **DE WITT PARK HISTORIC DISTRICT,** A square bounded roughly by properties fronting on E. Buffalo, E. Court, N. Cayuga, and N. Tioga Sts., 19th–20th C.. Primarily residential district located near commercial area includes city park and portions of the surrounding blocks; features 2–4-story residential, commercial, government, and religious structures of frame, brick, and stone in a variety of 19th–20th C. styles; notable are the Italianate Boardman House (1867, see also Boardman House, NY), the Beaux-Arts Classical Post Office (1910), and the Georgian Revival Williams-Fisher House (c. 1900). Area was developed by town's founder, Simeon DeWitt, in early-19th C.; park was then known as the Public Square; district is a focal point for many community activities. *Multiple public/private.*

Ithaca. **LEHIGH VALLEY RAILROAD STATION,** W. Buffalo St. and Taughannock Blvd., 1898. Brick, 1-story, modified rectangle, hipped roof, rear baggage wing and waiting platform; large iron freestanding clock at SE corner. Eclectic passenger station and adjacent passenger' cars renovated for restaurant. Built to serve trains, including the New York-Toronto Maple Leaf and various seasonal specials, that operated in city from 1828 until 1961. *Private.*

Ithaca. **MORRILL HALL, CORNELL UNIVERSITY,** Cornell University campus, 1866-1868, Henry W. Wilcox, architect. Rock-faced stone, 3 1/2 stories over high basement, rectangular, mansard roof, dormers, modillion cornice, large paneled interior chimneys, slightly recessed center section, 1st-story segmental arched windows, 2nd- and 3rd-floor round arched windows; renovated interior. Second Empire. Original building of Cornell University, founded and developed by Ezra Cornell and Andrew Dickson White as an institution where "any student can find instruction in any study"; school combined humanities and sciences, and was a land-grant college. *Private:* NHL.

Ithaca. **SECOND TOMPKINS COUNTY COURTHOUSE,** 121 E. Court St., 1854, John F. Maurice, architect. Brick, stuccoed; 2 1/2 stories, rectangular, gabled roof, similar N and S entrances with center compound pointed arched doorways surmounted by large lancet windows with dripstones and tracery, SW belfry, corner turrets, buttresses; N section of 2nd-story courtroom with classical detailing designed by William Henry Miller, local architect. Oldest Gothic Revival courthouse remaining in state. *County:* HABS.

Ithaca. **WHITE, ANDREW DICKSON, HOUSE,** 27 East Ave., 1871-1873, George Hathorne, William Henry Miller, Charles Babcock, successive architects. Brick, 2 1/2-story main section with connected units, irregular shape; roofline broken by jerkinhead dormers, high-pitched gables, and chimneys; center entrance in projecting tower enhanced by banded pointed arch and massive overhanging stone balcony above. Eclectic combination of Victorian styles. Built as home of Cornell University co-founder and first president, Andrew Dickson White; last remaining residence of Cornell's late-19th and early-20th C. "faculty row." *Private.*

Trumansburg. **CAMP, HERMON, HOUSE,** Camp St., 1845-1847, Thomas Judd, architect. Brick, 2-story central block flanked by 1-story wings, hipped roof with balustraded deck, 4 interior chimneys, full-height hexastyle portico with full entablature and parapet, center entrance. Greek Revival. Home of Hermon Camp, prominent 19th C. resident of Trumansburg. *Private; not accessible to the public.*

ULSTER COUNTY

DELAWARE AND HUDSON CANAL, *Reference—see Orange County*

Gardiner vicinity. **DECKER, JOHANNES, FARM,** SW of Gardiner on Red Mill Rd. and Shawangunk Kill, 1720's-1787. Stone, 1 1/2 stories, T-shaped, gabled roof with front shed extension over porch, 4 interior chimneys, gabled dormers; outbuildings include frame barn, carriage house, and icehouse; under restoration. Dutch colonial. Built by Johannes Decker, early settler. Excellent example of early New York Dutch architecture. *Private:* HABS.

Gardiner vicinity. **LOCUST LAWN ESTATE,** NY 32, SE of Gardiner, 18th–19th C.. Estate complex containing the stone Terwilliger House (1738); the Federal Col. Josiah Hasbrouck Mansion (1814); numerous outbuildings including the slaughterhouse, smokehouse, and carriage house; and an 18-acre bird sanctuary. Under restoration. Reflects growth and growing financial success of the occupants. *Private:* HABS.

Hurley. **HURLEY HISTORIC DISTRICT,** Hurley St., Hurley Mountain Rd., and Schoonmaker Lane, Late-17th–18th C.. Small town residential district contains a number of dwellings lining both sides of Main St.; features 1 1/2–2 1/2-story stone gabled dwellings, some with shed dormers and clapboarded gable ends constructed late-17th–18th C.; notable are Jan Van Deusen house (1723) with Dutch Colonial elements, temporary NY state capitol after the burning of Kingston in 1777; and the Hurley Patentee Manor (cottage 1696, main block 1745) with Dutch Colonial and Georgian elements, home of Cornelius Cool, colonial land estate agent. Town founded 1662 by Dutchand Huguenot settlers; soon taken over by English, but retaining Dutch customs and atmosphere. *Private:* NHL; HABS.

Kingston. **KINGSTON CITY HALL,** 408 Broadway, 1872–1873, Arthur Crooks, architect. Polychrome brick, 2 1/2 stories, modified rectangle, mansard roof, denticulated cornice, hipped dormers; front slightly projecting pavilion with projecting 4-story tower with pyramidal roof, entrance with transom and engaged columns at jambs, and pointed arched window above; rear projecting pavilion; sides with narrow center pavilions, each with entrance recessed within 1-story gabled entry; belt courses, rectangular and pointed arched windows, decorative sandstone panels beneath 3rd-story windows; gabled roof sections altered, 1927. High Victorian Gothic elements Center city landmark, expressive of city's growing economic importance during the canal and steamboat era. *Municipal.*

Kingston. **SENATE HOUSE,** NW side of Clinton Ave. near jct. with N. Front St., Late-18th C.. Brick and stone, 1 1/2 stories, modified L shape, gabled and hipped roof sections, 4 interior chimneys, shed dormers, corner porch; rebuilt after British burned original house in Oct. 1777; late-19th C. additions. State's first senate held its initial session in original 1676 house, Sept. 10, 1777. *State:* HABS.

Kingston. **WEST STRAND HISTORIC DISTRICT,** West Strand and Broadway, 19th C.. Waterfront district including the large Italianate Freeman building, the Mansion House Building (1854), and the West Strand Row containing 3–4-story brick attached Italianate structures with hipped or flat roofs, ornate cornice brackets, round and segmental arched windows with hood molds, and decorative brick and cast-iron work. Last remnant of city's early commercial center and business district that flourished after completion of the Delaware and Hudson Canal (see also Delaware and Hudson Canal, NY) in the late 1820's. *Multiple private.*

New Paltz. **HASBROUCK, JEAN, HOUSE,** Huguenot and N. Front Sts., 1694. Stone, 1 1/2 stories with attic, rectangular, steeply gabled roof with frame gables, interior chimneys, front center entrance with transom and small shed porch, side entrance with transom; original 1-room house enlarged, 1712. Flemish Colonial. Enlarged by merchant Jean Hasbrouck;

remained in family until 1899. Museum. *Private:* NHL; HABS.

New Paltz. **HUGUENOT STREET HISTORIC DISTRICT,** Huguenot St., 17th-18th C.. District containing 5 gabled stone dwellings—4 1 1/2-story structures, 2 with clapboarding in gable ends, and one 2 1/2-story structure (2nd story added late-18th C.); houses constructed late-17th-early-18th C. in Dutch Colonial style, some with later alterations; notable is the c. 1712 Jean Hasbrouck House (see also Jean Hasbrouck House, NY), unusually well preserved in its original form. Huguenot settlement (French and Walloon) founded 1677; town inc. 1785; council of 12 heads of families governed the settlement; families preserved Huguenot way of life by lack of intermarriage with their neighbors. *Multiple public/private:* NHL; HABS.

New Paltz. **LAKE MOHONK MOUNTAIN HOUSE COMPLEX,** NW of New Paltz, between Wallkill Valley on E and Roundout Valley on W, 1870-1902, Napoleon Le Brun, architect (1880's); James Ware, architect (later additions). 7500-acre recreational resort and woodland preserve. Focal point is Mountain House, large resort hotel typical of those in Catskills: frame and native stone construction; 3-7 stories, varying with rock cliff slope; varying roof styles including gabled and flat with parapet; unusual parlor wing (Ware, 1901) cantilevered over Lake Mohonk on huge steel trusses. Numerous resort structures. Quaker brothers Alfred and Albert Smiley acquired land and developed complex into noted resort and conference center. *Private.*

Rosendale vicinity. **PERRINE'S BRIDGE,** Off U.S. 87 over Wallkill River, 1844. Frame with vertical siding with clerestory openings; Burr arch truss of 138' single span, 17' wide, gabled roof, 12' clearance, bluestone abutments; repaired 1969. State's only true example of Burr arch patented in 1817 by Theodore Burr; transportation link between Rosendale and Esopus until 1932; now serves as footpath to a recreational facility. *County:* HABS.

West Park. **BURROUGHS, JOHN, RIVERBY STUDY,** Between NY 9W and the Hudson River, 1881. Log construction, 1 story, gabled roof, stone end chimney, bay window. Built as working quarters for John Burroughs, popular naturalist, whose prolific writings from 1865 to 1921 helped create a climate receptive to conservation in the U.S.; unchanged. *Private; not accessible to the public:* NHL.

West Park vicinity. **BURROUGHS, JOHN, CABIN (SLABSIDES)**, W of West Park, 1895. Log construction, 1 1/2 stories, rectangular, gabled roof with overhang over front porch, stone chimney. Built by John Burroughs, noted 19th C. naturalist, as retreat and summer residence. Here Burroughs wrote many of his essays included in *Ways of Nature* and *Bird and Bough*, and was visited by nearly 7000 guests, including President Theodore Roosevelt. *Private:* NHL.

WARREN COUNTY

ADIRONDACK FOREST PRESERVE, *Reference—see Clinton County*

Lake George. **OLD WARREN COUNTY COURTHOUSE COMPLEX,** Canada and Amherst Sts., 1845. Complex of 5 attached brick structures includes courthouse, judges' chambers, and jail; 1878 2-story facade with tower was added to 1845 1-story courthouse with front center entrance recessed under round arch, flared hipped roof with bacon striping and 2-stage clock tower, modillion cornice, machicolations, string courses; rear judges' chambers added 1878; 2-story jail and other structure added 1890's; county clerk's office built 1885, demolished in 1969 renovations; interior altered for adaptive use 1969. High Victorian Gothic elements. Growth of village of Lake George was spurred by expectations of a profitable trade route to Canada; county was created 1813; now provides space for research, planning, and museum facilities, fine example of adaptive use through cooperative state and local efforts. *Municipal.*

Lake George, Joshua's Rock. **OWL'S NEST (EDWARD EGGLESTON ESTATE)**, NY 9L, 1880's. Family estate complex. Includes the Homestead or main dwelling; Mellowstone (1883), a stone library with 2 large gabled dormers, each with a sunburst motif; a 1 1/2-story stone residence with large side gable containing 3 sunburst panels around a large lateral window; a wooden library; and cemetery. Stone dwelling and library built for one of America's earliest realistic novelists, Edward Eggleston, on land owned by his daughter and son-in-law; Eggleston was noted for his portrayal of American frontier life. *Private; not accessible to the public:* NHL.

WASHINGTON COUNTY

Fort Edward. **ROGERS ISLAND,** In Hudson River, W of Fort Edward, Woodland (1755–1763). Major military installation and medical facility for northern military activities during French and Indian War. Named for famous ranger leader, Maj. Robert Rogers, who used island as base of operations for raids on French. *Private.*

Schuylerville vicinity. **DERIDDER HOMESTEAD,** E of Schuylerville off NY 29,

18th-19th C.. Brick, 2 1/2 stories, rectangular, gabled roof, 2 interior end chimneys, off-center recessed entrance with transom and side lights; 1-story rear wing with 19th C. bracketed shed porch. Federal. Outbuildings include carriagehouse, barn, and broom factory. Home of the town's first settlers. *Private; not accessible to the public.*

Whitehall. **POTTER, JUDGE JOSEPH, HOUSE,** Mountain Ter., c. 1874, Almon Chandler Hopson, architect. Brick, stone facing; 2 1/2 stories, irregular shape, intersecting hipped and gabled roof sections, interior chimneys, gabled dormers, 3 bracketed porches, 4-story W clock tower with dormered pyramidal roof, 2 1/2-story S tower. Chateauesque. Built for Supreme Court Judge Joseph Potter. Converted to a restaurant, 1946. *Private.*

WAYNE COUNTY

Lyons. **BROAD STREET-WATER STREET HISTORIC DISTRICT,** 19th-20th C.. T-shaped commercial area along Erie Canal edge. Includes stone piers and buildings with cast iron storefronts and balconies and decorative cornices and window framing. Important is the Exchange Buildings, earliest documented commercial block of buildings. 19th C. character retained. *Private.*

Ontario. **BRICK CHURCH CORNERS,** Jct. of Brick Church and Ontario Center Rds., 19th-20th C.. Cluster of buildings and sites at road crossing, includes the North Methodist Church (1866) and the Pease-Micha house with its numerous outbuildings. Area first settled by the Pease family. Excellent remaining example of small rural settlement. *Multiple public/private.*

Palmyra. **EAST MAIN STREET COMMERCIAL HISTORIC DISTRICT,** Between Clinton and William-Cuyler Sts., 19th C.. Brick commercial district along main street of 19th C. canal town. Continuous rows of 2- and 3-story structures, many grouped in similarly treated blocks, with a variety of cornice and window detailing, and many cast iron shop fronts; Greek Revival Palmyrs Hotel, 1836-1837, dominates. Little altered district displays a typical 19th C. city business serving local residents and travelers. *Multiple private.*

Palmyra. **MARKET STREET HISTORIC DISTRICT,** Both sides of Market St. between Canal and Main Sts., 19th C.. One-block-long district includes residential and commercial structures; features 2-story frame detached dwellings or shops and 2-3-story attached brick and frame commercial buildings, some with cast iron storefronts; structures, which exhibit Greek Revival and Italianate elements, date primarily from 1830's to 1880's. Street was laid out in 1828 to link Main St. to the Erie Canal; economic activity lessened with decline of importance of canal. *Multiple public/private.*

WESTCHESTER COUNTY

Bedford. **BEDFORD VILLAGE HISTORIC DISTRICT,** 18th-19th C.. Town section embracing area founded by CT settlers, 1683. Planned in traditional New England village green scheme. Contains early burial area, 18th C. courthouse, 18th and 19th C. dwellings, and public and commercial buildings around common. Served as county seat until 1870; westward railroad construction diverted development and area was able to maintain 19th C. character. *Multiple public/private.*

Chappaqua. **OLD CHAPPAQUA HISTORIC**

DISTRICT, Quaker Rd., Late-18th–early-19th C.. Small residential area containing 12 simple frame structures clustered around a clapboarded 2-story frame meetinghouse. Displays excellent examples of rural vernacular domestic architecture. Developed as center of rural hamlet of Shapequaw, settled by Quakers in the mid-18th C. Retains colonial appearance. *Multiple public/private.*

Croton-on-Hudson. **VAN CORTLANDT MANOR**, U.S. 9 N of jct. with U.S. 9A, 1748–1749. Stone, 2 1/2 stories, modified L shape, hipped roof with deck, interior chimneys, gabled dormers, center entrance with transom, brick window surrounds with grotesque masks carved in keystones, simplified entablature; fine paneled interior; rear 1-story gabled and dormered sections, shed porch additions; related outbuildings. Restored. Georgian. Owned by Van Cortlandt family until 1889. Museum. *Municipal:* NHL.

Dobbs Ferry. **HYATT-LIVINGSTON HOUSE**, 152 Broadway, Late-17th–19th C.. Remains of 2 1/2-story frame Georgian style house; severely damaged by 1974 fire. House is believed to have served as Gen. George Washington's headquarters for a period in 1781. *Private; not accessible to the public:* HABS.

Greenburgh. **ODELL HOUSE (ROCHAMBEAU HEADQUARTERS)**, 425 Ridge Rd., 1732. Frame, shingling, and stone; 1 1/2–2-story sections, rectangular, gabled roof sections, interior chimneys, center entrance with transom in oldest center block, Dutch doors, mud and straw infill, corner fireplaces; 18th C. frame addition; 1850's stone addition; restored. Tenant farmstead on one of largest manors of time, Philipsburg Manor (see also Philipse Manor, NY); 1781 headquarters for Counte de Rochambeau, commander of the

French expeditionary forces during the Revolution. *Private.*

Hastings-on-Hudson. **CROPSEY, JASPER F., HOUSE AND STUDIO,** 49 Washington Ave., c. 1832. Stone basement, frame, board-and-batten siding; 1–1 1/2 stories over high basement on sloping site, irregular shape, gabled and hipped roof sections, interior chimneys, shed wall dormer, cross gables on front facade with carved bargeboards, front slightly projecting pavilion with entrance, front full-width wraparound porch with traceried braces to form stylized Tudor arches; original furnishings; studio with hipped roof added 1885. Gothic Revival. Home (1885–1900) of Jasper Cropsey, architect and Hudson River School artist. *Private.*

Katonah. **JAY, JOHN, HOMESTEAD (BEDFORD HOUSE)**, Jay St., 1787. Frame, clapboarding, wing end walls of stone; 2 1/2-story main block over high basement with 1-story wings, modified rectangle, gambrel and gabled roof sections, interior and interior end chimneys, front center entrance with transom and entablature with pilasters; full-width mainblock 1-story shed porch with balustrade wraps around to wing front facades, each with entrance (one false) with fanlight set within pediment; some original furnishings; 19th–20th C. additions; restored; outbuildings include overseer's brick cottage (1799), coachman's house, barns, and laundry building. Colonial format with Federal elements. Home of John Jay, an author of the *Federalist* essays and first Chief Justice of the U.S. Supreme Court; occupied by Jay's descendants until 1959. Museum. *State:* G.

Mount Vernon. **ST. PAUL'S CHURCH NATIONAL HISTORIC SITE,** Eastchester, c. 1765. Fieldstone, brick; 1 story, modified rectangle, gabled roof; projecting end tower with polygonal arcaded belfry, spire, and entrance with fanlight; side entrance, round arched windows; rear projecting gabled section; damaged and enlarged, 1787; restored to 1787 appearance, 1942. Georgian. Adjacent green site of denial of right to vote to Quaker group by Gov. William Cosby, later reported by printer John Peter Zenger in his *New York Journal*, an action for which he was tried and found innocent. *Private:* HABS.

Mount Vernon. **STEVENS, JOHN, HOUSE,** 29 W. 4th St., 1849. Frame, clapboarding; 2 1/2 stories, rectangular, gabled roof, interior end chimneys, denticulated cornice, front center entrance with transom and side lights; 1-story full-width hipped porch with denticulated cornice, Tuscan columns, and balustrade; front center 2nd-story window with cornice and side lights; original interior plasterwork and wooden and marble mantels. Greek Revival. Home of John Stevens, founder of Mount Vernon, an early suburban working-class community. *Municipal.*

New Rochelle. **PAINE, THOMAS, COTTAGE,** 20 Sicard Ave., 18th C.. Frame, shingling; 2 1/2 stories, L-shaped, gabled roof sections, interior chimneys; 1-story side wing with porch added, 1804; moved, 1909; saltbox rear extension. Home of Revolutionary propagandist Thomas Paine, author of *Common Sense*, *Rights of Man*, and *The Age of Reason*. *Private; not accessible to the public:* NHL; HABS.

North Tarrytown. **DUTCH REFORMED (SLEEPY HOLLOW) CHURCH,** N edge of Tarrytown on U.S. 9, c. 1700. Stone, 1 story, rectangle with 3-sided apsed end, gambrel roof, open belfry with pyramidal roof and spire, clapboarding on front gable; pointed arched doors and windows, 1837; altered, partially restored.

Washington Irving buried in adjacent cemetery. *Private:* NHL; HABS.

Ossining. **FIRST BAPTIST CHURCH OF OSSINING,** S. Highland Ave. and Main St., 1874. Brick, 1 1/2 stories, T-shaped, gabled roof sections, vents with tracery, interior end chimneys, traceried bargeboards, corner 3-stage tower with pyramidal roof and corner spires, pointed arched windows with trefoil tracery, side buttresses, perpendicular gabled structure at sanctuary end houses support facilities; baptistry added, schoolrooms added in undercroft. High Victorian Gothic elements. Central village landmark; church and village founded by Elijah Hunter. *Private.*

Ossining vicinity. **OLD CROTON DAM, SITE OF; NEW CROTON DAM,** N of Ossining on NY 129, 1837–1842, John B. Jervis (Old Croton Dam); 1893–1906, Alphonse Fteley, William R. Hill, J. Waldo Smith, and Walter H. Sears (New Croton Dam). Old Croton Dam (1837–1842), now submerged, consists of 50'-high trapezoidal section with rubble core surrounded by an impervious masonry facing of granite ashlar; New Croton Dam is 291'-high masonry dam of similar construction with buttresses, 2 stairways, and arched corbel table on downstream side, 2 pilasters on upstream side, and 19'-wide roadway carried on an arched steel bridge on top; originally constructed to incorporate an earthen dam, later removed and replaced with masonry construction; 97-acre landscaped park adjoins dam. Old Croton Dam was first major all-masonry dam in U.S., a prototype for others; New Croton Dam is highest and one of the last great masonry dams. *Municipal.*

Pelham Manor. **BOLTON PRIORY,** 7 Priory Lane, 1838. Stone, 2 stories, modified cross shape; hipped and gabled roof sections, partially crenelated; crenelated 4-story octagonal corner tower and 3-story square brick side tower. Gothic Revival. Depicted and described in 1841 by Andrew Jackson Downing in his *Theory and Practice of Landscape Gardening*, it helped introduce the Romantic Gothic Revival style to American domestic architecture. Home of Robert Bolton, American English-trained minister. *Private*.

Purchase. **REID HALL, MANHATTANVILLE COLLEGE (OPHIR HALL),** Manhattanville College, Purchase St., 1892 Stanford White, architect; Frederick Law Olmsted, landscape architect. Granite, 4 stories, modified L shape, flat roof with castelated parapet, main entrance block with wrap-around porch and projecting 5-story center tower with porte-cochere and entrance, W terrace; wings added by McKim, Mead, and White, 1912; upper stories and secondary halls altered to accommodate school needs. Built as residence for Whitelaw Reid, owner and editor-in-chief of the *New York Herald Tribune;* acquired by Manhattanville College, 1951. *Private*.

Purdys. **PURDY, JOSEPH, HOMESTEAD,** Jct. of NY 22 and 116, 1776. Frame, shingling and clapboarding; 1–2 1/2 stories, L-shaped, gabled roof sections, central chimney, bracketed cornice, front center double-door entrance with transom, full-width 1-story shed porch; porch added c. 1870; 1-story wings and shed structures added. Eclectic. Home of Joseph Purdy, member of the Purdy family, who founded the hamlet of Purdys and promoted industrial projects including a woolen mill. *Private*.

Rye. **WIDOW HAVILAND'S TAVERN,** Purchase St., 18th C.. Frame, clapboarding, front shingled in imbricated pattern; 2 1/2 stories, L-shaped, gambrel roof, 3 interior chimneys, full-width hipped porch, center entrance; side and rear additions. Served until 1830 as inn on post road between Boston and New York. *Municipal.*

Scarsdale. **HYATT, CALEB, HOUSE (CUDNER-HYATT HOUSE)**, 937 White Plains Post Rd., Mid-18th C.. Two structures connected at right angles: each frame with clapboarding, 2-2 1/2 stories, rectangular with gabled roof and interior chimney; each with 1-story entrance porch, one full-width; original 1-story dwelling (c. 1734-1754) raised to 2 stories c. 1836; later structure probably built before 1830; frame dependency. Colonial elements. Built as a tenant farmhouse, one of the few remaining buildings from early settlement period of Scarsdale and Eastchester. *Private.*

Somers vicinity. **SOMERS TOWN HOUSE (ELEPHANT HOTEL)**, Jct. of U.S. 202 and NY 100, 1820-1825. Brick over high granite foundation, 3 stories, modified rectangle, hipped roof with balustraded deck, 2 pairs of interior end chimneys; center entrance with transom, side lights, and small hipped portico; 3rd-story semicircular window, regular fenestration, small rear wing, statue of elephant in front of hotel. Federal. Main hotel in prosperous 19th C. town; built for Hachaliah Bailey, credited by P. T. Barnum as the "Father of the American circus;" housed 1805 meeting of showmen which resulted in the formation of the Association of the Zoological Institute, a major participant in circuses and the exhibition of animals for the next 50 years. *Municipal:* HABS.

Tarrytown. **LYNDHURST (JAY GOULD ESTATE)**, 635 S. Broadway, 1838, Alexander Jackson Davis, architect. Marble, 2-2 1/2 stories, irregular shape, gabled roof sections, numerous clustered interior chimneys, large turreted square towers, label molded pointed arched and rectangular windows, bay windows and oriels, stepped gables and gables with end parapets, cupola, battlemented porte-cochere; elaborate interior with wood sanded and painted to simulate stone, long gallery, hexagonal music room, vaulted ceilings; fine collection of furniture including Gothic pieces; enlarged 1864. One of best examples of picturesque Gothic Revival style and among the most famous buildings by noted architect A. J. Davis; built for New York mayor William Paulding as summer retreat; later home of Joy Gould, unscrupulous financier and railroad magnate and epitome of late-19th C. robber barons. Museum. *Private:* NHL.

Tarrytown vicinity. **SUNNYSIDE (WASHINGTON IRVING HOUSE),** Sunnyside Lane, c. 1656. Stone, 2 1/2 stories, irregular massing, gabled roof sections with stepped gables, interior chimneys with grouped diamond and circular stacks, square tower with bell-cast roof and cupola, entrance portico, weathervanes, dormers with scalloped bargeboards; product of extensive (1836-1849) remodeling of earlier house; restored. Eclectic elements. Irving, America's first writer of international repute, is remembered for his "Rip Van Winkle" and "The Legend of Sleepy Hollow." Museum. *Private:* NHL.

Upper Mills. **PHILIPSBURG MANOR,** 381 Bellwood Ave., c. 1683. Random stone, frame, clapboarding; 2 stories, rectangular, gambrel roof, large interior and interior end chimneys, front off-center entrance in frame wing with fanlight set partially within pediment; frame wing added 1785; restored 1943; outbuildings include old grinding mill and barn. Colonial elements. Erected by Frederick Philipse, First Lord of a manor of 90,000 acres; the main house was located a few miles away. Museum. *Private:* NHL.

Van Cortlandtville. **OLD ST. PETER'S CHURCH,** Oregon Rd. and Locust Ave., 1766–1767. Frame, clapboarding; 1 1/2 stories, rectangular, gabled roof with slight kick, front center entrance, round arched openings; pulpit opposite entrance on long side, gallery; restored 1964. Colonial elements. *Private:* HABS.

Yonkers. **PHILIPSE MANOR HALL,** Warburton Ave. and Dock St., Late-17th–mid-18th C.. Stone and brick, 2 1/2 stories, L-shaped, hipped roof with balustraded deck, 3 interior chimneys with corbeled caps, gabled dormers, center entrance on stone facade with fanlight and Doric portico, modillion cornice; brick side facade with 2 off-center entrances with fanlights, and full-width pent above 1st floor; fine interiors; original building extended during 18th C.; restored, early-20th C., 1970's. Georgian. Representative of Dutch manorial system in lower Hudson River valley; part of one of the most extensive manors in region; confiscated and sold when family remained loyal to Crown during Revolution. Museum. *State:* NHL.

Yonkers. **TREVOR, JOHN BOND, HOUSE (GLENVIEW)**, 511 Warburton Ave., 1876, Charles W. Clinton, architect. Rock-faced greystone, 2 1/2 stories, modified rectangle, flared hipped roof, flared hipped dormers, denticulated modillion cornice; front off-center slightly projecting tower with steeply pitched hipped roof, entrance with 1-story porch with truncated hipped roof; front side 2-story bay, ashlar sandstone belt courses and decorative rosettes; passage connects house to a recently-built concrete museum. Eclectic. Typical of many late-19th C. country residences built for financiers who wanted to own opulent estates within commuting distance of New York City. *Municipal.*

Yonkers. **UNTERMYER PARK,** Warburton Ave. and N. Broadway S of jct. with Odell Ave., 19th C.. Formal gardens containing small outdoor theater, columned pavilion, pergola, gazebo, and carriage house; all based on ancient Greek prototypes except for carriage house with hipped roof; free use of marble, Greek orders, and mosaics. Portion of estate of Samuel Untermyer, prominent early-20th attorney. *Multiple public/private.*

Yonkers and vicinity. **OLD CROTON AQUEDUCT,** Runs N from Yonkers to New Croton Dam, 1837–1842, John B. Jervis, chief engineer. Section of first major water supply system for New York City; includes nearly 26 mi. of original 38.09-mi. aqueduct, of which 85 percent is intact. Structural resources include 21 ventilating shafts, 4 gatehouses, 7 viaducts, 6 culverts, and the original maintenance buildings. General construction consists of concrete foundation, stone side walls, and brick interior facing and vaulting–8.5' high and 7.5' wide. Major engineering accomplishment when built; supplied water to NYC from 1842 to 1955; supplemented by new dam and aqueduct in late-19th–early-20th C. (see also High Bridge Aqueduct and Water Tower, and Site of Old Croton Dam; New Croton Dam, NY). To be developed into linear park system. *State:* HAER.

WYOMING COUNTY

Wyoming. **MIDDLEBURY ACADEMY,** 22 S. Academy St., 1817. Brick, 2 stories, rectangular, gabled roof, modillion cornice, front full-width tetrastyle Doric portico with pediment, lunette in tympanum, center entrance with fanlight, segmental arched windows; 1840 alterations included removal of one store and addition of portico; mid-20th C. renovations. Greek Revival. Important late-19th C. educational institution; now houses the Middlebury Historical Society. *Private.*

Wyoming. **WYOMING VILLAGE HISTORIC DISTRICT,** NY 19, 19th–early-20th C.. Small town center developed over 19th C., with about 70 structures, the main public ones arranged around a "green." The generally simple buildings include Federal and Greek and Gothic Revival structures, along with some turn-of-the-century eclectic buildings. Location of Middlebury Academy (see also Middlebury Academy, NY) in town gave the village an educational and cultural force unusual for a small village, as did the presence of several culturally-active wealthy families on the outskirts of town. *Multiple public/private.*

DIRECTORY OF NEW YORK STATE SERVICES
Key Word Underlined

AIRPORT DEVELOPMENT
Office: Department of Transportation, State Campus, Bldg. 4, Albany, 12232.

OFFICE FOR THE AGING
Office: Agency Bldg., Empire State Plaza, Albany, 12223.

AGRICULTURE AND MARKETS DEPARTMENT
Office: 50 Wolf Road, Albany, 12233.

ALCOHOLISM AND ALCOHOL ABUSE DIVISION
Office: 44 Holand Ave., Albany, 12229.

STATE ARCHIVES
Office: 10A46 Cultural Education Center, Empire State Plaza, Albany, 12230.

COUNCIL ON THE ARTS
Office: 80 Centre Street, New York City, 10013.

ATTORNEY GENERAL
Office: State Capitol, Albany, 12224.

AUDIT AND CONTROL DEPARTMENT
Office: Alfred E. Smith State Office Bldg., Washington Ave. and S. Swan Street, Albany, 12236.

BANKING DEPARTMENT
Office: Agency Bldg. 2, Empire State Plaza, Albany, 12223.

BUDGET DIVISION
Office: Executive Dept., State Capitol, Albany, 12224.

CHILD PROTECTIVE SERVICES
Office: 40 N. Pearl St., Albany, 12243.

CIVIL DEFENSE COMMISSION
Office: Public Security Bldg., State Campus, Bldg. 22, Albany, 12226.

CIVIL SERVICE DEPARTMENT
Offices: State Campus, Civil Service Bldg., Albany, 12239.

CLERK OF THE ASSEMBLY
Office: 407 State Capitol, Albany, 12224.

COMMERCE DEPARTMENT
Office: Twin Towers, 99 Washington Ave., Albany, 12245.

COMMUNITY AFFAIRS
Office: 162 Washington Ave., Albany, 12231.

COMPTROLLER
Office: Alfred E. Smith Office Bldg., Washington Ave., and S. Swan St., Albany, 12236.

CONSUMER PROTECTION BOARD
Office: 1000 Twin Towers, 99 Washington Ave., Albany, 12236.

CORRECTIONAL SERVICES
Office: 204 Correctional Services Bldg. 2, Albany, 12226.

COURT ADMINISTRATION
Office: 270 Broadway, New York City, 10007.

CRIMINAL JUSTICE SERVICES
Office: Executive Park Tower, Stuyvesant Plaza, Albany, 12203.

ECONOMIC DEVELOPMENT BOARD
Office: Alfred E. Smith Office Bldg., 17th Floor, Washington Ave. and S. Swan St., Albany, 12225.

ECONOMIC OPPORTUNITY DIVISION
Office: Department of State, 162 Washington Ave., Albany, 12231.

EDUCATION DEPARTMENT
Offices:
Higher Education: Cultural Education Center, Empire State Plaza, Albany, 12230.
Primary and secondary schools: State Education Bldg., Albany, 12234.

ELECTIONS BOARD
Office: Agency Bldg. 2, Empire State Plaza, Albany, 12223.

ENERGY
Office: Agency Bldg. 2, Empire State Plaza, Albany, 12223.

ENVIRONMENTAL CONSERVATION
Office: 50 Wolf Road, Albany, 12233.

FISH AND WILDLIFE DIVISION
Office: 50 Wolf Road, Albany, 12233.

FOOD INSPECTION SERVICES
Office: State Campus Bldg. 8, Albany, 12235.

FOREST RESOURCES MANAGEMENT
Office: 50 Wolf Road, Albany, 12233.

GENERAL SERVICES AGENCY
Office: Tower Bldg., Empire State Plaza, Albany, 12242.

GEOLOGICAL SURVEY
Office: 973 State Education Bldg. Annex, Albany, 12234.

HEALTH DEPARTMENT
Office: Tower Bldg. Empire State Plaza, Albany, 12237.

HOUSING AND COMMUNITY RENEWAL
Office: Two World Trade Center, New York City, 10047.
HUMAN RIGHTS DIVISION
Office: Executive Dept., Two World Trade Center, New York City, 10047.
INSURANCE DEPARTMENT
Office: Agency Bldg. 1, Empire State Plaza, Albany, 12233.
LABOR DEPARTMENT
Office: State Campus, Bldg. 12, Albany, 12240.
LEGLISLATIVE LIBRARY
Office: 337 State Capitol, Albany, 12230.
STATE LIBRARIAN
Office: Cultural Education Department, Empire State Plaza, Albany, 12230.
PROFESSIONAL LICENSING SERVICES
Office: Twin Towers, 99 Washington Ave., Albany, 12226.
LIQUOR AUTHORITY
Office: Two World Trade Center, New York City, 10047.
LOTTERY DIVISION
Office: Dept. of Taxation and Finance, Swan Street Bldg. Core No. 1, Empire State Plaza, Albany, 12223.
MENTAL HEALTH
Office: 44 Holland Drive, Albany, 12229.
MENTAL RETARDATION DEVELOPMENTAL DISABILITIES
Office: 44 Holland Ave., Albany, 12229.
MILITARY AND NAVAL AFFAIRS
Office: Public Security Bldg., State Campus, Bldg. 22, Albany, 12226.
MINERAL RESOURCES
Office: 50 Wolf Road, Albany, 12233.
DEPARTMENT OF MOTOR VEHICLES
Office: Swan Street Bldg., Empire State Plaza, Albany, 12228.
PARKS AND RECREATION
Office: Agency Bldg. 1 Empire State Plaza, Albany, 12238.
STATE PLANNING
Office: 162 Washington Ave., Albany, 12231.
STATE POLICE
Office: Public Security Bldg., State Campus, Bldg. 22, Albany, 12226.
PUBLICATIONS BUREAU
Office: 162 Washington Ave., Albany, 12231.
PROBATION DIVISION
Office: Tower Bldg., Empire State Plaza, Albany, 12233.

PUBLIC SERVICE COMMISSION
Office: Empire State Plaza, Albany, 12223.
PURCHASING DIVISION
Office: General Service, Tower Bldg., Empire State Plaza, Albany, 12242.
RAIL DIVISION
Office: Transportation Dept., State Campus, Bldg. 4, Albany, 12232.
EMPLOYEE'S RETIREMENT SYSTEM
Office: Alfred E. Smith Office Bldg., Washington Ave. and Swan Street, Albany, 12244.
SAFETY AND HEALTH DIVISION
Office: Labor Dept., Two World Trade Center, New York City, 10047.
SECRETARY OF STATE
Office: 162 Washington Ave., Albany, 12231.
SECRETARY OF THE SENATE
Office: 162 Washington Ave., Albany, 12231.
SECURITIES BUREAU
Office: Dept. of Law, Two World Trade Center, New York City, 10047.
SOCIAL SERVICES DEPARTMENT
Office: 40 N. Pearl St., Albany, 12243.
SOLID WASTE MANAGEMENT DIVISION
Office: 50 Wolf Road, Albany, 12233.
SUBSTANCE ABUSE SERVICES
Office: Executive Park South, Stuyvesant Plaza, Albany, 12203.
TAXATION AND FINANCE DEPARTMENT
Office: State Campus, Bldg. 9, Albany, 12227.
TOURISM DIVISION
Office: Commerce Dept., Twin Towers, Albany, 12245.
DEPARTMENT OF TRANSPORTATION
Office: State Campus Bldg. 5, Albany, 12232.
TREASURER
Office: Alfred E. Smith Office Bldg., Washington Ave. and Swan Street S., P.O. Box 7002, Albany, 12225.
VETERAN'S AFFAIRS DIVISION
Office: Executive Dept. Agency Bldg. 2, Empire State Plaza, Albany, 12223.
BUREAU OF VITAL RECORDS
Office: Tower Bldg., Empire State Plaza, Albany, 12237.
WASHINGTON OFFICE
Office of the Governor, 444 N. Capitol St., Washington, D.C. 20001.
PURE WATERS DIVISION
Office: 50 Wolf Road, Albany, 12233.

WORKER'S COMPENSATION BOARD
Office: 1949 N. Broadway, Albany, 12241.

YOUTH DIVISION
Office: Executive Dept., 84 Holland Ave., Albany, 12208.

THE CONSTITUTION

*[Preamble.] WE, THE PEOPLE of the State of New York, grateful to Almighty God for our Freedom, in order to secure its blessings, DO ESTABLISH THIS CONSTITUTION.

ARTICLE I
BILL OF RIGHTS

*[Rights, privileges and franchise secured; power of legislature to dispense with primary elections in certain cases.] Section 1. No member of this state shall be disfranchised, or deprived of any of the rights or privileges secured to any citizen thereof, unless by the law of the land, or the judgment of his peers, except that the legislature may provide that there shall be no primary election held to nominate candidates for public office or to elect persons to party positions for any political party or parties in any unit of representation of the state from which such candidates or persons are nominated or elected whenever there is no contest or contests for such nominations or election as may be prescribed by general law. (Amended by vote of the people November 3, 1959.)

[Trial by jury; how waived.] § 2. Trial by jury in all cases in which it has heretofore been guaranteed by constitutional provision shall remain inviolate forever; but a jury trial may be waived by the parties in all civil cases in the manner to be prescribed by law. The legislature may provide, however, by law, that a verdict may be rendered by not less than five-sixths of the jury in any civil case. A jury trial may be waived by the defendant in all criminal cases, except those in

---

*[Explanatory note. Section headings are enclosed in brackets throughout the constitution to indicate that they are not a part of the official text. Except where otherwise specifically indicated, the section has been re-enacted without change by the Constitutional Convention of 1938 and readopted by vote of the people November 8, 1938.]

which the crime charged may be punishable by death, by a written instrument signed by the defendant in person in open court before and with the approval of a judge or justice of a court having jurisdiction to try the offense. The legislature may enact laws, not inconsistent herewith, governing the form, content, manner and time of presentation of the instrument effectuating such waiver. (Amended by Constitutional Convention of 1938 and approved by vote of the people November 8, 1938.)

[Freedom of worship; religious liberty.] § 3. The free exercise and enjoyment of religious profession and worship, without discrimination or preference, shall forever be allowed in this state to all mankind; and no person shall be rendered incompetent to be a witness on account of his opinions on matters of religious belief; but the liberty of conscience hereby secured shall not be so construed as to excuse acts of licentiousness, or justify practices inconsistent with the peace or safety of this state.

[Habeas corpus.] § 4. The privilege of a writ or order of habeas corpus shall not be suspended, unless, in case of rebellion or invasion, the public safety requires it. (Amended by Constitutional Convention of 1938 and approved by vote of the people November 8, 1938.)

[Bail; fines; punishments; detention of witnesses.] § 5. Excessive bail shall not be required nor excessive fines imposed, nor shall cruel and unusual punishments be inflicted, nor shall witnesses be unreasonably detained.

[Grand jury; protection of certain enumerated rights; duty of public officers to sign waiver of immunity and give testimony; penalty for refusal.] § 6. No person shall be held to answer for a capital or otherwise infamous crime (except in cases of impeachment, and in cases of militia when in actual service, and the land, air and naval forces in time of war, or which this state may keep with the consent of congress in time of peace, and in cases of petit larceny, under the regulation of the legislature), unless on indictment of a grand jury, except that a person held for the action of a grand jury upon a charge for such an offense, other than one punishable by death or life imprisonment, with the consent of the district attorney, may waive indictment by a grand jury and consent to be prosecuted on an information filed by the district attorney; such waiver shall be evidenced by written instrument signed by the defendant in open court in the presence of his counsel. In any trial in any court whatever the party accused shall be allowed to appear and defend in person and with counsel as in civil actions and shall be informed of the nature and cause of the accusation and be confronted with the witnesses against him. No person shall be subject to be twice put in jeopardy for the same offense; nor shall he be compelled in any criminal case to be a witness against himself, providing, that any public officer who, upon being called before a grand jury to testify concerning the conduct of his present office or of any public office held by him within five years prior to such grand jury call to testify, or the performance of his official duties in any such present or prior offices, refuses to sign a waiver of immunity against subsequent criminal prosecution, or to answer any relevant question concerning such matters before such grand jury, shall by virtue of such refusal, be disqualified from holding any other public office or public employment for a period of five years from the date of such refusal to sign a waiver of immunity against subsequent prosecution, or to answer any relevant question concerning such matters before such grand jury, and shall be removed from his present office by the appropriate authority or shall forfeit his present office at the suit of the attorney-general.

The power of grand juries to inquire into the wilful misconduct in office of public officers, and to find indictments or to direct the filing of informations in connection with such inquiries, shall never be suspended or impaired by law.

No person shall be deprived of life, liberty or property without due process of law. (Amended by Constitutional Convention of 1938 and approved by vote of the people November 8, 1938; further amended by vote of the people November 8, 1949; November 3, 1959; November 6, 1973.)

[**Compensation for taking private property; private roads; drainage of agricultural lands.**] § 7. (a) Private property shall not be taken for public use without just compensation.

(c) Private roads may be opened in the manner to be prescribed by law; but in every case the necessity of the road and the amount of all damage to be sustained by the opening thereof shall be first determined by a jury of freeholders, and such amount, together with the expenses of the proceedings, shall be paid by the person to be benefited.

(d) The use of property for the drainage of swamp or agricultural lands is declared to be a public use, and general laws may be passed permitting the owners or occupants of swamp or agricultural lands to construct and maintain for the drainage thereof, necessary drains, ditches and dykes upon the lands of others, under proper restrictions, on making just compensation, and such compensation together with the cost of such drainage may be assessed, wholly or partly, against any property benefited thereby; but no special laws shall be enacted for such purposes. (Amended by Constitutional Convention of 1938 and approved by vote of the people November 8, 1938. Subdivision (e) repealed by vote of the people November 5, 1963. Subdivision (b) repealed by vote of the people November 3, 1964.)

[**Freedom of speech and press; criminal prosecutions for libel.**] § 8. Every citizen may freely speak, write and publish his sentiments on all subjects, being responsible for the abuse of that right; and no law shall be passed to restrain or abridge the liberty of speech or of the press. In all criminal prosecutions or indictments for libels, the truth may be given in evidence to the jury; and if it shall appear to the jury that the matter charged as libelous is true, and was published with good motives and for justifiable ends, the party shall be acquitted; and the jury shall have the right to determine the law and the fact.

[Right to assemble and petition; divorce; lotteries; pool-selling and gambling; laws to prevent; pari-mutuel betting on horse races permitted; games of chance, bingo or lotto authorized under certain restrictions.] § 9. 1. No law shall be passed abridging the rights of the people peaceably to assemble and to petition the government, or any department thereof; nor shall any divorce be granted otherwise than by due judicial proceedings; except as hereinafter provided, no lottery or the sale of lottery tickets, pool-selling, book-making, or any other kind of gambling, except lotteries operated by the state and the sale of lottery tickets in connection therewith as may be authorized and prescribed by the legislature, the net proceeds of which shall be applied exclusively to or in aid or support of education in this state as the legislature may prescribe, and except pari-mutuel betting on horse races as may be prescribed by the legislature and from which the state shall derive a reasonable revenue for the support of government, shall hereafter be authorized or allowed within this state; and the legislature shall pass appropriate laws to prevent offenses against any of the provisions of this section.

2. Notwithstanding the foregoing provisions of this section, any city, town or village within the state may by an approving vote of the majority of the qualified electors in such municipality voting on a proposition therefor submitted at a general or special election authorize, subject to state legislative supervision and control, the conduct of one or both of the following categories of games of chance commonly known as: (a) bingo or lotto, in which prizes are awarded on the basis of designated numbers or symbols on a card conforming to numbers or symbols se-

lected at random; (b) games in which prizes are awarded on the basis of a winning number or numbers, color or colors, or symbol or symbols determined by chance from among those previously selected or played, whether determined as the result of the spinning of a wheel, a drawing or otherwise by chance. If authorized, such games shall be subject to the following restrictions, among others which may be prescribed by the legislature: (1) only bona fide religious, charitable or non-profit organizations of veterans, volunteer firemen and similar non-profit organizations shall be permitted to conduct such games; (2) the entire net proceeds of any game shall be exclusively devoted to the lawful purposes of such organizations; (3) no single prize shall exceed two hundred and fifty dollars; (4) no series of prizes on any one occasion shall aggregate more than one thousand dollars; (5) no person except a bona fide member of any such organization shall participate in the management or operation of such game; and (6) no person shall receive any remuneration for participating in the management or operation of any such game. The legislature shall pass appropriate laws to effectuate the purposes of this subdivision, ensure that such games are rigidly regulated to prevent commercialized gambling, prevent participation by criminal and other undesirable elements and the diversion of funds from the purposes authorized hereunder and establish a method by which a municipality which has authorized such games may rescind or revoke such authorization. Unless permitted by the legislature, no municipality shall have the power to pass local laws or ordinances relating to such games. Nothing in this section shall prevent the legislature from passing laws more restrictive than any of the provisions of this section. (Amendment approved by vote of the people November 7, 1939; further amended by vote of the people November 5, 1957; November 8, 1966; November 4, 1975.)

No section 10 *(see footnote*)*

[Equal protection of laws; discrimination in civil

* Section 10 which dealt with ownership of lands, allodial tenures and escheats was repealed by amendment approved by vote of the people November 6, 1962.

rights prohibited.] § 11. No person shall be denied the equal protection of the laws of this state or any subdivision thereof. No person shall, because of race, color, creed or religion, be subjected to any discrimination in his civil rights by any other person or by any firm, corporation, or institution, or by the state or any agency or subdivision of the state. (New. Adopted by Constitutional Convention of 1938 and approved by vote of the people November 8, 1938.)

[**Security against unreasonable searches, seizures and interceptions.**] § 12. The right of the people to be secure in their persons, houses, papers and effects, against unreasonable searches and seizures, shall not be violated, and no warrants shall issue, but upon probable cause, supported by oath or affirmation, and particularly describing the place to be searched, and the persons or things to be seized.

The right of the people to be secure against unreasonable interception of telephone and telegraph communications shall not be violated, and ex parte orders or warrants shall issue only upon oath or affirmation that there is reasonable ground to believe that evidence of crime may be thus obtained, and identifying the particular means of communication, and particularly describing the person or persons whose communications are to be intercepted and the purpose thereof. (New. Adopted by Constitutional Convention of 1938 and approved by vote of the people November 8, 1938.)

No section 13 *(see footnote**)*

[**Common law and acts of the state legislatures.**] § 14. Such parts of the common law, and of the acts of the legislature of the colony of New York, as together did form the law of the said colony, on the nineteenth day of April, one thousand seven hundred seventy-five, and the resolutions of the congress of the said colony, and of the convention of the State of New York, in force on the

** Section 13 which dealt with purchase of lands of Indians was repealed by amendment approved by vote of the people November 6, 1962.

twentieth day of April, one thousand seven hundred seventy-seven, which have not since expired, or been repealed or altered; and such acts of the legislature of this state as are now in force, shall be and continue the law of this state, subject to such alterations as the legislature shall make concerning the same. But all such parts of the common law, and such of the said acts, or parts thereof, as are repugnant to this constitution, are hereby abrogated. (Formerly § 16. Renumbered and amended by Constitutional Convention of 1938 and approved by vote of the people November 8, 1938.)

No section 15 *(see footnote†)*

[**Damages for injuries causing death.**] § 16. The right of action now existing to recover damages for injuries resulting in death, shall never be abrogated; and the amount recoverable shall not be subject to any statutory limitation. (Formerly § 18. Renumbered by Constitutional Convention of 1938 and approved by vote of the people November 8, 1938.)

[**Labor not a commodity; hours and wages in public work; right to organize and bargain collectively.**] § 17. Labor of human beings is not a commodity nor an article of commerce and shall never be so considered or construed.

No laborer, workman or mechanic, in the employ of a contractor or subcontractor engaged in the performance of any public work, shall be permitted to work more than eight hours in any day or more than five days in any week, except in cases of extraordinary emergency; nor shall he be paid less than the rate of wages prevailing in the same trade or occupation in the locality within the state where such public work is to be situated, erected or used.

Employees shall have the right to organize and to bargain collectively through representatives of their own

† Section 15 which dealt with certain grants of lands and of charters made by the king of Great Britain and the state and obligations and contracts not to be impaired was repealed by amendment approved by vote of the people November 6, 1962.

choosing. (New. Adopted by Constitutional Convention of 1938 and approved by vote of the people November 8, 1938.)

[**Workmen's compensation.**] § 18. Nothing contained in this constitution shall be construed to limit the power of the legislature to enact laws for the protection of the lives, health, or safety of employees; or for the payment, either by employers, or by employers and employees or otherwise, either directly or through a state or other system of insurance or otherwise, of compensation for injuries to employees or for death of employees resulting from such injuries without regard to fault as a cause thereof, except where the injury is occasioned by the wilful intention of the injured employee to bring about the injury or death of himself or of another, or where the injury results solely from the intoxication of the injured employee while on duty; or for the adjustment, determination and settlement, with or without trial by jury, of issues which may arise under such legislation; or to provide that the right of such compensation, and the remedy therefor shall be exclusive of all other rights and remedies for injuries to employees or for death resulting from such injuries; or to provide that the amount of such compensation for death shall not exceed a fixed or determinable sum; provided that all moneys paid by an employer to his employees or their legal representatives, by reason of the enactment of any of the laws herein authorized, shall be held to be a proper charge in the cost of operating the business of the employer. (Formerly § 19. Renumbered by Constitutional Convention of 1938 and approved by vote of the people November 8, 1938.)

ARTICLE II
Suffrage

[**Qualifications of voters.**] Section 1. Every citizen shall be entitled to vote at every election for all officers elected by the people and upon all questions submitted to the vote of the people provided that such citizen is twenty-one †† years of age or over and shall have been a resident of this state, and of the county, city, or village for three months next preceding an election.

Notwithstanding the foregoing provisions, after January first, one thousand nine hundred twenty-two, no person shall become entitled to vote by attaining majority, by naturalization or otherwise, unless such person is also able, except for physical disability, to read and write English. (Amended by Constitutional Convention of 1938 and approved by vote of the people November 8, 1938; further amended by vote of the people November 2, 1943; November 6, 1945; November 6, 1951; November 8, 1966.)

[**Absentee voting.**] § 2. The legislature may, by general law, provide a manner in which, and the time and place at which, qualified voters who, on the occurrence of any election, may be absent from the county of their residence or, if residents of the city of New York, from the city, and qualified voters who, on the occurrence of any election, may be unable to appear personally at the polling place because of illness or physical disability, may vote and for the return and canvass of their votes. (Formerly § 1-a. Renumbered by Constitutional Convention of 1938 and approved by vote of the people November 8, 1938; amended by vote of the people November 4, 1947; November 8, 1955; November 5, 1963.)

[**Persons excluded from the right of suffrage.**] § 3. No person who shall receive, accept, or offer to receive, or pay, offer or promise to pay, contribute, offer or promise to contribute to another, to be paid or used, any money or other valuable thing as a compensation or reward for the giving or withholding a vote at an election, or who shall make any promise to influence the giving or withholding any such vote, or who shall

††Superseded by 26th amendment of U.S. Constitution. Pursuant to Chap. 918, N.Y. Laws of 1974, legislation was enacted giving 18-year-olds the right to vote.

make or become directly or indirectly interested in any bet or wager depending upon the result of any election, shall vote at such election; and upon challenge for such cause, the person so challenged, before the officers authorized for that purpose shall receive his vote, shall swear or affirm before such officers that he has not received or offered, does not expect to receive, has not paid, offered or promised to pay, contributed, offered or promised to contribute to another, to be paid or used, any money or other valuable thing as a compensation or reward for the giving or withholding a vote at such election, and has not made any promise to influence the giving or withholding of any such vote, nor made or become directly or indirectly interested in any bet or wager depending upon the result of such election. The legislature shall enact laws excluding from the right of suffrage all persons convicted of bribery or of any infamous crime. (Formerly § 2. Renumbered by Constitutional Convention of 1938 and approved by vote of the people November 8, 1938.)

[Certain occupations and conditions not to affect residence.] § 4. For the purpose of voting, no person shall be deemed to have gained or lost a residence, by reason of his presence or absence, while employed in the service of the United States; nor while engaged in the navigation of the waters of this state, or of the United States, or of the high seas; nor while a student of any seminary of learning; nor while kept at any almshouse, or other asylum, or institution wholly or partly supported at public expense or by charity; nor while confined in any public prison. (Formerly § 3. Renumbered by Constitutional Convention of 1938 and approved by vote of the people November 8, 1938.)

[Registration and election laws to be passed.] § 5. Laws shall be made for ascertaining, by proper proofs, the citizens who shall be entitled to the right of ·suffrage hereby established, and for the registration of voters; which registration shall be completed at least ten days before each election. Such registration shall not be required for town and village elections except by express provision of law. In cities and villages having five thousand inhabitants or more, voters shall be registered upon personal application only; but voters not residing in such cities or villages shall not be required to apply in person for registration at the first meeting of the officers having charge of the registry of voters; however, voters who are in the actual military service of the state or of the United States, in the army, navy, air force or any branch thereof, or in the coast guard, or inmates of a veterans' bureau hospital and voters who are unable to appear personally for registration because of illness or physical disability or because their duties, occupation or business require them to be outside the counties of their residence or, in the case of residents of the city of New York, their duties, occupation or business require them to be in a county outside such city; and a spouse, parent or child of such a voter in the actual military service or of such an inmate or of such a voter unable to appear personally for registration, accompanying or being with him or her, if a qualified voter and a resident of the same election district, and if outside the county of such election district, shall not be required to register personally. The number of such inhabitants shall be determined according to the latest census or enumeration, federal or state, showing the population of the city or village, except that the federal census shall be controlling unless such state enumeration, if any, shall have been taken and returned two or more years after the return of the preceding federal census. (Formerly § 4. Renumbered by Constitutional Convention of 1938 and approved by vote of the people November 8, 1938; amended by vote of the people November 6, 1951; further amended by vote of the people November 8, 1955; November 8, 1966.)

[Permanent registration.] § 6. The legislature may provide by law for a system or systems of registration whereby upon personal application a voter may be registered and his registration continued so long as he shall remain qualified to vote from the same address, or for such shorter period as the legislature may prescribe. (New. Adopted by Constitutional Convention of 1938 and approved by vote of the people November 8, 1938.)

[Manner of voting; identification of voters.] § 7. All elections by the citizens, except for such town officers as may by law be directed to be otherwise chosen, shall be by ballot, or by such other method as may be prescribed by law, provided that secrecy in voting be preserved. The legislature shall provide for identification of voters through their signatures in all cases where personal registration is required and shall also provide for the signatures, at the time of voting, of all persons voting in person by ballot or voting machine, whether or not they have registered in person, save only in cases of illiteracy or physical disability. (Formerly § 5. Renumbered and amended by Constitutional Convention of 1938 and approved by vote of the people November 8, 1938.)

[Bi-partisan registration and election boards.] § 8. All laws creating, regulating or affecting boards or officers charged with the duty of registering voters, or of distributing ballots to voters, or of receiving, recording or counting votes at elections, shall secure equal representation of the two political parties which, at the general election next preceding that for which such boards or officers are to serve, cast the highest and the next highest number of votes. All such boards and officers shall be appointed or elected in such manner, and upon the nomination of such representatives of said parties respectively, as the legislature may direct. Existing laws on this subject shall continue until the legislature shall otherwise provide. This section shall not apply to town, or village elections. Formerly § 6. Renumbered and amended by Constitutional Convention of 1938 and approved by vote of the people November 8, 1938.)

[Presidential elections; special voting procedures authorized.] § 9. Notwithstanding the residence requirements imposed by section one of this article, the legislature may, by general law, provide special procedures whereby every person who shall have moved from another state to this state or from one county, city or village within this state to another county, city or village within this state and who shall have been an inhabitant of this state in any event for ninety days next preceding an election at which electors are to be chosen for the office of president and vice president of the United States shall be entitled to vote in this state solely for such electors, provided such person is otherwise qualified to vote in this state and is not able to qualify to vote for such electors in any other state. The legislature may also, by general law, prescribe special procedures whereby every person who is registered and would be qualified to vote in this state but for his removal from this state to another state within one year next preceding such election shall be entitled to vote in this state solely for such electors, provided such person is not able to qualify to vote for such electors in any other state. (New. Added by vote of the people November 5, 1963.)

ARTICLE III
Legislature

[Legislative power.] Section 1. The legislative power of this state shall be vested in the senate and assembly.

[Number and terms of senators and assemblymen.] § 2. The senate shall consist of fifty members, except as hereinafter provided. The senators elected in the year one thousand eight hundred and ninety-five shall hold their offices for three years, and their successors shall be chosen for two years. The assembly shall consist of one hundred and fifty members. The assemblymen elected in the year one thousand nine hundred and thirty-eight, and their successors, shall be chosen for two years. (Amended by vote of the people November 2, 1937.)

*[Senate districts.] § 3. The senate districts described in section three of article three of this constitution as adopted by the people on November sixth, eighteen hundred ninety-four are hereby continued for all of the purposes of future reapportionments of senate districts pursuant to section four of this article. (Former § 3 repealed and replaced by new § 3 amended by vote of the people November 6, 1962.)

[Readjustments and reapportionments; when federal census to control.] § 4. Except as herein otherwise provided, the federal census taken in the year nineteen hundred thirty and each federal census taken decennially thereafter shall be controlling as to the number of inhabitants in the state or any part thereof for the purposes of the apportionment of members of assembly and readjustment or alteration of senate and assembly districts next occurring, in so far as such census and the tabulation thereof purport to give the information necessary therefor. The legislature, by law, shall provide for the making and tabulation by state authorities of an enumeration of the inhabitants of the entire state to be used for such purposes, instead of a federal census, if the taking of a federal census in any tenth year from the year nineteen hundred thirty be omitted or if the federal census fails to show the number of aliens or Indians not taxed. If a federal census, though giving the requisite information as to the state at large, fails to give the information as to any civil or territorial divisions which is required to be known for such

*At present there are 60 senate districts in accordance with Chapter 11, Laws of 1972.

purposes, the legislature, by law, shall provide for such an enumeration of the inhabitants of such parts of the state only as may be necessary, which shall supersede in part the federal census and be used in connection therewith for such purposes. The legislature, by law, may provide in its discretion for an enumeration by state authorities of the inhabitants of the state, to be used for such purposes, in place of a federal census, when the return of a decennial federal census is delayed so that it is not available at the beginning of the regular session of the legislature in the second year after the year nineteen hundred thirty or after any tenth year therefrom, or if an apportionment of members of assembly and readjustment or alteration of senate districts is not made at or before such a session. At the regular session in the year nineteen hundred thirty-two, and at the first regular session after the year nineteen hundred forty and after each tenth year therefrom the senate districts shall be readjusted or altered, but if, in any decade, counting from and including that which begins with the year nineteen hundred thirty-one, such a readjustment or alteration is not made at the time above prescribed, it shall be made at a subsequent session occurring not later than the sixth year of such decade, meaning not later than nineteen hundred thirty-six, nineteen hundred forty-six, nineteen hundred fifty-six, and so on; provided, however, that if such districts shall have been readjusted or altered by law in either of the years nineteen hundred thirty or nineteen hundred thirty-one, they shall remain unaltered until the first regular session after the year nineteen hundred forty. Such districts shall be so readjusted or altered that each senate district shall contain as nearly as may be an equal number of inhabitants, excluding aliens, and be in as compact form as practicable, and shall remain unaltered until the first year of the next decade as above defined, and shall at all times consist of contiguous territory, and no county shall be divided in the formation of a senate district except to make two or more senate districts wholly in such county. No town, except a town having more than a full ratio of apportionment, and no block in a city inclosed by streets or public ways, shall be divided in the formation of senate districts; nor shall any district contain a greater excess in population over an adjoining district in the same county, than the population of a town or block therein adjoining such district. Counties, towns or blocks which, from their location, may be included in either of two districts, shall be so placed as to make said districts most nearly equal in number of inhabitants, excluding aliens.

No county shall have four or more senators unless it shall have a full ratio for each senator. No county shall have more than one-third of all the senators; and no two counties or the territory thereof as now organized, which are adjoining counties, or which are separated only by public waters, shall have more than one-half of all the senators.

The ratio for apportioning senators shall always be obtained by dividing the number of inhabitants, excluding aliens, by fifty, and the senate shall always be composed of fifty members, except that if any county having three or more senators at the time of any apportionment shall be entitled on such ratio to an additional senator or senators, such additional senator or senators shall be given to such county in addition to the fifty senators, and the whole number of senators shall be increased to that extent.

The senate districts, including the present ones, as existing immediately before the enactment of a law readjusting or altering the senate districts, shall continue to be the senate districts of the state until the expirations of the terms of the senators then in office, except for the purpose of an election of senators for full terms beginning at such expirations, and for the formation of assembly districts. (Amended by vote of the people November 6, 1945.)

[**Apportionment of assemblymen; creation of assembly districts.**] § 5. The members of the assembly shall be chosen by single districts and shall be apportioned by the legislature at each regular session at which the senate districts are readjusted or altered, and by the same law, among the several counties of the state, as nearly as may be according to the number of their respective inhabitants, excluding aliens. Every county heretofore established and separately organized, except the county of Hamilton, shall always be entitled to one member of assembly, and no county shall hereafter be erected unless its population shall entitle it to a member. The county of Hamilton shall elect with the county of Fulton, until the population of the county of Hamilton shall, according to the ratio, entitle it to a member. But the legislature may abolish the said county of Hamilton and annex the territory thereof to some other county or counties.

The quotient obtained by dividing the whole number of inhabitants of the state, excluding aliens, by the number of members of assembly, shall be the ratio for apportionment, which shall be made as follows: One member of assembly shall be apportioned to every county, including Fulton and Hamilton as one county, containing less than the ratio and one-half over. Two members shall be apportioned to every other county. The remaining members of assembly shall be apportioned to the counties having more than two ratios according to the number of inhabitants, excluding aliens. Members apportioned on remainders shall be apportioned to the counties having the highest remainders in the order thereof respectively. No county shall have more members of assembly than a county having a greater number of inhabitants, excluding aliens.

*The assembly districts, including the present ones, as existing immediately before the enactment of a law making an apportionment of members of assembly among the counties, shall continue to be the assembly districts of the state until the expiration of the terms of members then in office, except for the purpose of an election of members of assembly for full terms beginning at such expirations.

In any county entitled to more than one member, the board of supervisors, and in any city embracing an entire county and having no board of supervisors, the common council, or if there be none, the body exercising the powers of a common council, shall assemble at such times as the legislature making an apportionment shall prescribe, and divide such counties into assembly districts as nearly equal in number of inhabitants, excluding aliens, as may be, of convenient and contiguous territory in as compact form as practicable, each of which shall be wholly within a senate district formed under the same apportionment, equal to the number of members of assembly to which such county shall be entitled, and shall cause to be filed in the office of the secretary of state and of the clerk of such county, a description of such districts, specifying the number of each district and of the inhabitants thereof, excluding aliens, according to the census or enumeration used as the population basis for the formation of such districts; and such apportionment and districts shall remain unaltered until after the next reapportionment of members of assembly, except that the board of supervisors of any county containing a town having more than a ratio of apportionment and one-half over may alter the assembly districts in a senate district containing such town at any time on or before March first, nineteen hundred forty-six. In counties having more than one senate district, the same number of assembly dis-

*At present there are 150 assembly districts in accordance with Chapter 11, Laws of 1972.

tricts shall be put in each senate district, unless the assembly districts cannot be evenly divided among the senate districts of any county, in which case one more assembly district shall be put in the senate district in such county having the largest, or one less assembly district shall be put in the senate district in such county having the smallest number of inhabitants, excluding aliens, as the case may require. No town, except a town having more than a ratio of apportionment and one-half over, and no block in a city inclosed by streets or public ways, shall be divided in the formation of assembly districts, nor shall any districts contain a greater excess in population over an adjoining district in the same senate district, than the population of a town or block therein adjoining such assembly district. Towns or blocks which, from their location may be included in either of two districts, shall be so placed as to make said districts most nearly equal in number of inhabitants, excluding aliens. Nothing in this section shall prevent the division, at any time, of counties and towns and the erection of new towns by the legislature.

An apportionment by the legislature, or other body, shall be subject to review by the supreme court, at the suit of any citizen, under such reasonable regulations as the legislature may prescribe; and any court before which a cause may be pending involving an apportionment, shall give precedence thereto over all other causes and proceedings, and if said court be not in session it shall convene promptly for the disposition of the same. (Amended by vote of the people November 6, 1945.)

[Definition of inhabitants.] § 5-a. For the purpose of apportioning senate and assembly districts pursuant to the foregoing provisions of this article, the term "inhabitants, excluding aliens" shall mean the whole number of persons. (New. Added by vote of the people November 4, 1969.)

[Compensation, allowances and traveling expenses of members.] § 6. Each member of the legislature shall receive for his services a like annual salary, to be fixed by law. He shall also be reimbursed for his actual traveling expenses in going to and returning from the place in which the legislature meets, not more than once each week while the legislature is in session. Senators, when the senate alone is convened in extraordinary session, or when serving as members of the court for the trial of impeachments, and such members of the assembly, not exceeding nine in number, as shall be appointed managers of an impeachment, shall receive an additional per diem allowance, to be fixed by law. Any member, while serving as an officer of his house or in any other special capacity therein or directly connected therewith not hereinbefore in this section specified, may also be paid and receive, in addition, any allowance which may be fixed by law for the particular and additional services appertaining to or entailed by such office or special capacity. Neither the salary of any member nor any other allowance so fixed may be increased or diminished during, and with respect to, the term for which he shall have been elected, nor shall he be paid or receive any other extra compensation. The provisions of this section and laws enacted in compliance therewith shall govern and be exclusively controlling, according to their terms. Members shall continue to receive such salary and additional allowance as heretofore fixed and provided in this section, until changed by law pursuant to this section. (Amended by Constitutional Convention of 1938 and approved by vote of the people November 8, 1938; further amended by vote of the people November 4, 1947; November 3, 1964.)

[Members; qualifications; not to receive certain civil appointments; acceptance to vacate seat.] § 7. No person shall serve as a member of the legislature unless he or she is a citizen of the United States and has been a resident of the state of New York for five years, and, except as hereinafter otherwise prescribed, of the assembly or senate district for the twelve months immediately preceding his or her election; if elected a senator or member of assembly at the first election next ensuing after a readjustment or alteration of the senate or assembly districts becomes effective, a person, to be eligible to serve as such, must have been a resident of the county in which the senate or assembly district is contained for the twelve months immediately preceding his or her election. No member of the legislature shall, during the time for which he or she was elected, receive any civil appointment from the governor, the governor and the senate, the legislature or from any city government, to an office which shall have been created, or the emoluments whereof shall have been increased during such time. If a member of the legislature be elected to congress, or appointed to any office, civil or military, under the government of the United States, the state of New York, or under any city government except as a member of the national guard or naval militia of the state, or of the reserve forces of the United States, his or her acceptance thereof shall vacate his or her seat in the legislature, providing, however, that a member of the legislature may be appointed commissioner of deeds or to any office in which he or she shall receive no compensation. (New. Derived in part from former §§ 7 and 8. Adopted by Constitutional Convention of 1938 and approved by vote of the people November 8, 1938; amended by vote of the people November 2, 1943.)

[Time of elections of members.] § 8. The elections of senators and members of assembly, pursuant to the provisions of this constitution, shall be held on the Tuesday succeeding the first Monday of November, unless otherwise directed by the legislature. (Formerly § 9. Renumbered by Constitutional Convention of 1938 and approved by vote of the people November 8, 1938.)

[Powers of each house.] § 9. A majority of each house

shall constitute a quorum to do business. Each house shall determine the rules of its own proceedings, and be the judge of the elections, returns and qualifications of its own members; shall choose its own officers; and the senate shall choose a temporary president and the assembly shall choose a speaker. (Formerly § 10. Renumbered by Constitutional Convention of 1938 and approved by vote of the people November 8, 1938. Amended by vote of the people November 5, 1963.)

[Journals; open sessions; adjournments.] § 10. Each house of the legislature shall keep a journal of its proceedings, and publish the same, except such parts as may require secrecy. The doors of each house shall be kept open, except when the public welfare shall require secrecy. Neither house shall, without the consent of the other, adjourn for more than two days. (Formerly § 11. Renumbered and amended by Constitutional Convention of 1938 and approved by vote of the people November 8, 1938.)

[Members not to be questioned for speeches.] § 11. For any speech or debate in either house of the legislature, the members shall not be questioned in any other place. (Formerly § 12. Renumbered by Constitutional Convention of 1938 and approved by vote of the people November 8, 1938.)

[Bills may originate in either house; may be amended by the other.] § 12. Any bill may originate in either house of the legislature, and all bills passed by one house may be amended by the other. (Formerly § 18. Renumbered by Constitutional Convention of 1988 and approved by vote of the people November 8, 1938.)

[Enacting clause of bills; no law to be enacted except by bill.] § 13. The enacting clause of all bills shall be "The People of the State of New York, represented in Senate and Assembly, do enact as follows," and no law shall be enacted except by bill. (Formerly § 14. Renumbered by Constitutional Convention of 1938 and approved by vote of the people November 8, 1938.)

[**Manner of passing bills; message of necessity for immediate vote.**] § 14. No bill shall be passed or become a law unless it shall have been printed and upon the desks of the members, in its final form, at least three calendar legislative days prior to its final passage, unless the governor, or the acting governor, shall have certified, under his hand and the seal of the state, the **facts** which in his opinion necessitate an immediate vote thereon, in which case it must nevertheless be upon the **desks** of the members in final form, not necessarily printed, before its final passage; nor shall any bill be passed or become a law, except by the assent of a majority of the members elected to each branch of the legislature; and upon the last reading of a bill **amendment thereof** shall be allowed, and the question upon its final passage shall be taken immediately thereafter, and the ayes and nays entered on the journal. (Formerly § 15. Renumbered and amended by Constitutional Convention of 1938 and approved by vote of the people November 8, 1938.)

[**Private or local bills to embrace only one subject to be expressed in title.**] § 15. No private or local bill, which may be passed by the legislature, shall embrace more than one subject, and that shall be expressed in the title. (Formerly § 16. Renumbered by Constitutional Convention of 1938 and approved by vote of the people November 8, 1938.)

[**Existing law not to be made applicable by reference.**] § 16. No act shall be passed which shall provide that any existing law, or any part thereof, shall be made or deemed a part of said act, or which shall enact that any existing law, or part thereof, shall be applicable, except by inserting it in such act. (Formerly § 17. Renumbered by Constitutional Convention of 1938 and approved by vote of the people November 8, 1938.)

[Cases in which private or local bills shall not be passed.] § 17. The legislature shall not pass a private or local bill in any of the following cases:

Changing the names of persons.

Laying out, opening, altering, working or discontinuing roads, highways or alleys, or for draining swamps or other low lands.

Locating or changing county seats.

Providing for changes of venue in civil or criminal cases.

Incorporating villages.

Providing for election of members of boards of supervisors.

Selecting, drawing, summoning or empaneling grand or petit jurors.

Regulating the rate of interest on money.

The opening and conducting of elections or designating places of voting.

Creating, increasing or decreasing fees, percentages or allowances of public officers, during the term for which said officers are elected or appointed.

Granting to any corporation, association or individual the right to lay down railroad tracks.

Granting to any private corporation, association or individual any exclusive privilege, immunity or franchise whatever.

Granting to any person, association, firm or corporation, an exemption from taxation on real or personal property.

Providing for the building of bridges, except over the waters forming a part of the boundaries of the state, by other than a municipal or other public corporation or a public agency of the state. (Formerly § 18. Renumbered and amended by Constitutional Convention of 1938 and approved by vote of the people November 8, 1938; further amended by vote of the people November 3, 1964.)

[Extraordinary sessions of the legislature; power to convene on legislative initiative.] § 18. The members of the legislature shall be empowered, upon the presentation to the temporary president of the senate and the speaker of the assembly of a petition signed by two-thirds of the members elected to each house of the legislature, to convene the legislature on extraordinary occasions to act upon the subjects enumerated in such petition. (New. Added by vote of the people November 4, 1975.)

[Private claims not to be audited by legislature; claims barred by lapse of time.] § 19. The legislature shall neither audit nor allow any private claim or account against the state, but may appropriate money to pay such claims as shall have been audited and allowed according to law.

No claim against the state shall be audited, allowed or paid which, as between citizens of the state, would be barred by lapse of time. But if the claimant shall be under legal disability, the claim may be presented within two years after such disability is removed. (Derived in part from former § 6 of Art. 7. Amended by Constitutional Convention of 1938 and approved by vote of the people November 8, 1938; further amended by vote of the people November 3, 1964.)

[Two-thirds bills.] § 20. The assent of two-thirds of the members elected to each branch of the legislature shall be requisite to every bill appropriating the public moneys or property for local or private purposes.

[Certain sections not to apply to bills recommended by certain commissioners or public agencies.] § 21. Sections 15, 16 and 17 of this article shall not apply to any bill, or the amendments to any bill, which shall be recommended to the legislature by commissioners or any public agency appointed or directed pursuant to law to prepare revisions, consolidations or compilations of statutes. But a bill amending an existing law shall not be excepted from the provisions of sections 15, 16 and 17 of this article unless such amending bill shall itself be recommended to the legislature by such commissioners or public agency. (Formerly § 23. Renumbered and amended by Constitutional Convention of 1938 and approved by vote of the people November 8, 1938.)

[**Tax laws to state tax and object distinctly; definition of income for income tax purposes by reference to federal laws authorized.**] § 22. Every law which imposes, continues or revives a tax shall distinctly state the tax and the object to which it is to be applied, and it shall not be sufficient to refer to any other law to fix such tax or object.

Notwithstanding the foregoing or any other provision of this constitution, the legislature, in any law imposing a tax or taxes on, in respect to or measured by income, may define the income on, in respect to or by which such tax or taxes are imposed or measured, by reference to any provision of the laws of the United States as the same may be or become effective at any time or from time to time, and may prescribe exceptions or modifications to any such provision. (Formerly § 24. Renumbered by Constitutional Convention of 1938 and approved by vote of the people November 8, 1938; amended by vote of the people November 3, 1959.)

[**When yeas and nays necessary; three-fifths to constitute quorum.**] § 23. On the final passage, in either house of the legislature, of any act which imposes, continues or revives a tax, or creates a debt or charge, or makes, continues or revives any appropriation of public or trust money or property, or releases, discharges or commutes any claim or demand of the state, the question shall be taken by yeas and nays, which shall be duly entered upon the journals, and three-fifths of all the members elected to either house shall, in all such cases, be necessary to constitute a quorum therein. (Formerly § 25. Renumbered by Constitutional Convention of 1938 and approved by vote of the people November 8, 1938.)

[**Prison labor; contract system abolished.**] § 24. The

legislature shall, by law, provide for the occupation and employment of prisoners sentenced to the several state prisons, penitentiaries, jails and reformatories in the state; and no person in any such prison, penitentiary, jail or reformatory, shall be required or allowed to work, while under sentence thereto, at any trade, industry or occupation, wherein or whereby his work, or the product or profit of his work, shall be farmed out, contracted, given or sold to any person, firm, association or corporation. This section shall not be construed to prevent the legislature from providing that convicts may work for, and that the products of their labor may be disposed of to, the state or any political division thereof, or for or to any public institution owned or managed and controlled by the state, or any political division thereof. (Formerly § 29. Renumbered and amended by Constitutional Convention of 1938 and approved by vote of the people November 8, 1938.)

[**Emergency governmental operations; legislature to provide for.**] § 25. Notwithstanding any other provision of this constitution, the legislature, in order to insure continuity of state and local governmental operations in periods of emergency caused by enemy attack or by disasters (natural or otherwise), shall have the power and the immediate duty (1) to provide for prompt and temporary succession to the powers and duties of public offices, of whatever nature and whether filled by election or appointment, the incumbents of which may become unavailable for carrying on the powers and duties of such offices, and (2) to adopt such other measures as may be necessary and proper for insuring the continuity of governmental operations.

Nothing in this article shall be construed to limit in any way the power of the state to deal with emergencies arising from any cause. (New. Added by vote of the people November 5, 1963.)

ARTICLE IV

EXECUTIVE

[**Executive power; election and terms of governor and lieutenant-governor.**] Section 1. The executive power shall be vested in the governor, who shall hold his office for four years; the lieutenant-governor shall be chosen at the same time, and for the same term. The governor and lieutenant-governor shall be chosen at the general election held in the year nineteen hundred thirty-eight, and each fourth year thereafter. They shall be chosen jointly, by the casting by each voter of a single vote applicable to both offices, and the legislature by law shall provide for making such choice in such manner. The respective persons having the highest number of votes cast jointly for them for governor and lieutenant-governor respectively shall be elected. (Amended by Constitutional Convention of 1938 and approved by vote of the people November 8, 1938; further amended by vote of the people November 3, 1953.)

[**Qualifications of governor and lieutenant-governor.**] § 2. No person shall be eligible to the office of governor or lieutenant-governor, except a citizen of the United States, of the age of not less than thirty years, and who shall have been five years next preceding his election a resident of this state.

[**Powers and duties of governor; compensation.**] § 3. The governor shall be commander-in-chief of the military and naval forces of the state. He shall have power to convene the legislature, or the senate only, on extraordinary occasions. At extraordinary sessions convened pursuant to the provisions of this section no subject shall be acted upon, except such as the governor may recommend for consideration. He shall communicate by message to the legislature at every session the condition of the state, and recommend such matters to it as he shall judge expedient. He shall expedite all such measures as may be resolved upon by the legislature, and shall take care that the laws are faithfully executed. He shall receive for his services an annual salary to be fixed by joint resolution of the senate and assembly, and there shall be provided for his use a suitable and furnished executive residence. (Formerly § 4. Renumbered and amended by Constitutional Convention of 1938 and approved by vote of the people November 8, 1938; further amended by vote of the people November 3, 1953; November 5, 1963; November 4, 1975.)

[Reprieves, commutations and pardons; powers and duties of governor relating to grants of.] § 4. The governor shall have the power to grant reprieves, commutations and pardons after conviction, for all offenses except treason and cases of impeachment, upon such conditions and with such restrictions and limitations, as he may think proper, subject to such regulations as may be provided by law relative to the manner of applying for pardons. Upon conviction for treason, he shall have power to suspend the execution of the sentence, until the case shall be reported to the legislature at its next meeting, when the legislature shall either pardon, or commute the sentence, direct the execution of the sentence, or grant a further reprieve. He shall annually communicate to the legislature each case of reprieve, commutation or pardon granted, stating the name of the convict, the crime of which he was convicted, the sentence and its date, and the date of the commutation, pardon or reprieve. (Formerly § 5. Renumbered by Constitutional Convention of 1938 and approved by vote of the people November 8, 1938.)

[When lieutenant-governor to act as governor.] § 5. In case of the removal of the governor from office or of his death or resignation, the lieutenant-governor shall become governor for the remainder of the term.

In case the governor-elect shall decline to serve or shall die, the lieutenant-governor-elect shall become governor for the full term.

In case the governor is impeached, is absent from the

state or is otherwise unable to discharge the powers and duties of his office, the lieutenant-governor shall act as governor until the inability shall cease or until the term of the governor shall expire. In case of the failure of the governor-elect to take the oath of office at the commencement of his term, the lieutenant-governor-elect shall act as governor until the governor shall take the oath. (Formerly § 6. Renumbered and amended by Constitutional Convention of 1938 and approved by vote of the people November 8, 1938; further amended by vote of the people November 8, 1949; November 5, 1963.)

[Duties and compensation of lieutenant-governor; succession to the governorship.] § 6. The lieutenant-governor shall possess the same qualifications of eligibility for office as the governor. He shall be the president of the senate but shall have only a casting vote therein. The lieutenant-governor shall receive for his services an annual salary to be fixed by joint resolution of the senate and assembly.

In case of vacancy in the offices of both governor and lieutenant-governor, a governor and lieutenant-governor shall be elected for the remainder of the term at the next general election happening not less than three months after both offices shall have become vacant. No election of a lieutenant-governor shall be had in any event except at the time of electing a governor.

In case of vacancy in the offices of both governor and lieutenant-governor or if both of them shall be impeached, absent from the state or otherwise unable to discharge the powers and duties of the office of governor, the temporary president of the senate shall act as governor until the inability shall cease or until a governor shall be elected.

In case of vacancy in the office of lieutenant-governor alone, or if the lieutenant-governor shall be impeached, absent from the state or otherwise unable to discharge the duties of his office, the temporary president of the senate shall perform all the duties of lieutenant-governor during such vacancy or inability.

If, when the duty of acting as governor devolves upon the temporary president of the senate, there be a vacancy in such office or the temporary president of the senate shall be absent from the state or otherwise unable to discharge the duties of governor, the speaker of the assembly shall act as governor during such vacancy or inability.

The legislature may provide for the devolution of the duty of acting as governor in any case not provided for in this article. (Formerly §§ 7 and 8. Renumbered and amended by Constitutional Convention of 1938 and approved by vote of the people November 8, 1938; further amended by vote of the people November 6, 1945; November 3, 1953; November 5, 1963.)

[Action by governor on legislative bills; reconsideration after veto.] § 7. Every bill which shall have passed the senate and assembly shall, before it becomes a law, be presented to the governor; if he approve, he shall sign it; but if not, he shall return it with his objections to the house in which it shall have originated, which shall enter the objections at large on the journal, and proceed to reconsider it. If after such reconsideration, two-thirds of the members elected to that house shall agree to pass the bill, it shall be sent together with the objections, to the other house, by which it shall likewise be reconsidered; and if approved by two-thirds of the members elected to that house, it shall become a law notwithstanding the objections of the governor. In all such cases the votes in both houses shall be determined by yeas and nays, and the names of the members voting shall be entered on the journal of each house respectively. If any bill shall not be returned by the governor within ten days (Sundays excepted) after it shall have been presented to him, the same shall be a law in like manner as if he had signed it, unless the legislature shall, by their adjournment, prevent its return, in which case it shall not become a law without the approval of the governor. No bill shall become a law after the final adjournment of the legislature, unless approved by the governor within thirty days after such adjournment. If any bill presented to the governor contain several items of appropriation of money, he may object to one or more of such items while approving of the other portion of the bill. In such case he shall append to the bill, at the time of signing it, a statement of the items to which he objects; and the appropriation so objected to shall not take effect. If the legislature be in session, he shall transmit to the house in which the bill originated a copy of such statement, and the items objected to shall be separately reconsidered. If on reconsideration one or more of such items be approved by two-thirds of the members elected to each house, the same shall be part of the law, notwithstanding the objections of the governor. All the provisions of this section, in relation to bills not approved by the governor, shall apply in cases in which he shall withhold his approval from any item or items contained in a bill appropriating money. (Formerly § 9. Renumbered by Constitutional Convention of 1938 and approved by vote of the people November 8, 1938.)

[Departmental rules and regulations; filing; publication.] § 8. No rule or regulation made by any state department, board, bureau, officer, authority or commission, except such as relates to the organization or internal management of a state department, board, bureau, authority or commission shall be effective until it is filed in the office of the department of state. The legislature shall provide for the speedy publication of such rules and regulations, by appropriate laws. (New. Adopted by Constitutional Convention of 1938 and approved by vote of the people November 8, 1938.)

ARTICLE V
OFFICERS AND CIVIL DEPARTMENTS

[Comptroller and attorney-general; payment of state moneys without audit void.] Section 1. The comptroller and attorney-general shall be chosen at the same general election as the governor and hold office for the same term, and shall possess the qualifications provided in section 2 of article IV. The legislature shall provide for filling vacancies in the office of comptroller and of attorney-general. No election of a comptroller or an attorney-general shall be had except at the time of electing a governor. The comptroller shall be required: (1) To audit all vouchers before payment and all official accounts; (2) to audit the accrual and collection of all revenues and receipts; and (3) to prescribe such methods of accounting as are necessary for the performance of the foregoing duties. The payment of any money of the state, or of any money under its control, or the refund of any money paid to the state, except upon audit by the comptroller, shall be void, and may be restrained upon the suit of any taxpayer with the consent of the supreme court in appellate division on notice to the attorney-general. In such respect the legislature shall define his powers and duties and may also assign to him: (1) supervision of the accounts of any political subdivision of the state; and (2) powers and duties pertaining to or connected with the assessment and taxation of real estate, including determination of ratios which the assessed valuation of taxable real property bears to the full valuation thereof, but not including any of those powers and duties reserved to officers of a county, city, town or village by virtue of sections seven and eight of article nine of this constitution. The legislature shall assign to him no administrative duties, excepting such as may be incidental to the performance of these functions, any other provision of this constitution to the contrary notwithstanding. (Amended by Constitutional Convention of 1938 and approved by vote of the people November 8, 1938; further amended by vote of the people November 3, 1953; November 8, 1955.)

[Civil departments in the state government.] § 2. There shall be not more than twenty civil departments in the state government, including those referred to in this constitution. The legislature may by law change the names of the departments referred to in this constitution. (Amended by Constitutional Convention of 1938 and approved by vote of the people November 8, 1938; further amended by vote of the people November 2, 1943; November 3, 1959; November 7, 1961.)

[Assignment of functions.] § 3. Subject to the limitations contained in this constitution, the legislature may from time to time assign by law new powers and functions to departments, officers, boards, commissions or executive offices of the governor, and increase, modify or diminish their powers and functions. Nothing contained in this article shall prevent the legislature from creating temporary commissions for special purposes or executive offices of the governor and from reducing the number of departments as provided for in this article, by consolidation or otherwise. (Amended by Constitutional Convention of 1938 and approved by vote of the people November 8, 1938; further amended by vote of the people November 7, 1961.)

[Department heads.] § 4. The head of the department of audit and control shall be the comptroller and of the department of law, the attorney-general. The head of the department of education shall be The Regents of the University of the State of New York, who shall appoint and at pleasure remove a commissioner of education to be the chief administrative officer of the department. The head of the department of agriculture and markets shall be appointed in a manner to be prescribed by law. Except as otherwise provided in this constitution, the heads of all other departments and the members of all boards and commissions, excepting temporary commissions for special purposes, shall be appointed by the governor by and with the advice and consent of the senate and may be removed by the governor, in a manner to be prescribed by law. (Amended by Constitutional Convention of 1938 and approved by vote of the people November 8, 1938; further amended by vote of the people November 7, 1961.)

No section 5 *(see footnote*)*

[**Civil service appointments and promotions; veterans' credits.**] § 6. Appointments and promotions in the civil service of the state and all of the civil divisions thereof, including cities and villages, shall be made according to merit and fitness to be ascertained, as far as practicable, by examination which, as far as practicable, shall be competitive; provided, however, that any member of the armed forces of the United States who served therein in time of war, who is a citizen and resident of this state and was a resident at the time of his entrance into the armed forces of the United States and was honorably discharged or released under honorable circumstances from such service, shall be entitled to receive five points additional credit in a competitive examination for original appointment and two and one-half points additional credit in an examination for promotion or, if such member was disabled in the actual performance of duty in any war, is receiving disability payments therefor from the United States veterans administration, and his disability is certified by such administration to be in existence at the time of his application for appointment or promotion, he shall be entitled to receive ten points additional credit in a competitive examination for original appointment and five points additional credit in an examination for promotion. Such additional credit shall be added to the final earned rating of such member after he has qualified in an examination and shall be granted only at the time of establishment of an eligible list. No such member shall receive the additional credit

---

* Section 5 which dealt with certain offices abolished was repealed by amendment approved by vote of the people November 6, 1962.

granted by this section after he has received one appointment, either original entrance or promotion, from an eligible list on which he was allowed the additional credit granted by this section. (Former section 6 repealed and new section approved by vote of the people November 8, 1949; amended by vote of the people November 3, 1964.)

[**Membership in retirement systems; benefits not to be diminished nor impaired.**] § 7. After July first, nineteen hundred forty, membership in any pension or retirement system of the state or of a civil division thereof shall be a contractual relationship, the benefits of which shall not be diminished or impaired. (New. Adopted by Constitutional Convention of 1938 and approved by vote of the people November 8, 1938.)

ARTICLE VI*
JUDICIARY

[**Unified court system; organization; process.**] Section 1. a. There shall be a unified court system for the state. The state-wide courts shall consist of the court of appeals, the supreme court including the appellate divisions thereof, the court of claims, the county court, the surrogate's court and the family court, as hereinafter provided. The legislature shall establish in and for the city of New York, as part of the unified court system for the state, a single, city-wide court of civil jurisdiction and a single, city-wide court of criminal jurisdiction, as hereinafter provided, and may upon the request of the mayor and the local legislative body of the city of New York, merge the two courts into one city-wide court of both civil and criminal jurisdiction. The unified court system for the state shall also include the district, town, city and village courts outside the city of New York, as hereinafter provided.

b. The court of appeals, the supreme court including

* New article adopted by vote of the people Nov. 7, 1961; repealing and replacing former article adopted Nov. 3, 1925, as amended.

the appellate divisions thereof, the court of claims, the county court, the surrogate's court, the family court, the courts or court of civil and criminal jurisdiction of the city of New York, and such other courts as the legislature may determine shall be courts of record.

c. All processes, warrants and other mandates of the court of appeals, the supreme court including the appellate divisions thereof, the court of claims, the county court, the surrogate's court and the family court may be served and executed in any part of the state. All processes, **warrants and other mandates of the courts or court of civil and criminal jurisdiction of the city of New York may,** subject to such limitation as may be prescribed by the legislature, be served and executed in any part of the state. The legislature may provide that processes, warrants and other mandates of the district court may be served and executed in any part of the state and that processes, warrants and other mandates of town, village and city courts outside the city of New York may be served and executed in any part of the county in which such courts are located or in any part of any adjoining county.

[**Court of appeals; organization; designations; vacancies, how filled.**] § 2. a. The court of appeals is continued. It shall consist of the chief judge, the six elected associate judges now in office, who shall hold their offices until the expiration of their respective terms, and their successors, who shall be chosen by the electors of the state and such justices of the supreme court as may be designated for service in said court as hereinafter provided. The official terms of the chief judge and elected associate judges shall be fourteen years from and including the first day of January next after their election. Five members of the court shall constitute a quorum, and the concurrence of four shall be necessary to a decision; but no more than seven judges shall sit in any case. In case of the temporary absence or inability to act of any judge of the court of appeals, the court may designate any justice of the supreme court to serve as associate judge of the court during such absence or inability to act. The court shall have power to appoint and to remove its clerk.

b. Whenever and as often as the court of appeals shall certify to the governor that the court is unable, by reason of the accumulation of causes pending therein, to hear and dispose of the same with reasonable speed, the governor shall designate such number of justices of the supreme court as may be so certified to be necessary, but not more than four, to serve as associate judges of the court of appeals. The justices so designated shall be relieved, while so serving, from their duties as justices of the supreme court, and shall serve as associate judges of the court of appeals until the court shall certify that the need for the services of any such justices no longer exists, whereupon they shall return to the supreme court. The governor may fill vacancies among such designated judges. No such justices shall serve as associate judge of the court of appeals except while holding the office of justice of the supreme court. The designation of a justice of the supreme court as an associate judge of the court of appeals shall not be deemed to affect his existing office any longer than until the expiration of his designation as such associate judge, nor to create a vacancy.

c. When a vacancy shall occur otherwise than by expiration of term, in the office of chief or elected associate judge of the court of appeals, the same shall be filled, for a full term, at the next general election held not less than three months after such vacancy occurs; and until the vacancy shall be so filled, the governor, by and with the advice and consent of the senate if the senate shall be in session, or if not in session, the governor may fill such vacancy by appointment. If any such appointment be made from among the justices of the supreme court, such appointment shall not be deemed to affect his existing office any longer than until the expiration of his appointment as such associate judge, nor to create a vacancy. If any such appointment of chief judge shall be made from among the associate judges, a temporary appointment of associate judge shall be made in like manner; but, in such case, the appointment shall not be deemed to affect his office of associate judge any longer than until the expiration of his appointment as chief judge, nor to create a vacancy. The powers and jurisdiction of the court shall not be suspended for want of appointment or election when the number of judges is sufficient to constitute a quorum. All appointments under this section shall continue until and including the last day of December next after the election at which the vacancy shall be filled.

[Court of appeals; jurisdiction.] § 3. a. The jurisdiction of the court of appeals shall be limited to the review of questions of law except where the judgment is of death, or where the appellate division, on reversing or modifying a final or interlocutory judgment in an action or a final or interlocutory order in a special proceeding, finds new facts and a final judgment or a final order pursuant thereto is entered; but the right to appeal shall not depend upon the amount involved.

b. Appeals to the court of appeals may be taken in the classes of cases hereafter enumerated in this section;

In criminal cases, directly from a court of original jurisdiction where the judgment is of death, and in other criminal cases from an appellate division or otherwise as the legislature may from time to time provide.

In civil cases and proceedings as follows:

(1) As of right, from a judgment or order entered upon the decision of an appellate division of the supreme court which finally determines an action or special proceeding wherein is directly involved the construction of the constitution of the state or of the United States, or where one or more of the justices of the appellate division dissents from the decision of the court, or where the judgment or order is one of reversal or modification.

(2) As of right, from a judgment or order of a court of record of original jurisdiction which finally determines an action or special proceeding where the only question

involved on the appeal is the validity of a statutory provision of the state or of the United States under the constitution of the state or of the United States; and on any such appeal only the constitutional question shall be considered and determined by the court.

(3) As of right, from an order of the appellate division granting a new trial in an action or a new hearing in a special proceeding where the appellant stipulates that, upon affirmance, judgment absolute or final order shall be rendered against him.

(4) From a determination of the appellate division of the supreme court in any department, other than a judgment or order which finally determines an action or special proceeding, where the appellate division allows the same and certifies that one or more questions of law have arisen which, in its opinion, ought to be reviewed by the court of appeals, but in such case the appeal shall bring up for review only the question or questions so certified; and the court of appeals shall certify to the appellate division its determination upon such question or questions.

(5) From an order of the appellate division of the supreme court in any department, in a proceeding instituted by or against one or more public officers or a board, commission or other body of public officers or a court or tribunal, other than an order which finally determines such proceeding, where the court of appeals shall allow the same upon the ground that, in its opinion, a question of law is involved which ought to be reviewed by it, and without regard to the availability of appeal by stipulation for final order absolute.

(6) From a judgment or order entered upon the decision of an appellate division of the supreme court which finally determines an action or special proceeding but which is not appealable under paragraph (1) of this subdivision where the appellate division or the court of appeals shall certify that in its opinion a question of law is involved which ought to be reviewed by the court of appeals. Such an appeal may be allowed upon application (a) to the appellate division, and in case of refusal, to the

court of appeals, or (b) directly to the court of appeals. Such an appeal shall be allowed when required in the interest of substantial justice.

(7) No appeal shall be taken to the court of appeals from a judgment or order entered upon the decision of an appellate division of the supreme court in any civil case or proceeding where the appeal to the appellate division was from a judgment or order entered in an appeal from another court, including an appellate or special term of the supreme court, unless the construction of the constitution of the state or of the United States is directly involved therein, or unless the appellate division of the supreme court shall certify that in its opinion a question of law is involved which ought to be reviewed by the court of appeals.

(8) The legislature may abolish an appeal to the court of appeals as of right in any or all of the cases or classes of cases specified in paragraph (1) of this subdivision wherein no question involving the construction of the constitution of the state or of the United States is directly involved, provided, however, that appeals in any such case or class of cases shall thereupon be governed by paragraph (6) of this subdivision.

[Judicial departments; appellate divisions, how constituted; governor to designate justices; temporary assignments; jurisdiction.] § 4. a. The state shall be divided into four judicial departments. The first department shall consist of the counties within the first judicial district of the state. The second department shall consist of the counties within the second, ninth, tenth and eleventh judicial districts of the state. The third department shall consist of the counties within the third, fourth and sixth judicial districts of the state. The fourth department shall consist of the counties within the fifth, seventh and eighth judicial districts of the state. Each department shall be bounded by the lines of judicial districts. Once every ten years the legislature may alter the boundaries of the judicial departments, but without changing the number thereof.

b. The appellate divisions of the supreme court are continued, and shall consist of seven justices of the supreme court in each of the first and second departments, and five justices in each of the other departments. In each appellate division, four justices shall constitute a quorum, and the concurrence of three shall be necessary to a decision. No more than five justices shall sit in any case.

c. The governor shall designate the presiding justice of each appellate division, who shall act as such during his term of office and shall be a resident of the department. The other justices of the appellate divisions shall be designated by the governor, from all the justices elected to the supreme court, for terms of five years or the unexpired portions of their respective terms of office, if less than five years.

d. The justices heretofore designated shall continue to sit in the appellate divisions until the terms of their respective designations shall expire. From time to time as the terms of the designations expire, or vacancies occur, the governor shall make new designations. He may also, on request of any appellate division, make temporary designations in case of the absence or inability to act of any justice in such appellate division, for service only during such absence or inability to act.

e. In case any appellate division shall certify to the governor that one or more additional justices are needed for the speedy disposition of the business before it, the governor shall designate an additional justice or additional justices; but when the need for such additional justice or justices shall no longer exist, the appellate division shall so certify to the governor, and thereupon service under such designation or designations shall cease.

f. A majority of the justices designated to sit in any appellate division shall at all times be residents of the department.

g. Whenever the appellate division in any department shall be unable to dispose of its business within a reasonable time, a majority of the presiding justices of the several departments, at a meeting called by the presiding justice of the department in arrears, may transfer any pending appeals from such department to any other department for hearing and determination.

h. A justice of the appellate division of the supreme court in any department may be temporarily designated by the presiding justice of his department to the appellate division in another judicial department upon agreement by the presiding justices of the appellate division of the departments concerned.

i. In the event that the disqualification, absence or inability to act of justices in any appellate division prevents there being a quorum of justices qualified to hear an appeal, the justices qualified to hear the appeal may transfer it to the appellate division in another department for hearing and determination. In the event that the justices in any appellate division qualified to hear an appeal are equally divided, said justices may transfer the appeal to the appellate division in another department for hearing and determination. Each appellate division shall have power to appoint and remove its clerk.

j. No justice of the appellate division shall, within the department to which he may be designated to perform the duties of an appellate justice, exercise any of the powers of a justice of the supreme court, other than those of a justice out of court, and those pertaining to the appellate division, except that he may decide causes or proceedings theretofore submitted, or hear and decide motions submitted by consent of counsel, but any such justice, when not actually engaged in performing the duties of such appellate justice in the department to which he is designated, may hold any term of the supreme court and exercise any of the powers of a justice of the supreme court in any judicial district in any other department of the state.

k. The appellate divisions of the supreme court shall have all the jurisdiction possessed by them on the effective date of this article and such additional jurisdiction as may be prescribed by law, provided, however, that the right to appeal to the appellate divisions from a judgment or order which does not finally determine an action or special proceeding may be limited or conditioned by law.

[Appeals from judgment or order; new trial.] § 5. a. Upon an appeal from a judgment or an order, any appellate court to which the appeal is taken which is authorized to review such judgment or order may reverse or affirm, wholly or in part, or may modify the judgment or order appealed from, and each interlocutory judgment or intermediate or other order which it is authorized to review, and as to any or all of the parties. It shall thereupon render judgment of affirmance, judgment of reversal and final judgment upon the right of any or all of the parties, or judgment of modification thereon according to law, except where it may be necessary or proper to grant a new trial or hearing, when it may grant a new trial or hearing.

b. If any appeal is taken to an appellate court which is not authorized to review such judgment or order, the court shall transfer the appeal to an appellate court which is authorized to review such judgment or order.

[Judicial districts; how constituted; supreme court.] § 6. a. The state shall be divided into eleven judicial districts. The first judicial district shall consist of the counties of Bronx and New York. The second judicial district shall consist of the counties of Kings and Richmond. The third judicial district shall consist of the counties of Albany, Columbia, Greene, Rensselaer, Schoharie, Sullivan, and Ulster. The fourth judicial district shall consist of the counties of Clinton, Essex, Franklin, Fulton, Hamilton, Montgomery, St. Lawrence, Saratoga, Schenectady, Warren and Washington. The fifth judicial district shall consist of the counties of Herkimer, Jefferson, Lewis, Oneida, Onondaga, and Oswego. The sixth judicial district shall consist o.' the counties of Broome, Chemung, Chenango, Cortland, Delaware, Madison, Otsego, Schuyler, Tioga and Tompkins. The seventh judicial district shall consist of the counties of Cayuga, Livingston, Monroe, Ontario, Seneca, Steuben, Wayne and Yates. The eighth judicial district shall consist of the counties of Allegany, Cattaraugus, Chautauqua, Erie, Genesee, Niagara, Orleans and Wyoming. The ninth judicial district shall consist of the counties of Dutchess, Orange, Putnam, Rockland and Westchester. The tenth judicial district shall consist of the counties of Nassau and Suffolk. The eleventh judicial district shall consist of the county of Queens.

b. Once every ten years the legislature may increase or decrease the number of judicial districts or alter the composition of judicial districts and thereupon re-apportion the justices to be thereafter elected in the judicial districts so altered. Each judicial district shall be bounded by county lines.

c. The justices of the supreme court shall be chosen by the electors of the judicial district in which they are to serve. The terms of justices of the supreme court shall be fourteen years from and including the first day of January next after their election.

d. The supreme court is continued. It shall consist of the number of justices of the supreme court including the justices designated to the appellate divisions of the supreme court, judges of the county court of the counties of Bronx, Kings, Queens and Richmond and judges of the court of general sessions of the county of New York authorized by law on the thirty-first day of August next after the approval and ratification of this amendment by the people, all of whom shall be justices of the supreme court for the remainder of their terms. The legislature may increase the number of justices of the supreme court in any judicial district, except that the number in any district shall not be increased to exceed one justice for fifty thousand, or fraction over thirty thousand, of the population thereof as shown by the last federal census or state enumeration. The legislature may decrease the number of justices of the supreme court in any judicial district, except that the number in any district shall not be less than the number of justices of the supreme court authorized by law on the effective date of this article.

e. The clerks of the several counties shall be clerks of the supreme court, with such powers and duties as shall be prescribed by law.

[Supreme court; jurisdiction.] § 7. a. The supreme court shall have general original jurisdiction in law and equity and the appellate jurisdiction herein provided. In the city of New York, it shall have exclusive jurisdiction over crimes prosecuted by indictment, provided, however, that the legislature may grant to the city-wide court of criminal jurisdiction of the city of New York jurisdiction over misdemeanors prosecuted by indictment and to the family court in the city of New York jurisdiction over crimes and offenses by or against minors or between spouses or between parent and child or between members of the same family or household.

b. There may be separate divisions of the supreme court established by the appellate division of the supreme court in each department for various classes of actions and proceedings.

c. If the legislature shall create new classes of actions and proceedings, the supreme court shall have jurisdiction over such classes of actions and proceedings, but the legislature may provide that another court or other courts shall also have jurisdiction and that actions and proceedings of such classes may be originated in such other court or courts.

[Appellate terms; jurisdiction.] § 8. a. The appellate division of the supreme court in each judicial department may establish an appellate term in and for such department or in and for a judicial district or districts or in and for a county or counties within the department and designate the place or places where such appellate term shall be held. Such an appellate term shall be composed of not less than three nor more than five justices of the supreme court who shall be designated from time to time by the appellate division of the supreme court in the department and who shall be residents of the department or of the judicial district or districts as the case may be.

b. Any such appellate term may be discontinued and re-established as the appellate division of the supreme court in each department shall determine from time to time and any designation to service therein may be revoked by the appellate division of the supreme court so designating.

c. In each appellate term no more tnan three justices assigned thereto shall sit in any action or proceeding. Two of such justices shall constitute a quorum and the concurrence of two shall be necessary to a decision.

d. If so directed by the appellate division of the supreme court establishing an appellate term, an appellate term shall have jurisdiction to hear and determine appeals now or hereafter authorized by law to be taken to the supreme court or to the appellate division other than appeals from the supreme court, a surrogate's court, the family court or appeals in criminal cases involving felonies prosecuted by indictment.

e. As may be provided by law, an appellate term shall have jurisdiction to hear and determine appeals from the district court or a town, village or city court outside the city of New York.

[Court of claims; jurisdiction.] § 9. The court of claims is continued. It shall consist of the eight judges now authorized by law, but the legislature may increase such number and may reduce such number to six or seven. The judges shall be appointed by the governor by and with the advice and consent of the senate and their terms of office shall be nine years. The court shall have jurisdiction to hear and determine claims against the state or by the state against the claimant or between conflicting claimants as the legislature may provide.

[County courts; judges.] § 10. a. The county court is continued in each county outside the city of New York. There shall be at least one judge of the county court in each county and such number of additional judges in each county as may be provided by law. The judges shall be residents of the county and shall be chosen by the electors of the county.

b. The terms of the judges of the county court shall be ten years from and including the first day of January next after their election.

[County court; jurisdiction.] § 11. a. The county court shall have jurisdiction over the following classes of actions and proceedings which shall be originated in such county court in the manner provided by law, except that actions and proceedings within the jurisdiction of the district court or a town, village or city court outside the city of New York may, as provided by law, be originated therein: actions and proceedings for the recovery of money, actions and proceedings for the recovery of chattels and actions and proceedings for the foreclosure of mechanics liens and liens on personal property where the amount sought to be recovered or the value of the property does not exceed six thousand dollars exclusive of interest and costs, provided, however, that the legislature, at the request of the county board of supervisors or other elective governing body in any county, may increase such amount in such county to any amount not exceeding ten thousand dollars exclusive of interest and costs; over all crimes and other violations of law; over summary proceedings to recover possession of real property and to remove tenants therefrom; and over such other actions and proceedings, not within the exclusive jurisdiction of the supreme court, as may be provided by law.

b. There may be separate divisions of the county court established by the appellate division of the supreme court in each department for various classes of actions and proceedings.

c. The county court shall exercise such equity jurisdiction as may be provided by law and its jurisdiction to enter judgment upon a counterclaim for the recovery of money only shall be unlimited.

d. The county court shall have jurisdiction to hear and determine all appeals arising in the county in the following actions and proceedings: as of right, from a judgment or order of the district court or a town, village or city court which finally determines an action or proceeding and, as may be provided by law, from a judgment or order of any such court which does not finally determine an action or proceeding. The legislature may provide, in accordance with the provisions of section eight of this article, that any or all of such appeals be taken to an appellate term of the supreme court instead of the county court.

e. The provisions of this section shall in no way limit or impair the jurisdiction of the supreme court as set forth in section seven of this article.

[Surrogate's courts; judges; jurisdiction.] § 12. a. The surrogate's court is continued in each county in the state. There shall be at least one judge of the surrogate's court in each county and such number of additional judges of the surrogate's court as may be provided by law.

b. The judges of the surrogate's court shall be residents of the county and shall be chosen by the electors of the county.

Constitution of New York

c. The terms of the judges of the surrogate's court in the city of New York shall be fourteen years, and in other counties ten years, from and including the first day of January next after their election.

d. The surrogate's court shall have jurisdiction over all actions and proceedings relating to the affairs of decedents, probate of wills, administration of estates and actions and proceedings arising thereunder or pertaining thereto, guardianship of the property of minors, and such other actions and proceedings, not within the exclusive jurisdiction of the supreme court, as may be provided by law.

e. The surrogate's court shall exercise such equity jurisdiction as may be provided by law.

f. The provisions of this section shall in no way limit or impair the jurisdiction of the supreme court as set forth in section seven of this article.

[Family court; organization; jurisdiction.] § 13. a. The family court of the state of New York is hereby established. It shall consist of at least one judge in each county outside the city of New York and such number of additional judges for such counties as may be provided by law. Within the city of New York it shall consist of such number of judges as may be provided by law. The judges of the family court within the city of New York shall be residents of such city and shall be appointed by the mayor of the city of New York for terms of ten years. The judges of the family court outside the city of New York, shall be chosen by the electors of the counties wherein they reside for terms of ten years.

b. The family court shall have jurisdiction over the following classes of actions and proceedings which shall be originated in such family court in the manner provided by law: (1) the protection, treatment, correction and commitment of those minors who are in need of the exercise of the authority of the court because of circumstances of neglect, delinquency or dependency, as the legislature may determine; (2) the custody of minors except for custody incidental to actions and proceedings for marital separation, divorce, annulment of marriage and dissolution of marriage; (3) the adoption of persons; (4) the support of dependents except for support incidental to actions and proceedings in this state for marital separation, divorce, annulment of marriage or dissolution of marriage; (5) the establishment of paternity; (6) proceedings for conciliation of spouses; and (7) as may be provided by law: the guardianship of the person of minors and, in conformity with the provisions of section seven of this article, crimes and offenses by or against minors or between spouses or between parent and child or between members of the same family or household. Nothing in this section shall be construed to abridge the authority or jurisdiction of courts to appoint guardians in cases originating in those courts.

c. The family court shall also have jurisdiction to determine, with the same powers possessed by the supreme court, the following matters when referred to the family court from the supreme court: habeas corpus proceedings for the determination of the custody of minors; and in actions and proceedings for marital separation, divorce, annulment of marriage and dissolution of marriage, applications to fix temporary or permanent support and custody, or applications to enforce judgments and orders of support and of custody, or applications to modify judgments and orders of support and of custody which may be granted only upon the showing to the family court that there has been a subsequent change of circumstances and that modification is required.

d. The provisions of this section shall in no way limit or impair the jurisdiction of the supreme court as set forth in section seven of this article. (Amended by vote of the people November 6, 1973.)

[**Discharge of duties of more than one judicial office by same judicial officer.**] § 14. The legislature may at any time provide that outside the city of New York the same person may act and discharge the duties of county judge and surrogate or of judge of the family court and surrogate, or of county judge and judge of the family court, or of all three positions in any county.

[New York city; city-wide courts, jurisdiction.]
§ 15. a. The legislature shall by law establish a single court of city-wide civil jurisdiction and a single court of city-wide criminal jurisdiction in and for the city of New York and the legislature may, upon the request of the mayor and the local legislative body of the city of New York, merge the two courts into one city-wide court of both civil and criminal jurisdiction. The said city-wide courts shall consist of such number of judges as may be provided by law. The judges of the court of city-wide civil jurisdiction shall be residents of such city and shall be chosen for terms of ten years by the electors of the counties included within the city of New York from districts within such counties established by law. The judges of the court of city-wide criminal jurisdiction shall be residents of such city and shall be appointed for terms of ten years by the mayor of the city of New York.

b. The court of city-wide civil jurisdiction of the city of New York shall have jurisdiction over the following classes of actions and proceedings which shall be originated in such court in the manner provided by law: actions and proceedings for the recovery of money, actions and proceedings for the recovery of chattels and actions and proceedings for the foreclosure of mechanics liens and liens on personal property where the amount sought to be recovered or the value of the property does not exceed ten thousand dollars exclusive of interest and costs, or such smaller amount as may be fixed by law; over summary proceedings to recover possession of real property and to remove tenants therefrom and over such other actions and proceedings, not within the exclusive jurisdiction of the supreme court, as may be provided by law. The court of city-wide civil jurisdiction shall further exercise such equity jurisdiction as may be provided by law and its jurisdiction to enter judgment upon a counterclaim for the recovery of money only shall be unlimited.

c. The court of city-wide criminal jurisdiction of the city of New York shall have jurisdiction over crimes and other violations of law, other than those prosecuted by indictment, provided, however, that the legislature may grant to said court jurisdiction over misdemeanors prosecuted by indictment; and over such other actions and proceedings, not within the exclusive jurisdiction of the supreme court, as may be provided by law.

d. The provisions of this section shall in no way limit or impair the jurisdiction of the supreme court as set forth in section seven of this article.

[District courts; jurisdiction; judges.] § 16. a. The district court of Nassau county may be continued under existing law and the legislature may, at the request of the board of supervisors or other elective governing body of any county outside the city of New York, establish the district court for the entire area of such county or for a portion of such county consisting of one or more cities, or one or more towns which are contiguous, or of a combination of such cities and such towns provided at least one of such cities is contiguous to one of such towns.

b. No law establishing the district court for an entire county shall become effective unless approved at a general election on the question of the approval of such law by a majority of the votes cast thereon by the electors within the area of any cities in the county considered as one unit and by a majority of the votes cast thereon by the electors within the area outside of cities in the county considered as one unit.

c. No law establishing the district court for a portion of a county shall become effective unless approved at a general election on the question of the approval of such law by a majority of the votes cast thereon by the electors within the area of any cities included in such portion of the county considered as one unit and by a majority of the votes cast thereon by the electors within the area outside of cities included in such portion of the county considered as one unit.

d. The district court shall have such jurisdiction as may be provided by law, but not in any respect greater than the jurisdiction of the courts for the city of New York as provided in section fifteen of this article, provided, however, that in actions and proceedings for the recovery of money, actions and proceedings for the recovery of chattels and actions and proceedings for the foreclosure of mechanics liens and liens on personal property, the amount sought to be recovered or the value of the property shall not exceed six thousand dollars exclusive of interest and costs.

e. The legislature may create districts of the district court which shall consist of an entire county or of an area less than a county.

f. There shall be at least one judge of the district court for each district and such number of additional judges in each district as may be provided by law.

g. The judges of the district court shall be apportioned among the districts as may be provided by law, and to the extent practicable, in accordance with the population and the volume of judicial business.

h. The judges shall be residents of the district and shall be chosen by the electors of the district. Their terms shall be six years from and including the first day of January next after their election.

i. The legislature may regulate and discontinue the district court in any county or portion thereof.

[Town, village and city courts; jurisdiction; judges.]
§ 17. a. Courts for towns, villages and cities outside the city of New York are continued and shall have the jurisdiction prescribed by the legislature but not in any re-

spect greater than the jurisdiction of the district court as provided in section sixteen of this article.

b. The legislature may regulate such courts, establish uniform jurisdiction, practice and procedure for city courts outside the city of New York and may discontinue any village or city court outside the city of New York existing on the effective date of this article. The legislature may discontinue any town court existing on the effective date of this article only with the approval of a majority of the total votes cast at a general election on the question of a proposed discontinuance of the court in each such town affected thereby.

c. The legislature may abolish the legislative functions on town boards of justices of the peace and provide that town councilmen be elected in their stead.

d. The number of the judges of each of such town, village and city courts and the classification and duties of the judges shall be prescribed by the legislature. The terms, method of selection and method of filling vacancies for the judges of such courts shall be prescribed by the legislature, provided, however, that the justices of town courts shall be chosen by the electors of the town for terms of four years from and including the first day of January next after their election.

[Trial by jury; trial without jury; claims against state.] § 18. a. Trial by jury is guaranteed as provided in article one of this constitution. The legislature may provide that in any court of original jurisdiction a jury shall be composed of six or of twelve persons and may authorize any court which shall have jurisdiction over crimes and other violations of law, other than crimes prosecuted by indictment, to try such matters without a jury, provided, however, that crimes prosecuted by indictment shall be tried by a jury composed of twelve persons, unless a jury trial has been waived as provided in section two of article one of this constitution.

b. The legislature may provide for the manner of trial of actions and proceedings involving claims against the state.

[Transfer of actions and proceedings.] § 19. a. The supreme court may transfer any action or proceeding, except one over which it shall have exclusive jurisdiction which does not depend upon the monetary amount sought, to any other court having jurisdiction of the subject matter within the judicial department provided that such other court has jurisdiction over the classes of persons named as parties. As may be provided by law, the supreme court may transfer to itself any action or proceeding originated or pending in another court within the judicial department other than the court of claims upon a finding that such a transfer will promote the administration of justice.

b. The county court shall transfer to the supreme court or surrogate's court or family court any action or proceeding which has not been transferred to it from the supreme court or surrogate's court or family court and over which the county court has no jurisdiction. The county court may transfer any action or proceeding, except a criminal action or proceeding involving a felony prosecuted by indictment or an action or proceeding required by this article to be dealt with in the surrogate's court or family court, to any court, other than the supreme court, having jurisdiction of the subject matter within the county provided that such other court has jurisdiction over the classes of persons named as parties.

c. As may be provided by law, the supreme court or the county court may transfer to the county court any action or proceeding originated or pending in the district court or a town, village or city court outside the city of New York upon a finding that such a transfer will promote the administration of justice.

d. The surrogate's court shall transfer to the supreme court or the county court or the family court or the courts for the city of New York established pursuant to section fifteen of this article any action or proceeding which has not been transferred to it from any of said courts and over which the surrogate's court has no jurisdiction.

e. The family court shall transfer to the supreme court or the surrogate's court or the county court or the courts for the city of New York established pursuant to section fifteen of this article any action or proceeding which has not been transferred to it from any of said courts and over which the family court has no jurisdiction.

f. The courts for the city of New York established pursuant to section fifteen of this article shall transfer to the supreme court or the surrogate's court or the family court any action or proceeding which has not been transferred to them from any of said courts and over which the said courts for the city of New York have no jurisdiction.

g. As may be provided by law, the supreme court shall transfer any action or proceeding to any other court having jurisdiction of the subject matter in any other judicial district or county provided that such other court has jurisdiction over the classes of persons named as parties.

h. As may be provided by law, the county court, the surrogate's court, the family court and the courts for the city of New York established pursuant to section fifteen of this article may transfer any action or proceeding, other than one which has previously been transferred to it, to any other court, except the supreme court, having jurisdiction of the subject matter in any other judicial district or county provided that such other court has jurisdiction over the classes of persons named as parties.

i. As may be provided by law, the district court or a town, village or city court outside the city of New York may transfer any action or proceeding, other than one which has previously been transferred to it, to any court other than the county court or the surrogate's court or the family court or the supreme court, having jurisdiction of the subject matter in the same or an adjoining county provided that such other court has jurisdiction over the classes of persons named as parties.

j. Each court shall exercise jurisdiction over any action or proceeding transferred to it pursuant to this section.

k. The legislature may provide that the verdict or judgment in actions and proceedings so transferred shall not be subject to the limitation of monetary jurisdiction of the court to which the actions and proceedings are transferred if that limitation be lower than that of the court in which the actions and proceedings were originated.

[Judges and justices; qualifications; eligibility for other office or service; restrictions.] § 20. a. No person, other than one who holds such office at the effective date of this article, may assume the office of judge of the court of appeals, justice of the supreme court, or judge of the court of claims unless he has been admitted to practice law in this state at least ten years. No person, other than one who holds such office at the effective date of this article, may assume the office of judge of the county court, surrogate's court, family court, a court for the city of New York established pursuant to section fifteen of this article, district court or city court outside the city of New York unless he has been admitted to practice law in this state at least five years or such greater number of years as the legislature may determine.

b. A judge of the court of appeals, justice of the supreme court, judge of the court of claims, judge of a county court, judge of the surrogate's court, judge of the family court or judge of a court for the city of New York established pursuant to section fifteen of this article who is elected or appointed after the effective date of this article may not:

(1) hold any other public office or trust except member of a constitutional convention or member of the armed forces of the United States or of the state of New York in which latter event the legislature may enact such legislation as it deems appropriate to provide for a temporary judge or justice to serve during the period of the absence of such judge or justice in the armed forces;

(2) be eligible to be a candidate for any public office other than judicial office or member of a constitutional convention, unless he resigns his judicial office; in the event a judge or justice does not so resign his judicial office within ten days after his acceptance of the nomination of such other office, his judicial office shall become vacant and the vacancy shall be filled in the manner provided in this article;

(3) hold any office or assume the duties or exercise the powers of any office of any political organization or be a member of any governing or executive agency thereof;

(4) engage in the practice of law, act as an arbitrator, referee or compensated mediator in any action or proceeding or matter or engage in the conduct of any other profession or business which interferes with the performance of his judicial duties.

c. Qualifications for and restrictions upon the judges of district, town, village or city courts outside the city of New York, other than such qualifications and restrictions specifically set forth in subdivision a of this section, shall be prescribed by the legislature, provided, however, that the legislature shall require a course of training and education to be completed by justices of town and village courts selected after the effective date of this article who have not been admitted to practice law in this state.

[**Vacancies; how filled.**] § 21. a. When a vacancy shall occur, otherwise than by expiration of term, in the office of justice of the supreme court, of judge of the county court, of judge of the surrogate's court or judge of the family court outside the city of New York, it shall be filled for a full term at the next general election held not less than three months after such vacancy occurs and, until the vacancy shall be so filled, the governor by and with the advice and consent of the senate, if the senate shall be in session, or, if the senate not be in session, the governor may fill such vacancy by an appointment which shall continue until and including the last day of December next after the election at which the vacancy shall be filled.

b. When a vacancy shall occur, otherwise than by expiration of term, in the office of judge of the court of claims, it shall be filled for the unexpired term in the same manner as an original appointment.

c. When a vacancy shall occur, otherwise than by expiration of term, in the office of judge elected to the citywide court of civil jurisdiction of the city of New York, it shall be filled for a full term at the next general election held not less than three months after such vacancy occurs and, until the vacancy shall be so filled, the mayor of the city of New York may fill such vacancy by an appointment which shall continue until and including the last day of December next after the election at which the vacancy shall be filled. When a vacancy shall occur, otherwise than by expiration of term on the last day of December of any year, in the office of judge appointed to the family court within the city of New York or the city-wide court of criminal jurisdiction of the city of New York, the mayor of the city of New York shall fill such vacancy by an appointment for the unexpired term.

d. When a vacancy shall occur, otherwise than by expiration of term, in the office of judge of the district court, it shall be filled for a full term at the next general election held not less than three months after such vacancy occurs and, until the vacancy shall be so filled, the board of supervisors or the supervisor or supervisors of the affected district if such district consists of a portion of a county or, in counties with an elected county executive officer, such county executive officer may, subject to confirmation by the board of supervisors or the supervisor or supervisors of such district, fill such vacancy by an appointment which shall continue until and including the last day of December next after the election at which the vacancy shall be filled.

[Court on the judiciary; removal or retirement of certain judges by appellate division; commission on judicial conduct.]
§ 22. a. Any judge or justice of any court in the unified court system may be censured, suspended or removed for cause, including, but not limited to, misconduct in office, persistent failure to perform his duties, habitual intemperance and conduct, on or off the bench, prejudicial to the administration of justice, or retired for mental or physical disability preventing the proper performance of his judicial duties after due notice and hearing as hereinafter provided.

b. The court on the judiciary shall be composed of five justices of the appellate division from judicial departments other than the judicial department in which the judge or justice who is before the court has been elected, appointed or designated to sit. The chief judge of the court of appeals shall appoint the members of the court and shall designate one member to preside or such appointment and designation shall be made by the senior associate judge of the court of appeals or as the legislature may provide in the absence, inability or disqualification of the chief judge of the court of appeals.

c. The affirmative concurrence of not less than three members of the court shall be necessary for removal, retirement, suspension or censure and the court may disqualify a judge or justice removed from office from again holding any public office of this state. Proceedings to remove or the removal of a judge or justice from office shall not prevent his indictment and punishment according to law. A judge or justice retired for disability in accordance with this section shall thereafter receive such compensation as may be provided by law.

d. The chief judge of the court of appeals may convene the court on the judiciary upon his own motion and shall convene the court upon written request by the governor or by a presiding justice of the appellate division, or an appellate division or upon the recommendation of the commission on judicial conduct, as hereinafter provided, or upon the written request of a judge or justice, whose censure, suspension or retirement has been recommended by the commission on judicial conduct, as hereinafter provided.

e. After the court on the judiciary has been convened and charges of removal or retirement have been preferred against a judge or justice, the presiding officer of the court on the judiciary shall, before a hearing on charges of removal for cause commences, give written notice to the governor, the temporary president of the senate and the speaker of the assembly of the name of the judge or justice against whom charges have been preferred, the nature of the charges and the date set for hearing these charges, which shall not be less than sixty days after the giving of such notice. Immediately upon receipt of such notice, the legislature shall be deemed to be in session for the purpose of this proceeding. If any member of the legislature prefers the same charges against the judge or justice concerned within thirty days after receipt of such notice and if such charges are entertained by a majority vote of the assembly, proceedings before the court on the judiciary shall be stayed pending the determination of the legislature which shall be exclusive and final. But a proceeding by the court on the judiciary for the retirement of a judge or justice for mental or physical disability preventing the proper performance of his judicial duties shall not be stayed.

f. The court on the judiciary shall have power to designate the attorney for the commission on judicial conduct to act as counsel to conduct the proceeding, to summon witnesses to appear and testify under oath and to compel the production of books, papers, documents and records before such counsel in advance of the trial and before the court upon the trial, to grant immunity from prosecution or punishment, as may be provided by law when the court deems it necessary and proper in order to compel the giving of testimony under oath and the production of books, papers, documents and records, and to make its own rules and procedures for the investigation and trial.

g. The court on the judiciary shall have such further powers and duties as may be provided by law.

h. The judges or justices while exercising the powers of a court on the judiciary shall serve without additional compensation but the legislature shall provide moneys by appropriation to meet the expenses of the court.

i. A judge or justice may not exercise the powers of his office while charged with a felony or while a proceeding for his removal or retirement by the court on the judiciary is pending. A judge or justice may not exercise the powers of his office nor receive his judicial salary upon pleading guilty to or being found guilty of a felony pending review of the conviction by a court of appellate jurisdiction.

j. An appeal may be taken by either the commission on judicial conduct or the respondent to the court of appeals by permission of such court from a final determination of the court on the judiciary.

k. There shall be a commission on judicial conduct, the organization and procedure of which shall be as the legislature shall provide. The commission shall receive and investigate complaints of the public with respect to the qualifications, conduct, or fitness to perform or the performance of the official duties of any judge or justice of any court within the unified court system and may, on its own motion, initiate investigations with respect to the qualifications, conduct, or fitness to perform or the performance of the official duties of any such judge or justice. The commission may either recommend to the chief judge of the court of appeals the convening of the court on the judiciary, for stated reasons, to hear and determine charges against a judge or justice, or determine that a judge or justice be censured, suspended or retired, as provided by law. The commission shall transmit any determination of censure, suspension or retirement to the chief judge of the court of appeals who shall give written notice of such determination to the judge or justice involved. Such judge or justice may either accept the commission's determination or make written request to the chief judge, within thirty days after receipt of such notice, for the convening of the court on the judiciary to hear and determine the charges, in which event the court on the judiciary may impose whatever disciplinary measures it may determine, including removal. If such judge or justice shall accept the commission's determination or shall not request the convening of the court on the judiciary, he shall thereupon be censured, suspended or retired by the commission in accordance with its findings. The jurisdiction of the commission on judicial conduct and the court on the judiciary over any judge or justice with respect to whom a complaint has been received or an investigation initiated shall continue notwithstanding the election, re-election, appointment or reappointment of such judge or justice to any other judicial office.

1. (1) The commission on judicial conduct shall consist of three persons appointed by the governor, one of whom must be a lawyer admitted to practice in the state and two of whom shall not be lawyers, justices or judges or retired justices or judges of the unified court system; one person appointed by the president pro tem of the senate; one person appointed by the minority leader of the senate; one person appointed by the speaker of the assembly; one person appointed by the minority leader of the assembly; and two persons appointed by the chief judge of the court of appeals, one of whom must be a justice of the appellate division of the supreme court and the other of whom must be a judge or justice of a court of record other than the court of appeals. None of the persons to be appointed by the legislative leaders shall be justices or judges or retired justices or judges of the unified court system.

(2) The persons first appointed by the governor shall have respectively one, two and three year terms as he shall designate. The persons first appointed by the chief judge of the court of appeals shall have respectively three and four year terms as he shall designate. The person first appointed by the president pro tem of the senate shall have a one year term. The person first appointed by the minority leader of the senate shall have a two year term. The person first appointed by the speaker of the assembly shall have a four year term. The person first appointed by the minority leader of the assembly shall have a three year term. Each member of the commission shall be appointed thereafter for a term of

four years. Commission membership of the judge or justice appointed by the chief judge shall terminate if such member ceases to hold the judicial position that qualified him for such appointment. Such membership shall also terminate if a member attains a position that would have rendered him ineligible for such membership at the time of his appointment. A vacancy shall be filled by the appointing power for the remainder of the term. (Paragraphs a through i amended and paragraphs j through l added by vote of the people November 4, 1975.)

[**Removal of judges.**] § 23. a. Judges of the court of appeals and justices of the supreme court may be removed by concurrent resolution of both houses of the legislature, if two-thirds of all the members elected to each house concur therein.

b. Judges of the court of claims, the county court, the surrogate's court, the family court, the courts for the city of New York established pursuant to section fifteen of this article, the district court and such other courts as the legislature may determine may be removed by the senate, on the recommendation of the governor, if two-thirds of all the members elected to the senate concur therein.

c. No judge or justice shall be removed by virtue of this section except for cause, which shall be entered on the journals, nor unless he shall have been served with a statement of the cause alleged, and shall have had an opportunity to be heard. On the question of removal, the yeas and nays shall be entered on the journal.

[**Court for trial of impeachments; judgment.**] § 24. The assembly shall have the power of impeachment by a vote of a majority of all the members elected thereto. The court for the trial of impeachments shall be composed of the president of the senate, the senators, or the major part of them, and the judges of the court of appeals, or the major part of them. On the trial of an impeachment against the governor or lieutenant-governor, neither the lieutenant-governor nor the temporary president of the senate shall act as a member of the court. No judicial officer shall exercise his office after articles of impeachment against him shall have been preferred to the senate, until he shall have been acquitted. Before the trial of an impeachment, the members of the court shall take an oath or affirmation truly and impartially to try the impeachment according to the evidence, and no person shall be convicted without the concurrence of two-thirds of the members present. Judgment in cases of impeachment shall not extend further than to removal from office, or removal from office and disqualification to hold and enjoy any public office of honor, trust, or profit under this state; but the party impeached shall be liable to indictment and punishment according to law.

[Judges and justices; compensation; retirement.]
§ 25. a. The compensation of a judge of the court of appeals, a justice of the supreme court, a judge of the court of claims, a judge of the county court, a judge of the surrogate's court, a judge of the family court, a judge of a court for the city of New York established pursuant to section fifteen of this article, a judge of the district court or of a retired judge or justice shall be established by law and shall not be diminished during the term of office for which he was elected or appointed. Any judge or justice of a court abolished by section thirty-five of this article, who pursuant to that section becomes a judge or justice of a court established or continued by this article, shall receive without interruption or diminution for the remainder of the term for which he was elected or appointed to the abolished court the compensation he had been receiving upon the effective date of this article together with any additional compensation that may be prescribed by law.

b. Each judge of the court of appeals, justice of the supreme court, judge of the court of claims, judge of the county court, judge of the surrogate's court, judge of the family court, judge of a court for the city of New York established pursuant to section fifteen of this article and judge of the district court shall retire on the last day of December in the year in which he reaches the age of seventy. Each such former judge of the court of appeals and justice of the supreme court may thereafter perform the duties of a justice of the supreme court, with power to hear and determine actions and proceedings, provided, however, that it shall be certificated in the manner provided by law that the services of such judge or justice are necessary to expedite the business of the court and that he is mentally and physically able and competent to perform the full duties of such office. Any such certification shall be valid for a term of two years and may be extended as provided by law for additional terms of two years. A retired judge or justice shall serve no longer than until the last day of December in the year in which he reaches the age of seventy-six. A retired judge or justice shall be subject to assignment by the appellate division of the supreme court of the judicial department of his residence. Any retired justice of the supreme court who had been designated to and served as a justice of any appellate division immediately preceding his reaching the age of seventy shall be eligible for designation by the governor as a temporary or additional justice of the appellate division. A retired judge or justice shall not be counted in determining the number of justices in a judicial district for purposes of section six subdivision d of this article.

c. The provisions of this section shall also be applicable to any judge or justice who has not reached the age of seventy-six and to whom it would otherwise have been applicable but for the fact that he reached the age of seventy and retired before the effective date of this article. (Subdivision b amended by vote of the people November 8, 1966.)

[**Temporary assignments of judges and justices.**]
§ 26. a. A justice of the supreme court may perform the duties of his office or hold court in any county and may

be temporarily assigned to the supreme court in any judicial district or to the court of claims. A justice of the supreme court in the city of New York may be temporarily assigned to the family court in the city of New York or to the surrogate's court in any county within the city of New York when required to dispose of the business of such court.

b. A judge of the court of claims may perform the duties of his office or hold court in any county and may be temporarily assigned to the supreme court in any judicial district.

c. A judge of the county court may perform the duties of his office or hold court in any county and may be temporarily assigned to the supreme court in the judicial department of his residence or to the county court or the family court in any county or to the surrogate's court in any county outside the city of New York or to a court for the city of New York established pursuant to section fifteen of this article.

d. A judge of the surrogate's court in any county within the city of New York may perform the duties of his office or hold court in any county and may be temporarily assigned to the supreme court in the judicial department of his residence.

e. A judge of the surrogate's court in any county outside the city of New York may perform the duties of his office or hold court in any county and may be temporarily assigned to the supreme court in the judicial department of his residence or to the county court or the family court in any county or to a court for the city of New York established pursuant to section fifteen of this article.

f. A judge of the family court may perform the duties of his office or hold court in any county and may be temporarily assigned to the county court or the family court in any county or to the surrogate's court in any county outside of the city of New York or to a court for the city of New York established pursuant to section fifteen of this article.

g. A judge of a court for the city of New York established pursuant to section fifteen of this article may perform the duties of his office or hold court in any county and may be temporarily assigned to the supreme court in the judicial department of his residence or to the county court or the family court in any county or to the other court for the city of New York established pursuant to section fifteen of this article.

h. A judge of the district court in any county may perform the duties of his office or hold court in any county and may be temporarily assigned to the county court in the judicial department of his residence or to a court for the city of New York established pursuant to section fifteen of this article or to the district court in any county.

i. Temporary assignments of all the foregoing judges or justices listed in this section shall be made by the appellate division of the supreme court of the department or departments concerned.

j. The legislature may provide for temporary assignments within the county of residence or any adjoining county, of judges of town, village or city courts outside the city of New York.

k. While temporarily assigned pursuant to the provisions of this section, any judge or justice shall have the powers, duties and jurisdiction of a judge or justice of the court to which assigned. After the expiration of any temporary assignment, as provided in this section, the judge or justice assigned shall have all the powers, duties and jurisdiction of a judge or justice of the court to which he was assigned with respect to matters pending before him during the term of such temporary assignment.

[Supreme court; extraordinary terms.] § 27. The governor may, when in his opinion the public interest requires, appoint extraordinary terms of the supreme court. He shall designate the time and place of holding the term and the justice who shall hold the term. The governor may terminate the assignment of the justice and may name another justice in his place to hold the term.

[Administrative supervision of court system.] § 28. The authority and responsibility for the administrative supervision of the unified court system for the state shall be vested in the administrative board of the judicial conference. The administrative board shall consist of the chief judge of the court of appeals, as chairman, and the presiding justices of the appellate divisions of the four judicial departments. The administrative board, in consultation with the judicial conference, shall establish standards and administrative policies for general application throughout the state. The composition and functions of the judicial conference shall be as now or hereafter provided by law. In accordance with the standards and administrative policies established by the administrative board, the appellate divisions shall supervise the administration and operation of the courts in their respective departments.

[Expenses of courts.] § 29. a. The legislature shall provide for the allocation of the cost of operating and maintaining the court of appeals, the appellate division of the supreme court in each judicial department, the supreme court, the court of claims, the county court, the surrogate's court, the family court, the courts for the city of New York established pursuant to section fifteen of this article and the district court, among the state, the counties, the city of New York and other political subdivisions.

b. The legislature shall provide for the submission of the itemized estimates of the annual financial needs of the courts referred to in subdivision a of this section to the administrative board of the judicial conference or to the said conference to be forwarded to the appropriating bodies with recommendations and comment.

c. Insofar as the expense of the courts is borne by the state or paid by the state in the first instance, the final determination of the itemized estimates of the annual financial needs of the courts shall be made by the legislature and the governor in accordance with articles four and seven of this constitution.

d. Insofar as the expense of the courts is not paid by the state in the first instance and is borne by counties, the city of New York or other political subdivisions, the final determination of the itemized estimates of the annual financial needs of the courts shall be made by the appropriate governing bodies of such counties, the city of New York or other political subdivisions.

[**Legislative power over jurisdiction and proceedings; delegation of power to regulate practice and procedure.**] § 30. The legislature shall have the same power to alter and regulate the jurisdiction and proceedings in law and in equity that it has heretofore exercised. The legislature may, on such terms as it shall provide and subject to subsequent modification, delegate, in whole or in part, to a court, including the appellate division of the supreme court, to the administrative board of the judicial conference, or to the judicial conference, any power possessed by the legislature to regulate practice and procedure in the courts. Nothing herein contained shall prevent the adoption of regulations by individual courts consistent with the general practice and procedure as provided by statute or general rules.

[**Inapplicability of article to certain courts.**] § 31. This article does not apply to the peacemakers courts or other Indian courts, the existence and operation of which shall continue as may be provided by law.

[**Custodians of children to be of same religious persuasion.**] § 32. When any court having jurisdiction over a child shall commit it or remand it to an institution or agency or place it in the custody of any person by parole, placing out, adoption or guardianship, the child shall be committed or remanded or placed, when practicable, in an institution or agency governed by persons, or in the custody of a person, of the same religious persuasion as the child.

[Existing laws; duty of legislature to implement article.] § 33. Existing provisions of law not inconsistent with this article shall continue in force until repealed, amended, modified or superseded in accordance with the provisions of this article. The legislature shall enact appropriate laws to carry into effect the purposes and provisions of this article, and may, for the purpose of implementing, supplementing or clarifying any of its provisions, enact any laws, not inconsistent with the provisions of this article, necessary or desirable in promoting the objectives of this article.

[Pending appeals, actions and proceedings; preservation of existing terms of office of judges and justices.] § 34. a. The court of appeals, the appellate division of the supreme court, the supreme court, the court of claims, the county court in counties outside the city of New York, the surrogate's court and the district court of Nassau county shall hear and determine all appeals, actions and proceedings pending therein on the effective date of this article except that the appellate division of the supreme court in the first and second judicial departments or the appellate term in such departments, if so directed by the appropriate appellate division of the supreme court, shall hear and determine all appeals pending in the appellate terms of the supreme court in the first and second judicial departments and in the court of special sessions of the city of New York and except that the county court or an appellate term shall, as may be provided by law, hear and determine all appeals pending in the county court or the supreme court other than an appellate term. Further appeal from a decision of the county court, the appellate term or the appellate division of the supreme court, rendered on or after the effective date of this article, shall be governed by the provisions of this article.

b. The justices of the supreme court in office on the effective date of this article shall hold their offices as justices of the supreme court until the expiration of their respective terms.

c. The judges of the court of claims in office on the effective date of this article shall hold their offices as judges of the court of claims until the expiration of their respective terms.

d. The surrogates, and county judges outside the city of New York, including the special county judges of the counties of Erie and Suffolk, in office on the effective date of this article shall hold office as judges of the surrogate's court or county judge, respectively, of such counties until the expiration of their respective terms.

e. The judges of the district court of Nassau county in office on the effective date of this article shall hold their offices until the expiration of their respective terms.

f. Judges of courts for towns, villages and cities outside the city of New York in office on the effective date of this article shall hold their offices until the expiration of their respective terms.

[**Certain courts abolished; transfer of judges, court personnel, and actions and proceedings to other courts.**] § 35. a. The children's courts, the court of general sessions of the county of New York, the county courts of the counties of Bronx, Kings, Queens and Richmond, the city court of the city of New York, the domestic relations court of the city of New York, the municipal court of the city of New York, the court of special sessions of the city of New York and the city magistrates' courts of the city of New York are abolished from and after the effective date of this article and thereupon the seals, records, papers and documents of or belonging to such courts shall, unless otherwise provided by law, be deposited in the offices of the clerks of the several counties in which these courts now exist.

b. The judges of the county court of the counties of Bronx, Kings, Queens and Richmond and the judges of the court of general sessions of the county of New York in office on the effective date of this article shall, for the remainder of the terms for which they were elected or appointed, be justices of the supreme court in and for the judicial district which includes the county in which they resided on that date. The salaries of such justices shall be the same as the salaries of the other justices of the supreme court residing in the same judicial district and shall be paid in the same manner. All actions and proceedings pending in the county court of the counties of Bronx, Kings, Queens and Richmond and in the court of general sessions of the county of New York on the effective date of this article shall be transferred to the supreme court in the county in which the action or proceedings was pending, or otherwise as may be provided by law.

c. The legislature shall provide by law that the justices of the city court of the city of New York and the justices of the municipal court of the city of New York in office on the date such courts are abolished shall, for the remainder of the term for which each was elected or appointed, be judges of the city-wide court of civil jurisdiction of the city of New York established pursuant to section fifteen of this article and for such district as the legislature may determine.

d. The legislature shall provide by law that the justices of the court of special sessions and the magistrates of the city magistrates' courts of the city of New York in office on the date such courts are abolished shall, for the remainder of the term for which each was appointed, be judges of the city-wide court of criminal jurisdiction of the city of New York established pursuant to section fifteen provided, however, that each term shall expire on the last day of the year in which it would have expired except for the provisions of this article.

e. All actions and proceedings pending in the city court of the city of New York and the municipal court in the city of New York on the date such courts are abolished shall be transferred to the city-wide court of civil jurisdiction of the city of New York established pursuant to section fifteen of this article or as otherwise provided by law.

f. All actions and proceedings pending in the court of

special sessions of the city of New York and the city magistrates' courts of the city of New York on the date such courts are abolished shall be transferred to the city-wide court of criminal jurisdiction of the city of New York established pursuant to section fifteen of this article or as otherwise provided by law.

g. The special county judges of the counties of Broome, Chautauqua, Jefferson, Oneida and Rockland and the judges of the children's courts in all counties outside the city of New York in office on the effective date of this article shall, for the remainder of the terms for which they were elected or appointed, be judges of the family court in and for the county in which they hold office. Except as otherwise provided in this section, the office of special county judge and the office of special surrogate is abolished from and after the effective date of this article and the terms of the persons holding such offices shall terminate on that date.

h. All actions and proceedings pending in the children's courts in counties outside the city of New York on the effective date of this article shall be transferred to the family court in the respective counties.

i. The justices of the domestic relations court of the city of New York in office on the effective date of this article shall, for the remainder of the terms for which they were appointed, be judges of the family court within the city of New York.

j. All actions and proceedings pending in the domestic relations court of the city of New York on the effective date of this article shall be transferred to the family court in the city of New York.

k. The office of official referee is abolished, provided, however, that official referees in office on the effective date of this article shall, for the remainder of the terms for which they were appointed or certified, be official referees of the court in which appointed or certified or the successor court, as the case may be. At the expiration of the term of any official referee, his office shall be abolished and thereupon such former official referee shall be subject to the relevant provisions of section twenty-five of this article.

l. As may be provided by law, the non-judicial personnel of the courts affected by this article in office on the effective date of this article shall, to the extent practicable, be continued without diminution of salaries and with the same status and rights in the courts established or continued by this article; and especially skilled, experienced and trained personnel shall, to the extent practicable, be assigned to like functions in the courts which exercise the jurisdiction formerly exercised by the courts in which they were employed. In the event that the adoption of this article shall require or make possible a reduction in the number of non-judicial personnel, or in the number of certain categories of such personnel, such reduction shall be made, to the extent practicable, by provision that the death, resignation, removal or retirement of an employee shall not create a vacancy until the reduced number of personnel has been reached.

m. In the event that a judgment or order was entered before the effective date of this article and a right of appeal existed and notice of appeal therefrom is filed after the effective date of this article, such appeal shall be taken from the supreme court, the county courts, the surrogate's courts, the children's courts, the court of general sessions of the county of New York and the domestic relations court of the city of New York to the appellate division of the supreme court in the judicial department in which such court was located; from the court of claims to the appellate division of the supreme court in the third judicial department, except for those claims which arose in the fourth judicial department, in which case the appeal shall be to the appellate division of the supreme court in the fourth judicial department; from the city court of the city of New York, the municipal court of the city of New York, the court of special sessions of the city of New York and the city magistrates' courts of the city of New York to the appellate division of the supreme court in the judicial department in which such court was located, provided, however, that such appellate division of the supreme court may transfer any such appeal to an appellate term, if such appellate term be established; and from the district court, town, village and city courts outside the city of New York to the county court in the county in which such court was located, provided, however, that the legislature may require the transfer of any such appeal to an appellate term, if such appellate term be established. Further appeal from a decision of a county court or an appellate term or the appellate division of the supreme court shall be governed by the provisions of this article. However, if in any action or proceeding decided prior to the effective date of this article, a party had a right of direct appeal from a court of original jurisdiction to the court of appeals, such appeal may be taken directly to the court of appeals.

n. In the event that an appeal was decided before the effective date of this article and a further appeal could be taken as of right and notice of appeal therefrom is filed after the effective date of this article, such appeal may be taken from the appellate division of the supreme court to the court of appeals and from any other court to the appellate division of the supreme court. Further appeal from a decision of the appellate division of the supreme court shall be governed by the provisions of this article. If a further appeal could not be taken as of right, such appeal shall be governed by the provisions of this article.

[**Pending civil and criminal cases.**] § 36. No civil or criminal appeal, action or proceeding pending before any court or any judge or justice on the effective date of this article shall abate but such appeal, action or proceeding so pending shall be continued in the courts as provided in this article and, for the purposes of the disposition of such actions or proceedings only, the jurisdiction of any court to which any such action or proceeding is transferred by this article shall be coextensive with the jurisdiction of the former court from which the action or proceeding was transferred. Except to the extent inconsistent with the provisions of this article, subsequent proceedings in such appeal, action or proceeding shall be conducted in accordance with the laws in force on the effective date of this article until superseded in the manner authorized by law.

No sections 36-a or 36-b.

[Effective date of certain amendments to article VI, section 22.] § 36-c. The amendments to the provisions of section twenty-two of article six as first proposed by a concurrent resolution passed by the legislature in the year nineteen hundred seventy-four and entitled "Concurrent Resolution of the Senate and Assembly proposing an amendment to section twenty-two of article six and adding section thirty-six-c to such article of the constitution, in relation to the powers of and reconstituting the court on the judiciary and creating a commission on judicial conduct", shall become a part of the constitution on the first day of January next after the approval and ratification of the amendments proposed by such concurrent resolution by the people but the provisions thereof shall not become operative until the first day of September next thereafter which date shall be deemed the effective date of such amendments. (New. Added by vote of the people November 4, 1975.)

[Effective date of article.] § 37. This article shall become a part of the constitution on the first day of January next after the approval and ratification of this amendment by the people but its provisions shall not become operative until the first day of September next thereafter which date shall be deemed the effective date of this article.

ARTICLE VII
STATE FINANCES

[Estimates by departments, the legislature and the judiciary of needed appropriations; hearings.] Section

1. For the preparation of the budget, the head of each department of state government, except the legislature and judiciary, shall furnish the governor such estimates and information in such form and at such times as he may require, copies of which shall forthwith be furnished to the appropriate committees of the legislature. The governor shall hold hearings thereon at which he may require the attendance of heads of departments and their subordinates. Designated representatives of such committees shall be entitled to attend the hearings thereon and to make inquiry concerning any part thereof.

Itemized estimates of the financial needs of the legislature, certified by the presiding officer of each house, and of the judiciary, certified by the comptroller, shall be transmitted to the governor not later than the first day of December in each year for inclusion in the budget without revision but with such recommendations as he may deem proper. (New. Derived in part from former § 1 of Art. 4-a. Adopted by Constitutional Convention of 1938 and approved by vote of the people November 8, 1938.)

[**Executive budget.**] § 2. Annually, on or before the first day of February in each year following the year fixed by the constitution for the election of governor and lieutenant governor, and on or before the second Tuesday following the first day of the annual meeting of the legislature, in all other years, the governor shall submit to the legislature a budget containing a complete plan of expenditures proposed to be made before the close of the ensuing fiscal year and all moneys and revenues estimated to be available therefor, together with an explanation of the basis of such estimates and recommendations as to proposed legislation, if any, which he may deem necessary to provide moneys and revenues sufficient to meet such proposed expenditures. It shall also contain such other recommendations and information as he may deem proper and such additional information as may be required by law. (New. Derived in part from former § 2 of Art. 4-a. Adopted by Constitutional Convention of 1938 and approved by vote of the people November 8, 1938; amended by vote of the people November 2, 1965.)

[**Budget bills; appearances before legislature.**] § 3. At the time of submitting the budget to the legislature the governor shall submit a bill or bills containing all the proposed appropriations and reappropriations included in the budget and the proposed legislation, if any, recommended therein.

The governor may at any time within thirty days thereafter and, with the consent of the legislature, at any time before the adjournment thereof, amend or supplement the budget and submit amendments to any bills submitted by him or submit supplemental bills.

The governor and the heads of departments shall have the right, and it shall be the duty of the heads of departments when requested by either house of the legislature or an appropriate committee thereof, to appear and be heard in respect to the budget during the consideration thereof, and to answer inquiries relevant thereto. The procedure for such appearances and inquiries shall be provided by law. (New. Derived in part from former §§ 2 and 3 of Art. 4-a. Adopted by Constitutional Convention of 1938 and approved by vote of the people November 8, 1938.)

[**Action on budget bills by legislature; effect thereof.**] § 4. The legislature may not alter an appropriation bill submitted by the governor except to strike out or reduce items therein, but it may add thereto items of appropriation provided that such additions are stated separately and distinctly from the original items of the bill and refer each to a single object or purpose. None of the restrictions of this section, however, shall apply to appropriations for the legislature or judiciary.

Such an appropriation bill shall when passed by both houses be a law immediately without further action by the governor, except that appropriations for the legislature and judiciary and separate items added to the governor's bills by the legislature shall be subject to his approval as provided in section 7 of article IV. (New. Derived in part from former § 3 of Art. 4-a. Adopted by Constitutional Convention of 1938 and approved by vote of the people November 8, 1938.)

[Restrictions on consideration of other appropriations.] § 5. Neither house of the legislature shall consider any other bill making an appropriation until all the appropriation bills submitted by the governor shall have been finally acted on by both houses, except on message from the governor certifying to the necessity of the immediate passage of such a bill. (New. Derived in part from former § 4 of Art. 4-a. Adopted by Constitutional Convention of 1938 and approved by vote of the people November 8, 1938.)

[Restrictions on content of appropriation bills.] § 6. Except for appropriations contained in the bills submitted by the governor and in a supplemental appropriation bill for the support of government, no appropriations shall be made except by separate bills each for a single object or purpose. All such bills and such supplemental appropriation bill shall be subject to the governor's approval as provided in section 7 of article IV.

No provision shall be embraced in any appropriation bill submitted by the governor or in such supplemental appropriation bill unless it relates specifically to some particular appropriation in the bill, and any such provision shall be limited in its operation to such appropriation. (New. Derived in part from former § 22 of Art. 3 and former § 4 of Art. 4-a. Adopted by Constitutional Convention of 1938 and approved by vote of the people November 8, 1938.)

[Appropriation bills.] § 7. No money shall ever be paid out of the state treasury or any of its funds, or any of the funds under its management, except in pursuance of an appropriation by law; nor unless such payment be made within two years next after the passage of such appropriation act; and every such law making a new appropriation or continuing or reviving an appropriation, shall distinctly specify the sum appropriated, and the object or purpose to which it is to be applied; and it shall not be sufficient for such law to refer to any other law to fix such sum. (New. Derived in part from former § 21 of Art. 3. Adopted by Constitutional Convention of 1938 and approved by vote of the people November 8, 1938.)

[Gift or loan of state credit or money prohibited; exceptions for enumerated purposes.] § 8. 1. The money of the state shall not be given or loaned to or in aid of any private corporation or association, or private undertaking; nor shall the credit of the state be given or loaned to or in aid of any individual, or public or private corporation or association, or private undertaking, but the foregoing provisions shall not apply to any fund or property now held or which may hereafter be held by the state for educational, mental health or mental retardation purposes.

2. Subject to the limitations on indebtedness and taxation, nothing in this constitution contained shall prevent the legislature from providing for the aid, care and support of the needy directly or through subdivisions of the state; or for the protection by insurance or otherwise, against the hazards of unemployment, sickness and old age; or for the education and support of the blind, the deaf, the dumb, the physically handicapped, the mentally ill, the emotionally disturbed, the mentally retarded or juvenile delinquents as it may deem proper; or for health and welfare services for all children, either directly or through subdivisions of the state, including school districts; or for the aid, care and support of neglected and dependent children and of the needy sick, through agen-

cies and institutions authorized by the state board of social welfare or other state department having the power of inspection thereof, by payments made on a per capita basis directly or through the subdivisions of the state; or for the increase in the amount of pensions of any member of a retirement system of the state, or of a subdivision of the state; or for an increase in the amount of pensions of any widow of a retired member of a teachers' retirement system of the state or of a subdivision of the state to whom payable as beneficiary under an optional settlement in connection with the pension of such member. The enumeration of legislative powers in this paragraph shall not be taken to diminish any power of the legislature hitherto existing.

3. Nothing in this constitution contained shall prevent the legislature from authorizing the loan of the money of the state to a public corporation to be organized for the purpose of making loans to non-profit corporations to finance the construction of new industrial or manufacturing plants, the construction of new buildings to be used for research and development, and for the purchase of machinery and equipment related to such new industrial or manufacturing plants and research and development buildings in this state or the acquisition, rehabilitation or improvement of former industrial or manufacturing plants in this state, including the acquisition of real property therefor, and the use of such money by such public corporation for such purposes, to improve employment opportunities in any area of the state, provided, however, that any loan by such public corporation shall not exceed forty per centum of the cost of any such project and the repayment of which shall be secured by a mortgage thereon which shall not be a junior incumbrance thereon by more than fifty per centum of such cost or by a security interest if personalty. (Formerly § 1. Derived in part from former § 9 of Art. 8. Renumbered and amended by Constitutional Convention of 1938 and approved by vote of the people November 8, 1938;

further amended by vote of the people November 6, 1951; November 7, 1961; November 8, 1966; November 6, 1973.)

[**Short term state debts in anticipation of taxes, revenues and proceeds of sale of authorized bonds.**] § 9. The state may contract debts in anticipation of the receipt of taxes and revenues, direct or indirect, for the purposes and within the amounts of appropriations theretofore made. Notes or other obligations for the moneys so borrowed shall be issued as may be provided by law, and shall with the interest thereon be paid from such taxes and revenues within one year from the date of issue.

The state may also contract debts in anticipation of the receipt of the proceeds of the sale of bonds theretofore authorized, for the purpose and within the amounts of the bonds so authorized. Notes or obligations for the money so borrowed shall be issued as may be provided by law, and shall with the interest thereon be paid from the proceeds of the sale of such bonds within two years from the date of issue, except as to bonds issued or to be issued for any of the purposes authorized by article eighteen of this constitution, in which event the notes or obligations shall with the interest thereon be paid from the proceeds of the sale of such bonds within five years from the date of issue. (Formerly § 2. Renumbered and amended by Constitutional Convention of 1938 and approved by vote of the people November 8, 1938; further amended by vote of the people November 4, 1958.)

[**State debts on account of invasion, insurrection, war and forest fires.**] § 10. In addition to the above limited power to contract debts, the state may contract debts to repel invasion, suppress insurrection, or defend the state in war, or to suppress forest fires; but the money arising from the contracting of such debts shall be applied for the purpose for which it was raised, or to repay such debts, and to no other purpose whatever. (Formerly § 3. Renumbered by Constitutional Convention of 1938 and approved by vote of the people November 8, 1938.)

[State debts generally; manner of contracting; referendum.] § 11. Except the debts specified in sections 9 and 10 of this article, no debt shall be hereafter contracted by or in behalf of the state, unless such debt shall be authorized by law, for some single work or purpose, to be distinctly specified therein. No such law shall take effect until it shall, at a general election, have been submitted to the people, and have received a majority of all the votes cast for and against it at such election nor shall it be submitted to be voted on within three months after its passage nor at any general election when any other law or any bill shall be submitted to be voted for or against.

The legislature may, at any time after the approval of such law by the people, if no debt shall have been contracted in pursuance thereof, repeal the same; and may at any time, by law, forbid the contracting of any further debt or liability under such law. (Formerly § 4. Renumbered and amended by Constitutional Convention of 1938 and approved by vote of the people November 8, 1938.)

[State debts generally; how paid; restrictions on use of bond proceeds.] § 12. Except the debts specified in sections 9 and 10 of this article, all debts contracted by the state and each portion of any such debt from time to time so contracted shall be paid in equal annual installments, the first of which shall be payable not more than one year, and the last of which shall be payable not more than forty years, after such debt or portion thereof shall have been contracted, provided, however, that in contracting any such debt the privilege of paying all or any part of such debt prior to the date on which the same shall be due may be reserved to the state in such manner as may be provided by law. No such debt shall be contracted for a period longer than that of the probable life of the work or purpose for which the debt is to be contracted, to be determined by general laws, which determination shall be conclusive.

The money arising from any loan creating such debt or liability shall be applied only to the work or purpose specified in the act authorizing such debt or liability, or for the payment of such debt or liability, including any notes or obligations issued in anticipation of the sale of bonds evidencing such debt or liability. (Derived in part from former § 4. Renumbered and amended by Constitutional Convention of 1938 and approved by vote of the people November 8, 1938.)

[Refund of state debts.] § 13. The legislature may provide means and authority whereby any state debt may be refunded if, when it was contracted, the privilege to pay prior to the date payable was reserved to the state and provided that the debt as thus refunded shall be paid in equal annual installments which shall be not less in amount than the required annual installments of the debt so refunded. (New. Adopted by Constitutional Convention of 1938 and approved by vote of the people November 8, 1938.)

[State debt for elimination of railroad crossings at grade; expenses; how borne; construction and reconstruction of state highways and parkways.] § 14. The legislature may authorize by law the creation of a debt or debts of the state, not exceeding in the aggregate three hundred million dollars, to provide moneys for the elimination, under state supervision, of railroad crossings at grade within the state, and for incidental improvements connected therewith as authorized by this section. The provisions of this article, not inconsistent with this section, relating to the issuance of bonds for a debt or debts of the state and the maturity and payment thereof, shall apply to a state debt or debts created pursuant to this section; except that the law authorizing the contracting of such debt or debts shall take effect without submission to the people pursuant to section 11 of this article. The aggregate amount of a state debt or debts which may be created pursuant to this section shall not exceed the difference between the amount of the debt or debts heretofore created or authorized by law, under the provisions of section 14 of article VII of the constitution in force on July first, nineteen hundred thirty-eight, and the sum of three hundred million dollars.

The expense of any grade crossing elimination the construction work for which was not commenced before January first, nineteen hundred thirty-nine, including incidental improvements connected therewith as authorized by this section, whether or not an order for such elimination shall theretofore have been made, shall be paid by the state in the first instance, but the state shall be entitled to recover from the railroad company or companies, by way of reimbursement (1) the entire amount of the railroad improvements not an essential part of elimination, and (2) the amount of the net benefit to the company or companies from the elimination exclusive of such railroad improvements, the amount of such net benefit to be adjudicated after the completion of the work in the manner to be prescribed by law, and in no event to exceed fifteen per centum of the expense of the elimination, exclusive of all incidental improvements. The reimbursement by the railroad companies shall be payable at such times, in such manner and with interest at such rate as the legislature may prescribe.

The expense of any grade crossing elimination the construction work for which was commenced before January first, nineteen hundred thirty-nine, shall be borne by the state, railroad companies, and the municipality or municipalities in the proportions formerly prescribed by section 14 of article VII of the constitution in force on July first, nineteen hundred thirty-eight, and the law or laws enacted pursuant to its provisions, applicable to such elimination, and subject to the provisions of such former section and law or laws, including advances in aid of any railroad company or municipality, although such elimination shall not be completed until after January first, nineteen hundred thirty-nine.

A grade crossing elimination the construction work for which shall be commenced after January first, nineteen hundred thirty-nine, shall include incidental improvements rendered necessary or desirable because of such elimination, and reasonably included in the engineering plans therefor.

Out of the balance of all moneys authorized to be expended under section 14 of article VII of the constitution in force on July first, nineteen hundred thirty-eight, and remaining unexpended and unobligated on such date, fifty million dollars shall be deemed segregated for grade crossing eliminations and incidental improvements in the city of New York and shall be available only for such purposes until such eliminations and improvements are completed and paid for.

Notwithstanding any of the foregoing provisions of this section the legislature is hereby authorized to appropriate, out of the proceeds of bonds now or hereafter sold to. provide moneys for the elimination of railroad crossings at grade and incidental improvements pursuant to this section, sums not exceeding in the aggregate sixty million dollars for the construction and reconstruction of state highways and parkways. (Amended by Constitutional Convention of 1938 and approved by vote of the people November 8, 1938; further amended by vote of the people November 4, 1941.)

[Sinking funds; how kept and invested; income therefrom and application thereof.] § 15. The sinking funds provided for the payment of interest and the extinguishment of the principal of the debts of the state heretofore contracted shall be continued; they shall be separately kept and safely invested, and neither of them shall be appropriated or used in any manner other than for such payment and extinguishment as hereinafter provided. The comptroller shall each year appraise the securities held for investment in each of such funds at their fair market value not exceeding par. He shall then determine and certify to the legislature the amount of each of such funds and the amounts which, if thereafter annually contributed to each such fund, would, with the fund and with the accumulations thereon and upon the contributions thereto, computed at the rate of three per centum per annum, produce at the date of maturity the amount of the debt to retire which such fund was created, and the legislature shall thereupon appropriate as the contribution to each such fund for such year at least the amount thus certified

If the income of any such fund in any year is more than a sum which, if annually added to such fund would, with the fund and its accumulations as aforesaid, retire the debt at maturity, the excess income may be applied to the interest on the debt for which the fund was created.

After any sinking fund shall equal in amount the debt for which it was created no further contribution shall be made thereto except to make good any losses ascertained at the annual appraisals above mentioned, and the income thereof shall be applied to the payment of the interest on such debt. Any excess in such income not required for the payment of interest may be applied to the general fund of the state. (Formerly § 5. Renumbered and amended by Constitutional Convention of 1938 and approved by vote of the people November 8, 1938.)

[Payment of state debts; when comptroller to pay without appropriation.] § 16. The legislature shall annually provide by appropriation for the payment of the interest upon and installments of principal of all debts created on behalf of the state except those contracted under section 9 of this article, as the same shall fall due, and for the contribution to all of the sinking funds heretofore created by law, of the amounts annually to be contributed under the provisions of section 15 of this article. If at any time the legislature shall fail to make any such appropriation, the comptroller shall set apart from the first revenues thereafter received, applicable to the general fund of the state, a sum sufficient to pay such interest, installments of principal, or contributions to such sinking fund, as the case may be, and shall so apply the moneys thus set apart. The comptroller may be required to set aside and apply such revenues as aforesaid, at the suit of any holder of such bonds. (Formerly § 11. Renumbered and amended by Constitutional Convention of 1938 and approved by vote of the people November 8, 1938.)

[**Authorizing the legislature to establish a fund or funds for tax revenue stabilization reserves; regulating payments thereto and withdrawals therefrom.**] § 17. The legislature may establish a fund or funds to aid in the stabilization of the tax' revenues of the state available for expenditure or distribution. Any law creating such a fund shall specify the tax or taxes to which such fund relates, and shall prescribe the method of determining the amount of revenue from any such tax or taxes which shall constitute a norm of each fiscal year. Such part as shall be prescribed by law of any revenue derived from such tax or taxes during a fiscal year in excess of such norm shall be paid into such fund. No moneys shall at any time be withdrawn from such fund unless the revenue derived from such tax or taxes during a fiscal year shall fall below the norm for such year; in which event such amount as may be prescribed by law, but in no event an amount exceeding the difference between such revenue and such norm, shall be paid from such fund into the general fund.

No law changing the method of determining a norm or prescribing the amount to be paid into such a fund or to be paid from such a fund into the general fund may become effective until three years from the date of its enactment. (Added by amendment approved by vote of the people November 2, 1943.)

[**Bonus on account of service of certain veterans in World War II.**] § 18. The legislature may authorize by law the creation of a debt or debts of the state to provide for the payment of a bonus to each male and female member of the armed forces of the United States, still in the armed forces, or separated or discharged under honorable conditions, for service while on active duty with the armed forces at any time during the period from December seventh, nineteen hundred forty-one to and including September second, nineteen hundred forty-five, who was a resident of this state for a period of at least six months immediately prior to his or her enlistment, induction or call to active duty. The law authorizing the creation of the debt shall provide for payment of such bonus to the next of kin of each male and female member of the armed forces who, having been a resident of this state for a period of six months immediately prior to his or her enlistment, induction or call to active duty, died while on active duty at any time during the period from December seventh, nineteen hundred forty-one to and including September second, nineteen hundred forty-five; or who died while on active duty subsequent to September second, nineteen hundred forty-five, or after his or her separation or discharge under honorable conditions, prior to receiving payment of such bonus. An apportionment of the moneys on the basis of the periods and places of service of such members of the armed forces shall be provided by general laws. The aggregate of the debts authorized by this section shall not exceed four hundred million dollars. The provisions of this article, not inconsistent with this section, relating to the issuance of bonds for a debt or debts of the state and the maturity and payment thereof, shall apply to a debt or debts created pursuant to this section; except that the law authorizing the contracting of such debt or debts shall take effect without submission to the people pursuant to section eleven of this article.

Proceeds of bonds issued pursuant to law, as authorized by this section as in force prior to January first, nineteen hundred fifty shall be available and may be expended for the payment of such bonus to persons qualified therefor as now provided by this section. (Added by amendment approved by vote of the people November 4, 1947; further amended by vote of the people November 8, 1949.)

[**State debt for expansion of state university.**] § 19. The legislature may authorize by law the creation of a debt or debts of the state, not exceeding in the aggregate two hundred fifty million dollars, to provide moneys for the construction, reconstruction, rehabilitation, improvement and equipment of facilities for the expansion and development of the program of higher education provided and to be provided at institutions now or hereafter comprised within the state university, for acquisition of real property therefor, and for payment of the state's share of the capital costs of locally sponsored institutions of higher education approved and regulated by the state university trustees. The provisions of this article, not inconsistent with this section, relating to the issuance of bonds for a debt or debts of the state and the maturity and payment thereof, shall apply to a state debt or debts created pursuant to this section; except that the law authorizing the contracting of such debt or debts shall take effect without submission to the people pursuant to section eleven of this article. (New. Added by vote of the people November 5, 1957.)

ARTICLE VIII

LOCAL FINANCES

[**Gift or loan of property or credit of local subdivisions prohibited; exceptions for enumerated purposes.**] Section 1. No county, city, town, village or school district shall give or loan any money or property to or in aid of any individual, or private corporation or association, or private undertaking, or become directly or indirectly the owner of stock in, or bonds of, any private corporation or association; nor shall any county, city, town, village or school district give or loan its credit to or in aid of any individual, or public or private corporation or association, or private undertaking, except that two or more such units may join together pursuant to law in providing any municipal facility, service, activity or undertaking which each of such units has the power to provide separately. Each such unit may be authorized by the legislature to contract joint or several indebtedness, pledge its or their faith and credit for the payment of such indebtedness for such joint undertaking and levy real estate or other authorized taxes or impose charges therefore subject to the provisions of this constitution otherwise restricting the power of such units to contract indebtedness or to levy taxes on real estate. The legislature shall have power to provide by law for the manner and the proportion in which indebtedness arising out of such joint undertakings shall be incurred by such units and shall have power to provide a method by which such indebtedness shall be determined, allocated and apportioned among such units and such indebtedness treated for purposes of exclusion from applicable constitutional limitations, provided that in no event shall more than the total amount of indebtedness incurred for such joint undertaking be included in ascertaining the power of all such participating units to incur indebtedness. Such law may provide that such determination, allocation and apportionment shall be conclusive if made or approved by the comptroller. This provision shall not prevent a county from contracting indebtedness for the purpose of advancing to a town or school district, pursuant to law, the amount of unpaid taxes returned to it.

Subject to the limitations on indebtedness and taxation applying to any county, city, town or village nothing in this constitution contained shall prevent a county, city or town from making such provision for the aid, care and support of the needy as may be authorized by law, nor prevent any such county, city or town from providing for the care, support, maintenance and secular education of inmates of orphan asylums, homes for dependent children or correctional institutions and of children placed in family homes by authorized agencies, whether under public or private control, or from providing health and welfare services for all children, nor shall anything in this constitution contained prevent a county, city, town or village from increasing the pension benefits payable to retired members of a police department or fire department or to widows, dependent children or dependent parents of members or retired members of a police department or fire department; or prevent the city of New York from increasing the pension benefits payable to widows, dependent children or dependent parents of members or retired members of the relief and pension fund of the department of street cleaning of the city of New York. Payments by counties, cities or towns to charitable, eleemosynary, correctional and reformatory institutions and agencies, wholly or partly under private control, for care, support and maintenance, may be authorized, but shall not be required, by the legislature. No such payments shall be made for any person cared for by any such institution or agency, nor for a child placed in a family home, who is not received and retained therein pursuant to rules established by the state board of social welfare or other state department having the power of inspection thereof. (Formerly § 10. Renumbered and amended by Constitutional Convention of 1938 and approved by vote of the people November 8, 1938; further amended by vote of the people November 3, 1959; November 5, 1963; November 2, 1965.)

[Restrictions on indebtedness of local subdivisions; contracting and payment of local indebtedness; exceptions.] § 2. No county, city, town, village or school district shall contract any indebtedness except for county, city, town, village or school district purposes, respectively. No indebtedness shall be contracted for longer than the period of probable usefulness of the object or purpose for which such indebtedness is to be contracted, to be determined by or pursuant to general or special laws, which determination shall be conclusive, and in no event for longer than forty years. No indebtedness hereafter contracted or any portion thereof shall be refunded beyond such period computed from the date such indebtedness was contracted. Indebtedness heretofore contracted may be refunded only with the approval of and on terms and conditions prescribed by the state comptroller, but in no event for a period exceeding twenty years from the date of such refunding.

No indebtedness shall be contracted by any county, city, town, village or school district unless such county, city, town, village or school district shall have pledged its faith and credit for the payment of the principal thereof and the interest thereon. Except for indebtedness contracted in anticipation of the collection of taxes actually levied and uncollected or to be levied for the year when such indebtedness is contracted and indebtedness contracted to be paid in one of the two fiscal years immediately succeeding the fiscal year in which such indebtedness was contracted, all such indebtedness and each portion thereof from time to time contracted, including any refunding thereof, shall be paid in annual installments, the first of which, except in the case of refunding of indebtedness heretofore contracted, shall be paid not more than two years after such indebtedness or portion thereof shall have been contracted, and no installment, except in the case of refunding of indebtedness heretofore contracted, shall be more than fifty per centum in excess of the smallest prior installment.

Notwithstanding the foregoing provisions, indebtedness contracted by the city of New York and each portion of any such indebtedness from time to time so contracted for the supply of water, including the acquisition of land in connection with such purpose, may be financed either by serial bonds with a maximum maturity of fifty years, in which case such indebtedness shall be paid in annual installments as hereinbefore provided, or by sinking fund bonds with a maximum maturity of fifty years, which shall be redeemed through annual contributions to sinking funds established and maintained for the purpose of amortizing the indebtedness for which such bonds are issued. Notwithstanding the foregoing provisions, indebtedness hereafter contracted by the city of New York and each portion of any such indebtedness from time to time so contracted for (a) the acquisition, construction or equipment of rapid transit railroads, or (b) the construction of docks, including the acquisition of land in connection with any of such purposes, may be financed either by serial bonds with a maximum maturity of forty years, in which case such indebtedness shall be paid in annual installments as hereinbefore provided, or by sinking fund bonds with a maximum maturity of forty years, which shall be redeemed through annual contributions to sinking funds established and maintained for the purpose of amortizing the indebtedness for which such bonds are issued.

Provision shall be made annually by appropriation by every county, city, town, village and school district for the payment of interest on all indebtedness and for the amounts required for (a) the amortization and redemption of term bonds, sinking fund bonds and serial bonds, (b) the redemption of certificates or other evidence of indebtedness (except those issued in anticipation of the collection of taxes or other revenues, or renewals thereof, and which are described in paragraph A of section five of this article and those issued in anticipation of the receipt of the proceeds of the sale of bonds theretofore authorized) contracted to be paid in such year out of the tax levy or other revenues applicable to a reduction thereof, and (c) the redemption of certificates or other evidence of indebtedness issued in anticipation of the collection of taxes or other revenues, or renewals thereof, which are not retired within five years after their date of original issue. If at any time the respective appropriating authorities shall fail to make such appropriations, a sufficient sum shall be set apart from the first revenues thereafter received and shall be applied to such purposes. The fiscal officer of any county, city, town, village or school district may be required to set apart and apply such revenues as aforesaid at the suit of any holder of obligations issued for any such indebtedness. (New. Adopted by Constitutional Convention of 1938 and approved by vote of the people November 8, 1938; further amended by vote of the people November 8, 1949; November 3, 1953.)

[**Local indebtedness for water supply, sewage and drainage facilities and purposes; allocations and exclusions of indebtedness.**] § 2-a. Notwithstanding the provisions of section one of this article, the legislature by general or special law and subject to such conditions as it shall impose:

A. May authorize any county, city, town or village or any county or town on behalf of an improvement district to contract indebtedness to provide a supply of water, in excess of its own needs, for sale to any other public corporation or improvement district;

B. May authorize two or more public corporations and improvement districts to provide for a common supply of water and may authorize any such corporation, or any county or town on behalf of an improvement district, to contract joint indebtedness for such purpose or to contract indebtedness for specific proportions of the cost;

C. May authorize any county, city, town or village or any county or town on behalf of an improvement district to contract indebtedness to provide facilities, in excess of its own needs, for the conveyance, treatment and disposal of sewage from any other public corporation or improvement district;

D. May authorize two or more public corporations and improvement districts to provide for the common conveyance, treatment and disposal of sewage and may authorize any such corporation, or any county or town on behalf of an improvement district, to contract joint indebtedness for such purpose or to contract indebtedness for specific proportions of the cost;

E. May authorize any county, city, town or village or any county or town on behalf of an improvement district to contract indebtedness to provide facilities, in excess of its own needs, for drainage purposes from any other public corporation or improvement district.

F. May authorize two or more public corporations and improvement districts to provide for a common drainage system and may authorize any such corporation, or any county or town on behalf of an improvement district, to contract joint indebtedness for such purpose or to contract indebtedness for specific proportions of the cost.

Indebtedness contracted by a county, city, town or village pursuant to this section shall be for a county, city, town or village purpose, respectively. In ascertaining the power of a county, city, town or village to contract indebtedness, any indebtedness contracted pursuant to paragraphs A and B of this section shall be excluded.

The legislature shall provide the method by which a fair proportion of joint indebtedness contracted pursuant to paragraphs D and F of this section shall be allocated to any county, city, town or village.

The legislature by general law in terms and in effect applying alike to all counties, to all cities, to all towns and/or to all villages also may provide that all or any part of indebtedness contracted or proposed to be contracted by any county, city, town or village pursuant to paragraphs D and F of this section for a revenue producing public improvement or service may be excluded periodically in ascertaining the power of such county, city, town or village to contract indebtedness. The amount of any such exclusion shall have a reasonable relation to the extent to which such public improvement or service shall have yielded or is expected to yield revenues sufficient to provide for the payment of the interest on and amortization of or payment of indebtedness contracted or proposed to be contracted for such public improvement or service, after deducting all costs of operation, maintenance and repairs thereof. The legislature shall provide the method by which a fair proportion of joint indebtedness proposed to be contracted pursuant to paragraphs D and F of this section shall be allocated to any county, city, town or village for the purpose of determining the amount of any such exclusion. The provisions of paragraph C of section five and section ten-a of this article shall not apply to indebtedness contracted pursuant to paragraphs D and F of this section.

The legislature may provide that any allocation of indebtedness, or determination of the amount of any exclusion of indebtedness, made pursuant to this section shall be conclusive if made or approved by the state comptroller. (Section added by vote of the people November 3, 1953. Paragraphs C-F added, next unnumbered paragraph amended, and three concluding unnumbered paragraphs added by amendment approved by vote of the people November 8, 1955.)

[**Restrictions on creation and indebtedness of certain corporations.**] § 3. No municipal or other corporation (other than a county, city, town, village, school district or fire district, or a river improvement, river regulating, or drainage district, established by or under the supervision of the department of conservation) possessing the power (a) to contract indebtedness and (b) to levy taxes or benefit assessments upon real estate or to require the levy of such taxes or assessments, shall hereafter be established or created, but nothing herein shall prevent the creation of improvement districts in counties and towns, provided that the county or town or towns in which such districts are located shall pledge its or their faith and credit for the payment of the principal of and interest on all indebtedness to be contracted for the purposes of such districts, and in ascertaining the power of any such county or town to contract indebtedness, such indebtedness shall be included, unless such indebtedness would, under the provisions of this article, be excluded in ascertaining the power of a county or town to contract indebtedness. No such corporation now existing shall hereafter contract any indebtedness without the consent, granted in such manner as may be prescribed by general law, of the city or village within which, or of the town within any unincorporated area of which any real estate may be subject to such taxes or assessments. If the real estate subject to such taxes or assessments is wholly within a city, village or the unincorporated area of a town, in ascertaining the power of such city, village or town to contract indebtedness, there shall be included any indebtedness hereafter contracted by such corporation, unless such indebtedness would, under the provisions of this article, be excluded if contracted by such city, village or town. If only part of the real estate subject to such taxes or assessments is within a city, village or the unincorporated area of a town, in ascertaining the power of such city, village or town to contract indebtedness, there shall be included the proportion, determined as prescribed by general law, of any indebtedness hereafter contracted by such corporation, unless such indebtedness would, under the provisions of this article, be excluded if contracted by such city, village or town. (New. Adopted by Constitutional Convention of 1938 and approved by vote of the people November 8, 1938.)

[Limitations on local indebtedness.] § 4. Except as otherwise provided in this constitution, no county, city, town, village or school district described in this section shall be allowed to contract indebtedness for any purpose or in any manner which, including existing indebtedness, shall exceed an amount equal to the following percentages of the average full valuation of taxable real estate of such county, city, town, village or school district:

(a) the county of Nassau, for county purposes, ten per centum;

(b) any county, other than the county of Nassau, for county purposes, seven per centum;

(c) the city of New York, for city purposes, ten per centum;

(d) any city, other than the city of New York, having one hundred twenty-five thousand or more inhabitants according to the latest federal census, for city purposes, nine per centum;

(e) any city having less than one hundred twenty-five thousand inhabitants according to the latest federal census, for city purposes, excluding education purposes, seven per centum;

(f) any town, for town purposes, seven per centum;

(g) any village for village purposes, seven per centum; and

(h) any school district which is coterminous with, or partly within, or wholly within, a city having less than one hundred twenty-five thousand inhabitants according to the latest federal census, for education purposes, five per centum; provided, however, that such limitation may be increased in relation to indebtedness for specified objects or purposes with (1) the approving vote of sixty per centum or more of the duly qualified voters of such school district voting on a proposition therefor submitted at a general or special election, (2) the consent of The Regents of the University of the State of New York and (3) the consent of the state comptroller. The

Constitution of New York 645

legislature shall prescribe by law the qualifications for voting at any such election.

Except as otherwise provided in this constitution, any indebtedness contracted in excess of the respective limitations prescribed in this section shall be void.

In ascertaining the power of any city having less than one hundred twenty-five thousand inhabitants according to the latest federal census to contract indebtedness, indebtedness heretofore contracted by such city for education purposes shall be excluded. Such indebtedness so excluded shall be included in ascertaining the power of a school district which is coterminous with, or partly within, or wholly within, such city to contract indebtedness. The legislature shall prescribe by law the manner by which the amount of such indebtedness shall be determined and allocated among such school districts. Such law may provide that such determinations and allocations shall be conclusive if made or approved by the state comptroller.

In ascertaining the power of a school district described in this section to contract indebtedness, certificates or other evidences of indebtedness described in paragraph A of section five of this article shall be excluded.

The average full valuation of taxable real estate of any such county, city, town, village or school district shall be determined in the manner prescribed in section ten of this article.

Nothing contained in this section shall be deemed to restrict the powers granted to the legislature by other provisions of this constitution to further restrict the powers of any county, city, town, village or school district to contract indebtedness. (New section approved by vote of the people November 6, 1951. Substituted for § 4, derived in part from former § 10, renumbered and amended by Constitutional Convention of 1938 and approved by vote of the people November 8, 1938.)

[**Ascertainment of debt-incurring power of counties, cities, towns and villages; certain indebtedness to be excluded.**] § 5. In ascertaining the power of a county, city, town or village to contract indebtedness, there shall be excluded:

A. Certificates or other evidences of indebtedness (except serial bonds of an issue having a maximum maturity of more than two years) issued for purposes other than the financing of capital improvements and contracted to be redeemed in one of the two fiscal years immediately succeeding the year of their issue, and certificates or other evidences of indebtedness issued in any fiscal year in anticipation of (a) the collection of taxes on real estate for amounts theretofore actually levied and uncollected or to be levied in such year and payable out of such taxes, (b) moneys receivable from the state which have theretofore been apportioned by the state or which are to be so apportioned within one year after their issue and (c) the collection of any other taxes due and payable or to become due and payable within one year or of other revenues to be received within one year after their issue; excepting any such certificates or other evidences of indebtedness or renewals thereof which are not retired within five years after their date of original issue.

B. **Indebtedness heretofore or hereafter contracted to provide for the supply of water.**

C. Indebtedness heretofore or hereafter contracted by any county, city, town or village for a public improvement or part thereof, or service, owned or rendered by such county, city, town or village, annually proportionately to the extent that the same shall have yielded to such county, city, town or village net revenue; provided, however, that such net revenue shall be twenty-five per centum or more of the amount required in such year for the payment of the interest on, amortization of, or payment of, such indebtedness. Such exclusion shall be granted only if the revenues of such public improvement or part thereof, or service, are applied to and actually used for payment of all costs of operation, maintenance and repairs, and payment of the amounts required in such year for interest on and amortization of or redemption of such indebtedness, or such revenues are deposited in a special fund to be used solely for such payments. Any revenues remaining after such payments are made may be used for any lawful purpose of such county, city, town or village, respectively.

Net revenue shall be determined by deducting from gross revenues of the preceding year all costs of operation, maintenance and repairs for such year, or the legislature may provide that net revenue shall be determined by deducting from the average of the gross revenues of not to exceed five of the preceding years during which the public improvement or part thereof, or service, has been in operation, the average of all costs of operation, maintenance and repairs for the same years.

A proportionate exclusion of indebtedness contracted or proposed to be contracted also may be granted for the period from the date when such indebtedness is first contracted or to be contracted for such public improvement or part thereof, or service, through the first year of operation of such public improvement or part thereof, or service. Such exclusion shall be computed in the manner provided in this section on the basis of estimated net revenue which shall be determined by deducting from the gross revenues estimated to be received during the first year of operation of such public improvement or part thereof, or service, all estimated costs of operation, maintenance and repairs for such year. The amount of any such proportionate exclusion shall not exceed seventy-five per centum of the amount which would be excluded if the computation were made on the basis of net revenue instead of estimated net revenue.

Except as otherwise provided herein, the legislature shall prescribe the method by which and the terms and conditions under which the proportionate amount of any such indebtedness to be so excluded shall be determined and no proportionate amount of such indebtedness shall be excluded except in accordance with such determination. The legislature may provide that the state comptroller shall make such determination or it may confer appropriate jurisdiction on the appellate division of the supreme court in the judicial departments in which such counties, cities, towns or villages are located for the purpose of determining the proportionate amount of any such indebtedness to be so excluded.

The provisions of this paragraph C shall not affect or impair any existing exclusions of indebtedness, or the power to exclude indebtedness, granted by any other provision of this constitution.

D. Serial bonds, issued by any county, city, town or village which now maintains a pension or retirement system or fund which is not on an actuarial reserve basis with current payments to the reserve adequate to provide for all current accruing liabilities. Such bonds shall not exceed in the aggregate an amount sufficient to provide for the payment of the liabilities of such system or fund, accrued on the date of issuing such bonds, both on account of pensioners on the pension roll on that date and prospective pensions to dependents of such pensioners and on account of prior service of active members of such system or fund on that date. Such bonds or the proceeds thereof shall be deposited in such system or fund. Each such pension or retirement system or fund thereafter shall be maintained on an actuarial reserve basis with current payments to the reserve adequate to provide for all current accruing liabilities.

E. Indebtedness contracted on or after January first, nineteen hundred sixty-two and prior to January first, nineteen hundred eighty-three, for the construction or reconstruction of facilities for the conveyance, treatment and disposal of sewage. The legislature shall prescribe the method by which and the terms and conditions under which the amount of any such indebtedness to be excluded shall be determined, and no such indebtedness shall be excluded except in accordance with such determination. (Derived in part from former § 10. Renumbered and amended by Constitutional Convention of 1938 and approved by vote of the people November 8, 1938; paragraph C further amended by vote of the people November 8, 1949, and November 6, 1951; paragraph A amended by vote of the people November 3, 1953; paragraph E added by vote of the people November 5, 1963 and amended November 6, 1973.)

[Debt-incurring power of Buffalo, Rochester and Syracuse; certain additional indebtedness to be excluded.] § 6. In ascertaining the power of the cities of Buffalo, Rochester and Syracuse to contract indebtedness, in addition to the indebtedness excluded by section 5 of this article, there shall be excluded:

Indebtedness not exceeding in the aggregate the sum of ten million dollars, heretofore or hereafter contracted by the city of Buffalo or the city of Rochester and indebtedness not exceeding in the aggregate the sum of five million dollars heretofore or hereafter contracted by the city of Syracuse for so much of the cost and expense of any public improvement as may be required by the ordinance or other local law therein assessing the same to be raised by assessment upon local property or territory (Derived in part from former § 10. Renumbered and amended by the Constitutional Convention of 1938 and approved by vote of the people November 8, 1938.)

[Debt-incurring power of New York city; certain additional indebtedness to be excluded.] § 7. In ascertaining the power of the city of New York to contract indebtedness, in addition to the indebtedness excluded by section 5 of this article, there shall be excluded:

A. Indebtedness contracted prior to the first day of

January, nineteen hundred ten, for dock purposes proportionately to the extent to which the current net revenues received by the city therefrom shall meet the interest on and the annual requirements for the amortization of such indebtedness. The legislature shall prescribe the method by which and the terms and conditions under which the amount of any such indebtedness to be so excluded shall be determined, and no such indebtedness shall be excluded except in accordance with such determination. The legislature may confer appropriate jurisdiction on the appellate division of the supreme court in the first judicial department for the purpose of determining the amount of any such indebtedness to be so excluded.

B. The aggregate of indebtedness initially contracted from time to time after January first, nineteen hundred twenty-eight, for the construction or equipment, or both, of new rapid transit railroads, not exceeding the sum of three hundred million dollars. Any indebtedness thereafter contracted in excess of such sum for such purposes shall not be so excluded, but this provision shall not be construed to prevent the refunding of any of the indebtedness excluded hereunder.

C. The aggregate of indebtedness initially contracted from time to time after January first, nineteen hundred fifty, for the construction, reconstruction and equipment of city hospitals, not exceeding the sum of one hundred fifty million dollars. Any indebtedness thereafter contracted in excess of such sum for such purposes, other than indebtedness contracted to refund indebtedness excluded pursuant to this paragraph, shall not be so excluded.

D. The aggregate of indebtedness initially contracted from time to time after January first, nineteen hundred fifty-two, for the construction and equipment of new rapid transit railroads, including extensions of and interconnections with and between existing rapid transit railroads or portions thereof, and reconstruction and equipment of existing rapid transit railroads, not exceeding the sum of five hundred million dollars. Any indebtedness thereafter contracted in excess of such sum for such purposes, other than indebtedness contracted to refund indebtedness excluded pursuant to this paragraph, shall not be so excluded.

E. Indebtedness contracted for school purposes, evidenced by bonds, to the extent to which state aid for common schools, not exceeding two million five hundred thousand dollars, shall meet the interest and the annual requirements for the amortization and payment of part or all of one or more issues of such bonds. Such exclusion shall be effective only during a fiscal year of the city in which its expense budget provides for the payment of such debt service from such state aid. The legislature shall prescribe by law the manner by which the amount of any such exclusion shall be determined and such indebtedness shall not be excluded hereunder except in accordance with the determination so prescribed. Such law may provide that any such determination shall be conclusive if made or approved by the state comptroller. (Derived in part from former § 10. Renumbered and amended by Constitutional Convention of 1938 and approved by vote of the people November 8, 1938. Paragraph D added by amendment approved by vote of the people November 8, 1949; paragraphs E and F added by vote of the people November 6, 1951. Former paragraph A deleted; subsequent paragraphs re-lettered A to E by amendment approved by vote of the people November 3, 1953.)

[**Debt-incurring power of New York city; certain indebtedness for railroads and transit purposes to be excluded.**] § 7a. In ascertaining the power of the city of New York to contract indebtedness, in addition to the indebtedness excluded under any other section of this constitution, there shall be excluded:

A. The aggregate of indebtedness initially contracted from time to time by the city for the acquisition of railroads and facilities or properties used in connection therewith or rights therein or securities of corporations owning such railroads, facilities or rights, not exceeding the sum of three hundred fifteen million dollars. Provision for the amortization of such indebtedness shall be made either by the establishment and maintenance of a sinking fund therefor or by annual payment of part thereof, or by both such methods. Any indebtedness thereafter contracted in excess of such sum for such purposes shall not be so excluded, but this provision shall not be construed to prevent the refunding of any such indebtedness.

Notwithstanding any other provision of the constitution, the city is hereby authorized to contract indebtedness for such purposes and to deliver its obligations evidencing such indebtedness to the corporations owning the railroads, facilities, properties or rights acquired, to the holders of securities of such owning corporations, to the holders of securities of corporations holding the securities of such owning corporations, or to the holders of securities to which such acquired railroads, facilities, properties or rights are now subject.

B. Indebtedness contracted by the city for transit purposes, and not otherwise excluded, proportionately to the extent to which the current net revenue received by the city from all railroads and facilities and properties used in connection therewith and rights therein owned by the city and securities of corporations owning such railroads, facilities, properties or rights, owned by the city, shall meet the interest and the annual requirements for the amortization and payment of such non-excluded indebtedness.

In determining whether indebtedness for transit purposes may be excluded under this paragraph of this section, there shall first be deducted from the current net revenue received by the city from such railroads and facilities and properties used in connection therewith and rights therein and securities owned by the city: (a) an amount equal to the interest and amortization requirements on indebtedness for rapid transit purposes heretofore excluded by order of the appellate division, which exclusion shall not be terminated by or under any provision of this section; (b) an amount equal to the interest on indebtedness contracted pursuant to this section and of the annual requirements for amortization on any sinking fund bonds and for redemption of any serial bonds evidencing such indebtedness; (c) an amount equal to the sum of all taxes and bridge tolls accruing to the city in the fiscal year of the city preceding the acquisition of the railroads or facilities or properties or rights therein or securities acquired by the city hereunder, from such railroads, facilities and properties; and (d) the amount of net operating revenue derived by the city from the independent subway system during such fiscal year.

The legislature shall prescribe the method by which and the terms and conditions under which the amount of any indebtedness to be excluded hereunder shall be determined, and no indebtedness shall be excluded except in accordance with the determination so prescribed. The legislature may confer appropriate jurisdiction on the appellate division of the supreme court in the first judicial department for the purpose of determining the amount of any debt to be so excluded. (New. Adopted by Constitutional Convention of 1938 and approved by vote of the people November 8, 1938.)

[Indebtedness not to be invalidated by operation of this article.] § 8. No indebtedness of a county, city, town, village or school district valid at the time of its inception shall thereafter become invalid by reason of the operation of any of the provisions of this article. (Derived in part from former § 10. Renumbered and amended by Constitutional Convention of 1938 and approved by vote of the people November 8, 1938.)

[**When debt-incurring power of certain counties shall cease.**] § 9. Whenever the boundaries of any city are the same as those of a county, or when any city includes within its boundaries more than one county, the power of any county wholly included within such city to contract indebtedness shall cease, but the indebtedness of such county shall not, for the purposes of this article, be included as a part of the city indebtedness. (Derived in part from former § 10. Renumbered and amended by Constitutional Convention of 1938 and approved by vote of the people November 8, 1938.)

[**Limitations on amount to be raised by real estate taxes for local purposes; exceptions.**] § 10. Hereafter, in any county, city, village or school district described in this section, the amount to be raised by tax on real estate in any fiscal year, in addition to providing for the interest on and the principal of all indebtedness, shall not exceed an amount equal to the following percentages of the average full valuation of taxable real estate of such county, city, village or school district, less the amount to be raised by tax on real estate in such year for the payment of the interest on and redemption of certificates or other evidence of indebtedness described in paragraphs A and D of section five of this article, or renewals thereof:

(a) any county, for county purposes, one and one-half per centum; provided, however, that the legislature may prescribe a method by which such limitation may be increased to not to exceed two per centum;

(b) any city of one hundred twenty-five thousand or more inhabitants according to the latest federal census, for city purposes, two per centum;

(c) any city having less than one hundred twenty-five thousand inhabitants according to the latest federal census, for city purposes, two per centum;

(d) any village, for village purposes, two per centum;

(e) any school district which is coterminous with or partly within or wholly within, a city having less than one hundred twenty-five thousand inhabitants according to the latest federal census, for school district purposes, one and one-quarter per centum; provided, however, that if the taxes subject to this limitation levied for any such school district for its first fiscal year beginning on or after July first, nineteen hundred forty-seven, were in excess of one and one-quarter per centum but not greater than one and one-half per centum, then for such school district the limitation shall be one and one-half per centum; or if such taxes were in excess of one and one-half per centum but not greater than one and three-quarters per centum for such fiscal year, then for such school district the limitation shall be one and three-quarters per centum; or if such taxes were in excess of one and three-quarters per centum for such fiscal year, then for such school district the limitation shall be two per centum. The limitation herein imposed for any such school district may be increased by the approving vote of sixty per centum or more of the duly qualified voters of such school district voting on a proposition therefor submitted at a general or special election. Any such proposition shall provide only for an additional one-quarter of one per centum in excess of the limitation applicable to such school district at the time of submission of such proposition. When such a proposition has been submitted and approved by the voters of the school district as herein provided, no proposition for a further increase in such limitation shall be submitted for a period of one year computed from the date of submission of the approved proposition, provided that where a proposition for an increase is submitted and approved at a general election or an annual school election, a proposition for a further increase may be submitted at the corresponding election in the following year. The legislature shall prescribe by law the qualifications for voting at any such election. In the event any such school district shall be consolidated with any one or more school districts, the legislature shall prescribe a limitation, not exceeding two per centum, for such consolidated district. Thereafter, such limitation may be increased as provided in this sub-paragraph (e). In no event shall the limitation for any school district or consolidated school district described in this sub-paragraph (e) exceed two per centum.

(f) Notwithstanding the provisions of sub-paragraphs (a) and (b) of this section, the city of New York and the counties therein, for city and county purposes, a combined total of two and one-half per centum.

The average full valuation of taxable real estate of such county, city, village or school district shall be determined by taking the assessed valuations of taxable real estate on the last completed assessment rolls and the four preceding rolls of such county, city, village or school district, and applying thereto the ratio which such assessed valuation on each of such rolls bears to the full valuation, as determined by the state tax commission or by such other state officer or agency as the legislature shall by law direct. The legislature shall prescribe the manner by which such ratio shall be determined by the state tax commission or by such other state officer or agency.

Nothing contained in this section shall be deemed to restrict the powers granted to the legislature by other provisions of this constitution to further restrict the powers of any county, city, town, village or school district to levy taxes on real estate. (Derived in part from former § 10. Renumbered and amended by Constitutional Convention of 1938 and approved by vote of the people November 8, 1938; further amended by vote of the people November 8, 1949; November 3, 1953; subparagraph (f) added by separate amendment approved by vote of the people November 3, 1953.)

[Application and use of revenues from certain public improvements.] § 10-a. For the purpose of determining the amount of taxes which may be raised on real estate pursuant to section ten of this article, the revenues received in each fiscal year by any county, city or village from a public improvement or part thereof, or service, owned or rendered by such county, city or village for which bonds or capital notes are issued after January first, nineteen hundred fifty, shall be applied first to the payment of all costs of operation, maintenance and repairs thereof, and then to the payment of the amounts required in such fiscal year to pay the interest on and the amortization of, or payment of, indebtedness contracted for such public improvement or part thereof, or service. The provisions of this section shall not prohibit the use of excess revenues for any lawful county, city or village purpose. The provisions of this section shall not be applicable to a public improvement or part thereof constructed to provide for the supply of water. (New section added by amendment approved by vote of the people November 8, 1949. Amended by vote of the people November 3, 1953.)

[Taxes for certain capital expenditures to be excluded from tax limitation.] § 11. (a) Whenever the city of New York is required by law to pay for all or any part of the cost of capital improvements by direct budgetary appropriation in any fiscal year or by the issuance of certificates or other evidence of indebtedness (except serial bonds of an issue having a maximum maturity of more than two years) to be redeemed in one of the two immediately succeeding fiscal years, taxes required for such appropriation or for the redemption of such certificates or other evidence of indebtedness may be excluded in whole or in part by such city from the tax limitation prescribed by section ten of this article, in which event the total amount so required for such appropriation and for the redemption of such certificates or other evidence of indebtedness shall be deemed to be indebtedness to the same extent and in the same manner as if such amount had been financed through indebtedness payable in equal annual installments over the period of the probable usefulness of such capital improvement, as determined by law. The fiscal officer of such city shall determine the amount to be deemed indebtedness pursuant to this section, and the legislature, in its discretion, may provide that such determination, if approved by the state comptroller, shall be conclusive. Any amounts determined to be deemed indebtedness of any county, city, other than the city of New York, village or school district in accordance with the provisions of this section as in force and effect prior to January first, nineteen hundred fifty-two, shall not be deemed to be indebtedness on and after such date.

(b) Whenever any county, city, other than the city of New York, village or school district which is coterminous with, or partly within, or wholly within, a city having less than one hundred twenty-five thousand inhabitants according to the latest federal census provides by direct budgetary appropriation for any fiscal year for the payment in such fiscal year or in any future fiscal year or years of all or any part of the cost of an object or purpose for which a period of probable usefulness has been determined by law, the taxes required for such appropriation shall be excluded from the tax limitation prescribed by section ten of this article unless the legislature otherwise provides. (New. Adopted by Constitutional Convention of 1938 and approved by vote of the people November 8, 1938; amended by vote of the people November 8, 1949, and by vote of the people November 6, 1951.)

[**Powers of local governments to be restricted; further limitations on contracting local indebtedness authorized.**] § 12. It shall be the duty of the legislature, subject to the provisions of this constitution, to restrict the power of taxation, assessment, borrowing money, contracting indebtedness, and loaning the credit of counties, cities, towns and villages, so as to prevent abuses in taxation and assessments and in contracting of indebtedness by them. Nothing in this article shall be construed to prevent the legislature from further restricting the powers herein specified of any county, city, town, village or school district to contract indebtedness or to levy taxes on real estate. The legislature shall not, however, restrict the power to levy taxes on real estate for the payment of interest on or principal of indebtedness theretofore contracted. (New. Adopted by Constitutional Convention of 1938 and approved by vote of the people November 8, 1938. Amended by vote of the people November 5, 1963.)

*ARTICLE IX
LOCAL GOVERNMENTS

Bill of rights for local governments.

Section 1. Effective local self-government and intergovernmental cooperation are purposes of the people of the state. In furtherance thereof, local governments shall have the following rights, powers, privileges and immunities in addition to those granted by other provisions of this constitution:

(a) Every local government, except a county wholly included within a city, shall have a legislative body elective by the people thereof. Every local government shall have power to adopt local laws as provided by this article.

(b) All officers of every local government whose election or appointment is not provided for by this constitution shall be elected by the people of the local government, or of some division thereof, or appointed by such officers of the local government as may be provided by law.

* New article adopted by amendment approved by the vote of the people November 5, 1963. Former Article IX repealed, except for sections, 5, 6 and 8 which were renumbered subdivisions (a), (b) and (c) respectively of new section 13 of Article XIII.

(c) Local governments shall have power to agree, as authorized by act of the legislature, with the federal government, a state or one or more other governments within or without the state, to provide cooperatively, jointly or by contract any facility, service, activity or undertaking which each participating local government has the power to provide separately. Each such local government shall have power to apportion its share of the cost thereof upon such portion of its area as may be authorized by act of the legislature.

(d) No local government or any part of the territory thereof shall be annexed to another until the people, if any, of the territory proposed to be annexed shall have consented thereto by majority vote on a referendum and until the governing board of each local government, the area of which is affected, shall have consented thereto upon the basis of a determination that the annexation is in the over-all public interest. The consent of the governing board of a county shall be required only where a boundary of the county is affected. On or before July first, nineteen hundred sixty-four, the legislature shall provide, where such consent of a governing board is not granted, for adjudication and determination, on the law and the facts, in a proceeding initiated in the supreme court, of the issue of whether the annexation is in the over-all public interest.

(e) Local governments shall have power to take by eminent domain private property within their boundaries for public use together with excess land or property but no more than is sufficient to provide for appropriate disposition or use of land or property which abuts on that necessary for such public use, and to sell or lease that not devoted to such use. The legislature may authorize and regulate the exercise of the power of eminent domain and excess condemnation by a local government outside its boundaries.

(f) No local government shall be prohibited by the

legislature (1) from making a fair return on the value of the property used and useful in its operation of a gas, electric or water public utility service, over and above costs of operation and maintenance and necessary and proper reserves, in addition to an amount equivalent to taxes which such service, if privately owned, would pay to such local government, or (2) from using such profits for payment of refunds to consumers or for any other lawful purpose.

(g) A local government shall have power to apportion its cost of a governmental service or function upon any portion of its area, as authorized by act of the legislature

(h) (1) Counties, other than those wholly included within a city, shall be empowered by general law, or by special law enacted upon county request pursuant to section two of this article, to adopt, amend or repeal alternative forms of county government provided by the legislature or to prepare, adopt, amend or repeal alternative forms of their own. Any such form of government or any amendment thereof, by act of the legislature or by local law, may transfer one or more functions or duties of the county or of the cities, towns, villages, districts or other units of government wholly contained in such county to each other or when authorized by the legislature to the state, or may abolish one or more offices, departments, agencies or units of government provided, however, that no such form or amendment, except as provided in paragraph (2) of this subdivision, shall become effective unless approved on a referendum by a majority of the votes cast thereon in the area of the county outside of cities, and in the cities of the county, if any, considered as one unit. Where an alternative form of county government or any amendment thereof, by act of the legislature or by local law, provides for the transfer of any function or duty to or from any village or the abolition of any office, department, agency or unit of government of a village wholly contained in such county, such form or amendment shall not become effective unless it shall also be approved on the referendum by a majority of the votes cast thereon in all the villages so affected considered as one unit.

(2) After the adoption of an alternative form of county government by a county, any amendment thereof by act of the legislature or by local law which abolishes or creates an elective county office, changes the voting or veto power of or the method of removing an elective county officer during his term of office, abolishes, curtails or transfers to another county officer or agency any power of an elective county officer or changes the form or composition of the county legislative body shall be subject to a permissive referendum as provided by the legislature.

Powers and duties of legislature; home rule powers of local governments; statute of local governments.

§ 2. (a) The legislature shall provide for the creation and organization of local governments in such manner as shall secure to them the rights, powers, privileges and immunities granted to them by this constitution.

(b) Subject to the bill of rights of local governments and other applicable provisions of this constitution, the legislature:

(1) Shall enact, and may from time to time amend, a statute of local governments granting to local governments powers including but not limited to those of local legislation and administration in addition to the powers vested in them by this article. A power granted in such statute may be repealed, diminished, impaired or suspended only by enactment of a statute by the legislature with the approval of the governor at its regular session in one calendar year and the re-enactment and approval of such statute in the following calendar year.

(2) Shall have the power to act in relation to the property, affairs or government of any local government only by general law, or by special law only (a) on request of two-thirds of the total membership of its legislative body

or on request of its chief executive officer concurred in by a majority of such membership, or (b) except in the case of the city of New York, on certificate of necessity from the governor reciting facts which in his judgment constitute an emergency requiring enactment of such law and, in such latter case, with the concurrence of two-thirds of the members elected to each house of the legislature.

(3) Shall have the power to confer on local governments powers not relating to their property, affairs or government including but not limited to those of local legislation and administration, in addition to those otherwise granted by or pursuant to this article, and to withdraw or restrict such additional powers.

(c) In addition to powers granted in the statute of local governments or any other law, (i) every local government shall have power to adopt and amend local laws not inconsistent with the provisions of this constitution or any general law relating to its property, affairs or government and, (ii) every local government shall have power to adopt and amend local laws not inconsistent with the provisions of this constitution or any general law relating to the following subjects, whether or not they relate to the property, affairs or government of such local government, except to the extent that the legislature shall restrict the adoption of such a local law relating to other than the property, affairs or government of such local government:

(1) The powers, duties, qualifications, number, mode of selection and removal, terms of office, compensation, hours of work, protection, welfare and safety of its officers and employees, except that cities and towns shall not have such power with respect to members of the legislative body of the county in their capacities as county officers.

(2) In the case of a city, town or village, the membership and composition of its legislative body.

(3) The transaction of its business.

(4) The incurring of its obligations, except that local laws relating to financing by the issuance of evidences of

indebtedness by such local government shall be consistent with laws enacted by the legislature.

(5) The presentation, ascertainment and discharge of claims against it.

(6) The acquisition, care, management and use of its highways, roads, streets, avenues and property.

(7) The acquisition of its transit facilities and the ownership and operation thereof.

(8) The levy, collection and administration of local taxes authorized by the legislature and of assessments for local improvements; consistent with laws enacted by the legislature.

(9) The wages or salaries, the hours of work or labor, and the protection, welfare and safety of persons employed by any contractor or sub-contractor performing work, labor or services for it.

(10) The government, protection, order, conduct, safety, health and well-being of persons or property therein.

(d) Except in the case of a transfer of functions under an alternative form of county government, a local government shall not have power to adopt local laws which impair the powers of any other local government.

(e) The rights and powers of local governments specified in this section insofar as applicable to any county within the city of New York shall be vested in such city.

Existing laws to remain applicable; construction; definitions.

§ 3. (a) Except as expressly provided, nothing in this article shall restrict or impair any power of the legislature in relation to:

(1) The maintenance, support or administration of the public school system, as required or provided by article XI of this constitution, or any retirement system pertaining to such public school system,

(2) The courts as required or provided by article VI of this constitution, and

(3) Matters other than the property, affairs or government of a local government.

(b) The provisions of this article shall not affect any existing valid provisions of acts of the legislature or of local legislation and such provisions shall continue in force until repealed, amended, modified or superseded in accordance with the provisions of this constitution.

(c) Rights, powers, privileges and immunities granted to local governments by this article shall be liberally construed.

(d) Whenever used in this article the following terms shall mean or include:

(1) "General law." A law which in terms and in effect applies alike to all counties, all counties other than those wholly included within a city, all cities, all towns or all villages.

(2) "Local government." A county, city, town or village.

(3) "People." Persons entitled to vote as provided in section one of article two of this constitution.

(4) "Special law." A law which in terms and in effect applies to one or more, but not all, counties, counties other than those wholly included within a city, cities, towns or villages.

ARTICLE X
CORPORATIONS

[Corporations; formation of.] Section 1. Corporations may be formed under general laws; but shall not be created by special act, except for municipal purposes, and in cases where, in the judgment of the legislature, the objects of the corporation cannot be attained under general laws. All general laws and special acts passed pursuant to this section may be altered from time to time or repealed. (Formerly § 1 of Art. 8. Renumbered by Constitutional Convention of 1938 and approved by vote of the people November 8, 1938.)

[**Dues of corporations.**] § 2. Dues from corporations shall be secured by such individual liability of the corporators and other means as may be prescribed by law. (Formerly § 2 of Art. 8. Renumbered by Constitutional Convention of 1938 and approved by vote of the people November 8, 1938.)

[**Savings bank charters; restrictions on trustees; special charters not to be granted.**] § 3. The legislature shall, by general law, conform all charters of savings banks, or institutions for savings, to a uniformity of powers, rights and liabilities, and all charters hereafter granted for such corporations shall be made to conform to such general law, and to such amendments as may be made thereto. And no such corporation shall have any capital stock, nor shall the trustees thereof, or any of them, have any interest whatever, direct or indirect, in the profits of such corporation; and no director or trustee of any such bank or institution shall be interested in any loan or use of any money or property of such bank or institution for savings. The legislature shall have no power to pass any act granting any special charter for banking purposes; but corporations or associations may be formed for such purposes under general laws. (Formerly § 4 of Art. 8. Renumbered by Constitutional Convention of 1938 and approved by vote of the people November 8, 1938.)

[**Corporations; definition; right to sue and be sued.**] § 4. The term corporations as used in this section, and in sections 1, 2 and 3 of this article shall be construed to include all associations and joint-stock companies having any of the powers or privileges of corporations not possessed by individuals or partnerships. And all corporations shall have the right to sue and shall be subject to be sued in all courts in like cases as natural persons. (Formerly § 3 of Art. 8. Renumbered and amended by Constitutional Convention of 1938 and approved by vote of the people November 8, 1938.)

[**Public corporations; restrictions on creation and powers; accounts; obligations of.**] § 5. No public corporation (other than a county, city, town, village, school district or fire district or an improvement district established in a town or towns) possessing both the power to contract indebtedness and the power to collect rentals, charges, rates or fees for the services or facilities furnished or supplied by it shall hereafter be created except by special act of the legislature.

No such public corporation (other than a county or city) shall hereafter be given both the power to contract indebtedness and the power, within any city, to collect rentals, charges, rates or fees from the owners of real estate, or the occupants of real estate (other than the occupants of premises owned or controlled by such corporation or by the state or any civil division thereof), for services or facilities furnished or supplied in connection with such real estate, if such services or facilities are of a character or nature then or formerly furnished or supplied by the city, unless the electors of the city shall approve the granting to such corporation of such powers by a majority vote at a general or special election in such city; but this paragraph shall not apply to a corporation created pursuant to an interstate compact.

The accounts of every such public corporation heretofore or hereafter created shall be subject to the supervision of the state comptroller, or, if the member or members of such public corporation are appointed by the mayor of a city, to the supervision of the comptroller of such city; provided, however, that this provision shall not apply to such a public corporation created pursuant to agreement or compact with another state or with a foreign power, except with the consent of the parties to such agreement or compact.

Neither the state nor any political subdivision thereof shall at any time be liable for the payment of any obligations issued by such a public corporation heretofore or hereafter created, nor may the legislature accept, authorize acceptance of or impose such liability upon the state or any political subdivision thereof; but the state or a political subdivision thereof may, if authorized by the legislature, acquire the properties of any such corporation and pay the indebtedness thereof. (New. Adopted by Constitutional Convention of 1938 and approved by vote of the people November 8, 1938.)

[Liability of state for payment of bonds of public corporation to construct state thruways; use of state canal lands and properties.] § 6. Notwithstanding any provision of this or any other article of this constitution, the legislature may by law, which shall take effect without submission to the people:

(a) make or authorize making the state liable for the payment of the principal of and interest on bonds of a public corporation created to construct state thruways, in a principal amount not to exceed five hundred million dollars, maturing in not to exceed forty years after their respective dates, and for the payment of the principal of and interest on notes of such corporation issued in anticipation of such bonds, which notes and any renewals thereof shall mature within five years after the respective dates of such notes; and

(b) authorize the use of any state canal lands and properties by such a public corporation for so long as the law may provide. To the extent payment is not otherwise made or provided for, the provisions of section sixteen of article seven shall apply to the liability of the state incurred pursuant to this section, but the powers conferred by this section shall not be subject to the limitations of this or any other article. (New. Added by vote of the people November 6, 1951.)

[**Liability of state for obligations of the port of New York authority for railroad commuter cars; limitations.**] § 7. Notwithstanding any provision of this or any other article of this constitution, the legislature may by law, which shall take effect without submission to the people, make or authorize making the state liable for the payment of the principal of and interest on obligations of the port of New York authority issued pursuant to legislation heretofore or hereafter enacted, to purchase or refinance the purchase of, or to repay advances from this state made for the purpose of purchasing, railroad passenger cars, including self-propelled cars, and locomotives and other rolling stock used in passenger transportation, for the purpose of leasing such cars to any railroad transporting passengers between municipalities in the portion of the port of New York district within the state, the majority of the trackage of which within the port of New York district utilized for the transportation of passengers shall be in the state; provided, however, that the total amount of obligations with respect to which the state may be made liable shall not exceed one hundred million dollars at any time, and that all of such obligations shall be due not later than thirty-five years after the effective date of this section.

To the extent payment is not otherwise made or provided for, the provisions of section sixteen of article seven shall apply to the liability of the state incurred pursuant to this section, but the powers conferred by this section shall not be subject to the limitations of this or any other article. (New section added by amendment Number 3 approved by vote of the people November 7, 1961.)

[**Liability of state on bonds of a public corporation to finance new industrial or manufacturing plants in depressed areas.**] § 8. Notwithstanding any provision of this or any other article of this constitution, the legislature may by law, which shall take effect without submission to the people, make or authorize making the state liable for the payment of the principal of and interest on bonds of a public corporation to be created pursuant to and for the, purposes specified in the last paragraph of section eight of article seven of this constitution, maturing in not to exceed thirty years after their respective dates, and for the principal of and interest on notes of such corporation issued in anticipation of such bonds, which notes and any renewals thereof shall mature within seven years after the respective dates of such notes, provided that the aggregate principal amount of such bonds with respect to which the state shall be so liable shall not at any one time exceed one hundred fifty million dollars, excluding bonds issued to refund outstanding bonds. (New section added by amendment Number 4 approved by vote of the people November 7, 1961. Formerly duplicate § 7 added by vote of the people November 7, 1961; renumbered and amended by vote of the people November 4, 1969.)

ARTICLE XI
EDUCATION

[Common schools.] Section 1. The legislature shall provide for the maintenance and support of a system of free common schools, wherein all the children of this state may be educated. (Formerly § 1 of Art. 9. Renumbered by Constitutional Convention of 1938 and approved by vote of the people November 8, 1938.)

[Regents of the University.] § 2. The corporation created in the year one thousand seven hundred eighty-four, under the name of The Regents of the University of the State of New York, is hereby continued under the name of The University of the State of New York. It shall be governed and its corporate powers, which may be increased, modified or diminished by the legislature, shall be exercised by not less than nine regents. (Formerly § 2 of Art. 9. Renumbered and amended by

Constitutional Convention of 1938 and approved by vote of the people November 8, 1938.)

[Use of public property or money in aid of denominational schools prohibited; transportation of children authorized.] § 3. Neither the state nor any subdivision thereof shall use its property or credit or any public money, or authorize or permit either to be used, directly or indirectly, in aid or maintenance, other than for examination or inspection, of any school or institution of learning wholly or in part under the control or direction of any religious denomination, or in which any denominational tenet or doctrine is taught, but the legislature may provide for the transportation of children to and from any school or institution of learning. (Formerly § 4 of Art. 9. Renumbered and amended by Constitutional Convention of 1938 and approved by vote of the people November 8, 1938. Formerly § 4, renumbered § 3 without change by amendment approved by vote of the people November 6, 1962; former § 4 repealed by same amendment.)

ARTICLE XII*
Defense

[Defense; militia.] Section 1. The defense and protection of the state and of the United States is an obligation of all persons within the state. The legislature shall provide for the discharge of this obligation and for the maintenance and regulation of an organized militia.

ARTICLE XIII
Public Officers

[Oath of office; no other test for public office.] Section 1. Members of the legislature, and all officers, executive and judicial, except such inferior officers as shall be by law exempted, shall, before they enter on the duties of their respective offices, take and subscribe the following oath or affirmation: "I do sol-

* New article adopted by vote of the people November 6, 1962; repealing and replacing former article adopted November 8, 1938.

emnly swear (or affirm) that I will support the constitution of the United States, and the constitution of the State of New York, and that I will faithfully discharge the duties of the office of ...., according to the best of my ability;" and no other oath, declaration or test shall be required as a qualification for any office of public trust, except that any committee of a political party may, by rule, provide for equal representation of the sexes on any such committee, and a state convention of a political party, at which candidates for public office are nominated, may, by rule, provide for equal representation of the sexes on any committee of such party. (Amended by Constitutional Convention of 1938 and approved by vote of the people November 8, 1938.)

[**Duration of term of office.**] § 2. When the duration of any office is not provided by this constitution it may be declared by law, and if not so declared, such office shall be held during the pleasure of the authority making the appointment. (Formerly § 3 of Art. 10. Renumbered by Constitutional Convention of 1938 and approved by vote of the people November 8, 1938. Formerly § 6, renumbered § 2 without change by amendment approved by vote of the people November 6, 1962; former § 2 repealed by same amendment.)

[**Vacancies in office; how filled.**] § 3. The legislature shall provide for filling vacancies in office, and in case of elective officers, no person appointed to fill a vacancy shall hold his office by virtue of such appointment longer than the commencement of the political year next succeeding the first annual election after the happening of the vacancy. (Formerly § 5 of Art. 10. Renumbered by Constitutional Convention of 1938 and approved by vote of the people November 8, 1938. Formerly § 8, renumbered § 3 without change by amendment approved by vote of the people November 6, 1962; former § 3 repealed by same amendment.)

[Political year and legislative term.] § 4. The political year and legislative term shall begin on the first day of January; and the legislature shall, every year, assemble on the first Wednesday after the first Monday in January. (Formerly § 6 of Art. 10. Renumbered and amended by Constitutional Convention of 1938 and approved by vote of the people November 8, 1938. Formerly § 9, renumbered § 4 without change by amendment approved by vote of the people November 6, 1962; former § 4 repealed by same amendment.)

[Removal from office for misconduct.] § 5. Provision shall be made by law for the removal for misconduct or malversation in office of all officers, except judicial, whose powers and duties are not local or legislative and who shall be elected at general elections, and also for supplying vacancies created by such removal. (Formerly § 7 of Art. 10. Renumbered by Constitutional Convention of 1938 and approved by vote of the people November 8, 1938. Formerly § 10, renumbered § 5 without change by amendment approved by vote of the people November 6, 1962; former § 5 repealed by same amendment.)

[When office to be deemed vacant; legislature may declare.] § 6. The legislature may declare the cases in which any office shall be deemed vacant when no provision is made for that purpose in this constitution. (Formerly § 8 of Art. 10. Renumbered by Constitutional Convention of 1938 and approved by vote of the people November 8, 1938. Formerly § 11, renumbered § 6 without change by amendment approved by vote of the people November 6, 1962; former § 6 repealed by same amendment.)

[Compensation of officers.] § 7. Each of the state officers named in this constitution shall, during his continuance in office, receive a compensation, to be fixed by law, which shall not be increased or diminished during the term for which he shall have been elected or appointed;

nor shall he receive to his use any fees or perquisites of office or other compensation. (Formerly § 9 of Art. 10. Renumbered and amended by Constitutional Convention of 1938 and approved by vote of the people November 8, 1938. Formerly § 12, renumbered § 7 without change by amendment approved by vote of the people November 6, 1962; former § 7 repealed by same amendment. Further amended as § 12 by vote of the people November 5, 1963.)

[**Election and term of city and certain county officers.**] § 8. All elections of city officers, including supervisors, elected in any city or part of a city, and of county officers elected in any county wholly included in a city, except to fill vacancies, shall be held on the Tuesday succeeding the first Monday in November in an odd-numbered year, and the term of every such officer shall expire at the end of an odd-numbered year. This section shall not apply to elections of any judicial officer. (New. Added by amendment approved by vote of the people November 2, 1965.)

No sections 9, 10, 11.

No section 12 *(see section 7).*

Law enforcement and other officers.

§ 13. (a) Except in counties in the city of New York and except as authorized in section one of article nine of this constitution, sheriffs, clerks of counties, district attorneys, and registers in counties having registers, shall be chosen by the electors of the respective counties once in every three years and whenever the occurring of vacancies shall require. Sheriffs shall hold no other office. They may be required by law to renew their security, from time to time; and in default of giving such new security, their offices shall be deemed vacant. But the county shall never be made responsible for the acts of the sheriff. The governor may remove any elective sheriff, county clerk, district attorney or register within the term for which he shall have been elected; but before so doing he shall give to such officer a copy of the charges against him and an opportunity of being heard in his defense. In each county a district attorney shall be chosen by the electors once in every three or four years as the legislature shall direct. The clerk of each county in the city of New York shall be appointed, and be subject to removal, by the appellate division of the supreme court in the judicial department in which the county is located. In addition to his powers and duties as clerk of the supreme court, he shall have power to select, draw, summon and empanel grand and petit jurors in the manner and under the conditions now or hereafter prescribed by law, and shall have such other powers and duties as shall be prescribed by the city from time to time by local law.

(b) Any district attorney who shall fail faithfully to prosecute a person charged with the violation in his county of any provision of this article which may come to his knowledge, shall be removed from office by the governor, after due notice and an opportunity of being heard in his defense. The expenses which shall be incurred by any county, in investigating and prosecuting any charge of bribery or attempting to bribe any person holding office under the laws of this state, within such county, or of receiving bribes by any such person in said county, shall be a charge against the state, and their payment by the state shall be provided for by law.

(c) The city of New York is hereby vested with power from time to time to abolish by local law, as defined by the legislature, the office of any county officer within the city other than judges, clerks of counties and district attorneys, and to assign any or all functions of such officers to city officers, courts or clerks of counties, and to prescribe the powers, duties, qualifications, number, mode of selection and removal, terms of office and compensation of the persons holding such offices and the employees therein, and to assign to city officers any powers or duties of clerks of counties not assigned by this constitution. The legislature shall not pass any law affecting any such matters in relation to such offices within the city of New York except on message from the governor declaring that an emergency exists and the concurrent action of two-thirds of the members of each house, except that existing laws regarding each such office shall continue in force, and may be amended or repealed by the legislature as heretofore, until the power herein granted to the city has been exercised with respect to that office. The provisions of article nine shall not prevent the legislature from passing general or special laws prescribing or affecting powers and duties of such city officers or such courts or clerks to whom or which functions of such county officers shall have been so assigned, in so far as such powers or duties embrace subjects not relating to property, affairs or government of such city. (Added by vote of the people November 5, 1963. Subdivisions (a), (b) and (c), formerly §§ 5, 6 and 8 of Art. 9.)

[**Employees of, and contractors for, the state and local governments; wages, hours and other provisions to be regulated by legislature.**] § 14. The legislature may regulate and fix the wages or salaries and the hours of work or labor, and make provisions for the protection, welfare and safety, of persons employed by the state or by any county, city, town, village or other civil division of the state, or by any contractor or subcontractor performing work, labor or services for the state or for any county, city, town, village or other civil division thereof. (New. Added by amendment approved by vote of the people November 5, 1963.)

ARTICLE XIV

Conservation

[**Forest preserve to be forever kept wild; certain highways and ski trails authorized; limited use for certain highways authorized; exchange of lands with the village of Saranac Lake and town of Arietta authorized for certain purposes.**] Section 1. The lands of the state, now owned or hereafter acquired, constituting the forest preserve as now fixed by law, shall be forever kept as wild forest lands. They shall not be leased, sold or exchanged, or be taken by any corporation, public or private, nor shall the timber thereon be sold, removed or destroyed. Nothing herein contained shall prevent the state from constructing, completing and maintaining any highway heretofore specifically authorized by constitutional amendment, nor from constructing and maintaining to federal standards federal aid interstate highway route five hundred two from a point in the vicinity of the city of Glens Falls, thence northerly to the vicinity of the villages of Lake George and Warrensburg, the hamlets of South Horicon and Pottersville and thence northerly in a generally straight line on the west side of Schroon Lake to the vicinity of the hamlet of Schroon, then continuing northerly to the vicinity of Schroon Falls, Schroon River and North Hudson, and to the east of Makomis Mountain, east of the hamlet of New Russia, east of the village of Elizabethtown and continuing northerly in the vicinity of the hamlet of Towers Forge, and east of Poke-O-Moonshine Mountain and continuing northerly to the vicinity of the village of Keeseville and the city of Plattsburgh, all of the aforesaid taking not to exceed a total of three hundred acres of state forest preserve land, nor from constructing and maintaining not more than twenty miles of ski trails thirty to eighty feet wide on the north, east and northwest slopes of Whiteface Mountain in Essex county, nor from constructing and maintaining not more than twenty miles of ski trails thirty to eighty feet wide, together with appurtenances thereto, on the slopes of Belleayre Mountain in Ulster and Delaware counties and not more than thirty miles of ski trails thirty to eighty feet wide, together with appurtenances thereto, on the slopes of Gore, South and Pete Gay mountains in Warren county, nor from relocating, reconstructing and maintaining a total of not more than fifty miles of existing state highways for the purpose of eliminating the hazards of dangerous curves and grades, provided a total of not more than four hundred acres of forest preserve land shall be used for such purpose and that no single relocated portion of any highway shall exceed one mile in length. Notwithstanding the foregoing provisions, the state may convey to the village of Saranac Lake ten acres of forest preserve land adjacent to the boundaries of such village for public use in providing for refuse disposal and in exchange therefore the village of Saranac Lake shall convey to the state thirty acres of certain true forest land owned by such village on Roaring Brook in the northern half of Lot 113, Township 11, Richards Survey. Notwithstanding the foregoing provisions, the state may convey to the town of Arietta twenty-eight acres of forest preserve land within such town for public use in providing for the extension of the runway and landing strip of the Piseco airport and in exchange therefor the town of Arietta shall convey to the state thirty acres of certain land owned by such town in the town of Arietta. (Formerly § 7 of Art. 7. Renumbered and amended by Constitutional Convention of 1938 and approved by vote of the people November 8, 1938; further amended by vote of the people November 4, 1941; November 4, 1947; November 5, 1957; November 3, 1959; November 5, 1963; November 2, 1965.)

[Reservoirs.] § 2. The legislature may by general laws provide for the use of not exceeding three per centum of such lands for the construction and maintenance of reservoirs for municipal water supply, and for the canals of the state. Such reservoirs shall be constructed, owned and controlled by the state, but such work shall not be undertaken until after the boundaries and high flow lines thereof shall have been accurately surveyed and fixed, and after public notice, hearing and determination that such lands are required for such public use. The expense of any such improvements shall be apportioned on the public and private property and municipalities benefited to the extent of the benefits received. Any such reservoir shall always be operated by the state and the legislature shall provide for a charge upon the property and municipalities benefited for a reasonable return to the state upon the value of the rights and property of the state used and the services of the state rendered, which shall be fixed for terms of not exceeding ten years and be readjustable at the end of any term. Unsanitary conditions shall not be created or continued by any such public works. (Derived in part from former § 7 of Art. 7. Renumbered and amended by Constitutional Convention of 1938 and approved by vote of the people November 8, 1938; further amended by vote of the people November 3, 1953.)

[**Forest and wild life conservation; use or disposition of certain lands authorized.**] § 3. 1. Forest and wild life conservation are hereby declared to be policies of the state. For the purpose of carrying out such policies the legislature may appropriate moneys for the acquisition by the state of land, outside of the Adirondack and Catskill parks as now fixed by law, for the practice of forest or wild life conservation. The prohibitions of section 1 of this article shall not apply to any lands heretofore or hereafter acquired or dedicated for such purposes within the forest preserve counties but outside of the Adirondack and Catskill parks as now fixed by law, except that such lands shall not be leased, sold or exchanged, or be taken by any corporation, public or private.

2. As to any other lands of the state, now owned or hereafter acquired, constituting the forest preserve referred to in section one of this article, but outside of the Adirondack and Catskill parks as now fixed by law, and consisting in any case of not more than one hundred contiguous acres entirely separated from any other portion of the forest preserve, the legislature may by appropriate legislation, notwithstanding the provisions of section one of this article, authorize: (a) the dedication thereof for the practice of forest or wild life conservation; or (b) the use thereof for public recreational or other state purposes or the sale, exchange or other disposition thereof; provided, however, that all moneys derived from the sale or other disposition of any of such lands shall be paid into a special fund of the treasury and be expended only for the acquisition of additional lands for such forest

preserve within either such Adirondack or Catskill park. (Formerly § 16 of Art. 7. Renumbered and amended by Constitutional Convention of 1938 and approved by vote of the people November 8, 1938; further amended by vote of the people November 5, 1957; November 6, 1973.)

[**Protection of natural resources; development of agricultural lands.**] § 4. The policy of the state shall be to conserve and protect its natural resources and scenic beauty and encourage the development and improvement of its agricultural lands for the production of food and other agricultural products. The legislature, in implementing this policy, shall include adequate provision for the abatement of air and water pollution and of excessive and unnecessary noise, the protection of agricultural lands, wetlands and shorelines, and the development and regulation of water resources. The legislature shall further provide for the acquisition of lands and waters, including improvements thereon and any interest therein, outside the forest preserve counties, and the dedication of properties so acquired or now owned, which because of their natural beauty, wilderness character, or geological, ecological or historical significance, shall be preserved and administered for the use and enjoyment of the people. Properties so dedicated shall constitute the state nature and historical preserve and they shall not be taken or otherwise disposed of except by law enacted by two successive regular sessions of the legislature. (New. Added by vote of the people November 4, 1969.)

[**Violations of article; how restrained.**] § 5. A violation of any of the provisions of this article may be restrained at the suit of the people or, with the consent of the supreme court in appellate division, on notice to the attorney-general at the suit of any citizen. (New. Derived from former § 7 of Art. 7. Adopted by Constitutional Convention of 1938 and approved by vote of the people November 8, 1938. Renumbered § 5 by vote of the people November 4, 1969.)

ARTICLE XV
CANALS

[**Disposition of canals and canal properties prohibited.**] Section 1. The legislature shall not sell, lease, abandon or otherwise dispose of the now existing or future improved barge canal, the divisions of which are the Erie canal, the Oswego canal, the Champlain canal, and the Cayuga and Seneca canals, or of the terminals constructed as part of the barge canal system; nor shall it sell, lease, abandon or otherwise dispose of any portion of the canal system existing prior to the barge canal improvement which portion forms a part of, or functions as a part of, the present barge canal system; but such canals and terminals shall remain the property of the state and under its management and control forever. This prohibition shall not prevent the legislature, by appropriate laws, from authorizing the granting of revocable permits for the occupancy or use of such lands or structures. (Formerly § 8 of Art. 7. Renumbered and amended by Constitutional Convention of 1938 and approved by vote of the people November 8, 1938.)

[**Prohibition inapplicable to lands and properties no longer useful; disposition authorized.**] § 2. The prohibition of sale, abandonment or other disposition contained in section 1 of this article shall not apply to barge canal lands, barge canal terminals or barge canal terminal lands which have or may become no longer necessary or useful for canal or terminal purposes; nor to any canal lands and appertaining structures constituting the canal system prior to the barge canal improvement which have or may become no longer necessary or useful in conjunction with the now existing barge canal. The legislature may by appropriate legislation authorize the sale, exchange, abandonment or other disposition of any barge canal lands, barge canal terminals, barge canal terminal lands or other canal lands and appertaining structures which have or may become no longer necessary or useful as a part of the barge canal system, as an aid to navigation thereon, or for barge canal terminal purposes. All funds that may be derived from any sale or other disposition of any barge canal lands, barge canal terminals, barge canal terminal lands or other canal lands and appertaining structures shall be paid into the general fund of the treasury. (Formerly duplicate § 8 of Art. 7. Renumbered and amended by Constitutional Convention of 1938 and approved by vote of the people November 8, 1938.)

[No tolls to be imposed; contracts for work and materials; no extra compensation.] § 3. No tolls shall hereafter be imposed on persons or property transported on the canals, but all boats navigating the canals and the owners and masters thereof, shall be subject to such laws and regulations as have been or may hereafter be enacted concerning the navigation of the canals. The legislature shall annually make provision for the expenses of the superintendence and repairs of the canals, and may provide for the improvement of the canals in such manner as shall be provided by law. All contracts for work or materials on any canal shall be made with the persons who shall offer to do or provide the same at the lowest price, with adequate security for their performance. No extra compensation shall be made to any contractor; but if, from any unforseen cause, the terms of any contract shall prove to be unjust and oppressive, the superintendent of public works may, upon the application of the contractor, cancel such contract. (Formerly § 9 of Art. 7. Renumbered and amended by Constitutional Convention of 1938 and approved by vote of the people November 8, 1938.)

[Lease or transfer to federal government of barge canal system authorized.] § 4. Notwithstanding the prohibition of sale, abandonment or other disposition contained in section one of this article, the legislature may authorize by law the lease or transfer to the federal government of the barge canal, consisting of the Erie, Oswego, Champlain, Cayuga and Seneca divisions and the barge canal terminals and facilities for purposes of operation, improvement and inclusion in the national system of inland waterways. Such lease or transfer to the federal government for the purposes specified herein may be made upon such terms and conditions as the legislature may determine with or without compensation to the state. Nothing contained herein shall prevent the legislature from providing annual appropriations for the state's share, if any, of the cost of operation, maintenance and improvement of the barge canal, the divisions thereof, terminals and facilities in the event of the transfer of the barge canal in whole to the federal government whether by lease or transfer.

The legislature, in determining the state's share of the annual cost of operation, maintenance and improvement of the barge canal, the several divisions, terminals and facilities, shall give consideration and evaluate the benefits derived from the barge canal for purposes of flood control, conservation and utilization of water resources. (Added by vote of the people November 3, 1959.)

ARTICLE XVI*
Taxation

[**Power of taxation; exemptions from taxation.**]
Section 1. The power of taxation shall never be surrendered, suspended or contracted away, except as to securities issued for public purposes pursuant to law. Any laws which delegate the taxing power shall specify the types of taxes which may be imposed thereunder and provide for their review.

Exemptions from taxation may be granted only by general laws. Exemptions may be altered or repealed except those exempting real or personal property used exclusively for religious, educational or charitable pur-

*[Entire article new. Adopted by Constitutional Convention of 1938 and approved by vote of the people November 8, 1938.]

poses as defined by law and owned by any corporation or association organized or conducted exclusively for one or more of such purposes and not operating for profit.

[**Assessments for taxation purposes.**] § 2. The legislature shall provide for the supervision, review and equalization of assessments for purposes of taxation. Assessments shall in no case exceed full value.

Nothing in this constitution shall be deemed to prevent the legislature from providing for the assessment, levy and collection of village taxes by the taxing authorities of those subdivisions of the state in which the lands comprising the respective villages are located, nor from providing that the respective counties of the state may loan or advance to any village located in whole or in part within such county the amount of any tax which shall have been levied for village purposes upon any lands located within such county and remaining unpaid.

[**Situs of intangible personal property; taxation of.**] § 3. Moneys, credits, securities and other intangible personal property within the state not employed in carrying on any business therein by the owner shall be deemed to be located at the domicile of the owner for purposes of taxation, and, if held in trust, shall not be deemed to be located in this state for purposes of taxation because of the trustee being domiciled in this state, provided that if no other state has jurisdiction to subject such property held in trust to death taxation, it may be deemed property having a taxable situs within this state for purposes of death taxation. Intangible personal property shall not be taxed ad valorem nor shall any excise tax be levied solely because of the ownership or possession thereof, except that the income therefrom may be taken into consideration in computing any excise tax measured by income generally. Undistributed profits shall not be taxed.

[**Certain corporations not to be discriminated against.**] § 4. Where the state has power to tax corporations incorporated under the laws of the United States there shall be no discrimination in the rates and method of taxation between such corporations and other corporations exercising substantially similar functions and engaged in substantially similar business within the state.

[**Compensation of public officers and employees subject to taxation.**] § 5. All salaries, wages and other compensation, except pensions, paid to officers and employees of the state and its subdivisions and agencies shall be subject to taxation.

ARTICLE XVII
SOCIAL WELFARE

[**Public relief and care.**] Section 1. The aid, care and support of the needy are public concerns and shall be provided by the state and by such of its subdivisions, and in such manner and by such means, as the legislature may from time to time determine. (New. Adopted by Constitutional Convention of 1938 and approved by vote of the people November 8, 1938.)

[**State board of social welfare; powers and duties.**] § 2. The state board of social welfare shall be continued. It shall visit and inspect, or cause to be visited and inspected by members of its staff, all public and private institutions, whether state, county, municipal, incorporated or not incorporated, which are in receipt of public funds and which are of a charitable, eleemosynary, correctional or reformatory character, including all reformatories for juveniles and institutions or agencies exercising custody of dependent, neglected or delinquent children, but excepting state institutions for the education and support of the blind, the deaf and the dumb, and excepting also such institutions as are hereinafter made subject to the visitation and inspection of the department of mental hygiene or the state commission of correction. As to institutions, whether incorporated or not incorporated, having inmates, but not in receipt of public funds, which are of a charitable, eleemosynary, correctional or reformatory character, and agencies, whether incorporated or not incorporated, not in receipt of public funds, which exercise custody of dependent, neglected or delinquent children, the state board of social welfare shall make inspections, or cause inspections to be made by members of its staff, but solely as to matters directly affecting the health, safety, treatment and training of their inmates, or of the children under their custody. Subject to the control of the legislature and pursuant to the procedure prescribed by general law, the state board of social welfare may make rules and regulations, not inconsistent with this constitution, with respect to all of the functions, powers and duties with which the department and the state board of social welfare are herein or shall be charged. (New. Derived in part from former § 11 of Art. 8. Adopted by Constitutional Convention of 1938 and approved by vote of the people November 8, 1938.)

[Public health.] § 3. The protection and promotion of the health of the inhabitants of the state are matters of public concern and provision therefor shall be made by the state and by such of its subdivisions and in such manner, and by such means as the legislature shall from time to time determine. (New. Adopted by Constitutional Convention of 1938 and approved by vote of the people November 8, 1938.)

[Care and treatment of persons suffering from mental disorder or defect; visitation of institutions for.] § 4. The care and treatment of persons suffering from mental disorder or defect and the protection of the mental health of the inhabitants of the state may be provided by state and local authorities and in such manner as the legislature may from time to time determine. The head of the department of mental hygiene shall visit and inspect, or cause to be visited and inspected by members of his staff, all institutions either public or private used for the care and treatment of persons suffering from mental disorder or defect. (New. Adopted by Constitutional Convention of 1938 and approved by vote of the people November 8, 1938.)

[Institutions for detention of criminals; probation; parole; state commission of correction.] § 5. The legislature may provide for the maintenance and support of institutions for the detention of persons charged with or convicted of crime and for systems of probation and parole of persons convicted of crime. There shall be a state commission of correction, which shall visit and inspect, or cause to be visited and inspected by members of its staff, all institutions used for the detention of sane adults charged with or convicted of crime. (New. Derived in part from former § 11 of Art. 8. Adopted by Constitutional Convention of 1938 and approved by vote of the people November 8, 1938. Amended by vote of the people November 6, 1973.)

[Visitation and inspection.] § 6. Visitation and inspection as herein authorized, shall not be exclusive of other visitation and inspection now or hereafter authorized by law. (New. Derived from former § 13 of Art. 8. Adopted by Constitutional Convention of 1938 and approved by vote of the people November 8, 1938.)

[Loans for hospital construction.] § 7. Notwithstanding any other provision of this constitution, the legislature may authorize the state, a municipality or a public corporation acting as an instrumentality of the state or municipality to lend its money or credit to or in aid of any corporation or association, regulated by law as to its charges, profits, dividends, and disposition of its property or franchises, for the purpose of providing such hospital or other facilities for the prevention, diagnosis or treatment of human disease, pain, injury, disability, deformity or physical condition, and for facilities incidental or appurtenant thereto as may be prescribed by law. (New. Added by vote of the people November 4, 1969.)

ARTICLE XVIII*
Housing

[**Housing and nursing home accommodations for persons of low income; slum clearance.**] Section 1. Subject to the provisions of this article, the legislature may provide in such manner, by such means and upon such terms and conditions as it may prescribe for low rent housing and nursing home accommodations for persons of low income as defined by law, or for the clearance, replanning, reconstruction and rehabilitation of substandard and insanitary areas, or for both such purposes, and for recreational and other facilities incidental or appurtenant thereto. (Amended by vote of the people November 2, 1965.)

[**Idem; powers of legislature in aid of.**] § 2. For and in aid of such purposes, notwithstanding any provision in any other article of this constitution, but subject to the limitations contained in this article, the legislature may: make or contract to make or authorize to be made or contracted capital or periodic subsidies by the state to any city, town, village, or public corporation, payable only with moneys appropriated therefor from the general fund of the state; authorize any city, town or village to make or contract to make such subsidies to any public corporation, payable only with moneys locally appropriated therefor from the general or other fund available for current expenses of such municipality; authorize the contracting of indebtedness for the purpose of providing moneys out of which it may make or contract to make or authorize to be made or contracted loans by the state to any city, town, village or public corporation; authorize any city, town or village to make or contract to make

* [Entire article new. Adopted by Constitutional Convention of 1938 and approved by vote of the people November 8, 1938.]

loans to any public corporation; authorize any city, town or village to guarantee the principal of and interest on, or only the interest on, indebtedness contracted by a public corporation; authorize and provide for loans by the state and authorize loans by any city, town or village to or in aid of corporations regulated by law as to rents, profits, dividends and disposition of their property or franchises and engaged in providing housing facilities or nursing home accommodations; authorize any city, town or village to make loans to the owners of existing multiple dwellings for the rehabilitation and improvement thereof for occupancy by persons of low income as defined by law; grant or authorize tax exemptions in whole or in part, except that no such exemption may be granted or authorized for a period of more than sixty years; authorize cooperation with and the acceptance of aid from the United States; grant the power of eminent domain to any city, town or village, to any public corporation and to any corporation regulated by law as to rents, profits, dividends and disposition of its property or franchises and engaged in providing housing facilities.

As used in this article, the term "public corporation" shall mean any corporate governmental agency (except a county or municipal corporation) organized pursuant to law to accomplish any or all of the purposes specified in this article. (Amended by vote of the people November 2, 1965.)

[Article VII to apply to state debts under this article, with certain exceptions; amortization of state debts; capital and periodic subsidies.] § 3. The provisions of article VII, not inconsistent with this article, relating to debts of the state shall apply to all debts contracted by the state for the purpose of providing moneys out of which to make loans pursuant to this article, except (a) that any law or laws authorizing the contracting of such debt, not exceeding in the aggregate three hundred million dollars, shall take effect without submission to the people, and the contracting of a greater amount of debt may not be authorized prior to January first, nineteen hundred forty-two; (b) that any such debt and each portion thereof, except as hereinafter provided, shall be paid in equal annual installments, the first of which shall be payable not more than three years, and the last of which shall be payable not more than fifty years, after such debt or portion thereof shall have been contracted; and (c) that any law authorizing the contracting of such debt may be submitted to the people at a general election, whether or not any other law or bill shall be submitted to be voted for or against at such election.

Debts contracted by the state for the purpose of providing moneys out of which to make loans to or in aid of corporations regulated by law as to rents, profits, dividends and disposition of their property or franchises and engaged in providing housing facilities pursuant to this article may be paid in such manner that the total annual charges required for the payment of principal and interest are approximately equal and constant for the entire period in which any of the bonds issued therefor are outstanding.

Any law authorizing the making of contracts for capital or periodic subsidies to be paid with moneys currently appropriated from the general fund of the state shall take effect without submission to the people, and the amount to be paid under such contracts shall not be included in ascertaining the amount of indebtedness which may be contracted by the state under this article; provided, however, (a) that such periodic subsidies shall not be paid for a period longer than the life of the projects assisted thereby, but in any event for not more than sixty years; (b) that no contracts for periodic subsidies shall be entered into in any one year requiring payments aggregating more than one million dollars in any one year; and (c) that there shall not be outstanding at any one time contracts for periodic subsidies requiring payments exceeding an aggregate of thirty-four million dollars in any one year, unless a law authorizing contracts in excess of such amounts shall have been submitted to and approved by the people at a general election; and any such law may be submitted to the people at a general election, whether or not any other law or bill shall be submitted to be voted for or against at such election. (Amended by vote of the people November 8, 1955; further amended by vote of the people November 5, 1957.)

[Powers of cities, towns and villages to contract indebtedness in aid of low rent housing and slum clearance projects; restrictions thereon.] § 4. To effectuate any of the purposes of this article, the legislature may authorize any city, town or village to contract indebtedness to an amount which shall not exceed two per centum of the average assessed valuation of the real estate of such city, town or village subject to taxation, as determined by the last completed assessment roll and the four preceding assessment rolls of such city, town or village, for city, town or village taxes prior to the contracting of such indebtedness. In ascertaining the power of a city, or village having a population of five thousand or more as determined by the last federal census, to contract indebtedness pursuant to this article there may be excluded any such indebtedness if the project or projects aided by guarantees representing such indebtedness or by loans for which such indebtedness was contracted shall have yielded during the preceding year net revenue to be determined annually by deducting from the gross revenues, including periodic subsidies therefor, received from such project or projects, all costs of operation, maintenance, repairs and replacements, and the interest on such indebtedness and the amounts required in such year for the payment of such indebtedness; provided that in the case of guarantees such interest and such amounts shall have been paid, and in the case of loans an amount equal to such interest and such amounts shall have been paid to such city or village. The legislature shall prescribe the method by which the amount of any such indebtedness to be excluded shall be determined, and no such indebtedness shall be excluded except in accordance with such determination. The legislature may confer appropriate jurisdiction on the appellate division of the supreme court in the judicial departments in which such cities or villages are located for the purpose of determining the amount of any such indebtedness to be so excluded.

The liability of a city, town or village on account of any contract for capital or periodic subsidies to be paid subsequent to the then current year shall, for the purpose of ascertaining the power of such city, town or village to contract indebtedness, be deemed indebtedness in the amount of the commuted value of the total of such capital or periodic subsidies remaining unpaid, calculated on the basis of an annual interest rate of four per centum. Such periodic subsidies shall not be contracted for a period longer than the life of the projects assisted thereby, and in no event for more than sixty years. Indebtedness contracted pursuant to this article shall be excluded in ascertaining the power of a city or such village otherwise to create indebtedness under any other section of this constitution. Notwithstanding the foregoing the legislature shall not authorize any city or village having a population of five thousand or more to contract indebtedness hereunder in excess of the limitations prescribed by any other article of this constitution unless at the same time it shall by law require such city or village to levy annually a tax or taxes other than an ad valorem tax on real estate to an extent sufficient to provide for the payment of the principal of and interest on any such indebtedness. Nothing herein contained, however, shall be construed to prevent such city or village from pledging its faith and credit for the payment of such principal and interest nor shall any such law prevent recourse to an ad valorem tax on real estate to the extent that revenue derived from such other tax or taxes in any year, together with revenues from the project or projects aided by the proceeds of such indebtedness, shall become insufficient to provide fully for payment of such principal and interest in that year. (Amended by vote of the people November 8, 1949.)

[**Liability for certain loans made by the state to certain public corporations.**] § 5. Any city, town or village shall be liable for the repayment of any loans and interest thereon made by the state to any public corporation, acting as an instrumentality of such city, town or village. Such liability of a city, town or village shall be excluded in ascertaining the power of such city, town or village to become indebted pursuant to the provisions of this article, except that in the event of a default in payment under the terms of any such loan, the unpaid balance thereof shall be included in ascertaining the power of such city, town or village to become so indebted. No subsidy, in addition to any capital or periodic subsidy originally contracted for in aid of any project or projects authorized under this article, shall be paid by the state to a city, town, village or public corporation, acting as an instrumentality thereof, for the purpose of enabling such city, town, village or corporation to remedy an actual default or avoid an impending default in the payment of principal or interest on a loan which has been theretofore made by the state to such city, town, village or corporation pursuant to this article. (Amended by vote of the people November 5, 1957.)

[**Loans and subsidies; restrictions on and preference in occupancy of projects.**] § 6. No loan or subsidy shall be made by the state to aid any project unless such project is in conformity with a plan or undertaking for the clearance, replanning and reconstruction or rehabilitation of a substandard and insanitary area or areas and for recreational and other facilities incidental or appurtenant thereto. The legislature may provide additional conditions to the making of such loans or subsidies consistent with the purposes of this article. The occupancy of any such project shall be restricted to persons of low income as defined by law and preference shall be given to persons who live or shall have lived in* such area or areas.

[**Liability arising from guarantees to be deemed indebtedness; method of computing.**] § 7. The liability arising from any guarantee of the principal of and interest on indebtedness contracted by a public corporation shall be deemed indebtedness in the amount of the face value of the principal thereof remaining unpaid. The liability arising from any guarantee of only the interest on indebtedness contracted by a public corporation shall be deemed indebtedness in the amount of the commuted value of the total interest guaranteed and remaining unpaid, calculated on the basis of an annual interest rate of four per centum.

[**Excess condemnation.**] § 8. Any agency of the state, or any city, town, village or public corporation, which is empowered by law to take private property by eminent domain for any of the public purposes specified in section one of this article, may be empowered by the legislature to take property necessary for any such purpose but in excess of that required for public use after such purpose shall have been accomplished; and to improve and utilize such excess, wholly or partly for any other public purpose, or to lease or sell such excess with restrictions to preserve and protect such improvement or improvements.

[**Acquisition of property for purposes of article.**] § 9. Subject to any limitation imposed by the legislature, the state, or any city, town, village or public corporation, may acquire by purchase, gift, eminent domain or otherwise, such property as it may deem ultimately necessary or proper to effectuate the purposes of this article, or any of them, although temporarily not required for such purposes.

*Word "in" appears twice in original.

[**Power of legislature; construction of article.**] § 10. The legislature is empowered to make all laws which it shall deem necessary and proper for carrying into execution the foregoing powers. This article shall be construed as extending powers which otherwise might be limited by other articles of this constitution and shall not be construed as imposing additional limitations; but nothing in this article contained shall be deemed to authorize or empower the state, or any city, town, village or public corporation, to engage in any private business or enterprise other than the building and operation of low rent dwelling houses for persons of low income as defined by law, or the loaning of money to owners of existing multiple dwellings as herein provided.

ARTICLE XIX
AMENDMENTS TO CONSTITUTION

[**Amendments to constitution; how proposed, voted upon and ratified; failure of attorney-general to render opinion not to affect validity.**] Section 1. Any amendment or amendments to this constitution may be proposed in the senate and assembly, whereupon such amendment or amendments shall be referred to the attorney-general whose duty it shall be within twenty days thereafter to render an opinion in writing to the senate and assembly as to the effect of such amendment or amendments upon other provisions of the constitution. Upon receiving such opinion, if the amendment or amendments as proposed or as amended shall be agreed to by a majority of the members elected to each of the two houses, such proposed amendment or amendments shall be entered on their journals, and the ayes and noes taken thereon, and referred to the next regular legislative session convening after the succeeding general election of members of the assembly, and shall be published for three months previous to the time of making such choice; and if in such legislative session, such proposed amendment or amendments shall be agreed to by a majority of all the members elected to each house, then it shall be the duty of the legislature to submit each proposed amendment or amendments to the people for approval in such manner and at such times as the legislature shall prescribe; and if the people shall approve and ratify such amendment or amendments by a majority of the electors voting thereon, such amendment or amendments shall become a part of the constitution on the first day of January next after such approval. Neither the failure of the attorney-general to render an opinion concerning such a proposed amendment nor his failure to do so timely shall affect the validity of such proposed amendment or legislative action thereon. (Formerly § 1 of Art. ·14. Renumbered and amended by Constitutional Convention of 1938 and approved by vote of the people November 8, 1938; further amended by vote of the people November 4, 1941.)

[Future constitutional conventions; how called; election of delegates; compensation; quorum; submission of amendments; officers; employees; rules; vacancies.]
§ 2. At the general election to be held in the year nineteen hundred fifty-seven, and every twentieth year thereafter, and also at such times as the legislature may by law provide, the question "Shall there be a convention to revise the constitution and amend the same?" shall be submitted to and decided by the electors of the state; and in case a majority of the electors voting thereon shall decide in favor of a convention for such purpose, the electors of every senate district of the state, as then organized, shall elect three delegates at the next ensuing general election, and the electors of the state voting at the same election shall elect fifteen delegates-at-large. The delegates so elected shall convene at the capitol on the first Tuesday of April next ensuing after their election, and shall continue their session until the business of such convention

shall have been completed. Every delegate shall receive for his services the same compensation as shall then be annually payable to the members of the assembly and be reimbursed for actual traveling expenses, while the convention is in session, to the extent that a member of the assembly would then be entitled thereto in the case of a session of the legislature. A majority of the convention shall constitute a quorum for the transaction of business, and no amendment to the constitution shall be submitted for approval to the electors as hereinafter provided, unless by the assent of a majority of all the delegates elected to the convention, the ayes and noes being entered on the journal to be kept. The convention shall have the power to appoint such officers, employees and assistants as it may deem necessary, and fix their compensation and to provide for the printing of its documents, journal, proceedings and other expenses of said convention. The convention shall determine the rules of its own proceedings, choose its own officers, and be the judge of the election, returns and qualifications of its members. In case of a vacancy, by death, resignation or other cause, of any district delegate elected to the convention, such vacancy shall be filled by a vote of the remaining delegates representing the district in which such vacancy occurs. If such vacancy occurs in the office of a delegate-at-large, such vacancy shall be filled by a vote of the remaining delegates-at-large. Any proposed constitution or constitutional amendment which shall have been adopted by such convention, shall be submitted to a vote of the electors of the state at the time and in the manner provided by such convention, at an election which shall be held not less than six weeks after the adjournment of such convention. Upon the approval of such constitution or constitutional amendment, in the manner provided in the last preceding section, such constitution or constitutional amendment, shall go into effect on the first day of January next after such approval. (Formerly § 2 of Art. 14. Renumbered and amended by Constitutional Convention of 1938 and approved by vote of the people November 8, 1938.)

[**Amendments simultaneously submitted by convention and legislature.**] § 3. Any amendment proposed by a constitutional convention relating to the same subject as an amendment proposed by the legislature, coincidently submitted to the people for approval shall, if approved, be deemed to supersede the amendment so proposed by the legislature. (Formerly § 3 of Art. 14. Renumbered and amended by Constitutional Convention of 1938 and approved by vote of the people November 8, 1938.)

ARTICLE XX
When to Take Effect

[**Time of taking effect.**] Section 1. This constitution shall be in force from and including the first day of January, one thousand nine hundred thirty-nine, except as herein otherwise provided. (Formerly § 1 of Art. 15. Renumbered and amended by Constitutional Convention of 1938 and approved by vote of the people November 8, 1938.)

DONE in Convention at the Capitol in the city of Albany, the twenty-fifth day of August, in the year one thousand nine hundred thirty-eight, and of the Independence of the United States of America the one hundred and sixty-third.

IN WITNESS WHEREOF, we have hereunto subscribed our names.

FREDERICK E. CRANE,
President and Delegate-at-Large

U. H. BOYDEN,
Secretary

AMENDMENTS APPROVED BY THE VOTE OF THE PEOPLE NOVEMBER 8, 1977

Effective January 1, 1978

AMENDMENT NO. 1

Article VI, sec. 2, subd. c (repealed); sec. 2 (amended); sec. 36-a (new):

§ 2. a. The court of appeals is continued. It shall consist of the chief judge [,] *and* the six elected associate judges now in office, who shall hold their offices until the expiration of their respective terms, and their successors, [who shall be chosen by the electors of the state] and such justices of the supreme court as may be designated for service in said court as hereinafter provided. The official terms of the chief judge and [elected] *the six* associate judges shall be fourteen years [from and including the first day of January next after their election].

Five members of the court shall constitute a quorum, and the concurrence of four shall be necessary to a decision; but no more than seven judges shall sit in any case. In case of the temporary absence or inability to act of any judge of the court of appeals, the court may designate any justice of the supreme court to serve as associate judge of the court during such absence or inability to act. The court shall have power to appoint and to remove its clerk. *The powers and jurisdiction of the court shall not be suspended for want of appointment when the number of judges is sufficient to constitute a quorum.*

b. Whenever and as often as the court of appeals shall certify to the governor that the court is unable, by reason of the accumulation of causes pending therein, to hear and dispose of the same with reasonable speed, the governor shall designate such number of justices of the supreme court as may be so certified to be necessary, but not more than four, to serve as associate judges of the court of appeals. The justices so designated shall be relieved, while so serving, from their duties

NOTE: Matter in *italics* is new; matter in brackets [ ] has been eliminated.

as justices of the supreme court, and shall serve as associate judges of the court of appeals until the court shall certify that the need for the services of any such justices no longer exists, whereupon they shall return to the supreme court. The governor may fill vacancies among such designated judges. No such justices shall serve as associate judge of the court of appeals except while holding the office of justice of the supreme court. The designation of a justice of the supreme court as an associate judge of the court of appeals shall not be deemed to affect his existing office any longer than until the expiration of his designation as such associate judge, nor to create a vacancy.

c. There shall be a commission on judicial nomination to evaluate the qualifications of candidates for appointment to the court of appeals and to prepare a written report and recommend to the governor those persons who by their character, temperament, professional aptitude and experience are well qualified to hold such judicial office. The legislature shall provide by law for the organization and procedure of the judicial nominating commission.

d. (1) The commission on judicial nomination shall consist of twelve members of whom four shall be appointed by the governor, four by the chief judge of the court of appeals, and one each by the speaker of the assembly, the temporary president of the senate, the minority leader of the senate, and the minority leader of the assembly. Of the four members appointed by the governor, no more than two shall be enrolled in the same political party, two shall be members of the bar of the state, and two shall not be members of the bar of the state. Of the four members appointed by the chief judge of the court of appeals, no more than two shall be enrolled in the same political party, two shall be members of the bar of the state, and two shall not be members of the bar of the state. No member of the commission shall hold or have held any judicial office or hold any elected public office for which he receives compensation during his period of service, except that the governor and the chief judge may each appoint no more than one former judge or justice of the unified court system to such commission. No member of the commission shall hold any office in any political party. No member of the judicial nominating commission shall be eligible for appointment to judicial office in any court of the state during the member's period of service or within one year thereafter.

(2) The members first appointed by the governor shall have respectively one, two, three and four year terms as he shall designate. The members first appointed by the chief judge of the court of appeals shall have respectively one, two, three and four year terms as he shall designate. The member first appointed by the temporary president of the senate shall have a one-year term. The member first appointed by the minority leader of the senate shall have a two-year term. The member first appointed by the speaker of the assembly shall have a four-year term. The member first appointed by the minority leader of the assembly shall have a three-year term. Each subsequent appointment shall be for a term of four years.

(3) The commission shall designate one of their number to serve as chairman.

(4) The commission shall consider the qualifications of candidates for appointment to the offices of judge and chief judge of the court of appeals and, whenever a vacancy in those offices occurs, shall prepare a written report and recommend to the governor persons who are well qualified for those judicial offices.

e. The governor shall appoint, with the advice and consent of the senate, from among those recommended by the judicial nominating commission, a person to fill the office of chief judge or associate judge, as the case may be, whenever a vacancy occurs in the court of appeals; provided, however, that no person may be appointed a judge of the court of appeals unless such person is a resident of the state and has been admitted to the practice of law in this state for at least ten years. The governor shall transmit to the senate the written report of the commission on judicial nomination relating to the nominee.

f. When a vacancy occurs in the office of chief judge or associate judge of the court of appeals and the senate is not in session to give its advice and consent to an appointment to fill the vacancy, the governor shall fill the vacancy by interim appointment upon the recommendation of a commission on judicial nomination as provided in this section. An interim appointment shall continue until the senate shall pass upon the governor's selection. If the senate confirms an appointment, the judge shall serve a term as provided in subdivision a of this section commencing from the date of his interim appointment. If the senate rejects an appointment, a vacancy in the office shall occur sixty days after such rejection. If an interim appointment to the court of appeals be made from among the justices of the supreme court or the appellate divisions thereof, that appointment shall not affect the justice's existing office, nor create a vacancy in the supreme court, or the appellate division thereof, unless such appointment is confirmed by the senate and the appointee shall assume such office. If an interim appointment of chief judge of the court of appeals be made from among the associate judges, an interim appointment of associate judge shall be made in like manner; in such case, the appointment as chief judge shall not affect the existing office of associate judge, unless such appointment as chief judge is confirmed by the senate and the appointee shall assume such office.

g. The provisions of subdivisions c, d, e and f of this section shall not apply to temporary designations or assignments of judges or justices.

§ 36-a. *The amendments to the provisions of sections two, four, seven, eight, eleven, twenty, twenty-two, twenty-six, twenty-eight, twenty-nine and thirty of article six and to the provisions of section one of article seven, as first proposed by a concurrent resolution passed by the legislature in the year nineteen hundred seventy-six and entitled "Concurrent Resolution of the Senate and Assembly proposing amendments to articles six and seven of the constitution, in relation to the manner of selecting judges of the court of appeals, creation of a commission on judicial conduct and administration of the unified court system, providing for the effectiveness of such amendments and the repeal of subdivision c of section two, subdivision b of section seven, subdivision b of section eleven, section twenty-two and section twenty-eight of article six thereof relating thereto", shall become a part of the constitution on the first day of January next after the approval and ratification of the amendments proposed by such concurrent resolution by the people but the provisions thereof shall not become operative and the repeal of subdivision c of section two, section twenty-two and section twenty-eight shall not become effective until the first day of April next thereafter which date shall be deemed the effective date of such amendments and the chief judge and the associate judges of the court of appeals in office on such effective date shall hold their offices until the expiration of their respective terms. Upon a vacancy in the office of any such judge, such* vacancy shall be filled in the manner provided in section two of article six.

AMENDMENT NO. 2

Article VI, sec. 28 (new) (former sec. 28 repealed):

§ 28. a. The chief judge of the court of appeals shall be the chief judge of the state of New York and shall be the chief judicial officer of the unified court system. There shall be an administrative board of the courts which shall consist of the chief judge of the court of appeals as chairman and the presiding justice of the appellate division of the supreme court of each judicial department. The chief judge shall, with the advice and consent of the administrative board of the courts, appoint a chief administrator of the courts who shall serve at his pleasure.

b. The chief administrator, on behalf of the chief judge, shall supervise the administration and operation of the unified court system. In the exercise of such responsibility, the chief administrator of the courts shall have such powers and duties as may be delegated to him by the chief judge and such additional powers and duties as may be provided by law.

c. The chief judge, after consultation with the administrative board, shall establish standards and administrative policies for general application throughout the state, which shall be submitted by the chief judge to the court of appeals, together with the recommendations, if any, of the administrative board. Such standards and administrative policies shall be promulgated after approval by the court of appeals.

Article VII, sec. 1 (amended):

Section 1. For the preparation of the budget, the head of each department of state government, except the legislature and judiciary, shall furnish the governor such estimates and information in such form and at such times as he may require, copies of which shall forthwith be furnished to the appropriate committees of the legislature. The governor shall hold hearings thereon at which he may require the attendance of heads of departments and their subordinates. Designated representatives of such committees shall be entitled to attend the hearings thereon and to make inquiry concerning any part thereof.

Itemized estimates of the financial needs of the legislature, certified by the presiding officer of each house, and of the judiciary, *approved by the court of appeals and* certified by the [comptroller] *chief judge of the court of appeals,* shall be transmitted to the governor not later than the first day of December in each year for inclusion in the budget without revision but with such recommendations as he may deem proper. *Copies of the itemized estimates of the financial needs of the judiciary also shall forthwith be transmitted to the appropriate committees of the legislature.*

Article VI, sec. 29, subd. b (amended):

b. The legislature shall provide for the submission of the itemized estimates of the annual financial needs of the courts referred to in subdivision a of this section to the [administrative board of the judicial conference or to the said conference] *chief administrator of the courts* to be forwarded to the appropriating bodies with recommendations and comment.

Article VI, sec. 7, subd. b repealed and subd. c relettered b; sec. 11, subd. b repealed and subds. c, d and e relettered b, c and d.

Article VI, sec. 26, subd. i (amended):

i. Temporary assignments of all the foregoing judges or justices listed in this section shall be made by the [appellate division of the supreme court of the department or departments concerned] *chief administrator of the courts in accordance with standards and administrative policies established pursuant to section twenty-eight of this article.*

Article VI, sec. 8, subds. a, b and d (amended):

a. The appellate division of the supreme court in each judicial department may establish an appellate term in and for such department or in and for a judicial district or districts or in and for a county or counties within [the] *such* department [and designate the place or places where such appellate term shall be held]. Such an appellate term shall be composed of not less than three nor more than five justices of the supreme court who shall be designated from time to time by the [appellate division of the supreme court in the department] *chief administrator of the courts with the approval of the presiding justice of the appropriate appellate division,* and who shall be residents of the department or of the judicial district or districts as the case may be *and the chief administrator of the courts shall designate the place or places where such appellate terms shall be held.*

b. Any such appellate term may be discontinued and reestablished as the appellate division of the supreme court in each department shall determine from time to time and any designation to service therein may be revoked by the [appellate division of the supreme court so designating] *chief administrator of the courts with the approval of the presiding justice of the appropriate appellate division.*

d. If so directed by the appellate division of the supreme court establishing an appellate term, an appellate term shall have jurisdiction to hear and determine appeals now or hereafter authorized by law to be taken to the supreme court or to the appellate division other than appeals from the supreme court, a surrogate's court, the family court or appeals in criminal cases [involving felonies] prosecuted by indictment or by * *information as provided in section six of article one.*

Article VI, sec. 20, subd. b, paragraph (1) (amended):

(1) hold any other public office or trust except *an office in relation to the administration of the courts,* member of a constitutional convention or a member of the armed forces of the United States or of the state of New York in which latter event the legislature may enact such legislation as it deems appropriate to provide for a temporary judge or justice to serve during the period of the absence of such judge or justice in the armed forces;

Article VI, sec. 20, subd. b, new paragraph added:

Judges and justices of the courts specified in this subdivision shall also be subject to such rules of conduct as may be promulgated by the chief administrator of the courts with the approval of the court of appeals.

* Word "an" evidently omitted.

Article VI, sec. 20, subd. c (amended):

c. Qualifications for and restrictions upon the judges of district, town, village or city courts outside the city of New York, other than such qualifications and restrictions specifically set forth in subdivision a of this section, shall be prescribed by the legislature, provided, however, that the legislature shall require a course of training and education to be completed by justices of town and village courts selected after the effective date of this article who have not been admitted to practice law in this state. *Judges of such courts shall also be subject to such rules of conduct not inconsistent with law as may be promulgated by the chief administrator of the courts with the approval of the court of appeals.*

Article VI, sec. 4, subd. e (amended):

e. In case any appellate division shall certify to the governor that one or more additional justices are needed for the speedy disposition of the business before it, the governor [shall] *may* designate an additional justice or additional justices; but when the need for such additional justice or justices shall no longer exist, the appellate division shall so certify to the governor, and thereupon service under such designation or designations shall cease.

Article VI, sec. 30 (amended):

§ 30. The legislature shall have the same power to alter and regulate the jurisdiction and proceedings in law and in equity that it has heretofore exercised. The legislature may, on such terms as it shall provide and subject to subsequent modification, delegate, in whole or in part, to a court, including the appellate division of the supreme court, *or* to the [administrative board of the judicial conference, or to the judicial conference] *chief administrator of the courts,* any power possessed by the legislature to regulate practice and procedure in the courts. *The chief administrator of the courts shall exercise any such power delegated to him with the advice and consent of the administrative board of the courts.* Nothing herein contained shall prevent the adoption of regulations by individual courts consistent with the general practice and procedure as provided by statute or general rules.

Article VI, sec. 36-a (new):

§ 36-a. *The amendments to the provisions of sections two, four, seven, eight, eleven, twenty, twenty-two, twenty-six, twenty-eight, twenty-nine and thirty of article six and to the provisions of section one of article seven, as first proposed by a concurrent resolution passed by the legislature in the year nineteen hundred seventy-six and entitled "Concurrent Resolution of the Senate and Assembly proposing amendments to articles six and seven of the constitution, in relation to the manner of selecting judges of the court of appeals, creation of a commission on judicial conduct and administration of the unified court system, providing for the effectiveness of such amendments and the repeal of subdivision c of section two, subdivision b of section seven, subdivision b of section eleven, section twenty-two and section twenty-eight of article six thereof relating thereto", shall become a part of the constitution on the first day of January next after the approval and ratification of the amendments proposed by such concurrent resolution by the people but the provisions thereof shall not become operative and the repeal of subdivision c of section two, section twenty-two and section twenty-eight shall not become effective until the first day of April next thereafter which date shall be deemed the effective date of such amendments and the chief judge and the associate judges of the court of appeals in office on such effective date shall hold their offices until the expiration of their respective terms. Upon a vacancy in the office of any such judge, such vacancy shall be filled in the manner provided in section two of article six.*

AMENDMENT NO. 3

Article VI, sec. 22 (new) (former sec. 28 repealed); sec. 36-a (new):

§ 22. a. *There shall be a commission on judicial conduct. The commission on judicial conduct shall receive, initiate, investigate and hear complaints with respect to the conduct, qualifications, fitness to perform or performance of official duties of any judge or justice of the unified court system, in the manner provided by law; and, in accordance with subdivision d of this section, may determine that a judge or justice be* admonished, censured or removed from office for cause, including, but not limited to, misconduct in office, persistent failure to perform his duties, habitual intemperance, and conduct, on or off the bench, prejudicial to the administration of justice, or that a judge or justice be retired for mental or physical disability preventing the proper performance of his judicial duties. The commission shall transmit any such determination to the chief judge of the court of appeals who shall cause written notice of such determination to be given to the judge or justice involved. Such judge or justice may either accept the commission's determination or make written request to the chief judge, within thirty days after receipt of such notice, for a review of such determination by the court of appeals.

b. (1) The commission on judicial conduct shall consist of eleven members, of whom four shall be appointed by the governor, one by the temporary president of the senate, one by the minority leader of the senate, one by the speaker of the assembly, one by the minority leader of the assembly and three by the chief judge of the court of appeals. Of the members appointed by the governor one person shall be a member of the bar of the state but not a judge or justice, two shall not be members of the bar, justices or judges or retired justices or judges of the unified court system, and one shall be a judge or justice of the unified court system. Of the members appointed by the chief judge one person shall be a justice of the appellate division of the supreme court and two shall be judges or justices of a court or courts other than the court of appeals or appellate divisions. None of the persons to be appointed by the legislative leaders shall be justices or judges or retired justices or judges.

(2) The persons first appointed by the governor shall have respectively one, two, three, and four-year terms as he shall designate. The persons first appointed by the chief judge of the court of appeals shall have respectively two, three, and four-year terms as he shall designate. The person first appointed by the temporary president of the senate shall have a one-year term. The person first appointed by the minority leader of the senate shall have a two-year term. The person first appointed by the speaker of the assembly shall have a four-year term. The person first appointed by the minority leader of the assembly shall have a three-year term. Each member of the commission shall be appointed thereafter for a term of four

years. Commission membership of a judge or justice appointed by the governor or the chief judge shall terminate if such member ceases to hold the judicial position which qualified him for such appointment. Membership shall also terminate if a member attains a position which would have rendered him ineligible for appointment at the time of his appointment. A vacancy shall be filled by the appointing officer for the remainder of the term.

c. The organization and procedure of the commission on judicial conduct shall be as provided by law. The commission on judicial conduct may establish its own rules and procedures not inconsistent with law. Unless the legislature shall provide otherwise, the commission shall be empowered to designate one of its members or any other person as a referee to hear and report concerning any matter before the commission.

d. In reviewing a determination of the commission on judicial conduct, the court of appeals may admonish, censure, remove or retire, for the reasons set forth in subdivision a of this section, any judge of the unified court system. In reviewing a determination of the commission on judicial conduct, the court of appeals shall review the commission's findings of fact and conclusions of law on the record of the proceedings upon which the commission's determination was based. The court of appeals may impose a less or more severe sanction prescribed by this section than the one determined by the commission, or impose no sanction.

e. The court of appeals may suspend a judge or justice from exercising the powers of his office while there is pending a determination by the commission on judicial conduct for his removal or retirement, or while he is charged in this state with a felony by an indictment or an information filed pursuant to section six of article one. The suspension shall continue upon conviction and, if the conviction becomes final, he shall be removed from office. The suspension shall be terminated upon reversal of the conviction and dismissal of the accusatory instrument. Nothing in this subdivision shall prevent the commission on judicial conduct from determining that a judge or justice be admonished, censured, removed, or retired pursuant to subdivision a of this section.

f. Upon the recommendation of the commission on judicial conduct or on its own motion, the court of appeals may suspend a judge or justice from office when he is charged with *a crime punishable as a felony under the laws of this state, or any other crime which involves moral turpitude. The suspension shall continue upon conviction and, if the conviction becomes final, he shall be removed from office. The suspension shall be terminated upon reversal of the conviction and dismissal of the accusatory instrument. Nothing in this subdivision shall prevent the commission on judicial conduct from determining that a judge or justice be admonished, censured, removed, or retired pursuant to subdivision a of this section.*

g. A judge or justice who is suspended from office by the court of appeals shall receive his judicial salary during such period of suspension, unless the court directs otherwise. If the court has so directed and such suspension is thereafter terminated, the court may direct that he shall be paid his salary for such period of suspension.

h. A judge or justice retired by the court of appeals shall be considered to have retired voluntarily. A judge or justice removed by the court of appeals shall be ineligible to hold other judicial office.

i. Notwithstanding any other provision of this section, the legislature may provide by law for review of determinations of the commission on judicial conduct with respect to justices of town and village courts by an appellate division of the supreme court. In such event, all references in this section to the court of appeals and the chief judge thereof shall be deemed references to an appellate division and the presiding justice thereof, respectively.

j. If a court on the judiciary shall have been convened before the effective date of this section and the proceeding shall not be concluded by that date, the court on the judiciary shall have continuing jurisdiction beyond the effective date of this section to conclude the proceeding. All matters pending before the former commission on judicial conduct on the effective date of this section shall be disposed of in such manner as shall be provided by law.

§ 36-a. *The amendments to the provisions of sections two, four, seven, eight, eleven, twenty, twenty-two, twenty-six, twenty-eight, twenty-nine and thirty of article six and to the provisions of section one of article seven, as first proposed by a concurrent resolution passed by the legislature in the year nineteen hundred seventy-six and entitled "Concurrent Resolution of the Senate and Assembly proposing amend-*

ments to articles six and seven of the constitution, in relation to the manner of selecting judges of the court of appeals, creation of a commission on judicial conduct and administration of the unified court system, providing for the effectiveness of such amendments and the repeal of subdivision c of section two, subdivision b of section seven, subdivision b of section eleven, section twenty-two and section twenty-eight of article six thereof relating thereto", shall become a part of the constitution on the first day of January next after the approval and ratification of the amendments proposed by such concurrent resolution by the people but the provisions thereof shall not become operative and the repeal of subdivision c of section two, section twenty-two and section twenty-eight shall not become effective until the first day of April next thereafter which date shall be deemed the effective date of such amendments and the chief judge and the associate judges of the court of appeals in office on such effective date shall hold their offices until the expiration of their respective terms. Upon a vacancy in the office of any such judge, such vacancy shall be filled in the manner provided in section two of article six.

AMENDMENT NO. 5

Article VII, sec. 8, subd. 2 (amended):

2. Subject to the limitations on indebtedness and taxation, nothing in this constitution contained shall prevent the legislature from providing for the aid, care and support of the needy directly or through subdivisions of the state; or for the protection by insurance or otherwise, against the hazards of unemployment, sickness and old age; or for the education and support of the blind, the deaf, the dumb, the physically handicapped, the mentally ill, the emotionally disturbed, the mentally retarded. or juvenile delinquents as it may deem proper; or for health and welfare services for all children, either directly or through subdivisions of the state, including school districts; or for the aid, care and support of neglected and dependent children and of the needy sick, through agencies and institutions authorized by the state board of social welfare or other state department having the power of inspection thereof, by payments made on a per capita basis directly or through the subdivisions of the state; or for the increase in the amount of pensions of any member of a

retirement system of the state, or of a subdivision of the state; or for an increase in the amount of [pensions] *pension benefits* of any widow *or widower* of a retired member of a [teachers'] retirement system of the state or of a subdivision of the state to whom payable as beneficiary under an optional settlement in connection with the pension of such member. The enumeration of legislative powers in this paragraph shall not be taken to diminish any power of the legislature hitherto existing.

AMENDMENT NO. 6

Article XIII, sec. 3 (amended):

§ 3. The legislature shall provide for filling vacancies in office, and in case of elective officers, no person appointed to fill a vacancy shall hold his office by virtue of such appointment longer than the commencement of the political year next succeeding the first annual election after the happening of the vacancy; *provided, however, that nothing contained in this article shall prohibit the filling of vacancies on boards of education, including boards of education of community districts in the city school district of the city of New York, by appointment until the next regular school district election, whether or not such appointment shall extend beyond the thirty-first day of December in any year.*

AMENDMENT NO. 8

Article VII, sec. 8, subd. 3 (amended):

3. Nothing in this constitution contained shall prevent the legislature from authorizing the loan of the money of the state to a public corporation to be organized for the purpose of making loans to non-profit corporations *or for the purpose of guaranteeing loans made by banking organizations, as that term shall be defined by the legislature,* to finance the construction of new industrial or manufacturing plants, the construction of new buildings to be used for research and development, *the construction of other eligible business facilities,* and for the purchase of machinery and equipment related to such new industrial or manufacturing plants [and], research and development buildings, *and other eligible business facilities* in this state or the acquisition, rehabilitation or improvement of former *or existing* industrial or

manufacturing plants, *buildings to be used for research and development, other eligible business facilities, and machinery and equipment* in this state, including the acquisition of real property therefor, and the use of such money by such public corporation for such purposes, to improve employment opportunities in any area of the state, provided, however, that *any such plants, buildings or facilities or machinery and equipment therefor shall not be (i) primarily used in making retail sales of goods or services to customers who personally visit such facilities to obtain such goods or services or (ii) used primarily as a hotel, apartment house or other place of business which furnishes dwelling space or accommodations to either residents or transients, and provided further that* any loan by such public corporation shall not exceed forty per centum of the cost of any such project and the repayment of which shall be secured by a mortgage thereon which shall not be a junior incumbrance thereon by more than fifty per centum of such cost or by a security interest if personalty, *and that the amount of any guarantee of a loan made by a banking organization shall not exceed eighty per centum of the cost of any such project.*

**AMENDMENT APPROVED
BY THE VOTE OF THE PEOPLE
NOVEMBER 6, 1979**

Effective January 1, 1980

AMENDMENT NO. 2

Article XIV, sec. 1 (amended):
Section 1. The lands of the state, now owned or hereafter acquired, constituting the forest preserve as now fixed by law, shall be forever kept as wild forest lands. They shall not be leased, sold or exchanged, or be taken by any corporation, public or private, nor shall the timber thereon be sold, removed or destroyed. Nothing herein contained shall prevent the state from constructing, completing and maintaining any highway heretofore specifically authorized by constitutional amendment, nor from constructing and maintaining to federal standards federal aid interstate highway route five hundred two from a point in the vicinity of the city of Glens Falls, thence northerly to the vicinity of the villages of Lake George and Warrensburg, the hamlets of South Horicon and Pottersville and thence northerly in a generally straight line on the west side of Schroon Lake to the vicinity of the hamlet of Schroon, then continuing northerly to the vicinity of Schroon Falls, Schroon River and North Hudson, and to the east of Makomis Mountain, east of the hamlet of New Russia, east of the village of Elizabethtown and continuing northerly in the vicinity of the hamlet of Towers Forge, and east of Poke-O-Moonshine Mountain and continuing northerly to the vicinity of the village of Keeseville and the city of Plattsburgh, all of the aforesaid taking not to exceed a total of three hundred acres of state forest preserve land, nor from constructing and maintaining not more than twenty miles of ski trails thirty to eighty feet wide on the north, east and northwest slopes of Whiteface Mountain in Essex county, nor from constructing and maintaining not more than twenty miles of ski trails thirty to eighty feet wide, together with appurtenances thereto, on the slopes of Belleayre Mountain in Ulster and Delaware counties and not more than thirty miles of ski trails thirty to eighty feet wide, together with appurtenances thereto, on the slopes of Gore, South and Pete Gay mountains in Warren county, nor from relocating, reconstructing and maintaining a total of not more than fifty miles of existing state highways for the purpose of eliminating the hazards of dangerous curves and grades, provided a total of no more than four hundred acres of forest preserve land shall be used for such purpose and that no single relocated portion of any highway shall exceed one mile in length. Notwithstanding the foregoing provisions, the state may convey to the village of Saranac Lake ten acres of forest preserve land adjacent to the boundaries of such village for public use in providing for refuse disposal and in exchange therefore the village of Saranac Lake shall convey to the state thirty acres of certain true forest land owned by such village on Roaring Brook in the northern half of Lot 113, Township 11, Richards Survey. Notwithstanding the foregoing provisions, the state may convey to the town of Arietta twenty-eight acres of forest preserve land within such town for public use in providing for the extension of the runway and landing strip of the Piseco airport and in exchange therefor the town of Arietta shall convey to the state thirty acres of certain land owned by such town in the town of Arietta. *Notwithstanding the foregoing provisions and subject to legislative approval of the tracts to be exchanged prior to the actual transfer of title, the state, in order to consolidate its land holdings for better management, may convey to International Paper Company approximately eight thousand five hundred acres of forest preserve land located in townships two and three of Totten and Crossfield's Purchase and township nine of the Moose River Tract, Hamilton county, and in exchange therefore International Paper Company shall convey to the state for incorporation into the forest preserve approximately the same number of acres of land located within such townships and such County on condition that the legislature shall determine that the lands to be received by the state are at least equal in value to the lands to be conveyed by the state.*

NOTE: Matter in *italics* is new

BASIL A. PATERSON
Secretary of State

DEPARTMENT OF STATE
Albany, NY 12231

IMPORTANT DATES IN NEW YORK

Annual Events in New York

January
    Snowfest, Skaneateles

February
    Winter Festival, New York City
    Winter Carnival, Cohocton, Monticello and Saranac Lake

March
    Spring Fling, Canandaigua
    Hofstra Univ. Jazz Festival, Hempstead
    Festival of Contemporary Music, New York City
    Festival of the Arts, Potsdam
    Brantling Winter Carnival, Sodus

April
    Spring Festival, Ithaca
    Foreign Language Festival, Jamaica
    State Maple Syrup Festival, Marathon
    Cultural Festival, New York City
    Eastern States Antique Fair, White Plains

May
    Dogwood Festival, Danville
    Long Island International Film Festival, Hempstead
    American Film Festival, New York City
    Fun Days, Norwich
    Arts and Crafts Fair, Oceanside
    Folk Song Festival, Petersburg
    Lilac Time Festival, Rochester
    Movies on a Shoestring Film Festival, Rochester
    Apple Blossom Festival, Williamson
    Celebration of Nations, Utica

June
Steuben County Dairy Festival, Bath
Exhibition of American Art, Chautauqua
Gerry Days, Elbridge
Newport Jazz Festival, New York City
Shakespeare Festival, New York City
International Computer Art Festival, New York City
Jazz in the Gardens, New York City
Colonial Days, Painted Post
Intercollegiate Regatta (rowing), Poughkeepsie
Northeast Craft Fair, Rhinebeck
Tournament of Drums, Rochester
Arts Festival, Roslyn
Saratoga Festival, Saratoga Springs
Music Festival, Southampton
Hudson Valley Folk Festival, Tarrytown
Creative Music Festival, Woodstock

July
Lake George Opera Festival, Glen Falls
Storm King Chamber Music Series, Cornwall
Music Festival, Forest Hills
Summer Music Festival, Glen Cove
Folk Music Festival, Huntington
Lewiston Festival, Lewiston
International Bach Society Festival, New York City
Music Festival, Pawling
Midsummer Faire, Petersburg
Summer Opera Festival, Port Jervis
Curbstone Art Festival, Rochester
Adirondack/Champlain Music Festival, Schroon Lake
Stony Brook Music Festival, Stony Point
Art Festival, Utica

August
Summer Music Festival, Chautauqua
Smoky Greens Bluegrass Festival, Fort Ann
Art Show, Hammondsport
Sauerkraut Festival, Phelps
Central New York Scottish Games, Syracuse
New York State Fair, Syracuse

September
Festival of Lights, Canadaigua
Fall Festival, Elmira
New York Dance Festival, New York City

New York Film Festival, New York City
Canal Town Days, Palmyra
"Fall-In", Ithaca
Grape Festival, Penn-Yan
Oktoberfest, Rochester

October
Oktoberfest, Canadaigua
Fall Foliage Festival, Cohocton
Festival of Arts, New York City (through May)
Community Carnival, Troy

November
Cornell Festival of Music, Ithaca
PRSA Film Festival, New York City

BIBLIOGRAPHY
TWO HUNDRED BOOKS ABOUT NEW YORK

Abbott, Edith, *Women in Industry,* New York, 1910.
Adams, C. F., *A Chapter of Erie,* Boston, 1869.
Albion, Robert G., *The Rise of New York Port, 1815-1860,* New York, 1970.
Alexander, D. S., *A Political History of the State of New York,* New York, 3 vols., 1906-09.
American Guide Series, *New York: A Guide to the Empire State* New York, 1940.
Andrews, Charles M., *The Colonial Background of the American Revolution,* New Haven, Conn., 1931.
Andrews, Edward D., *The Community Industries of the Shakers,* Albany, 1933.
Avery, Giles B., *Sketches of Shakers and Shakerism,* Albany, 1884.
Bacon, Edgar M., *The Hudson River from Ocean to Source,* New York, 1907.
Bailey, Rosalie F., *Pre-Revolutionary Dutch Houses and Families in Northern New Jersey and Southern New York,* New York, 1936.
Baker, Elizabeth F., *Protective Labor Legislation,* New York, 1925.
Barnes, Gilbert H., *The Anti-Slavery Impulse,* New York, 1933.
Barrus, Clara, *Life and Letters of John Burroughs,* Boston, 1925.
Beach, S. A., *Apples of New York,* Albany, 1905.
Beard, Charles and Mary R., *Rise of American Civilization,* New York, 1946.
Beauchamp, W. M., *History of the New York Iroquois,* Albany, 1905.
Becker, Carl L., *The History of Political Parties in the Province of New York,* 1760-76, Madison, Wis., 1909.
Beer, George L., *British Colonial Policy,* New York, 1907.
Benson, Adolph B., ed., *The America of 1750: Peter Kalm's Travels in North America,* 2 vols., New York, 1937.
Berger, Meyer, *Meyer Berger's New York,* New York, 1960.
Bliven, Bruce, Jr., *Battle for Manhattan,* New York, 1956.
—*New York,* New York, 1981.
—*Under the Guns:* New York, 1775-76, New York, 1972.
Bobbe, Dorothie, *DeWitt Clinton,* New York, 1933.
Bond, Elsie M., *Public Relief in New York State,* New York, 1938.
Bridenbaugh, Carl, *Cities in Revolt: Urban Life in America,* 1743-76, New York, 1955.
Brigham, A. P., *Glacial Geology and Geographic Conditions of the Lower Mohawk Valley,* Albany, 1929.
Burgess, Anthony, *New York,* New York, 1977.
Burroughs, John, *In the Catskills,* Boston, 1910.
Campbell, William W., *Annals of Tryon County; Or, the Border Warfare During the Revolution,* New York, 1924.
Canfield, William W., *The Legends of the Iroquois,* New York, 1902.
Carmer, Carl, *The Hudson,* New York, 1939.
—*Listen for a Lonesome Drum,* A New York State Chronicle, New York, 1936.
—*My Kind of Country,* New York, 1966.
—*The Tavern Lamps are Burning,* New York, 1964.
—*The Hudson,* New York, 1968.

Caro, Robert A., *The Power Broker: Robert Moses and the Fall of New York,* New York, 1974.
Carson, Russell, *Peaks and People of the Adirondacks,* Garden City, N. J., 1928.
Cheyney, Edward P., *Anti-Rent Agitation of the State of New York,* 1936-1946, Philadelphia, 1887.
Colden, Cadwallader, *History of the Five Nations,* New York, 1904.
Cole, G. W., *Early Library Development in New York State,* New York, 1927.
Commons, John R., *History of Labor in the United States,* 4 vols., New York, 1918-35.
Condon, Thomas J., *New York Beginnings,* New York, 1968.
Conway, Moncure D., *Life of Thomas Paine,* New York, 1892.
Cross, Whitney, *The Burned-Over District: The Social and Intellectual History of Enthusiastic Religion in Western New York,* 1800-50, Ithaca, 1950.
Crevecoeur, St. John de, *Letters from an American Farmer,* London, 1782.
Cummings, John, *Poor Laws of Massachusetts and New York,* New York, 1895.
Dangerfield, George, *Chancellor Robert R. Livingston of New York,* 1746-1813, New York, 1960.
Davidson, Marshall B., *Life in America,* 2 vols., Boston, 1951.
—*New York: A Pictorial History,* New York, 1977.
Davis, Elmer, *History of the New York Times,* 1851-1921, New York, 1921.
Day, R. E., ed., *Papers of Sir William Johnson,* Albany, 9 vols., 1921-39.
DeKay, James, *New York Natural History Survey: Zoology of New York,* 5 vols., Albany, 1842-44.
Dickens, Charles, *American Notes,* New York, 1842.
Donaldson, Alfred L., *A History of the Adirondacks,* New York, 1921.
Dowing, Andrew Jackson, *The Fruits and Fruit Trees of America,* New York, 1947.
—*The Architecture of Country Houses,* New York, 1850.
Dunlap, William, *A History of the American Theatre,* New York, 4 vols., New Haven, 1821-22.
Earle, Alice M., *Colonial Days in Old New York,* New York, 1896.
Eaton, E. H., *Birds of New York,* 2 vols., Albany, 1910-14.
Eberlein, H. D., *Manor Houses and Historic Homes of the Hudson Valley,* Philadelphia, 1924.
Edgell, George H., *American Architecture of Today,* New York, 1928.
Eldridge, Paul, *Crown of Empire,* New York, 1957.
Ellis, David M., and others, *A History of New York State,* Ithaca, 1967.
Ellis, David M., *New York, State and City,* Ithaca, 1979.
—*Empire State Report,* "Future of the Northeast," Albany, 1976.
Evans, John Henry, *Joseph Smith, an American Prophet,* New York, 1933.
Evers, Alf, *The Catskills: From Wilderness to Woodstock,* New York, 1972.
Fairchild, H. L., *Geologic Story of the Genesee Valley and Western New York,* Rochester, 1928.
Federal Writer's Project, *New York City Guide,* New York, 1939.
—*New York Panorama,* New York, 1939.
Flippin, E. O., *Rural New York,* New York, 1921.
Fitch, Charles E., *The Public School: History of Common School Education in the State of New York,* Albany, 1904.
Flexner, James T., *History of American Painting,* 3 vols., New York, 1937.
—*Young Hamilton: A Biography,* Boston, 1978.
Flick, Alexander C., ed., *History of the State of New York,* 10 vols., New York, 1937.

Bibliography

—*The Sullivan-Clinton Campaign in 1779,* Albany, 1928.
—*The American Revolution in New York, Its Political, Social and Economic Significance,* Albany, 1926.
Fox, Dixon Ryan, *Decline of the Aristocracy in the Politics of New York,* New York, 1918.
—*Caleb Heathcote: Gentleman Colonist, 1691-1721,* New York, 1926.
—*Yankees and Yorkers,* New York, 1940.
Gabriel, R. H., *The Evolution of Long Island,* New Haven, 1931.
Glazer, Nathan, with Maynihan, Daniel P., *Beyond the Melting Pot,* Cambridge Mass., 1963.
Godwin, Parke, *William Cullen Bryant,* New York, 1883.
Graham, Frank Jr., *The Adirondack Park,* New York, 1978.
Grant, Anne, *The Memoirs of an American Lady,* Albany, 1876.
Greene, Newlon, *History of the Mohawk Valley,* Gateway to the West, Chicago, 1925.
Hall, Captain Basil, *Travels in North America in the Years 1827-28,* London, 1829.
Halsey, Francis W., *The Old New York Frontier,* 1614-1800, New York, 1902.
Hamlin, Talbot, *The American Spirit in Architecture,* New Haven, 1926.
Hammond, J. D., *The History of Political Parties in New York, to 1840,* Syracuse, 1852.
Hensen, Marcus Lee, *The Atlantic Migration,* Cambridge, 1940.
Haring, H. A. *Our Catskill Mountains,* New York, 1931.
Harlow, Alvin F., *Old Towpaths,* New York, 1926.
Harper, Ida H., *The Life and Work of Susan B. Anthony,* 3 vols., Indianapolis, 1898-1908.
Headley, Rev. J. T., *Letters from the Backwoods and the Adirondack,* New York, 1850.
Hedrick, U. P. *History of Agriculture in the State of New York,* Albany, 1933.
Hicks, Granville, *The Great Tradition,* New York, 1835.
Hochschild, Harold K., *Township 34,* 7 vols., New York, 1952.
Hopkins, A. S., *Lake George,* Albany, 1939.
Horner, H. H., *Life and Works of Andrew Sloan Draper,* Urbana, Ill., 1934.
Howard, John T., *Our American Music,* New York, 1931.
Howat, John K., *The Hudson River and Its Painters,* New York, 1972.
Hungerford, Edward, *Pathway to Empire,* New York, 1935.
—*Men of Iron: History of the New York Central Railroad,* New York, 1938.
Hunt, George T., *Wars of the Iroquois,* New York, 1938.
Jackson, Harry F., *Scholar in the Wilderness: Francis Adrian Van der Kemp,* Syracuse, 1963.
Jameson, J. F., ed., *Narratives of New Netherland, 1609-1664,* New York, 1909.
Janvier, Thomas A., *Dutch Founding of New York,* New York, 1903.
Johnson, Clifton, *The Picturesque Hudson,* New York, 1910.
—*The Picturesque St. Lawrence,* New York, 1910.
Johnston, H.P., ed., *Correspondence and Public Papers of John Jay, 1763-1826,* 4 vols., New York, 1890-93.
Jones, Louis C., ed., *Growing up in the Cooper Country: Boyhood Recollections of the New York Frontier,* Syracuse, 1965.
Kalm, Peter, *Travels in North America,* London, 1770-71.
Kammen, Michael, *Colonial New York: A History,* New York, 1975.
Keller, Jane E., *Adirondack Park,* New York, 1978.

Kimball, Francis P., *New York—The Canal State,* Albany, 1937.
Klein, Milton M., *The Politics of Diversity,* New York, 1974.
Knight, Sarah, *The Private Journal of a Journey from Boston to New York... 1704,* Albany, 1865.
Kolodin, Irving, *The Metropolitan Opera* (1883-1939), New York, 1939.
Kouwenhoven, John A., *The Columbia Historical Portrait of New York,* New York, 1953.
La Follette, Suzanne, *Art in America,* New York, 1929.
Landon, Harry F., *History of the North Country,* Indianapolis, 1932.
Lathrop, Elsie L., *Early American Taverns,* New York, 1926.
Lincoln, C. Z., *Constitutional History of New York,* Rochester, 1906.
Linn, W. A., *Story of Mormonism,* New York, 1902.
Lodge, Henry Cabot, *Alexander Hamilton,* Boston, 1899.
Lydekker, John W., *The Faithful Mohawks,* New York, 1938.
Lyman, Susan E., *The Story of New York,* New York, 1935.
McKee, Samuel, *Labor in Colonial New York,* New York, 1964.
Mabie, Hamilton Wright, *The Writers of Knickerbocker New York,* New York, 1912.
Major, Howard, *The Domestic Architecture of the Early American Republic: The Greek Revival,* Philadelphia, 1926.
Meyer, B. H., with others, *History of Transportation in the United States Before 1860,* Washington, 1917.
Miller, John C., *Origins of the American Revolution,* Boston, 1943.
Morris, Lloyd, *Incredible New York,* New York, 1951.
Morison, Samuel E., *Samuel de Champlain,* Boston, 1972.
Nevins, Allan, *Herbert H. Lehman and His Era,* New York, 1963.
New York Historical Society, *Quarterly,* publications, 1969
Newland, David H., *The Mineral Resources of the State of New York,* Albany, 1921.
Niles, S. G., *The Hoosac Valley, Its Legend and Its History,* New York, 1912.
Nissonson, S. G., *The Patroon's Domain,* New York, 1937.
Nutting, Wallace, *New York Beautiful,* New York, 1927.
O'Brien, Raymond J., *American Sublime; Landscape Scenery of the Lower Hudson Valley,* New York, 1981.
Odell, G. C. D., *Annals of the New York Stage,* New York, 1927-39.
O'Donnell, Thomas F., *A Brief Description of the New Netherlands,* Syracuse, 1968.
Oppenheim, Samuel, *The Early History of the Jews in New York,* New York, 1909.
O'Reilly, Henry, *Settlement in the West; Sketches of Rochester,* Rochester, 1838.
Parker, A. C., *The Constitution of the Five Nations,* Albany, 1916.
Parker, Robert Allerton, *A Yankee Saint; John N. Noyes and the Oneida Community,* New York, 1935.
Parkman, Francis, *A Half-Century of Conflict,* Boston, 1892.
Phelps, Henry P., *Players of a Century, a Record of the Albany Stage,* Albany, 1880.
Phillips, McCandish, *City Notebook,* New York, 1974.
Pound, Arthur, *Johnson of the Mohawks,* New York, 1930.
Pritchett, V. S., *New York Proclaims,* New York, 1965.
Redway, Jacques W., *Making of the Empire State,* Boston, 1904.
Reid, W. Max., *Story of Old Fort Johnson,* New York, 1906.
The Mohawk Valley, New York, 1901.

Bibliography

Ritchie, William A., *The Archaeology of New York State*, Syracuse, 1969.
Rines, Edward P., *Old Historic Churches in America*, New York, 1936.
Roberts, Ellis H., *New York: The Planting and Growth of the Empire State*, Boston, 1887.
Schlesinger, Arthur M., *The Colonial Merchants and the American Revolution*, New York, 1918.
Schneider, Davis, *The History of Public Welfare in New York State*, 1609-1866, Chicago, 1938.
Sherwood, Sidney, *The University of New York: History of Higher Education in the State of New York*, Washington, 1900.
Silverstein, Barry and Krate, Ronald, *Children of the Dark Ghetto*, New York, 1975.
Simms, Jeptha R., *Trappers of New York*, Albany, 1851.
Simon, Kate, *Fifth Avenue: A Very Social History*, New York, 1978.
Smith, Alfred E., *Up To Now: An Autobiography*, New York, 1929.
Spaulding, Ernest W., *New York in the Critical Period, 1783-89*, New York, 1932.
Spiller, Robert E., *Fenimore Cooper, Critic of His Times*, New York, 1931.
Stokes, I. N. P., *The Iconography of Manhattan Island, 1498-1909*, 6 vols., New York, 1915-28. Reprinted, New York, in 1967.
Swiggett, Howard, *War out of Niagara: Walter Butler and the Tory Rangers*, New York, 1933.
Sylvester, N. B., *Indian Legends of Saratoga*, Troy, 1884.
Talese, Gay, *Fame and Obscurity*, New York, 1970.
Tarr, Ralph S., *The Physical Geography of New York State*, New York, 1902.
Thomas, A. C., and Thomas, R. N., *History of the Society of Friends*, New York, 1894.
Thompson, Benjamin F., *History of Long Island*, New York, 1918.
Thompson, John H., ed., *Geography of New York State*, Syracuse, 1966.
Towne, Charles Hanson, *Loafting Down Long Island*, New York, 1921.
Trollope, Mrs. F. M., *Domestic Manners of the Americans*, New York, 1901.
Van Wagenen, Jared, Jr., *The Cow*, New York, 1922.
—*Golden Age of Homespun*, Albany, 1927.
Van Wagner, Edith, ed., *Agricultural Manual of New York State*, Albany, New York State Dept. reports.
Van Sandt, Roland, *The Catskill Mountain House*, New York, 1966.
Van der Zee, Henri and Barbara, *A Sweet and Alien Land: The Story of Dutch New York*, New York, 1978.
Vanplanck, William E., *The Sloops of the Hudson*, New York, 1908.
Walsh, Raymond, C. I. O., *Industrial Unionism in Action*, New York, 1937.
Ward, Christopher, *The War of the Revolution*, 2 vols., New York, 1952.
Watson, Elkanah, *History of the Rise...of the Western Canals in the State of New York*, Albany, 1820.
Werner, M. R., *Tammany Hall*, New York, 1968.
Wheeler, Sherman, *New York's Port in History*, New York, 1915.
Whitford, Noble E., *History of the Canal System of the State of New York*, 1905, 1922.
Williams, Stanley, T., *The Life of Washington Irving*, New York, 1935.
Wilson, James G., ed., *The Memorial History of New York*, 2 vols., New York, 1892.
Wilstach, Paul, *Hudson River Landings*, Indianapolis, 1933.
Wissler, *Indians of Greater New York and the Lower Hudson*, 1950.

Index

--page numbers for illustrations are italicized.

Abercrombie, James, 141
 facing 141
Abolition, *see* Slavery
Accord, 229
Acid rain, 83, 193
Acra, 229
Addison, 229
Adirondacks, 62, 63, 68, 230
 Park Agency, 193
 preservation, 118
 state park, 187-92
 Uplands, 65
Afton, 230
Agfa-Ansco Corporation, 242
Agriculture,
 and soils, 79
 and the weather, 74
 prehistoric, 31-32
Akron, 230
Alabama, N.Y., 230
Albany, 6-7, 16, 198-203
 mayors, 198
Albany County, 231
 historical places, 361-73
Albany Regency, 100
Albion, 231
Alden, 231
Alexander, 231
Alexander's Ragtime Band, 148
Alexandria Bay, 231
Alfred, 231
Allegany, 231
Allegany County, 231
 historical places, 373-75
Allegany Reservation, 231-32
Allegeny River, 232

Allen, Ethan, 141-42
Alma, 232
Almond, 232
Altamont, 233
Altmar, 233
Altona, 233
Amagansett, 233
Amenia, 233
American Express Company, 161-62
Ames, 233
Amherst, 233
Amherst, Jeffrey, 143
Amityville, 233-34
Amsterdam, 234
Ancram, 234
Andes, N.Y., 234
Andover, 234
Angelica, 234
Angola, 234
Anthony, Susan B., 143-44,
 facing 140
Anti-masons, 53, 162
Anti-renters, 104
Antwerp, N.Y., 234
Appalachian Upland, 64, 67-70, 87
Arcade, 234
Archaic people, 25
Architecture, 6-7
Arden, 234
Ardsley, 235
Area of state, 60
Argyle, 235
Aristocracy in New York, 53
Arkport, 235

Arnold, Benedict, 46, 47, *facing 140*, 259
Art, in New York City, 213
Articles of Confederation, 14
Arts, 58-59
  in Syracuse, 223
Ashland, 235
Athens, N.Y., 235
Atlantic Beach, 235
Atlantic Coastal Plain, 70
Atlantic Monthly, 171
Attica, 235
Auburn, 236
Aurora, 236
Austerlitz, 236
Automobile, 252
Ava, 236-37
Avoca, 237
Avon, 237
Babcock, Dr. Stephen, 244
Babylon, 237
Bainbridge, 237
Bakers Mill, 237
Baldwinsville, 237
Ballston, 237
Ballston Spa, 237-38
Bangor, 238
Barker, 238
Barneveld, 238
Barton, 238
Baseball Hall of Fame, 255
Batavia, 238
Bath, 239-40
Bausch, John J., 217
Bayville, 240
Beacon, 240
Bear Mountain, *facing 186*
Bedford, 240
Belfast, 240
Bell, Alexander G., *facing 140*
Bellerose, 240
Bellport, 240
Belmont, 240
Bemus Point, 240
Bergen, 240
Berkshire, 240
Berlin, 241
Berlin, Irving, 148-49
Berne,Swett Bethel, 241
Bibliography, 719-23
Bingham, William, 241
Binghamton, 241-42

Bird, state, 5-6
Black, Frank Swett, 118
Black River, 242
Blacks, 151-52, 185-86
  settlements, 189
Blain, James G., 114
Blasdell, 243
Bloomer, Amelia J., 149
Bloomingburg, 243
Bluebird, 5-6
Bogs, 76
Borders, state, 60-61
Bouck, William C., 102-03
Brant, Joseph, 35-36, 150-51, *facing 140*
Brentwood, 244
Brewster, 244
Briarcliff Manor, 244
Bridgewater, 244
Brighton, 244
Brightwaters, 244
British control, 44, 92
  warfare in Revolution, 46-49
Broadalbin, 244
Broadway, 214
  at mid-century, facing 54
Brockport, 244
Brocton, 245
Bronx, 245
Bronx County, 245
  historical places, 375-77
Bronxville, 245
Brookfield, 245
Brookhaven, 245
Brooklyn, 245
Brooklyn Bridge, 213
  in 1880s, *facing 54*
Broome County, 245
  historical places, 377-78
Brown John, 189, *facing 140*
Brownville, 245
Brushton, 245
Buchanan, 246
Buffalo, 204-07, *facing 54, 186*
  mayors, 204
Burdett, 246
Burgoyne, General, 47, 201
Burial mounds, 26
Burke, 246
Burr, Aaron, 169

Index 727

Burroughs, John, 156-57
Byron, 246
Cabot, Sebastian, 9
Cairo, 246
Caledonia, 246
Callicoon, 246
Cambridge, 246
Camden, 246
Cameron, 246
Camillus, 246
Campbell, 246
Canaan, 246
Canajoharie, 246
Canals, 52, 81
Canandaigua, 247
Canandaigua Lake, 247
Canaseraga, 247
Canastota, 247
Candor, 247
Caneadea, 247
Canisteo, 247
Canton, 247
Cape Vincent, 247
Capitalists, see Tycoons

Capitol building, 6-7, 111,
  facing 186
  fire, 125
Carey, Hugh, 24, 59, 138-40
Carleton, Sir Guy, 280
Carlisle, 248
Carmel, 248
Carmer, Carl, 247
Carnegie, Andrew, 152-53,
  facing 140
Carpenter, Francis B., 279
Carthage, 248
Cary, Trumbull, 239
Cassadaga, 248
Castile, 248
Castle Clinton, 248
Castle-on-Hudson, 248
Castorland, 248
Catherine Montour, Queen, 300
Cato, 248
Catskills, 68, 248, 249
Cattaraugus, 249
  Indian Reservation, 249
Cattaraugus County, 249
  historical places, 378-79
Cayuga, 250
Cayuga County, 250
  historical places, 379-80

Cayuga Lake, 250
Cayuta, 250
Cazenovia, 250
Cedarhurst, 250
Celoron, 250
Centennial, 19
Centerville, 250
Central Park, 215
Central Square, 250
Chamber, Robert W., 244
Champlain, N.Y., 250
Champlain, Samuel de, 39, 155-
  56, 188, facing 140
Chateaugay, 250
Chatham, 250-51
Chaumont, 251
Chautauqua, 251
  Lake, 251
Chautauqua County, 251
  historical places, 380-82
Cheektowaga, 251
Cheese production, 290-91
Chemung, 251
  Canal, 255
Chemung County, 251
  historical places, 382
Chenango, Bridge, 251
  Canal, 241
  County, 251
    historical places, 383
  River, 251
Cherry Creek, 251
Cherry Valley, 251-52
Chester, 252
Chicago Canal, 100
Chittenango, 252
Christianity, and the Indians,
  32, 33
Church of Jesus Christ—Latter
  Day Saints, 184
Churchville, 252
Cicero, 252
Cincinnatus, 252
Civil War, 54, 105, 106, 108-09,
  166-67, 206, 211-12, 225
Claredon, 252
Clarence, 252
Clark, Myron, 107
Clarkson, 252
Claverack, 252
Clay, 252
Clayton, 252
Clayville, 252-53

Clemens, Samuel, 157-58, 262
Clermont, 164
Cleveland, Grover, 20, 113-14, 206, *facing 140*
Cleveland, N.Y., 252
Clifton Park, 253
Clifton Springs, 253
Climate, New York, 71-76
Climatic changes, 62
Clinton, 41, 253
Clinton County, 253
  historical places, 383-85
Clinton DeWitt, 3, 82, 96-97, 201, *facing 140*
Clinton Gov. George, 3, 91, 321
Clinton County, 253
Clintondale, 253
Clothing, 149
Clyde, 253
Clymer, 253
Cobleskill, 253
Cochecton, 253
Coeymans, 253
Cohocton, 253
Cohocton Park, 253
Cohoes, 253-54
Cold Brook, 254
Cold Spring, 254
Colden, 254
Colendonck, 224
Coll, Vincent, 248
Collins, 254
Colonial era, 39-46, 306
Colonial house, *facing 186*
Colonie, 254
Colton, 254
Columbia County, 254
  historical places, 385-90
Colvin, Verplanck, 190
Communal settlements, 320
Communism, 58
Communists, 21
Conesus, 254
Coney Island, 215
Conklin, 254
Conservation, 119, 190
  laws, 192
  soil, 80
Constable, 254
Constableville, 254
Constantia, 254
Constitution, federal, 48-49, 53
  amendments, 112
  Indian model for, 28, 311
  of 1821, 99
Constitution, state, 14, 543-714
Constitutional Convention of 1915, 128
Constitutional conventions (other), 23
Continental Congress, 14, 46
Cooper, James F., 159-60, 254-55, 327
Cooper, Judge William, 254
Cooperstown, 159, 254-55
Copake, 255
Copenhagen, N.Y., 255
Corfu, 255
Corinth, 255
Cornell, Alonzo B., 112-13
Cornell, Ezra, 160
Cornell University, 283
Corning, 255
Corning, Charles, 322
Corning, Erastus I, 255
Cornwall, 255
Cornwall on Hudson, 255
Cortland, 129, 255-56
Cortland County, 256
  historical places, 390-91
Cosby, William, 301
Covered bridge, *facing 186*
Coxsackie, 256
Cranberry Lake, 256
Croghan, 256
Crosby, Benjamin, 280
Croton-on-Hudson, 256
Crown Point, 256
Crugers Island, 256
Cuba, N.Y., 257
Cuddebackville, 257
Cuomo, Mario, 140
Curtiss, Glenn H., 148, 285
Cuyler, 257
Dairy industry, 290-91
Dana, Charles A., 270
Danforth, Maj. Asa, 220-21
Dannemora, 25
Dansville, 257
Davenport, 257
Dayton, 257
De Lancey, Etienne, 257-58
De Ruyter, 258
Debts, governmental, 59
Deferiet, 257
Dekanawida, 27, 232
DeLancey, 257-58

Delanson, 258
Delaware County, 258
 historical places, 391-92
Delevan, 258
Delhi N.Y., 258
Democracy, Indian, 28
Democratic party, 103, 106, 110, 181
Denmark, N.Y., 258
Depauville, 258
Depew, 258
Depew, Chauncey M., 268, 315
Depeyster, 258
Deposit, 258
Dewey, Thomas E., 133-34
Dewitt, 259
Diamond, Legs, 248
Discovery, 173
Discrimination, commission against, 134
Distant Early Warning System (DEW), 225
Divorce laws, 138, 185
Dix, John A., 124-25
Dobbs, or Dobbs Ferry, 259
Dolgeville, 259
Donegan, Thomas, 210
Doubleday, Frank N., 153-54
Douglass, Frederick, 219
Downing, Andrew Jackson, 154-55
Draft Laws, 106
Drainage systems, 63, 80-83, *map*, 84
Dresden, 259
Drumlins, *defined*, 69
Drums Along the Mohawk, 67
Duanesburg, 259
Dundee, N.Y., 259
Dunkirk, 259
Durham, 260
Durham, 260
Dutch, discrimination against English, 291
Dutch East India Company, 173
Dutch Hill War, 283
Dutch settlement, 10, 39-40, 44, 209, 224, 286, 320-21
Dutchess County, 260
 historical places, 392-99
Earlville, 260
East Aurora, 260
East Bloomfield, 260
East Greenbush, 260
East Hampton, 260

East Otto, 260
East Randolph, 260-61
East River, 261
East Rochester, 261
East Rockaway, 261
East Syracuse, 261
Eastchester, 260
Eastman, George, 160-61, 217, 219, *facing 140*
Eastman, Max, 256
Eaton, 261
Ecology, 83
Economic development, 51-52, 58
Eden, 261
Edmeston, 261
Education, Indians, 150
Education, public, 110
Education Act of 1965, 139
Edwards, 261
Eidlitz, Leopold, 7
Eisenhower Locks, *196*
Elba, 261
Elbridge, 261
Elizabethtown, 261
Ellenburgh, 261
Ellenville, 261-62
Ellicot, Joseph, 205, 238, 239
Ellicottville, 262
Ellington, 262
Ellis Island, 213, 262
Ellisburg, 262
Elma, 262
Elmira, 262-63
Elmira Heights, 263
Elmont, 263
Elmsford, 263
Emancipation Act of 1827, 185
Emancipation Proclamation, 152
Emerson, Ralph Waldo, 191
Emmons, Ebenezer, 190
Empire state, 3
Empire State Building, 129, 215 *facing 186*
Endicott, 263
English control, 35, 41, 306
 control of Albany, 201
English settlement, 11-14
Erie, Lake, 205
Erie Canal, 52, 82, 96, 102, 207, 221, 290, 325-26
Erie County, 206, 263
 historical places, 400-04
Erie-Ontario Lake Plain 69
Erin, 263

Esopus, 263
Esperance, 263
Essex, 263
Essex County, 263
  historical places, 404-06
Evans Mills, 263-64
Explorers, 155-56, 172-73
Fabius, 264
Factionalism, 53-54
'Fair Deal,' Truman's, 132
Fairfield, 264
Fair Haven, 264
Fairport, 264
Falconer, 264
Falls, N.Y.,264
Falls, formation, 64
Fallsburg, 264
Fargo, William G., 161-62
Farmingdale, 264
Farnham, 264
Fayette, 184, 264
Fayetteville, 264
Federalist papers, 49, 169
Fenton, Reuben Eaton, 109
Festivals, Indian, 29
  in New York towns, 715
Ficke, Arthur D., 279
Field, Cyrus W., 282
Fillmore, 264
Fillmore, Millard, 162-63, 206
Financial panics, 114
Fine, 264
Finger Lakes, 82, 264-65
  region, 283
Fire Island, 265
  national seashore, 194-95
Fish, Hamilton, 104-05
Fishers Island, 265
Fishing, 299, 308
Fishkill, 265
Five Nations, 27, 28-29, 170
  warfare, 33, 34
Flag, state, 4
Fleishmanns, 265
Floral Park, 265
Florida, N.Y., 265
'Flower City,' 217
Flower, Roswell Petibone, 116-17
Flower, state, 5
Flushing, 265
Fonda, 265-66
Food gathering, Indian, 30
Foote, Ebenezer, 258

Forest Hills, 266
Forest Hills Diary, 140
Forestport, 266
Forests, 76, 187-93
  management, 77
Forestville, 266
Fort Ann, 266
Fort Covington, 266
Fort Edward, 266
Fort Johnson, 266-67
Fort Nassau, 39
Fort Orange, 199
Fort Plain, 267
Fort Stanwix, 18, 44, 164, 325
Fort Ticonderoga, 142
Fourteenth Amendment, 144
Frankfort, 267
Franklin, 267
Franklin County, 267
  historical places, 407
Franklin Square, 267
Franklinville, 267
Fredonia, 267-68
Freedom, 268
Freeport, 268
Freeville, 268
French and Indian attacks, 41-42, 44
French and Indian War, 12, 35, 42, 142, 143
French forts, 34
French influence, 155-56, 200, 309
Friendship, 268
Frontier, New York, 50
Fuller, Thomas A., 7
Fulton, 268
Fulton County, 268
  historical places, 407-08
Fulton, Robert, 16, 163-64, *facing 140*
Fultonville, 268
Fur trading, 200, 309
Gainesville, 268
Galloo Island, 268
Galway, N.Y., 269
Ganeodaio, 36
Gansevoort, Peter, 164
Garden City, 154, 269
Gardiner, 269
Gardiners Bay, 269
Gardiners Island, 269
Gasoline rationing, 138
Gasport, 269
Gates, William A., 267

Index

Gedney, 269
Genesee Aqueduct, 217
Genesee County, 269
   courthouse, 239
   historical places, 408-10
Genesee River, 216, 269
Geneseo, 269
Geneva, 270
Genoa, 270
Gentleman's Magazine, 179
Geography, New York, 60-83
Geologic history, 62-65
Geology, 194
George II, 143
Georgetown, 270
German Flats, 277
German immigrants, 222, 309
   settlements, 290
Germantown, 270
Gerry, 270
Ghent, 270
Gibbons, Thomas, 256
Gilbertsville, 270
Gilboa, 270
Gilliland, William, 189
Glaciation, 64, 79, 194, 265
Glen Cove, 270-71
Glens Falls, 271
Gloversville, 271
Glynn, Martin Henry, 126
Gold market, 165
Gorham, 271
Goshen, 271
Gould, Jay, 165-66, *facing 140*
Gouverneur, 271
Government organization, 136
   state, 56-57, 543-714
   colonial, 45
Governors, New York, 92-140
   (listed), 90-91
Governors Island, 271
Gowanda, 271-72
Grafton, 272
Grand Canyon of the East, 69
Grand Island, 272
Grant, Ulysses S., 166-67
Granville, 272
Grape growing, 245, 301-02
Great Depression, 56, 130-31, 176, 212
Great Irish Famine, 52
Great Lakes, 306
Great Law, 29

Great Neck, 272
Great South Bay, 272
Great Spirit, 298
Great Valley, 272
Greece, N.Y., 272
Greeley, Horace, 211, 272, 276
Green Mountain Boys, 141-42
Greene, 272
Greene County, 272-73
   historical places, 410-11
Greenport, 273
Greenvale, 273
Greenville, 273
Greenwich, 273
Greenwich Village, 174, 214, 273
Greenwood, 273
Greenwood Lake, 273-74
Greig, 274
Groton, 274
Groveland, 274
Growing seasons, 74-75
Guggenheim Museum, *facing 186*
Guilderland, 274
Guilford, 274
Hadley, 274
Hagaman, 274
Halesite, 274
Half Moon, 172
Hamburg, N.Y., 274
Hamden, 175
Hamilton, 175
Hamilton, Alexander, 168, 169, *facing 140*
Hamilton County, 275
Hamlin, 275
Hammond, 275
Hammondsport, 275
Hampton, 275
Hancock, 275
Hand of God, English, 33
Hannawa Falls, 275-76, 320
Hannibal, N.Y., 276
Hannibal, Missouri, 157
Harbor Hill moraine, 70
Hardenbergh, Col. John, 236
Hardwoods, 77, 188
Harford, 276
Harpersfield, 276
Harriman, 276
Harriman, William A., 135-36
Harrison, 276
Harrisville, 276
Hartford, 276
   Treaty of 1780, 49

Hastings-on-Hudson, 276
Haverstraw, 277
Haviland, Dame Tamar, 327
Hearst, William R., 122
Hector, 277
Hempstead, 277
Henderson, 277
Henderson Harbor, 277
Hendrick King, 200
Hendy, John, 262
Hennepin, Father Louis, 306
Henrietta, 277
Herkimer, 277-78
Herkimer County, 278
 historical places, 412-15
Herkimer, Gen. Nicholas, 278
Hermon, 278
Herrings, 278
Heuvelton, 278
Hiawatha, 27, 169-70, 171, 232,
 facing 140
Higgins, Frank W., 121
Highland Falls, 278
Hill, David B., 299
Hill Cumorah, 183, 278
 formation, 65
Hill, David B., 115-16
Hillburn, 278
Hillsdale, 278-79
Hilton, 279
Hinsdale, 279
Historical Places, 361-536
Hiss, Alger, 23
Hobart, 279
Hodge, John, 291
Hoffman, John T., 110
Hogansburg, 279,
Holcomb, 279
Holland, N.Y., 279
Holland Patent, 279
Holland Purchase, 239
Holley, 279
Home Industrial Association, 301
Homer, 279
Honeoye Falls, 279
Hoosick, 279
 Falls, 279-80
Hopkinton, 280
Hornell, 280
Horseheads, 280
Horticulture, 154-55
Hough, Franklin B., 190
Housing, Indian, 31
 low income, *facing 140*

Howells, William D., 171-72
Hudson, 280
Hudson, Henry, 1, 39, 172-73,
 199, 209, 281
Hudson River, 224, 280-81
 falls, 280
 valley, 44, 67
Hudson-Mohawk Lowland, 66-67
Hughes, Charles E., 121-22, 123
Hume, 281
Humidity, 72, 78
Hunt, Washington, 105-06
Hunter, 281
Hunting, 30
Huntington, 281
Huntington, Ellsworth, 72
Hurley, 281
Huron tribe, 155
Hutchinson, Anne, 301, 315
Hyde Park, 281-82
Ice Age, 63-64, 79, 188, 194
Ice fishing, 319
Ice harvesting, 235
Ilion, 282
Immigrants, 212, 225, 242, 290,
Immigration, 52-53
Indian Lake, 282
Indian Reorganization Act, 319
Indians, 9, 25-37, 150, 298
 contributions to whites, 37
 reservations, 231-32, 249-50,
  309, 310-11, 318-19, 328-29
 settlement, 224
 tribes of New York, *map
  facing 25*
 warfare, *32*
*Industrial age, 147, 152-53, 178,
 207, 225, 236, 306*
Industrial revolution, 54-56
Inlet, 282
Interlaken, 282
*International Business Ma-
 chines (IBM), 242*
Inventors, 147-48, 177-78
Irish Republic, 126
Irondequoit, 282
*Iroquois, 27-29, 200, 232, 249,
 311, 328*
 Confederacy, 150, 220
Irving, Washington, 282
Irvington, 282
Ischua, 282-83
Island Park, 283
Islands, barrier, 194

Islip, 283
Italian immigrants, 132-33, 140, 175
Ithaca, 283
J.P. Morgan Company, 177
Jamaica, 283
James II, 41
Jamestown, 283-84
Jasper, 284
Jay, 284
Jay, John, 93-94
Jefferson, 284
Jefferson, Thomas, 169
Jefferson County, 284
  historical places, 415-17
Jeffersonville, 284
Jericho, 284
Jewett, 284
Jewish-Americans, 11, 131
  persecution of, 133
Jogues, Isaac, 199
'John Brown's Body,' 152
Johnsburg, 284
Johnson, Sir John, 266
Johnson City, 284
Johnstown, 284
Jordan, 284
Journal, Albany, 201
Journal, New York, 168, 201
June Bug, 148
Jungle, The, 183
Keene, 284
Keene Valley, 284-85
Keeney Nicholas, 288
Keeseville, 285
Kendall, 285
Kenmore, 285
Keuka Lake, 285
Kinderhook, 285
King, John A., 107-08
King William's War, 41
Kings County, 285-86
  historical places, 417-22
Kings Point, 286
Kingston, 286
Kipling, Rudyard, 154
Kirkwood, 286
Knickerbockers, 3-4
Knox, 286
Koch, Edward I., 173-74, facing 140
Kocherthal, Joshua, 302
Kodak Company, 161, 217-18

Labor, 55-56, 212, 301
Lackawanna, 286
Lacona, 286
LaFargeville, 286
La Fayette, 286-87
LaGuardia, Fiorello, 175, facing 140
Lake Champlain, 66, 82, 188
  battle at, 47
Lake Erie, 71, 81, 205
Lake George, 82, 287,
Lake Grove, 287
Lake Ontario, 81, 216
Lake Placid, 73, 287
Lake Pleasant, 287
Lakes, 205, 251, 282, 287, 292, 310, 313, 329
  Adirondack, 65, 83, 193
  and Rivers, 80-83
Lakeville, 287
Lakewood, 287
Lancaster, 287
Land clearing, 76
Landform regions, 65-71
Landscaping, 154-55
Languages, Indian, 29
Lansing, 287
Larchmont, 288
Latin American policy, 123
Laurens, 288
Lawrence, 288
Lawrence, Richard J., 193
Lawrenceville, 288
'Leatherstocking Tales,' 159
Lebanon, 288
Lebanon Springs, 288
'Legend of Sleepy Hollow,' 67
Legislature, state, 6
Lehman, Herbert H., 57, 131-32
Leicester, 288
Leisler, 41-42
Leisler, Jacob, 304
Lenni Lenape, 26-27, 320
Leon, 288
Leroy, 288
Lester, Horace and George, 242
Levittown, 288-89
Lewis, 289
Lewis, Gov. Morgan, 94-95, 289
Lewis County, 289
  historical places, 422-23
Lewiston, 289
Lexington, 289
Liberty, 289

734 Encyclopedia of New York

Lily, 149
Lily Dale, 289
Lima, 289-90
Lime, in soil, 80
Limestone, 290
Lindenhurst, 290
Lindley, 290
Lindsay, Mayor John, 174
Lisbon, N.Y., 290
Lisle, 290
Little Falls, 290
Little Valley, 291
Liverpool, 291
Livingston, 291
Livingston, Chancellor Robert, 256
Livingston County, 291
  historical places, 423-24
Livingston family, 235
Livonia, 291
Locke, 291
Lockport, 291
Locust Valley, 291
Lodi, 292
Log Cabin campaigns, 99
Lomb, Henry, 217
Long Beach, 292
Long Island, 292, 309
  Indian tribes, 318-19
Long Island City, 292
Long Island Sound, 70, 292
Long Lake, 292
Longfellow, Henry W., 171
Lorraine, 292
Louisiana Purchase Exposition, 126
Lowville, 292-93
Lumber industry, 76, 124, 192, 261
Lynbrook, 293
Lynch, Dominick, 325
Lyndonville, 293
Lyon Mountain, 293
Lyons, 293
Lyons Falls, 293
Lysander, 293
McDonough, 296
McGraw, 296
McKinley, William, 20
  assassination of, 119
Macedon, 293
Machias, 293
Macomb Purchase, 500

Macys Department Store, *facing 186*
Madison, 293
Madison County, 293
  historical places, 424-25
Madrid, 293-94
Mahopac, 294
Maine, 294
Malden on Hudson, 294
Malone, 294
Malverne, 294
Mamoroneck, 294
Manchester, 294
Manhasset, 294
Manhattan, 294-95. *See also* New York City
Manlius, 295
Mannsville, 295
Maple sugar, 6
Marathon, 295
Marcellus, 295
Marcy, 295
Marcy, William L., 100-01
Margaretville, 295
Marilla, 295
Marion, 295
Marriage customs, Indian, 28, 30
Martinsburg, 295
Maryland, N.Y., 295
Masonville, 296
Massapequa, 296
Massapequa Park, 296
Massawepie, 296
Massena, 296
Maybrook, 296
Mayfield, 296
Mayville, 296
Mechanicville, 296
Medina, 296-97
Mehta, Zubin, 213
Men of Men, *See* Iroquois)
Mendon, 296
Merchant Shipping Corporation, 135
Meredith, 297
Meridale, 297
Meridian, 297
Merriman, 297
Metcalf-Baker bill, 138
Mexico, 297
Middle Island, 297
Middleburgh, 297
Middleport, 297

Index

Middlesex, 297
Middletown, 297
Middleville, 297
Milford, 297-98
Military Tract, 49
Milk testing, 244
Milk trust barons, 128
Mill Neck, 298
Millay, Edna St. Vincent, 176
Millbrook, 298
Miller, Nathan L., 129-30
Millerton, 298
Millport, 298
Mineola, 298
Minerva, 298
Minetto, 298
Mining, 190, 221-22
Minoa, 298
Mirror Lake, 287
Missions, 289
Mohawk tribe, 298, 328
  in the Revolution, 43
Mohawk River, 67, 298
Mohegan Lake, 299
Moira, 299
Monroe, 299
Monroe County, 217, 299
  historical places, 426-32
Monroe Doctrine, 114, 123
Montauk, 299
  Confederacy, 318
Montauk Point, 299, *86*
Montezuma, 299
Montgomery, 299
Montgomery County, 299
  historical places, 432-35
Monticello, 299
Montour Falls, 299-300
Montreal, attack on, 142
Moody, Jacob S. and Martin, 329
Mooers, 300
Moravia, 300
Moreland Act, 122
Morgan, Edwin D., 108-09
Morgan, John P., 176-77
Moriah, 300
Mormons, 183-84
Morris, 300
Morris, Gouverneur, 271
Morris, Robert, 239
Morristown, 300
Morrisville, 300
Morse, Samuel F. B., 177-78,
  facing 140

Morton, Levi Parsons, 117
Morton Trust Company, 117
Mott, Lucretia, 185
Mount Kisco, 300
Mount Marcy, 300
Mount Morris, 300
Mount Vernon, 300-01
Mountains, 187
Munnsville, 301
Murray, Henry H. 'Adirondacks', 191
Musicians, 148
Myers, Carl and Carlotta, 267
Names, geographical, 2
Naples, 301-02
Nassau County, 302
  historical places, 435-38
National Parks, *map*, *197*
National Technical Institute for
  the Deaf, 139
National Woman Suffrage Association, 185
Natty Bumpo, 159
Natural gas, 69
'Nature Essay,' 157
Nelliston, 302
Nelsonville, 302
Neversink, 302
New Amsterdam, 40
New Amsterdam, in 1626-28, *38*
New Baltimore, 302
New Berlin, 302
New Bremen, 302
New City, 303
New Deal, 130-31, 182
New England Upland, 66
New France, 156
New Hartford, 303
New Haven, N.Y., 303
New Hyde Park, 303
New Lebanon, 303
New Lisbon, 303
New Netherlands, 10, 209
New Paltz, 303
New Rochelle, 304-05
New Scotland, 305
New Windsor, 305
New York City, 12, 20, 41, 174, 175, 209-15, 294-95, 438-66, *facing 186*
  bankruptcy, 140
  development, 54
  labor, 59
  mayors, 208

politics, 128, 168
in Revolutionary War, 48
transit, 24
New York Cotton Exchange, 131
New York County, 305
 historical places, 438-66
New York Mills, 305
New York World's Fair, 23
Newark, N.Y., 302
Newark Valley, 302
Newburgh, 302-03
Newcomb, 303
Newfane, 303
Newfield, 303
Newport, 304
Niagara County, 305
 historical places, 466-69
Niagara Escarpment, 81
Niagara Falls, 22, 207, 305-06, *facing 186*
Niagara River, 307
Nichols, 307
Nicknames, state, 3
Nicolls, Col. Richard, 40
Nor'easters, 71
Norfolk, 307
North Collins, 307
North Hudson, 307
North Norwich, 307
North Salem, 307
North Syracuse, 307
North Tarrytown, 307
North Tonawanda, 307-08
Northport, 307
Northville, 308
Northwest Territory, 151
Norwich, 308
Norwood, 308
Nova Scotia, 155
Nunda, 308
Nyack, 308
Oakfield, 308
Oaks, 77
Ocean Beach, 308
Oceanside, 308
Odell, Benjamin Barker, Jr., 120-21
Odessa, 308
Office of Civilian Defense, 182
Ogdensburg, 308-09
Oil, 180
 drilling, 68-69
 tariffs, 140
Oil Springs Indian reservation, 309

Old Age Pensions, 132
Old Westbury, 309
Olean, 309
Olympic Games, 287
Oneida, 309
Oneida County, 309-10
 historical places, 469-73
Oneida Lake, 310
Oneonta, 310, *87*
Onondaga, 310
 Lake, 221
 tribe, 169-70
Onondaga County, 310
 historical places, 473-78
Onondaga Indian Reservation, 310-11
Ontario, 311
Ontario County, 311
 historical places, 478-80
Orange County, 311
 historical places, 480-86
Orchard Park, 311
Orchards, 74-75
Organized crime, 134, 175
Oriskany, 311
Oriskany Falls, 311
Orleans County, 311
Orwell, 311-12
Ossining, 312
Oswegatchie, 312
Oswego, 312-13
Oswego County, 313
 historical places, 486-87
Otego, 313
Otisville, 313
Otsego County, 313
 historical places, 487-89
Otsego Lake, 313
Otselic, 313
Otto, 313
Ovid, 313
Owachira, 29
Owasco, 313
Owasco Lake, 313
Owego, 313-14
Oxford, 314
Oyster Bay, 314
Paine, Thomas, 304-05
Painted Post, 314
Painters, 285
Palatine Bridge, 314
Palatines, 302-03
Paleo-Indians, 25
Palmyra, 314

Index

Paris, N.Y., 314
Parish, 314
Parishville, 314
Patchogue, 314
Patterson, Matthew, 315
Patterson, N.Y., 315
Pavilion, 315
Pawling, 315
Peekskill, 315
Pelham, 315
Penfield, 316
Penn Yan, 316
Perry, 316
Perrysburg, 316
Peru, N.Y., 316
Petersburg, 316
Phelps, 316
Phelps, Oliver, 216
Phelps-Gorman Purchase, 247
Philadelphia, N.Y., 316
Phillipsburgh, 312
Philmont, 316
Phoenix, 316
Photography, 160-61
Physiographic regions of New York, *85*
Picquet, Abbet Francois, 309
Piercefield, 316
Piermont, 316
Pike, 316
Pine Hill, 316
Pioneers, 50
Piseco Lake, 316
Pitcher, 316-17
Pitcher, Nathaniel, 97-98
Pitt, William, 43-44
Pittsford, 317
Place Names, N.Y., 229-360
Plandome, 317
Platt, Zephaniah, 317
Plattekill, 317
Plattsburgh, 317-18
Pleasant Valley, 318
Pleasantville, 318
Pleistocene era, 63
  glaciation, 64
Plum Island, 318
Plymouth, 318
Poe, Edgar Allen, 178-07, *facing 140*
Poestenkill, 318
Poetry, 176
Poland, 318
Poletti, Charles, 132-33

Political machines, 55
Politics, New york, 57, 92-140
Pollution, air, 193
Polygamy, among Indians, 30
  among Mormons, 184
Pomona, 318
Pompey, 318
Pony Express, 162
Poospatuck Indian Reservation, 318
Population, 1, 24, 54, 61, *facing 197*
  colonial, 50-51
  distribution of, 69
  loss, in New York, 58
Port Byron, 319
Port Chester, 319
Port Henry, 319
Port Jefferson, 319
Port Jervis, 319-20
Port Leyden, 320
Port Washington, 320
Porter, Augustus, 306
Portland, 320
Portville, 320
Post Standard, Syracuse, 124
Potawatomie Executions, 151
Potsdam, 320
Pottery making, 26
Poughkeepsie, 320
Pound Ridge, 321
Prattsburg, 321
Prattsville, 321
Preble, 321
Precipitation, 72, 73, *map, 84*
Prehistory, 9, 25-37, 195
Prendergast, James, 283-84
Presidents, from New York, 54, 57, 98, 113-14, 118-20, 129, 130-31, 162, 167, 202, 206
Prison reform, 101
Prohibition, 21, 129, 132
  in 1850s, 107
  hideouts, 248
Prospect, 321
Provincial Congress of New York, 46
Public Service Commission, 56
Publishing, 153-54
Pulaski, 321
Pulteney, 321
Pure Food and Drug laws, 119, 183

Putnam County, 321
  historical places, 490
Putnam Valley, 321
Queens Borough, 322
Queens County, 322
  historical places, 491-92
Queensbury, 322
Quogue, 322
Racing legalization, 136
Radio City Music Hall, *facing 186*
Railroads, 52, 165, 225, 309
  state agency, 540
Rainbow Falls *facing 360*
Randolph, 322
Ravena, 322
Recreation, 192
Red Creek, 322
Red Hook, 323
Red Wing, 285
Redfield, 322
Redford, 322
Reed, John, 256
Reform movements, 53
Reforms, 95, 102, 115-16
  women, 143-44
Regions, New York, 61
  climatic, 75-76
  geographic, 65-71
  of soil, 78
Religion, 186
Remington, Eliphalet, 282
Remington, Frederic, 309
Remsen, 323
Rensselaer, 323
Rensselaer County, 323
  historical places, 492-99
Rensselaer Falls, 323
Rensselaerswyck, 199-200
Rensselaerville, 323
Republican party, 98, 108, 120
Reservations, Indian, 36
Revere Copper and Brass Company, 326
Revolutionary War, 13-15, 45, 46-49, 92, 93, 94, 141, 164, 168, 210-11, 262, 266, 304, 342, 357
  and Indians, 35, 36, 150
  treachery, 145-46
Rhinebeck, 323
Richburg, 323-24
Richfield Springs, 324
.Richford, 324

Richland, 324
Richmond, Dean, 238-39
Richmond Borough, 324
Richmond County, 324
  historical places, 499-502
Richmondville, 324
Richville, 324
Rip Van Winkel, 67
Ripley, 324
Riverhead, 324
Rivers, 281
Roads, colonial, 51
Roadside stand, *facing 186*
Robert, Moses, 325
Robinson, Lucius, 112
Rochester, 160-61, 216-21
Rockefeller, Gov. Nelson, 59, 136-37, 192
Rockefeller, John D., 179-80, *facing 140*
Rockefeller Center, 136, *facing 186*
Rockland County, 325
  historical places, 502-03
Rockville Centre, 325
Rodman, 325
Rome, 325-26
Romulus, 326
Ronkonkoma, 326
Ronkonkoma Moraine, 70
Roosevelt, 326
Roosevelt, Anna Eleanor, 181-82, *facing 140*
Roosevelt, Franklin D., 130-31, 281-82, *facing 140*
Roosevelt Theodore, 20, 157, 118-20, *facing 140*
Rose, 326
Roseboom, 326
Rosenberg, Julius and Ethel, 23
Rosendale, 326
Rosenthal, Herman, murder, 127
Roslyn, 326
Rossie, 326
Rotterdam, N.Y., 326
'Rough Riders,' 119
Round Lake, 326
Rouses Point, 326-27
Roxbury, 327
Rush, 327
Rushford, 327
Rushville, 327
Russell, 327
Rye, 327

Index

Sackets Harbor, 327
Safety and Health Division, state, 540
Sag Harbor, 327
Saint James, 327
Saint Johnsville, 328
St. Lawrence County, 328
  historical places, 511-12
St. Lawrence Power Development Commission, 133
St. Lawrence River, 328
  exploration, 155
St. Lawrence-Lake Champlain Lowland, 65-66
St. Regis Indian Reservation, 328
Salamanca, N.Y., 329
Salem, 329
Salina, 329
Saltaire, 329
San Remo, 329
Sanatoriums, 191
Sand Lake, 329
Sandy Creek, 329
Sangerfield, 329
Saranac, 329
Saranac Lake, 329-30
Saratoga, battle of, 48
Saratoga County, 330
  historical places, 503-06
Saratoga Lake, 330
Saratoga Springs, 330
Sardinia, N.Y., 331
Saturday Press, 158
Saugerties, 331
Saunders, William, 276
Savannah, 331
Savona, 331
Sayville, 331-32
Scarborough, 332
Scarsdale, 332
Schaghticoke, 332
Schenectady, 332-33
Schenectady County, 333
  historical places, 506-07
Schenevus, 333
Schoharie, 333
Schoharie County, 333
  historical places, 507-09
Schuyler, Peter, 14, 42, 200
Schuyler, Gen. Philip, 304
Schuyler County, 333-34
  historical places, 509
Schuyler Falls, 334
Schuylerville, 334

Scio, 334
Scotia, 334
Scottsville, 334
Sea Cliff, 334
Seal of the state, 4
Secretary of State, 5, 540
Secretary of the Senate, 540
Securities Bureau, state, 540
Sediments, 62
Selden, 334
Selden, George, 252
Senators, U.S., 88-89
Seneca County, 334
  historical places, 509-11
Seneca Falls, 334
  Women's Convention, *facing 54*
Seneca Lake, 335
Seneca Nation, 231-32, 249-50, 344
Sennett, 335
Settlement, of Adirondacks, 189
Settlement, post Revolutionary, 50
Seward, 335
Seward, William, 101-02, 236
Seymour, Horatio, 106-07
Shale, 79
Shandaken, 335
Shape, of state, 60
Sharon Springs, 335
Shelter Island, 335
Sherburne, 335-36
Sheridan, 336
Sherman, 336
Sherman Anti-Trust Law, 180
Silver Purchase Act, 115
Sherrill, 336
Shinnecock Bay, 336
Shinnecock Reservation, 336
Shipping, 19,.163, 307
Shirley, 336
Shoreham, 336
Shortsville, 336
Shroon Lake, 333
Shuckburgh, Dr. Richard, 323
Sidney, 336-37
Silk production, 338
'Silk Stocking' district, 174
Silver Creek, 337
Silver Springs, 337
Sinclair, Upton B., 182-83
Sinclairville, 337
Sing Sing Prison, 312
Six Nations, 310

Skaneateles, 337
Skiing in New York, *facing 360*
Slavery, 16, 54, 95, 102
  abolition, 105, 151, 184, 186, 334
  of Indians, 12
Slide Mountain, 337
Sloan, 337
Sloatsburg, 337
Smith, Alfred E., 57, 127-29
Smith, Claudius, 271
Smith, Joseph, 183-84, 230
Smith-Premier typewriters, 222
Smithtown, 337-38
  Bay, 338
Smyrna, 338
Snow, 72-73
Social organization, colonial 45
Social Services Department, state, 540
Sodus, 338
Sodus Point, 338
Softwoods, 77
Soils, 74, 78-80
Solid Waste Management Division, , 540
Solvay, 338
Somers, 338
Sound Beach, 338
South Dayton, 339
South Glens Falls, 339
South Huntington, 339
South Oyster Bay, 339
Southampton, 339
Southold, 339
Southport, 339
Speculator, 339
Spencer, 339
Spencerport, 339
Spiritualist monument, *facing 360*
Spring Valley, 339
Springs, mineral, 330, 335
Springville, 340
Springwater, 340
Squaw Island, 340
Stafford, 340
Stamford, 340
Stamp Act, 13
Standard Oil Company, 180
Stanton, Elizabeth Cady, 184-85
State Library, 539
State Planning agency, 539
State services, directory, 537-41

State symbols, 1-8
State University of New York, 242, 341
Staten Island, 340
Statue of Liberty, 117, 213, 340, *facing 186*
Steam shipping, 113, 163
Steel industry, 153, 286, 346
Stephentown, 340
Sterling, 340-41
Steuben County, 341
  historical places, 512
Stewart, Alexander T., 269
Stillwater, 341
Stockport, 341
Stockton, 341
Stony Brook, 341
Stony Point, 341
Stratford, 341
Stuyvesant, 341
Stuyvesant, Peter, 199, 286
Stylus, The, 179
Suburban growth, 218, 277, 288-89, 348
Suffern, 341
Suffolk County, 342
  historical places, 512-16
Suffrage, women's, 144, 186
Sullivan, Gen. John, 283
Sullivan County, 342
Sullivan-Clinton expedition, 36, 262, 314
Sulzer, William, 125-26
Summit, 342
Susquehanna River, 241
Swedish immigrants, 284
Sylvan Beach, 342
Syosset, 342
Syracuse, 220-23
Tammany Hall, 110, 125
Tannersville, 342
Tappan, 342
Tarrytown, 342
Taxation and Finance Dept., 540
Tayler, John, 98
Taylor, Zachary, 163
Tear-of-the-Clouds, 191
Technological developments, 22, 350
Telegraph, 147
Television, 22
Temperance, 107
  societies, 149
Temperature averages, 73-74

Index 741

Terryville, 343
Thayer, Maj. Sylvanus, 356
The Fuyck, 40
Theresa, 343
Thomas E. Dewey Thruway, 67, *227*
Thornwood, 343
Thousand Islands, 343, *facing 186*
Throop, Enos T., 99-100
Ticonderoga, 343
Tilden, Samuel, 55, 115, 111-12, 303, *facing 140*
Times Square, 215
Times-Union, Albany, 126
Tioga County, 343
  historical places, 516
Tivoli, 343-44
Tobacco industry, 242
Tompkins, Daniel D., 95-96
Tompkins County, 344
  historical places, 516-19
Tonawanda, 344
Tonawanda Indian reservation, 344-45
Tourism, 68, 305, 331
  state agency for, 540
Trade, British, 43
  Indian, 32
  with China, 146
Transportation, 51-52, 162, 205, 221-22, 224-25, 321
  improvements, 128
  state department, 540
  water, 312-13
Treasurer, state, 540
Treaties, with Indians, 344
Treaty of Paris, 13, 93
Treaty of Ryswyck, 42
Treaty of Utrecht, 42
Tree, state, 6
Tree growing, 74
Tribune, New York, 211
Troupsburg, 345
Troy, 345-46
Trudeau, Dr. Edward Livingston, 191, 329
Trumansburg, 346
Truth, Sojourner, 185-86 *facing 140*
Truxton, 346-47
Tuckahoe, 347
Tug Hill Upland, 70
Tully, 347

Tupper Lake, 347
Turin, 347
Tuscarora Indian Reservation, 347
Tuxedo Park, 348
Twain, Mark, *See* Clemens, Samuel
Tweed, William "Boss" M., 111, 212
Tweed Ring, 55, 111
Tycoons, 146-47, 152-53, 165-66, 176-77, 179-81
Tyrone, 348
U.S. Steel Corporation, 153
Ulster County, 348
  historical places, 519-23
Unadilla, 348
Underground Railroad, 186
Underhill, Capt. John, 291
Unemployment, 59
Union, 348-49
Union College, 333
Union Springs, 349
Unionville, 349
United Nations, 58, 182
  building, *facing 186*
Uplift, land, 63
Upper Bay, 349
Urbanization, 55
Utica, 349-50
Valatie, 350
Valhalla, 350
Valley Falls, 350
Valley Stream, 350
Van Buren, Martin, 98-99
Van der Donck, Adriaen C., 224
Van Etten, 350
Van Hoesen, Jan Frans, 280
Veeder, Albert, 234
Vegetation, native, 76-78
Vermont, 142
Vernon, 350
Verona, 350-51
Vestal, 351
Victor, 351
Voorheesville, 351
Waddington, 351
Walden, 351
Walker, Mary E., 313
Wall Street, 214
Walton, 351
Walworth, 351
Wampsville, 351
Wantaugh, 351

Wappinger Indian Confederacy, 304
Wappingers Falls, 351-52
War of 1812, 51, 100, 163-64
  battles, 317-18
Warren County, 352
  historical places, 523-24
Warrensburg, 352
Warsaw, 352
Warwick, 352
Washington County, 352
  historical places, 524-25
Washington, George, 47, 48, 53, 211, 357
Washingtonville, 352
Water power, 56, 128, 207, 281, 305-06
Water resources, 80-83
Waterford, 352
Waterloo, 352
Watertown, 352-53
Waterville, 353
Watervliet, 353
Wathatotarho, 170
Watkins Glen, 353
Watson, Thomas J., 242
Waverly, 353
Wayland, 353-54
Wayne County, 354
  historical places, 525-26
Webster, 354
Webster, Ephraim, 220
Weed, Thurlow, 201
Weedsport, 354
Weekly Journal, New York, 210
Welch, Dr. Thomas B., 355
Welfare, public, 56, 57
Wells, 354
Wells Fargo and Company, 162
Wells, Gardiner, 354
Wells, Henry, 319
Wellsburg, 354
Wellsville, 354
West Babylon, 354
West Bloomfield, 354
Westbury, 355
Westchester County, 355
  historical places, 526-35
Westerlo, 355
Western Union Telegraph Company, 113
Westfield, 355
Westford, 355
Westhampton Beach, 355

West Haverstraw, 355
West India Company, 39-40
West Monrie, 355
Westmoreland, 355
West Point Military Academy, 16, 94, 166, 355-56
Westport, 356
West Seneca, 356
West Winfield, 356
Wetlands, 76
Whigs, 101, 105
White, Horace, 123-24
White, Judge Hugh, 357
Whitehall, 356
White Plains, 356-57
Whitesboro, 357
Whitman, Charles S., 127
Whitman, Walt, 156
Whitney Point, 357
Wiard, Thomas, 238
Wildlife, 77, 188, 195
Willet, 357
Williamson, 357
Williamson, Col. Charles, 240
Williamstown, 357
Williamsville, 358
Williston Park, 358
Willsboro, 358
Wilmington, 358
Wilson, 358
Wilson, Charles M., 137-38
Wilton, 358
Windham, 358
Windson, 358
Winter Olympics, 73, 130
Winter weather, 73
Wisconsin glacier, 187
Wolcott, 358
Women's rights, 19, 53, 113, 143-44, 181-82, 184-85
  Convention of 1848, *facing 53*
Wood, James, 277
Wood, Fernando, 211
Woodhull, 359
Woodland culture, 26
Woodridge, 359
Woodstock, 359
  Music Festival, 24
Worcester, 359
Workman's Compensation Act, 122
World War I, 21, 55-56, 127, 212
World War II, 57-58, 131, 138, 173, 182, 225

Index

World's Columbian Exposition, 116
Wurtsboro, 359
Wyoming, N.Y., 359
Wyoming County, 359
 historical places, 535-36
Wright, Silas, 103
Y.M.C.A., 18
Yates, Joseph Christopher, 97
Yates County, 359
Yip, Yip, Yaphank, 149
Yonkers, 224-25
York, 359
Yorkshire, 359
Yorkville, 359-68
Young, John, 104
Youngstown, 360
Zenger, John Peter, 210, 301